FOR GOD AND KAISER

RICHARD BASSETT was staff correspondent for *The Times* in Vienna, Rome and Warsaw during the closing decade of the Cold War. His previous books include *Hitler's Spy Chief: The Wilhelm Canaris Mystery* (2012) and the highly acclaimed *Last Days in Old Europe* (2016).

T0317073

FOR GOD
AND
KAISER

THE IMPERIAL AUSTRIAN ARMY
FROM 1619 TO 1918

RICHARD BASSETT

YALE UNIVERSITY PRESS
NEW HAVEN AND LONDON

Copyright © 2015 Richard Bassett

First published in paperback in 2016

For information about this and other Yale University Press publications, please contact:
U.S. Office: sales.press@yale.edu   www.yalebooks.com
Europe Office: sales@yaleup.co.uk   www.yalebooks.co.uk

Typeset in Minion Pro by IDSUK (DataConnection) Ltd

Library of Congress Cataloging-in-Publication Data

Bassett, Richard.
   For God and Kaiser : the Imperial Austrian Army, 1619–1918/Richard Bassett.
     pages cm
   Includes bibliographical references and index.
   ISBN 978-0-300-17858-6 (cl : alk. paper)
   1.   Austria. Armee—History. 2.   Austria—History, Military.   I. Title.
   UA672.B37 2015
   355.009436'0903—dc 3
                                                                                   2014047021

A catalogue record for this book is available from the British Library.

ISBN 978-0-300-21967-8 (pbk)

10 9 8 7 6 5 4 3 2 1

Printed and bound by CPI Group (UK) Ltd, Croydon, CR0 4YY

For Gottfried Pils (Akad.Maler)

All the peoples of the monarchy have found a common home in the army. For that reason it has been enabled to accomplish so much.

The Emperor Charles I, 24 October 1918

CONTENTS

ILLUSTRATIONS

Plates

Maps

ACKNOWLEDGEMENTS

This book, so long in gestation, must inevitably count on the help and support of many individuals over many years. Though Habsburg history may no longer be taught to mainstream history undergraduates in the British Isles, there is still a corpus of expertise among our academics. I am indebted to Professor R. J. W. Evans of the University of Oxford for offering me some guidance on the career of Ferdinand II. He has illuminated a period of Central European History with which I have come to grips relatively late in my studies.

Professor Alan Sked of the LSE and Professor Roy Bridge of the University of Leeds were no less generous in helping me understand aspects of the Imperial and Royal Army in the nineteenth century and important details of Anglo-Austrian relations during the July crisis of 1914. In this context I should like also to thank Dr Paul Miller of the University of Birmingham who organised a fascinating 'Tagung' on the Habsburg Empire during the summer of 2012. I am grateful too to Dr John Warren who has also over recent years organised conferences on important Imperial Austrian themes. Dr Pavlina Bobič, doyenne of studies concerning her native Slovenia and the Habsburg army kindly devoted much time to showing me the impressive landscape and museums of Kobarid (Caporetto). My old college at Cambridge, Christ's, very generously granted me High Table privileges for the duration of the writing of this text and it is fair to say that this book has benefited enormously from the singular and stimulating intellectual environment which has long been the hallmark of the 'Custom of the Room'. At Cambridge I am also grateful for the advice of Will O'Reilly of Trinity Hall as well as Brendan Simms at Peterhouse. I am also most indebted to Dr Christopher Brennan, late of the LSE, and Miss S.R. Lim who very kindly strove to keep me abreast of the Modern European History Seminar, something of a Cinderella in the present Cambridge History Faculty.

I should perhaps also mention in England R.D.M.D. Danne, our virulently anti-Habsburg history master at school nearly fifty years ago, a man who combined all the high-mindedness of a Gladstonian liberal with the totalitarian instincts of the Soviet Comintern. Mrs Margaret Cross, Head of the History Department at St Peter's School Southbourne, was more objective and inspired her fourteen-year-old pupils to think about mid-nineteenth century Austria's position in Germany and Italy within the context of the legacy of the first Napoleon. Later, I was fortunate to enjoy some stimulating discussions with Professor Norman Stone whose extensive though acerbic knowledge of the subject he was always happy to share with me.

Another man to whose generous and kind support this book owes much is Dr Christopher Duffy, primus-inter-pares among the military historians of the Seven Years War. I am especially grateful to Dr Duffy for highlighting the significance of 5 June 1619. I have also benefited from conversations with his colleagues at the Royal Military Academy at Sandhurst, Dr Klaus Schmider and Dr Greg Frimont-Barnes. The details of Laudon's discussion with the Russian generals shortly before Kunersdorf were furnished by count Anton Wengersky whose knowledge and love of eighteenth-century military history have happily punctuated my many visits to Bavaria over the years. I am grateful to his son count Max Rechberg for continuing this tradition. His son-in-law, count Karl-Eugen Czernin whose friendship I have so long enjoyed, furnished me with many insights into Bohemian history as well as the role of the last Kaiser of Austria, Charles. I am especially grateful to his wife countess Fiona Czernin for supporting our happy discussions in Enzesfeld and Chudenice. Baron Lionel de Rothschild generously tried to help me clarify some details concerning Italy's entry into the Great War in 1915. I have also been helped by Dr Ilya Berkovich, the author of a fascinating imminent study on motivation in war, and Dr Martin Boycott Brown, the author of the widely acclaimed *Road to Rivoli*.

In Austria, I have no doubt that this book would never have seen the light of day were it not for the long years of friendship, stretching over thirty-five years, with Herr Gottfried Pils, my former neighbour in the Schubertstrasse in Graz. To him and his then employer, the Styria Verlag publishing house, I owe my first encounters with Austrians for whom the Imperial and Royal Army was an object of intense and scholarly interest. Herr Pils has more than amply responded to my request for illustrative material for this book. In Graz, too, I am also grateful for the insights of the late Dr Peter Altenburg and the late Dr Peter Schall.

In the beginning of my advanced Habsburg studies in the 1970s I might well say there was Herr Gottfried Pils but in those days Imperial Austrian military history meant the name first and foremost of Dr Johann Christoph

Allmayer-Beck, the then Director of the Heeresgeschichtlichesmuseum (HGM). On the occasions I met Dr Allmayer-Beck during the early 1980s, I was grateful to be able to absorb some of his truly exhaustive knowledge of the subject. Above all he was a master of concept and the drawing together of disparate strands. Later directors of the HGM have attempted with varying degrees of success to build on his work, and several of them have been helpful in the research for this book but I 'grew up' in my early twenties, so to speak, with many of Allmayer-Beck's interpretations of this story and they will be instantly recognisable to all those who work in his shadow.

Other Austrian historians including Hofrat Professor Peter Broucek were also of great assistance. Hofrat Broucek's encyclopaedic knowledge of the career of Marshal Radetzky was a gift I neither expected nor merited and for which I am deeply grateful. He very kindly took the time to read an early draft of this book and the text is as a result much improved. I am also particularly indebted to Dr Rudolf Jeřabek's help in the Kriegsarchiv especially with regard to tracing some hitherto little known but illuminating reports of the Imperial and Royal military attaché in Belgrade in 1914 Major Otto Gellinek. The late Professor Georg Eisler, that most patriotic of Austrians, shared much of his knowledge of k. (u.) k. (Imperial and Royal) affairs during a friendship of nearly twenty-five years (his father, the composer Hanns Eisler, had served in a Bosnian infantry regiment).

War is a terrible business, in Tolstoy's words: 'millions of men renouncing their human feelings and common sense'. What the young and indeed old men of these armies were forced to do is something few can empathise with. Yet the study of conflicts and campaigns paradoxically also sharply illuminates human nature and the role of the individual in a way which is often more immediate and compelling than other forms of historical enquiry. It is also one of the pleasures of military history that its study requires visits to past battlefields. In many cases they are long forgotten and difficult of access. In others they are well-tended places of extraordinary atmosphere and beauty. The walls of the famous Granary at Essling, the haunting silence of the Swiepwald near Königgrätz, the orchards at Austerlitz and at San Martino, the Piranesian ruins of Przemyśl; these are all repositories of collective memories which help to bring to life the events described in this book.

I am grateful to Marian Šveijda and Daniel Spička, old and loyal friends, for accompanying me on the trail of the 'Nordarmee' in Bohemia, and Nick Bence-Trower for driving me to Solferino. Richard Hudson, who also enjoys what Eric Hobsbawm has described as the 'incomparable advantages of a background in the old Austria', inspired a lightning visit (in every sense of the word) up the valley of the Isonzo.

Among military men, I am indebted to Field Marshal Lord Guthrie for exceptionally generously giving me his collection of books on the Imperial and Royal Army and to the late Lieutenant-General Sir Robin Carnegie, that fine cavalry officer and even finer man, for many happy discussions on the Dettingen campaign and the War of the Austrian Succession.

My thanks also go to my long-suffering agent Kate Hordern and my indefatigable editors Heather McCallum, Candida Brazil and Tami Halliday and, above all, to my former horn teacher and mentor Dr William H. Salaman without whose conscientious editorial scrutiny this text would never have been published. The Surveyor of the Queen's Pictures, Desmond Shawe-Taylor, arranged for me to examine the magnificent drawings and prints of the Habsburg army in the Royal Collection as well as the Lawrence portraits of the Archduke Charles, Prince Schwarzenberg and the Emperor Francis in the Waterloo Chamber at Windsor Castle. I should also like to take this opportunity to thank my dear friend Dr Raimund Kerbl who placed at my disposal his incomparable library of Austriaca in Salzburg and whose hospitality I have enjoyed over so many summers. I am also grateful to Hannah Landsman of the Jewish Museum in Vienna whose 2014 exhibition on the First World War was the outstanding Austrian contribution to the many commemorative events organised in Europe that year.

In life, geography and timing often play a greater role than birth and hierarchy. It was my very good fortune to have benefited quite fortuitously over the years from conversations with many for whom the Habsburg army was more than just a fading memory. When I arrived in Trieste in 1979, I had no inkling that I should meet and form a friendship with Gottfried von Banfield, until his death in 1986 the last surviving holder of the Military Order of Maria Theresa, and then the last man alive to have been personally decorated by Kaiser Franz Josef. I also enjoyed *en passant* between duties in Vienna and Budapest during the Cold War the frequent hospitality of the Benedictine monks at Pannonhalma in Hungary. The then assistant archivist, Dom Valentine, showed me many of the treasures of that foundation's magnificent library.

I am also grateful in Vienna to Fr. Christoph Martin, John Nicholson, Dr Claudia Lehner-Jobst, Gertraude Annemarie Felderer, Cristina Brandner-Wolfszahn, Ines and Mariano Felder; in Salzburg to Reinhold Gayer, Alfred Miller-Aicholz, Touschi Allés-Trautsmansdorff and Elisabeth Walderdorff. Katharina and Andrew Gammon and Campbell Gordon, as well as in Ischl, EHZ Markus von Habsburg pointed me in some helpful directions.

The late Count Lázló Szapáry (whose father as Austro-Hungarian Ambassador in St Petersburg declared war on the Tsar in 1914) and the late Charlotte Szapáry offered me great kindness over two decades as did the late

Stella Musulin (whose father-in-law drafted the famous 'Ultimatum' of 1914), the late Countess Sophie Nostitz (whose father was assassinated in Sarajevo in 1914) and Jean-Georges Hoyos, son of the Austrian diplomat tasked with acquiring a 'blank cheque' from Berlin in July 1914. I also owe a debt of gratitude to the late Prince Vincenz Liechtenstein who in the summer of 1982 with that characteristic kindness which was the hallmark of his all too brief life arranged with the late Stefan Amsüss for Her Imperial and Royal Majesty, the Empress Zita, to receive me in his parents' castle in Styria on her first visit back to Austria since 1919.

To my wife Emma-Louise and family for whom the demands of this book were at times rather consuming punctuation marks during holidays I am of course, like every married author, eternally grateful.

Im 'Bazar', 28 June 2014

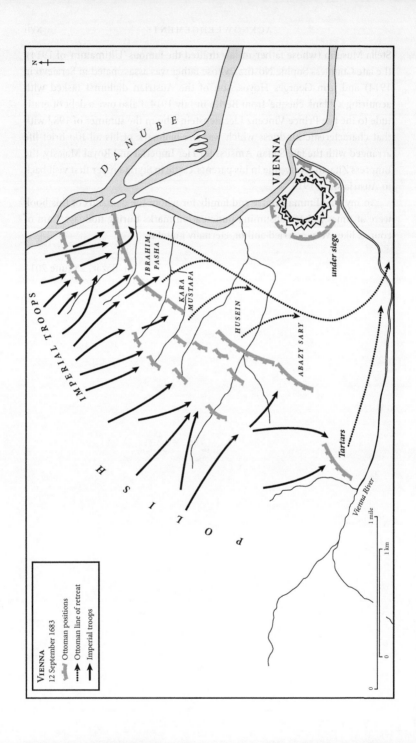

N←

DANUBE

VIENNA

under siege

IBRAHIM
PASHA

KARA
MUSTAFA

HUSEIN

ABAZY SARY

IMPERIAL TROOPS

Tartars

P O L I S H

Vienna River

1 mile

1 km

0

0

VIENNA
12 September 1683

▬▬▬ Ottoman positions
┈┈➤ Ottoman line of retreat
───➤ Imperial troops

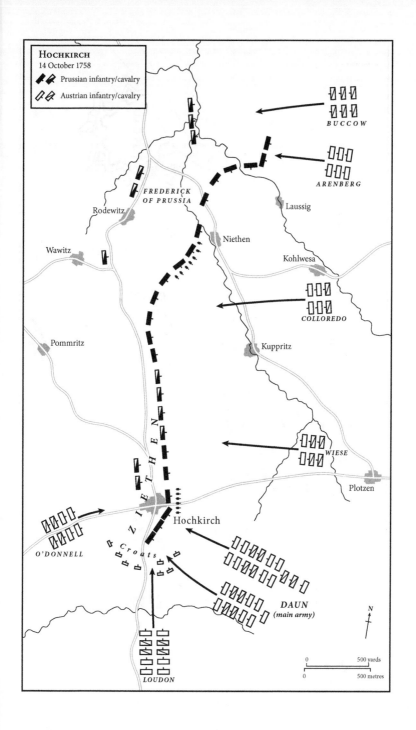

HOCHKIRCH
14 October 1758

Prussian infantry/cavalry
Austrian infantry/cavalry

BUCCOW

ARENBERG

FREDERICK
OF PRUSSIA

Rodewitz

Laussig

Wawitz

Niethen

Kohlwesa

COLLOREDO

Pommritz

Kuppritz

WIESE

Plotzen

ZIETHEN

Hochkirch

O'DONNELL

Croats

DAUN
(main army)

N

LOUDON

0   500 yards
0   500 metres

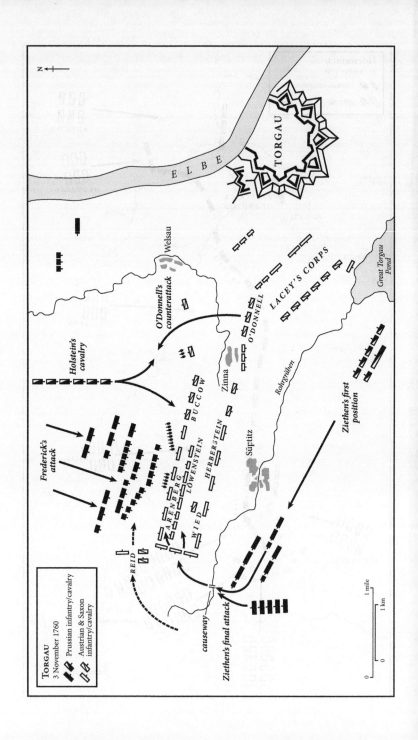

TORGAU
3 November 1760

Prussian infantry/cavalry

Austrian & Saxon infantry/cavalry

TORGAU

ELBE

Welsau

O'Donnell's counterattack

LACEY'S CORPS

Great Torgau Pond

Holstein's cavalry

O'DONNELL

BUCCOW

Zinna

Rohrgräben

Frederick's attack

HERBERSTEIN

Süptitz

Ziethen's first position

ARENBERG

LÖWENSTEIN

WIED

REID

Ziethen's final attack

causeway

0   1 mile

0   1 km

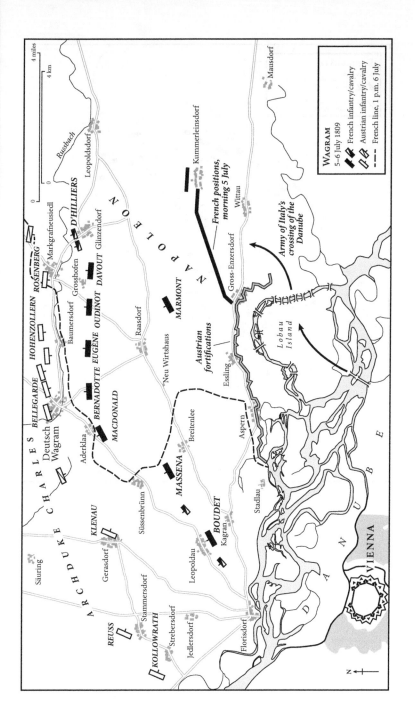

WAGRAM
5–6 July 1809

French infantry/cavalry
Austrian infantry/cavalry
French line, 1 p.m. 6 July

French positions, morning 5 July

Army of Italy's crossing of the Danube

Austrian fortifications

4 miles
4 km

N

ARCHDUKE CHARLES

NAPOLEON

D'HILLIERS
ROSENBERG
HOHENZOLLERN
BELLEGARDE
BERNADOTTE
EUGENE
OUDINOT
DAVOUT
MARMONT
MACDONALD
MASSENA
BOUDET
KLENAU
REUSS
KOLLOWRATH

Russbach
Leopoldsdorf
Markgrafneusiedl
Grosshofen
Glinzendorf
Baumersdorf
Raasdorf
Neu Wirtshaus
Deutsch Wagram
Aderklaa
Süssenbrünn
Breitenlee
Aspern
Essling
Stadlau
Kagran
Leopoldau
Gerasdorf
Stammersdorf
Streberdorf
Jedlersdorf
Florisdorf
Säuring
Kummerleinsdorf
Wittau
Gross-Enzersdorf
Mausdorf

Lobau Island

DANUBE

VIENNA

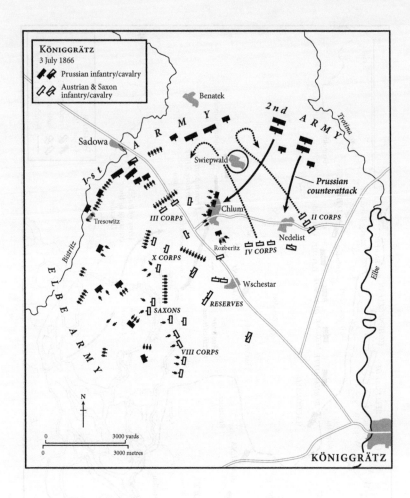

KÖNIGGRÄTZ
3 July 1866

Prussian infantry/cavalry

Austrian & Saxon infantry/cavalry

Benatek

2nd ARMY

Trotina

Sadowa

ARMY

1-st

Swiepwald

Prussian counterattack

Chlum

Tresowitz

III CORPS

II CORPS

Bistritz

Nedelist

Rozberitz

IV CORPS

X CORPS

ELBE

Wschestar

ARMY

SAXONS

RESERVES

Elbe

VIII CORPS

N

0   3000 yards

0   3000 metres

KÖNIGGRÄTZ

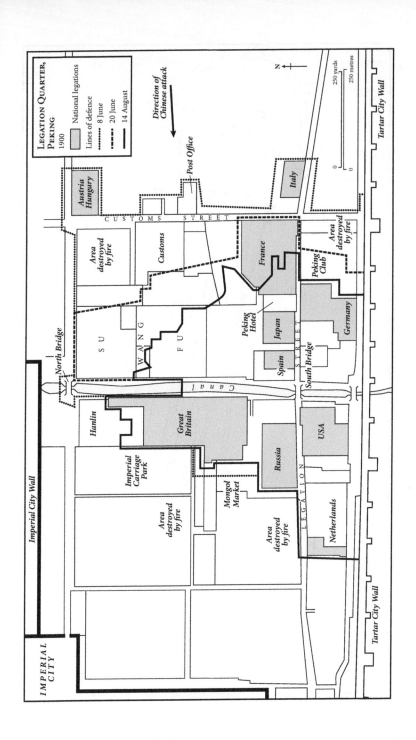

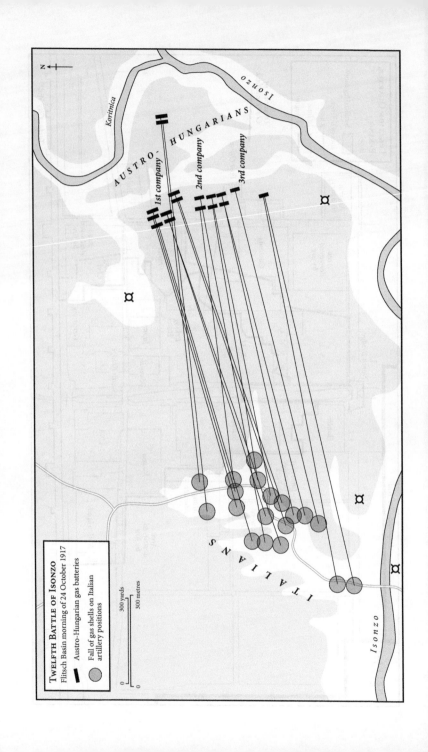

TWELFTH BATTLE OF ISONZO
Flitsch Basin morning of 24 October 1917

▬ Austro-Hungarian gas batteries

⬤ Fall of gas shells on Italian
artillery positions

Isonzo

Kortnica

AUSTRO - HUNGARIANS

1st company   2nd company   3rd company

ITALIANS

Isonzo

N

300 yards

300 metres

0

0

Introduction

'Austria', the Austrian writer Hermann Bahr wrote, 'has not been lucky with its biographers.'[1] If this is the case for Imperial Austria as a structure, it is also true for the Imperial and Royal Army whose efforts supported the empire for so many centuries. Perhaps it was Talleyrand who set the tone for later nineteenth- and twentieth-century disparagement with his famous quip that 'L'Autriche a la fâcheuse habitude d'être toujours battue'. ('Austria has the tiresome habit of always being beaten.')[2]

Nineteenth-century English liberals saw the white-coated troops as the symbol of the machinery which imprisoned peoples. Nowhere was this more marked than in Venice before 1866 where the Austrian officers with their military bands in St Mark's Square were a permanent affront to every liberal Englishman's sense of justice. The Austrian presence was regularly criticised by Ruskin and other influential personalities. Gladstone reinforced the message with his diatribe against Austria for never having done any good 'wherever she was'. As one historian noted: 'The white tunics of the Imperial and Royal Army became in the 19th century the very symbol of repression and autocratic rule.'[3]

In the twentieth century, the English liberal historians' conclusions were echoed by the school of German nationalist historians, many of whom were renegade Austrians who saw Austria as a part of Germany and six hundred years of Habsburg Austria as an historical error. The two schools seemed to link hands over a sea of Austrian military ineptitude. Even when the Germans and the British fell out during the twentieth century, on this one issue they could be guaranteed to agree. In 1917 the former Imperial German Chancellor von Bülow could observe that Germany 'would win the war' even if she emerged from it 'only with Austria'.[4] A.J.P. Taylor, certainly no admirer of Bülow, could portray the later annexation of Austria by Nazi Germany as the 'natural fulfilment of historical processes'.[5] Anthony Eden summed up this viewpoint in 1938 to a colleague at the Foreign Office who expressed regret at the swallowing up of Vienna by the Nazis: 'What is Austria? Five Habsburgs and a hundred Jews.'[6] On this point Eden agreed with Berlin; his words were later frequently and plausibly attributed to Hitler.

Later, in the 1960s, some British schoolchildren, studying history for public exams, were told the story of General 'Hyena' Haynau's flogging of innocent women in the campaigns against Hungarian and Italian insurgents in 1849. On a visit to London, the General had been recognised by some brewery workers in Southwark, who proceeded to throw Haynau into a barrel of ale. To this day the only monument connected with the Imperial Austrian army in England is a plaque in Southwark recalling these picturesque scenes which led to some hard words being exchanged between Queen Victoria and her Foreign Secretary Palmerston. A pub recalling happier days of the old Anglo-Austrian coalition against Napoleon, the 'Archduke Charles', in nearby Little Trafalgar Street, closed several years ago.

Haynau was a brute; in Radetzky's phrase, 'a razor to be used sparingly',[7] and may have deserved far worse than anything the brewers of London could inflict upon him. His inclusion in the 'Hall of Heroes' in the Vienna Arsenal still causes a frisson of unease for the historically aware English visitor but his elevation to one of the Austrian bogeymen in English folklore is a distortion, though one symptomatic of a wider attitude.

Even as patriotic an old Austrian as Lewis Namier could dismiss talk during the Second World War of Austria's 'historic mission' as 'good counter reformation stuff'.[8] For Namier's pupil, A.J.P. Taylor, Imperial Austria was by 1914 a 'corpse'.[9] Amputation or the removal of parts of the Empire to preserve the core 'was no longer possible. The patient was dead and amputation would have implied the possibility of survival.' While Taylor was still teaching at Oxford, this theme was expanded at Cambridge by a young Scot, Norman Stone, who delighted in the multiple absurdities of the k. (u.) k. (Imperial and Royal) army's last war. 'For in Vienna there was an immense gap – perhaps more than anywhere else between ideals and reality.'[10]

During five years' residence in Vienna, I too found the temptation to give vent to one's frustrations with Viennese methods irresistible. The workings of the Austrian temperament, climate and political culture on a young mind of the late 1970s were prone to emphasise the ridiculous at the expense of more dispassionate analysis. With the virulent partisanship of youth the bricks that were thrown at the edifice were large and heavy.

Time imparts perspective. This book sets out to explore whether the Habsburgs' army's reputation for inefficiency, incompetence, general unreliablilty, and even cruelty, is at all justified. Can the view that the Austrian armed forces were consistently weak and poorly led compared to most of their opponents really be proven? Were they hopelessly outclassed against Frederick's Prussians, or doomed to be routed by Napoleon and later Moltke? Did the Habsburg armies offer, as one historian recently noted, 'a truly lamenatable performance' in the First World War, crumbling and melting away?[11] How did an army of so many disparate national elements hold together for so long? What was the secret of the Habsburgs' armies' ability to serve one family in organising the states of Central and Eastern Europe into a coherent and secure single entity whose prosperity and security have been so difficult to replicate in modern times? In the process of answering these questions, a commonly accepted narrative can perhaps be enriched by an unfamiliar perspective on many critical events in modern European history.

The Habsburg army was certainly like no other in Europe. After the Theresian reforms, it achieved a level of cohesion and efficiency which, until the advent of Napoleon, was second to none. Everything the Empress Maria Theresa touched endured for more than a century. In many cases, institutions she founded have survived in Central Europe intact to this day. Burning disputes that tore apart the armies of other European states found a solution in the Austrian army. The French deployment of thousands of disgruntled Irish to fight against their English sovereign, as occurred at Fontenoy, could never have happened to troops from a Habsburg army. Like the state it defended, the Austrian army expressed the idea that dynastic, cultural, geographic and economic relations were more important than national identity. Even the rebellious Hungarians of 1848–49 were in theory at first fighting for their King, the Habsburg Emperor. The Imperial army was supranational. Among its ranks, members of twenty different nations, in return for knowledge of 86 German words of command, were vouchsafed equal treatment.

This army was often indifferent to the personal religious beliefs of its soldiers. The Habsburg dynasty may have been the backbone of the Counter-Reformation but its armed forces developed eventually into an institution that was truly multi-confessional. Many of Wallenstein's officers were not Catholics and under Maria Theresa (1717–80), Protestants enjoyed almost total equality of opportunity in her army. They would not enjoy such rights in civilian life until Joseph II (1741–90) introduced his Patent of Toleration in 1778. This did not mean that there were not factions within the army which inflamed tensions along confessional lines. There were traces of this under Charles VI (1685–1740) and even in the aftermath of Königgrätz in 1866.

Nevertheless, by 1918, the army's most highly decorated regiments were made up of Bosnian Muslims and Alpine Catholics, not infrequently commanded by Jewish officers and led by a general whose father had been a stalwart of the Serbian-Orthodox community. Under Kaiser Franz-Josef, anti-Semitism was a penal offence. The Emperor even intervened personally when he thought Jewish officers in his army were victims of discrimination. The Dreyfus affair, which demoralised the French military system in the late nineteenth century, could not have occurred in the Austrian army. The narrow exclusivity of the German army with its Prussian Junker officer caste – all Lutheran men with 'names like the sound of distant cannon fire' – was also alien to the Habsburgs' forces.

Religious tolerance, even in the days of the Josephinian Enlightenment, did not imply a totally secularist agenda. The dynasty's own piety was always expressed in the army's ethos and customs. The Habsburg army's rallying cry was 'With God and Kaiser for the Fatherland'. When the gifted Croat general Jellačić was made governor (Ban) of Croatia, his instalment speech was rich in devotional phrases invoking the Virgin Mary. Even as late as 1914, the Chief of the General Staff Conrad's public affair with a married woman cast a shadow over his relations with the heir to the throne, Archduke Franz Ferdinand.

Usually the army's relationship with the dynasty transcended confessional considerations. From the moment on 5 June 1619 that it saved the prayerful Archduke Ferdinand from the clutches of the Bohemian Protestant nobility, it sealed an unbroken bond between sovereign and soldier. Henceforth, the armed forces existed to serve the dynasty. The army would, if necessary, defend the Habsburgs against its own aristocracy. Right up to the end of its existence in 1918, the army's composition and way of making war were always subordinate to the interests of the Habsburg House.

Military strategy reflected this. No Austrian army could hazard trying to destroy its opponents if it ran the slightest risk of annihilation itself. Adventurous tactics posed a threat to the dynasty. Excessive daring or sponta-neous military gambles were not part of the Habsburg manual of warfare. The army always had to be able to fight another day, to defend the dynasty. War was not to be fought to the death of the last cavalry subaltern. The Napoleonic revolution in military tactics, especially its belief in the complete destruction of an opponent's capacity to fight, provoked a fundamental overhaul of the Habsburg military machine but, even under the Archduke Charles, the greatest of its generals, the Austrians never risked their army 'va banque'. Thanks to this strategy, the Habsburg army, in almost every war it fought, recovered from initial defeats, raised its game and became a more effective fighting machine. Between 1620 and 1918 it won more than 350 major victo-ries, a number far greater than its defeats.[12] It never suffered the fate of the

Prussian army at Jena in 1806, wiped out in an afternoon, and crippled for years as a fighting force.

The interests of the dynasty demanded much of its generals. The fate of Benedek, the hapless Austrian commander defeated by the Prussians at Königgrätz in 1866, reflected the unhesitating obedience the dynasty expected of its senior officers. Benedek had only accepted command at his Emperor's insistence. When he was made the scapegoat for the defeat, he never once criticised his sovereign or his brother officers, several of whom had disobeyed his orders. He accepted full responsibility for the debacle. He even threatened to divorce his wife if she did not stop complaining about the Emperor's shoddy treatment of him.

Following 1866, the army was re-equipped. By 1914, it had not fired a shot in anger for a generation. Unlike its Serbian and Russian opponents, the Austro-Hungarian army went into the First World War entirely unprepared to fight a modern war. It fought without interruption for more than four years, defying Entente expectations that it would quickly fall to bits through internal tensions and nationalist rivalries. It is only in the jagged peaks of the Dolomites that one can begin to appreciate the enormous feats of human endurance that these forces were called upon to perform. The barren limestone rock, splintered under shellfire, magnified a thousand times the effect of every shell burst. In sub-zero temperatures, soldiers tunnelled and counter-tunnelled through the ice to emerge facing each other at point blank range thousands of feet above the mountain floor. As one historian noted, 'one can be freshly amazed that Italians and Austrians alike managed to exist at all let alone fight in such conditions – and to marvel at historians and military critics who generalise comfortably about the poor fighting qualities of both armies'.[13]

The Habsburg army first took on a recognisable shape under Maximilian I (1459–1519) when the first infantry formations were created from mercenary Landsknechte (lit. serfs of the land). The late medieval tradition of single mounted combat still prevailed but uprisings in Flanders and Switzerland had shown that organised foot soldiers could defeat groups of knights. Maximilian encouraged the establishment of the Landsknechte, supplying them through a system of arsenals that radiated across his domains from Innsbruck to Graz and Vienna. We do not know when precisely the first of these infantry were raised, but by 1479 they had appeared on the battlefields of the Hussite wars and by 1486 Maximilian's campaigns in Italy saw their extensive deployment.

These soldiers often lacked discipline. They had no formal system of officers; no structured pyramid of command. After the Sack of Rome in 1527, the dynasty quickly realised that it did not have so much a loyal army as an armed mob. One way of enforcing discipline was to create a group of military leaders whose behaviour and personal qualities could impress and command the rank and file. The need for officers of the highest moral calibre suddenly became urgent. The moment of the aristocracy had arrived and 'adelmässig' (noble-like) men, who could organise and lead, were brought in to become the core of a new military system. By the eve of the Thirty Years War, cavalry and infantry regiments had begun to take shape under the guidance of a new generation of aristocratic officers who were increasingly expected to lead lives of exemplary conduct. At a time of religious upheaval, it was not a great leap for these officers to move towards a closer relationship with a devout Catholic dynasty, especially as there were in the first quarter of the seventeenth century huge material rewards to be reaped from confessional loyalty.

Both the army's opportune appearance on the 5 June 1619 and its later role during the second Siege of Vienna were depicted at the time, and subsequently, as iconic events in the defence of the Catholic faith.[14] Later, after 1848, the great Austrian statesman Prince Felix zu Schwarzenberg initiated a prestigious consular presence in Jerusalem to identify the shattered but recovering monarchy with its Catholic roots. Schwarzenberg dreamt of Austria as a Catholic superpower. From the beginning, the Habsburgs had embodied the obligations of a universal Catholic monarchy. Rudolf I (1218–91) demonstrated a piety which exalted him in comparison with other monarchs. His sucessors developed the tradition. Several popular Habsburg legends reinforced this. The story of how Rudolf I had encountered a priest carrying the Holy Sacrament was widely retold. Rudolf had offered the priest his horse to cross a raging stream and had then given him the animal as a present, because 'he did not wish to use a horse for fighting or hunting which had carried the Lord'.[15]

The oldest version of this tale was recorded less than fifty years after Rudolf's death in 1291. Later versions strengthened the special veneration of the Habsburgs for the Blessed Sacrament, building on Pope Urban IV's establishment of the Feast of Corpus Christi in 1264. This feast became one of the annual highlights of the military calendar under Charles V (1500–58). Charles, stunned at Henry VIII's execution of Thomas More and John Fisher, told Eliot, the British Ambassador: 'We should have willingly surrendered two of our richest kingdoms in order to have had two such men in our Empire'.[16]

Later, Austrian Catholics found Joseph II's 'sceptre both a prop and scourge'.[17] But for all his avowedly anti-clerical policies, even Joseph could not countenance removing the image of the Virgin from his army's battle-flags. His famous 1785 Edict granting the 'protection of the state' to Masonic lodges warned that he would not tolerate 'excesses harmful to religion'. Some battle-flags during the Josephinian period showed the Virgin crowned by the Trinity, implying that God's dominion over the world was in conjunction with the Habsburg Emperor's sovereignty.

Later Habsburg emperors preserved this idiosyncratic Catholicism, which for all its signs of outward devotion never yielded to Rome when the Vatican threatened the dynasty's interests. Prince Eugene's army was deaf to papal protests that it was occupying Vatican territory. Franz-Josef (1830–1916) did not hesitate to veto the Papal conclave's choice of pope in 1906 when he believed the cardinals had chosen an anti-Habsburg candidate. He also took exception to his nephew Franz Ferdinand openly supporting the cause of Catholic schools at the height of the German 'Los von Rom' (Away from Rome) movement. Paar noted that Franz-Josef would happily give up 'all his bishops' for three regiments of cavalry.

The last emperor, Charles, embraced, as much as any Habsburg, the traditional Catholicism of his House. As a young officer in the First World War, he never travelled without his personal prayer-stool. When he died on the island of Madeira in 1922 gazing from his sickbed at the Blessed Sacrament, a note was found on which he had written: 'in all things and at all times I have always asked God's guidance in resolving any challenge'.[18]

Such piety had consequences for the army as the First World War ended. Charles's decision to ignore offers of military support in 1918 undoubtedly hastened the army's disintegration. His empire had already all but broken up but he could have used some elements of his army to support his throne. Several units of the Isonzo army had prepared to march on Vienna to help him. The logistical planning was well advanced and the formidable Boroević had prepared the troops. But without a command from the dynasty, neither he nor the 'Kaiserliche Armee' could act. Charles, the closest any Habsburg has come to sanctity, saw his mission to be the welfare of his peoples. The deployment of the army would inevitably have provoked a civil war. That could never have been the last Habsburg Kaiser's preferred method. The Pietas Austriaca, which had been the catalyst in 1619 of the 'Kaiserliche' army's inception, proved, three hundred years later, capable of bestowing upon it the last rites.*

---

* A note on nomenclature: throughout this book I have used Kaiser and Emperor as interchangeable names for the ruling Habsburg. Some English readers associating the word Kaiser exclusively with Germany may initially be confused, but Kaiser was the title of the Habsburg emperors for several centuries before the German Hohenzollerns 'resurrected' the title for their new and very brief period of empire between 1870 and 1918.

As far as possible, I have kept English Christian names for the Habsburg personalities in the book. One obvious exception is Franz-Josef whose Austrian name, so much less ponderous than its English equivalent, was widely used by English observers even while he was alive. Austrian military personalities are without exception rendered in German. The same is true for Hungarians, although I have succumbed to the temptation to give Tisza István his English name: Stephen Tisza.

PART 1

THE HABSBURG CONNECTION

CHAPTER 1

The Kaiser's Cuirassiers

A DYNASTY SAVED

5 June 1619 and the 'Kaiserliche Armee'

The 'Kaiserliche Armee' (Emperor's army) was a name that stuck to the Habsburg forces until their dissolution in 1918. It was a title fashioned in the extraordinary crisis of June 1619. Before that moment no one had thought of the Habsburgs' troops as the personal property of the sovereign. A few dramatic moments changed all that and thenceforth a bond was formed between soldier and monarch which endured for three centuries. The strength of this new relationship was quickly tested in the Thirty Years War. When that conflict threw up in the shape of Wallenstein the greatest warlord of his time, the issue of loyalty became critical. The dynasty was eventually able to rely on its soldiers to eliminate the threat. By the end of this period the Kaiserliche Armee was an undisputed reality.

The first week of June takes Vienna in a haze of heat and dust. Throats become parched as the warm wind raises small clouds of dirt along roads and tracks. The Viennese, irritable at the best of times, fractiously push each other and the stranger aside, addictively and automatically seeking shade and shelter. While the clouds become darker the stifling humidity immobilises even the pigeons, which gather dozily on the surfaces of the dusty courtyards of the Hofburg, the Imperial palace whose apartments were, are and always shall be synonomous with the House of Habsburg.

In June 1619, Vienna had not yet reached its unchallenged position as capital of a great European empire. True, the Habsburgs had come a long way since 1218, when a modest count by the name of Rudolf had brought the family out of the narrow Swiss valleys of his birth and, through a series of battles and later dazzling dynastic marriages, had propelled a family of obscure inbred Alpine nonentities into the cockpit of Europe whence they would become the greatest Imperial dynasty in history. Other countries might have many families over the years to supply their monarchs – the case of England leaps to mind – but the story of Austria and the heart of Europe is really the story of one, and only one, family: the Habsburgs.

By the beginning of the seventeenth century, the Habsburgs as a world power were already past their zenith. The Empire 'on which the sun never set', with its domains across Spain, Latin America and Germany, had split into two on the retirement of Charles V in 1556. The Spanish domains had gone to Charles's son Philip II while the Austrian domains enmeshed with the fabric of the Holy Roman Empire had passed to Charles's nephew Ferdinand. Even England in 1554 when Philip married Queen Mary at Winchester Cathedral had seemed destined to be incorporated permanently into this family's system.

But while the Spanish domains were a more cohesive entity, the Austrian branch, assuming its 'historic' right to the crown of Charlemagne and the Holy Roman Empire, was a rich tapestry of principalities, Lilliput kingdoms and minor dukedoms in which different races owed their allegiance to the Holy Roman Emperor. The title was not hereditary, however much the Habsburgs may have thought it their own. The Emperor was elected by a council of seven princes who gathered at Frankfurt am Main. The Habsburg claim to this title, which from 6 January 1453 they perceived as almost a family right, arose from the possession of their crown lands in Central Europe and above all their title to the Kingdom of Bohemia. Although the Austrian Habsburgs could never really aspire to the global status their family had achieved under Charles V a generation earlier, they were to assume a powerful position in European history.

A half-century after the great division of Charles's Habsburg spoils, Vienna still had rivals. Graz to the south and east and Prague to the west and north were both cities of importance to the Habsburgs. In the latter Rudolf II, philosopher, astrologer and occultist, had set up his capital in 1583, tolerating the 'new' Reformation theologies. In the former, the Archduke Ferdinand after his childhood in Spain and a Jesuit education in Bavaria had ruled the Styrian lands of 'Inner Austria' in a different manner. Between these two very different poles of authority Vienna still had not yet come of age. But in the hot days of June 1619, Vienna was to establish now an unrivalled ascendancy, becoming for a few moments the fulcrum of a pivotal conflict.

On 5 June, as the soporific wind carried the dust across the Hofburg palace towards the great Renaissance black and red 'Swiss Gate', a heated exchange could be heard through the open shutters of the dark masonry above. A sullen and armed mob numbering about a hundred had gathered below to await the outcome of this exchange, intimidating the guards and cursing the name of Habsburg.

In the dark vaulted rooms above the Schweizer Tor the object of all this hostility sat at his desk, facing the mob's leaders, his frame defiant; his expression inscrutable. Diminutive in stature and stiff in countenance Archduke Ferdinand of Graz seemed unequal to the men who, unannounced, had burst into his rooms. These men were tall and rough; their hands large, bony and unmanicured. Their faces were twisted into angry and threatening expressions and the virtue of patience, if they had ever experienced it, was not uppermost in their minds.

They were a gang of Protestant noblemen who had defenestrated two of Ferdinand's representatives, Slawata and Martinic, from the great window of the Hradčany castle in Prague barely a year before, initiating the violent challenge to Habsburg authority which became the Thirty Years War. Their leader, Mathias Thurn, was a giant of a man who had used the pommel of his sword to smash the knuckles of his victims as they held on for dear life to the ledge of the window. That both men had cried for divine intervention and – *mirabile dictu* – had fallen safely on to dung heaps had not in any way been due to Thurn's going easy on them. Moderation was not his strongest suit. And now on this stifling day in Vienna, Thurn was again in no mood for negotiation. His large-boned fists crashed down on the desk in front of him. He may have been Bohemia's premier aristocrat but he was passionate, hot-headed and violent.

Martin Luther's 'Reformation' a hundred years earlier with its challenging practicalities, rejection of Papal corruption, increasing anti-Semitism and radical challenge to the authority of Rome had spread its tentacles across Germany into Bohemia and the new faith had fired the truculence and latent Hussite sympathies of the Bohemian nobility. Two hundred years earlier Jan Hus, the renegade Czech priest, had roused the Bohemians to revolt and he had been burned at the stake in Prague for heresy against the Catholic Church. Now, under Thurn, Hus's legacy of a Bohemian challenge to Catholic Habsburg authority had been reinvigorated with all the pent-up energy of the 'Reformation'. These sparks were literally about to set Europe ablaze.

Ferdinand of Graz

Ferdinand was a pupil of the Jesuits, one of the new orders established in 1540 by the Vatican to combat heresy and invigorate the Church. In 1595, at the age of 18, he had arrived in 'Reformation' Graz on Easter Sunday. When he celebrated Mass in the old faith that day, inviting the population to join him, he was dismayed to find that not a single burgher of Graz appeared. Styria at the end of the sixteenth century was overwhelmingly Protestant. Ferdinand with all the dignity of his upbringing showed no outward sign of disappointment but he immediately set about radically changing this state of affairs.

His Spanish upbringing and his devotion to the Jesuits could only produce one practical result. There were to be no half-measures. Ferdinand publicly proclaimed that he would rather live for the rest of his life in a hair shirt and see his lands burned to a cinder than tolerate heresy for a single day. Within eighteen months, Protestantism ceased to exist in Styria; every Protestant (and there were tens of thousands of them) was either converted or expelled, among the latter the great astronomer Kepler, who travelled to Prague. Every Protestant text and heretical tract was burned, every Protestant place of worship closed. Two weeks was allowed to the population to choose exile or conversion. As an exercise in largely bloodless coercion Ferdinand's measures have no equal. The Styrian nobility capitulated. When during the following Easters, Ferdinand celebrated Mass, the entire population of the city turned out to join him. To this day, as Seton-Watson, the historian of the Czechs and the Slovaks, observed, there is 'no more dramatic transformation in the history of Europe than the recovery of Austria for the Catholic Faith'.[1]

But in 1619 Vienna was not Graz and the Bohemian nobility with their Upper Austrian supporters were not to prove as pliant as their Styrian counterparts. On 5 June 1619, Ferdinand, now 41 years of age, might have been forgiven for believing his Lord had deserted him. Inside the palace, Ferdinand's supporters appeared demoralised and despondent. Ferdinand and his Jesuit confessor alone remained calm. For several hours, as they had awaited Thurn, the Archduke had prostrated himself before the cross. It seemed a futile gesture. The rest of Europe had already written Ferdinand off. France, the leading Catholic power, had withdrawn any offer of help. In Brussels, in the Habsburg Lowlands, members of Ferdinand's family spoke of replacing the 'Jesuitical soul' with the Archduke Albert, a man altogether less in thrall to the vigour of the gathering forces of the Counter-Reformation. Even Hungary, of which, like Bohemia, Ferdinand was theoretically King, appeared to be on the brink of open rebellion.

Ferdinand had abandoned his ill and dying son to hurry to Vienna from Graz towards the end of April in 1619 to meet the emergency in Bohemia head-on and rally the Lower Austrian nobility. But in the seven dry and hot weeks of the spring of 1619 his journey had been less of a pageant and more of a via dolorosa. Everywhere he had encountered refugees from Bohemia and Moravia where, following the defenestration, the rebels had seized church property. Many were monks and nuns from plundered churches and convents.

The Catholics, hunted out of Upper Austria, fell to their knees as their Emperor passed but few imagined this slight man could save them from the perils of their time. When Ferdinand reached Vienna at the end of May 1619, the hot weather had contributed to another pestilence to add to heresy: the plague.

As the Bohemian rebels, Starhemberg, Thurn and Thonradel smashed their way into the Hofburg they could be confident that all the strong cards were in their hands. How could this little Archduke hope to resist their demands? They would intimidate him and force him to sign documents that would restore their freedom to worship in the new faith, confirm their privileges and above all compel the hated Jesuits to leave the Habsburg crown lands of Styria and Bohemia. If he resisted, well the windows were large and high enough in the Hofburg and, as Thurn must have noticed with satisfaction as he raced up the stairs of the Schweizer Tor, there was no dung heap here to cushion a fall.

For what seemed might be the last time the Habsburg withdrew to his private oratory, and once again prostrate in front of the cross Ferdinand quietly prayed that he was 'now ready if necessary to die for the only true cause'.[2] But, Ferdinand added, 'if it were God's will that he should live then let God grant him one mercy: troops', and, he added as the noise rose without, 'as soon as possible'.[3]

As the Bohemian ringleaders burst into Ferdinand's rooms, one of their number, Thonradel, seized the collar of Ferdinand's doublet. According to one account, Thonradel forced the Archduke to sit down at his desk. Taking a list of their demands out of his own doublet, the rebel placed them on the desk in front of the Archduke and screamed in Latin: 'Scribet Fernandus!'

What would have happened next had these men remained undisturbed and allowed to continue this rather one-sided dialogue will never be known for at precisely this moment the sound of horses' hooves and the cracked notes of a distant cavalry trumpeter brought the confrontation to an abrupt halt.

As the clatter of horsemen wheeling below brought both the Archduke and his persecutors to the window, no one was arguably more surprised than Ferdinand. Below, to the consternation of the crowd, were several hundred Imperial cuirassiers under their colonel, Gilbert Sainte-Hilaire. The regiment was named after their first proprietary colonel: Count Heinrich Duval de Dampierre.

Sainte-Hilaire had been sent to the Archduke's aid by the only member of Ferdinand's family not to have deserted him: his younger brother, Leopold, from Tyrol. The cuirassiers had ridden hard from the western Alps and reached Vienna via Krems. Their timing was impeccable. Ferdinand straightened himself up and noticed that the confidence of even the most brutal of his opponents had evaporated. Thurn was too much of a realist to try to settle accounts with Ferdinand surrounded by loyal cavalry. As Sainte-Hilaire's men dismounted and with swords drawn raced up the stairs to the Habsburg, the rebels adopted almost instantly a very different mien. No more blood, they insisted, should be spilt. Thurn and his men bowed and withdrew.

Whatever the precise sequence of the encounter – and modern Jesuit historians challenge some of the details – there can be little doubt that had Ferdinand yielded that June day of 1619, the Counter-Reformation in his lands would have stalled and the Habsburgs would have ceased to play any further meaningful part in the history of Central Europe. With Bohemia and Lower Austria lost, the keys to Central Europe would have been surrendered. It is even likely that Catholicism would have become a minority cult practised north of the Alps only by a few scattered and demoralised communities.

For the army and the dynasty, the events of 5 June 1619 were no less critical. They had forged the umbilical cord which would bind them until 1918. Henceforth dynasty and army would mutually support each other. From this day there would be, for three hundred years, a compact between Habsburg and soldier, indivisible and unbreakable through all the great storms of European history. The army first and foremost would exist to serve and defend the dynasty.

For the next three centuries the generals of the Habsburg army would have the events of 5 June 1619 burnt into their subconscious and no commander would risk the destruction of his army, because without an army the dynasty would be put at risk. It was always better to fight and preserve something for another day than to risk all to destroy the enemy. This unspoken compact would snap only in November 1918 on the refusal of the last Habsburg monarch to use the army in a way that would risk their being deployed against his peoples.

The army benefited in many ways from these arrangements. As a symbol of this bond, Ferdinand II granted the Dampierre cuirassiers (and their successor regiments) the right to ride through the Hofburg with trumpets sounding and standards flying. Nearly two hundred years later, in 1810, the Emperor Francis I confirmed the privilege. The regiment could ride through Vienna and set up a recruitment office on the Hofburg square for three days. In addition the colonel of the regiment was to enjoy accommodation in the Hofburg palace whenever he wished and had the unique right of an unannounced audience with the Emperor at any time in 'full armour' ('unangemeldet in voller Ruestung vor Sr. Majestät dem Kaiser zu erscheinen').

These privileges were a modest recompense. The arrival of the Dampierre cavalry not only saved Ferdinand, it marked the turning of a tide. Five days later, on 10 June 1619 in Sablat near Budweis (Budějovice) in southern Bohemia, the Imperial forces under Buquoy defeated Mansfeld, the most able of the Protestant commanders, in the first Catholic victory of the conflict. This victory resonated throughout Europe and Ferdinand, having been written off barely a month earlier, now found himself receiving pledges of support not only from Louis XIII of France but from the many German princes who had earlier misinterpreted the winds of change blowing against the Habsburgs and had dismissed Ferdinand's claims to the title of Holy Roman Emperor.

This title to which the Habsburgs had been elected since the fifteenth century carried mostly prestige. The Empire itself was, for all its insistence on its links with Charlemagne and before him the old western Roman Empire, an incoherent tapestry of different entities. In a world where influence was as important as power, the presence of a Habsburg as Holy Roman Emperor gave that family a dominating say in the affairs of the Germans. If Ferdinand could secure the Imperial title, which became vacant on the death in 1619 of his more tolerant cousin Mathias, it would cut the ground from beneath those rebels who had opposed his receiving the crown of Bohemia in 1617 and the crown of Hungary in 1618, men who with reason feared the Catholic orthodoxy which was Ferdinand's touchstone.

Already, the Kurfürst (Elector) of Trier supported Ferdinand's claim to the leadership of the Holy Roman Empire. The Catholic League led by Maximilian of Bavaria also declared itself for Ferdinand. At the last moment, the news in the autumn of 1619 came from Prague that the rebels in a desperate step had elected as their king the Protestant Elector Palatine, Frederick, a 25-year-old Calvinist and mystic who believed in a Protestant Union of Europe. But it was too late: Ferdinand had been elected two days earlier unanimously (even with the votes of the Palatinate) as Holy Roman Emperor or Kaiser. The new Kaiser set about impressing his authority on his domains immediately.

The structure of Ferdinand's army: Wallenstein

In theory, Ferdinand, as Kaiser, had at his beck and call a Reichsarmee but this concept was not worth the paper on which it was written. The German princes who made up the patchwork of the Holy Roman Empire had long had local forces to support their own interests but the 'right' of the Kaiser to require the supply of a contingent was a frequent source of contention. The circumstances of the Reformation forced the Kaiser to appoint two Field Commanders, one Catholic and one Protestant.

Such contradictions did not make any easier the so-called *Simplum* whereby a minimum of 40,000 soldiers were in theory available to the Emperor. Other difficulties arose from the fact that the local nobility and the Church were reluctant to part with their staff and workers who contributed so much to the upkeep of their estates. As a result, the *Landesaufgebot* (contingent) rarely materialised.

Thus the Kaiser was really only able to establish his own army if he was prepared to finance it exclusively himself. But such an army required logistics and money, both of which were lacking as Ferdinand II at the beginning of his reign found himself confronted with a vast conflict.[4] Unsurprisingly he panicked and called for international support, thus helping transform a local dispute into a full-scale European war.

The presence of the 'usurper' Frederick of the Palatinate and his English wife, Elizabeth, daughter of James I of England (the Winter Queen, as she became known) on the throne of Bohemia further widened the conflict. Frederick's father-in-law sent two British regiments to support him though they never ventured beyond Berlin where they became, fortunately for Ferdinand, 'horribly drunk.'[5]

As these forces gathered against him, the absence of the essentials of war put the Habsburg in a precarious position. He had either to remain a dependant of the Catholic League, whose leader the King of Bavaria was a Wittelsbach and therefore also potentially a rival of the Habsburg family, or he had to make peace somehow with the rebels. Or there was a third way: he could find a warlord prepared to organise his war effort in return for Imperial 'favour'.

In Albrecht Eusebius Wallenstein (1583–1634), who was raised to the rank of Duke of Friedland in 1625, Ferdinand was fortunate to find a man who was prepared to build an army for the Emperor from entirely private funds. Wallenstein, the scion of a cadet branch of the Waldstein family, had fought against the Turks and had converted to Catholicism under Jesuit instruction. Marrying a wealthy widow with impeccable connections he had defected to the Imperial cause in 1619, shortly after Dampierre's cuirassiers had saved Ferdinand in Vienna.

Through the Jesuits, Wallenstein came to be trusted by the Archduke. The first encounter between this inscrutable monarch and the blunt warlord cannot have been easy for either party. Wallenstein had a reputation for violence: he had flogged half to death one of his servants when he was a student. Ferdinand, on the other hand had learnt from the events of June 1619 that in an age of violence he was defenceless without troops. Might Wallenstein be the answer to his prayers?

This 'soldier under Saturn', as a later biographer called him, as well as being the greatest commander of his age also offered the Habsburgs a way of making war which was truly new, relying on artillery and cavalry to an unprecedented extent. Discipline and leadership were organised along strict lines of command indifferent to the religious controversies of the time. In return Wallenstein sought not money, for Ferdinand's treasury was empty, but the one thing the Habsburg had in abundance, thanks to the turmoil in Bohemia: land and titles.

As the conflict in Bohemia progressed through the 1620s it provided a once in a lifetime opportunity for a radical reorganisation of wealth and a comprehensive redrawing of the aristocracy. The revolt of the Bohemian nobles brought the House of Habsburg the power of redistribution on a vast and hitherto unprecedented scale. It is estimated that some 670 estates changed hands as vast tracts of Bohemian territory were stripped from the rebels and given to 200 adventurers and officers prepared to embrace the Catholic faith. These included such men as the Friulan Collalto and Strassoldo, the Italian Gallas, Colloredo, Montecuccoli and Piccolomini (who received respectively Reichenberg, Nachod and Opočno) as well as such Celtic miscreants as Leslie and Butler (Neustadt and Hirschberg).

None benefited more from this unique redistribution than Wallenstein himself, who set about erecting at the heart of Europe, along the strategically vital Bohemian and Saxon frontier, a territory which would furnish him not only with prestige but with the wealth in agriculture and minerals needed to sustain a vast army. No costs were to be incurred by the Imperial house. All Wallenstein sought was the required charter of authority and the freedom to choose his officers and recruitment depots. The charter was quickly granted by Ferdinand, who also gave Wallenstein the impressive designation of 'General-Colonel-Field-Captain of the Imperial Armada'.

Armed with this title and his logistical genius, Wallenstein set about granting recruitment patents to various warlords and landowners who pledged to equip and dress their 'regiments', whereupon they would be assembled for the Kaiser's strategic wishes. At this point the Kaiser undertook to pay the soldiers. But even when the Kaiser failed to pay, Wallenstein, supported by a network of financiers, raised the vast sums necessary to create the conditions which enabled him to be the closest Europe north of the Alps had ever seen to the 'Condottiere' warlords of the early Renaissance. Throughout the 1620s, Wallenstein's financial architecture kept the bankers of Europe in business.

With money came a new organisation. Each regiment had its *Obristen* or colonels, each of whom was assigned an area for recruitment. The local civilian administration was ordered by the Emperor to support the recruitment as best they could. Once the recruits had received their 'hand-money' they were no longer under civilian law but governed by the rules of war. This system proved most effective but it led invariably to abuses. The financing of the system through the 1620s commercialised every aspect of the art of war. Equipment and soldiers became commodities to be speculated with by consortia of usually canny civilian tradesmen who well knew that the colonels had an interest in keeping their numbers of recruits as high as possible. Perhaps this explains why some accounts have tended to set the size of the armies at about 35 per cent above the actual figure.[6]

The feats of logistics hinted at here could not have been achieved without the help of the tax system, which fell with remarkable consistency through the 1620s on the crown lands of the House of Habsburg. For example, Upper Austria needed to pay 53,000 gulden (in modern values $53 million, at a rate of 10 gulden = $1,000). Silesia needed to finance the equipment for 28 regiments while in Lower Austria a poll tax was levied which cost every landowner 40, every priest 4, every doctor 30 and every craftsman 6 gulden. Even servants contributed, though only15 kreutzer (100 kr. = 1 gulden). In this way a regiment of foot soldiers cost about 260,000 gulden a year while a regiment of cavalry was 450,000 gulden a year, each regiment consisting of between 1,200 and 2,000 men. Each foot soldier cost the Kaiser 8 gulden while each cavalryman cost a staggering 20 Reichthaler ($20,000: 10 gulden = 1 Reichthaler). These costs were of course dwarfed by that of the new technology: artillery. Twelve guns and their crews cost at least 600,000 gulden a year.

Wages reflected rank but were modest. The Colonel received 185 gulden, his Lieutenant-Colonel 80 and so on down to the ordinary foot soldier who received 3.5 Reichthaler a year. According to a document dated 1623 from Znaim (Znojmo) each foot soldier received 2 pounds of bread, one pound of meat, 2 pints of beer or one pint of wine each day. A cavalry captain by contrast was entitled to 20 pounds of bread and 12 pounds of meat, two hens, half a sheep or cow, 8 pints of wine and 12 pints of beer (!). These 'rations' of 1623 contain the concluding sentence signed by Field Marshal Tilly that troops 'requiring more than this should pay for supplies out of their own money'.[7]

Tilly and the evolution of tactics

Count Jean Tserclaes Tilly (1559–1632) was another outstanding product of Jesuit training. First seeing service in Spain, the Walloon learnt the art of war from the age of 15, serving under the Duke of Parma in his war against the Dutch. In 1610, he was appointed commander of the forces of the Catholic League, established in 1609 as a loose alliance of Catholic principalities and minor states. Like Wallenstein, Tilly brought in important reforms, especially from his experience of the formidable Spanish infantry. Nicknamed the 'monk of war', he soon proved to be a highly capable organiser of infantry tactics, which were quickly adopted by Ferdinand's troops.

The infantry at this stage still consisted of pikemen and musketeers. The pikemen wore armour and carried a pike, which at that time was between 15 and 18 feet long, made of ash with a sharp metal point. Their officers carried shorter pikes with coloured ribbons. The musketeers were a kind of light infantry with a light metal helmet, later replaced by a felt hat. The heavy musket they carried needed to be rested on a wooden pole with an iron fork to be fired. The 'ammunition' was contained variously in a bandolier, a flask of gunpowder and a brass bottle of combustible material, the so-called *Zundkraut* as well as a leather bag containing small metal balls. A small bottle of oil was also carried to ensure that the 'alchemy' required to fire the weapon functioned smoothly. This was far from straightforward. A hint of the complexity of firing this primitive musket is given by the fact that ninety-nine separate commands were needed to fire and reload the weapon.

A further forty-one commands existed for dealing with the musket at other times. As this suggests, the need to increase the rate of fire and simplify the munitions were priorities for all commanders throughout the Thirty Years War. These problems would only be solved with the advent of the Swedes, who entered the fray against the Habsburg in 1630. They had a modern solution to many of these problems: the introduction of small cartridges wrapped in paper.

The only tactical unit at this time was the company, which was deployed in a large square made up usually of between 15 and 20 companies. This formation was 50 men deep with its flanks protected by 10 rows of musketeers. Despite much practice at marching to form such elaborate formations as the so-called 'Cross of Burgundy' or 'Eight-pointed Star', it takes little imagination to realise that manoeuvring in such formations was virtually impossible. The idea of marching to a single beat of the drum had still to be widely introduced and cohesive movement was only possible by extended rank.

Where Tilly proved so successful in organising infantry tactics, Wallenstein proved no less formidable in handling cavalry. Cavalry like infantry were divided into heavy and light. The heavy cavalry were cuirassiers and lancers, both armoured down to their boots. In addition to their main weapon, lancers were also armed with a sword and two pistols, symbols of their privileged status as bodyguards to the commanders in the field. The cuirassiers carried the heavy straight sabre or 'pallasch', which was designed to cut as well as thrust.

The horsed 'carabiniers' were organised as light cavalry as their only armour was a metal helmet and a light breastplate. Equipped with a shorter musket and 18 cartridges, these horsemen also carried pistols and a short sword. The dragoons were also equipped with a short musket and were indeed originally horsed musketeers. As the barrels of their muskets were often decorated with a dragon, they became known as dragoons. Deployed as advance guard cavalry they carried an axe with which, in theory, they could batter down doors and gates.

To these conventional groupings Wallenstein added new elements. An important part of the horsed advance guard was the 'ungrischen Hussaren', or Hungarian hussars. Together with the Croats they formed the irregular elements of the army who could be deployed to plunder and terrorise their opponents as well as perform scouting and reconnaissance.

The origin of the term 'hussar' to this day is a source of debate. The word most likely stems from the Slavic *Gursar* or *Gusar*. Other theories link the word to the German *Herumstreifender* or *Corsaren*; this last with its imagery of piracy perhaps being nearer to the truth than many a Hungarian would care to admit. Famous for giving their enemies no quarter, they became the nucleus of what would become the finest light cavalry in the world.

As with the infantry, the cavalry were grouped into companies. Often these were called *Cornetten* and hence the title of the junior officer of each such company was 'Cornet'. As these were formed into a square, the custom arose to call four of these companies a 'squadron' from the Italian *quadra*, meaning square. In theory every cavalry regiment consisted of ten companies each of a hundred riders but in reality no cavalry regiment had more than 500 men.

Drill of these formations was aimed at disordering infantry by charging the last 60 paces at the enemy's pikemen or cavalry. There was to be no firing from the saddle until the cavalry could 'see the white in the eye of the foe' ('Weiss im Aug des Feindt sehen thut').[8] Led by such Imperial officers as Gottfried Pappenheim, famous for his many wounds and refusal to be impressed by titles, or the redoubtable Johann Sporck, a giant of a man with hair like bronze, perhaps the most feared cavalry general of his time, the Imperial cavalry was trained in shock tactics relying on aggression and surprise to demoralise their opponents.

The artillery remained a strict caste apart. Each unit of artillery was in theory organised to have 24 guns of different calibre. Mortars and other guns were added to each unit. Every gun had as its team a lieutenant and eleven gunners. These were supported by the so-called *Schanzbauern* or Pioneers, who were organised into units as large as 300 under an officer of the rank of Captain. The unit had its own flag made of silk which displayed as its badge a shovel and its men were also skilled carpenters able to strengthen bridges, not just demolish them.

Imperialist versus rebel

Such an army for all its appearance was not in any way comparable to the armies of later years. There was no obvious way of telling one army from another. As any army advanced across the ravaged plains of Germany during the horrors of the Thirty Years War, it was accompanied by bands of irregulars, bandits and marauders, including spies and other n'er-do-wells who plundered the local landscape like locusts.

Armies learnt to distinguish each other by what would in modern parlance be called 'call signs'. At Breitenfeld in 1631, a battle which threw into sharp relief the energy and skill of the Swedes under their king, Gustavus Adolphus, the Imperialists under Tilly shouted 'Jesus-Maria' as they fought while the Swedes used the phrase: 'God with us'. As battles were fought and won, it became the custom to reward the officers and men with financial gifts. Thus after Lutzen, General Breuner was given 10,000 gulden while the brave Colloredo regiment was awarded collectively 9,200 gulden.

The names of the Imperial officers came from two sources. The aristocrats who had preferred to convert to Catholicism took full advantage of the political support Ferdinand offered them. Many of the names we encounter here for the first time will pop up again and again in our story: Khevenhueller, Trauttmannsdorff, Liechtenstein, Forgách, Eggenberg and Althan (these last two left behind them world-class works of architecture to commemorate their position and wealth: Schloss Eggenberg, on the outskirts of Graz, and Vranov – Schloss Frein – in Moravia). Then came a group whose careers were made in the long Turkish wars. These included not only Ferdinand's enemies Thurn, Hohenlohe, Schlick and Mansfeld, but a large number of his most important military commanders from Wallenstein downwards.

By 1620, Ferdinand was ready to move on to the attack. He now had no fewer than five separate armies with which to renew the offensive. Dampierre held Vienna with 5,000 men. Bucquoy was advancing along the Wachau with 21,000; from Upper Austria, the Duke of Bavaria, Maximilian, advanced alongside Tilly with 21,000, while a Spanish army invaded the Lower Palatinate. The previously Protestant lands of Lower Austria and Upper Austria were cleared of the rebels and more than sixty Protestant noblemen fled to Retz with their families. Half of these would be proclaimed outlaws. Both provinces had been recovered for Ferdinand and the Church with barely a shot being fired.

As the armies advanced into Lusatia and Moravia, the irregular forces of the Emperor began to introduce a far more brutal and indiscriminate warfare. Plundering, rape and other atrocities became widespread, especially among the Cossacks sent by the Polish Queen who was Ferdinand's sister. On the rebels' side Hungarian irregulars proved no less capable of atrocities and had in Ferdinand's own words 'subjected the prisoners to unheard of torture . . .' killing pregnant women and throwing babies on to fires.[9] Ferdinand would later note: 'So badly have the enemy behaved that one cannot recall whether such terror was the prerogative of the Turk.'[10]

These acts of cruelty set the tone for much of what occurred later. On 7 November 1620 Maximilian and Tilly finally reached the outskirts of Prague where they faced the new rebel commander, Prince Christian of Anhalt, who had taken up a potentially strong defensive position exploiting the advantage of the so-called White Mountain, in reality more of a hill, a few miles to the west of Prague.

Anhalt's forces consisted of about 20,000 men of whom half were cavalry. Some 5,000 of these were Hungarian light cavalry. His artillery consisted of only a few guns. The entrenching tools to convert his position into something more formidable never arrived. Thus was the stage set for destruction of the Bohemian rebels. The Imperial forces were superior in artillery, but more importantly in morale. The commanders were divided on what they should do next and it was only when an image of the Madonna whose eyes had been burnt out by Calvinist iconoclasts was brandished in front of Wallenstein's ally Bucquoy that he suddenly ordered the attack.

Anhalt deployed his cavalry but they made no impact on the Imperial horsemen and they fled after an initial skirmish. The Bohemian foot followed rapidly and even the feared Moravian infantry dissolved when Tilly appeared in front of them. The Battle of the White Mountain was over by early afternoon. The Imperial forces had suffered barely 600 casualties and the rebels more than 2,000 but what turned this skirmish into a decisive victory was Tilly's determination to keep up the momentum against a demoralised enemy. Prague, despite its fortifications, surrendered as rebel morale everywhere collapsed. Frederick joined the fugitives streaming out of the city to the east, leaving his crown behind him along with the hopes of a Protestant Europe. As the Czech historian Josef Pekař rightly observed, the Battle of the White Mountain was the clash between the German and Roman worlds and the Roman world won. Had the German world won, Bohemia would have rapidly been absorbed by Protestant Germany and Czech culture would have ceased to exist.[11]

For Protestantism, with the departure of the Winter King and his wife into exile in Holland, the tide of history which had seemed to run in the direction of the new faith in the sixteenth century now appeared to have turned irrevocably. Increasingly perceived as divisive, unhistorical and radical, Protestantism unsettled those who feared anarchy and extremism. The population of Prague sought refuge in the old certainties and comfortable verities of the Catholic Church and within a year the Jesuits had made the city into a bulwark of the Counter-Reformation.

As Professor R.J.W. Evans has pointed out, the demoralised forces of the new faith had little reply to the intellectual and practical solutions of the Society of Jesus.[12] Those who sought refuge in the occult and Rosicrucian view of the world were 'qualified at best only for passive resistance to the attacks of the Counter-Reformation'.

Moreover not only did Ferdinand's personal piety inspire his subjects through the widespread dissemination of the *Virtutes Ferdinandi II* penned by his Jesuit confessor Lamormaini,[13] but the international flavour of the new orders, like Ferdinand's army, was a powerful intellectual weapon. At the opening of the Jesuit University of Graz the inaugural addresses had been given in eighteen languages. When Ignatius Loyola had founded the Society of Jesus in 1540 he had from the beginning conceived it as a 'military' formation led by a 'general' who expected unhesitating obedience and the highest intellectual and spiritual formation among his recruits. These principles guided Ferdinand's vision of his army. The offensive of the intellect was supported by more practical steps. In 1621, all of the ringleaders of the Bohemian rebels were executed on Ferdinand's orders in the Old Town Square in Prague.

It was typical of Ferdinand II that while these 'Bohemian martyrs' were brought to the gallows, the Habsburg went on a pilgrimage to the great Marian shrine of Mariazell in his native Styria specifically to pray for their souls. In the years that followed, prayer and sword moved in perfect counterpoint for the Habsburg cause. If Ferdinand was the spearhead of spiritual revival, on the battlefield the corresponding military reawakening was to be organised by Wallenstein.

Wallenstein stood out from the newly minted nobility around Ferdinand because of his logistical skills, which he deployed with unrivalled expertise despite his physical disabilities. Plagued by gout which often forced him to be carried by litter, Wallenstein ceaselessly instructed his subordinates to organise his affairs to the last detail. Agriculture was virtually collectivised under his control to ensure that every crop and animal was nurtured efficiently to supply his armies. A fortunate second marriage to the daughter of Count Harrach, one of Ferdinand's principal advisers, brought him yet more support at court. In April 1625, Ferdinand agreed to Wallenstein raising 6,000 horsemen and nearly 20,000 foot soldiers. Wallenstein's force gave the Emperor freedom of manoeuvre. He now had formidable forces to counterbalance the armies of the Catholic League led by Tilly, who always showed signs of answering in the first instance to his Bavarian masters rather than to the Emperor Ferdinand.

Wallenstein's 'system'

At Aschersleben, Wallenstein created a depot for some 16,000 troops. More would follow. By 1628 the Imperial armies would number 110,000, of whom a fifth would be cavalry. From 1628, Wallenstein's prestige grew and he was given control of all forces in the Empire with the exception of those in the crown lands and Hungary. Many foreign soldiers of fortune, including English, Irish and Scottish officers and even well-known German Protestants such as Arnim, joined Wallenstein as the Imperial army rapidly expanded. Despite the religious feuds of his era, the 'Generalissimus' was indifferent to the faith of his commanders. What he valued above all was loyalty and ability.

Wallenstein is largely credited with mastering the logistics of war on a scale hitherto not achieved. By forcing officers to be responsible for the upkeep and pay of their men, Wallenstein obliged villages and towns to contribute to war, thus allowing the impoverished Ferdinand to wage war without regard to the sorry state of his treasury. By levying contributions from enemy states his forces occupied, Wallenstein systematised plunder. In addition, thanks to his own vast resources, he constructed an elaborate system of loans and financing to assist his hand-picked officers with their quotas and his senior commanders with their expenses. By 1628 a colonel in one of Wallenstein's regiments was receiving 500 florins (approx. $500) a week, more than an officer in other armies received in a month. The normal pay for a foot soldier was at this time barely 8 florins a month.[14]

The imposition on the local population defied both convention and even Imperial law. According to this soldiers could demand lodging but were expected to pay for food. In practice this was impossible, owing to the scale of Wallenstein's forces and their vast cohort of camp-followers. The villages and unfortified towns were ruined, with those houses refusing to pay levies often being torched. More funds could be acquired by 'tributes' from wealthy parts of the country, which could be exempted from supplying troops or occupation in return for large payments. Many of these sums were significant; for example Nuremberg paid half a million florins. But the cost, however great, was considered preferable to the destruction that accompanied occupation. Large swathes of Germany thus existed in a state of near-perpetual extortion in which Imperial decrees and laws appeared utterly overtaken by the rules of war. From Saxony to Brandenburg and Pomerania, from Mecklenburg to Württemberg expropriation became the order of the day. Elsewhere, in the crown lands, the 'Soldier Tax' became a weekly feature of urban life.

This 'system', such as it was, could be open to abuse. At a time of mercenary recruitment the commercial possibilities of all these activities were not lost along the many links of the chain. Bribes, 'Spanish' practices such as drawing supplies for non-existent soldiers, flourished in an era where the drawing up of accounts left much to be desired. Nor were these crimes the exclusive prerogative of any one army. For the populace of Germany, the Thirty Years War was truly a terrible era.

Elsewhere in the Habsburg domains taxation was used to preserve the great armouries in the cities of Inner Austria and maintain the Military Frontier which had developed in the late 1570s into a ragged line of frontier posts stretching some fifty miles alongside the Ottoman frontier. This was extended to include the approaches to Graz along the Drave around Varaždin and the area around Karlstadt (Karlovac) in Croatia proper as well as the three sections of the Hungarian frontier. Central funds from the Reichstag covered the costs of the principal garrisons (1.2 million florins a year) but elsewhere families were encouraged to take on the responsibility of particular areas of land, leading eventually to the creation of a warlike caste of military families with their own laws, customs and indeed dialect (Militärgrenze-Deutsch, for example 'Ist Gefällig' for 'Izvolite', which was heard around Koprivnica in eastern Croatia/Slavonia up to the mid-1970s).

That Wallenstein's 'system' was capable of functioning at all was the result of his bankers, notably Jan de Witte who deploying an extensive network raised money for Wallenstein in sixty-seven cities between London and Constantinople. The powerful financiers of the time, de Witte and Fugger, would lend to Wallenstein when they would never lend to a Habsburg, their fingers having been burnt too often in the past by Ferdinand's family's hopelessness with money. But the financial architecture these resourceful and able men now constructed was only possible through generous interest rates and as their financing system came more and more to resemble a giant pyramid scheme it could be sustained only by the sale of vast estates enabled by royal prerogative. Ferdinand dealt with Wallenstein's bills the only way he could – by ceding yet more land to the warlord.

The strategic tide was flowing in Ferdinand's direction. Everywhere the anti-Habsburg coalition was faltering. As the 1620s wore on, Tilly dealt with the Danes at Lutter where in 1626 for 700 casualties he routed an army under Prince Christian, inflicting thousands of dead, wounded and captured.

At one point the battle appeared to be turning in the Danes' favour but the dispatch of 700 of Wallenstein's heavy cavalry turned the tables with dramatic effect.

Wallenstein meanwhile had negotiated a truce with the Hungarian rebel leader Gabor Bethlen, a zealous Calvinist who claimed to have read the Bible twenty-five times and who had led an anti-Habsburg insurrection one of whose victims indeed had been the cavalry officer Dampierre. But though the Hungarian Protestants harboured many grievances against the Habsburgs, without external support there was little they could hope to achieve.

At the same time the Danes had retreated, leaving Saxony and Silesia to Wallenstein's mercy. In May 1627 Wallenstein received the Duchy of Sagan instead of 150,850 florins owed to him by the Emperor, who now continued to write off any further debts to Wallenstein through granting him land. Titles fell to Wallenstein as rapidly as his opponents on the battlefield. He was elevated to Reichsfurst (with its concomitant right of access to the Emperor) and enfeoffed as a duke (Mecklenburg). Even his own coinage began to circulate, to the irritation of the court in Vienna.

The 'Lion of the North'

Inevitably such material riches aroused jealousy. In addition, by 1629 Wallenstein's army had reached three times the size of Tilly's. He bestrode the stage of Central Europe increasingly independent in mind and actions. Moreover, with wealth and prestige he began to turn on those who had supported him. He opposed the Jesuits and in particular their plans to support the Edict of Restitution (later passed in March 1629) whereby they sought to return all property confiscated from the Church back to its lawful owners. This, more than anything, undermined Ferdinand's confidence in his warlord. Wallenstein had grown weary of war and religious sectarianism and his decisions increasingly showed an independence of his Imperial master that could not go unnoticed. At a time when the Counter-Reformation seemed everywhere triumphant his was a lone voice of pragmatism. In 1627, Wallenstein was 'retired' and his own finances began to crumble. Unable to pay his bankers' interest charges he sold property at knock-down prices and, worse, began to borrow at extortionate rates.

Ferdinand hesitated to name a successor. The army, bereft of its leader, became demoralised and paralysed. To deal with this Ferdinand reduced its size to a more manageable 40,000. All his domains would pay a tax to secure the upkeep of the force. In the event of a shortfall, commanders such as Tilly were permitted to levy contributions

Despite his Bavarian masters, Tilly was the ideal candidate to succeed Wallenstein. But he now faced a new escalation in the conflict. As the Protestant cause appeared to wither, a new champion entered the struggle. Gustavus Adolphus of Sweden seeing the danger of a Catholic triumph across the German lands entered the war in 1630. A gifted strategist, backed by the skilled gunsmiths who had made Swedish artillery a byword for excellence, the 'Lion of the North' brought northern discipline and money into the conflict just as the terrible Siege of Magdeburg by Tilly was entering a dramatic phase. This great city, a bastion of the Protestant cause, had become the anvil on which the Imperial hammer was being forged.

Unfortunately the Swede came too late to save Magdeburg: large parts of the city centre were set alight with terrible consequences for its civilian population, whose wholesale slaughter would go down in history as synonymous with the atrocities of the war.[15] There is no escaping the fact that 20,000 of Magdeburg's population perished; and a census taken two years later gave the population as a modest 449.

The news of the atrocities of Magdeburg would be carried across all of Europe, a symbol of the appalling conflict, which by now was more than twelve years old. Determined to avenge Magdeburg, Gustavus Adolphus began to make life for Tilly and the Imperialists very hot indeed. The 'king of snow and ice' had not 'melted under the German sun' as Ferdinand's advisers had promised. At the Battle of Breitenfeld in 1631 Tilly's forces were routed by a combined Swedish and Saxon force which displayed much more pliability of movement than Tilly had expected. The dashing Imperial commander Pappenheim lay wounded in seven places, once more taken for dead.[16]

The fall of Frankfurt on the Oder in April 1631 focused the Imperial mind and Ferdinand began to negotiate with Wallenstein to return. The document reappointing the Generalissimus has not survived, victim perhaps of the sanguinary circumstances of the warlord's death.[17] But we know that Wallenstein was again invested with far-reaching military powers, bordering on dictatorship, though in theory all senior appointments in his army were still subject to Imperial approval.

Only the desperate situation of the Emperor in Germany would have compelled Ferdinand to reinstate Wallenstein. But with Tilly's death on 30 April 1632, the way was clear for Wallenstein to assume unchallenged command of all the Imperial armies. A new regime of training was instigated to reflect the latest tactics of musket volleys and smaller units that the Swedes had introduced. At Steinau, the newly returned commander bided his time as the Swedes began to concentrate all their forces. Angry and impatient missives flew from Vienna demanding action. But to these Wallenstein simply replied that he was teaching the Swedish King a 'new way of making war'. By bottling up the Swedes around Nuremberg, he prevented Gustavus from breaking out until some 29,000 of the Swede's troops had perished from disease and hunger. On 7 November Gustavus halted at Erfurt and decided to force a confrontation with his Imperialist pursuers and at Lützen in 1632 the long-awaited battle between these two masters of the art of war began.

From the beginning Wallenstein displayed superior generalship: securing his right flank with lines of musketeers and moving his cavalry across his front as need arose. A screen of Croats posted by Wallenstein soon dispersed when the fog lifted to reveal two ranks of the Swede's infantry advancing, their pikes lowered towards Wallenstein's defensive positions around the town. After several hours – the Swedes knew only the tactic of frontal assault – around the Imperial centre both armies began to lose cohesion. Wallenstein had earlier ordered Pappenheim to join the main bulk of his forces as soon as possible. On receiving Wallenstein's written orders, Pappenheim had ridden through the night; his arrival with reinforcements rallied the Croats and a counter-attack pushed the balance of the battle slowly in Wallenstein's favour.

Gustavus Adolphus immediately saw the crisis and riding at the head of some cavalry sought to deflect Pappenheim's charge. An earlier wound had deprived the Swedish King of the ability to wear armour. He had in any case always declared that 'God will be my armour'. The absence of a cuirass as he closed with the most violent cavalry in Europe proved fatal. As the Swedish King rode to rally his infantry he was shot and killed, the news of his death rapidly sowing dismay among the Swedish ranks.

But Wallenstein had lost his nerve; he had suffered more than 3,000 casualties as a result of the aggressive Swedish tactics and abandoning his guns he decided to withdraw. At almost the same time, the Swedes, who had lost nearly 6,000 men, were about to retreat when a prisoner told them their opponents were already leaving the battlefield. Thus ended the inconclusive Battle of Lützen, later hailed as a great Swedish victory, though in reality it was a stalemate memorable for the death of the great Gustavus on one side and the loyal Pappenheim on the other. When Wallenstein's men undid Pappenheim's bloodstained tunic, his orders from Wallenstein, drenched in his own blood, fell to the ground (and have survived to this day). The loyal lieutenant had barely read them before thrusting them into his pocket and galloping off to his General.

Wallenstein's use of Croats as skirmishers was innovatory and he would deploy them to harry Arnim (who had changed sides yet again) as he retreated through Lusatia. At Steinau, Thurn surrendered, as did the fortresses of Glogau and Liegnitz. Wallenstein's cavalry began to overrun the Pomeranian lands to the east and north of Berlin. But in the teeth of these undoubted successes, Wallenstein began to lapse into a strange inertia only partly explained by later writers as caused by his obsession with the occult.[18]

Wallenstein's horoscope

Though Rome denounced magic there is little evidence to suggest that the Inquisition strayed north of the Alps.[19] In fact, although magic was a suspect word and many books were on the Index, the works of the great European magicians were readily available and one Jesuit even advised study of some of the texts.[20] The study of the occult was widespread in Ferdinand's army. One of the Imperial generals, Montecuccoli, apparently knew the writings of the magician Robert Fludd almost by heart.[21] Certainly in Central Europe contemporary magical literature was considered almost mainstream. The Habsburgs led the way in the study of the mysteries of nature. As Professor Evans observes: 'Nowhere is the truth more clearly demonstrated that Counter-Reformation learning committed itself heavily in the illicit arts, the better to find out how illicit they really were.'[22]

The great Protestant teacher of the astronomical and astrological arts, Johann Kepler, expelled from Graz by Ferdinand II, was formally employed by Wallenstein to prepare his horoscopes from 1628. Kepler had already worked on them for Wallenstein as early as 1608. One of these horoscopes still survives. It notes that the beginning of the month of March 1634 would prove 'very difficult' for the horoscope's subject.[23]

Whatever the reasons for Wallenstein's sudden lack of energy, Vienna interpreted his unresponsiveness in the most sinister light possible. It did not help that the warlord had not spoken to the Emperor since 1628 or that the Jesuits still harboured resentment towards him. Rumours that Wallenstein sought a compromise peace that would be hostile to the Emperor's interests flourished and from such rumours it was not difficult to deduce the line of reasoning that the warlord was guilty of treason.

The factor that decided Wallenstein's fate was one created to maximise the distrust between warlord and monarch. Wallenstein consistently refused to allow the Emperor's son to assume command in his armies. He thus struck at the very foundation of the monarchy, its legitimacy and hereditary prerogatives. No other action could so plainly challenge Ferdinand's beliefs, position and, above all, authority. Wallenstein's actions were a direct attack on the Emperor's rights. Above all, they threatened the compact sealed in June 1619 that hot Vienna day when Dampierre's horse had saved the dynasty. The later historian Heinrich Ritter von Srbik empathised with Ferdinand; such a challenge justified no compromise; the response had to be 'extreme'.[24]

On 11 January 1634, the snow fell heavily in Graz. At the remarkable schloss which Ferdinand's trusted adviser Count Eggenberg had just built to an astrological design at the heart of which was a so-called 'Planetary Room', Ferdinand took soundings from his closest circle. Eggenberg perhaps explained that his new castle had four towers for each of the seasons and 365 windows, one for each day of the year. Twelve of these, on the *piano nobile*, symbolised the months of the year. Here in this temple to seventeenth-century occult rationalism the decision to eliminate Wallenstein once and for all was finally agreed.[25]

At the same time, while these dark discussions proceeded in Styria, the army and its officers were no less unimpressed by their leader's listlessness that winter of 1634. Piccolomini, an Italian who had done well out of the redistribution of the Bohemian estates, was ambitious to replace Wallenstein. He began a careful campaign against him. When Wallenstein released the Protestant rebel leader Thurn, the very man who embodied the challenge to Habsburg authority, it was a decision taken expressly against the Emperor's orders. The officers did not have to wait long for the signal from their sovereign.

Piccolomini organised the gang of Scottish and Irish officers who were to form the murder squad. Their ringleaders were to be Leslie, Gordon and Devereux. On 24 January 1634 Ferdinand signed the critical document. It reminded the officers of their allegiance to the monarch and released them from Wallenstein's service. As the warlord realised what was happening, he rode to Eger to seek the shelter of his erstwhile Swedish opponents. There on 24 February 1634, in the upper storey of the still beautifully preserved Pachabel house, Wallenstein immobilised by fatigue and gout took to his bed. He had with him four trusted aides who, he knew, would lay down their lives for him. Vienna seemed far away; the support of the Swedes and Saxons nearby.

Three of these men, Terzka, Ilow and Kinsky were invited to dine at a banquet in the Eger fortress nearby. With no thought of treachery they accepted, hanging their swords behind them on the wall. For an hour they ate and drank until their host, the smooth-tongued Leslie, at a prearranged signal nodded and his accomplices burst in with drawn swords shouting 'Vivat Fernandus!' The table was overturned and the windows smashed as the three men loyal to Wallenstein tried to defend themselves. Kinsky died unarmed and only Terzka recovered his sword from the wall to give a good account of himself. Before he was clubbed and stabbed he had managed to break Devereux's sword and kill three of his assailants. The floor was slippery with mingled wine and blood as the assassins grimly set out for Wallenstein's quarters barely five minutes' walk away. On the way they came across Wallenstein's fourth aide, Captain Niemann and cut him down.

Oblivious to these events, Wallenstein slept uneasily in his bed mulling no doubt what he would say to the Swedes when he offered himself up to their protection the following day. Although they had slaughtered four of the general's aides, on reaching Wallenstein's room, at first none of the three chief conspirators dared face alone the sick man who had once held the great armies of Europe in his hand. Leslie and Gordon held back and it was left to Devereux, his hand bleeding from where Terzka had broken his sword to continue the mission. As his sword was useless he seized a halberd and hurried on.

It was just after eleven o'clock. Wallenstein had just taken a cool drink from one of his servants and his boots and sword and coat lay far from his bed. The first note of alarm was the sound of the guard being overpowered in the court-yard below and then a few seconds later the muffled cry of the servant, followed by the sinister thud of his falling body on the stairs. Wallenstein, interpreting these strange noises correctly, pulled himself slowly up and tried to stand as Devereux burst into the room, eyes ablaze. The General began to mouth the word 'Quarter?'

'Faithless rebellious old villain!' the Irishman cried before plunging the halberd into Wallenstein's chest. The terrible weapon pierced the old General, sticking out of his shoulder blades more than a foot. Like a felled tree Wallenstein crashed sideways and lay still.[26]

Many of these assassins later received estates as well as cash for their part in the murder though only Leslie would become a figure of any note in the upper ranks of the new aristocracy. It is perhaps not without significance that all of the principal conspirators would meet hideous deaths within five years of the murder, either on the battlefield or at the hands of the plague.

Wallenstein's lands were broken up and redistributed. If the rank and file officers hoped that they would benefit from the removal of their erstwhile leader they were in for a disappointment. The elaborate financial system, not for the last time in Habsburg military history, bereft of the apex of the pyramid, collapsed, precipitating bankruptcy and impoverishment for scores of young officers who had depended on Wallenstein for all their capital.

The austerities of financial collapse were for Ferdinand of secondary importance. 'Ah my Wallenstein!' cried Ferdinand when the commander's collar of the Golden Fleece was returned to him by one of the murderers on 2 March. 'They painted him blacker than he was,' he murmured, before, characteristically, ordering 3,000 Masses to be said for the repose of his soul. The greatest warlord of the seventeenth century had fallen victim to that one trait no Habsburg could ever forget or forgive: disloyalty. A later Habsburg Kaiser would famously quip when told that one of his subjects was a staunch patriot: 'But is he a patriot for me?' With Wallenstein's murder, Ferdinand reaffirmed the ground rules that had to exist between the dynasty and the army. However indissoluble the compact between dynasty and army, however much they needed each other, the latter existed to serve the former.

Ferdinand moved swiftly to make his son and heir, Ferdinand, the new commander-in-chief. Gallas, an unimpressive subordinate of Wallenstein, was made second in command. The dismemberment of the Wallenstein estates did much to preserve discipline among senior officers who might have been resentful. There was no need for a great purge of the senior ranks; all the evidence pointed to Wallenstein having posed unique challenges to Imperial authority, which were not widely supported.

Before his death Wallenstein and the troops he commanded had ensured that whilst Germany might never be united in his lifetime, it would at least be able to exist without the patronage of Sweden. Thanks to the Imperial troops no Scandinavian country would ever again play any meaningful role in the affairs of Germany.

The subsequent Imperial victory with Spanish help at Nordlingen confirmed these new arrangements. But that which Wallenstein had feared now came to pass. With the weakening of Sweden, France felt compelled to throw tens of thousands of men into the fray. Cardinal Richelieu did not wish Habsburg power to dominate Europe. To safeguard a favourable balance of power for Paris, the Cardinal brought France into the conflict and Germany became again one great battlefield of foreign ambitions.

With the death of Ferdinand II in 1637, his son was elected Kaiser Ferdinand III. The new Emperor, like his father, was a product of Inner Austria – he had been born in Graz and educated there by the Jesuits. He showed some interest in the Jesuits' intellectual and practical solutions to the issues of the time and, like Wallenstein, was not uninterested in the hermetic world. But war would continue to dominate his affairs until, with Germany ravaged, he was forced step by step to accept the policies Wallenstein had implicitly urged upon his father fourteen years earlier. The Edict of Restitution of 1629 was abandoned and the young Emperor had to fight to save what he could before peace came in 1648 through sheer exhaustion.

By the time the Treaty of Westphalia was signed in 1648, millions had died in a war which appeared to have weakened the Holy Roman Empire by splitting its constituent parts into separate states whose reunification would only be achieved partially two hundred years later. The 'Christian, general and permanent' peace it intended to establish offered a new basis for relationships in Europe, though it would end neither conflicts nor wars. The principle of a state's sovereignty, while laudable in its establishment, remains even to this day one of the most violated foundations of international relations. Peace did not imply that the Habsburgs' armies could retire. As Tolstoy later noted: 'it was necessary that millions of men in whose hands the real power lay – the soldiers – should consent to carry out the will of those weak individuals.'[27]

Neither Ferdinand III nor his successor Leopold I, who became Emperor in 1658 following the premature death of his elder brother, stinted on their armies. The Habsburgs appeared increasingly committed to a permanent state of two-front warfare: against France in the west and the Ottomans in the east. The compact forged in June 1619 was set to endure.

Sporck and Montecuccoli

Germany was a wasteland. Sweden chose to turn her attention to Poland and in 1657 had occupied Polish territory as far south as Cracow. It was left to the formidable Sporck to raise the siege. In his 58th year he still signed himself Sporck though countless titles and privileges had been showered upon him. Together with Montecuccoli his troops cleared Poland of the enemy, his cavalry becoming the scourge of the Swedes on the flat terrain of Pomerania.

It was in fighting the enemy to the east, the Ottomans, that Sporck was to gain his most enduring laurels. The Turks had erupted into Transylvania and captured Grosswardein (Nagyvárad), plundering and torching the beautiful landscape until the villages were deserted, sinister ruins. Sporck with his 'hair gleaming like iron', later immortalised by Rainer Maria Rilke in his magnificent epic poem 'Die Weise von Liebe und Tod des Cornets Christoph Rilke',[28] was to save Christendom again.

The logistics that had kept Sporck's cavalry well equipped a decade earlier were no longer available. Against a superior and vigorous force, his troops fell back. The Sultan exploited this weakness to abrogate the fifty-year-old peace treaty the Ottomans had signed with the Habsburgs. Such was the vigour with which the Ottomans advanced that, having turned Transylvania into a wasteland, they now began to penetrate as far as Silesia and Moravia before wintering in Belgrade to prepare for their next drive into Hungary. Suddenly the threat to Central Europe of a major Turkish incursion began again to become tangible.

Not for the last time the Ottomans had over-extended themselves. The year 1664 opened with the chance for the Kaiser's forces to regroup and reorganise. This respite enabled Sporck to build up his forces so that with the advent of spring their numerical inferiority had been largely eliminated. By the time the Ottomans attempted to force a crossing of the river Raab in order to menace Styria, Sporck was sufficiently reinforced to be able to drive them back with loss at Kormend. With the river between them, both armies shadowed each other until on 1 August 1664 they clashed spectacularly further upstream at St Gotthard.

By the time this great battle was fought, the Habsburgs had found another capable general in the form of Raimondo Montecuccoli (1609–80). This gifted strategist famously said, paraphrasing St Augustine, that in order to wage war 'you need three things: money, money and money'. It fell to Montecuccoli to command the forces at St Gotthard.[29] At first they could not withstand the sheer frenzy of the Ottoman attack. The Austrian centre was cleverly split by the Janissaries and Montecuccoli began to fall back, ordering one final counter-attack to be spearheaded by Sporck's cavalry. When Sporck received the order he rode to the head of his riders, removed his helmet, dismounted and knelt before them. In a loud voice he shouted: 'Almighty Generalissimus above us! If you do not wish to help your Christian children at least do not support the Turkish dogs! Just watch on and you will get your joy.'

For nearly three hours Sporck's men fought hand to hand with the Turkish horsemen. Eyewitnesses recalled years later how Sporck fought like a madman, his helmet and breastplate covered in blood, until after a while the Turkish wing began to weaken. Finally panicking, it crumbled, sending the rest of the Ottoman troops into disarray.[30] At this moment Montecuccoli moved his infantry against the Ottoman centre and seized the Turkish bridgehead.

In 1664 at St Gotthard, the Ottomans were crushed by a composite force of French, German and Imperial troops. For 1,000 casualties, Montecuccoli had inflicted more than 14,000 losses on the Turks. So dazzling was this victory that the Ottomans immediately signed a peace treaty that was to guarantee a cessation of formal hostilities for twenty years. It was a fitting triumph for Montecuccoli whose writings on war (*Dell'arte militare*) illustrated his intellectual as well as leadership qualities. He was responsible for persuading his contemporaries that the era of the pikeman was now finally over. Under Montecuccoli, the Imperial forces were reorganised in accordance with his masterly treatise. His principles, often imitated later, corresponded to those of his Imperial masters and arguably all great generals down the ages. They were to be incorporated into the mentality of the Habsburg military:

> God's help to be implored at all times/cultivate the counsel of experienced and loyal men/never miss the right moment/avoid contradictory orders/ assign tasks only to those who have the capability and will to perform them/in significant danger display cheerfulness/Be always ahead of the enemy/Know your forces, the terrain and the enemy/observe carefully secrets when reaching decisions/maintain discipline by rewarding the good and punishing the bad/Cultivate self-control.[31]

With skill and insight Montecuccoli also reorganised the Habsburg armaments industry so that weapons could be made cheaply and efficiently. In doing this he brought weapons manufacture to the town of Steyr, whose name would become synonymous with excellent firearms well into present times.

In addition to these innovations Montecuccoli also recommended a new structure for the infantry, namely the battalion. He advised that battalions be formed by combining companies of men drawn from the same territories. He further suggested the formation of a reserve Landwehr, the erection of barracks for the quartering of troops in peacetime and the introduction of grenadiers as elite units, as well as other ideas which were well in advance of their time and which reflected the scientific and magical interests he had inherited from his uncle.[32] The standing army under Montecuccoli began to take form as the unit of military force of the future whose training would become a priority of the dynasty.

Montecuccoli retired from active service in 1676 and would die four years later as the result of a riding accident. At his own request he was buried without pomp or circumstance. His place as Generalissimus was taken by a worthy successor, Charles of Lorraine, who would within ten years enter the pantheon of Habsburg war heroes in a campaign much closer to home.

The army that had begun this period emerging from an earlier era of mercenary warfare was undeniably a formidable force. The loyalty of its officers was unquestioned – Wallenstein's execution had proved that. Under Montecuccoli it had been reorganised and equipped to face not only European enemies but also the Ottoman hordes. As the seventeeth century moved towards its close the Kaiserliche Armee had become a formidable instrument.

CHAPTER 2

For God and Emperor

THE RELIEF OF VIENNA

The Siege of Vienna remains to this day one of the great set pieces of Austrian and indeed European history. From a tactical point of view its significance lies entirely in the defensive brilliance of the Austrian Stadtkommandant, Starhemberg, and the subsequent character of the city's relief by a multi-national force. In terms of military prestige, its effects were more widely felt. Vienna had withstood an ordeal no major European city had ever experienced. Austria's role as a bulwark of Christendom was loudly proclaimed and its army celebrated for saving Europe. In fact the laurels were to be shared with the soldiers of other nations, notably the Poles, but the events of 1683 burnished the reputation of the Habsburgs' armed forces, giving them confidence to face the struggles ahead, especially to the east.

The swamp-like conditions of the Danube islands and the flat Hungarian plain still evoke the landscape captured by Rilke's great poem: 'The Way of the Love and Death of Cornet Christoph Rilke': 'And courage has become so tired and desire so great. There are no more hills, hardly a tree. Nothing stirs.'[1]

It was on such a summer morning in 1683 that a sinister realisation slowly stole over an Austrian cavalry vedette sent out to reconnoitre the lands east of Győr, which marked the western marches of that turbulent baked land known as Hungary. Peering through the midsummer haze, wary of the illusions of the notorious 'fata morgana' across the Hungarian plain, they saw on the horizon a small cloud of dust. Turning to ride back towards Győr, they paused after a minute to look back, assuming the cloud would have evaporated. In the dry midday heat they could be forgiven their illusion. But as they stretched in their saddles the cloud had not disappeared. Rather, it had grown in size. As Rilke wrote: 'Everything was bright but it was not day.' Campaigning along Austria's eastern marches sharpened military tactics and senses.[2]

The riders turned away quickly; they knew that they had been afforded a glimpse of something that was not a mirage or some other trick of the sun. For all its picturesque majesty, this cloud was a mortal threat to the world they knew. An entire civilisation was on the march; an Ottoman army immense in size and ambition, confident in its military and scientific prowess, was about to demonstrate a new form of terror for the peoples of Central Europe. Its aim was simple: it was not territorial or diplomatic, though these were of course minor factors. No, the unalloyed objective of the Janissaries who marched with their muskets shouldered and their scimitars unsheathed was uncomplicated: the extermination of Christianity as a force in the Danube lands. To achieve this they would have to organise the destruction of the hated House of Habsburg. Time and again this house had stood opposed to their expansion. Less than a hundred years earlier, the illegitimate son of Charles V, Don John of Austria had annihilated the Ottoman fleet at Lepanto in 1572 in a victory widely attributed at the time to the divine intervention of 'Our Lady of Victory' mobilised by a million rosaries.

Kaiser Leopold I

More or less at the same time as the vedette turned away, some miles further west in more shaded country, the Habsburg Emperor Leopold I rode out to the hunt in the Vienna woods. Leopold I (1640–1705) had been destined and educated for the Church. He had become heir only after his elder brother Ferdinand III's early death brought on by the stresses and strains of the post-Wallenstein world in 1655.

The inbreeding of generations gave the Habsburg all the classic family physical traits in an extreme form. His face was long and narrow. His eyes were large and in most portraits of him somewhat weary. The nose was long and slightly hooked and the famous Habsburg lip – a protruding lower lip – was accompanied by a long, pointed, almost jutting chin. This was the man whom destiny had chosen at least nominally to 'save Christendom from the infidel'; or at least much of that part over which he ruled. Like his brother and his predecessors, Leopold was a product of the Jesuits' education. In this Habsburg the notion that he was to be answerable only to God and his confessor was deeply ingrained, but that did not mean he was a simple-minded crusader.

As 1683 opened, Leopold spent six months overseeing intense diplomacy to shore up his efforts to keep what he knew was a large invading army of Ottomans away from his realm. But neither Leopold nor his court seriously reckoned on invasion from the east until it was almost too late. Preoccupied with the power of their great rival France, their focus was not unnaturally directed towards the west and the Rhine.

Montecuccoli's great victory at St Gotthard barely twenty years earlier in 1664 had resulted in the Treaty of Vasvar, which was intended to preserve the peace between Habsburg and Ottoman for at least twenty years. But intrigue on the part of Louis XIV of France, keen on a policy of encirclement of his Habsburg rival, had stirred up the Ottomans and a Hungarian revolt under Tököly against the Emperor had been supported by the Pasha of Buda. In 1682 the Ottoman Sultan Mehmed IV, advised by Kara Mustafa his Grand Vizier since 1676, chose to disregard the Treaty of Vasvar and prepare for war with Leopold.

Leopold kept abreast of these developments through ambassadors and advisers, and did what he could to play for time. His commitments against the French who were menacing the lowlands did not encourage him to provoke conflict in the east. He hoped diplomacy and a system of fortifications would keep his eastern enemies at bay and certainly far from Vienna. But the Military Frontier had not yet reached the apogee of tribal administration and efficiency that was to become the envy of military scholars throughout Europe. The Karlovac and Varaždin 'Generalats' were barely even the nucleus of a system of garrison strongholds from which the arts of counter-insurgency were later honed and perfected.

In February 1683, the quartermasters had drawn up an inventory of all the troops under Leopold's command and the lists were impressive. Little more than a generation earlier the Imperial armies had entered the great conflicts of the Thirty Years War with barely a standing formation save the Maradas Cuirassier regiment and Dampierre's cavalry who had famously rescued Ferdinand II from the rebel Protestants besieging the Hofburg.

Leopold's army: Charles of Lorraine and the 'affair at Petronell'

The Habsburgs' forces were now substantial: 45 companies of infantry in nearby Moravia and 48 more in distant Silesia, totalling 10,000 cavalry and nearly three times as many infantry. This was before one counted the forces around Graz, western Hungary and the Military Frontier. As Leopold issued new patents of nobility new regiments were formed. Further units were in the western part of his empire facing off threats from Louis XIV. Altogether Leopold had at least 50,000 effective troops.

But on this sultry day when the stillness of the landscape under the baking sun belied the challenges ahead, an unhappy portent cast a long shadow over Leopold's mood. Messengers began to arrive in Vienna from the east, feverish with excitement. Contrary to the accepted wisdom of the preceding weeks, the Ottomans had pushed beyond the Leitha hills and had had the temerity to enter Ungarisch Altenburg with a vast force barely a few miles down the Danube.

So complete was the surprise inflicted by this Turkish movement that the defenders of Hungarian Altenburg were prevented from destroying the bridge over the Danube. It began to look as if an aggressive patrol was in fact the vanguard of at least 30,000 disciplined troops coming up fast to encircle the Imperial commander Charles of Lorraine and his modest force of dragoons and infantry stationed nearby in order to annihilate them before striking rapidly in the direction of Vienna. Ominously, large clouds of dust to the west suggested that more Turks had crossed further upstream.

Charles of Lorraine (1643–90) had not been Leopold's undisputed choice to command the Imperial forces gathered around Vienna. A disenfranchised duke whose territories had been seized by France, Lorraine had married Leopold's niece and was therefore on intimate terms with the ruling family. But Lorraine had been ill for months before the spring of 1683 and though he had served with distinction at the Battle of St Gotthard, his appointment as commander-in-chief in 1675 had been controversial. He was competent and what he lacked in imagination he had made up for in loyalty to his sovereign, since the murder of Wallenstein a generation earlier a key factor engraved on every Habsburg's consciousness. Lorraine's plan had been to force the Turks into a pitched battle around the Hungarian fortress of Győr. The events at Altenburg shattered these designs as Charles's own rearguard was suddenly attacked with energetic ferocity by squadrons of Tatars.

But Lorraine was not a fearful man. Leopold had chosen him precisely because the Habsburg monarch, the 'small Herr in red stockings' as Carlyle called him, was no warrior king. He did not see himself in the mould of a Sobieski and needed someone to discharge this kind of martial spirit on his behalf. Lorraine was courageous and nothing showed this more sharply than his action on this day in July. On being brought news of his rearguard's predicament he immediately turned back and, with every cavalryman he could muster, reached the sloping ground on the banks of the Danube at Petronell where the present day schloss of the Abensberg-Trauns is to be seen. There he mounted a strong counter-attack shouting at his subordinates not to dishonour the Imperial standard by retreating.

The Turks broke off the skirmish, leaving thirty-five dead on the field.[3] The Habsburg casualties ran into the low hundreds. Lorraine was 'victorious' but messengers from his camp reached Vienna with vivid tales of Turkish hordes. Leopold inspected his regiments, including the Mansfeld-Colloredo and

Scherffenberg, smartly attired in bleached grey with blue facings but, their uniforms and professional appearance notwithstanding, the Emperor decided it was time for his family and the court to evacuate. That evening the eleventh-century crown of St Stephen, the unique and priceless symbol of Hungarian sovereignty, was taken under heavy guard to accompany him on his westward journey along the Danube towards Linz.

Belatedly Lorraine's intelligence apparatus, such as it was, finally confirmed what Leopold had intuited. The Turks had left barely 10,000 troops to invest Györ and the rest of the Ottoman forces, now estimated as 80,000 strong, were pushing remorselessly straight towards him and the eastern approaches to Vienna.

Ernst Rüdiger Starhemberg organises the defence

On the evening of 8 July Lorraine entered Vienna with Ernst Rüdiger Starhemberg, who had been appointed three years earlier as Stadtkommandant. Starhemberg had already taken steps to strengthen the city's fortifications. With the Turks barely hours away he issued draconian instructions for manpower.

According to contemporary reports Starhemberg possessed a fiery and courageous nature and this had long been put to military service, first against the Turks, but also later against the French. It was in these campaigns that his energy and toughness became apparent. The son of the wealthy representative of Lower Austria, he did not depend on local favours for either riches or position. Typical of the newly minted aristocracy that had replaced the Protestant nobility vanquished at the Battle of the White Mountain, his family owed its allegiance first and foremost to the crown rather than to the land or peoples of their estates. The Counter-Reformation had dramatically changed the composition of the Austrian aristocracy. It was now made up of generals and their families, who formed a reliable layer of obedience immediately below the extended family of the dynasty. In 1683, Starhemberg needed neither title (though he was at this stage a count) nor rank to organise the defence against the Turk. His orders have come down to us as a model of how a military commander prepares a civilian population for the rigours of a siege.

The first priority of Starhemberg's orders was men. He demanded manpower and that it present itself on the ramparts by 4 a.m. the next day. When these did not suffice a further order demanded 500 more able-bodied men to present themselves within 24 hours and, if these did not appear, 'extreme measures' would 'be applied'.[4] Additional barricades were constructed, as were palisades by the outer fortifications; the counterscarp was strengthened and the moat deepened. The population of Vienna responded enthusiastically to Starhemberg's orders and the preparations began.

During the following two days Lorraine and Starhemberg discussed the logistics of war. Starhemberg insisted like any sensible commander that his troops be paid regularly. His garrison would soon grow to 10,000 regular infantry and dismounted cavalry as well as some 4,000 members of the City Guard including companies made up of students and bakers.

Meanwhile, Lorraine's forces, outside the city, now consisted of 14 foot regiments and eight Cuirassier regiments reinforced by five Dragoon regiments and five further regiments of Croats. (When the eventual relief force appeared only 21,000 out of the 89,000 would be Imperial troops.) These could be paid from a variety of potential sources but for the garrison the need for regular generous payment was far more pressing. A defence force of 20,000 men was a modest force with which to confront the 80,000 of Kara Mustafa.

In the meantime Starhemberg was told that just 30,000 florins remained in the military *Schatzkammer* (treasury) and none of this would be available for the payment of the soldiers. Starhemberg insisted that he would need at least 40,000 florins a month for the punctual payment of his men. To resolve this impasse a number of rich seams were tapped from a variety of sources.

First of these was the property of the Archbishop of Esztergom whose treasury had been brought to his palace in Vienna in the Himmelpfortgasse and with its plate and jewels was valued at over 400,000 florins.[5] The Bishop of Wiener-Neustadt, Kollonits, a Knight of St John, swiftly moved to 'access' these. Kollonits was undoubtedly one of the most energetic men behind the success of the defence, convinced as he was that this was a great emergency in which there was no time to stand on privilege or wealth. The aristocracy did what it could: Prince Schwarzenberg left 1,000 litres of wine, and several other important personages who were unable to leave with their treasures also found their property impounded. Kollonits was the prime instigator in seizing these treasures. No doubt his role in the Court Inquisition fifteen years earlier, in which he had played a significant part in the Leopoldine expulsion of the Jews from Vienna in 1670, afforded him a cavalier approach to property rights.

The small community of Jewish traders had worshipped at the 'New Synagogue' in what is today Vienna's second district, the Leopoldstadt. Kollonits had overseen the transformation of the synagogue into the church of St Leopold, whose first priest had been Kollonits's personal adviser. The expulsion of the Jewish community according to the official Order in Council of 27 February 1670 had been based partly on the widespread suspicion that they had communicated during the last hundred years with the enemy, the Turks, illegally, thus threatening the 'security' of Vienna (the original of many later dubious accusations and of course resurrected as a new variation on a baleful theme with relish during the terrible days of March 1938).

In a wonderful twist of irony Kollonits, along with the rest of Vienna, would come to depend on one of the last surviving members of that Jewish community. Fortunately for Kollonits and the Viennese, and indeed for the Habsburgs and Europe, the expulsion order of 1670 had not been implemented against all Jews. One, but only one, survived and he was – until Samson Wertheimer entered the city of Vienna on 2 December 1684, a few weeks after the siege had been raised – the only Jew official records recall as registered in the city. His name was Samuel Oppenheimer and he came to personify the so-called 'Hof Jude' or 'Court Jew' who enjoyed special privileges and Imperial protection.

Samuel Oppenheimer mobilises the 'sinews of war'

The so-called upper class of Jews living in Vienna gradually grew after the siege was raised, and they constituted in total 1,346 in a census made in 1699.[6] But in 1683 Samuel Oppenheimer was alone and he made a significant contribution to ensuring that the funds Kollonits sequestered were transformed into the vital munitions and supplies the Imperial forces would need. Moreover, he contributed out of his own purse considerable sums, which provided crucial help in financing the campaign against the Turks for years to come. He was the most brilliant in the long series of men who would serve as the Habsburg army's quartermaster.

One of the Imperial documents conferring on Oppenheimer the privilege of access to and protection by the Emperor Leopold has survived in parts.[7] It is dated 2 June 1691. It notes that the privilege of Imperial protection is conferred by the Emperor Leopold 'in view of the 16 years [dating back to 1675] of unbroken service in supplying the Imperial armies with food, munitions and war materials'. It further acknowledges the 'notable' sums of money which Oppenheimer also donated 'especially in the wars against the Turks and the French' before warning that anyone violating Herr Oppenheimer's rights under the document will face an immediate fine of 30 golden crowns and 'the Imperial displeasure' ('die Kaiserliche Ungnade'), a significant threat in the last decade of the seventeenth century.

The importance of Oppenheimer to the Imperial cause in 1683 is difficult to quantify in detail but we know that as Kollonits and Starhemberg were in their own different ways supporting the preparations for the siege, Oppenheimer was working on the supply of munitions. Two weeks after Starhemberg returned to Vienna, several ships belonging to Oppenheimer laden with grenades and other ordnance made their way to Linz from the west, for use by the Imperial armies gathering to relieve Vienna. A further 26,000 grenades would reach Linz in early September, again transported along the Danube by Oppenheimer's ships. He was in frequent contact with the Jewish Gompertz family in Saxony and his links with Gompertz helped to raise further funds.

Perhaps the most poignant indication of Oppenheimer's significance for the military machine of the Habsburgs was that with his death in 1703 the entire Habsburg state finances fell almost immediately into disarray and state bankruptcy ensued. This default Oppenheimer had staved off for the last few years by financing the Habsburg military machine with millions of his own money and constructing an elaborate credit system whose precarious and labyrinthine tentacles stretched across most of Europe. The system was kept afloat by dint of Oppenheimer simply remaining alive. In this sense he indeed personified the adventurous risk-taking that marked capitalism in the era of the 'Hochbarock'.[8]

While Oppenheimer attended to the provisioning of war materiel, by 11 July Starhemberg had been reinforced by Imperial troops under Leslie's command and his garrison was coming together. He had now more than 12,000 men at his disposal, of whom 10,000 were regular troops. Thanks to the efforts of Kollonits and Oppenheimer, these were fed, paid and well equipped.

Among the officers were disparate spirits, by no means all Catholics. The De Souches regiment, who fell in their dozens, fearlessly leading sorties from the Burg Ravelin near the present-day Albertina during the later stages of the siege, had been founded by Count Ludwig de Souches who was a Huguenot from an impoverished minor aristocratic family. At the other end of the spectrum was a regiment drawn from more than a dozen bakeries in the city that would manfully defend the Loebel bastion not far from the present-day Burgtor under a scorched standard bearing the image of the Virgin Mary which can still be seen today in their livery hall in the Josefstadt.

The second half of the seventeenth century had seen not only the forma-tion of a standing army for the Habsburgs but also a degree of uniformity in attire and weaponry. Factories and workshops had been established under the supreme Council of War to achieve this. The core of both Lorraine and Starhemberg's infantry regiments were the musketeers, who carried no body armour but a matchlock musket which fired a small metal ball about 20 millimetres in circumference along a smooth barrel and had a range of 150–200 metres. For close-quarters fighting a 'plug bayonet' fitted into the barrel of the musket.

In addition to these devices, the infantry had another weapon of consider-able importance that would play a large and useful role during the siege: the hand grenade. Some were made of bronze or iron but in the Imperial and Royal Army were more often of thick glass and filled with black gunpowder. Montecuccoli had already introduced tall men who could vigorously hurl these grenades over long distances as 'grenadiers', a word that would soon become a synonym for elite troops the world over.

Their opponents however also knew the value of grenades and the Ottomans who were not only equipped with guns and, at that time, potentially even more lethal archery, also had their own hellish variation: burning sulphur balls. These early forerunners of chemical warfare were indeed deadly crystal balls: round vessels of glass containing sulphurous substances that started fires and filled the air with suffocating fumes. Grenades became an everyday feature of the siege and could be deployed with terrifying effect.

Lorraine's cavalry had not changed much in appearance and organisation since the Thirty Years War. The cuirassiers were the shock cavalry, armoured and equipped with the heavy 'pallasch' and occasionally also a carbine. The dragoons, a cross between the musketeers and cavalry of the religious conflicts earlier in the century, were by 1683 a recognised cavalry unit armed with pistols, muskets and sabres but not armoured.

In addition to these there were the Croat cavalry who until 1688, when they were incorporated into the Imperial forces as the Habsburgs' first Hussar regiments, served as irregular light cavalry. These were mostly men of the eastern marches: brilliant horsemen, like their Turkish opponents they spurned any armour that could slow them down. Like their Ottoman opponents they favoured the light curved sabre (often known in Britain as the 'mameluke's sword'), which with its simple pommel-free ivory handle would become the weapon of choice for light cavalry throughout the world during the coming century.

These were joined eventually by the Polish cavalry, whose equipment was unique in Europe at that time, including five-metre-long lances and 'hussar wings' (an early example of psychological warfare as the noise emitted by these feathered wings on charging was a terrifying hiss).

For the defenders of Vienna such dashing units were unavailable so Starhemberg concentrated on the infantry regiments that would form the nucleus of his defence. Other measures were hastily implemented. All bells were silenced except the one in the tower of St Stephen's Cathedral, which was to be used as a signal in calling men to the walls in an emergency. The tower of the cathedral was the principal lookout of the defenders, commanding, as it still does today, an uninterrupted view around the city.

As troops of Tatar cavalry approached as close to the city as the New Favorita gardens (today the Theresianum), Starhemberg gave orders to create a glacis (artificial slope) with clear views for the defenders to fire on their attackers. The housing was demolished and cleared away.

Starhemberg had issued orders earlier for these buildings to be destroyed but to no effect. On 12 July he personally oversaw the firing of the entire area. A conflagration burned to tinder the whole space between the counterscarp and the *Vorstädte* (suburbs). By the evening of the 13th with most of the glacis clear, reports came in of cavalry skirmishes. Firing began against some Turks who impudently rode up towards the Kärtnerbastei (near the present-day Vienna State Opera).

The siege begins

Starhemberg began deploying his infantry in depth along the counterscarp (by the present-day Hofburg). At the same time the suburbs of Mariahilf and the Alsergrund, Währing and Rennweg, all beyond the walls, were gutted to ensure that no protection or shelter was afforded to the attackers

At approximately 8 p.m. on 15 July two letters were delivered to Starhemberg from the Ottoman lines demanding the immediate surrender of the city. Kara Mustafa had risked an unauthorised large-scale raid but he meant to see it through. The letters were ignored. Starhemberg redoubled his efforts to complete his defences, which at this stage were by no means finished. Every family was enjoined to lay in a supply of food sufficient to last it for at least one month under penalty of expulsion from the city. Gunpowder was placed in the basements of the churches; all windows were walled up with solid masonry to prevent ignition by sparks.

Twenty-four hours before the Ottoman camps appeared around the city, Starhemberg gave the order to tear up all paving stones so that these too could be used to strengthen the defence points, and also to lessen the risk of the attackers' artillery ordnance shattering the stone surfaces and causing greater numbers of casualties through fragmentation. Feverish activity prevailed as Vienna's inhabitants realised that there was now no alternative to a siege. As the population toiled through the night a grim silence descended on the city.

Barely a day later, the Turks had established their encampment and their batteries opened fire, raining all manner of pyrotechnics on the besieged. From now on the fortifications erected around Vienna by Sebastian Schrantz and Starhemberg's modest garrison were all that stood between European civilisation and the forces of annihilation. Fortunately Schrantz had done his work well: the bricks of the bastions were so hard that even two hundred years later the construction of the Vienna U-Bahn was held up for weeks by the resilience of the lower courses.

On the first afternoon of the siege a fire broke out near the Schottenbastei. This soon began to spread towards the Arsenal then, as now, a fine building situated on the western side of the Am Hof complex. The suspicion of sabotage was rife and several of the crowd were set upon often with violent, even fatal, consequences until the civil guard restored order and the fire, perhaps helped by a change of wind, was extinguished. The Turks meanwhile began digging ditches towards the bastions.

In less than 48 hours, these ditches afforded cover for Turkish activities within range of the fortifications. On the 15th, Starhemberg was wounded by a Turkish ball, which kept him for the next few days at home. From his bed he ordered a counter-attack, which was successful, and the preparation of the bastions to house batteries that could silence the Ottoman guns. Far on the other side of the city, Starhemberg's cavalry broke up an attack by Janissaries streaming across from the Prater Island roughly where today the famous 'Big Wheel' (*Riesenrad*) now stands. Fortunately that sector of his defence was reinforced by the proximity of the river, which allowed the Viennese batteries to play upon the Turks almost with impunity. This forced the Ottomans to concentrate on the dry ground to the south of the city.

A sortie led by Guido Starhemberg, a kinsman of the commander, and two companies of Mansfeld infantry brought back the first prisoners. The news from these was sobering for they told of a besieging army of more than 100,000 including over 20,000 Janissaries.

On 20 July more ominous news was brought by refugees from the suburbs. The village of Petersdorf (Perchtoldsdorf) had surrendered the preceding day after receiving a guarantee of safe passage for its inhabitants. This guarantee had at once been violated on the surrender of the village, and all its inhabitants were put to the sword.

Against this dismal news there came the following day a more promising message from Charles of Lorraine: a relief of the city was being prepared. However, spirits had barely lifted on hearing this piece of encouraging news when a few hours later a message was received from Baron Kunitz, an Austrian envoy to the Sultan who had been allowed to accompany the Turkish besieging force on its journey from Constantinople to Vienna. This stated flatly that the Turks expected the city to fall within a few days.

In this emotional see-saw Starhemberg remained aloof and detached. Each day he gave orders which implied preparations for a long siege. Livestock was plundered from outlying districts and brought into the city to ensure that food supplies remained adequate and further sorties were ordered to slow development of the Turks' trench system.

The explosion of two Turkish mines on 23 July provoked a fierce fight around the counterscarp which lasted several hours before the Turks retired leaving a hundred dead and several hundred wounded. The following night, a contemporary noted, the 'enemy was more silent than usual'.[9]

So far Starhemberg had held his nerve and could be satisfied with the performance of his garrison in the first ten days of the siege. Casualties had been relatively light. The discipline of his troops had held and the civilian population, once battle was joined, had pulled together to support the defence. Along with the good provisioning and supplies, morale was high.

The army's Madonna and the infidel's mines

In the Michaelerkirche just behind the most exposed and critical bastion a votive portrait of the Madonna which had been spirited into the church from the outlying endangered suburb of Mariahilf a few weeks earlier was 'exposed' for public veneration. Every evening nearly every member of the garrison would pass by for spiritual support. The portrait, barely ten inches high, was a copy of the famous Lukas Cranach the Elder's portrait of the Madonna and Child. The painting is still to be found in the chapel in the Mariahilf church in Vienna and is venerated to this day.

The siege now settled down into a certain routine, according to contemporary accounts, in which the daily climax was a mid-afternoon assault by the Turks on the fortifications around the Burg bastion.[10]

By far the greatest danger came from the Turks' mines and the defenders began to neutralise these in addition to the sorties mentioned above by a systematic programme of countermining. Modern visitors to Vienna have few reference points to help them imagine the siege. The great walls and counterscarps are all gone, pulverised not by any invading army but by the far more destructive guns of nineteenth-century capitalism which created Europe's most famous and grandest *Ringstrasse* (ring road) from the 1850s. Only the Albertina standing proudly with its equestrian statue of the Archduke Albrecht gives a hint of the heights from which the defenders fought.

Fortunately for today's visitor, a sizeable legacy of the great underground labyrinth which was created to countermine the Turkish encroachments is still visible. The Ezsterhazy Keller, under the Freyung, provides, in its deepest recesses, rooms well below the street, which evoke more powerfully than anywhere else in modern Vienna the atmosphere of Starhemberg's underground defences.

At 5 p.m. on 26 July, the defenders burrowed from here towards the glacis and exploded a countermine in front of the Burg Ravelin. This failed to have the desired effect and a heavy Turkish attack was launched on the Ravelin and repulsed with more difficulty than hitherto. Ten Turks clambered over the palisades. They were swiftly piked and bayoneted by the defenders.

About the same time an arrow fired into the city contained a curious text. Written in a few lines of Western script, it claimed to be a message from the Imperial ambassador attached to the Ottoman besieging force saying that the Duke of Lorraine had wanted a few days earlier to organise a cease-fire. There was much debate over the truth and origins of this message.

Starhemberg dismissed it as yet another ruse and gave orders for the Turkish wounded to be slaughtered ('und noch halb-lebenden geschunden'). Three days later a Turkish mine exploded with great dramatic effect, covering the members of the Mansfeld regiment holding the palisades in that sector with earth. Fortunately no follow-up attack materialised and the infantry repaired the damage swiftly without distraction.

By now, with the churches filled with the wounded and dying within the city, and the area below the ramparts littered with the fallen of the enemy, Vienna was girdled with bands of putrefying carcasses of men, camels, horses and oxen. They fringed the walls, polluted the moat and in the summer heat produced a stench which, according to contemporary accounts, was almost unendurable.

As August dragged on, a concentrated night attack by the Turks towards the Graben ditch was fought back, but with considerable casualties, including Count Leslie, the kinsman of one of Wallenstein's assassins. Starhemberg on this day, exhausted from the heat and struggle, fell sick and retired again to bed. The mood in the city had become more anxious. A Lieutenant Gregorowitz, disguised in Turkish clothes was sent just before midnight out of the city with an urgent message for Lorraine demanding immediate help.

The following day the largest mine the Turks had deployed so far exploded. It ripped the silence of the early morning in front of the Burg bastion, sending several of the defenders into the air and opening a gap in the Graben ditch through which the Turks poured. Only a violent sortie led by the City Guard recovered the ground.

Conditions for the defenders were deteriorating distinctly and to add to the pressures now facing the garrison, crippling dysentery began to take hold. On 9 August strict sanitary measures were introduced to contain the outbreak. New burial grounds were dug near the Augustinian church as the existing mass graves within the city walls were full.

The resourceful Kolschitzky is sent to find help

On the 13th a dramatic thunderstorm gave the garrison a brief respite. Another messenger, Raitz Kolschitzky, was sent to Lorraine, dressed in oriental clothes and accompanied by his manservant, Stephan Serhadly. Kolschitzky is generally credited with the introduction to the city of that staple *sine qua non* of Viennese life: coffee. In fact this intrepid Pole who had lived among the Ottomans and knew their language and manners so well that he could pass among them unnoticed did not open the first coffee house in Vienna and died impoverished, though not unforgotten thanks to a fine contemporary print of him in his disguise.[11]

A week later, Kolschitzky returned with reliable intelligence concerning the relief force. The King of Poland together with the rest of his forces was expected within the next eight days. Buoyed up by this news, the defenders sent the agreed sign, a smoke signal, that Kolschitzky had got safely through the Turkish lines and returned to the city.

The following day Kolschitzky's manservant returned with bad news. As the Turks had destroyed all the Danube bridges, Lorraine was forced to retire to Tulln further down the Danube where a new bridge would be constructed. Lorraine hoped to relieve the garrison in ten days. Starhemberg ordered six rockets to be fired to signal the servant's safe return but he was more aware than anyone else how difficult the next ten days were likely to prove because the besiegers were tightening the noose, torching the outlying villages, reducing Kagran, Stammersdorf and Langenzersdorf to ashes.

For the first time, Starhemberg ordered chains to be erected across the streets behind the Loebelbastei while all the city gates were barricaded. Two deserters, simply described in contemporary accounts as musketeers, were condemned to death. The following day a strong sortie led by 300 men of the Scherffenberg and De Souches regiments pushed the Turks a few yards back and the sound of distant cannon appeared to herald the promise of the relief force.

For both sides the crisis of the battle was rapidly approaching. On 26 August two Turkish mines were exploded at the Ravelin and part of the wall towards the Michaelerkirche was also detonated. Another strong attack was again beaten back with heavy loss. Despite these setbacks, the Turks continued their preparations for a breakthrough and their artillery fire, though still ineffective, was stepped up in pace. From now on large parts of the day and increasingly the night were punctuated by Turkish cannonades.

On Friday 27 August, a sortie by Baron Spindler ended disastrously with a score of dead, including the unfortunate Baron and countless more wounded. On the same day, deserters, already condemned to death, were hanged on the Neue Markt 'pour encourager les autres'. Between 11 p.m. and midnight more than 36 rockets were fired and new messages were sent to Lorraine. They were terse and to the point: 'Send help NOW immediately. Situation desperate.'[12]

The Turks meanwhile began to direct their artillery on the symbol of the city's vitality and obduracy, namely the soaring tower of St Stephen's Cathedral. The days were a continuous series of thunderous cannonades, punctuated by mines exploding around the Ravelin, followed by the ubiquitous attempt to storm the counterscarp, beaten off usually with heavy loss on the part of the attackers. The Turkish assaults became more and more desperate; often they would storm the Ravelin three times in one day.

On the last day of August some Turks were found to have tunnelled into the cellars below the Rossmarkt, well into the interior of the city. Their severed heads were brought to Starhemberg, who the following day sent Kolschitzky to Lorraine with another desperate plea. Two days later and the Ravelin was largely in Turkish hands; a sortie by a young officer with fifty civil guards failed to weaken the Ottoman grip and resulted in large numbers of Austrian casualties. Starhemberg could content himself that evening only with the rockets fired from the Bisamberg, confirming his emissary's safe arrival. Prayers were offered up for deliverance at every street corner.

The day after, a series of cloudbursts announced the first of the autumn rains. The rain proved more effective than either Charles of Lorraine or Starhemberg in slowing down the activities of the attackers. Under cover of the downpour the Dupigny regiment undertook a sortie for food and returned with thirty-two head of cattle, horses and a wagon of supplies. Starhemberg ordered the meat to be divided among the wounded. At the same time the commandant ordered his troops to withdraw from the last section of the Burg Ravelin. It was no longer tenable. As the troops withdrew behind the bastion the faint chinks and noises of the excavations of the Turks could be clearly heard.

Fortunately for the defenders the rain continued, but at three in the afternoon on 4 September the Turks finally exploded a mine with devastating effect, demolishing part of the Burg bastion so recently vacated by Starhemberg's men. At first there was absolutely nothing to be seen, then a broad cloud began to envelop the section of the wall. Four thousand Janissaries under the leadership of the Grand Vizier himself had been prepared for this moment. With an appalling scream they now charged, to be met by two lines of disciplined infantry in grey and behind them another line of the city guard.

Every officer of the garrison, with his troops, was rushed to the scene to stem the breach, a deployment helped by the fact that the change of guard had been taking place at precisely the time the mine exploded. Some 3,000 infantrymen engaged the besiegers in desperate hand-to-hand fighting. Gradually, the Turks were beaten back, Starhemberg himself leading the last reserves after almost two hours of incessant fighting. The ground was littered with nearly

700 corpses, the majority of whom were Ottoman. That evening more rockets than usual were fired to signal the city's distress, a practice that continued virtually every night.

It was not until a week later on 8 September that the Ottomans once again launched a large attack. Again this was beaten back, but the Viennese losses were heavy and Starhemberg knew that his men could not hold out for very much longer. He now ordered all able-bodied burghers to turn out with their arms to form two last reserves; one to be stationed in the Freyung near the Schottentor. Barricades were erected across all the streets. A beating of mass drums summoned the beleaguered citizenry to their stations. Starhemberg ordered six artillery batteries to be placed at strategic points to form a last redoubt. Finally at midnight another dozen distress rockets were fired from the cathedral tower.

The relief force and Sobieski arrive

For the next two days few of the defenders slept. During the day they noticed that the Turkish troops were beginning to regroup towards the Kahlenberg. On 10 September another mine exploded under the Burg Bastei. But there was no follow-up. Starhemberg's men, every nerve stretched to breaking point, assembled for what they believed would be their last stand, but the attack never came. The following day artillery fire and infantry attacks along the Burg Bastei continued but the defenders noted that these had slackened in intensity. The crisis was over. The besiegers were now preoccupied with another foe. The King of Poland, Sobieski, had arrived and Charles of Lorraine was preparing to attack.

Lorraine had completed the concentration of his forces around Tulln on 9 September, some days later than he had hoped in his earliest messages to Starhemberg. The disparate nature of the troops – Bavarians, Saxons and Poles as well as Franconians and Austrians – had provoked logistical challenges; the Turks' destruction of the bridges over the Danube had also not helped. There then followed the usual haggling over command. It was finally agreed that the Imperial forces would be under Lorraine's overall command but that the Poles under their king, Sobieski, would form the right wing. In this way no sovereign prince (or his representative) was in danger of any perceived slight. As king, Sobieski might have been expected to have pulled rank, but his was an elected monarchy and his overall command would not have been acceptable to many of those present.

Sobieski has come down to us as the embodiment of the vigorous hero of Polish chivalry. He certainly kept his promise to help Kaiser Leopold but we can be sure that negotiations with him were difficult and protracted. In one respect he appears to have shared the cause of the Austrians with enthusiasm. He was, like every Pole of distinction, a devotee of Roman Catholicism. This combined with his military talents – he had led the Poles to a crushing victory over the Turks ten years earlier at Chocim – and the knowledge of Ottoman ways that had undoubtedly arisen from his role as Polish envoy to their court made him a powerful ally for Lorraine.

Lorraine was in any event accustomed to the challenges occasioned by the differing nationalities of the coalition force. Like any Habsburg commander then and indeed until 1918 he would be perfectly accustomed to and knowledgeable of the diverse national traits and languages of a multinational army.

Lorraine organised the chain of command with tact and skill. What he lacked in naked aggression he more than compensated for in diplomacy and intelligence. To avoid disputes, command was devolved along the lines of the different units taking part. Thus the 11,300 men of the Bavarian Elector were commanded by his representative, Field Marshal Degenfeld. Count Waldegg commanded some 9,000 Swabians and the Elector of Saxony commanded his 9,500 troops. Also present and under autonomous commands were the Duke of Brunswick with 600 men, and a junior representative of the House of Hanover, later to become George I of England.

Sobieski's troops numbered some 25,000, mostly cavalry, with Charles of Lorraine's contingent numbering roughly the same. The total relief force was made up of 65,000 men and about 165 artillery pieces. By the evening of 11 September, the plan for these troops to descend from their position high in the Vienna woods was finalised. Both Lorraine and Sobieski reckoned on at least two to three days of fighting and did not imagine that they could relieve the city in one decisive attack. Sobieski in particular foresaw great difficulties for his cavalry and predicted a bitter resistance on the part of the Turks at the foot of the Vienna woods. The two generals could not have guessed that their opponent Kara Mustafa would in fact divide his weakened forces, sending only a part of his troops towards the relief force, a movement observed by the defenders two days earlier. The first Turkish line of defence was erected between Maria Brunn and Kahlenbergerdorf. Behind this a second line was prepared but the allies struck first at dawn. After Mass on the Kahlenberg or, if Austrian accounts are to be believed, on the Leopoldsberg (three hundred years later the exact location of the allies' Mass still could not be agreed upon by Poles and Austrians), the order to attack was given.

First engaged was Lorraine's left wing and then soon afterwards his centre. Both encountered significant resistance. Slowly the Turks surrendered their positions one after the other; only at Heiligenstadt and Nussdorf did they manage some local successes. By midday it looked as if they would make a stand between Krottenbach and Döblingerbach and here the Poles, finally emerging from the tight terrain and mini defiles of the Wienerwald, had the advantage. Unlike the Imperial centre and Lorraine's left wing, the Poles had not engaged the enemy but had used the time to bring their horsemen slowly down through the woods to emerge as fresh shock troops.

Before them lay Vienna and an opportunity too good to miss. As the Turkish lines momentarily wavered the entire right wing of Lorraine's forces, including Sobieski's 25,000 cavalry, charged home through the vineyards and fields of Hernals. At the same time in an inspired tactic Lorraine's left wing pushed through towards his right to force the Turks in front of him in the direction of the Poles.

The manoeuvre worked beautifully and the Turks, fearful of the thousands of horseman now thundering towards them, began to flee. Two squadrons of Imperial dragoons led by the Margrave of Baden reached the Schottentor around 5 p.m. only to be attacked by hundreds of Janissaries who in a desperate final effort had tried to storm the Schottenbastei. Starhemberg, seeing the Margrave's predicament, ordered one last sortie and his infantry rescued the surrounded cavalry.

With this last furious encounter the siege was over. Ottoman military power was not only defeated; it was broken. Even the Janissaries sought only how to flee and save their lives. Kara Mustafa, surveying the scene from what is now the Josefstadt, briefly contemplated death; he knew all too well how his defeat would be rewarded at home. But even he decided on flight. It would delay only briefly his end at the hands of the Sultan's executioner's silken garrotte upon his eventual return to the Ottoman court.

After sixty-one days of bitter siege, Vienna was free. The reputations of many great and soon to be great Austrian families were burnished here with baptismal fire. A Habsburg-led force had saved Europe from the infidel. The courts were dazzled by the news. Even in London the town criers announced the details of the 'heroic' siege. The political consequences were no less vivid: it was a turning point in European history. Austrian power relentlessly moved east to fill the vacuum left by Ottoman withdrawal. For the Viennese the memory of the siege would remain part of their collective subconscious even four centuries later.

The opportunities created for the Habsburg army heralded a new era in its development. In a world of Imperial expansion no Habsburg ruler would wish to rely on anything but a professional and well-equipped army. Austrian white was beginning to arrive.

CHAPTER 3

'The noble knight'

PRINCE EUGENE AND THE WAR OF THE
SPANISH SUCCESSION

The 'first age of heroes'

Confidence, that critical of military factors, allowed the Habsburgs' army to assume the offensive rapidly. As it rolled the Turks out of central and eastern Europe, the army became better disciplined and organised. It was to become by the end of this period more than capable of holding its own against any force in the world, thanks in no small part to that dazzling architect of Habsburg military power, Prince Eugene.

A young, not very prepossessing or especially handsome youth had arrived in Vienna that autumn of 1683. Small even by the standards of his time, this man appeared almost crippled to his contemporaries, who found the idea that he might want to make soldiering his career risible. His manner was taciturn but his pride was Olympian and indeed he had much to prove. He had been spurned in his quest for a military career by the court of Louis XIV and his rage at this humiliation was unquenchable. When he arrived in Vienna he made enemies at court almost by blinking but Kaiser Leopold recognised early on that here indeed was a soldier of potential, though it is unlikely that even Leopold realised the full extent of the military genius whose spindly frame stood before him.

Eugene of Savoy like many a patriotic 'old' Austrian did not possess a drop of what today would be called Austrian blood. By birth he was Italian and his temperament and his rapidity of decision constituted what were once considered typical Latin traits. By upbringing he was French and this invested him with his limitless and rigid devotion to revenge and his obsessive detestation of the French monarch Louis XIV. When many years later, after France had come to regret all too painfully its rejection of Eugene, a message from the French court gingerly enquired whether Eugene after all might consider serving France and said that a dazzling career awaited him in the service of Louis XIV. The Prince of Savoy demonstrated that he neither forgot nor forgave: 'I should like to accept the invitation to return to France,' he replied, 'but only at the head of an invading army to occupy it.'[1]

Eugene had arrived with Lorraine's polyglot relief force and had performed bravely with energy and imagination at the raising of the great siege. He was a natural choice to take a commission and perform a role in the pursuit of the Turkish hordes. With Vienna saved and the besiegers in full flight it was tempting to see the Ottoman lands as wide open for reconquest. Vienna would no longer be a border city on the fracture line of two empires, she would take her place – and this was the strategic significance of 1683 – at the heart of an immense domain protected from Islamic intrusion by a vast hinterland. This hinterland first and foremost was Hungary.

Asia, Metternich later quipped, began on the Landstrasse in Vienna, and though the Landstrasse hardly existed in 1683 the dusty tracks to the east of the Austrian city created (as they do even today) the sense of a limitless expanse stretching far into an unknown world. Only the fortresses offered punctuation marks on the horizon and one by one these would have to be captured or destroyed. From 1683 to 1699 the war against the Turks would pitilessly roll the Ottomans out of Hungary. But these were hard campaigns and, as so often happens after moments of euphoria, they suffered at first from excessive zeal and inadequate preparation.

On 27 September 1683, Lorraine's cavalry entered the great fortress of Pressburg, but further east at Barkan the Turks caught the Polish hussars in an ambush which only Lorraine's rapid deployment of his dragoons en masse prevented turning into a rout. The following month, the fortress of Esztergom, later to become the seat of the Hungarian bishops, was occupied and returned to the Habsburgs after eighty years of Ottoman suzerainty and a siege of six days. It really did seem as if nothing could stop the Imperial troops, and the news the same week of Kara Mustafa's execution for failing to take Vienna raised morale further. By 1684, a coalition of the Venetian Doge, the Habsburg Emperor and the King of Poland pledged to wage continuous war against the Turk. With the capture of Visegrad in June the route to Buda, the key to western Hungary, was open.

But Buda, or as the Austrians called it, Ofen, was a formidable obstacle. Its ramparts were as thick as Vienna's, but unlike that city it lay not on a flat plain but on a dramatic rocky hill above the Danube, dominating the surrounding landscape with its citadels and towers. A vast fleet of barges and supply vessels was sent from Vienna down the Danube to provision the siege forces with artillery and other weapons and victuals.

The Ottomans proved no less tenacious than the Viennese and after a year Lorraine broke off the siege as his troops were decimated by the terrible 'Morbus Hungaricus' or swamp fever, which persuaded the patriotic and influential priest Marco d'Aviano to advise Lorraine that the siege should be lifted, if only temporarily. By the time the siege was resumed a few months later, the Turks had used the interval to strengthen their defences and once again the Habsburg troops, though now reinforced by Prussians and Bavarians, found they could make little impact on the fortress. Only with the arrival of new guns in June 1686 did the siege resume progress and a breach on the Gellért side of the fortifications allow the Bavarians to gain a foothold. After several days of fierce combat, during which Prince Eugene's hand was pierced by an arrow fired at close range near the main gate, the city's defenders began to tire.

A summons by Lorraine to the Turkish commander to surrender brought the reply that Buda would be defended 'until my last gasp of breath'. Meanwhile the Imperial War Council had agreed that the capture of Buda would not bring offensive operations against the Turks to an end. A new war aim had been formulated and this was nothing less ambitious than 'the annihilation of the Ottoman Empire'. A fresh artillery barrage a few weeks later breached the main gate and the Imperial troops poured in, wreaking havoc on all traces of humanity they could find, including women and children. Only with considerable difficulty did Lorraine get his men under control as the pent-up bloodlust of months took over and hundreds of innocent civilians were slaughtered with the greatest brutality and mutilation.[2] Of the 13,000-strong Ottoman garrison, barely 2,000 survived.

With the fall of Buda in 1686 the great Hungarian plain and the Danube routes to Belgrade were open and Leopold, true to his alliance with both the King of Poland and Venice, pushed his forces south and east. The following year, at the Battle of Nágyharsány, the defeat of the Hungarians by the Turks at Mohács, a century and a half earlier, was avenged and a year after that Belgrade was stormed.

The capture of Belgrade was a triumph which rang the church bells throughout the Habsburg lands. It was the jewel in a campaign of conquest that had pushed Habsburg power hundreds of miles down the Danube. But in the uncertainty of war, which made Belgrade change hands with increasing frequency over the coming century, the Ottomans launched a vigorous counter-attack. The great city fell to the Ottomans the following year and the Habsburg forces' grip began to weaken, beset by indifferent leadership and Ottoman tenacity. Eugene had returned west to Austria's second front, the war against his hated foe Louis XIV, and it was only when peace was concluded in early 1697 that Eugene returned to Hungary.

His reputation preceded him. Against France Eugene had demonstrated that swiftness of movement which he had learnt during his campaigning against the Turks. It was to make him famous; the Siege of Cuneo was raised virtually as soon as the besieging French heard the Prince was riding to that town's relief. He had also learnt, as Wallenstein had at the beginning of the century, that his cavalry, well handled, were some of the finest the world had ever known.

The bridge at Zenta

But it was to be back on the eastern front at Zenta in 1697 that Eugene, now commander-in-chief, was able to harness all his military experience to deal a crippling blow to the Ottoman Empire. In the fifteen years since the Siege of Vienna, his army had become better equipped and trained to deal with their eastern foe. Against an enemy that was formidable in hand-to-hand combat and deadly in its use of the 'arme blanche', the Imperial infantry had learnt the hard way to close ranks and maintain fire discipline. Those units that failed to move swiftly could face immediate destruction. Contemporary accounts are littered with descriptions of Imperial infantry cut to pieces for failing to form a line before the enemy was within 20 paces of them. Eugene imposed new training regimes which forced his men to react much more quickly. Eugene invested his troops with a keen sense of the need for speed almost as if his own sense of movement had been sharpened by his encounters with the Ottomans. After the slow, methodical warfare on the plains of Piedmont his lightning-like thought processes relished the fast-moving demands of eastern warfare. In Hungary he almost allowed himself to be led by instinct rather than planning. Nothing expressed this more vividly than his actions in the second week of September 1697, which culminated in Zenta.

On 11 September one of Eugene's scouts caught a solitary pasha out riding without an escort. After failing to get any information from him the Prince ordered his Croat horsemen to draw their swords and prepare to cut off the pasha's head, a command which unsurprisingly focused the Turk's mind more acutely than had Eugene's earlier request.

The pasha began to explain: Ottoman forces were at that very moment crossing the Tisza river at Zenta, not many miles from where they stood. On closer questioning, the prisoner thought it would take the best part of the day to effect the crossing. The pasha's life was spared but Eugene immediately leapt into the saddle and rode with his hussars to Zenta, ordering the rest of his army to follow him at once. Eugene realised that he had been given a unique chance to win a great victory. By the time he arrived at Zenta, with the bulk of his cavalry, although the Ottomans had strongly entrenched the entry to the bridge their army was still crossing the river.

Eugene immediately had his cavalry attack the entrenchments in close formation, achieving almost complete surprise. The Turkish defenders panicked and began to withdraw on to the bridge, where they were overcome by indescribable confusion and terror. Attempts to rally failed and, as Eugene's infantry came up an hour later with the artillery, the entrenchments were stormed and volley after volley was poured into the mass of Turks on the bridge. His artillery pounded the forces on the other side of the river. Within six hours the devastation was complete. Twenty thousand Turks lay dead or wounded and more than 10,000 had been drowned as the crowded bridge collapsed under Austrian shellfire. Eugene lost just 350 men. So dazzling was this victory that the victors captured not only the Sultan's seal, treasury and harem (some eighty strong) but also the entire Ottoman baggage train, including nearly a hundred camels.

The Treaty of Karlowitz and the reorganisation of the Military Frontier

The political consequences were no less dramatic. Within less than eighteen months the Treaty of Karlowitz was signed, on 26 January 1699, ending centuries of Ottoman power in Central Europe. Turkey was obliged to surrender Hungary and even parts of Bosnia, which Eugene had raided returning, according to a contemporary account, with 'many beautiful Turkish women'. The picturesque land of Transylvania though nominally independent would henceforth be governed by Austrian appointees. At a stroke the entire eastern frontier of the Habsburg Empire had been shifted many hundreds of miles to the east. Even the Military Frontier, the fortified borderlands between the two empires, had to be reorganised to incorporate these new territorial acquisitions.

Originally created, as we have seen, in 1553 as a form of cordon sanitaire running from Senj across Sisak to Durdevac, the Military Frontier had been financed by the Styrian nobility and administered by the War Council in Graz. From the 1630s, the Habsburgs had encouraged immigration from the Turkish provinces, offering the privilege of internal self-administration and freedom of religion for the settlers along the Military Frontier so that many Serbs of Orthodox religion found refuge in what gradually became one long, armed encampment where every tenth inhabitant was under arms.

After the Treaty of Karlowitz this frontier was now vastly expanded to include Lower Slavonia, Illyria and the Banat. New units of locally recruited cavalry known as Serežan were engaged for piquet and police duties among a population that was extremely mixed but, thanks to the continuous skirmishing, increasingly made up of resourceful and practical men, natural warrriors often capable of rising rapidly through the ranks. This huge extension of the Military Frontier would feed the tactics and manpower of the Balkans into the Imperial standing army for its campaigns in the coming century, giving Austrian arms a reputation for dash and style.

Politically, Karlowitz marked decisively the decline of one empire and the rise of another. Throughout south-eastern Europe Christians rejoiced at the fall of the Turkish oppressors. Optimism and euphoria abounded. From Mount Athos a group of Orthodox monks made a pilgrimage all the way to Vienna to lay at the feet of the Emperor Leopold a beautiful icon of the Virgin Mary. They were convinced that within months the Imperial armies would liberate the entire Balkan peninsula.

It was not to be. Left to their own devices, no doubt Leopold and Eugene would have seen Karlowitz as a brief armistice. They contemplated pushing the Turks further back and reconquering, again, Belgrade, left by the Treaty of Karlowitz in Turkish hands. But the completion of this particular 'Austrian mission' in the east was never to happen, though several wars would still be fought against the Ottomans throughout much of the next years. It would be more than a century before the monks of Athos and Greece were, in Metternich's memorable phrase, 'condemned to life', and then Austria would play no significant role in the struggle for Greek independence.

War with France

Austria, secure to the east, now turned towards her other great 'mission' whereby she contributed forcefully to the balance of power in Europe. This mission meant that she could not be indifferent to the activities of Louis XIV of France.

The issue of who would succeed to the Spanish throne at the beginning of the eighteenth century after the death in 1700 of the infirm and childless Charles II, son of Philip IV, was not one any Austrian Habsburg could regard with Olympian detachment. When Louis XIV proposed uniting the Spanish with the French throne the response could only be war. Not for the last time would Austria become the lynchpin of a coalition whose aim was to prevent mainland Europe from falling under the dominance of a single power.

While shifting the focus of the Austrian Habsburgs dramatically from the east to the west, the War of the Spanish Succession would provide the world with extravagant confirmation that as a military power the Habsburg armies were a force to be reckoned with. Hard though it might be to imagine a more dazzling victory than Zenta, Prince Eugene was about to demonstrate with the

Duke of Marlborough his brilliance even more impressively than he had on the parched plains of Hungary. The small Bavarian village of Blindheim, not far from the banks of the Upper Danube, was surrounded by lush grass and fertile fields.

In the war that was coming, Kaiser Leopold did not find it easy to ally himself with the Protestant maritime powers, England and the Netherlands. But the world had changed and it was a sign of Leopold's intelligence as a monarch that he possessed the ability to realise that he must adapt to the new circumstances and draw the correct conclusions from events. He was, understandably, outraged by the Pope's support of France, whose diplomatic machinations had taken every advantage of Leopold's difficulties in the east. With the Ottomans defeated, Leopold did not flinch for a moment from defending the interests of his house and from entering battle for the Spanish inheritance even though in military strength and statesmanship he was far inferior to his French cousin. (Louis XIV, like Leopold, was also the son of a Spanish Habsburg mother.)

The war began in a rather understated way on the north Italian plain near Legnagno. A French army under the dry and unimaginative Nicolas Catinat had occupied and fortified the Rivoli defile above Verona to ensure that a patchwork of Italian possessions remained loyal to Louis XIV. Catinat was encouraged by the court to demonstrate boldness and defeat the Habsburg troops as soon as possible should they descend from the Tyrol. Unfortunately for Catinat, Eugene was at the summit of his abilities in 1701 and his troops, fresh from the war of movement and energy in the east, were as keen as their commander to gain ascendancy over their French enemy as soon as possible. Eugene raised the old military art of the feint to new levels of sophistication. The Italian campaign of 1701–2 was subsequently overshadowed by the glittering victories of Blenheim and Oudenarde but this opening of the war revealed all Eugene's armies' qualities which later were so admired by the Duke of Marlborough.

As Catinat was expecting Eugene to approach via Rivoli, the Imperial commander wasted no time sending out messages *en clair* that this was precisely what he was doing. At one point Eugene proved so successful in giving the impression that he was entering Italy along the Adige that even his corps commanders believed this was their planned route. In fact Eugene had long decided to descend on the Italian plain through Vicenza further to the east. By guaranteeing Venetian property and keeping a firm grip on his troops to ensure that the agreements with the Veneto land-owning families were respected, the secret was well kept. Any soldiers found looting were summarily executed, much to the relief of the locals, who gradually came to welcome the

Imperial troops and prefer them to their French foes. A key part of Eugene's great success in masking his real intentions was the support of the Venetians of the plain whose understandable antagonism to a foreign army was power-fully reduced not least by Eugene's excellent relations with the local clergy. By 27 May Catinat had to report to Paris that, despite his 'vigilance', Eugene had succeeded in reaching the Venetian plains without giving battle.

Where Eugene was bold, Catinat was cautious and in a fierce cavalry engagement on the Mincio, Eugene forced the French to retreat over the Oglio in a strange series of manoeuvres which is sometimes called the Battle of Carpi. The news of this engagement, coupled with the fact that the army of Louis XIV had not, contrary to popular belief, defeated or even hindered Eugene's deployment, was enough for Paris to sack the hapless Catinat and send the aged Villeroi to replace him.

Villeroi in his early seventies was an experienced general but, at this stage of his career, rich years at court had sapped his appetite for risk. 'It is difficult,' Louis XIV said later to him, 'at our stage of life to have much luck.'[3] As soon as he was established on the plains of Lombardy, Eugene set about constructing a powerfully defensive position in front of the fortress town of Chiari. He was aware that the French would be encouraged to take the offensive and his plan now was to create an anvil of such strength that the hammer-blows of the French would prove incapable of making any serious impression. For supplies he raided the estates of the wealthy Mantuan aristocracy while giving strict orders that the possessions of the less well off inhabitants were to be untouched.

The position at Chiari was well suited to Eugene's ends. Streams protected his forces on three sides and the earthworks he set about constructing with the fortress at his rear offered no scope for surprise cavalry attacks. His infantry was arranged into a solid line three ranks deep. Thus drawn up they waited until the French infantry had dressed their lines and advanced to within 15 paces. At this moment they let fly three volleys of such withering effect that within an hour Villeroi had suffered nearly 3,000 casualties.

The news of the French defeat resounded around Europe, emboldening the maritime powers to sign the second treaty of the Grand Alliance. The Austrian infantry had proved capable of being stubborn in defence and were well drilled against what were then considered to be the finest foot soldiers in Europe.

The seizure of Cremona

Villeroi fell back on Cremona, where events took a picturesque turn. After five months of careful consolidation following his victory at Chiari, Eugene again took the offensive. His army was still well provisioned and disciplined. He had executed forty-eight soldiers for looting houses around Mantua and, continuing his excellent relationship with the local clergy, had been informed by a Father Cossoli, a priest in Cremona, of a secret route into that town via one of the sewerage canals.

While Eugene formed two columns to approach the two main gates of the town before dawn, he detached 400 soldiers under an intrepid Scot, Captain Francis Macdonnell, to enter the town by this clandestine route, await the quiet moment before dawn, then emerge and open the gates from within. The plan was executed the night before the first day of February when temperatures were low enough to prevent the worst of the vermin and stench of the canal from demoralising Macdonnell's men as they crouched awaiting their moment to strike.

The Austrians achieved complete surprise. One gate was seized and more than a thousand French soldiers were slaughtered in their beds as one of Eugene's columns entered the town. Villeroi himself was captured and, it is said, was only saved from being bayoneted in his bed by the quick-witted Macdonnell.[4] Villeroi promptly offered Macdonnell not only a commission but an entire regiment in the French army if he would return to France with him, but the Scottish officer politely refused.

The news of Villeroi's capture spread through the town as the morning wore on. But Eugene had not reckoned with the 600 men of two Irish regiments in the French service commanded by Dillon and Burke. One of the Austrian columns approaching from the other side of the river Po had been delayed. The Po Gate and the Citadel roused by the firing in the rest of the town had not been overwhelmed as Eugene had planned. They were held by men of the Dillon regiment and the Irish took up a strong position around the Citadel, giving the Austrians their first check of the day. Even fierce hand-to-hand fighting failed to dislodge them. At first Eugene ordered Villeroi to tell the Irish to lay down their arms but Villeroi merely shrugged and, pointing to his surrendered sword lying on the floor, observed: 'I should be delighted to oblige but I am no longer in command here.'[5]

Eugene then asked Macdonnell to tell the Irish that they would all be slaughtered if they did not surrender immediately and that greater honour and improved pay and conditions awaited them in the Austrian service where many Irishmen had made splendid careers as officers. To this ultimatum the Irish replied that their pride was insulted by so 'ungenerous an offer' which they felt was 'unworthy of a great prince' who would 'surely know the true value of honour and loyalty'. As an added expression of their 'disappointment' they felt compelled to keep Macdonnell prisoner.

The Austrians resumed the attack but without much success. After two hours of fierce fighting Eugene gradually realised that without his second column entering the Po Gate he could not dislodge the Irish and that with every minute that passed the town which at dawn had fallen into his hands as a prize would become, with the imminent approach of a large French relief force, a trap. By mid-afternoon Eugene broke off the action. Well might he later report that Cremona had been 'taken by a miracle; lost by an even greater one'.

Aside from the Irish heroics – Louis XIV would increase their pay and honour them generously on their return to France – it had been a bad day for French arms. Eugene's withdrawal and the subsequent inconclusive action at Luzzara in no way detracted from the lustre that surrounded his leadership and the quality of his troops. Louis XIV realised that his taunting of the 'Abbé Eugene' and his refusal to offer the Prince a commission in the French army all those years ago had been an expensive gesture.

Nevertheless, whatever the vicissitudes of the campaigns in northern Italy, along the Rhine French arms and those of their allies, the Bavarians, were victorious. There, one German town after another trembled at the thought of the almighty French army. If French prestige were to be destroyed it would have to be here.

Marlborough and Eugene cooperate

The presence of the Bavarians – for neither the first nor the last time on the side of the Habsburg's enemies – implied a threat to the crown lands and even Vienna. Eugene was hastily recalled and though there is some controversy over the exact authorship of the plan that was next devised, it is clear that Eugene immediately saw that the army of the maritime powers under Marlborough would need to travel from the distant Lowlands all the way down the Rhine to the valley of the Upper Danube if the French threat was to be met.

Marlborough's march to the Danube is rightly seen as one of the great feats of his generalship. Eugene had grasped immediately on his return to Vienna as head of the Imperial War Council that the junction of his forces and Marlborough's in the valley of the Upper Danube was the best way to defend the Habsburg marches. He wrote to Marlborough suggesting he withdraw his forces from the northern to the southern sphere of war and by happy coincidence Marlborough's judgement 'exactly coincided' with his own.[6]

This was the first sign of the strong sympathy between the two men whose relationship was to be so critical for Europe over the next six years. Where Eugene was mercurial in mood, neurotic and highly strung, the more stolid Marlborough enjoyed more earthy pleasures. Despite their different temperaments and attitudes they formed a partnership that is still considered one of the most successful in the history of modern warfare. Their combined talents all but destroyed France as a military power, and their personal differences were sublimated in their respect for each other's military skill.

Marlborough's execution of the march to the Danube was faultless, keeping the French guessing that an attack was being prepared against Alsace until it was too late for the French marshal Tallard to stop the British, Danish and Dutch troops reaching the Danube. Eugene performed a no less notable 'ruse' in marching his men during the same days, over similar terrain. He also gambled on the French army in Alsace misinterpreting his intentions and left a small screen of troops to engage in much activity along the Rhine while he stole away. At the same time a network of Austrian spies in a campaign of calculated disinformation reported that Eugene's troops were heading for Rottweil to the west. Eugene's movements in fact were contrived to give the French every reason to think he was to remain in the neighbourhood of the Upper Rhine. Raising the Siege of Villingen he ordered the breaches to be repaired. In every order and disposition he appeared determined to remain where he was. His movements were arranged with 'a masterly penetration of his enemy's mind'.[7]

Leaving some eight battalions at Rottweil, he headed off towards the valley of the Neckar with about 15,000 troops. These he had chosen for their mobility and nearly one third were cavalry: his best cavalry, including the formidable cuirassiers, then considered among the elite of the Habsburg troops. Suddenly from the moment Eugene reached Tübingen a curious thing happened. All this open and rather unhurried activity ceased. Eugene and his 15,000 men abruptly, and to the consternation of the French spies, simply disappeared. Behind him a fog of rumours and ill-considered reports, contradictory and fantastic, were all that was left. Eugene headed towards Höchstädt on the Danube and would soon be within shouting distance of his ally.

As had been the allies' intention all along, Marlborough now aimed to disrupt the freedom of movement of the Franco-Bavarian force under Marcin and the Elector of Bavaria, who were centred on Augsburg, threatening the approaches to Vienna. The Franco-Bavarians reacted with predictable hostility and began marching north to threaten Marlborough's supply line. The Franco-Bavarians would cut this supply line once they reached the northern bank of the Danube and so they obliged Marlborough to march in parallel with them back north. Unwittingly, this only brought Marlborough closer to Eugene.

On 8 August the Franco-Bavarians were approaching the Danube crossing at Dillingen when Tallard was suddenly brought intelligence that Eugene was on the other side at Höchstädt with 39 squadrons and 20 battalions. Eugene's rapid and secret march had achieved the utmost success. He had been helped by the slowness of communications of those times: a message could barely cover a hundred miles and might take several days to arrive. Movements could be disguised by a combination of disseminating contradictory messages and carefully planted cavalry screens.

In this case the effect on the morale of the Franco-Bavarians was dramatic. With no inkling of his existence Eugene had brought reinforcements the size of a third of Marlbrough's forces to within striking range. Moreover, as the reports confirmed, Eugene's leadership had ensured that these were all disciplined and highly trained troops serving under a soldier whose name was already invested with the prestige of countless battle honours. Eugene's sudden appearance not only transformed the equation of power on the Upper Danube but it allowed Marlborough, who had been finding his ally, 'Turkish' Louis of Baden, something of a trial, a perfect opportunity to rid himself of this narrow-minded pedant and dispatch him to the Siege of Ingolstadt.

One serious obstacle remained before these two commanders could effect the junction of their forces: the Danube. On the same day that Tallard was apprised of Eugene's arrival, the Savoy Prince crossed the Danube to hold a council of war with his English ally. Marlborough agreed that the northern bank of the river was the key to his lines of communications and so dispatching 3,000 of his cavalry to follow Eugene back, he began preparing for the rest of his army to cross the river.

Blenheim

Eugene's position was perilous, as he was barely a day's march away from a Franco-Bavarian force that was three times the size of his own. An urgent message to Marlborough spurred the Englishman to march his infantry through the night. Before dawn on 11 August Marlborough had crossed the river at Merxheim with twenty battalions while a further column was crossing the river at Donauwörth. By the afternoon of the following day the two allies were together at the head of an army of 52,000 men made up of Danes, Hessians, Austrians, English, Prussians and Dutch. Marlborough's achievement was all the greater for the fact that his artillery arrived only by the following day.

The French and their Bavarian allies chose to deny Marlborough further progress along the Danube, convinced that rather than risk an indecisive action the allies would retreat northwards along their lines of communication. A strongly fortified position, the lynchpin of whose right flank would be the village of Blindheim five miles away from where Eugene and Marlborough stood, was prepared by Tallard and the Elector. But if the French and Bavarians thought Marlborough would shun battle they were mistaken. At two in the morning of Wednesday 13 August, the allies broke camp and began their march westwards towards Blenheim, as Marlborough's scouts called the village of Blindheim. Eugene and Marlborough had surveyed the battlefield from the church tower of Tapfheim the day before and, despite the care with which the French were laying out their position, it was clear that it was a battleground made for a bold frontal attack.

By seven o'clock the allied columns began to deploy in line about a mile away from the Franco-Bavarian position still shrouded in the early morning mist. Eugene's troops took rather longer to arrive on the allies' right flank because the hills of Schwennenbach and French artillery made their deployment far from painless. The ground was 'so embarrassed with brambles, hedges and other encumbrances that there was no marching by columns'.[8] By half past twelve the Prince was ready and within an hour the entire line on both sides was engaged.

From the beginning Eugene had subordinated himself to Marlborough and both men had agreed that the key to the French position lay between the villages of Blindheim and Oberglauheim. Eugene's task was to hold the numerically superior forces of the Elector and Marcin while Marlborough attacked the French line on the allied left flank and centre. The French centre was weak; too many regiments had been crammed into Blindheim but when the first attack went in against the village, Marlborough's forces were repulsed, with heavy loss.

In contrast to the war of movement and dynamic ebb and thrust familiar to those who had served Eugene in the east, the initial phase of the battle here was a textbook example of that perfection of restraint with which the disciplined armies of the eighteenth century fought in western Europe. When a distance little longer than a cricket pitch separated the advancing English from the French palisades a volley from the defenders crashed out, felling one in three of the attackers. Still the British regiments, obedient to their officers, reserved their fire until their leading officer gave the agreed signal by touching the woodwork of the outer palisade with his sword, whereupon they too volleyed but failed to make any impact on the carefully constructed defences.

Any attempt to turn the French line from here was doomed to failure and Marlborough, who had lost a significant part of his force in the failed attempt to storm the village, renewed his attack against the weaker French centre, this time with more success. His cavalry, though inferior in number and stationary, saw off a violent attack by the French Gens d'Armes elite household cavalry, an event which later analysts of the battle would regard with significance as indicating that the French cavalry were in a less robust form than might have been expected. Despite the tremendous feats of arms performed by the infantry,

Blenheim would be decided by cavalry and in particular the cavalry of Prince Eugene, which was comprised, though by no means exclusively, of several regiments of Austrian horsemen (Lobkowitz, Styrum and Fugger's Dragoons and Cuirassiers).

Eugene's infantry brigade made up of Prussians and Danes initially carried much before them but soon the Franco-Bavarian numbers began to tell and by about 2.30, Eugene's position was becoming desperate as the enemy cavalry and artillery began to shatter his lines. The pressure of these attacks mounted and first the Prussians and then the Danes began to withdraw behind the little Nebel stream. Eugene was about to commit his reserves to stem this crumbling edifice of his infantry, which threatened to engulf his entire wing, when a message from Marlborough arrived asking for urgent cavalry reinforcements as his centre came under renewed pressure from repeated French cavalry attacks. All Marlborough's centre was pressed and shaken. His cavalry had just been caught while still in the disorder of forming on the further bank of the Nebel. Here was the crisis of the battle and had the French commanders comprehended it correctly they would no doubt have deployed their reserves – idle and unused around Blenheim – to roll the English centre back across the river and slaughter it in the marshy land beyond.

It is the most remarkable testament to the powerful bond Eugene and Marlborough had formed during their very brief acquaintance that at the moment when Eugene's own forces appeared to be facing their greatest peril of the day, he, without hesitating, ordered Fugger's brigade of heavy cavalry to ride immediately to Marlborough's aid. Eugene knew the battle would be decided on Marlborough's front and with his swiftness of thought lost not a second in ordering support to his embattled ally.

Fugger, scion of a wealthy family from Augsburg which though situated in Bavaria was a 'Reichstadt' and therefore no friend of the Elector of Bavaria, was not a man to be trifled with. He had earlier rejected a plea from the Dutch infantry for help on the ground, that he answered only to Prince Eugene. Now he needed no further prompting and made haste to correct his earlier reserve towards his allies. The three squadrons of his own cuirassiers plus three further squadrons of the Lobkowitz Cuirassiers reinforced by some of Styrum's Dragoons came thundering across the battlefield and crashed into the French cavalry in flank, permitting Marlborough's demoralised Dutch infantry – who were about to be swept away – to reform.

As in so many battles, the line between utter defeat and outright victory was extremely thin. In less than twenty minutes the great threat to the allies' centre had been resolutely met, thanks to the discipline of a few hundred fresh Austrian cavalry engaged with the rapidity of perception that was their commander's hallmark. The French cavalry were literally ridden off the battle-field first by the Austrians and then by a counter-charge of Marlborough's united cavalry. It was as if the tables had been turned in a few minutes. The pressure was now on the French with their line crumbling and their powerful right wing still holding Blenheim but bottled up and isolated, unable to affect the outcome of the battle.

As Tallard would later poignantly write: 'I saw one instant in which the battle was won; if the cavalry had not turned and abandoned the line.'[9] The French centre was exposed by the rout of the French cavalry. Further weak-ened, it severed into two disconnected parts. Tallard and the Elector of Bavaria lacked the empathy of their opponents and they made little attempt to coordi-nate. Blenheim itself surrendered as darkness fell, adding 10,000 prisoners to the 12,000 casualties on the Franco-Bavarian side.

The political consequences of this day were even more significant than the character of the military success. It was the first great defeat Louis XIV had suffered and utterly destroyed all the stratagems with which he had dreamt of menacing Vienna and advancing a Franco-Bavarian force along the valley of the Danube. It sealed in blood the bond between Catholic Vienna and Protestant London and between Marlborough and Eugene. At the same time it put paid to any chance of a Hungarian insurrection and threw the Bourbons on to the defensive. For five years the myth of French invincibility would remain shattered until on the great palisades of Malplaquet the French defence recovered its stubbornness.

After Blenheim the two victors went their own ways. While Marlborough, after due adulation in London, defeated the French in another great though more modest victory at Ramillies, Eugene returned to Vienna to be feted by a grateful court. Both men were lavishly rewarded. In Vienna in addition to a fine Palais near the cathedral along the Himmelpfortgasse, the Prince was given ground to construct the magnificent Schloss Belvedere under the design of Lukas von Hildebrandt. Further east on the Marchfeld, the hauntingly beautiful Schloss Hof, immortalised by Canaletto, was another gem to be added to the victor's laurels. Eugene, the unlikely warrior whose fearless courage bordered on hysteria on the battlefield, became a great patron of the arts and the Belvedere remains to this day one of the great triumphs of Austrian baroque.

The Siege of Turin: Oudenarde and Malplaquet

It was not to be long before the sound of the guns would take Eugene on the road to war again. He was determined not to allow the year of 1706 to pass without some great action. It was time to deal with Louis XIV's ambitions on the Italian peninsula again. Checked on the Danube and in the Lowlands after his defeat at Ramillies, Louis wanted to undermine the Habsburgs' allies around Turin. The French invested the city and occupied the surrounding land and Alpine foothills.

Another army would have to make its way from the Alpine fastnesses of the Tyrol down to the Piedmontese foothills. Eugene marched with only 24,000 mostly Austrian and German troops across the Alps, ascending mountains and crossing rivers through country occupied by his enemies. To everyone's astonishment he arrived in time to relieve the besieged garrison, venturing an attack on the French at four o'clock in the morning on 7 September 1706 notwithstanding his inferiority in equipment and numbers. The French were prepared and their artillery decimated Eugene's front ranks until the Prussians on Eugene's left wing under Prince Leopold of Dessau broke through the French entrenchments on their third attempt and put their obstinate opponents to the bayonet. This encouraged Eugene's right wing, made up of Palatinate and Gotha troops, leavened with some Württemberg regiments, to push forward. At the same time Count Daun who commanded the garrison erupted from the citadel with several thousand troops, further disordering the French lines that were now pressed upon two fronts.

The Prussians mounted the ramparts first and in a letter to Zinzensdorf, Eugene generously acknowledged the Prussians' valour noting: 'The Prince of Anhalt has once more done wonders with his troops at Turin. I met him twice in the thickest fire and in the very front of it, and, I cannot conceal it, that in bravery, and especially in discipline his troops have far surpassed mine'.[10]

The raising of the Siege of Turin added further laurels to Eugene's reputation, and although the Prussian infantry under his command had distinguished itself, the Austrian garrison had also fought with great vigour and courage. The confusion of the French had greatly increased as a result of their rear line being attacked by Daun, whose troops wounded the senior French commander, Marcin and the Duke of Orleans. Marcin, who was captured, died the following day. His troops left more than 5,000 dead on the battlefield and twice as many wounded. Barely 16,000 survivors fled over the Alps into France, all that remained of an army which had at one point been reckoned at nearly 60,000 strong. The abandoned supplies were stupendous. More than 200 cannon[11] and 80,000 barrels of powder as well as standards and treasure fell into Eugene's hands.

The strategic effects were even more spectacular as the French rapidly lost one place after another in Italy and were forced to conclude a general capitulation according to the terms of which they evacuated Italy entirely. On hearing the news of Turin, Marlborough wrote: 'It is impossible to express the joy it has given me but I really love this Prince [Eugene]. This glorious act must bring France so low that . . . with the blessing of God we have such peace as will give us quiet for all our days.'[12] By 1707 France had lost a third of the Spanish inheritance she claimed and the Habsburg Emperor had secured Lombardy and the Netherlands by the two great battles of the previous year.

On 11 June 1708 at Oudenarde, the two allied commanders again formed an invincible duo, Marlborough's mood visibly lifting when he was joined by Eugene after a string of British losses in Flanders. Their opponents, the Dukes of Burgoyne and Vendôme could not abide each other. Once again at a critical moment in the battle, Eugene's cavalry rode against their old opponents, the French Household dragoons, though with less effect this time. Nevertheless, the left wing of the allies under Eugene never let Marlborough down and this great battle was won, as at Blenheim, because of the cohesion of command.

Oudenarde opened the way for Eugene to attack and take by storm the citadel of Ryssel, hitherto regarded as impregnable. France was now utterly humbled north as well as south of the Alps and the dreadful winter of 1708 forced her into further concessions though not as many as Eugene and Marlborough desired. Both men agreed not only that no single possession of the House of Austria should be in French hands but that Louis XIV should assist in expelling his own grandson Philip from Spain. Not even defeated France could bear such extreme humiliation, and war began again. In the Netherlands the great armies limbered up for another sanguinary struggle.

At the outset of the great Battle of Malplaquet, Eugene received a graze to the head from a passing shot. It was almost an omen, because this victory was more bitterly contested than any other in the campaigns to date. The French retired from the field exhausted but in good order. They had given a good account of themselves and had shown resilience when pushed. Their defensive position, the bloc, was formidable and this battle cost Marlborough many of his finest regiments. The French were not pursued by Eugene's horse which in one final melee had fought their opponents to a standstill but were themselves so exhausted that they were incapable of harassing the French further.

It was to be the last of the great duo's victories but they could look back on an undefeated partnership that had restored the balance of power to the Continent. Nonetheless, Malplaquet marked the point at which France would be pushed no more. France sued for terms and one by one her network of fortresses was surrendered but the complete destruction of France was no longer deemed possible and any plans for a march on Paris to fulfil the promise of total revenge were abandoned after the Tories took over in London and Marlborough was recalled and dismissed. With the death of the Emperor

Joseph I on 17 April 1711 all enthusiasm on the part of England to support Austria began to wane.

Eugene's military reforms and Austrian white

Eugene was keen to incorporate lessons learnt from his campaigning next to Marlborough. In his role as President of the Imperial War Council, he had initiated a number of reforms to the Imperial forces which further emphasised the distinctive character of the army he had led to victory in both eastern and western theatres of war.

His experience of all three military branches had led him to the firm conviction that a greater degree of uniformity was necessary if efficiency was to be maintained and even improved. He had been impressed by many aspects of Marlborough's war machine, not least the steadfastness of his infantry and its fine drill. He had also seen at first hand the hardiness of the Prussians under his command and their stoical ability to survive the fiercest of attacks. Above all, Eugene's experience of effective cavalry screens in his campaigns with Marlborough and the great value of mounted scouts in his campaigns against the Ottomans encouraged him to favour the development of light cavalry.

It is interesting to note that according to at least one authority (Ottenfeld)[13] the Austrian cavalry officers were deliberately chosen to include a small but significant proportion of soldiers who had risen through the ranks. Eugene, whose detestation of all things to do with Louis XIV's military machine was legendary, strongly believed that one of the defects of the French military system was that its officer caste was too remote from its other ranks. An officer cadre that was drawn too exclusively from one narrow level of society bred complacency and inertia. It was important that the 'best families' produced a great share of the officer corps but the social distance between the French cavalry officer and his troopers was in Eugene's view simply too wide.

These views would have a long-term effect on the social make-up of the Habsburg officer corps. Unlike that of France or, notably, Prussia whose officer corps was exclusively drawn from the Junker families, it would not be bound entirely by the hierarchy of social origins. Even the British army was domi-nated well into the twentieth century in its upper echelons by the Anglo-Irish Protestant ascendancy: most of the field marshals of the Second World War were from Ulster. The Austrian army at this stage in its development embraced diversity and social mobility.

Eugene also addressed the issue of recruitment of all arms with a reforming zeal. He consolidated the system whereby regiments recruited in particular areas (*Bezirk*). He was convinced that local people who knew or were related to each other would fight best together in the same regiment. The regiment should recruit 'the relatives and people who are known' to men already serving.

Eugene also insisted on the highest possible standards of physical appearance. 'Manly faces and a good figure' were among his requirements. Convicted criminals and deserters were banned from recruitment, the latter on account of the inevitability that they 'having deserted once will certainly desert again'.[14] Because an army had many requirements in its day-to-day activities in peacetime, Eugene believed that priority should also be given to craftsmen in the recruitment process. Above all, where possible the men should be 'good young people from good homes'.

The reforms bore fruit and accompanied a significant expansion in the numbers of regiments in the Habsburg forces. Between 1697 and 1710 Infantry regiments increased from 29 to 40 in number. Each regiment was composed of 12 companies, each of 150 men. Cavalry expanded too. By 1711 the seven Cuirassier and one Dragoon regiment of the decade earlier had been increased to 20 Cuirassier regiments, 12 Dragoon regiments and, notably, five Hussar regiments.

This new establishment demanded a concomitant overhaul of military expenditure. In 1699 Leopold I had initiated a system whereby part of each soldier's pay was retained for equipment and uniform costs. Officers continued to pay for their own full dress and battle equipment and uniforms. Pay was standardised between regiments, the normal daily rate for an infantryman being two and two-thirds kreutzer and, for a cavalry soldier, 5 kreutzer. The pay was increased in the ranks as and if the soldiers received promotion to non-commissioned rank (e.g. corporal: 4 kreutzer). The captain detailed to oversee regimental payments was instructed to ensure each soldier was given a receipt (*Zettel*) detailing all deductions from his pay for equipment. This is an early example of the bureaucracy that became a hallmark of all things military for the Habsburgs.

Alongside these financial innovations, Prince Eugene and the Imperial War Council attempted to introduce more consistency in the regimental uniforms, still largely at this stage in the hands of the regimental colonels. As 'pearl grey' wool was the cheapest and easiest material to conserve, this colour, which under the Danubian sun bleached easily to a lighter shade of off-white, began to be more and more widely adopted. It was still not by any means ubiquitous until in 1707, on 28 December, Eugene, as President of the War Council, issued a decree allowing only three regiments (Osnabrück, Bayreuth and Wetzel) to wear green or blue. Six months later, on Leopold's death, the new Emperor, Joseph I, approved an order insisting on 'bleached grey' for all regiments with the exception of the garrisons of Prague and Gross-Glogau. By the winter of 1708 most regiments had adhered to these regulations and the traditional picture of the Austrian soldier in white with facings of various shades of blue and red became more widespread.[15]

Like Field Marshal Daun later, under Maria Theresa, Eugene believed the soldier would look after his uniform better if he considered it to be his own. But compared to the uniforms of England and France Austrian service dress was not only less ornate but generally of cheaper quality. This economy underlined the severe financial restraints that governed military outlay and in which the remarkable career of Samuel Oppenheimer alluded to earlier during the Siege of Vienna also played a role. On Oppenheimer's death in 1703 the state finances with which he had shored up Eugene's campaigns against the Turks went bust and drastic cuts had to be made to all areas of military expenditure.

The new Emperor Joseph I (crowned in 1705) strongly supported Eugene's policies. Joseph was very different from his father even in appearance – he looks to have been one of the few pre-modern Habsburgs not to have had the typical Habsburg lip. Fair-haired and blue-eyed, he was strikingly handsome. An enthusiast for the arts, he was also fascinated by the science of war. He supported religious toleration and coming to an understanding with the Hungarians. But the Magyars could not trust a Habsburg and their predilection for violent rebellion cast a constant shadow over Joseph's reign. It was manifested in the form of a peasant war in which a people's army under the leadership of Ferenc Rákóczi brought death and destruction to parts of Silesia and Moravia. This rebel made it with his men virtually to the gates of Vienna until he was defeated by the shock of trained troops. The Hungarian revolt, though decisively put down by General Heuster, was followed – to the Hungarians' great surprise, by a peace of dazzling magnanimity.

Joseph was advised by brilliant men who had detested the unwieldiness of his father's administration, and his brief six-year reign, as well as being marked by clemency and tolerance, was characterised by reforming zeal and a proud indifference towards the Francophile Pope. When Clement XI threatened to excommunicate Prince Eugene who was about to encamp on papal territory, Joseph recalled that Comacchio on the Po delta had originally been an Imperial domain and promptly ordered Eugene to occupy it without delay.

Joseph's efforts to develop his and Eugene's ideas for the army came into constant conflict with financial realities. At one point in 1708 Eugene in exasperation wrote acidly to Count Zinzendorf, Joseph's Foreign Minister: 'the troops have not been paid in August a single kreutzer. I leave it to Your Excellency to imagine how the men can be saved from their inevitable collapse.'[16] These constraints especially affected the recently expanded cavalry regiments. Despite these problems, Eugene's reforms were strongly supported by Joseph. As an archduke, he had fought in Eugene's army with some distinction. Reform proceeded as fast as Imperial bureaucracy would permit. As well as recruitment, uniform and organisation, the President of the Imperial War Council also addressed the issue of tactics.

Although some historians have dwelt on the influence of the Turkish wars on the Austrian army's campaigns in western Europe, Eugene appears always to have regarded the two spheres of war as separate.[17] In fact he insisted on a firm separation between the tactics to be used against the Ottomans and those used against western European armies. For example he gave clear instructions that against the Turks his cavalry should always form three lines to protect against the shock surprise tactics of the Ottomans, whereas against western European cavalry his horsemen were to be drawn up in only two lines.[18] A cavalry veteran himself, on becoming President of the Imperial War Council one of the first steps Eugene took was to increase the establishment of the Dragoon regiments from ten to twelve companies.

Noting the need in the western sphere for formal arrangement of his cavalry, Eugene also set the exact distances between his units. The two lines were to be no more than five paces apart and the horses similarly spaced in the line. The positioning of the kettledrums, trumpeters and 'lifeguard' or reserve squadron were all carefully considered.

In 1711, shortly before Joseph I died tragically young of smallpox, he and Eugene had further agreed to strengthen the cavalry by the incorporation of grenadier companies among the dragoons. These were, like the infantry grenadiers, not formed into separate units but were elite companies of existing regiments. At more or less the same time the Cuirassier regiments were to be reinforced by the addition of carbine-equipped companies who were given the short carbine with a socket bayonet.

Charles VI : The last embers of Spanish inheritance

The new Emperor was Joseph's brother, Charles VI, on whose account the War of the Spanish Succession had been waged. The maritime powers, having fought to prevent the crowns of Spain and France uniting, had no wish for the crowns of Spain and Austria to be reunited by a single Habsburg, and thus the new Tory government in London broke off the alliance with Vienna.

By the terms of The 'Great Betrayal', as the series of treaties concluded in Utrecht in 1713 were called in Vienna, the Spanish crown was awarded to a Bourbon after all, on condition that no individual could be King both of France and Spain. France as a military power was humbled and Austria gained suzerainty over the Spanish Netherlands, Naples, Milan and Sardinia, this last soon to be swapped for Tuscany. At the Habsburg Kaiser's request, the treaty confirmed a token of gratitude for Prussia's support in the war. Henceforth the Prussian Elector would be allowed to style himself 'King in Prussia'.

But, Spain or no Spain, Austria was great even though she did not have in her new Kaiser, Charles, a great Emperor. Charles VI, in appearance, resembled his father Leopold. In character, he was imbued with the stiffness of the seventeenth-century Spanish Habsburgs. In 1703, after he had been proclaimed King of Spain, he travelled as Charles III through Holland and landed at Portsmouth where Marlborough conveyed him to an audience with Queen Anne at Windsor. From this meeting we have the charming portrait of an eyewitness, Rapin:

> The court was very splendid and much thronged; the queen's behaviour towards him was very noble and obliging. The young king charmed all present; he had a gravity beyond his age, tempered with much modesty. His behaviour was in all points so exact that there was not a circumstance in his whole deportment that was liable to censure.[19]

But Rapin's account also noted the outlines of a certain Hispanic severity: 'He paid an extraordinary respect to the queen and yet maintained a due greatness in it. He had the art of seeming well pleased with everything without so much as smiling once all the while he was at court, which was three days. He spoke but little and all he said was judicious and obliging.'

This demeanour though correct was not necessarily calculated to impress. He felt all the aspects of Habsburg Spain's greatness very keenly. Moreover, he lacked his late brother's open-minded tolerance of non-Catholics; hence his scrupulously correct but cool behaviour at the English court described above. So it was no surprise that the loss of Spain was traumatising for one who had seemed destined to rule as King. In Vienna during the long fogs of the winter months and their fierce biting winds, he thought of recreating the Spanish Escorial in the great monastery of Klosterneuburg on the banks of the Danube. To this day, Klosterneuburg's domes show in the splendour of their decoration the power of Charles's dreams. This Hispanic mentality meant that Charles rarely considered the army he had inherited. He placed more faith in diplomats than in soldiers. His indifference towards the army was born of bitter experience. After all, he had lost Spain even though Habsburg armies had fought with success.

Moreover, his experience in Spain, a great seafaring nation, stimulated Charles to seek compensation. Now north of the Alps and serving as monarch of largely landlocked territories, he favoured the advice of Spanish navigators and merchants rather than his Austrian generals. The great port of Trieste was encouraged to be the entrepôt of the Habsburg lands and the Imperial and Royal East India Company set about the foundation of a trading empire which, within a generation, showed all the signs of being able to rival that of the great maritime nations. At Britain's request, for supporting the Pragmatic Sanction the company was later disbanded.[20]

Charles VI remained defined by the sudden loss of Spain and his reign was overshadowed by the neurotic fear that his House would also lose the empire in the east unless he took concrete steps to ensure that his successor could inherit his realm without challenge. To this end he issued the Pragmatic Sanction in 1713, the year of the Utrecht treaty. This domestic edict was to ensure the succession for Charles's children, as yet unborn, in preference to the daughters of Joseph I. It established the right of sole inheritance by the eldest son or, if no sons existed, by the eldest daughter. By its terms, the Austrian Habsburg line was finally freed from the possibility of a divided inheritance.[21]

Once his eldest child, Maria Theresa, was born in 1717, Charles began seeking the recognition of the European powers for the Sanction but this process was not only unhappy in its constant genuflection to the wishes of other nations but it involved Vienna in many harmful concessions.

Eugene's final triumph: boldly by battery besieges Belgrade

The birth of Maria Theresa coincided with Eugene's arguably most spectacular feat of arms. In the same year, Eugene crowned his military career and retook Belgrade. In 1715, the Turks had broken the Treaty of Karlowitz and declared war against the Venetians and besieged Corfu. When the Venetians appealed to the Emperor, as a guarantor of the Karlowitz treaty, for help, Charles brushed aside appeals from the Porte and dispatched Eugene to Hungary at the head of a small army including many veterans of his campaigns against the French. In addition, thanks to the settlement of Szatmár with the Hungarians, many Hussar regiments were suddenly available, an indispensable light cavalry arm which Eugene respected and admired. Well screened from an Ottoman army of more than twice his size he camped at Peterwardein, whose fortifications erected by him in an earlier campaign the Turks had not destroyed. Without delaying, the following morning he deployed his cavalry to attack. Eugene's horsemen surrounded the wings of his enemy and after some stubborn resistance initially by Janissaries began to encircle the Ottoman army while Eugene personally led his infantry into the Turkish centre.

At the same time six gunboats on the Danube, deployed by Eugene, opened fire and the Peterwardein garrison made up largely of Serbs poured out to take part in the slaughter. The Grand Vizier who commanded the Ottomans was killed and Eugene captured more than 250 artillery pieces, 50 standards and immense treasures. By three o'clock, more than 30,000 Turks lay dead on the field near Karlowitz where the treaty had been signed seventeen years earlier.

Eugene now proceeded to invest and capture Temesvár (Timişoara), the key to the Banat and the last of the ancient dependencies of Hungary retained by the Turks, before moving on to besiege Belgrade. Belgrade was a formidable obstacle: the Belgrade garrison was 30,000 strong, it had supplies for at least two months and its strategic importance meant that it would receive assistance from other parts of the Ottoman Empire. Indeed, after two months of fruitless investment, Eugene's forces found themselves pinned by a relief force into the marshy ground between the Danube and the Save where, exposed daily to enemy fire and fever, their morale began to decline rapidly. The Turkish relief force kept up the pressure and was soon threatening Eugene's main line of communication over the Save. At the same time their lines pressed closer and closer. Eugene was in danger of becoming trapped in the feverish delta of the confluence of the two great rivers below the Belgrade fortress of Kalemegdan.

Calling a council of war Eugene urged a general attack under cover of darkness as the only means of retrieving the situation. His commanders supported him and the following night he personally inspected every outpost of his forces to give refreshment and support to his weary men ahead of the attack. His forces numbered 60,000 men but of these a third was on the other side of the Save so that he had barely 40,000 men with whom to attack a force reckoned at more than 200,000, the largest army the Sultan had sent west since the Siege of Vienna. The attack was scheduled for the following midnight and was to be preceded by a mortar bombardment.

The explosions caused chaos and many casualties but thick fog disorientated the attackers and although they achieved a degree of surprise, their opponents rallied, with the result that Eugene's forces were in danger of being thrown back in total confusion. A couple of hours later the sun rose, dispelling the fog. Instantly Eugene saw the crisis as his right wing was in danger of being outflanked by the Ottomans. Placing himself in front of his second line of infantry, sword in hand, he summoned his cavalry and charged the enemy and, though wounded, his example rallied his troops, who pressed forward and drove the Ottomans back with wild cries of 'We will conquer or die!' This infantry attack proved successful and Eugene's men, seizing the enemy cannon, turned and fired them into the disordered Ottomans. Once again imminent defeat had been turned into victory and so precipitate was the Turkish retreat that many were crushed to death in the stampede.

Belgrade thus once more fell to the Austrians and by the Treaty of Passarowitz, the following year in 1718, a truce of twenty-five years was signed and the Austrians secured much Balkan territory, including the Banat, which comprised parts of Serbia, Bosnia and Romania.

But though the Treaty of Passarowitz cemented the reputation of Austrian arms at its zenith, subsequent military commitments proceeded less gloriously. Many of these were undertaken as a result of the demands of the other powers in return for supporting the Pragmatic Sanction. The campaigning to the west and the east proved less successful than a generation earlier and it left the reputation of the Imperial forces much diminished.

First Saxony demanded participation in the ill-fated War of Polish Succession. Then Russia demanded renewed hostilities against the Turks. England needed no help in wars but simply insisted on the Ostend trading company and the Imperial and Royal East India Company being disbanded. All of these events had unhappy consequences for the Habsburg domains.

The army neglected

Eugene saw the need to keep the army strong but Charles preferred to pour money into projects like the Klosterneuburg monastery and the magnificent Karlskirche rather than the equipment and drill of his troops. The Karlskirche, completed in 1737, the year after Eugene's death, was the architectural expression of Habsburg political and religious rule, fusing Greek and Roman elements with motifs drawn from the Ottoman Empire. Conceived by Fischer von Erlach, it remains to this day the masterpiece of Austrian baroque. But by 1737 this building – envisaged as the crowning glory of a style long associated with the Counter-Reformation – seemed only to reflect hubris and fiction. The state was on the verge of bankruptcy and the spoils of so many of Eugene's victories were to be thrown away on the foolish new Turkish war.

In the Polish war, Austria was isolated from her traditional ally England though once again she faced the French and their Bavarian allies. Countless manoeuvres and skirmishes went on, with a battle at Clausen near Trier which saw the Hussars fight bravely against heavy odds. But this was indecisive, as was a more sanguinary engagement at Crocetta in 1734 near Parma.

The so-called Russo-Austrian-Turkish War was also pointless for Austria. It culminated in a major Austrian defeat at Banja Luka. A Turkish army under the command of Ali Pasha, son of a Venetian doctor and a Turk and a veteran sirdar of the Persian wars not only surprised the Habsburg forces besieging the town but in a single day's fighting routed them so comprehensively that barely a few hundred out of some 15,000 Austrians and Grenzer (recruited from the borders) made it back up the Morava valley.

Banja Luka occurred one year after Prince Eugene had died in 1736 and it was a sinister portent of problems to come for the House of Austria. A little later, an Austrian army under Wallis was routed near Belgrade at the Battle of Krotzka by a well-prepared Ottoman army that showed every sign of learning from its past mistakes. Though Wallis withdrew his forces in good order, he was compelled to surrender the following day.

The blow to Austrian prestige was colossal. In the years since Eugene had taken Belgrade, the Habsburg forces had begun to atrophy under his successors. The infantry and cavalry were still excellent but the commanders had become courtiers rather than military leaders. Wallis was brought back to Vienna in disgrace, court-martialled and imprisoned. (He would be released three months later by the new Habsburg monarch, Maria Theresa.)

In the closing months of his life Charles VI had worked tirelessly to receive recognition for his Pragmatic Sanction. This much-misunderstood document did more than serve to secure his domains through the female line over the claims of earlier Habsburg heirs. The Pragmatic Sanction also vouchsafed the inseparable and indivisible nature of the Habsburg territories. But however impressive the language, as an exercise in statecraft it was folly compared to the modernisation of an army. Despite Eugene's earlier reforms, the army was losing ground to new tactics and better-trained rivals. Charles secretly seemed to know this, which was why he placed so much trust in the diplomatic support of the Great Powers. He thought to shore up his possessions and his succession on a rock of legal and diplomatic agreement. In this he was encouraged by countless obsequious placemen and courtiers.

Charles VI's upbringing under the eye of Prince Liechtenstein, the Master of the Household had been unfortunate. Liechtenstein, the exception to the rule in this otherwise talented family, was of 'mean intellect, pedantic knowledge and obsessed with alchemy'.[22] Charles was a poor judge of character and his choice of Liechtenstein's nephew, Altheim, as confidant gave inordinate influence to a cunning intriguer whose judgement was as shaky as Charles's. In Altheim's case it was married to vaulting ambition. Altheim's creatures soon filled many of the high positions of state and, as tends to happen when nepotism is not tempered by ability, the rot quickly set into the fabric of empire. Only Eugene gave Charles the advice he needed: that France was recovering; that England was an essential ally for the Habsburgs and that Spain was the dream of the past; that a strong army was worth a dozen Pragmatic Sanctions.

Earlier, when Eugene had briefly taken the field in the campaign in northern Italy, a young Prussian prince had been attached to Eugene's staff and he carefully noted the failure of the Austrian commanders to respond rapidly to the great warlord and the lumbering deployment of the Habsburg infantry in the siege campaigns. Like Eugene fifty years earlier, this youth seemed at first glance unsuited to war. He too was highly strung but he watched the Austrian Generalissimus like a hawk and would later write of Eugene that 'everything I know about war, I learnt from that great man'.

The young Prussian's name was Frederick and the House of Austria would not have long to wait to see him prove just how well he had digested the lessons he had imbibed from the last months of Eugene's career.

CHAPTER 4

'Our Blood and Life'

THE GREAT EMPRESS

The death of Eugene: Austria's military weakness

The period unfolding opens with Austria's army weak and poorly led. The policies of Charles VI left his inheritance vulnerable to pillage and invasion. Yet by the time his daughter's husband was crowned Holy Roman Emperor, Austria and her armies had proved more than capable of surviving a war waged by many enemies. That such progress was possible from such inauspicious beginnings was the result of one young woman's tenacity and courage.

The death of Prince Eugene on 20 April 1736 at the age of 73 came mercifully before the debacle of Wallis on the approaches to Belgrade. The Generalissimus fortunately did not live to see the Treaty of Belgrade (1739) sign away nearly all he had won twenty years earlier at Passarowitz. As his faculties faded, Eugene was dimly aware that the formidable army he had done so much to create was now enfeebled and complacent; its weakness caused largely by a combination of Imperial over-expansion and somnolent leadership.

Every honour was paid on his death to the memory of Eugene. After his death, his heart was sent to Turin and at the interment in the cathedral of Vienna, Charles VI and the principal members of his court assisted incognito at the ceremony. The pall was borne by sixteen generals and full Imperial honours were given in the course of three days of solemnities.

The army the Generalissimus left behind him was now bitterly divided by rivalries, notably over the character of Eugene's able protégé Friederich Heinrich Seckendorf (1673–1763) who as a Protestant aroused some hostility and intrigue. Seckendorf's critical reports of conditions prevailing among the troops in the Balkans were treated with suspicion and resentment. Writing to Bartenstein, one of the most influential of the courtiers and a man who had risen high in court circles from relatively modest origins, he noted, 'Some companies of my regiment in Belgrade are thrust into holes where a man would not put even his favourite hounds and I cannot see the situation of these miserable and half-starved wretches without tears,' concluding: 'these melancholy circumstances portend in case of war the loss of these fine kingdoms with rapidity'.[1]

Nor were Seckendorf's strictures limited to the condition of the ranks. With a boldness that could not endear him to the snake pit of Charles's court he informed the Emperor, 'some of your generals are so incapable of discharging the duties of their station that Your Imperial Majesty must countenance the loss of his crown and sceptre'. Charles half-heartedly supported these views and allowed Seckendorf to introduce some reforms, but these were watered down by the military council. Meanwhile huge amounts of effort and vast sums from his treasury were given over to securing diplomatic recognition of the Pragmatic Sanction. In contrast, the army atrophied under parsimony and inertia.

Two years later in 1740 with Charles's death, the direct male line of the House of Austria became extinct. Charles's eldest daughter Maria Theresa succeeded with her husband Francis Stephen of Lorraine, who had had to cede his patrimony of Lorraine to win the hand of the Habsburg heiress as her consort. As Bartenstein had warned Francis Stephen, 'No surrender; no Archduchess.'

All Charles's energies had been devoted to ensuring that his daughter would be recognised as Queen of the Habsburg crown lands and that her husband would as a Habsburg consort be elected 'King of the Romans', implying that he would eventually be crowned Holy Roman Emperor. The thought that only a credible army could offer such a guarantee was seemingly lost on Charles and his advisers. They realised that Austria with her far-flung territories and weak administration was unlikely to survive the shock of a major war but in their efforts to put their trust in the Sanction and hope for the best they gravely miscalculated.

Maria Theresa and the new Prussian king: a study in contrasts

In the crisis that unfolded, Maria Theresa was to develop into the most impressive monarch of the eighteenth century. An unashamed innovator and moderniser despite her personal conservatism, she left her mark on every area of her realms. There would be no later Austrian or indeed Central European economic, administrative, public health, legal, educational or military institution that did not in some way trace its roots to her energetic reforming zeal and retain the imprint of her measures even centuries later. She also bore her husband sixteen children, observing, 'One cannot have enough of them. In this matter I am insatiable.'[2]

This great tribal mother, the icon for so many Central European aristocratic families for centuries afterwards, also redefined the relationship between the Habsburg monarchy and her peoples. She injected a new style of sovereignty into the Imperial house, eliminating the 'forbidden zone' that had surrounded the person of earlier Habsburg rulers in Vienna. She became truly popular with her subjects. During her reign nearly all vestiges of the Spanish Habsburgs' elaborate and formal mystique were dismantled.

All these achievements would have been remarkable at any time in the history of Europe, even during a phase of relative tranquillity, but it is all the more astounding that a 23-year-old monarch brought this to fruition after inheriting a throne which was virtually bankrupt (only 100,000 florins were in the treasury and these were mostly pledged to the dowager Empress); a court which was bereft of good advisers; and an army of barely 30,000 effectives which was desperately in need of reform precisely at a time when the majority of her neighbours had come to the conclusion that the Austrian Habsburg realms were ripe for violent dismemberment.

Despite the Pragmatic Sanction, Prussia, France and Spain harboured hostility towards the new Empress. In addition, her cousin and nearest neighbour, Charles Albert of Bavaria was about to challenge her family's succession to the Imperial title. We have noted that this had been held almost without interruption by a Habsburg for more than three centuries, and was regarded as an almost mystical element of prestige in German-speaking lands. Barely had Charles VI been buried in 1740 when an envoy arrived from Munich to announce that Charles Albert 'could not acknowledge the young queen as the inheritress and successor of her father because the House of Bavaria had legitimate claims to the hereditary provinces'.[3]

Behind Bavaria stood, of course, the old *Erbfeind* France, which had encouraged the Bavarians to pursue this spurious claim. The Electors of Cologne and the Palatinate gave additional support, the latter sending a letter through the public post addressed to the 'Archduchess' Maria Theresa, a calculated impertinence. The King of Spain, even more archly, gave her no other title than Grand Duchess of Tuscany. As it became increasingly obvious that Maria Theresa's inheritance would be disputed by most of her neighbours, the young sovereign's advisers gave further proof of their enfeeblement. In the words of an eyewitness, 'The Turks seemed to them already in Hungary, the Hungarians already in arms, the Saxons in Bohemia and the Bavarians approaching the gates of Vienna.'[4] Before these various challenges could be

settled, another even more striking blow was about to be aimed from the direction of Prussia. Frederick II, the new King in Prussia,* was without doubt an
unusual personality.

He had mounted his throne in the same year as the young Austrian archduchess. As a child he had been forced to witness the execution of his favourite
friend and lover on the orders of his father and he had turned his precocity into
a powerful weapon of resistance to his father's conventional morality. Frederick
played the flute, composed music, read and discoursed with such revolutionary
writers as Voltaire and embraced the mid-eighteenth-century 'Enlightenment',
or at least some of its philosophical points of view. Brought up constantly rebel-
ling against the straitjacket of Prussian *Nüchternheit* (lit. sobriety), he was the
epitome of selfish, histrionic and unbridled egotistical arrogance.

As we have seen, he had served with the Imperial troops and had learnt
much from contact with the great Eugene. He had seen at first hand the quality
of the Austrian army and with the exception of its light cavalry he had not been
impressed. His father had left him a treasury with some eight million 'dollars'†
more than enough money to wage two campaigns. Frederick had also
inherited an army of 80,000 whose infantry was certainly at that time already
reckoned to be the most consistently drilled and courageous of any in the
world. These were powerful supports for any young monarch but Frederick
also had vaulting ambition. He openly admitted he 'wanted to make an impact'.
Austria, now placed in the hands of a young, inexperienced girl surrounded by
incompetent advisers, defended by an army long past its best with officers of
notable mediocrity, was a target too irresistible to miss. He certainly failed to
grasp the measure of Maria Theresa; and of Francis Stephen, whom he
described as like a man given over to the pleasure of the hunt, 'content to leave
his realms, like a Gasthaus, to his wife to run'.[5]

Frederick coveted Silesia, one of Austria's wealthiest provinces: with its rich
mineral deposits, it was the treasury of Bohemia. Geographically it pointed
like a salient into the marches of Brandenburg with which it shared a common
frontier of some forty miles. Moreover, its population was partly Protestant
and might even – so Frederick fantasised – welcome the Lutheran Prussians.

Without warning – at this stage the Prussian King was an enthusiastic
correspondent and disciple of Voltaire – Frederick marched into Silesia. He
proclaimed it his in a manifesto which, riddled with pretensions and

---

* It is a common error in texts to refer to Frederick in 1740 as the King of Prussia. This was a hereditary
title of the Polish monarchs and was not 'available' to Frederick until 1772, when the partition of that
unfortunate land in which he joyfully participated initiated the process of erasure that eventually
deleted Poland from the map of Europe.
† Thalers: owing to the Austrian pronouciation of 't' as 'd' corrupted to 'dollars'. About half a billion US
dollars in today's money.

half-truths, laid claim to various principalities dating back to 1507 and, later, the Thirty Years War. Frederick gambled. Strangely, given the adulation of later biographers, not least in England, this strategy was not only destructive, it was also utterly devoid of long-term rational analysis. Later Frederick would admit with all the arrogance of an Enlightenment intellectual that 'Ambition, the opportunity for gain, the desire to establish my reputation – these were decisive, and thus war became certain.'[6] As Macaulay later noted: 'On the head of Frederick is all the blood which was shed in a war which raged in every quarter of the globe . . . In order that he might rob a neighbour whom he had promised to defend, black men fought each other on the coasts of Coromandel and red men scalped each other by the great lakes of North America.'[7]

Unfortunately for Frederick, his opponent was not a frivolous, light-headed 'Wienerin' of just simple easy charm and temperament. In Maria Theresa Frederick encountered a woman of singular intelligence and fortitude. He was to discover that beneath the rococo grace, redolent of *Schlagobers* and *Gemütlichkeit*, there was steel, and something else: a concept utterly alien to Frederick – integrity. A brief anecdote, much quoted, perhaps gives us the measure of the woman. One morning studying state documents over breakfast, she spilt a drop of coffee on one of the pages after dipping her customary *kipfel* into the cup. The sovereign ringed the offending mark with ink and scrupulously wrote in her neat hand in the margin that the stain was hers, for which she offered apologies.[8] Frederick possessed neither integrity nor humility. Indeed, the 'greatness' of Frederick's character for all its histrionics and drama does not in many points maintain its superiority when placed in comparison with that of his most tenacious opponent.

Frederick calculated that his campaign would be swift and easy, with the 'Rape of Silesia' accomplished in weeks. In fact the swift little campaign he so gaily embarked upon was to condemn him to a lifetime of often desperate fighting at ruinous expense in blood and treasure. 'Fighting Maria Theresa,' he would later moan, 'is like dying a thousand times a day.'

Before it was all over more than twenty-five years later Prussia, not Austria, was on the verge of total extinction, saved only by what must have seemed the miraculous death of his other determined foe Elizabeth of Russia. The Prussia that survived just held on to Silesia but she was bankrupt, a basket case: her economy ruined and her manpower decimated. Even as a military leader Maria Theresa could claim superiority. After all, she bequeathed an army immensely stronger than the one she had inherited, so unlike the ruined armies of Frederick. Prussia's military power indeed was so drained that a generation later Napoleon could wipe it out in less than an afternoon on the plains of Jena and Auerstadt. Unlike Austria which would fight five coalition wars against

Napoleon, Prussia's weak efforts before 1813 showed that the shattered legacy Frederick left his country would take more than a generation to heal, and then only thanks to the presence of a unique combination of single-minded men.[9]

Silesia seized: Mollwitz

The beginning for Frederick, as for many a later megalomaniac, was promising. He achieved total surprise; neither his ambassadors nor his relations were informed. Just before his troops entered Silesia in 1741, he sent an ambassador to the Austrian court with a draft convention offering support for Maria Theresa in the struggle to defend her other kingdoms if Prussia were ceded Silesia. This was merely a gesture and he did not expect it to be received in Vienna as anything more. But Maria Theresa's refusal even to receive the Prussian envoy, Count Gotter, while Prussian troops menaced her possessions caused dismay in Berlin, where the hope of an eventual settlement after the initial incursion ran high.

The few Austrian troops – barely 3,000, the majority of whom were invalids or raw recruits under Maximilian von Browne in Silesia – were swiftly routed; a few fortresses, their defences decayed after years of neglect, held out but Frederick arrived at the head of 20 battalions and 36 squadrons on Christmas Eve, entering Breslau (today Wroclaw in Poland), the capital of Silesia on New Year's Day. Though at first the Prussians were greeted by the Protestant majority, they swiftly seized the revenues of the province to pay for the equipment of the entire Prussian army. Maria Theresa noted acidly that its revenues hitherto had barely covered the expense of two of her Cuirassier regiments. Browne was driven back to Moravia. The so-called strongest fortification, Glogau, put up some resistance but it had a garrison of just 1,178 troops, of whom half were retired invalids, and just 17 guns.

Maria Theresa was let down not only by her advisers in this moment. Long-standing allies were equally fickle. Holland and England both counselled accommodation with Frederick. George II was especially afraid of a conflagration with France. He also feared that his native Hanover, or as he termed it his 'country seat', would be overrun by Prussia if he supported Austria. Russia and Poland, which had initially pledged troops, swiftly backtracked while acknowledging the integrity of the Austrian cause. Of the 'Pragmatic Sanction' there was no more talk. The young sovereign was learning an important lesson in European power politics: that weakness only brings out the worst in governments. It is said that when she finally received from her counsellors a correct appreciation of precisely how dire the financial and military straits in which she found herself were, she left the room and, alone, burst into tears.

It did not help that her two most experienced generals, Wallis and Neipperg, were languishing in jail following the debacle in Turkey of the previous year, which had resulted in their being court-martialled. Maria Theresa moved swiftly to liberate them and Neipperg marched at the head of a sizeable force in March 1741 to eject the Prussians. The Prussian army by the first week in April, rejoined by Frederick, came face to face with the Austrians under Neipperg at Mollwitz. It was to be Frederick's first taste of military action in all its raw brutality and it was a deeply unpleasant experience for the Prussian monarch.

The series of wars that had closed Charles VI's reign had highlighted Austria's military weakness. It is therefore surprising that, given the abuses and disorders rampant in the Habsburg forces, the Austrians gave as good an account of themselves at Mollwitz as they did. The battle was certainly far from a foregone conclusion. The superb drill of the Prussian army was viewed with a certain disdain by the Austrians. After all, had not their own army been trained on the battlefield rather than the drill square? The Austrian officer corps was less cohesive socially and ethnically. Also, in its love of frivolity, sardonic wit and *Milde und Munifizenz* (Mildness and munificence), it was far removed from the class of tough, small-time landowners bred on the barren windswept Lutheran estates of Prussia who officered Frederick's army. Neipperg their commander exuded black humour and was much admired for his repartee.[10] His luck on the field of battle that April day would require it.

The initial Austrian manoeuvre took the Prussians by surprise. But Neipperg, rather than precipitate an attack with troops wearied from their march, chose to take up a defensive position around Mollwitz. Neipperg was not expecting an attack when late on the morning of 10 April he was informed that the Prussian columns were 'uncoiling' over the snowy fields. General-Leutnant Roemer, one of Neipperg's more resourceful commanders immediately perceived the need to screen the Austrian infantry as it came into position and swiftly brought six regiments of cuirassiers forward where they shielded the main part of Neipperg's force. At this stage the Prussian artillery opened fire on the stationary cavalry who, after receiving casualties, were ordered by Roemer to charge the right wing of the Prussian cavalry that had just come into view. The Prussian horsemen proved no match for the Imperial cuirassiers. An Austrian officer later recalled:

> The Prussians fought on their horses stationary and so they got the worst of every clash. The extraordinary size of their horses did them no good at all – our cavalry always directed their first sword cut at the head of the enemy horse; the horse fell, throwing its rider to the ground who would then be cut down from behind. The Prussian troopers have iron crosses set

inside their hats. These were splintered by our swords which made the cuts deadlier still. I might add that we had been ordered to sharpen most of our swords before the action and now their edges looked like saws.[11]

The exposed right wing of Frederick's army began to crumble as Roemer's men charged home. It was at this moment that Frederick, seized by panic as the Imperial cavalry penetrated his artillery park, decided to flee the conflict, leaving Schwerin to take charge. Schwerin acted swiftly to restore order on his right flank and hastily moved up three battalions, which in perfect drill formed a line and began to volley the disordered Austrian cavalry. Three times Roemer charged this Prussian line and each time his horsemen were repulsed, the last charge killing their commander. Unsupported by the Austrian infantry who were demoralised by the firepower of the Prussians, the Austrian cavalry fell back. Frederick's infantry, though he was not there to see it, had not let their sovereign down. The Austrians, including Neipperg, had seen nothing like it. For every one volley the Austrian infantry loosed, the Prussians returned five. The effect was, after an hour, decisive.

'Our infantry kept up a continuous fire,' wrote an Austrian eyewitness, 'but could not be made to advance a step. The battalions sank into disorder, and it was pathetic to see how the poor recruits tried to hide behind one another so that the battalions ended up thirty or forty men deep, and the intervals became so great that whole regiments of cavalry could have penetrated between, even though the whole of the second line had been brought forward into the first.'[12]

Neipperg withdrew, his confidence in his troops almost as shattered as the morale of his men. The casualties for both sides together amounted to over 9,000, a figure regarded as considerable. Mollwitz had proved no simple victory for the Prussians and strategically it achieved little immediately. Frederick was unwilling to risk a second battle. Its effect on the Habsburg forces was nonetheless crushing.[13]

Accounts of the weak showing of the Austrian infantry could not be entirely attributed to their being 'made up of recruits, peasants and other poor material'.[14] Maria Theresa would later write:

You would hardly believe it but not the slightest attempt had been made to establish uniformity among our troops. Each regiment went about marching and drilling in its own fashion. One unit would close formation by a rapid movement and the next by a slow one. The same words and orders were expressed by the regiments in quite different styles. Can you wonder that we were invariably beaten in the ten years before my accession? As for the condition in which I found the army, I cannot begin to describe it.[15]

But though Mollwitz had hardly 'cleared' Silesia for the Prussians, news of the Prussian victory travelled across Europe, further encouraging various courts to deny the basis of the Pragmatic Sanction. In fact had Prussia lost Mollwitz the war and the bloodshed of the next two decades would have ended there and then; but fate decreed otherwise. While the Saxon army prepared to invade Bohemia, the French and the Bavarians advanced into Upper Austria. The dismemberment of the once 'indivisible realms' appeared inevitable.

Maria Theresa refuses to yield: the 'King' of Hungary

Calm resignation reigned at court. Somehow, under new rulers, the estates of the high aristocracy would survive. Life would go on and Maria Theresa would surely come to terms with just remaining an important Archduchess. Outside her domains no one preached appeasement more vigorously than England. A certain Mr Robinson was instructed by London to represent the dangers of failing to settle with Frederick. He was urged by the British government to 'expiate on the dangerous designs of France ... of the powerful combination against Austria'.[16] But Mollwitz notwithstanding, Maria Theresa refused to yield. She listened patiently to Robinson but dismissed him with the words: 'not only for political reasons but from conscience and honour I will not consent'.[17]

It was only with the greatest of difficulty that Maria Theresa found advisers of backbone prepared to share her defiance. The news in June that Frederick had signed a treaty with France only made them rarer. Nevertheless, a handful stepped forward in the moment of crisis. Unsurprisingly we encounter yet again the name of Starhemberg but also Bartenstein and Khevenhueller, the grandson of Montecuccoli. In the moment of supreme trial the families that had had some connection with the Great Siege of Vienna in another moment of danger for the House of Austria two generations earlier once more stepped forward. But there were others, notably Count Emanuel Silva-Tarouca, a Portuguese aristocrat who never learnt German but became a kind of personal 'coach' to the Empress, advising her on every detail of her actions.[18]

Another of these was an elderly shrewd Magyar by the name of Johann Pálffy, the Judex Curiae (Judge Royal) and the man whose moral authority in Hungary would prove Maria Theresa's greatest support in this troubled year of 1741. Pálffy combined the qualities of statesmanship with the personal courage of a more martial calling. He too, like Starhemberg, had a name interwoven with battle honours, including the Great Siege of Vienna. He had taken part in most of the wars the Habsburgs had fought since then and had been wounded many times. He had also shown himself a keen diviner of the mysteries of the Hungarian temperament, negotiating the Peace of Szatmár with the insurgent

Ráckóczi. At the same time, as a former Ban (viceroy) of Croatia, no one knew the mentality of that warlike people better than Pálffy.

Pálffy, like Khevenhueller was in the 'sunset' phase of his life in his late seventies – he would die in 1751. Nevertheless, he was deeply impressed by the young woman he served and saw that an approach to the Hungarian nobility was one of the keys to strengthening her position. It would also enable the Magyars to cement their own position advantageously vis-à-vis the Imperial house.

In accordance with Hungarian tradition, Maria Theresa would have to be crowned 'King' of Hungary (the Hungarian Constitution did not recognise a queen). The same tradition required then, as it would for nearly two more centuries, that the monarch mount a horse and ascend the 'Royal Mount' of Pressburg,* some miles east of Vienna. Wearing the historic robes of St Stephen and the famous crown with its crooked cross, the sovereign was expected to take the slope at a brisk canter and, with the ancient drawn sabre of the Hungarian kings, point in turn to the four points of the compass, swearing to defend the Hungarian lands.

The story of the events of that 25 June in Pressburg and later in September have been much embroidered but we have, thanks to the hapless Mr Robinson – returned from his fruitless task to help Maria Theresa find a compromise with Frederick – a vivid eyewitness account of that day which gives us something of the flavour:

> The coronation was magnificent. The Queen was all charm; she rode gallantly up the royal mount and defied the four corners of the world with the drawn sabre in a manner to show she had no occasion for that weapon to conquer all who saw her. The antiquated crown received new graces from her head and the old tattered robe of St Stephen became her as well as her own rich habit.[19]

It was a good beginning to the eternally delicate Habsburg–Magyar relationship. Later that day as she sat down to dine in public without the crown, her looks, invested as they were with what one writer called 'an air of delicacy occasioned by her recent confinement', became 'most attractive, the fatigue of the ceremony diffused an animated glow over her countenance while her beautiful hair flowed in ringlets over her shoulders'.[20]

A little later on 11 September, having summoned the states of the Magyar diet to a formal assembly and once again wearing the crown, she appealed in Latin, the language of aristocratic Hungary at that time, to her audience, proclaiming in the language of the Roman Emperors, her speech:

---

* Today Bratislava is in Slovakia (Poszony in Hungarian)

The disastrous situation of our affairs has moved us to lay before our most dear and faithful states of Hungary the recent violation of Austria. I lay before you the mortal danger now impending over this kingdom and I beg to propose to you the consideration of a remedy. The very existence of the Kingdom of Hungary, of our own person, of our children and our crown are now at stake! We have been forsaken by all! We therefore place our sole resource in the fidelity, the arms and the long tried immemorial valour of the Hungarians.[21]

The original of this speech exists and it is without doubt one of the most fascinating documents in eighteenth-century Central European history. It shows everywhere the young Queen's hand over-working (in Latin!) the text of the original much less emotional speech prepared by her advisers. The word 'poor' for example is scratched out and replaced with the word 'disastrous'. In almost every paragraph this girl, barely out of her teens, crosses out some anodyne formulation, replacing it with a more stirring phrase or word. Like a composer carefully judging structure and climax she transformed by a series of amendments a good speech into a brilliant one. As was to be so often the case, her instincts did not let her down.

What happened next is immortalised in countless paintings. Moved by the pleas of this young, helpless woman, the Hungarian nobles drew their sabres and pointing them into the sky cried: 'Vitam nostrum et sanguinem pro Rege nostro consecramus' ('Our Life and Blood we dedicate to our King!').

The drawing of swords was part of the ceremonial though clearly on this occasion injected with great passion. Who could resist the call of chivalry when articulated with such grace, and with feminine distress? Within a month Hungary had declared the 'comprehensive insurrection', pledging to take up arms to enter the war.

Even today we can sense the pulling of male emotional heart strings at which Maria Theresa so excelled in a letter to Khevenhueller penned around this time and sent with an accompanying portrait of herself and her son: 'Here you have before your eyes a Queen and her son deserted by the whole world. What do you think will become of this child?'[22] In the first spontaneous response to this passionate outpouring of emotion on the part of the Magyars, it was estimated that perhaps as many as 100,000 men would flock to the cause. In the event it was to be a much more modest contribution, but significant nonetheless. Three new regiments of Hussars were raised, the first clad in exquisite chalk blue and gold, in the name and ownership of Prince Paul Eszterhazy.[23]

Habsburg irregulars: the Pandours

In addition, six regiments of infantry were raised. As well as the Hungarians there came another group of volunteers: the Pandours. These brigands, often the natives of the 'wrong side' of the Military Frontier, followed their leader, the gifted Baron Trenck. This Trenck is not to be confused with his kinsman who was initially in the Prussian service and whose memoirs were widely read in the eighteenth century. The Austrian Trenck pledged a unit of irregulars, a *Freikorps* (Free Corps) numbering about 1,000 to Maria Theresa's aid.

These irregulars were welcomed into the Imperial service even though they possessed no conventional officer corps but a system whereby each unit of fifty men obeyed a 'Harumbascha'. All the Pandours, Harumbaschas included, were paid 6 kreutzer a day out of Trenck's own estates, a pitiful sum. This was certainly not enough for any semblance of a uniform and their appearance was highly exotic. When they appeared in Vienna at the end of May 1741, the 'Wienerische Diarium' could write:

> Two Battalions of regular infantry lined up to parade as the Pandours entered the city. The Irregulars greeted the regulars with long drum rolls on long Turkish drums. They bore no colours but were attired in picturesque oriental garments from which protruded pistols, knives and other weapons. The Empress ordered twelve of the tallest to be invited with their officer to her Ante-Room where they were paraded in front of the dowager Empress Christina.[24]

Neipperg found the Pandours rather raw meat. He was unused to the ways of the Military Frontier. On several occasions while campaigning he had to remind them that they were 'here to kill the enemy not to plunder the civilian population'. The Pandour excesses soon provoked Neipperg into attempting to replace Trenck. The man chosen for this daunting task was a Major Mentzel who had seen service in Russia and was therefore deemed to be familiar with the 'barbaric' ways of the Pandours. Unfortunately, some Pandours fell upon Mentzel as soon as news of his appointment was announced and the hapless Major only escaped with his life after the intervention of several senior Harumbaschas and Austrian officers.

Mentzel, notwithstanding this indignity, was formally proclaimed commander of the Pandours, whereupon a mutiny took place which only Khevenhueller, a man of the Austrian south and therefore familiar with Slavic methods, could stem by reinstating Trenck under his personal command. At both Steyr and Linz, the Pandours in their colourful dress decorated with heart-shaped badges and Turkic headdresses would distinguish themselves against the Bavarians. Indeed, by the middle of 1742 the mention of their name alone was enough to clear the terrain of faint-hearted opponents. Within five years they would be incorporated into the regular army though with an order of precedence on Maria Theresa's specific instruction 'naturally after that of my Regular infantry regiments'.[25] At Budweis (Budejovice) they captured ten Prussian standards and four guns.

The crisis was far from over. While Khevenhueller prepared a force to defend Vienna, the Bavarians gave the Austrian capital some respite by turning north from Upper Austria and invading Bohemia. By November, joined by French and Saxon troops, this force surprised the Prague garrison of some 3,000 men under General Ogilvy and stormed into the city largely unopposed on the night of 25 November. To deal with these new threats, Maria Theresa using Neipperg as her plenipotentiary had signed an armistice with Frederick at Klein Schnellendorf. She realised that her armies were in no condition to fight Bavarians, Saxons, French and Prussians simultaneously.

Maria Theresa received the news of Prague's surrender with redoubled determination. In a letter to Kinsky, her Bohemian Chancellor she insisted: 'I must have Grund and Boden and to this end I shall have all my armies, all my Hungarians killed off before I cede so much as an inch of ground.'[26]

Charles Albert the Elector of Bavaria rubbed salt into the wounds by crowning himself King of Bohemia and thus eligible to be elected Holy Roman Emperor. The dismemberment of the Habsburg Empire was entering a new and deadly phase. Maria Theresa was now only Archduchess of Austria and 'King' of Hungary.

The election of a non-Habsburg 'Emperor' immediately provided a practical challenge for the Habsburg forces on the battlefield. Their opponents were swift to put the famous twin-headed eagle of the Holy Roman Empire on their standards. To avoid confusion Maria Theresa ordered its 'temporary' removal from her own army's standards. The Imperial eagle with its two heads vanished from the standards of Maria Theresa's infantry to be replaced on both sides of the flag with a bold image of the Madonna, an inspired choice, uniting as it did the Mother of Austria with the Mother of Christ and so investing the 'Mater Castrorum' with all the divine prestige and purity of motive of the Virgin Mary.

Another development followed: because Maria Theresa's forces could no longer be designated 'Imperial' there emerged the concept of a royal Bohemian and Hungarian army which became increasingly referred to for simplicity's sake as 'Austrian'. The name would stick. When less than five years later Maria Theresa's husband was crowned Holy Roman Emperor, Europe had become accustomed to referring to the Habsburg armies as the Austrians.

A glimmer of hope appeared as Khevenhueller cleared Upper Austria of the Bavarians and French. He blockaded Linz, which was held by 10,000 French troops under Ségur. And by seizing Scharding on the Inn he deprived the unfortunate French garrison of all chance of relief from Bavaria. The Tyroleans showed their skill at mountain warfare and ambushed one Bavarian force after another, inflicting fearful casualties. On the day that Charles Albert of Bavaria was elected Holy Roman Emperor, Khevenhueller sent the Bavarian upstart an unequivocal message: he occupied his home city of Munich and torched his palace.

Charles of Lorraine assumes command

Prince Charles of Lorraine, Francis Stephen's brother and the descendant of the Charles of Lorraine who had played such an important part in raising the great Siege of Vienna, took command of the main Austrian force, hitherto under Neipperg. It was his first independent command and the fun-loving Prince, if contemporary accounts are to be believed, was uncouth, loud and a poor judge of character. It was quickly revealed that he was far from competent as a military commander. To Lorraine's surprise and in breach of the treaty he had just signed at Klein Schellendorf, Frederick moved into Moravia, launching a full invasion of that picturesque province in February and linking arms with the French and Saxons in southern Bohemia. By the 19th he was at Znaim (Znojmo) barely a day and half's march from Vienna.

Several thousand light cavalry were sent towards Vienna to scout and pillage. The panic in the Austrian capital was immense. Once again several prominent families contemplated flight but wiser counsels prevailed. Austria's enemies could not agree on their shares of the spoils and Frederick, aware that he was overstretched, withdrew to a strong position in northern Bohemia. Here, eventually, Lorraine, after much prodding from Vienna, attacked at a village called Chotusitz. Once again the Austrian cavalry fought magnificently, overwhelming the opposing horse and driving it from the field. As the Austrian cavalry plundered the Prussian camp all was set for significant victory if the Austrian infantry could behave with cool discipline and attack. Unfortunately a certain over-zealous Colonel Livingstein had the idea of setting fire to Chotusitz, oblivious to the fact that the flames and smoke would effectively bring any attack to a halt and give the Prussian defence time to reform and hold their ground.

After four hours of heavy fighting Charles ordered his troops to withdraw. This they did in good order, having captured fourteen standards. The Prussians remained masters of the battlefield but their casualties were, at 7,000, no fewer than the Austrians'. The Prussian cavalry had been so severely handled that it was no longer an effective fighting force. This was not the crushing victory Frederick, who had finally distinguished himself during the battle by his courage and quick reactions, had wanted to support his demands for northern Bohemia.

The Prussians had been saved by the inability of their opponents to take advantage of at least three opportunities to crush them. Once again the Austrians for all the indifference of their leadership and discipline had proved themselves to be no easy enemy. Moreover the severity of the Prussian losses highlighted the asymmetry in manpower upon which both armies relied. The Austrians could draw on far greater numbers for recruitment and Chotusitz illustrated vividly Frederick's dilemma were he to continue hostilities. As Count Podewils, Frederick's courtier elegantly noted with regard to Austria, only 'some lovely feathers had been torn from its wings'. The bird was 'still capable of flying quite high'.[27]

The situation in Bohemia was moving rapidly in Austria's favour. The moment for rapprochement had arrived. Podewils signed the preliminaries at Breslau and Prussia gained Upper and Lower Silesia together with Glatz. The later Treaty of Berlin confirmed that only a sliver of Silesia around Troppau and Jaegersdorf was kept by Austria but Bohemia was secured and the Habsburg armies could now turn their full weight against their other enemies, notably the French.

These under Broglio had already retreated from Frauenberg, their baggage falling into the hands of Lobkowitz's light cavalry. Seeking shelter in Písek, a French corps was compelled to surrender when a detachment of Nadasti's Hussars, mostly Croats, swam across the river with sabres in their mouths and climbing on each other's shoulders scaled the walls and first surprised and then began massacring the garrison.

Broglio sought to bring his harassed forces to Prague but here the condition of the French garrison was pitiable. Meanwhile, the coalition against Maria Theresa was breaking up. The Saxons no longer wished to be involved and the French and Bavarians had been outmanoeuvred on the Danube by Khevenhueller. Opinion in London and other parts of Europe was belatedly but finally rallying to Austria. The success of her armies and the character of her defiance added to the diplomatic awareness that only the House of Austria could check the ambitions of the House of Bourbon. With the removal of Walpole, the Austrian party once again was in the ascendant in London and large supplies of men and money were voted in parliament to support Maria Theresa. In Russia a new government watched how Prussia was developing with increasing scepticism.

At the same time in Italy, where both French and Spanish forces threatened Maria Theresa's inheritance, a significant Austrian army assisted by the Royal Navy and the fine troops of the King of Sardinia drove their opponents out of Savoy, Parma and Modena. The Austrians here were commanded by Count Abensburg-Traun, governor of Lombardy and one of the more elderly of Maria Theresa's generals. But though not in his prime, Traun was an able tactician and even Frederick admitted that the 'only reason Traun has not defeated me is because he has not faced me on the battlefield'.[28]

Traun had served as adjutant to Guido Starhemberg and as Khevenhueller noted:

> From this experience he learnt how to conduct marches and plant camps with foresight and acquired the art of holding the defensive with inferior forces. Defensive operations were in fact his forte and he had few rivals in this respect. . . . The soldiers were very fond of him because he cared for their welfare and they invariably called him their 'Father'. So generous was he towards his officers and the men that in later years he had almost nothing to live on and was virtually compelled to contract his second marriage so as to obtain a housekeeper and nurse.[29]

All these successes offered the chance to conclude peace but Maria Theresa rejected all the overtures of the French. In front of the entire court she answered the French proposals with fighting words:

> I will grant no capitulation to the French Army; I will receive no proposition or project. Let them address my allies!

When one of her courtiers had the temerity to refer to the conciliatory tone of the French General Belle-Isle, she exclaimed:

> I am astonished that he should make any advances; he who by money and promises excited almost all the princes of Germany to crush me. . . . I can prove by documents in my possession that the French endeavoured to excite sedition even in the heart of my dominions; that they attempted to overturn the fundamental laws of the empire and to set fire to the four corners of Germany; and I will transmit these proofs to posterity as a warning to the empire.[30]

The Siege of Prague continued and the French troops bottled up in the city became more and more desperate. Broglio escaped in disguise and Belle-Isle was left to effect the retreat. This he accomplished largely because of the incompetence of Prince Lobkowitz who, taking up a position with his army beyond the Moldau river, left only a small detachment of hussars to observe the French. Belle-Isle took full advantage of Lobkowitz's complacency and stole away leaving only the sick and wounded. Eleven thousand infantry and 3,000 cavalry were thus extricated and passed some thirty miles through open country without receiving the slightest check.

In Prague even the wounded, amounting to some 6,000, rejected Lobkowitz's furious demand for unconditional surrender. Their enterprising leader Chevert warned he would set fire to the city if he was not granted the full honours of war and Lobkowitz to his credit yielded, encouraged perhaps by the fact that his own magnificent palace with its priceless treasures would be the first to go up in flames.

But Belle-Isle had entered Germany at the head of 40,000 men and he returned to France with only 8,000, humiliated and a fugitive, a sorry outcome when an easy conquest had been anticipated.

The Second Silesian War and the 'Pragmatic Army', 1744–1745

Although France had been humiliated and Bohemia liberated, French forces still threatened the Habsburg claims further to the west. England's change of mood supported the creation of what became known as the Pragmatic Army, so named because it was to protect the Pragmatic Sanction, made up of Austrians, British and Hanoverian contingents brought together with the sole aim of excluding French influence from the Imperial possessions, a kind of anti-Bourbon league. With Maria Theresa triumphant in virtually every part of Europe and the British eager to reduce France's power, hostilities were far from over.

The British aim was, according to Austria's minister Wasner in London, 'nothing less than to chase the House of Bourbon from Italy to return Lorraine to the House of Lorraine and to round off a bit the states of Her Majesty to compensate in that way for the sacrifices she had just made to the King of Prussia.'[31]

Austria had indeed risen phoenix-like from the ashes. By 1743 Maria Theresa could survey a wholly changed situation. Other than Silesia, her domains were intact and far from facing dismemberment. Now it was she who threatened her enemies with nemesis. Even Frederick could not rest easy despite Prussia growing by more than 50 per cent through the incorporation of Silesia. It would only be a question of time before a revivified Austria sought to recover Silesia and Frederick, by his machinations with his allies, had made himself one of the most distrusted men in Europe.

The successful campaigns of the early part of 1742 had reversed the disappointments of the last years. Maria Theresa had received the crown of the Kingdom of Bohemia, though she wisely referred to it as a 'fool's cap'. With the arrival of the Pragmatic Army in Germany in the spring of 1743, the stage was set for a formidable threat to the French. At this juncture the Pragmatic Army was commanded by Lord Stair, with Count Aremberg leading the sizeable Austrian contingent as his chief of staff. Of the 20,000 Austrian troops the majority were infantry from the Austrian Netherlands. While Prince Lobkowitz moved out of Bohemia to tie down the French troops in the Upper Palatinate, Maria Theresa's husband stumbled upon a Bavarian force near Braunau and defeated it soundly at Simbach. A few days later Daun took the town of Dingolfing from the French before uniting with Lobkowitz to march to Landau further down the Isar. For the inhabitants of these beautiful lands the presence of marauding armies once again offered few benefits. As the French retreated they pursued a scorched earth policy and while the Austrians pursued, their Croat irregulars showed equally little mercy, in one case, at Dingolfing slaughtering the inhabitants of an entire village.

Munich fell (again) to the Austrians and the electorate of Bavaria was given up entirely to Austrian administration, its armies neutralised and its bureaucrats, supposedly in appearance at least, loyal to Vienna. By the summer the Pragmatic Army now camped on the Rhine was awaiting the arrival of George II of England to take command. Its condition had deteriorated with inactivity and it was decided to withdraw it towards Dettingen. Noailles, the French commander camped across the river, rapidly conceived a plan to block his opponent's line of retreat between the Spessart hills and the river Main.

All was prepared by the French commander for a masterly stroke that would have at the very least humiliated if not destroyed the Pragmatic Army under the English sovereign. But so eager was one of Noialles's commanders, the Duke of Grammont to charge the enemy that he committed the cardinal error of ordering his troops to cross the river at Dettingen and so at a stroke ensure that the swampy ground which had been in front of him was now behind him. Grammont's move changed the entire logistical premise of the French plan. From having sought to use the marshy terrain to pin down the allies and crush them, the French now found themselves uncomfortably close to their opponents. Their artillery, which had been happily enfilading the allies as they retreated on Dettingen, now ceased firing to avoid hitting Grammont's troops. At this point the Hanoverian and British troops began to fall back under a charge by the Maison du Roi cavalry and three lines of British infantry were broken only to be stabilised when three

Austrian regiments composed mostly of tough Flemish stock filled the gap and held their ground along the fourth British line.[32]

King George II now led a series of cavalry attacks which pushed the French back on to Dettingen, where his artillery completed their defeat. Dettingen could have turned the tables on the allies in an afternoon but instead it further placed the French on the defensive and the Pragmatic Army crossed the Rhine. Their casualties, at 4,000, had been twice that of their opponents but it was a less sanguinary battle than either Mollwitz or Chotusitz.

In the winter of 1743, a defensive alliance was signed between Austria and Saxony. Maria Theresa still sought war. She prepared for an attack on Alsace, a region with historic Habsburg connections, and had drawn up a bold plan for the conquest of Naples. Unfortunately the Austrian army under the indifferent leadership of Lobkowitz in Italy had deteriorated under the influence of the enervating climate and recreational pleasures of the Roman Campagna. A small Spanish army surprised and routed their outposts at Velletri. A later attempt to capture Charles VII of Spain while he was visiting the area ended in fiasco, the Spanish monarch finding time to escape while the Austrians took to plundering the local citizenry. This so-called Second Battle of Velletri saved the Bourbons' Neapolitan possessions and confirmed Lobkowitz as one of Maria Theresa's least gifted generals.

Meanwhile north of the Alps, Frederick, recalling his failure to take Bohemia and anxious that a Pax Austriaca in Europe would be the prelude to a renewed attack on his ill-gotten gains of Silesia, conceived a plan to repeat the attempt on Bohemia. Skilful diplomacy would revive the alliance with Louis XV and the Bavarian monarch who still held the Imperial crown. This would ensure that Austrian forces thinly stretched across the Netherlands and along the Rhine would be unable to march to reinforce Austrian troops to the east. Little over a hundred years before a Prussian army would eject Austria from her leadership of Germany at Königgrätz, Frederick was attempting something similar, though with the added Frederician dimension of naked avarice and lust for territorial expansion, in this case for the rich crown lands of Bohemia.

For her part, Maria Theresa still refused to recognise the Bavarian usurper as emperor and contemptuously rejected the diet of Frankfurt. She did not conceal her resolution to appropriate Bavaria. Moreover, with England and Saxony she would dismember Prussia and humble France.

The Franco-Prussian alliance was built on the solid blocks of Maria Theresa's determination to recover Silesia and Lorraine for her house. Lorraine like Alsace was a region of dubious loyalty to France. However, the incursion of an army of 70,000 Austrians drew a vigorous French response. No fewer than four armies began manoeuvring into position to force the Austrians to withdraw when, on 15 August, Frederick with his usual love of subterfuge declared war on Austria, vowing with France to renew the task of Austrian dismemberment and to conquer Bavaria, Bohemia and Hanover.

On the same day some 80,000 Prussian troops began entering northern Bohemia. It was, Frederick lied, 'just a pre-emptive attack' as 'Austria was certainly preparing to recover Silesia'. The invasion was above all 'protective'. Frederick in his distaste for the truth even went so far as to say that the invasion of Bohemia would offer 'repose for Europe'.[33]

The real reason was that, with Austrian designs in northern and southern Italy blocked, and her possessions in the Netherlands under threat, Maria Theresa's main army was more than 400 miles away. It was an irresistible opportunity for the rapacious Prussian King, though once again he had underestimated his foe and, perhaps more importantly, overestimated his ally.

Three Prussian columns descended on the outnumbered Austrian garrison of Prague and, after a brief siege in which the Marian column on the old town square was hit but not extensively damaged by Prussian artillery, the city surrendered. Nevertheless, help for the Austrians was at hand. Another appeal to Hungarian chivalry produced another levy en masse and 40,000 Hungarians flocked to the Imperial colours. At the same time, thanks to the sudden illness of Louis XV, the French army allowed the Austrians under Lorraine to escape back across the Rhine with only a few trifling attacks on his rearguard. By 22 October more than 75,000 troops were marching towards Frederick, carefully coordinated by Count Traun who, deploying Fabian tactics, relentlessly harassed and confused his opponents.

The Prussian King retreated but goaded by Austrian irregulars, including the terrible Pandours, the Prussian monarch's once disciplined infantry withdrew in disorder. His garrisons surrendered and the tough Bohemian peasantry fell upon his outposts with a ferocity born of an enduring hatred for the *Saupreissen* (pig-Prussians). Disease completed their work and the Prussian military machine collapsed, disintegrating in front of the King's eyes. In desperation Frederick sued for peace but Maria Theresa was implacable. He rapidly realised that only a total evacuation of Bohemia could stave off disaster. Abandoning (again) his army he withdrew to Silesia leaving the beleaguered Prussian troops of Prague to march out to the jeers and stone-throwing of the populace and stagger north to Silesia. But even here there was no respite, and by Christmas all of Upper Silesia had been recovered by the Austrians. The Prussian army entering Bohemia in this 'protective' action lost 30,000 men.

To reinforce the sense of Austrian triumph there was also good news from Bavaria where Charles, succumbing to a violent attack of gout on hearing from one of his domestic servants the news of an Austrian victory, expired on 20 January 1745. The Bavarian who had usurped the Holy Roman Imperial title left a 'memorable example to his posterity not to aspire to a dangerous pre-eminence without power or resources or those transcendent abilities which so arduous a situation required'.[34]

On his deathbed he testified to his regret that he had brought ruin to himself and his country to become 'an Imperial pageant in the hands of France'. He urged his son to renounce any claim to the Imperial title and come to an agreement with Maria Theresa as soon as possible.

Meanwhile in Italy, the Piedmontese expelled the Bourbons with the help of some Austrian regiments, largely composed of Croats. Unsurprisingly, Frederick now desperately wanted peace but again this was to prove elusive.' Never has a crisis been greater than mine,' he wrote. 'Pray for help from my lucky star.'[35] The sentiment was well expressed. The new British government of the Whigs was pro-Austrian and granted £200,000 to Vienna and a contingent of Hanoverian troops. There was even talk of partitioning Prussia, though Maria Theresa noted with her usual practical realism that 'before dividing up the bear's skin it is necessary first to kill it'.[36]

The Prussian recovery

Bavaria hesitated before coming to an accommodation with Vienna and on 21 March 1745 two gifted generals, Batthány assisted by Browne, launched a veritable blitzkrieg against the armies of the Electorate. Within a few weeks every Bavarian garrison in his way had fled or surrendered. At Pfaffenhofen, a small French army under Ségur made a stand. In fierce hand-to-hand fighting among the houses the Pandours reinforced their formidable reputation by slaughtering every French soldier they could find whether wounded or not. The intensity of the close-quarters fighting was something new and the French casualties were unusually high. As Ségur retreated, his troops' discipline almost collapsed as the Pandours assisted by some Hussar squadrons menaced the French army's rear and flanks. Only nightfall brought Ségur any respite. Of his 6,500 troops barely 2,000 survived.

Unsurprisingly, the peace party in Munich gained the upper hand over those Bavarians who wished to continue the struggle, especially as the Austrians once again entered the city as victors. Within a week, the Elector of Bavaria had agreed to recognise the Pragmatic Sanction and sign the Treaty of Füssen.

Although the treaty was a great celebration of Austrian arms, cementing Bavarian recognition of Maria Theresa's claims, it was also lenient. With her usual masterly insights into the temper of the southern Germans, Maria

Theresa wrote to the Elector: 'Everything which is harmful has its origins in the division of our two houses.' In return for these words Bavaria like Saxony would move into the anti-Prussian camp and recognise Maria Theresa's husband as the new Holy Roman Emperor. Maria Theresa had vanquished the last pretender to the Habsburg inheritance. Above all, with Bavaria knocked out there was no longer geographical cohesion to the Franco-Prussian cooperation. From now on Austria would engage in two entirely separate wars in different theatres against enemies who, though united by a common distaste for the House of Austria, were no longer able to form a cohesive alliance. Nevertheless, just as this moment when all seemed to be running in Maria Theresa's favour, everything began to go wrong.

First at Fontenoy though the Austrian contingent of the Pragmatic Army consisted of only eight squadrons of dragoons and hussars, the gifted Maurice de Saxe outwitted an inexperienced Duke of Cumberland and, in one of the most decisive battles of the entire War of the Austrian Succession, crushed the British infantry. The victory was enduringly traumatic for the British: Irish regiments had fought magnificently – on the French side. But for Vienna it was relatively unimportant. Indeed, Frederick summed up its significance for his struggle with Austria, saying that it had 'no more advantage than the capture of Pekin'.

Then less than a month later at Hohenfriedberg, an entire Austrian army supported by the Saxons, both under Charles of Lorraine, fell into a brilliantly conceived and executed trap of the Prussians. Lorraine's ascendancy had been hitherto unstoppable. Characteristically he had claimed much of the credit for Austria's success and predictably this had led to hubris, which in turn had brought back to Austrian arms the twin demons of sluggishness and complacency; vices which would so often cast a long shadow over the Habsburg military effort.

As usual Frederick's strategy was accompanied by some skilful disinformation and above all the technical discipline of his infantry. 'To catch the mice we must set a trap,' Frederick remarked and this he proceeded to do superbly. First he marched some troops west to suggest that he had no stomach for a fight. Then he used his newly reorganised cavalry. Impressed by the Magyar horsemen of his opponents Frederick had at last recruited some hussars from the dissident Hungarians. These he deployed to screen his real movements. Finally he had a network of agents spread the rumour that he himself was ill and in no mood to offer battle.

As he entered Silesia this was precisely what Lorraine wanted to hear. As he rested near Landeshut in scattered formation with his Saxon allies, his cavalry screen undertook no detailed reconnaissance and in fact were not even near their horses when the battle started.

Frederick had under cover of darkness (and ordering his men to leave their campfires burning) marched his men some four miles across the Austrian front and at five in the morning launched an attack on the Saxons. 'Kein Pardon an den Sachsen' (No Pardon for the Saxons) was the order of the day in revenge for the fickle friendship the Saxons had offered Frederick in deserting their alliance. The Prussians would indeed take few prisoners that day.

After two hours the Prussian horse had ridden their Saxon opponents off the field. Fired up by its easy success against the demoralised Saxon infantry, the Prussian cavalry proved more energetic and pressed home three vigorous attacks against the Austrians. The first two the Austrians saw off with ease but the third strangely demoralised and eventually broke them and they fled. For the first time in an Austro-Prussian battle, the Prussian horse were both battle-hardened and superior. They even captured the Austrian general Berlichingen who, surveying his captors with a scornful glance, asked with typical Austrian hauteur: 'Do I really have to be taken by a mob like this?'[37]

No one had expected the Austrian cavalry to be outfought. With near-mechanised efficiency the Prussian infantry unmolested by the dreaded Austrian cavalry calmly advanced to within virtual point-blank range of the Austrian lines drawn up in front of them between the villages of Guntersdorf and Thomaswaldau. But now it was the turn of the Prussian infantry to be surprised. Though utterly unprotected, the Austrian line discharged two devastating volleys and advanced. For a further half an hour the Austrian infantry proved it could be formidable in defence and might even have held its own had not a sudden gap in the Prussian line opened to allow the Bayreuth Dragoons to charge the infantry, with unfortunate consequences for the Austrians.

Within twenty minutes the two Austrian lines and the flower of five infantry regiments, some 25 battalions, had been trampled or cut to pieces by a mere 1,500 horsemen. The losses were by the standards of the time, both in quantity and ratio, appalling for the Austrians. Lorraine left over 10,000 men on the battlefield in dead, wounded and prisoners while the Prussian losses were barely a fifth that number. Sixty-six standards and scores of guns as well as a vast amount of booty including eight pairs of silver kettledrums fell into Prussian hands. Four Austrian commanders had been killed and several generals were captured. Lorraine summed it up with untypical candour: 'At Hohenfriedberg, we have suffered a total defeat in one of the finest positions you could imagine.'

Charles withdrew into Bohemia to lick his wounds and reorganise his shattered army. With reinforcements his confidence gradually returned and his light cavalry and irregulars began to harass the Prussians. Nadasti the gifted Hungarian hussar commander soon had the Prussians in his sights. No longer 'blind', Lorraine together with the Hungarian conceived a plan to roll the Prussian army up from the west by a bold attack.

Unfortunately the time that elapsed between the plan and its execution was too long and the real 'surprise' attack came from the Prussians who, despite a devastating artillery barrage, wheeled with perfect discipline to effect a 90-degree change of front, leaving them parallel with their enemy. Once again, the Prussian cavalry rode the Austrian horse off the battlefield. The Battle of Soor confirmed the Prussian superiority in the cavalry arm. Prince Lobkowitz was so infuriated by the failure of his dragoons to counter-charge the Prussians he shot three of his own officers immediately for cowardice before himself falling into a ditch as his demoralised troopers were overrun.

The Hungarian hussars proved no more reliable. Charging home, they reached through to the Prussian camp where they then wasted valuable time at the climax of the battle when they could have sown confusion in the rear ranks of the Prussians by plundering Frederick's tent, capturing his hound and his silver (but ignoring his letters and orders). Lack of discipline and coordination were the key features of the Austrian effort and, though not as bloody a battle as Hohenfriedberg, the results were the same. After three failed advances the Prussian infantry stormed the key position to the Austrian left, the Graner Koppe, held by six battalions and no fewer than fifteen elite grenadier companies and sixteen guns. At virtually the same time, the Austrian centre began to crumble and Lorraine ordered a withdrawal. Under a skilfully covered retreat organised by a young officer called Daun, the Austrians retired in mostly good order.

But the trend at Hohenfriedberg had been confirmed. The Austrian cavalry had proved deficient and the Austrian infantry though courageous could not match its Prussian opponents man for man. Soor had shown that a Prussian army inferior in numbers could still defeat the Austrians. There were now hard lessons to be digested for the Habsburg military machine. As Frederick wrote: 'If the Austrians could not beat me at Soor I shall never be beaten by them'.[38] This was to prove a little over-confident.

But in 1745 Frederick's victories strengthened the peace party in Vienna and as England in the throes of the Jacobite rebellion was desperate to have an Austrian ally that could devote undivided attention to dealing with the mortal foe France, the news of Soor gave the diplomats the opening they needed. On 25 December Silesia was signed over to Frederick, together with the county of Glatz. This was a colossal sacrifice in every way: a hard-working population in excess of 1,220,000 people and many rich mineral deposits. Maria Theresa pledged not to resort to arms to recover this jewel in her crown, and indeed when hostilities were resumed once again a decade later it was she who kept her word and Frederick who once again committed the aggression.

The year 1745, which had started so promisingly for the Habsburg cause, ended with Austria's armies north of the Alps demoralised and exhausted. In the Netherlands the cause fared little better. British support was compromised by the emergency at home over the Stuarts, which distracted them for many months to come. In the Dutch provinces the Francophile party gained more momentum and was sceptical of the arrangements with Austria. Only the election of Maria Theresa's husband Francis to the Imperial crown offered some recompense. The proud Imperial double-headed eagle could be returned to the colours and standards of the Austrian troops and Austrian prestige reinforced by the symbolism of the crown of Charlemagne.

In Italy under the imaginative leadership of Prince Wenzel Liechtenstein the Austrians retook Milan and Parma and won a convincing victory at Piacenza over the Spanish and French. The Austrian infantry and cavalry proved more than equal to the Bourbons' forces and indeed Wenzel's interest in artillery served the Austrians well that day. For only 700 fatalities the Austrians inflicted more than 15,000 casualties (including prisoners) on their opponents.

Austrian setbacks

This victory secured Milan and for the rest of the year the Austrians were left to attempt to suppress the Genoese whose city the Austrians, much to the chagrin of their ally Charles Emmanuel of Sardinia-Piedmont, had occupied. The occupation of Genoa under Botta d'Adorno was not a glorious chapter for Austrian arms. Indeed, the ease with which he had entered the city was something of a stroke of luck. But this highly resourceful population was exhausted and eager for radical reform, including nothing less than a new political system that would disenfranchise the oligarchic patriciate. But the great patrician families of Genoa were not to be dislodged so easily.

The Austrian occupiers behaved with such crass vindictiveness that something had to give. On the evening of 5 December 1746 when an Austrian officer peremptorily demanded some help to remove a mortar that had fallen into a ditch the locals looked sullenly on and then began to throw stones. The Austrians withdrew under this hail of projectiles but within hours the protests had spread to other parts of the city and the cry of 'Libertà' went up, rapidly followed by the more menacing cry of 'Armati' (weapons). Botta could not believe what was happening but the uprising erupted, driving him from the city and leaving more than 2,000 of his troops prisoners. Well might the French Consul write: 'Nothing like this has ever been seen.' Maria Theresa was outraged but she wisely replaced the incompetent Botta with the more capable

Schulenburg. Few mourned Botta's departure: 'he should have been hanged years ago,' commented the British minister Hardwicke.[39]

Maria Theresa looked forward to seeing her claims on the Bourbon possessions in the peninsula, notably Naples, vindicated. But disaster in the Netherlands tempered these plans. The Battle of Laffeldt sealed the reputation of Maurice de Saxe as Europe's leading general, tricking a numerically superior Pragmatic Army under Cumberland in a superbly coordinated attack which left the English troops cut off from their Austrian allies, whose cavalry only just managed to cover the English retreat. French losses were double that of the allies, making it the largest and bloodiest battle of the War of the Austrian Succession. By now Austrian arms were exhausted. Her enemies were not much better off and every belligerent looked for a way to escape the relentless bloodshed and logic of combat. In Italy Browne, no stranger to the hardships of war, was also tired of the slaughter.

The Peace, which was signed at Aix La Chapelle in 1748, gave Austria a much-needed respite. Maria Theresa could survey most of her armed forces with some degree of satisfaction. Though her armies had been overtaken dramatically by the Prussians towards the end, they had served their purpose of defending the dynasty. No one could question the power, prestige and existence of the Casa Austria. France, which had sought to 'annihilate Austria' (in Belle-Isle's phrase), found out in Upper Austria and Bohemia that her arms could not in any way even begin to achieve this. At the same time the old 'Imperial' army had emerged briefly in the course of the war as the 'Austrian' army. Following the coronation of Maria Theresa's husband as Emperor, its return to the Imperial insignia fused both terms unequivocally for the next century.

But the series of conflicts collectively known as the War of the Austrian Succession had been bloody in the extreme. The civilian dislocation was enormous. The so-called age of civilised warfare had seen appalling atrocities carried out by all the belligerents. The British army in the Rhineland pillaged churches and regularly burned villages. The Prussians occupied Saxony and Bohemia with exceptional severity, administering what one historian has called 'exemplary brutalities' while the French were equally capable of barbarous behaviour towards civilians. The Austrians despite all Maria Theresa's efforts to imbue her troops with a different spirit to that of 'merciless Prussia' were no less capable of atrocities and her irregular troops, especially the Pandours, came to be known for their pitiless violence towards civilians. Along the Ligurian coast regular Austrian troops behaved almost as badly though they did not dismember civilians with the enthusiasm of their irregular comrades in arms. Such behaviour was rarely authorised and was not typical, but it was not infrequent and rarely was it punished. (The estimate of deaths arising from the War of the Austrian Succession has been put as high as five million.)[40]

During the next eight years Maria Theresa would demonstrate that she was both a courageous monarch and a zealous reformer of military methods and organisation. When the Austrians next marched into battle it would be with an army that was no longer dissipated and weary, lacking in discipline and energetic leadership. By 1756, Maria Theresa would have an army that was indeed full of strength and life. Moreover the negotiations leading up to the Peace of Aix La Chapelle brought about subtle changes in the attitude of Austria towards the rest of Europe. The great Empress had not only survived mortal threats to her inheritance; she had without doubt strengthened her domains. She had shown an uncanny ability to promote able men and she was now about to reap the benefits of these instincts.

Count (later Prince) Wenzel Kaunitz (1711–93) Austrian chancellor from 1753, though at this stage only a relatively minor diplomat, saw clearly that France would have more to offer the Habsburgs than England whose armies had been, with the odd notable exception, unimpressive on the battlefields of Europe and defeated so many times by the French in the Lowlands. England's money had always been given with strong strings attached.

Maria Theresa characteristically offered Kaunitz some practical advice: 'It is better to rely on one's own strength in the future than to beg for foreign money and thereby remain in eternal subordination.'[41] Kaunitz took the hint. The support of non-Catholic Britain, accompanied as it was with the full panoply of hypocrisy and cynicism masquerading as 'pragmatism', left Maria Theresa cold. Her husband who had spent time in London and had been inducted into English Freemasonry by Lord Chesterfield[42] was also unimpressed by London's performance. But to effect a realignment with France would require nothing short of a truly dramatic reversal of alliances. Fortunately for Austria, and unfortunately for Frederick and Prussia, Kaunitz was to prove more than capable of realising this. This diplomatic gambit would be accompanied by a comprehensive overhaul of the Habsburg armies.

CHAPTER 5

Austria Resurgent

THERESIAN MILITARY REFORMS

Maria Theresa's armies had survived the shock of invasion from three sides. They had often fought bravely but they had shown little sign of being able to inflict a major defeat on the Prussians. The reforms they underwent in the run-up to the Seven Years War improved their morale and effectiveness dramatically. When hostilities were renewed, Prussia faced a Habsburg army of altogether different calibre.

Prince Liechtenstein and the modernisation of the Austrian artillery

On 8 February 1748, a distinguished group of senior officers met in Vienna to coordinate military reform. Under the presidency of Lorraine, the detailed work was to be carried out by Liechtenstein and Harrach with the support of Wenzel Wallis with two gifted officers, Daun and Schulenburg. Of these, Liechtenstein and Daun were perhaps the most enterprising. The former was an Alpine prince whose rank, wealth and status were, as it is for his descendants to this day, on a different level to that of the high Austrian aristocracy. (The fabulous wealth of the Liechtenstein family was founded, according to legend, on the secret of the Philosopher's Stone.) With their uniquely corrupt vowels inflecting their speech, their enormous height and practical materialist outlook at once both realist and solemn, the Liechtensteins consequently were always far removed from the atmosphere and frivolity of the Austrian court. Field Marshal Joseph Wenzel Liechtenstein was no exception and it was no coincidence that the arm requiring the highest quotient of intelligence, the artillery, fell to his responsibility. Wounded at the head of his Dragoon regiment at the Battle of Chotusitz, Liechtenstein had been very impressed by the 82 well-served Prussian guns, which had compared so well with the antiquated

Austrian cannon. With his active military career cut short by his wounds he was determined to devote the rest of his life to giving the Habsburgs the best artillery in Europe.

Assisted by his immense private wealth – not a ducat needed to come from the Austrian treasury to finance his experiments – he invited at his own expense the foremost artillerists of Europe to advise him: Alvson from Denmark, the brothers Feuerstein from Kolín, Schröeder from Prussia, 'Fire Devil' Rouvroy from Saxony and even the formidable Gribeauval from France. By the time Liechtenstein had finished his reorganisation a few years later Austrian artillery would be established as among the finest in Europe, a reputation that would more or less endure until 1918. All these later successes were built on the foundation stone of Liechtenstein's reforms in the 1750s.

These reforms had a geographical and ethnic dimension to them for Liechtenstein soon realised that artillery could not be left to ordinary soldiers of no education. In a move which was to prove far-seeing and have significant consequences for the development of the Central European arms industry later in the twentieth century, the Prince established the home of the Habsburg artillery arm unequivocally once and for all in Bohemia. He knew that the Bohemians of mixed German and Czech race were not only the quickest wits in the Empire but that they combined resilience with toughness, humour with imagination, practicality with energy and above all a sense of theatre with coolness under fire. How did he know this? He knew this because vast tracts of Bohemia and Moravia belonged to his family, who administered them with tremendous care and intelligence. Truly can it be said that Bohemia elevated the House of Liechtenstein to something beyond mere Alpine aristocracy. Placing the artillery headquarters in Budweis, he also ensured that his artillerists were paid a third more than the rank and file infantry.*

When Wenzel Liechtenstein began his work, there were only 800 trained artillerists in the Habsburg army. By 1755 there were three artillery brigades made up of some 33 companies.[1] In addition Artillery Fusilier regiments were created to assist the gunners in moving and defending the guns. As well as these a munitions corps and mining company were established. The artillery 'park' was also increased, with 768 3-pounder guns and several batteries of 6-pounder cannon. At Ebergassing near Vienna the cannon foundry was 'modernised' with a new range of horizontal drilling machines invented by a Swiss mechanical but illiterate genius called Jacquet. By the end of Maria

---

* The Liechtenstein estates in Bohemia and later Moravia were indeed so immense that for many years after the 'Velvet Revolution' in 1989 the thorny issue of restitution prevented Prague even entering into basic diplomatic relations with the principality of Liechtenstein.

Theresa's reign there were more than 600 heavy 6- and 12-pounder pieces and the artillery arm numbered nearly 15,000 men. Standardisation of wheels and other parts of the guns was an important feature of the new weapons.

Drill and exercise were the natural concomitants of this huge increase in firepower and Liechtenstein insisted on full-scale training at least twice a week. By 1772, also by Imperial decree, a brown uniform with red facings was established to distinguish the corps from the white-coated rank and file infantry. Maria Theresa noted – she always took a keen and practical interest in these details – 'it is important for the uniform to be conspicuous but not more expensive'. More than a century later at the 1900 Paris Exhibition a modern version of this brown and red uniform would win the first prize for combining elegance and practicality.

Not only were the uniforms distinctive, the levels of rank were also unique, with archaic titles such as *Buchsenmeister* (gunner) or *Alt-Feuerwerker* (second lieutenant) or *Stuckhauptmann* (captain) or *Stuckjuncker* (first lieutenant). The artillery was in its atmosphere more a medieval guild of kindred spirits with its own rituals and language than a conventional regiment of the army. Promotion to officer rank was strictly meritocratic and almost always proceeded from within the corps. Candidates were first trained in the Budweis artillery depot where they were schooled in geometry, ballistics, hydraulics and the science of fortification.

In 1757 the artillery Reglement (Regulations) noted: 'We must seek in the artillery to encourage the men in their duties more through a love of honour and good treatment than through brutality, untimely blows and beatings.'[2]

In addition to these reforms, the Empress, on Liechtenstein's advice, established institutes (Witwen und Waisen Confraternität) to look after the families of artillerists, especially widows and orphans in Prague, Kolín and Landshut.[3] At the same time Liechtenstein introduced a radical overhaul of ordnance. Anton Feuerstein as head of the Feld Artillerie Corps sought to pare weight down to a minimum by shortening and lightening barrels. Gun carriages also benefited from this practical approach. He established a common axle and just two types of wheel for all artillery pieces. This uniformity meant that spares could be made available in the event of breakdown.

Moreover, each gun was given a number which in turn was painted on every item of equipment down to the mop-cum-rammer to help every soldier identify with his artillery piece, for 'both officers and men feel their honour is engaged when taking a close interest in the upkeep of their equipment and ammunition. Thus the entire ordnance is most carefully engaged.'[4]

Above all, to ensure an instantly recognisable and practical appearance the gun carriages and wheels were to be painted in the Imperial colours, *schwarzgelb* (black and gold, or rather yellow), with the result that this application of oil paint offered 'much better protection than before against damp and other climatic conditions. In this way 'the greater durability of the wood repays the cost many times over'. Not even Austrian gunpowder was immune from Liechtenstein's zealous reforms. Renowned for its combustibility and strength, it was made even more effective when packaged in linen cartridges which were bound together with a sabot.*

The linen surface of the cartridge was then painted with a covered paste and finally coated with white oil paint. Thus the powder was compressed tightly together for maximum effect.

Cavalry reform

Though far less radically innovative than the Liechtenstein reforms of the artillery, the spirit of reform permeated all other arms. This included even that part of the Austrian army which justifiably enjoyed a high reputation: the cavalry, though the reforms were on balance less successful than those in other arms, perhaps because of the cavalry's innate conservatism.

The peace establishment of 1748 reduced the strength of the cavalry regiments from 1,000 to 800 men. The cavalry were divided into four distinct units: Cuirassiers, Dragoons, Chevauxlegers and Hussars. The Hussars along with the other units of irregular cavalry maintained their distinctive traditions and uniforms but in the case of the regular cavalry Maria Theresa soon made it clear that she expected greater uniformity in dress. 'Gleichheit in der Montur' became the watchword and the cavalry regiments needed this more than the infantry on account of the expense of their dress. It cost 7 florins to dress a grenadier but 56 florins to kit out a cuirassier. The independence of the officers in their appearance was especially anathema to the Empress. In 1749 she issued a decree which forbade discrepancy in horse furnishing. The amounts of gold and silver used had to be identical for all regiments.

The few Chevauxleger regiments tried to balance the preponderance of hussars with a non-Hungarian light cavalry unit. Because of their rarity they soon became something of an elite formation, distinguished by their green tunics (a legacy of the Low Countries) and red or black facings. Later Maria Theresa's son Joseph II would, in imitation of Frederick of Prussia's many portraits in uniform, regularly wear the green uniform of Colonel of his regiment of the First Chevauxlegers (die 'Schvolay', as they were called colloquially

---

* Another Bohemian quality. 'We are a nation of chemists.' The Czech skill in explosives was all too apparent during the Cold War. Semtex was invented not far from Prague.

in Viennese dialect). With Joseph's elevation on his father's death to 'co-regent' in 1765, this regiment was issued with dashing light green tunics and poppy-red cuffs, and straw-coloured breeches for officers.

Some other cavalry regiments managed to negotiate exceptions to the cloak of Theresian uniformity that was now descending on them. Each time it was the Empress personally who decided. The Latour Dragoons in commemoration of their exploits were allowed to wear green and were granted an exemption from the prevailing fashion of moustaches. The Savoy Dragoons, who had distinguished themselves equally heroically on campaign after much intercession by their colonel Count Lyndon (the model perhaps for the hero of Thackeray's novel, *Barry Lyndon*) were allowed the unique privilege in the Austrian army of wearing red with black facings. Maria Theresa when questioned about this indulgence in a formal report simply scribbled laconically: 'Lyndon's regiment is good'.[5]

Maria Theresa's personal equestrian skills gave her particular insights into the use of light cavalry but her commonsense observations often were the source of much irritation among conservative military men. Her 'suggestion' that all her cavalry regiments present arms in identical fashion caused consternation, especially among her Hussar regiments that were equipped with carbines. On another occasion she complained that there were increasingly too many words in the phrases of command. 'The shorter the better,' she insisted. Another time she was unimpressed by one especially effete aspect of cavalry drill and immediately penned the command that it be abolished, noting: 'It is important to change this as it strikes me as decidedly unmilitary.'[6]

Nor were the Empress's strictures confined to the parade ground; she immersed herself in the study and practical application of cavalry tactics. During a long debate on the efficacy of cavalry firing in formation she observed: 'With regard to the cavalry firing from the saddle I do not take it very seriously' ('Ich halt' nicht viel').[7]

Other points she was quick to make included the obvious but at the time much-debated issue of whether cavalry needed drummers. Drums were an important part of the irregular cavalry, which had taken them on from the long-standing traditions of the Ottoman drum horses they had faced on the Military Frontier. The Empress thought them 'completely unnecessary' and strongly urged more trumpeters.

At every point she was determined to cut down the influence of the Inhaber (proprietary) colonels while raising the standing of the officer corps in Austrian society as a whole. As her senior commanders found out, no detail seemed too insignificant to escape her attention, whether it was the make of riding gloves, particular shades of green as facing colours, the use of powder in the hair or the cut of riding boots. On all these things the Empress had an opinion.

The Hussars

Issues of cost were no less relevant to the Hussar regiments. The eight regular regiments of hussars on the army list when the Empress succeeded to her domains had consisted each of ten companies of 100 men. Strangely assorted groups of 'enthusiasts' had been raised by the Transylvanian and Hungarian magnates as part of the 'Insurrectio' following Maria Theresa's dazzling Pressburg appearance. The Empress was determined, once peace was secured, that these too be reduced to a coherent order.

But the very qualities, noted by the historian H. G. Mirabeau in his famous work on the Prussian military system, which were to be found in the Hussars made them less amenable to conventional organisation. Mirabeau pointed out in 1788 that 'The Hungarian has an inborn spark and a natural inclination towards stratagems. He lives in a country which abounds in horses. He learns to be a horseman in childhood and having nothing better to do in that half savage land, he teaches his horse all sorts of tricks ... with this kind of upbringing, the Hungarian becomes a perfect light cavalryman without any further training. . . .'[8]

With 'this kind of training', Mirabeau hinted, attempts at administrative conformity were difficult to digest. The code of regulations for the Hussars was identical to that of the regular 'German' cavalry. For the first time all the regiments now received regular pay, thus in theory eliminating the 'need' for extended plunder which gave the Hussars along with their legendary swordsmanship (one French head split into four pieces with one blow) such a fearsome reputation.

But the hussars proved difficult to tame and one observer noted there were scarcely twenty officers in the entire French army who had not been victims of Maria Theresa's hussars' lust for plundering. Despite the extravagance and cost of their uniform, the hussars successfully resisted any attempt to reduce their opulence or breadth of colour. Although the Empress introduced strict rules on the length and cut of dolmans and cloaks, she utterly failed to impose, as she had decreed, the single colour of sapphire blue on all pelisses and dolmans. Even attempts to impose a common sabre with a blade uniformly 32 inches long and one and a half inches wide failed miserably. In practice the colonels would often supply sabres that varied from the regulations. The feudal system in Hungary reinforced the proprietary colonels, who often saw their regiments as extensions of their own prestige and estates, even to be kitted out by their local tailor, often Jewish. Entire factories of uniform-makers grew up in the Austrian frontier marches between Vienna and Györ. To this day the ornate headdress of the Spanish Riding School is made by the descendants of one of these artisans.

These industrious men also supplied the sabretaches and shabraques and other details of 'horse furniture' bearing the colonel's crest rather than the royal or Imperial cipher. Hussar guidons were equally expressive of this. While the *Leibstandarte* (sovereign standard) bore the double-headed eagle on one side and the Virgin Mary on the other, the regimental standard replaced the image of the Madonna with the Colonel's monogram.

In keeping with these distinctions, there was no attempt either to make Hungarian saddles conform with those of the rest of the cavalry. Hussar saddles and stirrups were light, the latter worn very short so that spurs were consequently positioned near the side of the horse's chest, a practice which unsurprisingly made both riders and mounts somewhat jittery. But this well expressed the nervous neurotic energy that invested everything these soldiers did. The fashion of never powdering hair but dressing it in plaits that reached down to the waist reinforced the general exoticism of this branch.

Tales of the exploits of these horsemen spread far and wide and in 1743 Frederick sent a secret envoy to Vienna to bribe and cajole some Hungarians to come to Berlin and train up some regiments into passable imitations of the genre under Zieten and a Hungarian renegade by the name of von Halasz. At first these efforts met with mixed success but later, under Seydlitz, dramatic results were achieved and, as we saw earlier, by the Battle of Soor the Prussian hussars had become a match for the real thing.

Infantry reform

With regard to the infantry, the need for reform was far more pressing. Compared to the forced marches and parade ground precision of the Prussians the Austrian infantry were felt to be dogged and courageous but less agile and inventive. Such was the zeal with which successive reforms were introduced that at times all 44 regiments of infantry of the line which Maria Theresa had inherited in 1740 appeared to be in a permanent state of work in progress. Breakdown of companies, size of regiments, and numbers of grenadiers assigned to each regiment, as well as tactics, drill and dress, were constantly shifting under a veritable avalanche of experiments.

By 1769, the structure of the Austrian infantry had evolved into single regiments totalling 2,000 men each. These were broken down into three battalions and two Grenadier companies of between 120 and 150 men each. At first these grenadier companies were armed with grenades but gradually they came to be used as shock troops, the tallest and bravest in the regiment distinguished by their lofty bearskin headdress, general air of arrogant ferocity and curved sabres worn by all the men. As an added refinement the stocks of their muskets were of polished walnut as opposed to plain beechwood for the Fusilier infantry.

As the reputation of the Inhaber of the regiment often rested largely on the size and appearance of these men, attempts to combine the Grenadier companies into a single regiment or even into tactical units failed miserably at first. Nevertheless as one contemporary, Cognazzo, observed, 'in our army it does a man good simply to give him a bearskin. He is less inclined to desert and will fight better.'[9]

Gradually the idea of combining these elite companies as ad hoc formations began to gather momentum, and the reforms of the infantry after 1748 certainly made it easier to detach each regiment's two grenadier companies. This would be implemented with devastating effect on the battlefields of the next war. Pay and conditions meanwhile were improved, especially for subaltern officers, though the rich detailing of their uniforms inevitably caught the Empress's eye and on 5 June 1755 she ordered that there should be 'more economy in excess details'. Uniforms therefore came to be marked by simplicity and great modesty among the rank and file, relying on their elegance of cut and colour for effect in contrast to the heavier more ornate uniforms of Prussia and England, let alone France. In order to distinguish in the fog of battle one set of white-coated combatants from those of another country (for example France) the custom grew of adding a sprig of oak leaves in summer months or pine needles in the winter months as a *Feldzeichen* to each soldier's headdress, a tradition that would outlive the abolition of white tunics more than a century later and remain synonymous with Habsburg service.

The modern reader might well question how white or pearl grey undyed wool could be a practical uniform for parades and battles. In fact undyed wool could be brought up with pipe clay to a dazzling white, while blue, red and green coats all lost their colour after a little wear owing to the deficiencies of eighteenth-century dyes. The Habsburg white was therefore an eminently practical colour and no attempt was made to change it. Regiments were distinguished by shades of red, green, orange, yellow, blue and black in the facing colour, and increasingly in the colour of their buttons.

In 1765, a new shorter and lighter infantry uniform was introduced following Maria Theresa's injunction that the old uniform was unsatisfactory: 'One of my principal ambitions is and always shall be,' she wrote, 'to make such arrangements as will promote the upkeep of the private soldier and alleviate his duties. Bearing this in mind I have decided to try out a new kind of uniform among my infantry regiments which will give the ordinary soldier's body better protection against cold and wet and yet be no heavier to wear.'[10]

The greatcoats that could be issued with this lighter uniform were a welcome comfort against inclement weather (and the last item any deserter chose to part with). But these improvements had followed years of failed attempts to shorten Austrian infantry coats in the teeth of opposition from vested interests. Thus fifteen years earlier Podewils had noted that Maria Theresa's attempts to change uniforms by shortening coats had been frustrated by officers who had submitted vastly inflated costs for providing tents which 'of course' would be necessary if the coats had less material to protect their wearers from the vagaries of the weather.

'They grossly exaggerated the expense of the covers of the pack horses to carry them and of the men to look after the horses so that the total bill reached an enormous sum and it was easy for them to persuade the Empress to give up the idea.'[11] Reforms of uniform in the infantry were accompanied by a complete modernisation of weaponry. In 1748, six regiments were rearmed with a musket designed by Johann Schmied, a lowly official with a creative mind. The gun proved effective but easily breakable. It was better than the 1722 muzzle-loading smooth bore musket with which the Austrians hitherto had been equipped. In 1754, Liechtenstein applied his considerable intellect to the problem and formed a commission of officers to examine the Schmied musket and three other muskets made by the Penzeneter factory. The best of each weapon was now integrated into the so-called Comissflinte which was able to deliver as consistently as the much-admired Prussian muskets. To ensure this was the case, all moving parts were to be kept 'Mirror bright' (*Spiegel glänzend*).

This addiction to polish had unfortunate consequences. As Cognazzo observed:

> We polished our weapons unceasingly and in the course of time the barrels became so thin that after a few live rounds they were liable to burst and melt. . . . Many regiments scarcely got off eight or ten volleys before we saw hundreds of these beautiful gleaming muskets lying useless on the ground.[12]

Maria Theresa also immersed herself in the shortcomings of her infantry's drill, as was highlighted early on in the war at Mollwitz. In 1749 when peace offered a respite to address these deficiencies she issued a proclamation: 'It has come to Our notice that Our Imperial infantry possesses neither a uniform drill nor consistent observation of military practice. These two shortcomings not only give rise to various disorders but promote a dangerous harmful and damaging situation . . .'.[13]

Browne, Neipperg and Eszterhazy had all compiled their own drill manuals, while an earlier manual of 1737 was virtually ignored. The Military Reform Commission lost no time in attempting to impose some uniformity on infantry drill. In 1749 it published the *Regulament und Ordnung des gesammten Kaiserlich-Königlichen Fuss-Volcks* (Infantry drill regulations) drawing on much of these earlier manuals, old administrative manuals and indeed several conversations Maria Theresa had with a retired Prussian officer called Doss.

When Frederick heard of this manual's existence he ordered his Ambassador in Vienna to acquire a copy, but in vain. The Prussian Ambassador noted that though every regiment was in possession of the book, 'the penalty for communicating its contents is nothing less than dishonourable discharge. For this reason neither I nor any of the other foreign envoys have been able to obtain a copy.'[14]

The drill and deployments – though modified notably after the Seven Years War and in the midst of the Napoleonic Wars in 1805 – remained largely in use up until the time of Radetzky and beyond, thus showing how these Theresian articles of military conduct endured for more than a hundred years. The *Regulament* laid down four lines of infantry to be drawn up, with the 'tallest and best looking' in the front line. The first in conventional fashion dropped to one knee when preparing to volley. The fourth line was a reserve and stood with shouldered muskets.

When receiving cavalry the first two rows of troops were expected to stand with bayonets pointed towards the horses' chest and head while the third line aimed at the riders. *Schrott* (shotgun) cartridges were considered most effective at close range against cavalry. The bayonet charge as an isolated tactic was relatively rare, though some Austrian generals such as Khevenhueller fondly nurtured the notion of infantry storming positions without firing a shot. This tactic became more usual a generation or so later (e.g. the Young Guard taking Plancenoit at the *pas de charge* in 1815, or the struggle for Aspern in 1809).

It was still far more common for infantry to fire at each other from a range of a hundred paces or less until one side broke and withdrew. The Austrians aimed to fire five rounds a minute. While this was possible on the parade ground, it proved far more difficult in battle conditions. Moreover the muskets were inaccurate and the Austrian drill remained complex compared to that of the Prussians.

The *Regulament* was extravagantly detailed in prescribing the correct drill for all occasions. For example, there were no fewer than 27 pages on a soldier's conduct on Good Friday and exhaustive rules for a soldier on duty accepting a glass of wine while in uniform. But less effective rules were laid down for actually training the men for battle. A paucity of NCOs, the backbone of any army, meant that in some battles several platoons were not allowed to be incorporated into the line of battle because they did not know how to load and fire.

Officer recruitment: The Wiener Neustadt Military Academy

Nevertheless, the reforms gathered pace. To reinforce the prestige of the officer corps and create a more homogeneous body, the Empress felt the existing state of officer recruitment left much to be desired. Nepotism was rife, but not all young men of good family were necessarily suitable for the job. The Hungarian commander, Eszterházy, was quick to note: 'The recruiting officer may be assured that nobody in the regiment will thank him for bringing in unsuitable cadets.'[15]

Good manners, a pleasant countenance and good physical appearance were only part of the equation. Maria Theresa was determined that the officers should be formally trained. It was Haugwitz, one of her most astute advisers who, after a trip to Carinthia where he had seen countless young nobles wasting their time in hunting and drinking, came up with the idea of a military academy. Already in 1746, the Empress had founded the Theresianum as a *collegium nobilum* to educate a cadre of future administrators and civilian servants of the state. Like everything she established, this institution endured and was to provide the elite of Central Europe and the Balkans for more than a century to come. Encouraged by the institution's success, it was time to explore the possibilities of a military version. Like the Theresianum, Imperial property was put at the disposal of the project.

The site chosen was twenty-five miles south of Vienna at Wiener Neustadt. There a small castle in Imperial hands was converted into an 'aristocratic cadet school' (*Adelige Kadettenschule*). The decree issued by Maria Theresa on 14 December 1751 retained the meritocratic traditions of the Austrian officer class. Significantly, it envisaged an officer *training* academy, not a finishing school. The name Military Academy was confirmed in 1765. To ensure that no ethnic group was left out, the decree was communicated to all commanding officers of general rank and above in the crown lands, including Hungary, Transylvania, Italy and the Netherlands. Moreover, this racial diversity was to be complemented by a degree of social mix. The decree envisaged a corps of cadets divided into two companies each of 100 men. One company was reserved for young aristocrats while the second was the preserve of sons of senior officers who might or might not have been ennobled. In practice, as the Theresian reforms gathered pace, the raising of the prestige of the officer corps meant that all officers with thirty years' service were routinely ennobled. In certain cases the award of the Maria Theresa Order automatically conferred elevation to the nobility. But this class of officer was socially a very different creature from the well-born scions of the *Hochadel* (high aristocracy).

The tensions between the graduates of these two companies would be a recurring theme in later years, especially in the run-up to and aftermath of Königgrätz. Duties were identical and in both companies the cadets were admitted at the age of 14 with all costs met from state funds. To prepare boys for entry into the academy a kind of preparatory school (*Vorschule*) was established for boys between the ages of 8 and 13. (This Theresian division of schooling survives to this day in England.)

To oversee the academy, Maria Theresa appointed no less a figure than Leopold Daun (1705–66), one of the most gifted of her generals, soon to be the scourge of the Prussians and the butt of Frederick's most venomous abuse ('the anointed fat pig of Kolín' was one of the more printable insults Frederick used in describing Daun). Daun was a typical product of soldierly aristocratic ancestry: conventional, professional, reliable and courageous. What he lacked in imagination he made up for in tenacity.

As a medal struck commemorating the foundation shows, the religious dimension in the young officers' training was not forgotten: it is inscribed with the words: MILITARIS INSTITUENDAE IVVENT SACRUM VOLVERUNT. Moreover, the first manual for the recruits included a list of days when confessions could be heard, and when other rites of the Catholic Church would be performed, with detailed instructions for Mass on Sundays and feast days as well as timetables of religious education and music instruction for church chorales. The fledgling officer corps were under no illusions that the loyalty they owed the Imperial House was rivalled only by their loyalty to the Almighty. Indeed, as the banners richly embroidered with Marian and Habsburg images on the battlefield showed, these were but two sides of the same fabric.

While the cadets' routine each day consisted of lessons and exercises including fencing, riding and dancing, each officer was expected to be fluent in at least four languages including German, Czech, French and Italian. The initial twelve cadets graduated in 1754, the first of what would become a steady stream. As the delightful series of gouaches of Bernhard Albrecht, a Viennese artist of the time, show in a later period, life for the cadets was a mixture of discipline and entertainment. Behind the doors of the academy was a world different to anything outside. Yet as Albrecht's paintings illustrate, winter ice-skating was a *sine qua non* of cadet life.

Reform of the Hofkriegsrat

At the highest levels of the Imperial administration the Hofkriegsrat was overhauled no less zealously to oversee all these reforms. Again Daun was the key figure to preside over change. The Hofkriegsrat has rightly been called the 'most notorious and least understood of Habsburg military institutions'.[16] Founded by the Emperor Ferdinand in 1556, this unwieldy inner sanctum of military counsels was presided over by Count Harrach when Maria Theresa came to the throne. Its thirty-six nominal members enjoyed support staff in excess of a hundred largely inexperienced clerks who had been parked in the organisation often because no other part of the Habsburg administration could, or would, accommodate them.

This bureaucratic leviathan exercised a shadowy influence over recruitment, pay, all quartermaster affairs as well as fortifications, military law and even foreign policy. Relations with Russia and Turkey were its preserve until 1742 and 1753 respectively.

There were, confusingly, other organisations that also in theory dealt with these matters, notably the Chancellery with regard to foreign affairs and the Obrist-Proviantamt with regard to supplies, but the long paper trail of bureaucracy generally ended with a *Referat* (report) sitting on a desk in one of the many scattered offices of the Hofkriegsrat. If it was not dealt with, it were then filed and duplicated. The most enormous amount of time and energy were thus devoted to the most insignificant of problems. Reports were demanded of all regiments and units sometimes even on a fortnightly basis. These may have been read or may simply have been filed and stamped. One thing was certain: they were never thrown away.

By an instruction of 23 March 1745, Maria Theresa ordered a dramatic streamlining of the Hofkriegsrat. The number of counsellors was cut to eleven and an attempt was made to make the organisation less byzantine. Military justice became the preserve of a separate Justizkolleg and the quartermaster functions broke loose with the establishment of a General-Kriegs-Kommissariat (which inevitably proceeded to wage relentless bureaucratic warfare with the Hofkriegsrat).

More root and branch reform had to wait until after the Seven Years War but, even in its slightly improved state, the Hofkriegsrat still managed to introduce an unwelcome element of complexity into the Austrian military machine, which arguably would be a symptom of Austrian military affairs for generations to come.

A Corps of Engineers, created on the suggestion of Charles of Lorraine, was more rapidly successful. On the 6 February 1747, the Hofkriegsrat published a *Referat* recommending that a new corps be responsible for fortifications. The corps would be made up of four brigades comprising Hungarians, subjects of the Austrian Netherlands, 'German', and Italian ('Welsch') soldiers. Its pro tem commander would be General Paul Ferdinand Bohn. Each brigade would have a pioneer company but mining specialists were to remain attached to the artillery. In this way Maria Theresa hoped 'finally to regulate the Engineer Corps' ('entlich das ingeniurs corpo zu regulirn').

Military medical services: Gerard van Swieten

Another area also in dire need of reform was the army's medical services. On 29 January 1744 the chief physician of the army, an Irishman named Brady, penned a blistering critique of the organisation, noting how he was denied access to hospitals and control of medication and how a state of utter anarchy appeared to prevail with regard to military medical staff postings and essential supplies.

As Protomedicus, Brady in theory was the apex of the military medical service pyramid but he felt utterly ignored until one of Maria Theresa's gifted advisers, her personal physician, Gerard van Swieten (1700–72) took up his cause. Van Swieten was a brilliant medical man with a burning mission to bring scientific progress to the Habsburg Empire. Commissioned by the Empress to investigate tales from Moravia of vampires, he brought the clarity of science to bear on such phenomena even if it came into conflict with vested interests. As Maria Theresa's personal physician he persuaded the Empress to consume less by the simple but illuminating measure of ordering one of her footmen to fill each evening a silver bowl with the equivalent of what she had eaten that day. This practice rapidly led to the Empress eating less, with a consequent improvement in her physical and mental health.

Van Swieten, like Kaunitz and Lacy, another gifted officer, and so many of the highly capable men Maria Theresa came to surround herself with, were undeniably men of the Enlightenment even though she herself found the spirit of the intellectual Enlightenment far from congenial and her son Joseph's fascination with 'philosophy' deeply disturbed her unintellectual character. It was especially disappointing that Joseph adopted attitudes of cold irony and sarcastic wit, which clearly paid Frederick the compliment of imitation.

'For my part,' she wrote, 'I do not like anything that smacks of irony. Nobody is ever improved by it. . . . I think it is incompatible with loving one's neighbour.'[17]

But Van Swieten, whose son would also rise to great eminence in the Austrian court, was undoubtedly a gifted man. It was the Empress's great quality that she never let intellectual arguments interfere with her judgement of people. Instinct and intuition ruled her mind. Maria Theresa was more than happy to entrust the challenge of medical reform to Van Swieten. Later she handed authority over the entire medical system of her lands to this man who, further equipped with her unstinting support, became the enabler of all Brady's suggestions.

Van Swieten went further than Brady could have hoped. He completely reconstructed the medical faculty of the University of Vienna, thus establishing its worldwide reputation, which would endure for centuries. At the same time, thanks to these reforms, only doctors who had passed this faculty's examinations were permitted to enter the military. Field orderlies were also now subject to professional examination in anatomy and physiology. Hitherto they had simply had their certificates of medical training bought for them by officers eager to reward a retired servant or other lackey. In a short time, a corps largely made up of quacks and amateurs and conforming to no regulation were trained and disciplined, then put on a professional foundation that quickly became the envy of other European armies.

Regimental surgeons, established as a military rank already in 1718, could not now absent themselves from their regiments during campaigns. Each company had at least one medical orderly fully trained in drawing blood, applying bandages and lancing boils. During battle a fire was made of leaves and straw which discharged a column of smoke to indicate the position of the surgeon and his dressing station; increasingly, reliable older men were deployed as orderlies; musicians as stretcher-bearers.

A similar enlightened approach imbued the regulations of military chaplains who, as well as saying Mass, were officers capable of exercising considerable moral authority. Protestants and Orthodox members were permitted free exercise of their religion and a regulation posted in 1769, but clearly in practice earlier, wisely noted:

> Religion is something you should never speak about. Rather it is something you should strive to live by. Upon pain of severe and unfailing punishment we forbid any behaviour which may create ill feeling between those of different faiths. (*Reglement für die Sämmentlich-Kaiserlich Königliche Infanterie 1769*)

All these reforms were more or less implanted in a period of eight years, the brief interlude between the wars of the Austrian Succession and the Seven Years War. The proof of their success was to be widely demonstrated in the coming conflict when Frederick would ruefully observe on the battlefield: 'unfortunately these are no longer the old Austrians'.

Prince Kaunitz prepares for war

It was in 1753 that the Empress appointed Count Anton Wenzel Kaunitz to the position of her first minister. Kaunitz was in his 43rd year; able, intelligent, patient and above all loyal to his Imperial mistress. In addition to these qualities he was possessed of the greatest gifts necessary for diplomacy, namely incorruptible integrity, negotiating skill, impenetrable secrecy and profound dissimulation masked by open charm and candour.

Kaunitz had already in the run-up to Aix-la-Chapelle quietly and discreetly questioned the existing diplomatic arrangements which, as almost a foundation of European diplomacy, pitched Austria against France and aligned England with Vienna. It was perhaps while strolling one afternoon through his magnificent park and arboretum in Moravia that an original idea struck him. Maria Theresa had already expressed her frustration with the status quo of the diplomatic line-up. He saw that with the emergence of the King in Prussia as a rival, France rather than England would be of more use as an ally. France's armies were stronger, her generals better, and conditions and terms might be less demanding and hectoring than those of London, whose arrogance and materialism were wearing Austria's patience thin. Vienna, it should be remembered, had already conceded much to London. Her flourishing trade companies with the East had been surrendered as a condition of English support in 1740. The Ostend and East India Companies had had the potential to be a major commercial force for the Habsburgs but they were quietly closed down with barely a murmur.

English cash had come with so many conditions that Maria Theresa was determined to have a degree of financial independence. Above all, a developing tension, fed by relatively small disputes, fuelled a breakdown in trust. The language used by British envoys was deemed harsh and unfair in Vienna. The Austrian minister in London was snubbed and criticised. Communication between the two courts degenerated into 'a paper war', in the English historian William Coxe's phrase. The details of the Barrier Treaty whereby Austria was supposed to fund foreign troops to guard her fortresses in the Austrian Netherlands added fuel to these disagreements.

The reversal of the alliances

Kaunitz had already seen the possibilities and his presence earlier in Paris gave him the opportunity to soften up the French court further, not least through contact with the influential mistress of the French King, Madame de Pompadour. Here Kaunitz deployed flattery, opening a correspondence between the French Marchioness and his own Empress which so indulged the Frenchwoman that she became the most ardent supporter of an Austro-French alliance. From the beginning Maria Theresa fully supported Kaunitz's vision of a dramatic 'Renversement des alliances'.

Recalled to Vienna, Kaunitz pursued his policy with vigour. He worked hard to lull London into believing the ancient alliance was solid while inflaming tensions wherever possible between Prussia and England. Gradually London began to suspect Austrian intentions but Kaunitz still managed to temporise. In order to secure France, Kaunitz had to break with England but he dare not do this without having assured himself of France's support. The negotiations on troop numbers in the Netherlands proved fertile ground for spinning things out. As the Duke of Newcastle had pointed out, the Austrian Netherlands was 'a kind of common country' shared by Austria, Britain and the Dutch. It was also London's commercial door to the Continent.

In 1755 matters came to a head and the Empress listed her grievances against the English court and the maritime powers, noting that she 'has never had the satisfaction of seeing her allies do justice to her principles'. Further, she responded to London's claims that England had spent so much blood and treasure to support the House of Austria by pointing out: 'to those efforts England owes its present greatness, riches and liberty'.

London's statesmen began to realise something was moving and peremptorily demanded a guarantee of military aid to Hanover in the event of French aggression, to 'display the real intentions of the court of Vienna'. Kaunitz simply referred them to the Empress's note, knowing full well that this would provoke the King of England to turn to Prussia and thus assist further the rupture between Berlin and Paris.

The nurturing of an alliance with France was only the keystone of Kaunitz's new diplomatic architecture. He intended to secure more allies to destroy the King in Prussia. To this end his negotiations with Russia promised parts of Prussia and Pomerania to the Empress Elizabeth in return for a Russian army descending on Frederick. In another set of negotiations, part of Pomerania was vouchsafed to Sweden in return for a Swedish army crossing the Prussian frontier. Saxony, the arch-enemy of Prussia, would also join in the war.

Kaunitz at this stage could not know if this deadly constellation would prove fatal for Prussia or even guarantee the return of Silesia but if this remarkable diplomatic revolution could be achieved he realised that the war which would follow from it would annihilate Frederick's armies and, if not utterly destroy his country of barely five million, it would almost certainly prevent Prussia from menacing Austria and indeed Europe for a hundred years. From his sleepy baroque castle in Moravia, from which avenues lined with fruit trees spread out for miles in the direction of Vienna, Kaunitz polished and worked on his plan.

These negotiations were conducted with great secrecy. At a suitable moment, and with the Empress's backing, Kaunitz summoned the Council of State to announce his plans to the ministers and the Emperor. Maria Theresa feigned ignorance of the entire stratagem, aware that Kaunitz's proposal was not only brilliantly unorthodox but likely to incur considerable disapproval. Once again Maria Theresa was supporting wholeheartedly a gifted man whose intellectual vision was infinitely greater than her own. Her judgement of character as in the case of Van Swieten was, however, faultless: Kaunitz was the diplomatic genius of the age.

When the day came for Kaunitz to propose his plan, he had barely announced his intentions when the Emperor, Maria Theresa's husband Francis Stephen, rising up with great emotion brought his fist firmly down on the table and exclaimed, 'Such an unnatural alliance is impracticable and shall never take place.' The monarch instantly left the room. This was not a promising beginning but Maria Theresa was nothing if not mistress in her own house and she encouraged Kaunitz to proceed with the details in Francis's absence. After affecting much interest, the Empress resolved to bring her husband round and spoke with such enthusiasm for Kaunitz's plans that no minister dared to contradict them.

In the event London panicked and signed a treaty with Prussia in January affording Maria Theresa the moral high ground of accusing England of 'abandoning the old system' first with this new Convention of Westminster. On 13 May 1756 she expressed her disappointment with England to the British envoy. Not by one breath did she admit that two weeks earlier at Versailles Austria and France had signed their own treaty whereby Austria promised to defend French dominions in Europe (though maintaining neutrality towards England), while France was to aid Austria without any exception. France and Austria, enemies for three hundred years now found themselves, to their own astonishment, placed in close proximity and all the rules of political calculation hitherto held as immutable were at one stroke demolished. In modern parlance Kaunitz and Maria Theresa had really thought 'outside the box'.

Not that it should be imagined Prussia was to be an innocent victim in all this. Frederick had already admitted 'I very much should like to tear Bohemia away from her' and he envisaged a renewal of hostilities that would destroy Habsburg hegemony once and for all. Prussia would take Bohemia, Bavaria would revive her claims to Upper Austria and Tyrol, France would dismember the Netherlands and Sardinia would absorb Lombardy.

Fortunately for Austria, Frederick, whatever his talents, possessed none of the gifts of Kaunitz. The King in Prussia soon realised that the Convention of Westminster was a fatal diplomatic blunder that had bought him neither time nor a credible ally on the mainland of Europe. England could not help Prussia against the deadly alliance that was threatening to encircle Frederick. There was no naval dimension to renewed campaigning in Silesia and not even any British troops to create a distraction.

Only a preventative war launched with rapidity could possibly stave off the fatal constellation gathering around his country and thus Frederick, like Germany in 1914, was to launch a quick assault on a neighbour, in this case Saxony, in the hope of seizing the initiative in a multi-front war. Frederick saw that Austria had not completed her preparations and so determined to fight a limited campaign to knock out his most implacable foe. With Vienna humbled, the coalition against him would fall apart. Demanding an unambivalent statement of Habsburg intentions, he received as he expected an utterly unsatisfactory response. Maria Theresa simply replied: 'In the present crisis I deem it necessary to take measures for the security of myself and my allies which tend to the prejudice of no one.' Austria had no intention of violating any treaty but neither would she bind herself by any promise which might prevent her acting 'as circumstances required'.

This was all Frederick needed. The Prussian Canton system of conscription efficiently and rapidly brought Frederick's army up to about 150,000 men. Speed and aggression were the watchwords of this force and its supreme commander. Meticulous planning was another quality. The destruction of Saxony was to be accompanied by a merciless but premeditated pillaging of its resources to support the Prussian war effort. Of the country's 6 million thaler annual revenue 5 million were to be sequestered for the Prussian military machine. This annual 'tribute' alone would secure the survival of the Prussian economy and represented a third of the total of the Prussian war effort. The Prussian army moved swiftly at the end of August 1756 to occupy Dresden and bottle up the Saxon army in the fortress of Pirna. In a matter of days the Kingdom of Saxony was looted and systematically stripped of her wealth.

Frederick's personal responsibility for the destruction and exploitation that followed was immense. His vindictiveness was unlimited towards those who had crossed him and he appears to have taken great delight in ordering the Prussian Freikorps' detonation of the Saxon statesman, Count Brühl's schloss, with the proviso of course that it should appear that he knew nothing of the pillage. Even the British representative at Frederick's court commented after the wanton sacking of Hubertsburg castle that these actions demonstrated 'a meanness that I am really ashamed to narrate'.[18]

The Prussian irruption into Saxony was the price Maria Theresa appeared willing to pay to maintain the moral high ground and show up Frederick as an unambiguous aggressor and breaker of treaties. But Frederick, who had published his own manifestos of half-truths and dubious history, was uninterested in such niceties. He pushed on into Bohemia hoping to compel the Saxons in Pirna to give up any hope of relief, capturing Teschen and Aussig an der Elbe (Dečin and Usti nad Labem in modern Czech) along the north-western Bohemian frontier. To counter this audacious move was an Austrian army of 32,465 troops supported by a corps of some 22,000 under Piccolomini, all of them under the newly promoted Field Marshal Maximilian Ulysses Browne.

Browne's defence of Bohemia

Browne's task was initially to relieve Pirna but Frederick's blitzkrieg made the defence of Bohemia his first priority. A plan was devised to check and hold the Prussians in an engagement while relief to the Saxons was organised through the difficult but picturesque terrain of the mountains of 'Saxon Switzerland' via a 'flying column'. On 1 October 1756, Browne skilfully deployed a force of Croatian irregulars on the tangled slopes of the volcanic Lobosch hill. Behind this was the right flank of his army but most of his troops were cunningly concealed behind the marshy banks of the Morellen stream. The Prussian King fell for the trap. Believing the Croats were simply the rearguard of an army moving away from him he ordered the Duke of Bevern to clear the hill and thus enable the rest of the Austrian army to be attacked in the flank.

The Battle of Lobositz that ensued was to remain a bitter memory for Frederick for the rest of his life. As Bevern advanced to drive the Croats from their positions, he was met by a murderous rapid fire from skirmishers in concealed positions, which brought his infantry to a standstill. If this was not enough to do more than irritate Frederick, he was suddenly given a vivid example of the progress made with Liechtenstein's artillery reforms. As Frederick ordered his cavalry to chase what he thought was a retreating Austrian cavalry division, the Austrian horsemen led their Prussian pursuers directly on to the guns of the Habsburg batteries drawn up behind the Morellen stream. These opened fire with case at 300 paces with devastating effect. The Prussian horse was cut down in a matter of seconds and soon fled in utter disorder. It could not be rallied, even when Frederick ordered his own infantry to fire at them to prevent them throwing his entire centre into disarray.

A second cavalry charge fared little better and as the fog cleared around midday Frederick became demoralised. He was aware that his heavy cavalry had ceased to exist as an effective fighting arm so he promptly removed himself from the battlefield, leaving Field Marshal Keith to save what could be saved. The Croats were now being supported by regular Austrian units under Lacy and the Prussian infantry attack stalled and began to waver. But at this moment, as so often in warfare, the fate of individuals decided the day. Lacy was wounded and carried from the battle, with a dispiriting effect on his troops. Keith seeing the Austrian offensive falter organised a vigorous counter-attack and began rolling up the Austrian infantry. Browne seeing his advance guard in difficulties ordered them to withdraw, covering it with the main part of his force, which effectively halted any attempt by the Prussians at pursuit and brought the battle to an end. Prussian casualties were noticeably higher than the Austrian losses, which were computed at 2,873.[19] Keith had saved the day for Frederick and his army was in undisputed possession of the battlefield once Bevern had driven out the remaining Croats, but it had been at a terrible cost.

As an officer attached to Frederick noted:

> On this occasion Frederick did not come up against the same kind of Austrians he had beaten in four battles in a row. He was not dealing with people like Neipperg or the blustering Prince Charles of Lorraine. He faced Browne who had grown grey in the service and whose talent and experience had raised him to one of the heroes of his time. He faced an artillery which Prince Liechtenstein had brought to perfection at his own expense. He faced an army which during ten years of peace had attained a greater mastery of the arts of war.[20]

Meanwhile Browne stole away with 9,000 men through the wooded hills on the left bank of the Elbe and in a series of impressive forced marches, unheard of in an Austrian army of five years earlier, arrived opposite the Saxon troops. But these were too demoralised to provide any opportunities to rally and they consistently failed to communicate with Browne, forcing him to return to Bohemia. Shortly after this the Saxons surrendered to the Prussians, giving Austro-Saxon cooperation a very poor name.

Frederick had hoped to establish his winter quarters but the Battle of Lobositz despite the Frederician propaganda had in fact been a draw. Browne now commanded the country around Frederick's forces and used his irregular troops to harry and plunder Prussian lines of communication so that the King in Prussia had little choice but to withdraw his army back to Saxony for the winter. The Austrian army had certainly not failed its first test.

The Saxon army on the other hand met a fate which was considered highly innovative for the time. It was simply incorporated into the Prussian army.

Only the officers were allowed the 'choice' between swearing loyalty to Prussia and incarceration. This step, heartless, bold and cynical, caused protests even in Prussia. Frederick saw them off with the comment: 'I take pride in being original.' In fact, from a practical point of view, it would turn out to be a grave error. The Saxons proved notoriously unreliable in battle fighting for their Prussian masters. More than two-thirds deserted while the incorporation of a nation's entire fighting force into new uniforms, oaths and drills under Prussian command was rightly and widely seen at the time as sinister proof of Prussian expansionary tendencies.

Moreover, in France any lingering sympathy for Frederick was strongly dissipated by his behaviour in Saxony. The Dauphin after all was married to the daughter of the Elector. But Frederick was like many cruel cynics utterly oblivious to the effects of his behaviour. Nowhere was this to have more devastating consequences for him than with regard to Russia. Lulled by the wildly over-optimistic reports of the incompetent and boorish British envoy Charles Hanbury Williams, Frederick was encouraged to think that bribing the Russian minister Bestuzhev would secure Russian neutrality. On Hanbury's advice he ordered the transfer of the payment and even denuded his units in East Prussia, so convinced was he by the Englishman's dispatches. On Christmas Day the news, an unwelcome Christmas present, arrived. The payment notwithstanding, Russia was preparing to put an army of 100,000 into the field against Prussia the following spring.

Frederick invades Bohemia again

Again Frederick was persuaded that Bohemia was the key to his strategy. He had to seize the initiative and commit his entire army to nothing less than a four-pronged invasion of Bohemia to deliver, in his words, the 'Grand Coup'. On 18 April 1757 this formidable invasion force crossed the frontier at four points, causing panic and consternation throughout Bohemia. The 'final reckoning' between the two pre-eminent dynasties of the German speaking lands was at hand.

After some debate, one Austrian army under Charles of Lorraine fell back on Prague to await the arrival of another, under Daun. So concerned was Kaunitz at the turn of events and disagreements between Lorraine and his brilliant subordinate Ulysses Browne that he set off with his personal physician from Vienna to Prague to instil some sense of coherence into Austrian strategy, which seemed to be crumbling before Prussia's blitzkrieg. But Kaunitz left too late. On 6 May two Prussian armies effected their conjunction and now were marching on Prague to face an outnumbered foe.

Lorraine and Browne would have to fight alone without Daun. They drew up their troops east of Prague where today the heavily built up suburb of Žižkov runs along raised ground. Frederick ordered his infantry to shoulder muskets to speed up their march and outflank the two Austrian lines but Browne immediately spotted the movement and deployed his second line in a 90-degree shift to confront the Prussians, opening fire on the massed Prussian infantry still in the act of deployment. Several Prussian regiments were completely overwhelmed and the Saxon regiments broke and fled. As Field Marshal Schwerin attempted to rally his infantry he fell in a hail of musket balls from the Austrian line which, in parade ground drill, was advancing and halting to fire a volley every fifty seconds. The Austrian artillery meanwhile had come into action and was rapidly depleting the Prussian infantry who were bogged down in soft wet ground.

At this point it looked as if the Prussians would be thrown back. Frederick once again fled the battlefield, blaming stomach cramps and fearing the worst, but Browne fell from his horse wounded by a cannonball and the Austrian attack faltered. The Prussian cavalry led by Ziethen's 'new' Hussars showed that there was not much difference in quality between the imitation and the real thing. Striking the Austrian cavalry in the flank, the Prussians scattered their opponents and opened a gap in the angle between the Austrian infantry's original and new lines. The crisis of the battle had arrived and Charles of Lorraine fainted at this moment with chest pains and had to be carried from the field. The Austrian attack ground to a halt and by mid-afternoon, faced with a weakening front, the regimental commanders chose to conduct a fighting withdrawal into the city, covered by cavalry. Thanks to the near suicidal rearguard action of the Austrian cavalry somehow the army avoided annihilation and retreated successfully behind the walls of the city. Once again the Prussians had won but their casualties were higher than the Austrians' (14,400 compared to the Austrians' 13,400, of whom nearly 5,000 were prisoners).

Frederick, recovering from his brief panic, was confident that the Siege of Prague would be completed before any Austrian reinforcements could arrive and he interpreted the news of Kaunitz leaving Vienna as a sure sign that the Austrian Chancellor was coming to negotiate personally with him. Despite his extravagant powers of self-deception, Frederick was not utterly negligent, and he dispatched a screen of 25,000 men under Bevern to watch for any Austrian relief force.

On 7 May the relief force and its commander Daun were greeted by a fanfare announcing Kaunitz's arrival. The two men had great confidence in each other and agreed a strategy to relieve Lorraine in Prague by retreating first to Kolín where forces could be gathered to give Daun the capacity to engage the Prussians on his own terms. Kaunitz would return to Vienna immediately to organise the reinforcements. Both men were critical of the sluggish concentration of Lorraine's early movements and realised that the next weeks could decide the fate of their monarchy.

Kaunitz arrived back in Vienna on the morning of 11 May and went straight in his muddied boots to the Empress, brushing past the near-apoplectic protests of the Court Chamberlain, Khevenhueller who was, like so many of his family, unimpressed by any departure from official protocol. The *Konferenz 'in mixtis'* of privy councillors and War Cabinet members cooled their heels while Kaunitz spent two hours with Maria Theresa apprising her of the details of the reverse at Prague and the urgent need to reinforce Daun.

The Chancellor drew up an 18-point plan to reinforce Daun, which was rapidly endorsed by the Empress and thus implemented without further delay. Within two weeks Daun's force numbered more than 50,000 men and 156 guns. By the end of the first week of June he could even risk taking the offensive, and orders to this effect were dispatched from Vienna.

The Golden Sun of Kolín: birthday of the monarchy

But Frederick had not been idle and his cavalry screen had observed the build-up of Daun's forces. The Prussian King determined to crush the Austrians before the force grew any larger. The name Daun at this stage of the war meant very little to Frederick, who perhaps recalled the names of some of the senior Austrian officers who had overseen the military reforms of the previous years. The Austrians were in any event, he fervently imagined, demoralised after Prague and could be easily crushed.

Daun's advance guard probed the Prussian screen and at Kuttenberg (Kutna Hora) a fierce firefight developed, news of which determined Frederick to act decisively against the Austrians, who had concentrated in a strong position in the hills south of the so-called Kaiserstrasse which linked Prague with Vienna, a few miles west of Kolín. In the weeks since the battle at Prague, Daun had worked hard with his naturally cautious temperament to rebuild morale among the stragglers who had swelled his ranks. His preparation was meticulous and, if the fate of the House of Habsburg was to be decided that day, he was not prepared to leave anything to chance.

Frederick's scouts soon convinced him that Daun's position was far too strong to face a frontal attack, so Frederick indulged his passion for rolling up his opponents' flanks by devising a strategy whereby his army would march along the Kaiserstrasse under the eyes of the Austrians and simply conduct a flanking manoeuvre west of Kolín. His plan decided, Frederick retired for the evening. Rising with the sun the following day, the 18th, he climbed the church tower near the Inn of 'the Golden Sun' (Zlati Sunce) to find to his consternation that Daun had anticipated his plans and had reinforced his flank overnight so that his line now ran east–west overlooking the Kaiserstrasse, and was centred on the village of Chocenitz (Chocenice).

Undeterred, Frederick ordered his infantry forward. One by one the Prussian regiments, the brass plates of their mitre caps glinting in the sun, advanced up the steep gradient towards the village of Křehoř, the key to the new Austrian right. It was a dry and hot day, and by early afternoon the temperature had soared into the eighties. The volleys of the Austrian infantry prevented any real breakthrough and when the pressure seemed to become dangerous Daun shifted Wied's division to his right to reinforce his unbroken lines there.

Frederick seeing this, or at least the vast dust clouds kicked up by this movement, now committed a cardinal error and ordered a frontal attack to smash what he imagined must be Daun's denuded centre. Some later historians have claimed that Frederick did not intend a frontal attack and that his orders were misinterpreted by subordinates. In any event the results were sobering for the Prussians. As an Austrian officer present that day wrote:

> The Austrians saw nothing of the Prussians save their brass caps through the thick corn and as soon as these brave but doomed men had climbed one third of the steep slope with unspeakable difficulty they were met and thrown back by the regular volleys of the infantry and a frightful rain of canister from the batteries which maintained a cross fire from every side.[21]

The slaughter of the Prussians was truly terrible in front of Daun's line but the battle was far from over. The oak wood, just south of Křehoř, became a fulcrum of destruction as Hulsen's Prussian infantry tried and failed to drive a mixed force of Croat irregulars and several Austrian Grenadier companies out of the wood and press on to the village. The grenadiers in particular delivered rolling volleys by platoon 'just as if they had been on the drill square'. A contemporary noticed the veteran grenadiers reminding one another to 'keep aiming a little lower'.

To the west the Prussian corps under Tresckow advanced, only to be completely repulsed by the disciplined volley fire of three Austrian regiments: Botta, Baden and Hoch und Deutschmeister. The Deutschmeister, later to become the 'House' regiment of Vienna, had been largely recruited in the German provinces where the 'Knights of the German Order' were headquartered under their titular head the so-called *Hochmeister*. Though transferred to Vienna, recruits from this part of Germany were still regularly drawn to the regiment on account of its elite status. The regiment was distinguished by sky blue facings and an almost familial sense of loyalty, and its morale was extremely high. With ammunition running short, its commanding officer Count Soro, wounded but with sword in hand ordered the men to fix bayonets and led them into Tresckow's infantry with great effect. At a time when there were no decorations or medals for the ordinary rank and file, their heroism on this day would be repaid later when the Empress personally distributed the *Gratifikations* money to them. They would receive a higher proportion than any other regiment present at Kolín that day.

While this was taking place in the west, Starhemberg's division began to increase the pressure around the oak wood. The time was nearly six o' clock and the intensity of the battle showed no sign of waning. Both sides knew the moment of decision was near and Daun reorganised his troops with cool rapidity. There was barely a line of infantry effective enough to withstand the next assault and the troops were so low on ammunition that the order was given to the drummer boys to cut open the tops of their drums and fill them with ammunition from the pouches of the dead and wounded and redistribute it as quickly as possible.

Shortly after 6.30 the Prussian Guard led six other regiments in a final effort against Daun's centre. It was the seventh attack the Prussian infantry had put in that hot day and few on either side were under any illusion that the crisis of the battle was now at hand.

Sources to this day argue as to what happened next. Some insist that Daun, seeing how desperate the situation was and imbued with the caution that was his second nature, ordered preparations for a withdrawal and told his staff to communicate to his regimental commanders a rallying point to his rear. But as the staff officers spread the message, so engaged was the Austrian line in the struggle that the command was simply ignored or disobeyed because, in the heat of the moment, disengagement seemed the wrong decision. For once the poor logistics of Austrian military communications, a recurring theme in this book, was actually helpful.

One unit that was ordered to cover withdrawal was that of the de Ligne Dragoons but their colonel, stupefied by the request, rode up to the commander and asked Daun if he could not lead his reserve cavalry at the advancing Prussians. The de Ligne Dragoons were recruited from the French-speaking Netherlands and wore distinctive dark blue coats of almost Prussian hue. They did not wear moustaches and Daun nonchalantly surveying their officers told their commander that if he really thought 'these blancs becs' could achieve anything they could by all means attack. The tone of dismissive scepticism was well calculated. It was an insult the de Ligne were determined to avenge. As their commanding officer relayed the words to his men the regiment charged through a gap in the Austrian lines at the head of six other regiments of reserve cavalry and took Bevern's six Prussian battalions in the flank. The shock was palpable. Heads were severed by sabres, colours cut down and captured and as the Prussians belatedly attempted to form square they were ridden down by the dragoons possessed with almost satanic bloodlust.

The Prussian infantry crumbled and those who could not flee lay down to avoid the whirling blades of their enemy. Frederick's army, exhausted and unsupported by their cavalry, began to collapse. As so often in a battle, barely fifteen minutes divided the moment of seemingly inevitable victory and over-whelming defeat. The Prussians saw it all unfold before their very eyes. Never had an army of Frederick's known such a crushing reverse.

Daun could have turned this decisive defeat into a rout but he did not order a pursuit though he had several regiments of cavalry under Nadasti available for the purpose. Perhaps, as one writer has commented, he simply did not wish 'the sun to go down on his anger'.[22] More likely he did not perhaps see the need to take any further risk. The Prussians had been beaten and the work of reform had borne fruit. Austria could indeed claim a great victory.

Just how great a victory, Daun was only just beginning to appreciate. The news, which reached Maria Theresa two days later, caused universal rejoicing. The Order of Maria Theresa, from then onwards the supreme military decoration of the Habsburgs, was established with its birthday firmly anchored to 'Kolín Day', 18 June. Until the Empire fell in 1918 this order was to retain its prestige as one of Europe's most coveted awards for gallantry.

Daun was nominated Commander of the Order though contrary to popular belief he was not to be its first candidate for recognition. That privilege was to fall to the luckless Charles of Lorraine, whose career, now compre-hensively overshadowed by Daun, needed some *douceur* to accompany his imminent and well-deserved demotion from the status of overall commander.

CHAPTER 6

Mater Castrorum

Kolín shattered the myth of Prussian invincibility. It also changed the view in the German lands of Maria Theresa. Her armies marched to victory and as the number of these mounted and Prussia was gradually laid to waste it was hard not to see the Empress as a Mater Castrorum, Mother of War. As Frederick bitterly recalled, waging war against Maria Theresa was like 'dying a thousand times a day'.[1]

The King in Prussia had experienced a dramatic reversal of fortune. From seemingly being about to complete the destruction of one Austrian army holed up in Prague and the marginalisation of another under Daun, he had been totally defeated, with great destruction of men and materiel. Austria, recently so vulnerable, had been saved. It was no hyperbole when Maria Theresa presented Daun's son with a map of Bohemia on which the name of Kolín was entered in gold lettering. The map's golden case bore the inscription in the Empress's hand:

> Toutes les fois que vous regarderez cette carte géographique, souvenez vous de la journée où votre père a sauvé la Monarchie. [Every time you look at this map, remember the day your father saved the monarchy.][2]

Prussian losses were immense. Following on the death of his mentor Schwerin in the earlier battle Frederick might be forgiven for thinking his stars were not in a favourable alignment. The expensive 'victory' at Prague had cost him more than 12,500 casualties. Defeat at Kolín had cost him another 14,000. These were losses Prussia could ill afford. Maria Theresa's allies now bestirred themselves with an ominous unity of purpose. With two French armies crossing the Rhine, a Swedish army advancing on Pomerania and a Russian force headed for East Prussia, the very existence of Frederick's kingdom was now open to question.

At the court in Vienna the language spoken envisaged not only the crushing of Prussia but its dismemberment. Silesia and Glatz would revert to the Habsburgs, Magdeburg and Halberstadt were to be given to the King of Poland, Ravensberg to the Elector Palatine and most of Prussian Pomerania to the Swedes. Frederick would rue the day he hazarded his 'rape of Silesia'. A month later at Gabel, another 2,000 Prussians fell into the Austrians' hands as prisoners. A week later on 26 July, thanks to the 'inexperience and imbecility' of the Duke of Cumberland, an Anglo-Hanoverian force was defeated by the French at Hastenbeck.[3]

Frederick dashed back to Prussia, his usual energy proving too much for Charles of Lorraine who wasted several days failing to organise a dynamic pursuit. In the Prussian King's absence a number of blows were struck. Early in September at Moys a stiffly contested skirmish between three Prussian regiments and a composite force of Austrian grenadiers and other infantry ended in another Austrian victory and the death of another senior Prussian general, Winterfeldt. Close to the King, Winterfeldt was a man on whom Frederick had relied for the defence of Silesia.

Meanwhile a small Austrian army of 3,500 men, under General-Leutnant Andreas Hadik, which had taken up position in Lusatia, was ordered to carry out a reconnaissance in force towards the Prussian capital. Hadik reached Berlin in five days and found the city undefended. He exacted a considerable financial tribute. Much treasure was plundered although the 'beautiful' set of ladies' gloves, with the city arms embroidered on them, which he was later widely reputed to have given to Maria Theresa, appears to have been only a tale to stir up Austrian patriotism. It was good propaganda but Hadek did not linger. He withdrew his men with great speed to avoid Frederick's approaching forces. The raid was a humiliation Prussia was keen to avenge but at that moment Frederick seemed to possess neither the means nor the manpower to achieve this.

Everywhere Frederick's men were on the run or caught off guard. Even Keith in Saxony had to take refuge in Leipzig when an allied army largely made up of Germans and French troops under the Austrian veteran Field Marshal, the Prince of Saxe-Hildburghausen erupted into Saxony. The fortress of Schweidenitz also yielded 6,000 Prussian prisoners after being stormed by Nadasti's Grenadiers. After Schweidenitz, Breslau – the key to southern Silesia – also fell to the Austrians.

The need for a negotiated peace appeared imminent, were Frederick to survive. If his problems in Saxony and Silesia were not enough, a Russian army had in August defeated a Prussian force at Gross-Jaegersdorf. The Russians enthusiastically began laying large tracts of East Prussia to waste.

But the King in Prussia was all too aware that negotiations without some cards in the hand were a waste of time. His forces were scattered and small but somehow he had to win some battles. Frederick chose the weakest of his foes to deal with first. At the village of Rossbach he annihilated a French army under Soubise which had effected a junction with the Reichsarmee under Hildburghausen. The only units on the allied side to acquit themselves honourably that day were the two attached Austrian regular Cuirrasier regiments, of Trautmannsdorff and Bretlach. The rest, in Hildburghausen's phrase, 'all ran like sheep'.[4] Rossbach was over in less than half an hour and the Prussian casualties numbered only 165 dead. But this engagement secured Saxony, and the morale-boosting effect on Frederick was immense.

Charles of Lorraine received the news of Rossbach nonchalantly. He was determined to win the laurels of victory that had been granted to Daun at Kolín. Confirmed again as commander-in-chief, in the teeth of Kaunitz's opposition, Lorraine was anxious to prove his worth. But he lacked Daun's skill at positioning and strategic grasp. Although he outnumbered Frederick almost two to one, he left much of his artillery at Breslau and even appears to have believed Frederick would prove a soft target. Against the advice of his most senior officers Lorraine was determined to give battle.

Lorraine routed at Leuthen

On the morning of 5 December 1757 Lorraine prepared his army over a wide front, placing Württemberg and Bavarian regiments on his left flank. The long lines of infantry appeared 'endless'.[5] At first the Prussians marched north and so Charles strengthened his right wing. But from where Charles and his staff stood a fold in the ground prevented their seeing the Prussian dispositions. They did not notice Frederick order his infantry to change direction and march south. The lie of the land concealed this change from Lorraine brilliantly and although he was alerted by messengers from Nadasti, who was in charge of the weakened left wing, he failed to respond.

To the Prussians' disbelief, their infantry could calmly dress their lines after their march and advance almost unnoticed. Drawing up in line, their first volley caused the startled Württembergers to break and flee. Five minutes later a second volley dispersed the Bavarians. In barely fifteen minutes Lorraine's left flank had vanished. Some 12,000 men were in headlong retreat. Denuded of cavalry, Lorraine's flank was rapidly reinforced by infantry from the right but the confusion and disorder were total and by the time the Austrian cavalry arrived it was too late. The Austrian cavalry commander Lucchesi was killed and panic set in. The village of Leuthen became a mass of Austrian infantry struggling to form coherent lines. In less than three hours it was over. Entire Austrian regiments surrendered en masse. Victory was absolute. The Austrian losses, including prisoners, exceeded 21,000, a third of Lorraine's entire army.

If Kaunitz needed any ammunition to ensure Lorraine's long overdue removal from command, Leuthen provided all he needed. Not even Maria Theresa's husband, Charles's brother, could save him now. Lorraine had rejected Daun's advice to choose a strongly entrenched position. Even in the depths of despondency he failed to recognise his own incompetence. The Emperor hinted twice and the Empress waited until on 16 January 1758 she drafted a letter even Charles of Lorraine could not fail to understand. Daun would assume command.

As a *douceur* Charles was to be decorated with the new Order of Maria Theresa, before rather than after Daun, as had originally been planned. Charles would also enjoy the distinction of being appointed the newly established Order's first master. Thus were the protocols of Europe's most distinguished order of merit suborned to soothe the ego of a complacent and mediocre prince, one whose arrogance had dissipated in an afternoon the warm afterglow of the 'glorious sun' of Kolín.

For Frederick, notwithstanding the laurels of Leuthen, it was strategically insignificant. The battle did not rid him of the Austrians 'completely'. At first he hoped Vienna would seek peace but he underestimated the determination and tenacity of the Mater Castrorum and her chief adviser Kaunitz. Alarmed courtiers in Vienna responded to Prussian incursions into Moravia by packing their bags but Kaunitz and his Empress were Frederick's most implacable opponents and did not for a moment contemplate leaving the capital. They knew that Austria, unlike Prussia, was rich in resources of manpower and materiel.

Frederick moved south, threatening almost the approaches to Vienna and investing the key to Moravia, the fortress of Olmütz. At the same time Daun gathered his corps commanders around Skalitz and began the work of restoring the shattered morale of the Habsburg army after Leuthen. He appointed Lacy as chief of staff and a comprehensive training for staff officers was implemented. Infantry tactics were also overhauled. New recruits poured in from all over the Empire. The success of combining Grenadier companies into larger formations of shock troops was drilled into the units. By the spring of 1758 Daun had redeployed into Moravia, even reinforcing the garrison at Olmütz, provoking Frederick acidly to say, 'I cannot believe these are Austrians! They must have learnt to march!'[6]

In June a Prussian resupply column of 4,000 troops with ammunition and provisions to reinforce the besiegers of Olmütz set out from Silesia. It was ambushed by a force led by a taciturn but capable officer called Loudon at Domstadl (Domašov) and routed. Ziethen, the Prussian cavalry commander sent to escort the convoy with 3,000 hussars was completely overpowered by two of Loudon's irregular cavalry regiments. Nearly 4,000 Prussians were killed, wounded or captured and more than a hundred wagons seized. The Austrian losses of only 600 attested to the success of Loudon's guerrilla war tactics and the ferocity of his troops.

A few days later when the news reached Frederick he raised the siege and withdrew. The Austrians were approaching slowly but relentlessly and they commanded the area east of the Morava. Frederick had to admit, if only in private, that he had been outmanoeuvred by Daun. This realisation was disguised in the usual ritual dressing-down of his subordinates. Ziethen was accused of having 'dawdled' his way with the convoy. Balbi, his chief engineering and siege warfare officer was publicly humiliated. 'It was impossible to imagine all the horrible things he said to me,' he later recalled.[7]

Frederick was determined to bring the Austrians to battle because, with one eye on the Russian incursion into Prussia, as he noted, 'If we beat the Austrians we will have nothing to fear from the others.'[8] Frederick hoped for a decisive engagement near Königgrätz (Hradec Králové) but Daun, ever the master of positioning, refused to offer battle except on his terms. The complaints from Vienna and even some of his subordinate commanders became ever more strident so that he had to write a long letter to his Empress defending his apparent slothfulness:

> God knows I am no coward but I shall never set my hands to anything which I judge to be impossible or to the disadvantage of Your Majesty's service.[9]

Frederick felt he had to abandon his plans to bring Daun to battle and was compelled to retreat into Silesia and deal with the Russians who had already occupied Königsberg, the capital of East Prussia. At the battle of Zorndorf in August, Frederick encountered a Russian army made up in his words of 'ferocious and infamous brigands'. The battle was dominated by Seydlitz's cavalry, which snatched a victory of sorts from the tough Russian infantry. Frederick dubbed the Russians 'scum', but they had annihilated a third of his army. Both Prussia and Russia claimed Zorndorf as a victory. Indeed, both armies failed miserably in the bloodletting to achieve their strategic objectives: Prussia failed to force a Russian withdrawal and Fermor, the Russian commander, was powerless to pursue the withdrawing Prussians.

By the end of August Daun had decided on a plan to enter Lusatia and combine with the Russians. The plan was approved and Kaunitz instructed

Daun to proceed with unprecedented vigour. Russia would be unwilling to persist if it did not see evidence of Austrian aggression. A battle, even one that was not decisive, was urgently needed, in Kaunitz's view.

The news of Zorndorf ended all hopes of the Austrians effecting a junction with the Russian army. Daun advanced from Görlitz to Stolpen, covering the 120 kilometres in ten days but Frederick, in yet another demonstration of the Prussian army's superiority in forced marches, covered 180 kilometres in barely seven days. Arriving just north of Dresden on 10 September the Prussian King assembled an army totalling nearly 45,000 men. Confidently he announced that, 'if his fat Excellency of Kolin (*Die dicke Excellenz*) would only perform for me the honour of sticking out his neck, I shall be ready to smash it off'.[10]

Apprised of the King's arrival, Daun who had planned to attack called the offensive off. Frederick's arrival had changed the forces now arrayed against the Habsburg armies and Daun was never one to rush into something he did not meticulously plan. In Vienna criticism of this caution reached fever pitch. Kaunitz was anxious and the Empress wrote on 24 September urging Daun to undertake a decisive operation 'at all costs if an unfavourable peace was to be avoided'.[11] By 13 October a heated discussion in Vienna examined a 'Cabinet directive' signed by the Emperor urging Daun 'to look seriously for an opportunity to give battle'. Even if Daun was not successful, it was vital for action if France and Russia were not to drop out of the coalition against Prussia.

Hochkirch's street of blood

But Daun would not be hurried. As he sat encamped near Stolpen in October, Frederick tried to provoke him out but each time the Austrians slipped away. As the court discussed the wording of the directive to their commander, Daun had on his own come to the conclusion that the moment was now finally propitious for attack.

Publicly, Frederick expressed only contempt for the Austrian. Daun's way of waging war seemed designed to irritate the Prussian King for he was a master of position and detail. As Duffy has noted in his magisterial survey of Maria Theresa's army, Daun's caution was tempered by sudden bursts of inspiration from his energetic commanders such as Lacy or Loudon. 'It was just when the Field Marshal's [Daun's] slow uncoiling lulled Old Fritz [Frederick] into the deepest torpor that Daun was apt to listen to the bold counsel of someone like Lacy.' Just such a moment was imminent.

Lacy and Loudon, in their different ways, were examples of how the Empress Queen managed to surround herself with talented men of very different backgrounds and temperaments. Lacy, the consummate courtier of

Irish extraction complete with 'fascinating manners' was the perfect foil in so many ways to his contemporary Gideon Loudon, the descendant of an Ayrshire family that had settled in Livonia in the fourteenth century.[12] Where Lacy was charming and witty, Loudon was taciturn and introspective, only really coming to life in the drama of battle. Yet whatever their differences, both men were now about to complement each other perfectly in the campaign that was unfolding.

Frederick arranging his army east of Dresden was aware that Daun was blocking his access to Silesia and he moved his forces gingerly towards it. Frederick's right flank was anchored around the village of Hochkirch, which sat on elevated ground defended by a battery of artillery and six battalions. The nearby woods were seething with Loudon's Pandours and other irregular troops. The Prussian commander, Keith, remarked of the Prussians' exposed position: 'If the Austrians allow us to remain peacefully here they deserve to be hanged.' To which Frederick dismissively replied: 'True, but I hope they fear us more than the hangman.'[13]

Keith was not alone in having misgivings about Frederick's contempt for the Austrians. His quartermaster Marwitz refused to pitch his tents in such an exposed position but was promptly put under arrest. Frederick may have been further lulled into thinking 'Die dicke Excellenz' would not attack him as Daun's espionage service had been successful in 'turning' one of Frederick's spies. The spy returned to the Prussian lines explaining that Daun would never undertake so uncharacteristic an action as a surprise attack.

The spy was perhaps right. It was Franz Moritz Lacy, that eccentric officer, later to be buried with his horse in the woods above Vienna, who persuaded Daun. Lacy devised a plan whereby a large part of the Austrian army would steal away in the night to reappear a few hours later in a star-shaped formation of columns whose epicentre was Frederick's exposed salient on the spur at Hochkirch. Everything was done to lull the Prussians into a false sense of security, with even the Austrian tents and tent fires maintained in their existing positions. According to one witness, a large number of woodsmen were encouraged to cut trees while loudly calling out to each other and singing songs. For several days Daun had reconnoitred the ground eager to see every detail before the attack. On one of these occasions, coming under fire from a Prussian piquet he listened as his cavalry commander Serbelloni dismissed the whizz of musketry as 'only flies'. A moment later Serbelloni's hand was shattered by a ball. Daun turned and noted quietly: 'Yes flies; but they seem to bite.'[14]

The Austrian infantry was to seize the village entrenchments by stealth. The attack would begin as the village church struck five and artillery would be brought up to blast the main square and street to pieces shortly afterwards. As the church bell rang, the entrenchments guarding the village were rushed by Croat irregulars, who bayoneted the sentries and began cutting the tent ropes of the encampments. As the tents collapsed, the Croats began systematically bayoneting the writhing mass of trapped humanity within. Total surprise was achieved and the streets literally ran red with blood as the Croats proceeded, quietly murdering the sleeping soldiery along what became known as the Blutgasse, in memory of these sanguinary events.

At six, with just the first glimmer of the dawn beginning in the east, the Austrian artillery opened up and the fifteen pieces of Prussian artillery in the village were turned against the disorientated Prussian survivors. Entire regiments of Prussians were slaughtered, as those who managed to escape their tents in vain struggled to form two lines back to back to deal with the attacks from all sides. The din of gunfire and cannon shot mingled with the clash of steel and cries of the wounded. Fog and smoke combined to give the morning an unreal light in which only the brass plates of the Prussian grenadiers' mitre caps offered any sense of who was foe and who was friend. Amidst all this confusion the flash of artillery fire illuminated for an instant the white coats of the Austrians remorselessly advancing to the cries of their officers.

As the Prussian generals and their officers endeavoured in the confusion to command, the slaughter was dreadful. The Prince of Brunswick pointed with his sword – only to have, a few seconds later, his head carried away by a cannonball. The veteran and brave Keith who had foreseen attack made a vain attempt to clear the village. He fell with two musket balls through his chest while advancing at the head of some hastily assembled grenadiers. Prince Maurice of Dessau and a dozen other senior Prussian officers were also badly wounded in the first hour of battle.

The Prussian infantry was not the finest infantry in Europe for nothing, and while other armies certainly would have disintegrated under these shocks, it rallied. The Prussian cavalry under Ziethen made a spirited counter-attack against the Austrian left to gain time for withdrawal. Ziethen's Hussars were eventually beaten off by Loudon's Hussars but not before Frederick, at the head of three brigades, had attempted to outflank Daun. This effort bought time for the Prussians but was soon countered by such a solid wall of infantry fire that only the bravery of Frederick's hussars rescued him from certain death as his horse was shot from beneath him yards from the Austrian lines.

By ten o'clock it was clear to Frederick that it was time to save what could be saved and he ordered a full-scale withdrawal. This was accomplished in remarkable order partly owing to the timidity of the Austrian 'pursuit' and the fierce firepower retreating disciplined Prussian infantry could bring to bear on those who followed them. This blunted the teeth of even the most aggressive Austrians while the Croats and irregulars were tempted as usual to pillage the Prussian camp rather than risk their lives against a retreating foe.

And what pillage there was. A third of Frederick's army was dead or dying. The entire Prussian artillery park of 101 guns had been captured along with most of their tents and baggage and more than thirty standards. Most of the Prussian generals were wounded or dead, including Keith, Frederick's most distinguished comrade in arms.

Keith's body was carried off the street and left, covered in a Croat's cloak, lying on the floor in the church of Hochkirch. Later that afternoon, Daun and Lacy entered the church and, sensing the cloak covered a Prussian officer, Daun stooped down and uncovered the dead man's face. He recoiled in horror as he immediately recognised his distinguished opponent. Lacy simply said 'That is my father's best friend', before both men burst into tears.

The completeness of the Austrian victory was marred by a characteristic failure to follow through. But Austrian casualties had not been light. The fighting had been bloody and fierce and the Prussians had sold themselves dearly. More than 7,000 Austrians were dead or wounded and Daun rejected Lacy's proposal to launch a new attack. Frederick admitted that Hochkirch had been 'a disaster' and that he was 'a beaten man'. In Vienna, the news of Hochkirch occasioned much rejoicing. Honours and riches were showered on Daun, including a gold sword from the Tsarina of Russia.

The humbling of Frederick: Kunersdorf

By 1759 Maria Theresa's hopes were justifiably high. Her armies had proved their worth under Daun. France, Sweden and Russia had all mobilised forces and the heartlands of Prussia began to look distinctly vulnerable. The Prussian King was also showing signs of wear and tear. Though barely 46, he was, according to the British envoy in Berlin, 'an old man lacking half his teeth, with greying hair, without gaiety or spark or imagination'.[15]

Gout and flu debilitated him throughout the winter and in appearance he took on a slovenly mien – not helped by his reluctance to change his uniform, which gradually became moth-eaten and covered in food stains. He had lost his best generals, his closest friends, and the casualty rate among his subalterns was as high as 70 per cent in many regiments. Several of his regiments had virtually ceased to exist as the native Prussian manpower simply dried up. Yet still he had not knocked Austria out of the war.

Writing to Frederick of Brunswick on Christmas Eve, the Prussian King noted: 'Do not expect big things. We are thoroughly dilapidated and our defeats as well as our victories have robbed us of the flower of our infantry.'[16]

Composing a lengthy military assessment in December he noted that the Austrians had raised their game. Of all Prussia's enemies, including France and Russia, Austria's soldiery was now regarded by Frederick as his most formidable opponent. The Russians were 'wild and incompetent' and the French 'experienced but careless'. Only the Austrians had become consistently a most professional adversary. This was high praise from their greatest enemy and proof that under Maria Theresa's reforming zeal the army and its leadership had improved dramatically. The improvements were consistent across all three arms and forced the Prussians to rethink their tactics.

Frederick noted that it had become impossible to attack the Austrians frontally in closed order, owing to their skill in choosing their positions and the improvement in their artillery. In addition, their skill at concealment and guerrilla warfare had made it virtually impossible to receive prior intelligence of their movements. Austrian superiority in light cavalry and irregular infantry was also duly noted. Despite frequent attempts to imitate these formations, it had proved, with the notable exception of Ziethen's Hussars, utterly impossible to replicate the tactics and skirmishing skill of the 'Grenzer'.

Put quite simply, the Prussians, if they were to beat the Austrians, had no option but to become more like the Austrians. Only on the open plains of Eastern Prussia could Prussian discipline and firepower still retain an advantage but even there the deterioration in the Prussian army, in contrast to the qualitative improvement in the Austrian forces, meant that this principle was no longer immutable. New Prussian recruits were now of a hue very different from that of Frederick's original grenadiers. Some were dragooned from hostile and unreliable states such as Saxony; others came from Mecklenburg where they were often more or less kidnapped into service along the lines so eloquently described by Thackeray in his masterpieces *Henry Esmond* and *Barry Lyndon*.

So much for the men. The recruitment of junior officers was even more difficult as the rigid social cohesion, traditionally the dominating factor in selection of Prussian officers, could no longer be imposed in the light of the heavy casualties of the previous year. There simply were not enough sons from the traditional landowning families to go round. To Frederick's consternation, he realised he would have no choice but to recruit from the ranks of the bourgeoisie, a class whose devotion to materialism, he was convinced, rendered them mentally and spiritually 'unfit' for the honourable profession of arms. Once the war was over, Frederick would spend the remaining years of his reign purging the army of the last of this 'objectionable material'.

Frederick's recruitment for the coming campaign would be saved by Austria's decision to exchange prisoners, but although he was back up to his usual strength of 125,000 men under arms by March, they were not the same quality as his troops of earlier campaigns. In contrast, through his careful and cautious campaigning, Daun had preserved an army that could now be reinforced easily to total some 140,000 men. Thanks to the reforms of the previous fifteen years, it was becoming a far more efficient body of troops in every way. Taxes and the emergence of a new caste of talented commanders supplied the material to wage war. By contrast Frederick had to resort to debasing the thaler coinage to achieve the same results. On 4 December 1758, the Empress awarded thirty-three Knights' Crosses of the new Order of Maria Theresa. These senior officers were to form the apex of a pyramid of a new and dynamic officer corps whose talent was not limited, like that of its Prussian opponents, to one narrow stratum of society.

Daun, ever cautious, was determined to await the Russians, and their progress was slow. Once again, Kaunitz had to prod the victor of Kolín and Hochkirch into more decisive action. Kaunitz saw that the highly favourable diplomatic constellation in which Austria found herself was unlikely to be repeated. Moreover, just in case Daun felt Habsburg war aims were confined to the recovery of Silesia, he expounded in a note to the commander a more profound objective: a post-war environment without the evil of 'remaining armed beyond our means and burdening loyal subjects with still more taxes rather than granting relief from their burdens'.[17]

Preserved in the Kriegsarchiv of Vienna this is another one of those remarkable documents of the eighteenth century. In it Kaunitz displays his far-seeing intellect and humanity. He warns that without victory Austria and then all the nations of Europe would have no option but to introduce a militarist form of government 'in the Prussian manner' until 'finally the whole of Europe would be subjected to this unbearable burden ... this and other evil consequences can only be prevented by weakening the King in Prussia ....' Kaunitz argued that Prussian militarism and European civilisation were incompatible. The Imperial statesman was concerned with more than the geopolitical interests of Austria. Nothing less than the 'happiness of the human species', to use his phrase, was at stake.

As the Russians advanced into Pomerania all Daun felt obliged to do was to send Loudon to join them with a modest force of 24,000 hand-picked troops. These included several of the best regiments in Maria Theresa's army. Frederick knew it was vital to prevent this junction of the Russian and Austrian armies and his scouts apprised him of Loudon's progress. On 22 July he set out, in his own words, 'to settle all this Loudon hysteria' and by the 29th he was less than two miles behind the Austrian. But once again the superiority of Austrian screening tactics prevented Frederick from knowing what was really happening.

A diversionary force under Hadik persuaded the Prussians that they were the bulk of Loudon's force while Loudon slipped away to link up with the Russian commander Soltikow. Soltikow had expected all of Daun's army rather than just the auxiliary corps under Loudon but the two men soon settled their differences. Loudon, who spoke fluent Russian as well as German, French and English, was dismayed at the position Soltikow's troops occupied. In Loudon's view the Russians were facing the wrong direction to anticipate the imminent arrival of the Prussian King. Loudon persuaded the Russians to cross the Oder and form a strongpoint along a series of small hills above the village of Kunersdorf.

Frederick determined on swift action. He knew that he had to beat the combined Austro-Russian force before Daun eventually appeared with 30,000 reinforcements. The key to the left of the allied position was the so-called Mühlberg. After a cursory inspection of the terrain, Frederick decided on a flanking operation preceded by an artillery bombardment of the utmost severity. At 11.30 more than 200 Prussian guns opened up on the Russian left flank, decimating the troops on the Mühlberg. Despite the fact that his infantry had completed several exhausting forced marches to reach the position north-east of Kunersdorf, Frederick immediately committed them to the attack.

The Prussians marched up the steep gradient of the Mühlberg, their drums and pipes playing. Sensing the fragility of his men, Soltikow asked Loudon for reinforcements and twelve companies of Austrian Grenadiers were rushed to the Mühlberg. They were too few and too late. After an hour's bitter close-quarter fighting, the Russians and Austrians were forced to withdraw. The battle seemed to be a certain victory for the Prussians and the postillion bearing the good news of 'victory' was sent off to Berlin.

But here, as so often in war, a commander overreached himself. Frederick saw the brutal reality that, although he had dislodged the allied left, the bulk of his opponents' forces had still not been committed. If he was to secure outright victory and, in his own words, 'be rid of these people once and for all', he would have to attack the allied centre around the Grosse Spitzberg, the second hill on the allied front which also anchored Soltikow's right wing. To achieve this, his exhausted troops would have to march down into shallow ground and then advance once again up another steep gradient.

While Frederick brought up his artillery to the Mühlberg to prepare for the new assault, Soltikow asked Loudon for the bulk of his forces to reinforce the Spitzberg. Unhesitatingly, Loudon moved all his remaining infantry, save for a small rearguard, and began to prepare two defensive lines on the Spitzberg across a relatively narrow front. As the Prussians advanced, they were met by a series of withering volleys, which completely disordered their formation. Five times they re-formed and advanced, only to be crushed by a hail of musketry. As the Austrian artillery came into action with canister, the so-called 'Kuhgrund' between the two hills became a slaughterhouse.

To regain momentum, Frederick now ordered his dashing cavalry commander Seydlitz to charge the allied lines from the south, but the Austrian artillery smoothly changed front and in less than fifteen minutes completely shattered Seydlitz's attack, the able cavalry commander falling wounded at the head of his men.

The charge had panicked the Russians positioned on the Judenburg slope of the Spitzberg. They began to fall back and abandon their artillery. Loudon's infantry and gunners rushed to the position and turned the guns on the Prussian infantry, which was marching up barely 150 paces away. Opening fire with grapeshot, the Austrian gunners mowed down entire ranks of the attacking Prussians. It was the first of the many 'miracles' the Austrians were to perform that day.

Once again the Prussian infantry re-formed to take the Spitzberg. Loudon now brought up his entire grenadier force and in the hand-to-hand fighting that followed, the Prussians were pushed back at the point of the bayonet. By 4.30 p.m., the Prussian infantry attacks were spent and only the remnants of Seydlitz's cavalry under von Platen remained to either cover the retreat or launch one last desperate effort. Although he had had two horses killed beneath him and his gold snuffbox had stopped a musket ball travelling towards his heart, Frederick continued to believe in a last supreme gamble. He ordered von Platen, who had replaced the wounded Seydlitz, to launch a cavalry charge at the allied right wing now denuded of its Austrian infantry regiments, which had been fed into the struggle around the Spitzberg.

During all this time, Loudon had not been inactive. Galvanised by the sublime terrors of warfare, which invigorated this repressed and shy man with an energy unknown even to his admirers in peacetime, he gathered together his cavalry. These were too few to stop the Prussians and he urgently asked for Russian reinforcements. As he saw von Platen's Prussians forming up, he was delighted to find his request unhesitatingly granted and several Russian regiments of Lancers, Hussars and even Cossacks trotted calmly to take up position behind his own Chevauxlegers and Dragoons. The resulting force must have appeared mesmerisingly exotic in their mixture of white, blue and green uniforms. Loudon placed himself at the head of his first line of chevauxleger, drew his sword, and cantered towards von Platen's men.

Austrian cavalry tactics made much of the first blow of the regulation heavy cavalry 'pallasch' on contact with a mounted opponent, being a downward cut to the horse's head with the upward 'return' cut – if performed correctly – catching the trooper's neck and head as his mount stumbled.

Loudon's charge offered ample opportunity for this to be put into practice. Russian cavalry tactics were less codified but the Cossacks' lances were about to make a no less bloody debut on the European battlefield.

Von Platen's cavalry took the attack as best they could but they were still forming up for their own charge. As they were nearly stationary, the sudden impact of Loudon's first line smashed right through them, leaving exposed the struggling mass of Frederick's infantry. Ridden over first by their own fleeing horsemen, the Prussian foot soldiers could barely close ranks before Loudon's men cut them to pieces.

An earlier Prussian army might have seen off the attack but these raw recruits panicked and fled. Many would be found the following day on their faces, their backs torn open by the cut of Loudon's cavalry's sabres. As the Prussian left wing disintegrated, Loudon now rode across to the Mühlberg to complete the rout of the Prussian infantry there. But the Prussians on the Mühlberg had seen all too clearly the fate that awaited exposed infantry attacked by Loudon's cavalry. They took to their heels in a general 'sauve qui peut' which even Frederick could not stem as he rode from one part of the battlefield to another to stop the rout. At one point surrounded by Cossacks, he was only rescued from certain capture by the help of an enterprising young Prussian officer named von Prittwitz and 200 hastily gathered hussars.

Even by the standards of Kolín and Hochkirch, this was victory on the grandest of scales. There was no orderly retreat or withdrawal, no sanctuary in a well-executed rearguard as at Hochkirch. Never before had Frederick's armies suffered so overwhelming and crushing a defeat. Frederick's entire artillery park of 178 guns was captured. More than 21,000 of his soldiers were casualties and barely 3,000 of his army, less than a tenth of his original force, were capable of any coherent formation. Loudon, a man whom Frederick had rejected for Prussian service years earlier, could never have dreamt of a more complete revenge.

'I believe all is lost,' Frederick wrote that evening, adding with a flourish of the melodramatic: 'Adieu forever.' Kunersdorf had been lost largely because of Frederick. He had decided the tactics, and the decision to continue the assault was entirely his. Frederick unlike his opponent, the Empress, was not known for accepting personal culpability. He would later blame his infantry, noting: 'The battle would have been won if the infantry had not collapsed.' To ram home the point, this idol of the Enlightenment ordered that every soldier who had fled the battlefield and returned later to the colours was to be flogged with 20 strokes of the cane. Thus, the darling of Prussian 'progress' was convinced, might the morale of his soldiers be improved.

Austria triumphant: Maxen and Landshut

Frederick ordered the evacuation of the royal family from Berlin but he need not have worried because he was about to be saved by the petty jealousies of his opponents. Loudon was widely seen as the hero of the hour but his Russian counterpart was left with the uncomfortable feeling that Vienna was happy to fight on to the last Russian. The allied casualties had also been enormous. Soltikow complained that his two battles had cost him 27,000 men and that were he to win another victory on such terms he would have no choice but to return to Moscow 'alone with a truncheon' to confront his Empress.

The moment for the Austrians to combine with their Russian allies and take Berlin came and went. Daun had barely established his communications with Soltikow when Frederick's brother Henry rose in his rear and began raiding Bohemia. Frederick meanwhile, recalling his able subordinate Kleist with 5,000 men from Pomerania, began rebuilding his army so that he soon sat astride the Frankfurt (Oder)–Berlin highway with another new army of 30,000 men and a fresh artillery park.

Meanwhile in Saxony the Prussian garrison of Dresden fell to an Austrian corps under Macquire but Prince Henry of Prussia's perfectly executed withdrawal to Torgau persuaded Daun that he should deal with Saxony first because Frederick had resumed command of combined Prussian forces now numbering about 57,000 men. Against this Daun had an Austro-Imperial army of 80,000 but experience showed that the Imperials, the troops of the various German princedoms, were more a liability than an asset. Their performance at Rossbach had not been followed by any programme of reform and their commanders were on the whole men of indifferent ability and extreme timidity. To Vienna's dismay Daun felt he could not attack Frederick's strong defensive position at Torgau and he contemplated evacuating to Bohemia for winter quarters. But for Frederick whose contempt for Daun bordered on the pathological this was not enough. The 'Fat Consecrated Excellency' (Daun had been recently invested with a papal decoration) who had 'accumulated all the symbols of human vanity about him' needed to be 'sent packing with a colossal kick up his ass'.[18]

To administer the 'colossal kick' Frederick sent a corps of 15,000 men under General Finck to take up a position on a strategic plateau south of Dresden near the small town of Maxen from where it could harass the Austrian rear and accelerate Daun's surrender of Dresden and withdrawal to Bohemia. But Daun, whatever his critics might say, was not blind to his opponent's dynamism. Moreover, Lacy saw that the steep valleys and dense forests offered an opportunity and Daun was soon persuaded.

As at Hochkirch, Daun carefully reconnoitred the ground and arranged an attack from four directions with the greatest secrecy and stealth. Stealing away with 40,000 troops in the dead of night from Dresden he brought cavalry and artillery into position despite the driving sleet and ice. Lacy struggled to find a route through the heavily forested and broken country but got into position by the morning of 20 November. Finck and his Prussians found themselves surrounded by three Austrian columns and a detachment of the Reichsarmee. Once again, Frederick's commands, issued in the teeth of both Finck's and many other officers' reservations, had brought the Prussians to the brink of disaster. Earlier when Finck had protested Frederick had simply dismissed him in the third person, the ultimate in German linguistic contempt: 'See to it that he is gone from here.'

By mid afternoon the Austrian artillery began to open up on Finck's positions which, duly softened up, were then carried at bayonet point by a spirited charge of Austrian grenadiers. Finck withdrew and took up a new position in an attempt to organise an escape to Frederick. But Finck's repeated attempts to inform Frederick of his predicament had all been intercepted by the Croat screen, which completely isolated Frederick from any news of events at Maxen. As dawn broke the following day, Finck decided to surrender rather than risk the utter annihilation of his force. For 900 casualties the Austrians had captured 14,800 men, 549 officers including 16 generals, and 71 artillery pieces.

Maxen secured Austria's position in Saxony. When he heard the news, Frederick was dumbfounded. As usual he blamed others for what had been his own *folie de grandeur*. Finck, in Austrian captivity, was curtly informed that his career in the Prussian army was at an end and that the surrender of an entire Prussian corps was an 'unheard of precedent'. He was told that a court-martial and dismissal awaited him once hostilities were at an end. His fellow generals with one exception, Wunsch, were also dismissed. All the Prussian regiments present at Maxen were declared to have incurred the King's displeasure, remaining disgraced and the object of the King's *Ungnade* until the day Frederick died.

The 'Finckenfang' (lit. *Finck* – snare) was another brilliant victory for the Austrians. A month later a small skirmish near Meissen brought a further 1,500 prisoners to the Austrians under Beck for the cost of barely 200 casualties. Frederick had failed to push the Austrians out of Saxony and his own material losses were staggering. Only the relentless debasement of the Prussian coinage enabled him to survive the winter financially. That and the subsidies of the English were all that stood between Prussia and extinction because, as Frederick's brother noted, 'He has thrown us into this cruel war. . . . Since the day that he joined my army he has spread confusion and misfortune . . . every-thing is lost through Frederick.'[19]

The spring of 1760 brought renewed vigour to the Austrian military effort. Kaunitz was adamant that the Prussians needed to be destroyed rather than just contained. Prussia was on its knees and there was to be no relaxation of pressure. Aggression, not defensive posturing, was needed, and the man most obviously suited to spearhead this was Loudon, the solemn but brave corps commander at Kunersdorf. Loudon was convinced that Frederick's forces could be divided and annihilated. He proposed tersely to Kaunitz that this could be done through a bold move into Silesia whose long-suffering populace were now to witness yet another Austrian incursion.

While the main armies under Daun and Frederick watched each other in Saxony, Loudon took off with 50,000 men against General Fouqué's much smaller force around Landshut. Once again Loudon's irregulars and Grenzer performed sterling service in preventing any news of his intentions reaching the Prussian high command. The screen they formed around Loudon's move-ment gave the Austrians almost a cloak of invisibility. Poor Fouqué had to guess at what was going on until Loudon invested the great fortress of Glatz well to his north whereupon Fouqué's Prussians had to fall back and quit their mountain position to protect the Silesian capital of Breslau.

Fouqué's retreat infuriated Frederick, who recklessly ordered him back noting, 'My generals do me more harm than the enemy, because they always move the wrong way.'[20]

Fouqué, all too aware of the fate of Finck at Maxen, was determined to avoid such ignominy. He returned to Landshut, ejected the small 600-man garrison Loudon had left there and prepared for war. Austere and determined, Fouqué was not universally popular among his officers but he was nothing if not a realist. He predicted: 'I foresee my destruction and that of a lot of brave men.' He was further away than ever from any other Prussian troops and could hardly fail to escape destruction if the Austrians showed any energy.

With Loudon in charge, they did this with a vengeance. Breaking off the siege at Glatz, he resolved to wipe out Fouqué immediately. On 23 June, Loudon assembled 30,000 men around the Prussian force of 11,000 and attacked at dawn. A cavalry attack was repulsed by Prussian squares in superb style with parade ground company volleys halting each wave of horsemen. But this unequal contest could only end one way and, as the Prussians fell back with their usual discipline contesting every inch of ground for nearly eight hours, the sheer weight of Austrian numbers began to tell. Fouqué's horse was shot beneath him and had he not been rescued by a company of Jaeger he would have been bayoneted by the advancing Austrian infantry. Even so, an hour later again in the thick of the melee he was wounded badly and was about to be finished off by an Austrian hussar when an Austrian cavalry officer, Colonel Voit, recognised him and seeing his wounded state took him under his charge and saved him.

Voit, an officer in the Loewenstein Dragoons, brought up his own beautifully saddled remount for the wounded Prussian who at first declined the offer, noting that 'the blood will spoil your fine horse furnishings', to which Voit replied with old Austrian courtesy: 'It will become far more precious when it is stained with the blood of a hero.'[21]

As the Prussians ran out of ammunition, they began to surrender and by midday barely 1,500 of them, mostly cavalry, had managed to escape by cutting their way through the Austrian right wing. Some 2,000 Prussians had been killed and nearly 8,000 prisoners, including two other generals, were taken along with 68 artillery pieces and countless flags and standards. Fouqué's forces had been annihilated and Silesia lay wide open. But the Prussians had sold themselves dearly and Loudon's casualties were more than 3,000, though fatalities were less than 800. Frederick, through his own tactical misjudgement, had lost another army.

Once again Frederick placed the blame on others and determined to obliterate the memory of this defeat in a grand *coup de main* against Daun before he could unite with Loudon. Frederick proceeded to execute a series of forced marches but his infantry was not as fit as it once was and hundreds of men dropped out under the strain. As the British envoy Mitchell noted, Frederick blamed 'the army he had [which] was not equal in goodness to what he had brought into the field the former years, that one part of his troops were fit only to be shewn at a distance to the enemy'.[22]

'A picture of hell': Liegnitz and Torgau

Frederick laid siege to Dresden but, while he destroyed large civilian parts of the city, a crime well documented in the paintings of Bellotto, he made no impact on Macquire's garrison. Moreover Lacy with his nimble skill began to harass the Prussian supply lines, on one occasion capturing as many as thirty-six Prussian reinforcement boats and securing some 8,000 prisoners. On hearing of Loudon's successful investiture of Glatz, Frederick broke off the Dresden siege and moved to Silesia where he hoped Daun would pursue him and offer battle on Frederick's terms, but the 'consecrated fat Excellency' was, unsurprisingly, unwilling to comply. Loudon, meanwhile, took Glatz by storm, capturing its garrison and 200 cannon for fewer than 180 casualties. Frederick was outraged and the Prussian garrison commander, the unfortunate Bartolomei d'O, was the object of a furious diatribe from the royal pen. On leaving Austrian captivity after the war, d'O was court-martialled and executed.

Loudon marched on the Silesian capital Breslau where he awaited his allies, the Russians. Frederick hotly pursued by Daun sped towards Silesia, so setting the stage for what was widely expected to be the final triumph of Austrian arms over their foe. Daun would have more than 90,000 troops under his command to Frederick's 30,000 and with his usual mixture of caution and brilliance Daun began planning a vast convergence attack, rightly described as a kind of 'monstrous Maxen writ large'. Even the Russians seemed likely to join in.

Frederick's options were becoming limited. Harassed mercilessly by Loudon's light troops and with Daun and Lacy astride his path, he took up a position near Liegnitz. But the lessons of Hochkirch had been digested and Frederick was unwilling to pitch his tents so close to the Austrians for more than 24 hours. Keeping campfires burning in the Austrian manner and ordering his troops to move silently, he marched towards his brother Henry in the north-east and rearranged his camp on the heights of Puffendorf. Loudon – who had been given the task of outflanking Frederick by crossing the Katzenbach five miles downstream of Liegnitz so that he could attack Frederick in the rear – found to his consternation that the position the Prussians had occupied twenty-four hours earlier had suddenly changed. As soon as Loudon advanced towards the eminences of Puffendorf south of Liegnitz he suddenly found himself facing not Frederick's rearguard as he had expected but the King's vanguard, behind which stood the entire Prussian army. Two furious assaults by the Austrian infantry against a powerful Prussian artillery line broke down and by 4 a.m. Loudon ordered a withdrawal. His cavalry covered this in great style, routing two Prussian regiments that had found themselves exposed while attempting pursuit without cavalry support.

The Austrian withdrawal was indeed conducted with a parade ground efficiency which even caught the eye of Frederick, who commended their example to his officers saying: 'Except for the bodies lying about you would think they were marching off the drill square.'[23]

While all this was going on, Daun followed by Lacy had discovered the original Prussian camp deserted. On hearing an hour later of the setback to Loudon, he called off the action. Loudon was unamused. His single corps of 25,000 men had for more than three hours engaged most of the Prussian army and had been badly mauled. Ten thousand of his men lay wounded or dead and he had lost more than 3,000 as prisoners and 82 pieces of artillery. More importantly, the unique opportunity to crush Frederick had been lost and the road to Breslau now was open to the Prussians. The frustration of Loudon and the other Austrian generals was palpable. Lacy was ordered to take a corps and raid Berlin with the Russians. The feeble Berlin garrison offered no resistance to these forces and on 9 October 1760 Lacy entered Berlin, retaking various trophies captured from the Austrians in earlier campaigns and exercising much care and attention in the preservation of private property. At Potsdam, a Hungarian general, Ezsterházy, could not resist helping himself to a fine writing desk for Lacy and one of Frederick's flutes as a souvenir for another Austrian officer, O'Donnell.

At Charlottenburg the Russians with some help from Austrian irregulars were less restrained and were described as 'marching knee-deep in shattered Meissen' until three days later news of Frederick returning to Berlin encouraged them to abandon the city.

Daun perceived that future operations would revolve once again around Saxony. Crossing the Elbe, he joined Lacy's men while Loudon, nursing his resentment at having been left in the lurch at Liegnitz, was left smouldering like a not so dormant volcano in Silesia. Kaunitz wrote to reassure Loudon that the defeat had been but a 'matter of chance', a view incidentally shared by Frederick, who noted it was 'a mere scratch'.[24] While Daun linked arms with Lacy, Frederick approached Wittenberg and moved swiftly to occupy Leipzig. He knew he had to attack Daun and that a decisive victory could bring to an end the war which Prussia could barely afford.

For once both armies, at around 56,000, were equally matched. Frederick after his usual swift reconnaissance – he knew this terrain well – was convinced that he could execute a brilliant outflanking manoeuvre against the Austrian forces by marching through the woods round the Austrian right flank and then falling on their rear. To convince the Austrians that this was nothing serious, a huge diversionary attack against the Austrian left flank would be executed by a corps under the newly promoted general Ziethen.

On 3 November, as dawn broke, three Prussian columns made their way through the thick forest that masked them from the Austrian front. The passage through the forest was not easy; the paths were confusing and Frederick's troops became disorientated, which caused delay so that it was not until 1 p.m. that Frederick's vanguard emerged from the woods to take up their positions.

By that time Daun had espied what Frederick was up to and had taken precautionary measures. He moved his infantry rearguard to form a westward-facing flank, many of his regiments reversing their fronts. More critically, he rearranged his artillery park. One of the consequences of this movement was that the village of Stuptiz became the key to the Austrian rearguard. As the Prussian vanguard emerged from the woods it was met in clear ground by no fewer than 275 guns of the Austrian artillery firing along hastily marked lines covering all the exits from the woods. As Frederick himself appeared in the woods with ten regiments of his finest infantry, he was received with such a destructive hail of fire that whole lines of his best grenadiers were 'swept away as if by a thunderbolt'.[25] This murderous fire proceeded without interruption, preventing the Prussian artillery or indeed cavalry from deploying. The Prussian dead piled up denying any opportunity to manoeuvre. Well might a later writer narrate of how 'Daun received the Prussians with a cannonade such as had never been experienced since the invention of gunpowder'.[26]

It was certainly the largest cannonade deployed in the history of land warfare until that time and, as a Prussian survivor later plausibly recalled, it really did present them with a 'picture of hell'. Nearly two-thirds of Frederick's grenadiers were slaughtered as they attempted to form ranks long before they had managed to fire off a single shot. Frederick declared to those around him that he had never witnessed in his entire life such carnage, and once again Frederick's uniform was holed by a grazing shot though again without any material effect. The Prussian King was despondent. He had lost many armies in the past but it still pained him to see his best regiments being massacred in front of him without the slightest impact on the Austrian defensive positions.

The cannonade halted to allow three Austrian infantry regiments to put in a counter-attack but this gave Frederick the opportunity to bring up sixteen fresh battalions which, brushing the Austrian infantry aside, advanced in a renewed frontal assault. But this was cut up by the Austrian artillery fire long before it gained the Austrian line, with a slaughter and futility worthy of the Western front in the First World War.

Daun's front actually became stronger as the battle raged because both his flank generals, Sincere and Wied, fed in their troops to attack the third suicidal Prussian attack in the flank. This time eleven Prussian battalions were annihilated. On touching the Austrian heights, they were driven right back to the woods by volleys from Daun's Grenadier companies drawn up with parade ground calm on two sides of the Prussian attack. At this moment the Prussian cavalry under the Prince of Holstein galloped up to the Austrian position and was about to overwhelm two infantry regiments when a spirited cavalry charge of Austrian cuirassiers under O'Donnell disorientated them, giving Daun's infantry time to form square and drive off the Prussian horse with several well aimed volleys. For the Austrians victory seemed all but certain. But Daun had been wounded in the foot and he retired from the battlefield two hours later with blood pouring from his boot, to have his wound dressed at Torgau. At around 6 p.m. a messenger was sent to Vienna to give the Empress the news of a great victory.

On being wounded, Daun had passed command to O'Donnell. As he retired from the battlefield, Daun heard firing from the direction of Stuptiz and he immediately sent a messenger to Lacy warning him to watch Stuptiz for any signs of a Prussian threat. It will be recalled that Ziethen, the Prussian cavalry commander, had been tasked with effecting a diversionary attack against the Austrian left flank. Ziethen, seeing that his diversion was not achieving very much, had decided to rejoin his master and moved his corps towards Frederick's embattled position. Ziethen had no idea that Frederick had in fact shifted so far to the west until well past four o'clock when a courier arrived from Frederick ordering Ziethen to relieve the pressure by some new diversion against Stuptiz.

Ziethen hastened to comply, leaving his entire cavalry on his right to keep Lacy in the dark about his intentions. Lacy received Daun's warning but believed that the heights at Stuptiz were well defended. Indeed, as Ziethen's infantry scrambled up the village slopes they were met with artillery fire almost as deadly as that which had faced Frederick. But the Austrian position had been weakened here because troops had been drawn off to deal with Frederick. Two of Ziethen's assaults were driven off but the chance discovery of a sheltered causeway unguarded by the Austrians allowed a third attempt succeed. It gave Ziethen an opportunity to come closer to his master's forces. As darkness fell, Ziethen's movements were masked. The opposing commanders had quitted the battlefield to write their reports, Frederick seated on the steps of the altar in the church at Elsnig, and Daun in Torgau recovering from his wound.

Not for the last time would a relatively junior Prussian officer, now acting on his own initiative, rescue victory from the jaws of defeat in a battle with the Austrians. As Ziethen's men came up on to the higher western end of the Stuptiz village, the noise of the firing travelled across to the remnants of the main Prussian army north of the ridge which was commanded by General Hulsen. Frederick, who imagined the battle lost, had just ordered Hulsen to withdraw his shattered survivors. At this moment a Major Gaudi persuaded Hulsen to disregard Frederick's command and gather what troops he could for another assault. The time was now after 9 p.m. but Hulsen, encouraged by the noise of the fierce firefight opposite him, sent in a scratch force under General Saldern to link up with Ziethen. Ziethen's force, in the best tradition of the cavalry, though six hours late, had arrived in the nick of time. The Austrian position was about to be transformed from one of impregnability to one of vulnerability.

As the fighting died down towards eleven, with both armies on the Stuptiz ridge, the news of the Prussian arrival at Stuptiz was brought to Daun. He immediately perceived the mortal threat now facing his armies. He ordered Lacy to reconnoitre another defensive position but by two in the morning it was clear no such position could be found. Daun, seeing that his army faced renewing the struggle with two Prussian forces united astride his rear lines, ordered a withdrawal across the Elbe to Dresden. This was to be conducted in silence through Torgau, barely a few hundred yards from the Prussians.

So effectively was this carried out that three and a half hours later the Prussians were preparing for a fresh action completely oblivious to the fact that their enemy had withdrawn. When shortly after six Frederick rode out in the dawn light to survey the battlefield he found it completely abandoned and his troops lined up to greet him with cries of 'Hurrah!' Lacy, who was blamed for the entire debacle, covered Daun's withdrawal effectively and the exhausted Prussians were in no mood to offer a pursuit. Again the Prussian casualties were much higher than those of the Austrians. The exact number when Frederick was told was sufficiently disconcerting for the King to say to his informant: 'It will cost you your head if this number gets out.' The exact number was a Prussian state secret until well into the nineteenth century. Modern research suggests Prussian losses were as high as 24,000 men. This against 2,000 Austrian fatalities.[27]

Torgau was thus an expensive victory and a limited one. Frederick was glad it had prevented a greater tragedy and that Saxony would afford him winter quarters before the next campaign season but he was under no illusions. In his official communiqué after the battle he noted with an unprecedented newly found respect for his adversary that '... it was obvious that Daun's wound helped us win the battle'.[28] Daun's prestige certainly suffered in the aftermath of Torgau but he was irreplaceable despite the fact that, as Duffy notes, the Habsburg monarchy pursued the most egalitarian policies of officer recruitment and promotion in Europe. But neither O'Donnell nor Loudon was acceptable to the senior officers. Only one man combined social prestige with a reputation for professionalism and that was Daun.

Daun wanted no further offensive operations and took up the reins of command again in 1761 on condition that the army remained in a strong defensive position around Dresden. He even begrudged Loudon's corps its raiding potential and he hoped to reduce it in numbers. Kaunitz thwarted this plan. With the Empress, Kaunitz expected great things of Loudon.

Inaction seemed the order of the day for 1761. Both armies were tired and Frederick needed yet again to rebuild a new army after the losses at Torgau. Meanwhile Kaunitz's diplomacy continued to work overtime to bring Russian forces into Silesia. The illness of the Russian Empress and the growing influence of the Tsarevich, the future Peter III, gave Russian policy an ambivalence that was not supportive of Austrian stratagems. Kaunitz came to realise that Russia was more interested in peace than war. Moreover, Frederick had bribed a Russian officer, Tottleben, into being a willing spy. General Tottleben wished to serve in the Prussian army after the war, and was prepared to give Frederick details of Austro-Russian military plans in return for money. Fortunately for the Austrians, as 1761 wore on, their inability to reach any effective agreement with the Russians meant that by the time Tottleben's treason was discovered no agreement had been reached. It was clear to Kaunitz that the anti-Austrian party in Moscow was gaining momentum. The Tsarevich was an outspoken admirer of Frederick, though in this he was not alone. To Maria Theresa's horror, her son Joseph was also showing alarming signs of becoming a devotee.

The Russians were still to be reckoned with. Combining finally with Loudon in Silesia they effectively bottled up Frederick in his camp at Bunzelwitz in the environs of Striglau. But a lasting Austro-Russian agreement still proved elusive and Frederick was able to take advantage of the disharmony of his opponents and slip the leash. He immediately began menacing Loudon's lines of communication with Bohemia.

Loudon moved with his customary energy to disoblige Frederick. On the night of 1 October he took Schweidnitz by storm with twenty battalions of his own infantry and 800 wildly inebriated but fierce Russians who hurling themselves recklessly on to the defensive ditches formed with their corpses a veritable green bridge over which the Austrians poured. Within three hours the garrison had surrendered and the supposedly most modern fortress in Central Europe had fallen without a single shot from any of its 200-odd guns.

Frederick was stupefied: 'nearly unbelievable,' he commented. With the capture of Schweidnitz, Loudon had secured for the first time in the war the provisioning of an Austrian army that would enable it to winter in Silesia. Not since 1740, Silesia, the most contested province on earth, was de facto in the hands of the Austrians. As the year drew to a close, Frederick and Prussia's fate looked again increasingly desperate. In London the British support for Frederick began to waver. Hostilities with Spain seemed imminent and London was reluctant to fight two wars. Moreover, George II's wife, Charlotte of Mecklenburg-Strelitz, was appalled at Frederick's treatment of her home-land, which he had plundered of manpower and wealth in characteristic fashion. To the east, the Russians captured Kolberg. Great tracts of Pomerania and Neumark were now largely in Russian hands.

Had Austria been able launch one colossal final effort, there is no doubt that Prussia would have been all but wiped off the face of the map as 1762 approached. Frederick's resources had shrunk significantly and as the King himself admitted: 'Unless some miracle happens, I do not see how we can be saved.' Less than a month later, on 6 January he could only write: 'the time for miracles is over, all that remains is deadly reality'.[29]

The 'miracle' of Brandenburg

In fact miracles began to occur with almost biblical profusion in the first weeks of the year. First a financial crisis that had been gathering for months suddenly flared up and dramatically compromised the Austrian war effort. Under the strain of war, the national debt had increased sharply, as had taxes. The court had no desire to go down the Prussian route of a debased currency, so savings of a most draconian kind needed to be implemented at once. From the beginning of 1762 cuts were imposed on the army. Each regiment was reduced by two companies. The generals protested, as did Maria Theresa's husband, and her son Joseph, who penned the first of many memorandums on military affairs but all to no avail. The army was brought back to its peace-time establishment. This was still a highly disciplined force but it made the chances of aggressive action against Frederick far less likely. By clipping the wings of the Habsburg military–industrial complex, to use a later phrase, the Austrian treasury had indeed made peace far more likely.

Then on 5 January there occurred the death of the Russian Empress Elizabeth, Frederick's most determined and hated opponent. The new Tsar, Peter III, had been marginalised by his aunt and so it was not perhaps surprising that new policies appeared. Nowhere were these changes more dramatic than in the realms of military and foreign affairs. Peter, who liked to refer to Frederick mischievously as 'the King my master', immediately sent a message to Frederick asking him to participate in a 'new enterprise'. Frederick took the hint, released all his Russian prisoners and sent a trusted envoy, von der Goltz, with a diamond-encrusted Order of the Black Eagle to bestow on the new young Tsar.

Peter's 'new enterprise' was nothing less than a joint Prussian–Russian offensive against Austria. He offered an auxiliary corps, a guarantee of Silesia and Glatz and a proposal to surrender all claims on Russian-occupied Prussian territory. This subordination of Russian interest to Prussian concerns spelt challenges for Kaunitz and all his policies. From a military perspective, the effects of this policy were extensive. With the Russian evacuation of East Prussia, Frederick's diminished resources were suddenly reinforced by a huge increase in available manpower and all the financial possibilities of the province that now could be harnessed to Frederick's crippled machinery of war. Moreover, the release of Prussian prisoners from Russian captivity brought the return of many experienced officers and men.

Suddenly Frederick's position was looking altogether more positive. So confident did he become that he drew up an ambitious plan to send a raiding force through the Carpathians to link up with an army of 6,000 Tatars who would push towards Vienna. Once in the Austrian capital, Frederick ordered that they should 'commit more excesses than usual ... so that they can see the flames in Vienna as ... the inhabitants are reduced to wild screams and disorder'.[30]

Fortunately for the Viennese, the Tatars of the Crimea never appeared and the Prussian Werner came up against a superior blocking force under Beck and beat a hasty retreat to Silesia. There Frederick's confidence led him to think that he could walk into Schweidnitz *à la* Loudon and, pushing forward into Moravia, force the Austrians to accept humiliating terms.

The defence of Schweidnitz

But Daun, aware that the fortress was the key to Austria's position in Silesia, as usual had chosen to position his forces around Schweidnitz with consummate skill and all of Frederick's attempts to outflank him or catch him off guard failed. Daun's army was not what it had been. The new cuts to the establishment had taken their toll and the winter had been crippling for the Austrians encamped in Silesia despite Loudon's capture of Schweidnitz. Daun himself, though still a master in any war of positioning, had lost the appetite for attack.

Nevertheless, his army of observation prevented Frederick from laying siege to the fortress and the Prussian King determined that only with the help of the Russian auxiliary corps promised by Peter could he dislodge Daun. Events meanwhile continued to throw up surprises. On 18 July Frederick was summoned to an urgent meeting with the Russian corps commander Chernysev. There was dramatic news from Moscow. Frederick could hardly believe his ears as the Russian general calmly told him that unfortunately there had been 'an incident' in the Russian capital. Peter had been deposed by his wife Catherine and was under arrest. The new Empress had immediately ordered the alliance with Prussia to be declared null and void, though she wished the two countries to remain 'on friendly terms' and would honour the peace treaty between Berlin and Moscow.

In a grand improvisation Frederick decided to make use of the Russian corps still 'available' to him. He hoped to persuade Daun that this force threatened the Austrian centre. While Daun fussed about that, Frederick would in fact march the bulk of the Prussian army undetected towards the Austrian right wing, north-east of Burkersdorf.

The Prussians burst upon the Austrian right wing at its weakest point where the Austrian general Kelly commanded 5,000 men. After a tenacious defence, Kelly was forced to withdraw, with devastating strategic consequences for Daun as his communications with Schweidnitz were now cut and nothing could prevent Frederick investing the town.

The defence of Schweidnitz was to go down in Austrian military history as a heroic chapter. The fortress Frederick hoped would fall in a week held out for sixty-three days. How could it take so many weeks to recapture something 'we lost in two hours'? Frederick ranted. Thanks to the skill and tenacity of the garrison's mining officers, especially a young captain by the name of Pabliczek, the Prussians had to contest every inch of the glacis. The sorties organised by the Austrians, of which the most famous was by a dashing Leutnant Waldhütter ('der hübsche Waldhütter', the handsome Waldhütter), harassed the Prussians constantly.

The garrison commander Guasco also had at his disposal one of the best engineering officers of his day, General Gribeauval, as well as a fiery bunch of younger Irish officers including Tom Caldwell and Bernard MacBrady, who at one stage resorted to scythes to repel the Prussian attackers. Each day the Austrians thought up some countermine or sortie to give their besiegers little rest. This ceaseless war of nerves brought its rewards. After three and a half weeks, the Prussian officer overseeing the engineering works, Lefebvre, had a total mental collapse and had to retire from the siege to spend the rest of the war in an asylum.

Guasco's little command had done more than enough to salvage Austria's military honour and so when his magazine was finally detonated by the Prussians an exchange of cipher messages with Daun followed, affording him the possibility of surrendering honourably. Guasco finally surrendered on 9 October. His stout defence had inflicted 3,000 casualties on the Prussians. Guasco and eighteen of his officers would go into captivity knowing that they had been awarded *in absentia* the coveted Military Order of Maria Theresa.

Meanwhile another 'miracle' began to work its magic for Frederick. Kaunitz, his most dangerous diplomatic opponent, suddenly fell seriously ill. When he recovered several weeks later he appeared to have lost his earlier belligerence and urged peace. With his usual ingenuity, he began to construct a way in which Saxony might serve as an intermediary. Frederick's response was quite simple. What, he demanded, did Austria mean by the term 'equitable peace'? For Prussia nothing less than the *status quo ante* was acceptable. Eventually, after some wrangling over Glatz, Austria agreed. The Saxons, desperate to be rid of the Prussians, capitulated on all points. The Peace of Hubertusburg restored the frontiers of Prussia, Austria and Saxony to where they had run before the war.

Six years of war had cost Austria nearly half a million men. Prussian casualties were far higher and Prussia both as a state and military machine was a wasteland at the conclusion of the war, while Austria's arms enjoyed a high reputation. The Empress would never again be thought of as a 'passive victim' and as Prince Albert of Saxony observed: 'her armies in which the first princes of Germany reckoned it was an honour to serve, returned to her lands after the years of war in a stronger and finer state'.[31] The Mater Castrorum had indeed earned her title.

CHAPTER 7

The Army and the Josephinian Enlightenment

The great victories of the Seven Years War not only thwarted a coalition of attempts to annihilate Austria as a great power, it also gave Austrian arms a prestige unrivalled in Europe. There was no danger of complacency setting in, as in earlier times, because Maria Theresa's son Joseph was a man in a hurry. Everything had to be improved and strengthened to stand the test of the storms he could see were coming. The army was not spared his zealous interference, although whether it emerged from these ministrations stronger is questionable.

Character of Joseph II

The Capuchin Crypt is entered through a rather nondescript building in modern Vienna, its austere outlines the result of modest Capuchin piety and twentieth-century war damage. Compared to the brilliant baroque churches nearby of Hildebrandt or Fischer von Erlach, it is the Austrian capital's masterpiece of understatement. Here, beneath the simple entrance with its iron doors, lie the tombs of the Habsburgs. The final resting hall of the Emperors is still alive with tradition. As recently as 2011 the last Austrian crown prince to have been born into the Empire, Archduke Otto, was carried there in a procession attended by nearly 200,000 mourners.

In death, as in life, the tension between Maria Theresa and her son Joseph was enduring. Both may have received the same last rites and burial solemnities but there is no more vivid testament to the character differences between mother and son than their respective tombs in the Capuchin Crypt. Where Maria Theresa's is the most opulent and ornate construction, bursting out of its domed chamber with magnificent carvings depicting her great military victories, her son's simple copper and wooden coffin with its faded inscription seems in every way designed to contrast with the pomp and grandeur of Maria Theresa's sarcophagus. The simple inscription runs: 'Here lies the body of Joseph II who failed in everything he tried to achieve.' In death, as in life, Joseph wanted to demonstrate that he was different.

Joseph had what modern psychoanalysts would term a love–hate relationship with his mother. Spoilt, precocious, highly-strung and philosophically curious, he was that recurring figure in European history: the frustrated intellectual crown prince. Chafing at the bit, he was impatient with the pieties of his mother, the structures of his empire and above all the state of his armies. To his mother's consternation he loved sarcasm and irony ('too many notes' was his comment on Mozart's *Die Entführung*). He admired Frederick of Prussia, adored his cold, ruthless approach to *Staatspolitik* and military matters. To Maria Theresa's dismay, he was an ardent believer in the Enlightenment and even dabbled in the doctrines of the 'Supreme Being'. The high baroque Catholicism of the Jesuits and the ornate panoply and rituals of the Pietas Austriaca were anathema to him. He found the *Gemütlichkeit*, emotional intelligence and maternal instincts of his mother embarrassing and incomprehensible.

Deprived of personal emotional fulfilment – his much-loved first wife and child both died young – he immersed himself in his work. A certain emotional frigidity and temperamental harshness became more pronounced. He was horrified when, shortly before her death, Maria Theresa visited the military academy at Wiener Neustadt and sat some of the younger cadets on her knee, wistfully observing: 'Is it not a shame that this will be our last time together?'[1]

Such displays of emotion and heart were not part of the zeitgeist for Joseph. The two monarchs' outlook on humanity was fundamentally divergent. While Joseph analysed with clinical rigour all the challenges his peoples posed for his domains, Maria Theresa simply replied to his criticisms: 'You would have to kill me to prevent my trying to do good.'[2] Like Frederick of Prussia, Joseph was a believer in the rational philosophy of Voltaire. Like Frederick, he wished to be portrayed constantly in uniform. Already at the age of nine he had reprimanded Count Haugwitz, a military reformer, and warned him to 'lay off my own regiment [1st Chevauxleger] with your meddling reforms'.[3] In fact Haugwitz's reforms would count for nothing compared to the 'reforms' Joseph would prepare as co-regent from 1765 and have implemented by the time of his mother's death in 1780.

Convinced that it was his destiny to modernise his empire and to prepare its armies for the challenges ahead, Joseph scorned tradition as he rushed ahead into radical reforms. No walk of life or entity or religious or racial group was immune from his reforming zeal. The army and the Church were at the top of his list. His supporters noted that his keen intelligence saw what was coming and his haste was essential to ensure that the explosion about to occur in Paris in 1789 did not happen in Vienna first. His detractors simply saw this obsession to intrude into every walk of Imperial life as the misdirected energy of the greatest egotist of his age, in an admittedly competitive field.

It was Mozart who perhaps best captured the tension between Joseph and Maria Theresa. In *The Magic Flute* the Empress with her simple verities and disdain for hermetic philosophy and the occult is wittily portrayed as the 'Queen of the Night', while Joseph II is clearly in Mozart's mind in the character of Sarastro, as much a control freak as Joseph in his attempts to promote a new order where all is regulated by his own arbitration.

Already as co-regent from 1765 when his father died, Joseph's influence on the two pillars of the state was dramatic. Unsurprisingly, the Jesuits felt the change of direction first. Joseph had met the Capuchin friar Garganelli in Rome. Impressed by his humble origins and simple attire, Joseph asked 'Who are you?' The future Pope Clement XIV replied 'A poor priest in the uniform of St Francis.'[4]

This austerity appealed to Joseph. It appealed even more that Clement was pliant. In 1767, the monarchs of Catholic Europe bullied the spineless pontiff into ordering the Jesuits' suppression. Joseph cheered them on. What had begun in Portugal at the behest of powerful interests concerned at the Jesuits' growing power, especially among the poor in Latin America, led, by the late 1770s, to the confiscation of most Jesuit property in Europe. Ironically only the avowed atheist, Prussian Frederick, offered them sanctuary in his kingdom, thus ensuring the Society's survival and the excellent education of his newly acquired Catholic Silesian subjects. If the 'military order' of the Church could be subjected to such 'reforms' what fate lay in store for the army? Nervously the army watched as Joseph devoted his reforming passions to the Church.

Once he became Emperor in 1780 far worse followed for the Church. Joseph set out on a secularisation programme without parallel in Central Europe until the imposition of communism after 1945. From the 1950s to the 1980s, communist leaders in Central Europe re-enacted Joseph's policies, especially with regard to the suppression of the orders in Hungary, Moravia and Bohemia. But even their energy proved a pale imitation of Joseph's zeal.

In Lombardy, while Joseph created a bureaucracy that would be the envy of the rest of Italy, he closed virtually every convent irrespective of its social and charitable activities. Only the Ursuline teaching order was exempt. He banned pilgrimages, religious festivals (save for a very few), stripped the clergy of many of their privileges and closed 1,143 religious institutions with disastrous social consequences for tens of thousands of poorer Italians.[5]

On the other hand, Joseph permitted freedom of worship for other religions and allowed groups of more than 3,000 to construct their churches as long as they could demonstrate they had the capital to maintain them. He also issued edicts of tolerance that permitted certain rights to the Jewish population. But Joseph was no real friend of any of these other religions. From 1780, Jews had to adopt German names, often associated with trees and flowers, thus ensuring they were instantly recognisable by the state.[6] By granting Jews special status, some would argue, he institutionalised their segregation from the community and provided a powerful building block for future anti-Semitism. Joseph's efforts aimed at assimilation but proved an early warning of the inherent contradictions of such policies.[7]

Joseph's tolerance of Masonic lodges was a neurotic, obsessive desire to have no potentially subversive element in his domains unregulated by his state apparatus. His patent granting freedom to Masonic lodges in December 1785 was hedged with restrictions and contained the ominous phrase 'bringing them under the protection of the state'.[8] The army was directly affected by this as several younger officers, including the later famous Marshal Radetzky entered such societies at this time. Joseph II saw himself as the apex of a broad structure of state administration whose tentacles were everywhere. Liberty could never degenerate into licence under Joseph, as all liberty was put at his service. He himself admitted this when he wittily said: 'Nothing would give me more pleasure than to command free men.'[9]

By the time of his death, this absolute monarch had anticipated and fulfilled most of the demands of the French Revolutionary Council that were made ten years later. In modern terms he could be regarded as an archeytypal 'enlightened despot'.

Josephinian military reform

Such reforming zeal could not fail to treat military structures with equal irreverence. But the army, unlike the Church, could not be cowed by the arrival of a new energised bureaucracy preaching reform. It had its own bureaucratic structures and these proved surprisingly resilient. The clash between what was called then rational enlightenment and what we would call today 'military tradition' was predictably piquant. As always with Joseph, there was no gentle calibration or moderation.

First on the block was the traditional Austrian white tunic. For reasons of expense the Hofkriegsrat had in 1775 authorised research into various shades of grey. When it was discovered that a darker 'grey in grey' lasted up to a third of the amount of time longer than off-white, Joseph II promptly ordered several regiments to adopt the colour. The new uniforms were unpopular and were to be made up in the factories of Stockerau not far from Vienna. There, discussion as to whether 'pike grey' or 'wolf-grey' was the suitable replacement failed to arrive at any agreement and this slowed down the experiment among the unfortunate units chosen to wear the new attire. During this delay, there were opportunities for further brakes to be applied. There were widespread complaints of shabbiness and unreliable wear and tear. The officers instinctively played for time, another Habsburg quality. After a few years the idea was quietly dropped. Having survived Joseph's critical focus, the white tunic would endure for another hundred years until the breech-loading rifle of the Prussian infantry at Königgrätz achieved in an afternoon what a reforming Emperor failed to change in a decade.

The survival of the white tunic was an isolated triumph for the traditionalists. Keen at all times to emulate Frederician military practices, Joseph had the infantry reorganised along cantonal lines as in Prussia. As of June 1769, each regiment was numbered. But this was just the beginning. As Joseph had pointed out in his first ever memorandum in May 1761: 'We should not reduce our forces; rather we must dismantle the luxury and excesses of an unaffordable system.'[10]

The rights of the Inhaber proprietary colonels, including their privilege of setting the facing colour of their regiment, were now curtailed in favour of the regimental colonels. Court dress for generals and senior officers was replaced by uniforms, as befitted the servants of the 'first servant' of the Austrian state. Joseph, who now posed as the 'soldier-Kaiser', and was himself in uniform most days, affected a military vocation. 'To be a soldier has always been my profession and favourite occupation,' he insisted, despite his eminent unsuitability for the profession of arms, to be proved all too vividly during his short life.[11]

Following a long reconnaissance trip to Bohemia in 1766, Joseph had already noted the need to appoint new inspector-generals for cavalry, infantry and artillery. He now set about selling all his estates in Bohemia and Hungary to raise the money necessary to aid the next wave of reforms. With Daun's death in 1766, Lacy, by now a field marshal, moved to centre stage as Inspector-General of infantry and showed an aptitude for organisation and pedantic detail that suited Joseph's plans well.[12]

'The Queen of Arms'

The expensive Swiss Guard was abolished; the Staff reorganised. Conscious of the superb drill of the Prussian foot soldier, Joseph declared the infantry to be the 'Queen of Arms'.[13] As in the Khevenhueller Reglement a generation earlier, great emphasis was placed on the appearance of the infantry soldier. The 57 line regiments were exhorted to maintain the highest standards of personal smartness and hygiene. They were implored to change shirts at least twice a week. Collars were to be neatly unobtrusive and uniform and weapons were to be rigorously inspected each Saturday. Colonels of regiments were required to know the names of all their officers while the adjutant was to know also the names of all NCOs and 'reliable' other ranks of the regiment.

Nor were the line regiments the only branch of the infantry to be 'regulated'. The officer's stick, the symbol of his authority, henceforth was to have a simple unadorned top and its application with regard to punishment of soldiers was to be strictly regulated. Officers were to wear more modest uniforms and boots of similar quality to those of the NCOs. All excessive ornamentation was to be removed. Epaulettes were banned and officers' uniforms were to resemble more closely in cut and cloth those of the other ranks. Even the Grenzer infantry regiments were brought into the new military machine and incorporated into the line infantry, losing many of their colourful distinctions of dress.

The grenadier companies which during the Seven Years War had temporarily been formed into grenadier battalions were now regrouped into 19 units of battalion strength. Five were to be recruited from Bohemia, three from Moravia, three from Hungary and one each from Styria and the other Austrian duchies and Transylvania. Given that these units contained the fittest and tallest men in the Austrian army it is interesting to note that proportionately the greatest number were recruited from the Czech lands. This would appear to dispel the modern presumption that Bohemia's only contribution to soldiery was the infamously unreliable 'Good Soldier Schwejk'.

Lacy's Infantry Reglement contained 15 specific points with regard to the grenadiers, which underlined their elite status. No recruit could join a grenadier unit without a 'completely unblemished' military record of service in a line infantry regiment. In appearance they had to be at least six feet tall and *grenadiermässig* (lit. grenadier-measured) in terms of physical fitness and countenance.

The different companies that made up the battalions retained their infantry regiment distinctions of buttons and facing colours. This was another triumph of Josephinian rationalisation. For the first time all facing colours (*Egalisierungsfarben*) were precisely stipulated so that between 1766 and 1798 a rigid system of *Egalisierung* (lit. equalisation) was established. Groups of four regiments, two 'German' and two Hungarian, shared the same *Egalisierungsfarbe* but were distinguished from each other by their buttons, white or gold metal; and their trousers, blue or white.

The 'box of colours' (*Farbkastel*)

The facing colours included five shades of red, from the rich 'Pompadour scarlet' to 'Brick red' via 'Ponceauroth', 'Alizarinrot' and 'Carmoisroth' (pumice red, Alizarin red and carmine red), two (later three) shades of blue, three shades of green, two shades of Lacy's favourite colour, yellow (including the splendidly named *Schwefelgelb*: sulphur yellow), violet, orange, rose-pink, chocolate and black. Some of these colours quickly became associated with certain elite regiments. For example *Kaisergelb* (Imperial yellow) was given to the House regiment of Graz, sky blue to the House regiment of Vienna, pink to Trieste, chocolate to Carinthia, canary-orange to Salzburg, black to Linz, etc.

As the colours of this scheme were imposed with what Victor Adler later called 'absolutism softened by incompetence (*Schlamperei*)',[14] there were examples of logistical challenges being met ingeniously by regiments as the occasion demanded. In 1770, one infantry regiment, number 41 (Plunket), successfully petitioned to be released from its *Egalisierungsfarbe* of dull brick red in favour of the more arresting sulphur yellow. This was achieved rapidly in a matter of a few weeks until someone pointed out that the regiment's grenadier companies had not been informed of the change and that, while the tunics could be replaced, no one had thought about their bearskins, whose peaks on their reverse bore the relevant *Egaliserungsfarbe*. A quick-witted official – whose name has not been recorded but who clearly had on his desk the entire *Schematismus* (schedule) of the Josephine army with the positions of each grenadier company – organised a swap with the nearby Kolowrat grenadiers stationed in Pressburg whose bearskins bore sulphur yellow distinctions. These were now collected and loaded on to barges. Thus was the machinery of the Josephinian state suborned into the service of the appearance of a few Imperial grenadiers.[15] Only in one respect were the grenadiers lacking in privilege: their musical ensembles or bands. These bandsmen were, in contrast to the rest of the army, not permitted to enjoy any uniform other than that of their regiment and the ornate distinctions associated with line infantry musicians were denied them.

Virtually no detail of military life was left unregulated in the Josephinian era. Soldiers were told precisely how to greet a civilian of rank and were banned from eating or drinking in the street. A new headdress, made of black felt, the forerunner of the British stovepipe shako later to be immortalised at Waterloo, was introduced on cost grounds to replace the tricorn hat for the line infantry. The precise dimensions of tents were prescribed and chaplains were exhorted to watch vigilantly over the morals of their regiments and report any incident of *Weibgsindel* (female irregularities). As was to be expected, the chaplains were given a peculiarly Josephinian twist to the inter-pretation of their faith. With the exception of Easter when the full 'Fear of God' was to be put into the minds of the men, the chaplains were instructed not to encourage 'any open discussion of religion'.

The most individual arm of the army, the cavalry, felt this wind of austere reform especially keenly. The number of cavalry regiments was significantly reduced and in a drive for economy the number of regimental standards was cut by half. The drum horses of all Cuirassier and Hussar regiments were abol-ished and all cavalry furniture was henceforth to bear the simple Imperial cipher rather than the Inhaber's more costly and ornate family crest. The Chevauxleger regiment Loewenstein which had the privilege of riding in parade with a pair of ornate kettledrums it had captured from the Prussians in 1758 at Wisternitz was promptly deprived of these 'luxuries' and warned of further cuts to its expenditure to come. But despite all these efforts, military expenditure continued to rise. In 1711 it had totalled 22,248,871 florins. By 1790 this sum had increased, taking into account inflation, by 13 per cent.[16]

In 1768 two carabiner cavalry regiments were created out of dragoon and cuirassier components. In 1769 the cavalry were reduced to a total of 45 regi-ments: 15 cuirassier, 10 dragoon, 10 hussar, 2 chevauxleger, 2 carabiner, 5 Grenzhussar, 1 Wallachian dragoons. The hussars felt these reforms keenly and a notable deterioration in their performance was observed in comparison to that of their confrères serving Berlin who learnt how to intervene decisively in full-scale battles as well as traditional hussar work.

Reforms were equally vigorous in the artillery. With the exception of the guns in the Netherlands forts, all Austrian artillery was now grouped into three field regiments, centred on Vienna, Prague and Olmütz. The old ranks, such as Stückhauptman (lit: Bit-Captain), peculiar to the artillery, were abol-ished and distinctions were brought into line with general ranks in the army. Even before his accession to the throne, the co-regent Joseph could write to his mother in 1775 plausibly insisting, 'Nothing of the old army remains.'[17]

As his reign proceeded, the wave of reforms became a torrent. A new medal for military valour, the Tapferkeitsmedaille, was introduced in 1789 for non-commissioned ranks. A new red–white–red flag was authorised for the Austrian Navy (it was to last until 1918 and as the national flag to the present day) while the headquarters of the Imperial War Council was transferred to the Josephinium from its old quarters near the old Arsenal, Am Hof.

In the sphere of military medicine, Austria led the world as Joseph, following this one time in his mother's footsteps, arranged for his own personal physician Giovanni von Brambilla to continue the reforms of the military medical service. In 1785, a military-medicine academy was established that would prove important for the development of medicine. The academy would not only provide support for the soldier in the closing years of the eighteenth century, it would lay the foundations for the establishment of scientific and ethical principles in the medical profession.

Incorporation of Lancers: the Partition of Poland

A portrait of Joseph II in 1788 surrounded by his staff at Minkendorf, the new military training ground, shows a small group of cavalry hitherto not part of the regular Austrian army even though Schiller referred to them thirty years later in his great 'Wallenstein' drama. They are instantly identifiable by their headdress and tunics as a group of Polish lancers, making their first appearance in the Austrian army. Their presence was the direct consequence of the Partition of Poland in 1772. This sorry affair, which Maria Theresa's instincts persuaded her to resist but which, as Frederick of Prussia acidly noted, caused her 'despite all her weeping to participate in', was an act of political violence unprecedented even by the 'standards' of eighteenth-century diplomacy.

We have seen how Joseph had weakened the Pietas Austriaca through his religious reforms, which stressed the material and commercial to the detriment of the spiritual. This countered directly the ethos of his mother. Maria Theresa personally believed she owed her throne to nothing less than a miracle. She was fond of saying: 'I ascribe this by no means to my virtue but exclusively to God's grace'.[18]

She was therefore highly distressed at the thought of Austria, already the victim of such realpolitik, becoming a willing predator of a defenceless neighbour. But in the end, she consented and paved the way for that intellectual climate which permitted nothing less than the liquidation of one of the oldest states of Europe whose kings had played a prominent part in saving Austria and Europe from the Ottomans.

When Augustus III of Poland died in 1765 leaving only a young grandson, the Kingdom of Saxony, having held the throne of Poland for sixty-six years, was deprived of its privileges in Polish affairs. Both Russia and Prussia stepped forward to fill the vacuum. The subsequent election of Stanislaus Poniatowski to the Polish throne only emphasised further the disarray of the ever-quarrelsome Polish aristocracy. In a move which was to set an unhappy precedent, Joseph ordered the occupation of the Zipser valleys at the foot of the Carpathians by Austrian troops in 1770. Two years later Russia and Prussia agreed to follow where Joseph had led and helped themselves to considerable slices of Polish territory. This presented Austria with a dilemma: to join in, against all the scruples of the Empress, or to permit Russia and Prussia to indulge in aggrandisement that could only menace Austrian interests.

A later historian noted that the system 'had become so superficial, so miserable and absurd that they lost sight altogether of the principle that a just equilibrium and the permanent safety of all can only be secured by the inviolable preservation of the rights of nations. The partition of Poland was the formal renunciation itself of that system of equipoise and served as the precursor of all those great revolutions and later dismemberments ... which during a space of five and twenty years were the means of convulsing Europe to her very foundations'.[19] It allowed Frederick, finally, to style himself 'King of Prussia'.

The First Partition of Poland was a bloodless affair for the Austrians. Hadik occupied Galicia without opposition in the summer of 1772. Twelve years later, in 1784, the first Polish Lancer units were established, followed a year later with a third *Pulk* or division. Each regiment was 300 strong and uniformed in the Polish national-guard style of plastron tunic, shapka headdress, and a lance with a detachable pennant of gold and black: the Habsburg colours. Officers were slightly more richly attired but were not permitted epaulettes.

In 1787, for political reasons, notably a certain distrust of the Polish and Ruthene (Ukrainian) population, the Lancer units were abolished as a separate entity and divided up among the Chevauxleger regiments as Lancer squadrons, where they would remain until Joseph's death in 1790. They were reformed into individual Lancer units in 1791.

Jaeger and sharpshooters

Another unit, perhaps even more relevant for the shape of warfare to come, was also organised on a more stable footing. These were the sharpshooters or 'Jaeger' (lit. hunters), as they were called, who were now grouped for the first time into their own formations. Their keen marksmanship was supplemented by a new form of light infantry. These, together with the Grenzer sharpshooters, were equipped with a remarkable shotgun with an over-and-under barrel system in which the upper barrel fired smooth-bore cartridges and the lower barrel fired along a rifled barrel.

In addition to these sophisticated shotguns, 20,000 of which were manufactured by various gunsmiths throughout the Empire, reforms brought other new weapons of high precision. The Crespi carbine of 1771 which was 123cm long and 19mm calibre was innovatory and the leading rapid-fire carbine of the age. The brothers Crespi demonstrated it to Joseph in 1771 and after initial highly successful tests 2,351 pieces were made in Ferlach (today in Carinthia and still one of the world's leading suppliers of precision shotguns). The carbines were issued to the two carabineer regiments and the elite Chevauxleger Regiment Nr 1. With a firing rate of three shots a minute, they were considered superior to the *Vorderlader* (front-loading) carbine with which hussars were issued.[20]

Other related developments were smokeless ammunition and a repeating rifle making partial use of the Girardoni system.[21] Until 1798, when a new model musket was introduced for the infantry, the line infantry used the standard infantry musket manufactured in Steyr in Upper Austria at a cost of between 5 and 7 gulden per piece.

Frederick, rejoicing in his title 'King of Prussia' now that the Partition of Poland had done away with the Polish monarchy, was invited to inspect the Austrian troops in Neustadt. Dressed discreetly in an Austrian uniform (Divisa Austriaca), he knew well how to flatter Joseph, complimenting him on his reforms and referring to the Austrian troops as 'Prussians in white coats'.[22]

The 'potato war' and the creation of Josephstadt

The 'new' Habsburg army however was to be deprived of any real warlike activity in the conventional sense. The 'Potato War' (*Kartoffelkrieg*: so called because the soldiers survived the winter only by digging up potatoes with their bayonets) or, as it was known more formally, the 'War of the Bavarian Succession', saw a series of brilliant manoeuvrings by an Austrian army whose mobilisation was accomplished with a skill and speed that suggested Joseph's reforms had taken root. But this war, which was supposed to help Austria annex Bavaria, saw neither battles, sieges nor any real engagements. While Europe trembled at the thought of the impending clash of two great armies yet again on the Bohemian plains as Frederick mobilised to counter Austrian pretensions, the two great armies simply glowered at each other.

Eventually, after some mild skirmishing between both armies' irregular troops, Frederick, despite his enjoying for once a significant superiority in numbers, withdrew. Maria Theresa had secretly communicated a desire for peace. Her treasury was pleading imminent poverty. The *status quo ante* was the result, though Maria Theresa felt the Treaty of Teschen, which once again had brought hostilities to an end, one of the happiest treaties she had ever signed. Frederick had proved 'so reasonable'. Was Frederick's reluctance to force a crisis a sign of his maturity? Or was it rather his awareness, confirmed by his reconnaissance of the Austrian positions, that his adversary was technically and materially far better equipped?

Certainly the winter wrought havoc among Frederick's troops while, thanks to Lacy's skilful logistics, the Austrians seemed to want for little. In this sense the Austrian deployment was masterly as it saw off the Prussian threat without real hostilities. It made it more attractive for Frederick to withdraw with his forces than engage the Austrians, something that would have been unheard of a generation earlier.

Moreover, the preparations for the war had seen a dramatic upsurge in Austrian patriotism. As a keen British observer resident in the Austrian capital, William Wraxall had commented:

> Vienna has now been transformed into an arsenal. Every day new regiments arrive. . . . Nothing can convey a more striking idea of the greatness of the House of Austria, the magnitude of its resources, the extent of its dominion . . . than the scene to which I am daily a witness.[23]

In another important respect the *Kartoffelkrieg* over the Bavarian succession influenced Habsburg military thinking. The campaign threw into sharp relief just how important it was to reinforce the line of the Upper Elbe in northern Bohemia. Accordingly in 1780, on 3 October, the foundation stone of a new fortress town, whose architecture would comprise one vast late neoclassical barracks divided into streets surrounded by a horseshoe of ramparts, was laid at Pless. Designed in the French style by General Ludwig du Hamel de Querlonde, Josephstadt took nine years to build at a cost of 10.5 million gulden. The new city would offer its burghers certain privileges. At Lacy, Loudon and Hadik's request Josephstadt would enjoy the status of a 'free city' in its dealings with the Imperial bureaucracy.

Josephstadt or Josefov as it is called in Czech to this day is a remarkable survival of late eighteenth-century military town planning. Its streets arranged around the central town square and its neoclassical garrison church offer a crisp and suitably austere Josephinian masterpiece of pantheistic solemnity. Far more homogeneous in architectural style than Potsdam, more martial than Verona or the fortresses of the Quadrilateral in northern Italy, Josephstadt is one of the eighteenth century's military architectural wonders of the world.

Like other great fortresses, Josephstadt would never serve any function in war. It was insignificant until the Red Army made it their principal garrison in Bohemia during the Cold War. (Its sister fortress, Theresienstadt, would have its name defiled by the appalling use it was put to by the Nazis in the Second World War as a transit camp for their Jewish victims and part of the complex to implement the horrors of the Holocaust.)

The lure of the east

As Joseph's brief reign developed, military consideration became fixated on events to the east. Within a year of his succession, in 1781, Joseph formed a defensive alliance with Catherine of Russia. When the Turks declared war on Russia, Austria, under the terms of this agreement, mobilised 30,000 men, though neither Kaunitz nor Joseph had any desire to see Russia in Constantinople. Meanwhile Joseph's own ambitions for territorial aggrandisement began to seize his imagination. Wallachia, Bosnia, the recovery of Serbia: all these fruits of conquest danced before his fevered eyes.

Instead of just being satisfied with his alliance commitments, Joseph moved to put an entire army into the field against the Ottomans. Declaring war on 9 February 1788, Joseph mobilised more than a quarter of a million men, including 37,000 cavalry and 900 guns. Never before had Austria waged war on so broad a front, more than 1,350 kilometres long and stretching deep into the Bukowina. Lacy, now firmly Joseph's favourite, envisaged his forces spread in a great arc covering the Austrian monarch's entire southern frontier. Never was such an ambitious plan devised by a more mediocre strategist. Confronted with anything grander than the logistics and issues of supply, Lacy was hopelessly out of his depth. The Turks could choose their targets at will and under aggressive leadership took full advantage of Lacy's strategic weaknesses.

The campaign inevitably developed into a fiasco. Two attempts to storm Belgrade failed miserably. Disease and hunger began to reduce the ranks of the troops and undermine morale. At Orsova, an Austrian battalion under Stein was surrounded and after twenty-one days forced to surrender. Shortly afterwards in September, Joseph and Lacy agreed to take up a defensive position in the valley of Caransebeş despite the advice of all their senior officers that they should attack the nearby Turks immediately and regain the initiative. On 21 September some hussars picked a fight with some Grenzer troops from the Banat and the casualties that ensued in the subsequent firefight were vastly increased when panic seized hold of the encampments in the face of an imminent Turkish attack. These events scattered Joseph's staff. Joseph, abandoned by aides and escort, emulated his idol Frederick's earlier behaviour on the battlefield, and galloped away from his fleeing soldiers. Later when he reproached his staff for having deserted him, one of them mischievously replied: 'We used our utmost endeavours to keep up with your Imperial Majesty but our horses were not as fleet as yours.'

The Emperor's camp was abandoned along with most of the artillery park. This all fell into Turkish hands. Coming on the heels of events earlier at Meadia where an entire Austrian corps under Wartensleben was annihilated, panic soon spread across the entire Military Frontier into Hungary. Within a few months the most powerful army Austria had ever put into the field was reduced under its 'enlightened' Emperor to a disease-ridden, demoralised force fighting a rearguard action on its own territory. The Banat and Transylvania were scorched by the pursuing Turks.

This was not the campaign Joseph had imagined. He could not emulate the glories of the Prussian soldier-king. His resources exhausted and his generalship utterly discredited, Joseph resorted to desperate measures. Ill and distracted by the news of an uprising in the Austrian Netherlands he retired to Buda. In the face of all these setbacks, he called for Loudon, whom he had neither employed nor consulted hitherto. To compensate for such foolish neglect of the taciturn commander, he ordered a diamond-encrusted and emerald Knight Commander's cross of the Order of Maria Theresa to be made. This he bestowed on the now 73-year-old Loudon. Loudon was by no means unhappy to be brought out of retirement and he did not nurse any resentment for Joseph's earlier treatment of him. As Loudon proceeded in triumph across the Empire towards the military frontier, his presence alone raised morale among the shivering remnants of Joseph's armies.

To replenish his forces, Joseph now took another radical step. Sick and feverish, he transferred from Buda to Vienna in the December snows. Broken, without possessions, racked by the illness that within months would kill him, he organised a comprehensive conscription of manpower that represented a huge and unprecedented intervention by the state into the affairs of the private sphere.

Introduction of conscription: Loudon takes Belgrade

For the first time the conscription for front-line units applied also to Jews (Maria Theresa had always opposed this, observing acidly that 'here the frontiers of tolerance are reached', and that the question of Jews serving in the army was unmentionable ('kann keine Rede sein')).[24]

Not only were they now eligible to be called up, but their houses, like everyone else's, were numbered and their villages catalogued and delineated. Jews initially had only been allowed to serve in logistics and support functions and only in Galicia, but in 1789, under the pressure of the Turkish wars, this was extended to all branches of the services.

Joseph II understood the importance of the 'small men' and his recruiting machine not only conscripted front-line soldiers but hairdressers, footmen, bakers and candlestick makers, widening the cultural make-up of the army. An authoritarian bureaucracy administered a microcosm of the Empire which reflected its social diversity, though the officer class came to be dominated increasingly by the aristocracy.

The experiment was not a success everywhere. Conscription in Hungary almost triggered a revolution. Its imposition in Tyrol was so unpopular among the fiercely independent men of those valleys that shortly before his death Joseph had to rescind all forms of recruitment there.

Meanwhile, the war continued. Led by Loudon, the Austrians showed that under professional leadership they were still a first-rate fighting force. Within days of taking over command, he defeated the Turks at Dubica and took the fortress there. At Novi and Berbir, Loudon defeated the Turkish armies again. Securing the strategically important village of Šabac, he moved swiftly to invest Belgrade.

On 8 October 1789 Belgrade was finally stormed thanks partly to a newly created 'Bombardier corps' which shattered Turkish resistance in an artillery bombardment of immense ferocity. For Joseph, Loudon's taking of Belgrade could not have come at a more opportune moment. 'I am speechless' ('Mir fehlt die Worte') he wrote to Loudon and, returning to Vienna, he ordered a Te Deum to be sung in the cathedral. It was to be Joseph's last public appearance.[25]

Joseph's armies under Loudon and Prince Coburg continued their run of success in the Balkans. On 10 November Coburg occupied Bucharest and around this time a talented young adjutant of Lacy's by the name of Radetsky began to make a name.

The Lowlands revolt

In northern Europe events continued to distract Joseph. The uprising in the Austrian Netherlands that had begun two years earlier now gathered momentum. With reason Joseph wrote to the Prince de Ligne, a native of the Lowlands: 'Your country has killed me .... the loss of Ghent my agony; the surrender of Brussels my death'.[26]

This revolt was again a violent reaction to Joseph's administrative reforms. As always with Joseph, these were comprehensive. They aimed at the total deconstruction of the Austrian Netherlands' autonomy. The new cadres of state administrators whom Joseph sent to take over were resented and seen as the advance guard of a bureaucratic despotism of which Joseph was the High Priest. General Murray, the Austrian commander only kept the peace by quietly repealing all Joseph's measures and generally disobeying his orders, a circumstance Joseph became swiftly aware of after his return to Vienna.

Furious that the Imperial will had been subverted in this way, Joseph replaced Murray with D'Alton, a martinet of the utmost inflexibility, and ordered that his decrees be applied with renewed vigour. As news of the spreading insurrection reached him, advice in favour of leniency was spurned. 'The flame of rebellion can only be extinguished by blood,' this so-called 'liberal' and 'enlightened' monarch said.[27]

The trigger for conflagration was one of the new 'reforms' Joseph had wished on the famous university town of Louvain. It involved the establishment of a 'General Seminary'. Hitherto Louvain had dedicated its institutions to the propagation of the Catholic faith. The university was now ordered to permit instruction in other religions. These 'impolitic innovations' were nothing less than incendiary in the context of the university's well-known devotion to the Holy See.

To rub salt into the wounds, Joseph ordered half of the university's professors to be sacked, replacing them with foreigners who were independent of the clergy. The result of all this was predictable: Louvain erupted in revolt. Bishops and clergy joined in the tumult and order was restored only with the help of the military. But this was merely the beginning. As the class of new administrators began to implement the new laws they were met with civil disobedience on a colossal scale. Tax collectors were shunned and cooperation with the elements of the bureaucracy was withdrawn as clergy and laity linked hands over a sea of Josephinian reforms.

In Louvain the foreign professors were driven from the university and the 'General Seminary' closed down. All Brabant assumed the national cockade and the military authorities were forced to make immediate concessions. Embarrassed as he was by the Turkish debacle, Joseph moved swiftly to lull the representatives of the Belgian states into a false sense of security so that he could strike at them once matters assumed a more favourable outcome in the east. Receiving the delegates, he expressed his utmost displeasure noting, after they had spoken, that 'the great dissatisfaction that I feel from all the late proceedings in my Belgic provinces cannot be effaced by a vain parade of words'.[28]

However, the Emperor insisted that he was willing to make concessions and would suspend some of his projects. This had the desired effect of persuading the states to compromise and the rebels to lay down their arms.

But Joseph had no intention of granting any meaningful concessions. Count Trautmannsdorff was ordered to the region as governor and commanded to remove gradually all disaffected persons from any positions of authority while supporting D'Alton's build-up of military resources. The 'General Seminary' was to be re-established, by force if necessary. Matters came to a head when this demand was presented to the Council of Brabant. In an attempt to overawe the rebels, D'Alton, who had been boasting of restoring order to the provinces in a few months, drew up his artillery outside their building and paraded his troops.

The council refused to be impressed by this display of force and as D'Alton's men became the focus of an ever more hostile crowd, they opened fire, killing six people. D'Alton ordered the council house to be occupied but at this moment Trautmannsdorff, seeing that a bloodbath was imminent, ordered the troops to stand down and said they had been deployed without his authorisation.

When news of these events reached Vienna, Joseph decorated the officer who had given the order to open fire and encouraged D'Alton to proceed with more vigorous measures. This D'Alton did at Louvain, where his troops slaughtered many of the students who resisted the re-establishment of the 'General Seminary' and expelled all refractory members of the university, including the Rector who was banished for three years. Through three Imperial edicts, Joseph formally dissolved the ancient constitution which for centuries had guaranteed the judicial rights of the provinces, and he instigated a bureaucratic reign of terror.

If Joseph had hoped to quell these provinces with his combination of military force, constitutional diktat and duplicity he was doomed to failure. In nearby Paris, events were setting an example for those whose rights were perceived to have been injured. The outbreak of the French Revolution in 1789 sent shock waves across Europe. In the nearby Netherlands the effect was especially electrifying. Less than five weeks after the constitution was suspended a full-scale armed revolt ensued. The Habsburg soldiers were attacked on the streets, the organs of the judiciary plundered and prisoners released. Violence broke out in every town and at Diest, a volatile crowd led by monks expelled all the magistrates and their infantry escort.

Meanwhile the Emperor was denounced and, under van der Noot, an armed force was trained up by former officers in the Imperial service who had served during the Seven Years War. One of these was van der Mersch, who led 3,000 men, mostly armed with pitchforks, to Turnhout. There he surprised the well-armed force of 28,000 under General Schroeder. To everyone's astonishment, he put them to rout, securing a victory that was promptly proclaimed a miracle by the accompanying monks. On a more practical level, the abbots of the provinces' richest monasteries now organised themselves to provide the finances necessary to secure arms.

With his numbers and resources increased by this initial success, van der Mersch sent a force to take Ghent and, with local help, it succeeded in capturing some artillery. Bruges and other towns now declared for the rebels while D'Alton and Trautmannsdorff pursued conflicting policies. Overwhelmed by events, D'Alton was forced to conclude a brief armistice, his troops so demoralised that mass desertions began to decimate his numbers. On 11 December D'Alton surrendered Brussels.

Thus, Joseph's last attempts to convert his multifaceted monarchy into a single administrative province ended in humiliation. He himself admitted he was a 'fanatic for the welfare of the state'. The armed forces were a pillar of that state and had to endure their own fair share of the Emperor's 'enlightened despotism'. At the same time the 'revolutionary era' in warfare that had already in America given its first intimations of trends to come had not in Austria's case created a 'revolutionary' army, save perhaps if we include the timely introduction of Jaeger units.

A few months after Joseph's death in 1790, peace with Turkey was signed at Sistowa. Meanwhile Brussels was retaken a year after it was surrendered without a shot being fired. England, Holland and Prussia, alarmed at the dramatic turn of events in Paris, had all withdrawn their support for the rebels. The new Emperor, Leopold II (1747–92), Joseph's younger brother, in contrast to his predecessor's autocratic temperament, was a pacifist and a genuine reformer, whose earlier government of Tuscany to this day is seen as a model of liberal administration. He lacked Joseph's all-consuming pride and sense of mission. He had inherited above all from his mother the gifts of moderation and moved swiftly to douse the flames which, as Joseph lay dying, seemed about to consume all of the 'Enlightened' monarch's domains. Joseph died a disappointed and broken man, an unforgettable example of the road to hell being paved with good intentions.

Leopold lacked Joseph's brilliance but also his fanaticism. He would reign for barely two years, but he ably resolved the crises that had clouded the last weeks of Joseph's life. True to his liberal principles, the revolution which had broken out in Paris met initially with Leopold's approval but he was not to live long enough to see the storm fully played out. That experience was to fall to Joseph's nephew Francis, Leopold's eldest son. Despite its initial lacklustre performance, the army would bear the brunt of this storm. Almost uniquely among the continental powers it did not collapse under the strain, and such resilience can be attributed to the Josephinian and Theresian reforms but above all to Leopold's ability to bring stability back to the Habsburg lands just as the entire Europen continent began to seethe.

PART 2

REVOLUTION AND REACTION

CHAPTER 8

The Army and the French Revolution

The army Joseph II had bequeathed was not as capable as that which he had inherited from his mother. Joseph's ceaseless meddling and obsession with state control had demoralised the army as much as it had all other walks of Austrian life. The army breathed a sigh of relief on Joseph's demise. The new Emperor, Leopold, appeared to usher in a period of domestic calm, free from foreign adventure. But one year before Joseph's death, Paris had erupted in revolution and, as Joseph had foreseen, it was unlikely that its ripples would not be felt in his empire.

The storm that broke in Paris in 1789 had long been predicted by Joseph II. His sister, after all, was Marie Antoinette. He was in a great hurry to reform every walk of Imperial life, to shield his empire from the impending explosion he knew was coming. It is ironic that Joseph's self-styled fanaticism for the welfare of the state stimulated revolt in his own provinces. Joseph meant well and he had impeccable Enlightenment credentials, but not even these could persuade Benjamin Franklin to meet him when the two coincided briefly in Paris. Joseph was a Habsburg autocrat and the staunch republican could not countenance a meeting, much to the former's regret.

Leopold II repairs the fabric

Joseph's successor Leopold lowered the temperature with his considerable understanding and intelligence. Shortly before his accession, Leopold wrote a heartfelt letter to his favourite sister, Marie-Christine, outlining his interpretation of that much-abused word 'sovereignty'.

> I believe that the sovereign, even one who has inherited his position is only the delegate and representative of his people for whom he exists; to whom

he must devote all his work and care. I believe that every country should have a legally defined relationship of contract established between the people and the sovereign which limits his power so that when the sovereign does not observe the law he actually forfeits his position (which is granted to him only under that condition) and it is no longer anyone's duty to obey him. . . .[1]

It would be Austria's tragedy that this model of an enlightened ruler would only reign for two years before succumbing to illness. But in those two brief years he achieved much, calming the empire which under his predecessor had bridled at so much indigestible reform. As regards the army, Leopold's reign offered a welcome respite of stability after the frenetic pace of change of the last ten years. Leopold devoted relatively little of his energy to military reform; earlier, in Tuscany, he had disbanded the army and navy. This neglect was benign. The Imperial Austrian army which was to face the Revolutionary forces of France was largely that bequeathed by Joseph. Over the following twenty-three years, these forces would wage no fewer than six wars against Revolutionary and Napoleonic France, a record unequalled by any other European state.

By the time of Leopold's death in 1792, the army consisted of 268,129 men, a formidable force but well below the peacetime establishment of 1787 when Austria had 304,628 men under arms. In organisation the army consisted of 70 line infantry regiments, 34 cavalry regiments (40,324 men) and 10 batteries of artillery which together with four further gun companies made up a force of some 13,560 artillerists.

Despite the reforms of Joseph aiming at greater uniformity, recruitment was still subject to certain inconsistencies. Thus Hungarians could not join 'German' (i.e. officered by German-speaking Austrians) cavalry regiments. In addition there were no corps or brigade structures. This would prove a great disadvantage in the coming conflict, where French military tactics began to evolve rapidly in a more dynamic and modern form as their 'People's Army' took shape.

Austrian cavalry tactics remained formalised in the eighteenth-century mould of outflanking infantry or acting as a reserve for pursuit or defence. Infantry, with the exception of the recently established Jaeger, continued also to be drilled along formal lines. Whatever these deficiencies, the Austrian army would fight in no fewer than 264 engagements from the Baltic to the Adriatic, from Zurich to the hills of Moravia over the coming years, and emerge as victor in 168 of them. The military historian of the period is fortunate in having an eyewitness account of the appearance of some of these troops penned by Goethe:

> There are three battalions of the Manfredini regiment stationed here . . . the men are all remarkably consistent in height and appearance mostly having small slanted eyes, long mouths and narrow brows. Their noses are short but not stub and have fine nostrils; their appearance is enriched by a countenance of understanding and the lively sprig of daily fresh oak-leaves which adorn their helmets. Their drill is swift and efficient . . . . they are Bohemians I think. . . .[2]

In fact the Manfredini regiment recruited mainly from Moravia, with some recruits drawn from Zamość in Austrian Galicia, but Goethe's prose illustrates well the flavour of the Austrian infantryman and is informative as Goethe goes on to describe the French soldiers who occupied Frankfurt after the Austrians withdrew:

> The French soldiers were the opposite of the Austrians. Where the Austrian uniforms were practical and simple, the French uniforms are luxurious and full of superfluous details. . . .

Not everyone agreed with Goethe. One contemporary Austrian officer by the name of Crone noted on reading Goethe's words: 'I am amazed that a Goethe could write this. The men in the Austrian regiment are so different especially the officers who come from all nations: French Belgian, Walloon, English, Luxemburg, Poles, Croats, Irish, Hungarians, Swedes, Italians etc.'[3]

Similar in countenance or not, this was the infantry that was about to face the fury of the revolutionary storms gathering across the European skyline. The Queen of France, Marie Antoinette, was Leopold's sister. Her arrest in 1792 and further indignities were deliberately calculated by the Jacobins to focus the attention of the populace on an external threat. Rumours of Austrian machinations were given wide credence as a carefully orchestrated campaign reminded the French people that their historic enemy was, and would always be, the House of Austria. When the revolutionary Brissot rose to address the French Assembly in the early weeks of 1792, his message was simple: 'The mask is fallen,' he said. 'Your real enemy is known . . . . it is the Habsburg Emperor . . . he, I repeat, he is your true enemy.'

The fateful decision was now taken to send an ultimatum to Vienna demanding that Austria 'live in peace' with France. Full satisfaction of this was to be given by 1 March if a state of war was to be avoided. Kaunitz's reply was dignified and moderate but the clamour for war was all that rose from the Assembly when it was read. Once again Brissot harangued the Assembly on the theme of Austrian interference. But before matters could develop any further, the Emperor Leopold died in his forty-fourth year.

The new Emperor Francis

Leopold's son, the new emperor Francis (1768–1835), was cut from very different cloth. It is the fate of the monarchical system to rely on the principle of primogeniture and at this moment of supreme need, had this principle been temporarily suspended, the crown might have passed to one of Francis's two highly gifted brothers, Charles or John. Both these men would become famous; the first as (after Napoleon), the most gifted military commander of his age, the second as the inheritor of Leopold's enlightened ideas of government and the value of local tradition in building a new relationship between its peoples and the dynasty.

In contrast to his intellectually gifted brothers, Francis II of the Holy Roman Empire (later to be Francis I of Austria) was reserved, distrustful and generally considered 'untalented'. At a time when everything around him was throbbing with the fervour, drama and adventure of the revolutionary age, Francis was conservative, understated, and undistinguished to the point of blandness. Entire systems were being challenged and destroyed. To east and west nations and the map of Europe were beginning to be remade. To these events Francis could never be indifferent but not for a moment did he view them in any other way than in terms of a mortal threat to his dynasty. His view of life and the world was totally unaffected by the zeal and breadth with which his tutors had taught him in that abundance of broad intellectual training which marked the late eighteenth-century upbringing of Habsburg princes.

But Francis was not without qualities. He was a survivor. Stoic, he certainly enjoyed that great Habsburg virtues of perseverance and courage in adversity. Like Maria Theresa he trusted his instincts, and his instincts (like hers) told him to be wary of the Enlightenment, modern philosophy, intellectual brilliance and, above all, nationalism. This Kaiser cultivated almost to extremes the weary cynicism and lethargic manner that was to become one of the hallmarks of the later high Austrian aristocracy in the century to come. After the crushing defeat at Austerlitz he sent a terse message to his wife noting with a hint of boredom, 'The battle has not gone well today.'

His love of simplicity and homeliness, the hallmarks of the Biedermeier age his reign of forty-five years encapsulated, disguised a tough, unyielding temperament. Beneath the cosy visits to the greenhouses at Schönbrunn where he loved to 'potter about' and his supposedly spontaneous delight in 'dropping in' on the kitchens to help make toffee and chocolate-dipped meringues there was a darker, more neurotic side. In the gloomy dungeons of his summer Wasserschloss of Laxenburg, a fake castle of faux-medieval splendour, complete with moat, on the outskirts of Vienna, the young Emperor erected a mordant amusement to while away moments of frustration. A life-size suit of armour complete with helmet and sword was carefully placed attached to strings that led to a pulley beneath a floorboard, whose surface was so arranged that if stamped upon firmly the suit of armour would suddenly spring to life briefly shaking and clanking its arms and sword.

This macabre device would afford the 'Bieder [cosy] Franz' some comfort as he paced these rooms in solitude. Austria's many defeats at the hands of France, the early deaths of each of his four wives, the marriage of his daughter to Napoleon after the defeat of 1809, the mental impairment of his son and heir; he bore all these vicissitudes with dignity and calm, perhaps partly as a beneficial outcome of this therapeutic divertissement in the Laxenburg dungeon.

Meanwhile, the ultimatum sent to Vienna expired and France, still nominally ruled by a King who was Francis's uncle, declared war on Austria. An alliance with Prussia negotiated by Leopold three weeks before his death now automatically came into force and a largely Prussian army under the Duke of Brunswick advanced on Paris. In a proclamation aimed at intimidating their opponents, the Prussians vowed, *in extremis*, to burn Paris to the ground and to put all their opponents to the sword. It was language unlikely to appeal to their audience. The French rallied to their colours with passionate outrage in an early example of the 'Levée en masse' which characterised the 'Nation in arms'. When it came to intimidation, the armies of France would show they needed no lessons from Berlin.

At Valmy some 40,000 Prussians were stopped in their tracks by a numerically inferior force, thanks largely to the skill of the French artillery. Goethe was on hand to witness the debacle and observed: 'we are all witnesses of the birth of a new era in the history of Europe'. In truth the Prussian army had not really recovered from the ravages of the Seven Years War and in organisation and leadership it was a shadow of the force it had once been. The renewal of Prussian arms would take almost another generation.

Though it was late in the campaigning season, the French commander, Dumouriez, now turned his attention to the Austrian Netherlands. At Jemappes on 6 November 1792, a small vastly outnumbered Austrian force under the Duke of Sachsen-Teschen, and with the Archduke Charles in his first baptism of fire commanding the right wing, was attacked in bold style by the French, fired up by their Prussian victory. The paucity of Austrian forces underscored the swiftness with which the French had seized the initiative. Despite its modest numbers, the Austrian army was far better led than the French and, though outnumbered nearly four to one, it fought heroically for six hours before falling back in disciplined order, inflicting heavy casualties on its opponents. Although 13,000 Austrians faced 43,000 French, they inflicted more than 2,000 casualties. Austrian fatalities were 304.[4]

The French euphoria over Jemappes was to be short-lived. Meanwhile, in a flush of excitement triggered by victory over the detested arch-enemy, the destructive energy of the Revolution reached new heights. In early 1793, Marie Antoinette's husband was executed on the scaffold of the guillotine. The murder of Louis XVI ignited a fire of revulsion and horror throughout Europe. Vienna realised the seriousness of the situation and mobilised to put a formidable force into the field to recover her position in the Netherlands. A few months later at Neerwinden, a still numerically inferior but well-equipped Austrian army under Coburg ejected the French from the Austrian Netherlands in a dazzling demonstration of what disciplined Austrian infantry could achieve. Faced with the same vigorous storming tactics the French had deployed at Jemappes, the Austrian infantry coolly received each onslaught with murderous volleys.

The defeat was crushing and Dumouriez, well aware what fate awaited him at the tender mercies of his Jacobin masters once the news of his defeat reached Paris, passed over to the ranks of the Austrians. Assisted by reinforcements from England under the Duke of York, they pressed forward towards Paris. At Famars, the insubordination and poor judgement of the Duke of York allowed his French opponents under Dumouriez's successor, Dampierre, to slip the noose that the Duke of Coburg was erecting. But the French were again defeated. It is one of the ironies of Austro-French relations that the French commander should bear the name of the Habsburg officer who had saved the dynasty generations earlier. Demoralised and indifferently led, Dampierre's army fell back, leaving the road from Valenciennes to Paris wide open.

The Emperor Francis made plans to travel to the front to encourage his victorious army. A Spanish army crossed the Pyrenees and began ravaging parts of southern France. Holland joined in. To the superficial observer, Revolutionary France appeared on the brink of defeat. But at that time France was Europe's superpower demographically. Her population had far outstripped that of her rivals in less than a generation. By 1792 the population of France was approaching 30 million and had risen by almost a third in barely a generation. Fuelled by the revolutionary fervour of the time, volunteers to defend France were not in short supply.

In October at Wattignies a two-day bloody encounter once again saw the Austrians inflict heavy casualties on their opponents but Coburg was forced to raise the Siege of Mauberge and the immediate Austrian threat to Paris was averted. Marie Antoinette had been kept a prisoner as a possible bargaining chip for negotiations with the Austrians and was now deemed expendable. The

Emperor Francis in any event was in no mood for negotiations even if his aunt's life was at stake. It was now Marie Antoinette's fate to follow in the steps of her husband. Her calm demeanour and dignified bearing on the scaffold impressed even her persecutors. She apologised to the executioner for inadvertently stepping on his foot. Huge black clouds drifted across the Paris skyline as she mounted the block; the crowd fell silent as the sun was suddenly hidden by a cloud. As the blade fell, there were no immediate cries of satisfaction. In death Marie Antoinette had shown she was a true child of the Great Empress.

The following spring at Tourcoing, an Anglo-Austrian army reinforced by Dutch troops was defeated by a gifted Frenchman by the name of Pichegru. A certain lethargy on the part of the Austrian commander, Clerfayt, combined with poor staff-work by the officers around the recently arrived Austrian Emperor, prevented the more energetic Archduke Charles and his troops reaching the battlefield in time.

A month later at Fleurus, poor staff-work again dogged a coalition army under Coburg. In fifteen hours of struggle, described by the later French Marshal Soult, then a young lieutenant, as 'the most desperate fighting I ever witnessed', the Austrian and Dutch troops, supported by the Duke of York, fought doggedly, inflicting once again immense casualties on their opponents. Compared to 208 allied fatalities, more than 5,000 Frenchmen were left dead or dying on the battlefield. But the French forces prevailed, thanks to General Jourdan's skill and tenacity in marshalling his often ill-disciplined troops. Jourdan was helped by the first known use of aerial surveillance, thanks to the intrepid balloonists of his newly formed French Aerostatic Corps. They manned L'Entreprenant giving Jourdan exact details of the movements of Coburg's five columns. (L'Entreprenant's sister balloon L'Intrépide was captured by Coburg at the Battle of Würzburg in 1796 and is on display in the Austrian Military Museum.) This new technology proved decisive for it meant that Jourdan knew precisely where to place his troops to take advantage of any weaknesses in the allies' cohesion.

Suddenly, as if the door France had been pushing against had swung open, Europe appeared unlocked for the armies of Revolutionary France. In panic the Dutch flooded the dykes but a freezing winter two months later merely converted the waters into solid ice highways for the invading army. The Dutch Republic was dissolved and Amsterdam occupied, while the Austrian Netherlands, that most tiresome possession of the Habsburgs, was irretrievably seized from Vienna and occupied by France. The Austrian army had fought well, on the whole, but it was facing a new style of warfare with techniques that were novel and unfamiliar.

Not even along the Rhine was there any respite. An encounter between an Austro-Prussian force and the French at Kaiserslautern in May pushed the French back but was inconclusive. A second, more sanguinary affair in which an outnumbered Austrian force beat off eight French attacks before finally succumbing to the ninth gave the French the momentum they needed to push for all German territory along the left bank of the Rhine. Coblenz and Cologne fell to the French in rapid succession. Holland withdrew from the conflict and a humbled Prussia concluded a separate peace. Not for the last time in the coming twenty years of war against France did Austria now stand alone on the Continent, though supported financially by England.

Remaking the art of war: Napoleon, Guibert and the Archduke Charles

The French renewed their offensive in 1796. Three armies converged to push the Austrians out of Germany and Italy and force Vienna to terms. While one of these made for Würzburg and Franconia, another returned to the Black Forest and Swabia. More significant was the third Revolutionary army. This made for Piedmont and northern Italy and was led by the 25-year-old son of a Corsican lawyer. His name, which the world and the Austrians in particular would come to know all too well, was Napoleon Buonaparte.

Napoleon's military genius has been much discussed. His outstanding qualities might be summarised as an instinct for strategy; an intellectual appreciation of the science of war, especially the power of intelligently deployed artillery; and an unparalleled ability to inspire his men. To these gifts could be added sheer good luck, the *coup d'oeil* of every great commander on the battlefield, and an energy almost bordering on the frenetic. It is less frequently mentioned that Napoleon, as a personality of the Enlightenment, was heavily influenced by the thoughts of leading military intellectuals, one of whom was Jacques Antoine Hippolyte, comte de Guibert.[5]

Guibert's treatise, *Essai general de tactique* on a 'new' way of waging war published in 1771 in Paris (and then ten years later in London) was discussed initially only by a very few military men but its ideas travelled across the Atlantic to America, where they were first put into practice towards the end of the American War of Independence. Guibert's treatise envisaged a 'citizens' army', intensely patriotic and capable of huge sacrifices to sustain its efforts. Napoleon and other revolutionary thinkers were attracted to this idea of the nation in arms. But this was not all. The second strand of Guibert's thinking was the concept of more mobile armies, unencumbered by trains and magazines but living off the land. This was the negation of the eighteenth-century concept of supply encampments provisioning armies, rather than the hapless civilian populace. This idea too held enormous appeal for Napoleon. Moreover, in the fertile plains of Lombardy he had the perfect landscape to try out these new tactics. As he would find later when he advanced into far less fertile Austria, nowhere perhaps furnished such a rich and plentiful supply of provisions for his army than Lombardy.

A new way of waging war was about to burst on to the unsuspecting generals of the anti-French coalition. That the Habsburg army was able to withstand these assaults would be largely due to the abilities and personality of the Emperor Francis's brother, the Archduke Charles.

In any other age, against any other opponent there can be no doubt that Charles would have been seen as the most gifted and outstanding military commander of his time. It was Charles's fate to be born into the era of Napoleon though it was Austria's good fortune to have such an able general at its disposal during this exceptionally challenging period. Where Francis was intellectually somnolent, Charles exuded ideas and theories. An epileptic, Charles was vigorous, handsome and courageous; his sensual features, strong nose, generous lips all pointed to a vivid personality. But for the accident of birth he might have proved the greatest revolutionary of them all. But as an Austrian officer and a Habsburg, his loyalty lay first and foremost to his House. Every military decision he took always had this unhesitating obedience as its subtext.

Until now we have only seen the Archduke in a cameo role during the Flanders campaign but as Napoleon laid siege to Mantua, the key to Austria's position in northern Italy, the emergency for Austria became extreme. The aged Austrian general Wurmser, an early member of one of the Josephinian lodges, had lost much of his Enlightenment fire. He was forced to march south to relieve the situation in Mantua, leaving the road to Vienna open to the armies of the Republic. Charles suddenly found himself given independent command north of the Alps.

In Italy, Napoleon experienced something remarkable for the leader of an anti-clerical supposedly 'godless' Republican army. The devoutly Catholic northern Italians, still smarting with rage from the sequestration and dissolution of hundreds of their monasteries inflicted upon them a few years earlier by Joseph II's 'reforms', rushed to welcome the invaders with open arms. Not only the progressive middle classes but also the peasantry saw Napoleon as a force for improvement even though his agenda was to demonstrate elements of aggressive secularisation. Napoleon's staggering ease in his march through Italy was the direct result of earlier Habsburg policies. The French were greeted as liberators despite the terror and excesses of the Revolution in Paris. The hapless Lombardy peasants were pathetically grateful to be delivered from the zealous rationalism of the late Josephismus with all its petty and pedantic bureaucratic impositions. Even though their enthusiasm dimmed, as the full effects of a starving army living off their land and stealing their art treasures became obvious, their support for the Austrians was never to return. In this matter at least, Joseph II had not 'failed' to do his work.

Another terrible scourge was to afflict the Austrians and the French alike: malaria. On 1 October 1796 Napoleon would write to the Directory in Paris noting that of his 18,000 casualties, 14,000 were sick on account of the swamp fevers prevalent around Mantua. By the time Mantua finally fell to the French, the garrison had lost no fewer than 10,000 men to malarial illnesses. These were unprecedented figures for losses arising from sickness in European warfare.

Having invested Mantua, Napoleon suddenly found the road to the south unblocked. The sorely stretched resources of the Republican war machine were to be replenished with the fine art and treasures of the quaking Italian provinces as they rushed to make peace with the French warlord. Even the Pope would hurry to pay the invaders 21 million francs and a hundred of his finest paintings to head off the threat of occupation.

While this dramatic military landscape dominated south of the Alps, to the north the Archduke Charles, two years younger than Napoleon, demonstrated in a series of brilliantly executed movements that the Habsburg armies were still a potent force. At Amberg, and then a little later at Würzburg, he routed Jourdan in a masterly display of tactical deception. Leaving a screen of 30,000 men across Jourdan's front, he rapidly marched 27,000 troops to fall upon the French general's rearguard with such violence that the entire army of the Meuse took to its heels and did not stop running until it reached the Lower Rhine several days later. Austrian casualties numbered barely 350 while the French lost more than 2,500 men. The French general Moreau and his army of the Rhine had hoped to take advantage of Charles's distraction, but Moreau soon had to abandon his efforts in Franconia and effect as rapid a retreat as possible to prevent the Archduke annihilating his forces.

The Archduke Charles would prove his mettle again and again in the coming years, though intrigues and jealousy prevented his being given the supreme command during the next coalition war. Charles's talents in the military field always made him the object of court resentment. Many mediocre officers insinuated that Charles's success was a threat to the Emperor who, lacking any great talents himself, resented the popularity and brilliance of his brother. He need not have worried. Intellectually and morally Charles was an outstanding personality. The later first 'conqueror' of Napoleon was in almost every way a figure out of the antique pantheon of heroes. His integrity and self-discipline saw off not only his brother's intrigues against him but even Napoleon's mischievous 'offer' of the Bohemian throne at Stammersdorf in 1805.[6]

Charles was also a formidable military reformer. His writings on military science, which even in the abridged version run to six volumes, reveal a remarkable synthesis of practical experience on the battlefield with the dictums of German philosophy and classical literature. Moreover, in his three-volume *Grundsätze der Strategie* (Foundations of Strategy) he developed a theory of war that is equal in every way to that of Clausewitz and is perhaps even superior to it in its inherent objectivity.[7]

Charles's ability to be completely objective as a critic of the art of war was vividly illustrated when the ponderous Viennese censors wanted to suppress an anonymously published volume of his work. The pedantic bureaucrat explained that the work could not be published because the unknown author had indulged in sharp criticism of the Archduke Charles's generalship!

Charles's victories at Amberg and Würzburg slammed the door Paris had opened and gave the Republic pause for thought. After the debacle at Amberg, Jourdan resigned his command. For Paris to conclude a suitable peace she had to menace Vienna. Checked in Germany, the Republic needed to take Austria's possession in Italy as a hostage in the bargaining ahead. Paris could only offer Vienna an armistice once events south of the Alps enabled her third army to threaten the Austrian heartlands. On the Italian front the Austrians, working at first with their Piedmontese allies, experienced a more challenging campaign. While a strong Austrian force under Beaulieu moved towards the French in front of Genoa, another force began to gather around Mantua, the key Austrian strongpoint in Lombardy. This formidable Austrian fortress was the most important of the bridgeheads that allowed Austria to control Lombardy.

The Austrian forces in Lombardy were, as we have seen, commanded by Field Marshal Count Wurmser, then in his 74th year. After his successes against the French at Mannheim, supporting the Archduke Charles, he was expected to make light work of the French Armée d'Italie. His name was associated then with military valour, not the incompetence with which it was later connected, perhaps unfairly.

Austrian setbacks in Italy

Austria's forces in Italy consisted of three disparate elements. First, there were the remnants of the Italian-based troops whose morale was low after days of enforced marches keeping up with a far more energetic enemy. Then there were the grenadier battalions, together with Jaeger and other infantry units, mostly crack troops that Wurmser had brought with him from the Rhine. To these could be added a Freikorps under Gyulai. This unit included several Grenzer units under a tough Croat called Vukassovich.

These forces were supplemented by the third element: units that had taken part in the recent and bloodless Third Partition of Poland and had absolutely no experience of warfare at all but had marched from Galicia far north of the Carpathians. Because the Italian marshy terrain was considered unsuitable for cavalry, Wurmser had only one regiment of lancers and a few squadrons of hussars. Thus the traditionally superior arm of the Austrian war machine was not to play a significant role in the struggles ahead. Not only were many of the troops inexperienced, but the quality of some of the officers was mixed. The years of Josephinian change had exacted a toll. The new political climate also affected morale. As one officer wrote at the time:

> The infantry officers especially argue rather a lot, are politicised and give vent to improper and reprehensible views in front of the men. The generals set the example. From where does this come? Well in part from our misfortunes but above all from the poor selection of officers; too many soldiers of fortune, over-promoted N.C.O.s. . . . Moreover the ruinous system of promotion by seniority means we do not have any generals and few colonels of ability . . . . this stifles talent, discourages merit and removes all boldness. . . . We do not have anyone who is inventive among our highest in rank.[8]

The campaign in Italy began on Sunday 10 April 1796 with General Beaulieu mobilising two columns to drive the French from Genoa where Napoleon was engaging Austria's allies, the Piedmontese. Beaulieu's attack was poorly coordinated and the absence of cavalry blinded the Austrian High Command to what their opponents were doing. The Austrian grenadiers of Argenteau's column marched three times up the redan at Monte Negino only to fail to dislodge the French. The Croat Grenzer troops then suffered heavy casualties at the same point. After a day of this, Argenteau had to accept that his men could not storm the position. The failed Austrian offensive now afforded Napoleon a chance to concentrate his forces in Carcare where the link between Beaulieu's two columns was at its weakest.

As Napoleon's forces arrived, Argenteau immediately ordered the retreat, to avoid being surrounded. But his rearguard came under heavy attack and at Castelazzo a battalion of Austrian infantry, moving with parade ground precision was virtually annihilated by superior numbers of skirmishing light infantry. Two other battalions retreating down the valley of Montenotte were almost cut to pieces by these new mobile tactics of their opponents. On the nearby hill of Monte Pra the infantry regiment Alvinczi – under Oberst Adorian and Oberst Nesslinger who displayed great 'composure and determination' – was reduced to one company. The French threatened the nearby village of Dego, the key to Beaulieu's two columns' lines of communications.

Austrian casualties were over a thousand: the official Austrian figures give 162 killed and 114 wounded but would appear to have been understated, though they add that 409 were missing. Given the violence of the fighting experienced by certain units, it seems likely that about 1,000 casualties, including prisoners, was the tally for the Austrians that day. Argenteau himself wrote to Beaulieu after the battle: 'I was almost completely destroyed . . . my losses are extremely great.'[9]

As Argenteau wrote in his report to Beaulieu, the small hamlet of Dego was 'now in the greatest danger'. In the village, the Austrian commander Rukavina sent an urgent message to Argenteau: 'In the name of God come immediately with your troops.' But Argenteau was in no condition to send support and, with rather typical diffidence, he explained to Rukavina that it was best for the troops in Dego to await orders.

The mood in the French camp was more buoyant but, for once, Napoleon did not move against Dego with his customary energy. A force of about 1,500 Austrian soldiers and Piedmontese grenadiers (*Granatieri di Sardegna*) retreated to the fortress of Cosseria where, on being called to surrender, the Sardinian colonel Del Carretto famously told the French envoy: 'Know that here are Grenadiers of Sardinia, and the Grenadiers of Sardinia never surrender'. Three murderous assaults were repulsed and as ammunition ran low the defenders hurled rocks and stones at their attackers. Augereau, the French commander was seen sitting with his head in his hands muttering: 'This blasted castle will send us back to the Riviera.'[10]

Meanwhile Argenteau ordered various units to support Dego but his orders were not models of clarity and his instructions to Vukassovich contained the phrase 'create a diversion towards Dego tomorrow morning'. The Croat colonel received the message around six in the morning and assumed that as he was eight hours' march from Dego, the order referred to the following morning. He therefore set off with no particular urgency.

Meanwhile, Cosseria had finally surrendered and nothing stood in the way of a final French assault on Dego. This hamlet of some 300 houses had been fortified as well as the Austrian units holding it could manage. Eighteen field guns were placed at strategic positions. Rukavina, in some pain from a wound, chose to retire and leave the defence in the hands of a young Piedmontese officer by the name of Avogadro who, having arrived only the day before, had not the faintest knowledge of either the area or the forces at his disposal. The battle raged all day and the defenders gave a good account of themselves until, after nearly twelve hours of fighting, sheer weight of numbers forced the Austrians to retreat. As the French finally managed to close, the defenders took to their heels. A group of Croats holed up in the castle ransacking the wine cellars was quickly overpowered but the French followed their example. A long night of pillage began as discipline broke down. Houses were looted and food and drink hastily absorbed as the mixed-up French units ran amok, unresponsive to their officers. As a thick fog and torrential rain such as only northern Italy in April can experience took hold, the victorious troops slept off their excesses in a drunken reverie, failing to post either sentries or lookouts.

It was just before daybreak that the dilatory Vukassovich and his Habsburg troops finally appeared. His 3,000 men, mostly Grenzers but supported by two battalions of regular infantry, fell on the sleeping village and began slaughtering every Frenchman they could find. Vukassovich's Croats from the Carlstadt provinces of the Military Frontier had possibly heard from their fathers tales of Hochkirch and they knew exactly what to do. For three hours with pistol, knives and bayonets Vukassovich's men did their work, using the cover of the weather to wreak havoc with stealth and surprise.

Hundreds surrendered rather than face certain death and by ten o'clock the majority of the French commanders were dead or wounded and most of the French troops were in full tilt retreat. By midday the French had abandoned the village, and the recently captured Austrian guns were now turned against their fleeing numbers. Panic spread down the lines and the French commander, Masséna, in bed with a beautiful Italian mistress at an inn on the road less than a mile away, was forced to run out of the house in nothing more than his nightshirt.

Masséna could not arrange a renewed assault until early in the afternoon and the French had to fight all over again for Dego. For ten hours Vukassovich's men fought on, but the reinforcements which alone could have stabilised the Austrian line failed to appear. By 6 p.m., the Austrian position was deteriorating fast; Vukassovich's men had been either fighting or marching without break for nearly twenty hours. It was time to leave. With their customary skill, the Croats withdrew as silently as they had arrived, covered by the Grenadiers, who retreated in good order leaving their opponents too exhausted to pursue. Although the French promptly returned to looting, this time they posted sentries. The men of the Military Frontier had left their visiting card and it would be some time before Napoleon was confident that the Austrians were really departing.

By these actions Napoleon had divided the Austrians from their Piedmontese allies. He turned swiftly to eliminate the weaker of his foes, the Piedmontese. This was accomplished during the ensuing twelve days in a series of sharp actions. Cuneo and Alessandria, two fortresses once thought impregnable, fell like ripe fruit into French hands, and the King of Piedmont sued for peace. Austria was now alone.

On 28 April Napoleon informed the Directoire:

> Tomorrow I shall march against Beaulieu. I shall force him to recross the Po. I shall cross it immediately afterwards. I shall take the whole of Lombardy and before a month is over I hope to be in the mountains of the Tyrol, meet the army of the Rhine and in cooperation take the war into Bavaria.[11]

The Directoire however was not a reactive institution and in the coming weeks it would give their 'Citizen General' detailed instructions on how he was to proceed and, in particular, his political as well as military objectives.

Here Napoleon faced a contradiction that would become more marked as the campaign proceeded. On the one hand, his martial instincts married to the concepts of Guibert envisaged the destruction of the Austrian army in Lombardy and the securing of that rich land to hold as a hostage in future negotiations. On the other hand, the ideas of the Revolution brought in their wake a certain dynamic which was developing its own momentum. There would be no bargaining chip if the hostage were so consumed by revolution that it was ablaze and wrecked.

As the campaign proceeded this challenge began to feature more and more in the commander's mind. Moreover, there was the religious dimension to the conflict as well. The Austrian army was the defender not only of the *Ancien Régime* but also inevitably of the values of one of its major props: the rights and privileges of the clergy and the Catholic Church. Their standards still displayed the Madonna and their soldiers were arguably the guardians of the Catholic faith. Along the Rhine it was the objective of the Directoire to cement the ideas of the Revolution by a programme of radical secularisation. This programme would sweep away the century-old rights and privileges of the Church and utterly transform the Prince-Bishopric states, disenfranchising their sovereigns and stripping them of their wealth.

In a letter to Napoleon from the Directoire intoxicated by his success and after their meeting on 3 February, the case against the Catholic Church was explicit.[12]

> Citizen General!
>
>   In considering the obstacles that stand in the way of the consolidation of the French Constitution, the Executive Directoire has come to the

conclusion that the Roman religion is the one of which the enemies of freedom can for a long time to come make the most dangerous use. You are too intelligent, Citizen General, not to have realised, just as we have, that the Roman religion will always be an irreconcilable enemy of the Republic, firstly by its very essence and secondly because its ministers and votaries will never forgive the Revolution for attacking its wealth and the influence of its ministers as well as combating the beliefs and habits of its followers.

There is one thing however probably no less essential for attaining this end, and that is the destruction if possible of the centre of the unity of the Roman Church. ... The Directoire Executive therefore asks you to do everything possible ... to destroy the Papal government.[13]

The Austrian military reverses conceal the subtlety of Thugut's diplomacy

Thus Austria was fighting for more than just issues of territorial integrity. Indeed, as a solid and dynamic empire long made up of many far from cohesive provinces, the Habsburg Empire could easily afford to affect an Olympian detachment towards its lands. Duchies, voivods, cities all came and went in the interests of the dynasty. The question for Austrian statesmen was, as always, to examine what possibilities the fluidity of the situation offered to the House of Austria. Military defeats did not necessarily mean nemesis or even amputation. The subtlety of Austrian policy was perhaps never more amply demonstrated than in its reaction to the resounding defeats her armies suffered.

It is clear from the Austrian Foreign Minister Baron Thugut's instructions to Gherardini, his minister in Piedmont, that from the spring of 1796 Austria was secretly preparing the ground for an exchange of territories when the day came to make peace with Paris. This was done with complete though concealed indifference to her sole remaining ally, Britain. Thugut had studied his craft at the feet of Kaunitz and he knew that allies were often unreliable. They were either 'too petulant (Britain), too greedy (Prussia) too volatile (Russia), too faint hearted (the German and Italian states) or too weak (Spain) to help Austria'.[14] Thugut subscribed to the view that, for the dynasty's survival in such turbulent times, lines of communication had to be tightened and geographical anomalies removed. The Austrian Lowlands, which had been preserved under Habsburg rule at the expense of so much blood and treasure, would have to be given up, as would perhaps even Lombardy, another territory which was relatively remote from the Habsburg centre.

Johann Amadeus de Paula Thugut (1736–1818), though considered by his enemies a terrible *intrigant* (plotter), was a remarkable man. The son of a lowly military official – following some reports, he was even an orphan and had been purchased from a convent – Thugut had according to general if unsubstantiated wisdom captivated Maria Theresa when he was a child, on being asked to row her across the Danube. Maria Theresa with her instinctive eye for young male intelligence was so impressed by the bright-eyed boy that she paid for him to study at her recently opened Imperial School of Oriental Studies where his hard-working brilliance soon led to his being posted as dragoman to the embassy in Constantinople. In fact, like so many great servants of the dynasty before him, Thugut (or Thuegutt, as he was christened in Linz) was another outstanding product of a Jesuit education. As the first Director of the Imperial School of Oriental Studies was also a Jesuit his potential was not only recognised but developed.

Thugut like many upon whom greatness is thrust had his fair share of vices. He was proud, secretive and all too aware that he was not of the aristocratic establishment that surrounded him. Whatever the origins of his Imperial preferment, one thing was clear: he had begun his studies as a *Bettelstudent* (beggar-student). Though not given to extravagance, he nevertheless needed funds, and the need for money was amply met by the French secret service, which on the direct instructions of Louis XV paid him an annual pension of several million francs. In the more intimate society of eighteenth-century Europe such 'treachery', as no doubt a later generation would call it, could be tolerated if it brought benefits. France and Austria, after all, had allied with the aim of bringing about the marriage of Marie Antoinette to the future Louis XVI. Thugut's remuneration by his French contacts might have been viewed as giving Vienna insights into Louis XVI's court as reconciliation continued. The use of the highly placed agent who works for both sides is of course the staple of modern espionage fiction. In any event Thugut's effortless rise from virtually penniless boatboy to Foreign Minister of the most powerful court in Europe refutes the myth that social mobility is an exclusively modern phenomenon.[15]

Later, Thugut's many enemies were quick to point to his failings. His successor after 1801, Metternich, noted with aristocratic disdain that Thugut was never destined for high office, pointing out in a private paper: 'The ministry of Baron Thugut shows only a succession of blunders and false calculations.'[16] But Thugut, like many diplomats, saw opportunities in military campaigns, and made his preparations accordingly.

On crossing the Po, Napoleon moved rapidly to reduce, once and for all, Mantua, the key to and symbol of Austrian authority in Lombardy. At the end of July the Austrian relief army of Wurmser began to move. It was divided into three corps. On the right, General Quasdanovich marched round the northern end of Lake Garda with 20,000 men and, skirting the western edge, descended on Salo and Brescia. The rest of the army was divided into two columns. One, under Wurmser, was to march along the right of the Adige to attack the positions at Montebaldo while the second, under Davidovič, was to descend along the left bank of the Adige and, passing through Ala, to arrive in front of Verona.

Wurmser, by dividing his troops, was engaging in an over-elaborate eighteenth-century style of warfare. In any other battle of that century the two armies opposed to each other would have engaged in lengthy manoeuvres, giving battle from time to time in engagements of varying duration and different degrees of violence but rarely decisive while their governments continued to negotiate. Napoleon had no time for this. Startled by the compliance of the Italians it took him some time to realise that they would not join in support of their Austrian masters if he struck a decisive blow quickly. Above all, his army needed quick success if it were to retain morale. Thus the clash between *Ancien Régime* and Revolution was also the clash of two different military mindsets moving at entirely different tempi. Wurmser, understandably for a man of his age, had concocted a complex and conventional scheme that might have worked against lesser French generals. Against Napoleon it was doomed.

It was also questionable whether Mantua at this stage needed reinforcement. Her manpower had been depleted by malaria from the surrounding marshes and lakes which were the perfect breeding ground for the disease's vector. But it had at this stage sufficient supplies to hold out and an arsenal of 500 pieces of artillery. Thanks to its control of water levels in the lakes through various locks, the defenders could only be attacked along a very narrow front. At this stage Napoleon had no siege artillery.

On 5 August, after a number of inconclusive engagements, Wurmser's forces finally gathered and engaged Napoleon on the last hills near Castiglione which sloped down from the Garda lake to the Po valley. In a brilliantly executed feint, Napoleon forced the Austrians to weaken their right wing to strengthen their centre. Masséna commanding the French left saw the prize and attacked the Austrian flank under Davidovič with such vigour that Wurmser was almost forced to fall back in utter disorder. Speed had doubled the force of mass; this first application of the Guibert doctrine almost annihilated the Austrians.

An enterprising young Austrian officer, Colonel Weidenfeld, at the head of 3,000 troops coming up from Peschiera, immediately saw what was happening and, leading his men from the front, energetically attacked Masséna in the flank, disordering his attack and allowing Davidovič – who by then had had two horses shot from beneath him – to withdraw in reasonably good order. Weidenfeld was awarded the Maria Theresa Order for his bravery in preventing 'total disorder' and allowing Davidovič to make his retreat safely to Valeggio.[17]

Three more attempts were made by the Austrians to relieve Mantua and each furnished Napoleon with a glorious new victory to his name. Only the third attempt under Alvinczi, another long-in-the-tooth general, who had replaced Wurmser on the latter's decision to join the garrison at Mantua, gave Napoleon any pause for thought – first at Calliano where Davidovič's corps led by Grenzer troops routed Vaubois and then at Caldiero, arguably Napoleon's first defeat. Here Alvinczi's advance on Verona from the east was coordinated with Davidovič's progress from Trient, and a strong force by Masséna and Augereau was held by one Austrian army until another could come up to crush them. The Austrian infantry fought well and only the arrival of darkness saved the French from a serious defeat.

Bassano, Arcole and Rivoli made the reputation of Napoleon as a military commander even if Caldiero underscored the fact that it was far from over. For an empire as solid as Austria's, even the defeat at Rivoli was but a pinprick. At times indeed the Austrians gave such a good account of themselves that morale in the French army sank to considerable depths. After Caldiero, Napoleon fully expected his mauled troops to be slaughtered the following day but Austrian passivity, not for the last time, saved him. Again, on the eve of Arcole, Napoleon's brother wrote to his family saying, 'We all expect the morrow to bring defeat.'[18]

Such despair underlines the fact that while the War of the First Coalition has come down to us as an unbroken string of magnificent French victories, its relatively brief and violent course was slightly more mixed. Napoleon's generals, Masséna and Augereau both experienced the tenacity of the Austrians and it is not clear that had the French forces been left entirely to the command of these men, they would have won any of the battles that were fought.

But Napoleon used tactics that involved both greater movement and a break with the old eighteenth-century tradition of engagement by manoeuvre. At Castiglione, the Austrians were especially discomforted by their opponent's bold use of artillery. In this case a 12-gun battery under Marmont was rolled close to the Austrian flank on the Monte Medolano and fired with deadly effect for twenty minutes, allowing two battalions of French grenadiers to storm the hill, the key to the Austrian left wing. Such rapid and effective close coordination of artillery and infantry was unprecedented.

Similarly, with each day that passed after Caldiero and without the Austrians making any offensive move, Napoleon realised that retreat was what his opponents expected of him. But if he did what was *not* expected of him, a counter-stroke might prevent the opposing forces gathered against him from combining to destroy him. Meanwhile, the Austrian High Command took it for granted that if there were no French retreat, their enemy would stay put and then fight a defensive battle against the Austrians' superior numbers.

Only Napoleon perhaps could have found the way out of this extreme situation. He rejected all thought of retreating to the Adda river behind him and as the Austrians continued to fail to follow up their victory his contempt for his opponents grew. He rushed his troops to menace the Austrian lines of communications at precisely the place where the road back to the Alps was at its most narrow and vulnerable, Arcole. An attack here, at this vital nerve point, was bound to provoke a reaction.

The key was the bridge over the Adige and for two days the Austrians clung on to it until under cover of darkness it finally fell to French light infantry who braved the shallow waters to attack the Austrians from the flanks. When a small detachment of French cavalry was sent to find a crossing and menace the Austrian troops its trumpeters sounded its bugles so loudly near the Austrian rear that absolute panic set in and Alvinczi withdrew, forcing Davidovič to match his withdrawal for fear of being abandoned to fight Napoleon alone.

Mantua falls

Seven weeks later in the cold January moonlight, Napoleon frustrated the fourth and final Austrian attempt to relieve Mantua. Approaching Verona again from Trient, Alvinczi drove back a French force under Joubert stationed between Rivoli and La Corona, causing panic among Napoleon's subordinates, who were about to give orders to retire. Arriving at two in the morning, under a gleaming moon, Napoleon countermanded the order and repositioned his troops.

When the action resumed shortly after daybreak, Joubert had been reinforced by Masséna with some artillery. The initial Austrian attacks were repulsed but eventually a spirited attack by some Hungarian grenadiers began to turn Masséna's west flank.

Meanwhile Quasdanovič was making good progress against Joubert, and Napoleon moved up some artillery swiftly to steady the defence. This was to prove decisive. Firing canister at close range, the French gunners brought Quasdanovič's attack to a halt. A lucky artillery shell hit the Austrian ammunition wagons. On the other flank, the Austrians misjudged their timing and came up against withering crossfire and, after some desperate fighting, surrendered.

By 5 p.m. that afternoon the Battle of Rivoli for the Austrians was lost. A further day of fighting against an inferior Austrian force under Provera which almost reached Mantua resulted in a further Austrian defeat at La Favorita and the capture of La Corona. Alvinczi retreated towards Trient, having lost in two days of fighting half his men, mostly as prisoners. The debacle, truly astounding by the standards of the time, made what followed three weeks later inevitable: the surrender of Mantua after its eight-month ordeal. These events not only sealed Napoleon's reputation as the most feared general of the age, but freed him to menace the Austrian heartlands.

Rather than risk their lines of communication with Tyrol being cut, the Austrians had no choice but to fall back while the French pressed rapidly into the Habsburg crown lands. Mantua had surrendered on 2 February and, although Wurmser was allowed all the honours of war, he died a broken man a few months later. Together with his staff and all officers of field rank, the commander was permitted a 600-strong escort back to the Austrian lines. By far the greatest part of his garrison had succumbed to malaria and this more than anything had made the fortress untenable. Some 15,000 prisoners and 60 captured regimental colours were escorted back to Paris by the French. But Napoleon had advanced too rapidly after Rivoli, impelled as much by political as by military considerations.

He was keen to leave Italy because he sensed growing civil unrest. It was important to have an agreement with Vienna before the ideas of *fraternité* and *egalité* set the whole of Lombardy alight, destroying the most important bargaining chip he had. At the Tagliamento river, the Archduke Charles, who had been rushed south on news of Mantua's fall, organised a strong defence which gave the shattered remains of the Austrian army time to retreat in good order, thus preserving something for future campaigns closer to home.

As Napoleon raced towards the Austrian capital, his scouts penetrated as far as the Semmering Pass, which on a clear day overlooked the Viennese plain. But his lines of communication became more and more precarious. Styria was not fertile Lombardy and his army's supplies were dwindling. Moreover, Austria had many armies, and Napoleon had so dangerously over-extended himself that a determined aggressive action might have finished his career prematurely. Vienna had other plans. History generally accepts that after four defeats and the final surrender of Mantua, the Emperor Francis wanted peace to recover at least something of his composure after the whirl-wind of the last ten months so, in 1797, preliminaries were signed in the remote Styrian mining town of Leoben.

The Vienna court's policies were in fact more calculated. Thugut, as we have seen, was a passionate believer that for Austria to survive in the time of revolution its domains would have to be more cohesive. Appendages such as Lombardy and the Austrian Netherlands contained the risk of Imperial over-extension and could not be defended with the same ease as territory that was contiguous. Why not reach an accommodation with Revolutionary Paris and surrender the remote Netherlands and even Lombardy in return for territories closer to home? Chief of these was the Republic of Venice, one of Italy's richest and most fertile regions. Cohesion would mean that the struggle – and Thugut was under no illusions as to the inevitability of this – could be renewed under more favourable conditions.

Thugut could not openly suggest this because Austria's ally and army paymaster, England, might object. Venice and her domains along the Adriatic controlled one of England's routes to the east. As Napoleon came closer to Vienna a parallel set of negotiations began between Thugut and Paris. To the outside world Austria, humbled and humiliated, would be forced to accept the crushing dictates of a military superpower. For a few individuals in Paris and Vienna, the story was more complex. Austria would emerge stronger rather than weaker from all this. Such a deal could only be struck if the world accepted that Vienna had been humbled by the military genius of Napoleon and forced to surrender her territories. This would neutralise England's potential opposition by stressing Vienna's helplessness and by offering the Directoire the prestige of having brought her most detested foe to her knees and, even more importantly, by having won the important concession of Revolutionary France being a legitimate partner in negotiations.

Reconfiguring the Habsburg monarchy

In reality, Thugut was keen to reconfigure his Imperial master's inheritance to take advantage of geographical reality. The Court of Vienna and the Directoire came to an understanding to eliminate Venice and to make the world believe that the peace, about to be concluded at the expense of Venice, had been dictated to the monarchy of the Habsburgs by the Revolution.

The most illustrious of the European dynasties had presented the Revolution with a much-needed if spurious trophy. Moreover, Buonaparte was rescued from the abyss into which he had fallen when pursuing the Archduke Charles only by extraordinary circumstances created by the men who were in on the secret of the 'intrigue which brought together the Vienna Cabinet and the Paris Directory'.[19] Thugut had earned his French pension as well as his Austrian one.

At the preliminaries at Leoben, Vienna surrendered the Austrian Netherlands which had cost so much blood throughout the previous century and also Lombardy, with the city of Milan. In return, the century-old Republic of Venice which had been occupied by Napoleon was abolished and granted, with her eastern territories of Istria and Dalmatia, to Vienna. The remodelling of the map of Europe had begun, but this partition of northern Italy between France and Austria was one from which only Austria would benefit.

With the annexation of Venetia, Austria would extend from the Danube to the Po, dominating both sides of the Alps, a huge and formidable entrenched camp. France on the other hand would have in Italy, outside her natural frontiers, an erratic and sporadic republic to protect. The monstrous octopus of Italian anarchy clung to Napoleon, compelling his return. Fits of revolutionary fury were breaking out everywhere under various guises: an insurrection in Venice; incessant disturbances in Lombardy; a permanent state of riot in Genoa and Piedmont; Naples and the Papal States in a state of extreme agitation.

Thugut took advantage of all these distractions to prepare his diplomatic coup. He dealt carefully with London's increasingly frantic enquiries, disingenuously instructing his Ambassador in London to tell the British government that Vienna was resisting all French attempts at Leoben to break the Austro-British alliance. At no time did Thugut authorise his Ambassador to communicate any of the preliminaries to the English government. The Ambassador was to stress that London could be assured that none of the preliminaries would be allowed to contain 'any clause which might bring about in the future a dissolution of our alliance with Great Britain'.[20]

To add to London's frustration, Thugut instructed his envoy to inform the British government that if Austria did not succeed in concluding peace, England must realise the necessity of paying more abundant and more regular subsidies to Austria. Nothing demonstrates more dazzlingly the brilliance of Thugut's Ottoman training as a humble dragoman in Constantinople a generation earlier than the way in which he ran rings around his master's opponents and outwitted Austria's most powerful ally.

Napoleon had not conquered Austria; he had only induced her to discuss a partition of territories much more favourable to Austria than France but these truths could never be admitted by either the Directoire or Napoleon. The humbling of Austria, the great victory at Rivoli, the battles won in the months earlier, the fall of Mantua: all an adventure? Napoleon had to remain in the opinion of the world the conqueror of Italy even while Italy was escaping from him on all fronts. He had to remain the vanquisher of Austria even while he was about to double her power. The Habsburg army had collaborated in all this. It remained a powerful and unvanquished force and as such cast a dark cloud over French options.

Leoben opened a period of five months of negotiations punctuated by various parts of northern Italy exploding to keep Napoleon distracted. The concessions from the French side grew: islands in the Adriatic; the rich and strategically importantly placed Prince-Bishopric of Salzburg; another ecclesiastical jewel, Passau. Still Thugut stayed his hand. He had to extract as much as he could to strengthen Austria for the next round. There could be no question of Vienna disarming. On the contrary, Austria must rearm because, as

Thugut saw more clearly than his allies, Revolutionary France was, even in the eyes of this far from religious man, an almost satanic creation. It would require all the resources of the Habsburgs to withstand its demonic energy. Napoleon had proved by his policies and warfare without rules in Italy that he was addicted to an almost diabolical lust for destruction and disorder. England, demoralised by news of the preliminaries, was suffering from one of her fits of recurrent weakness, and sought peace with Paris. If Austria was to continue the struggle alone it must emerge as strong as possible from any treaty to be signed.

When England finally signalled it would conclude a separate peace with Paris, Thugut, aware that the alliance hung by a thread, knew he too must conclude a definitive peace. By now reality had briefly descended on the Directoire who were waking up to the full extent of Napoleon's concessions. They ordered the preliminaries to be changed. The talks moved to Friuli, where Napoleon was ordered to obtain all he had renounced at Leoben. But if he had failed at the gates of Vienna a few months earlier, how could he possibly prevail now? The Austrian army had not been destroyed. True to its traditions it remained a chip on Thugut's bargaining table. The Treaty of Campo Formio was signed in the splendid Villa Manin at Passeriano in 1797.

Thanks to this treaty, Austria would remain in Venice for two generations, enjoy the benefits of the most formidable and defensible harbour in the eastern Mediterranean, Cattaro, until 1918, and, even today, in the early years of the twenty-first century, she retains Salzburg. Vienna complained that she was the victim of force but her adversary had allowed her to seize territories that made her the most powerful factor on the continent of Europe. Well might a later writer ask: 'Where was force and where was weakness? Who was the victor and who was the vanquished?'[21]

The Peace of Campo Formio of 1797 was, as Thugut predicted, to be but a brief interlude in the era of conflict that was to blight Europe over the coming years. Thugut knew that the Austrian army and Austrian finances needed a breathing space. The disastrous Turkish wars and then the campaigns in the Lowlands, let alone the huge efforts of the last eighteen months against Napoleon, required funding. The treasury needed replenishing and the army needed rebuilding.

The army takes stock: The 1798 *Adjustierungsvorschrift*

For the Austrian army it was indeed a moment to reflect on what had gone wrong in Italy and which reforms of tactics were now necessary. The practices of Guibert, the callous breaking of the rules of 'civilised' warfare, required a response. The Archduke Charles began to apply his considerable intellectual talents to thinking about new strategies to counter the innovative techniques of warfare used by the armies of Revolutionary France, now rapidly increased by the Levée en masse.

More formally, the Emperor and the ever-byzantine Aulic Council (Hofkriegsrat) focused on 'essentials'. That meant first and foremost adapting the army's appearance to the new era. The *Adjustierungsvorschrift 1798* is a formidable document. Born in the aftermath of Napoleon's victories in Italy and the surrender of Mantua, it is a clear attempt to breathe new life into an army fighting a modern war with an antique mentality.

The language alone was remarkable. Given that it bore the Imperial imprimatur it offered neither subtlety nor nuance in its condemnation of sloppy practices which by implication had cost the Imperial House so much blood and treasure in the fertile lands of the Po valley. The document was designed to shake the army out of its complacency and it brooked no argument.

For example the tendency of officers to wear items of civilian dress was described as a 'dangerous delusion' and a practice that not only 'did not father a military spirit' but was to be systematically 'stamped out' (*ausgerottet*). All luxury was to be eschewed and generals were not to appear in front of their men without their coats 'fully buttoned'. Wigs were considered especially egregious and on these, along with the precise profile of officers' porte-epée sword knots, the appropriate dimensions of command sticks and the amount of hair permissible under headdress, the new regulations were rigorous in attempting to impose a strict uniformity.

Visually the most significant development of the new uniform regulations was the phasing out of the old casquet headdress with its raised front (soon to be embraced and improved by the British army) in favour of a more impressive classical Roman-style helmet with a black and yellow crest. The crest was made of wool for other ranks and silk for the officers. Field and staff officers were to be equipped with helmets whose crests were made of a more luxurious 'unturned' silk.

The helmet, which was to be an imposing six-and-a-half *Zoll* high (16 inches), fitted the Josephinian legacy of relentless crusade towards total uniformity. It was to be worn by cavalry and infantry, and even Jaeger units, alike. Its front was adorned with a brass plate bearing the Imperial cipher. Ironically, this headdress would constitute one of the most expensive items of attire in the history of the Austrian army and would within ten years be replaced by a cheaper bell-topped shako.

While these regulations were implemented, Austria not only rearmed, she attempted to tie the dynasty to the army more closely. The Archduke Charles and his brother the Archduke John were both seen as figures to be exploited by the Emperor to raise the prestige of his House while at the same time ensuring that his own personal position remained uncompromised by any reversal in the fortunes of war. Thugut was convinced that in this way a certain counter to the prevailing zeitgeist could be organised to make sure the dynasty survived the storms that clearly were coming. That these tempests were on their way was the legacy of Campo Formio and a French army which needed to be supported by the loot and resources of countries outside France.

Austria had not been defeated. She had lost a few frontier battles but was still strong enough to bar an invading army. With Austria undefeated, Italy remained unconquered and the Napoleonic creation of the Cisalpine Republic as a satellite of France in northern Italy in 1797 remained vulnerable and flawed.

As a quid pro quo for digesting Venice, Austria had recognised the Cisalpine Republic where, by the order of the Directoire, Napoleon had declared the 'people' sovereign on 29 June. But in the new state, liberty after three *coups d'état* was equated with secularisation and the new regime of the Cisalpine Republic degenerated into arbitrary acts of violence and despotism. The earlier work of Joseph II was now brought to its logical conclusion: monasticism was abolished, the Papacy attacked, the churches and clergy pillaged. All religious orders were suppressed and all church property confiscated in two months of 1798. The secularisation of Italy was a tremendous revolution, again offering Vienna a great challenge: how could Austria tolerate Venetia continuing to apply the principles of the *Ancien Régime* alongside a revolutionary despotism aimed at driving the Catholic Church out of existence? These two systems could not survive side by side without an explosion. Thugut's diplomacy had made certain that Campo Formio was the beginning of an immense general war, which would only end at Waterloo nearly twenty years later.

CHAPTER 9

From Marengo to Austerlitz

THE SECOND AND THIRD COALITION WARS

Although Austria's armies had a mixed record against Napoleon, the fact remained that her forces were the only reliable ally England possessed. If Revolutionary France was to be contained, the Austrian army was the only instrument capable of doing so. The army continued to be in the forefront of every campaign. That it survived the hammer blows that now rained down upon it was a tribute to the long-lasting effect of reforms a generation earlier.

Barely was the ink dry at Campo Formio than Britain, Russia, Naples and Turkey began to see the ambitions of Revolutionary France in an ever darker light. As these countries drew together, it was apparent that the key to any credible coalition against Napoleon remained Austria. After much promise of gold on the part of London, Austria on 22 June 1799 formally signed a new alliance with Britain.

This war would bring new areas of campaign for the French, notably Egypt. For Austria, Italy would continue as a major theatre of hostilities. But the French remained obsessed with the Rhine. They therefore threatened Germany, which brought them inevitably into conflict with Vienna.

The Swiss campaign

In the event, when war came, it was Switzerland that was to be the first battle-field to draw blood. Then as now, the Alpine lands were a strategic factor. They offered Paris the chance to cut the shortest lines of communication between the Austrian forces on the Danube and the Austrian army on the Po. Moreover, a strong position in Switzerland could always threaten any plans the allies might have for the invasion of southern France. An army of about 30,000 men under Masséna pushed east into the Engadine but soon faced a much stronger

Austrian force under Hoetze and Bellegarde, a capable general of Saxon extraction. At Feldkirch the French were repulsed in some style. This encouraged the Swiss, unenthusiastic about the French occupation, to rise up and threaten Masséna's lines of communication.

Meanwhile the French general Jourdan, nicknamed by his soldiers 'the anvil' on account of his always being beaten, crossed into the Black Forest at Basle where he promptly found himself face to face with the Archduke Charles at the head of 60,000 seasoned troops. On 21 March 1799, the Archduke attacked near Stockach, sending Jourdan reeling back towards the Rhine. At the crisis of this battle, the Archduke put himself at the head of six battalions of Hungarian grenadiers and twelve squadrons of cuirassiers in order to break up the attack on his right flank. It was an early sign of that complete disregard for his own person which became one of Charles's hallmarks as a military leader. This physical courage was to be a feature of the Archduke's generalship as much as his intellectual qualities.

Although the Austrians had fought well, it was their superiority in numbers that had, more than anything, carried the day. The Austrian grenadiers, formed into powerful elite tactical units following recent reforms, performed well. Notwithstanding his personal bravery, the Archduke was persuaded to relinquish the leadership of this attack to Karl Aloys zu Fürstenberg fifteen minutes after it started. Fürstenberg was promptly felled by case shot, forcing the Archduke to resume command.

Jourdan's losses were about 5,000. The hotly contested woods of Stockach had cost the Austrians several thousand casualties as well. In typical Austrian style Charles contented himself with having put the French Army of the Rhine out of action rather than pursuing it and destroying it. To risk a battle when one's opponents were already demoralised and defeated was not the Habsburg style and the Hofkriegsrat Aulic Council decreed that crossing the Rhine was too risky an operation. The Archduke was ordered to await reinforcements from Bellegarde and the arrival of Korsakow's Russian corps. Jourdan was in any event already a broken man. Masséna on taking over the remnants of his army was horrified at the condition in which he found the troops.

Six weeks later, strengthened and reinforced, the allies renewed their attacks on the French positions around Zurich and the Archduke's army crossed the Rhine near Constance. The French could not face such a concentration of forces and by mid-June the Austrians were in Zurich and the French had been driven off the St Gotthard Pass. Here the Archduke halted once again, though for practical reasons. His opponent, Masséna, had been reinforced and had constructed a formidable defensive position on the Limmat behind Zurich. Reconnoitring the position, Charles saw immediately that to storm it would cost him many casualties. Critics of the Archduke in Vienna had already begun to play on the tensions between him and his brother the Emperor. Charles felt he could not risk putting a foot wrong with the cream of the Habsburg army if he was to enjoy the support of the court and government. Ideally, Charles envisaged a convergence attack but the other prong of this scheme, General Hadik's men, had just been sent to join the Russians in northern Italy.

In Italy meanwhile the French were also checked. Schere, leading a fumbling attack on Vero, was beaten off by Kray at Magnano in the first week in April. By 6 April the French were behind the Mincio and by the 12th they had fallen back behind the Adda. In Rome and Naples, French troops were ordered to evacuate. Everywhere the military genius of Napoleon was absent, and indifferent leadership compromised French arms. When the Russian Suvorov joined Kray with his 30,000 men the allies could deploy 90,000 men and the Russian was made commander-in-chief. Napoleon was unimpressed; he described Suvorov as having the soul but not the brain of a great commander.[1]

On 21 April Serurier's division, left imprudently on the left bank of the Adda, was attacked by Suvorov and the Austrians. In a brisk action at Cassano, the French were virtually annihilated by an Austrian cavalry charge led by Melas, a talented officer and a Greek born in Transylvania. Once again the Austrian cavalry, in particular the Chevauxleger squadrons, proved that they were the most formidable horsed arm in Europe. Everywhere, the French fell back, heading for the safety of the Ligurian Alps. By late May, the Russians were in Turin, having defeated the French with Austrian help at the ferocious Battle of Novi.

At Novi, the French under Joubert effectively deployed their new tactic of mobile skirmishing infantry. The Austrian grenadiers were repeatedly driven back by swarms of French sharpshooters carefully positioned around their exposed flanks as they advanced. It fell to a young Austrian colonel who was Melas's adjutant to see and suggest that the key to the French position was the right flank and ask for two brigades (Mitrovsky and Loudon) to help storm the position. This movement late in the day finally disordered the French whose commander Joubert fell with a bullet through his head just where the fighting was at its most violent. The Loudon Brigade of Grenadiers took their objectives at the point of the bayonet spurred on by the young colonel whose name was already becoming a legend: Radetzky.

In his official bulletin to the Emperor, Melas brought this name to wider attention:

I can find neither the words nor the expressions which can do justice to the courage and heroism of the army on this day. ... Finally I cannot fail to mention to his Majesty the conduct of Lieutenant Colonel Count Radetsky who in so many moments displayed decisiveness, courage and restless energy and in this battle organising and leading the attack columns which contributed significantly to our victory.[2]

Meanwhile another French force under Macdonald, which had evacuated Naples and attempted to menace the allied lines of communication, was caught by a combined Russo-Austrian force under Suvorov at Trebbia. In nearly three days of fierce fighting Macdonald lost more than 10,000 men and nearly all his guns. After barely three months, the French position in Italy had crumbled. In July both Alessandria and Mantua, which had been defended by French garrisons, had surrendered. Novi and Trebbia simply completed the picture of Gallic gloom.

Fortunately for the French, the old evil of malaria had once again sapped the Russian and Austrian soldiers' strength and, for the moment, exhaustion prevented pursuit. Moreover, as was often to happen between the Russians and the Austrians, there emerged tensions at the level of command. Relations between Suvorov and Melas were cordial and the Russian made much use of the staff infrastructure the Austrian High Command put at his disposal but the allies moved at a slower pace than their opponents. Their failure to prevent Macdonald escaping with the remnants of his defeated army to join up again with Moreau showed that the Austrian military command had not digested the lesson that the new era of war exacted a high price for lethargy.

Moreover, there were political difficulties. Thugut in Vienna was unamused to hear that Suvorov single-handedly had restored the Piedmontese monarchy. Vienna was also understandably cautious at the prospect of invading France. A vigorous thrust towards Grenoble might have brought the entire edifice down but Vienna as usual was concerned with her own long-term interests, and these dictated action nearer to home. If there were to be an invasion of France then it would have to be through the old Austrian crown lands of Lorraine so that, when the time came to make another peace, these provinces could be under Habsburg occupation.

Archduke Charles withdrawn: Napoleon returns

Thus the fateful decision was taken to shift the bold Archduke Charles away from Zurich where he had achieved so much and move him back to the tributaries of the Rhine. In his place would come the Russians under Korsakow, a far less gifted commander than Suvorov. This weakening of the allies in Switzerland essentially doomed the coalition. As a British diplomat observed, 'le vrai général' in Austria was not Melas or the Archduke but Thugut.[3]

A British expeditionary force of perhaps no more than 25,000 men might at this stage have ended the war, but no such force materialised and Masséna's brilliant delaying tactics gave Buonaparte time to develop his strategy of threatening both the Danube valley and northern Italy. The stage was set for the moment when Napoleon returned from his triumphs in the shadows of the Pyramids and political victory in Paris to assume control over the armies he had led to victory barely a year earlier.

While the Archduke returned with his troops towards Mannheim, Mássena saw his chance. He faced only 45,000 Austro-Russian troops and the Russian contingent was inferior in quality and leadership. Mássena had been re-inforced and he now commanded 70,000 troops. On 25 September he attacked his opponents arranged in front of Zurich and sent them reeling. The French hold on Switzerland was consolidated further by movements that neutralised Suvorov's and Korsakow's attempts to renew the offensive.

Had the international situation been a conventional one, a negotiated peace might at this stage have been possible but Napoleon needed a dazzling military victory to shore up his domestic success after his elevation to First Consul. His regime needed glory as well as order to survive. Moreover, in Thugut he had a diplomatic adversary who was unwilling to concede defeat even if it meant the prosecution of a 'war to the knife'. Events were all moving in Napoleon's favour. The Russian–Austrian relationship was deteriorating as Thugut's war aims were perceived by the Russians to have let them down in Switzerland. Thugut had become annoyed with his Russian partners over Piedmont and these feel-ings were reciprocated when the Austrians claimed Ancona. The Tsar had had enough of Austrian friction. He abruptly instructed his generals to begin their withdrawal. Russian troops would cease to be a relevant factor by February 1800. By holding Switzerland, the French had frustrated any attempt to invade the south of France.

The Austrians still possessed two fine armies in the field. That under Melas in northern Italy numbered nearly 110,000 men, while under Kray, in southern Germany, there was an even stronger force of 145,000. Napoleon would need to destroy one of these if his aims were to be realised. As their destruction would open the road to Vienna, the forces of Kray were Napoleon's preferred target. But political problems soon arose over this.

Chief of these was Moreau, who commanded the French Army of the Rhine. He was both stubborn and unimaginative. Even after the events of Brumaire, Napoleon's position was not so powerful that he could remove as prestigious a commander as Moreau. Moreover as First Consul there was a legal issue as to whether Napoleon could hold command in the field. Therefore Napoleon tried to foist on to Moreau his plan for the destruction of Kray by a swift march to outflank and annihilate the Austrian right wing. But Moreau found the strategy too bold and risky. As Napoleon wrote later from St Helena, 'Le plan que Moreau ne comprend pas'[4] would have to be executed in northern Italy, very much Napoleon's second choice, as a victory there was unlikely to end the war.

While Moreau advanced along the Danube sluggishly, Napoleon entered Italy along the most difficult and westernmost of the passes, the St Bernard. He had hoped to cross using the lower passes of the Simplon and St Gotthard but Melas was on the move and he could not risk debouching on to Melas's troops. Moreover, if he was to rescue all that was left of the army of Italy at Genoa and Suchet's forces on the Var, time was of the essence. Moreau meanwhile pushed Kray back, capturing some of his depots and taking some 12,000 Austrian troops prisoner. But the decisive battle was skilfully avoided by Kray, who kept his army together in a well-executed withdrawal that deprived Moreau of the 'battle without a morrow' which was always Napoleon's aim.

In Italy, Melas's troops were thinly spread with some 30,000 of his men pinned down by Suchet on the Var. A further 25,000 of his troops invested Genoa.This made it difficult for Melas to cover all the passes. Apart from a brisk defence at the formidable fortress of Bard where Captain von Bernkopf's garrison held out for ten days from 21 May until 1 June, Melas's troops held the Val d'Aosta lightly. The news of Bernkopf's heroic stand did not reach Melas until Napoleon had managed to pass the bulk of his army over the Alps. When Bernkopf finally surrendered, Napoleon razed the fortress to the ground.

Marengo: a battle won

As the day of 14 June dawned, Melas's troops were completing their concentration on the Scrivian plain near the village of Marengo. Melas knew his business well. He was old enough to remember the relevant lessons of the Seven Years War and under him the Habsburg army demonstrated that it had lost none of its ability to mislead its opponents. A successful Austrian strategy of disinformation hoodwinked Napoleon completely. Fires were lit to give the impression that Melas was retreating towards Genoa. A number of 'agents' and 'deserters' found their way to Napoleon with tales of extremely low morale among the Austrian officers. The French pickets barely a few hundred yards away from the Austrian front line heard signs of movement at night but assumed it was the Austrians retreating. Even when the Austrian artillery opened up at dawn Napoleon believed it was simply a diversion to cover their withdrawal.

After an earlier engagement at Montebello, Melas had sent a trusted spy by the name of Toli to report to Napoleon on 11 June that the Austrians were extremely despondent and were only thinking of retreat. Primed deserters reinforced the message, including a prisoner whom Napoleon personally interrogated. This particular deserter was an émigré cavalry officer still wearing his Bourbon decorations, and his tale of Austrian 'ruin' was believed by Napoleon with near-disastrous consequences for him. Napoleon was therefore blissfully unaware of the forces deploying against him. He detached two divisions, one to watch the Po crossing, the other, commanded by Desaix, to march towards Novi in case Melas withdrew towards Genoa. The Austrians by then had seen the French dispositions around Marengo and, organising his army into three columns to cross the river Bormida at daybreak on the 14th, Melas promptly attacked with overwhelming force.

At first none of the French piquets could believe what was happening. As the Austrian columns marched out of their bridgehead in front of Alessandria with flags flying and bands playing, it became ominously clear that this was not the expected prelude to an Austrian withdrawal. Surprised and divided, Napoleon's men were within hours fighting for their lives against a much larger force. Melas throughout showed considerable tactical flair and by 11.30 a.m., with Ott's division threatening to outflank the French, the Austrian General Staff felt confident their opponent's centre was about to break.

This battle, so decisive and important for Napoleon, ironically was a small one with barely 60,000 troops committed in total by both sides. By the standards of the later Napoleonic Wars it was a modest affair; 'one of the smallest battles we ever fought,' Radetzky recalled, though its political consequences were to be enormous.[5]

Austrian confidence was justified as the grenadier battalions of Splenyi and the Chevauxleger cavalry of the Lobkowitz regiment had both distinguished themselves in the morning during spirited attacks, notwithstanding a murderous fire put up by the French around the village of Marengo which was protected by the Fontanone river. Radetzky suggested a flank attack on the village across one of the streams and Melas ordered Zach to execute it. But in the first sign of that mental and physical weariness which was to have such devastating consequences for the Austrians later that day, Zach, who had been on unbroken night watches for three days, was so exhausted that, having fallen asleep, he could not be roused quickly. It took him, Radetzky recalls, some time to 'pull himself together and wake up'.[6]

The flank attack finally went in with great elan before noon. At one stage the Jaeger and the grenadiers of the Splenyi regiment crossed the river Fontanone running over the backs of seventeen tough pioneers who formed a human bridge for forty-five minutes. Their success caught Napoleon by surprise and he tried in vain to deploy his guns. Much of his artillery, however, had been held up crossing the Alps thanks to the tenacious defence at Bard by Bernkopf's men. By two in the afternoon the French centre was broken and Napoleon reluctantly conceded that he would have to fall back if he was to avoid the kind of annihilation he usually reserved for his opponents. Melas, leading a charge of the Kaiser Chevauxlegers personally (with Radetzky at his side), sealed the fate of Napoleon's centre, which was forced to construct hastily a fighting withdrawal.

The French Consular Guard, Napoleon's reserve, was committed and demonstrated the value of shock troops. They first fought stubbornly against an attack by Austrian dragoons, before seeing off the grenadiers of Splenyi. Finally surrounded, they formed a hollow square against the Austrian artillery. This 'granite redoubt', as Napoleon later called it, bought valuable time, but at great cost. Of the 800-strong Consular Guard more than 300 fell in less than an hour.

By 3 p.m., seeing the French lines beginning to break, Melas considered the battle won. Marengo was occupied and his grenadiers were triumphantly waving the debris that the French troops had abandoned on the field. French shakos were raised as trophies on the ends of Austrian muskets and bayonets. The units that had poured into Marengo now lost cohesion as they began plundering the abandoned French equipment. They had been fighting without respite for more than six hours.

Their 71-year-old commander, Melas, was also weary. Throughout the battle he had demonstrated an energetic front-line leadership which had been admired by many of the younger Austrian officers. He had taken part in two cavalry charges. Two horses had been shot from beneath him and one of his falls had left his arm severely bruised. As he picked himself up and regarded the battlefield, the General could be forgiven for thinking the battle won. Everywhere he looked, all he could see were the backs of the French infantry carrying out a forced retreat covered by their reserves.

Having been in the saddle for eight hours, and exhausted, he decided to retire from the battle, so he handed over command to his subordinates Kaim and Zach to organise the pursuit. Melas's orders were clear: they were to destroy as much of the French army as possible with artillery and cavalry before they crossed the river Scrivia. Unfortunately, many of the Austrian generals, seeing their commander abandon the battle presumably to pen a letter to Vienna giving news of a great victory, followed his example.

Melas might be forgiven for underestimating his opponent. Napoleon's military career lay mostly in the future but the Austrian made the unforgivable error of believing a battle was won when, in reality, it was far from over. It was Torgau all over again, only this time there was no Daun to extricate the Austrians from their fate.

There is no doubt that a determined and energetic pursuit by Zach with his cavalry would have crushed Napoleon before Desaix arrived so dramatically an hour later to turn the tide of battle. But Zach was still exhausted and had been cat-napping yet again when Melas ordered him to take over command. Indeed it was only with the greatest of difficulty that Zach was woken up. His bleary-eyed countenance did not augur well for an energetic pursuit. Meanwhile, rather than let his cavalry and artillery pursue the French, Kaim wasted much time bringing the units in and around Marengo to a semblance of parade ground order. As the Wallis regiment belatedly advanced up the road towards San Giuliano supported by the Liechtenstein Dragoons and artillery, the French began to organise a new line from which to attack the Austrians.

Marengo: a battle lost

While Zach struggled with his exhaustion, on the French side, a youthful, exuberant officer called Desaix, who had been deployed far away from Marengo, had heard the artillery fire of the battle. Immediately, he decided to disobey his orders and march his troops to the sound of the guns. He now arrived to greet Napoleon with the famous words: 'This battle is completely lost. But there is time to win another.'[7] As the Austrians slugglishly organised a pursuit column, Desaix reordered his division to attack them. Another young and gifted officer, Kellermann, with barely 400 cuirassiers, charged the leading elements of the Austrian column in the flank with devastating effect just as they were reeling from Desaix's initial counter-attack. Marshal Marmont recalls in his memoirs how the Austrian grenadiers of the Lattermann regiment were cut to pieces while thousands of Austrian cavalry looked on, seemingly mesmerised and frozen to their position barely a hundred yards distant.[8]

Rarely in military history has a hastily improvised cavalry charge proved more effective. Marmont later said that three minutes earlier and the charge would have been repulsed, while three minutes later it would have come too late and Lattermann's grenadiers would have broken Desaix's assault. As Kellerman's first squadron crashed into the Austrian flank, Desaix fell dead from a musket ball. But he had lived long enough to see the first fruits of his work. When the peaks of the tall Austrian grenadier hats had crested the slight ridge ahead of San Giuliano, the 9th Light Infantry had hurtled towards them with drums beating the *pas de charge* and with bayonets fixed. At the same time Marmont's artillery had opened up on them with canister. The effect was dramatic. The grenadiers staggered and fired a volley, and it was Kellerman's good fortune to strike the grenadiers in the flank ten seconds after they had discharged this volley. Caught in the act of reloading, the grenadiers were defenceless. As the semi-official Austrian account drily noted: 'This attack, unexpected and executed with surprising swiftness, threw the Austrian infantry into disorder and dispersed it after a short resistance; many men were cut down.'[9]

Under this murderous three-arm assault, coordinated to perfection, the rest of the Austrian column recoiled and then appeared frozen to the ground. A young grenadier ensign was bayoneted and his colour seized as his fellow soldiers looked on in amazement, seemingly paralysed. Behind them, one of their artillery wagons exploded. The Wallis regiment then broke and fled while the grenadiers continued to be slaughtered by Kellerman's Cuirassiers.

More French cavalry arrived and one trooper seized the astounded Zach by the throat. The Liechtenstein Dragoons who should have immediately grasped the opportunity to counter-attack the French cavalry also seemed rooted to the spot by the sudden transformation of events. As some of Kellerman's horse charged them they simply fled in terror, stampeding the ranks of the Pilati cavalry brigade who were attempting to ride to the rescue of the infantry. They found themselves surrounded by French cavalry reinforcements organised by Murat and galloped away in panic. Until this moment, the Austrian cavalry had still been regarded as the finest in Europe. Their pitiful performance, coming so suddenly at this stage of the battle, would rankle for generations to come. Even Radetzky in the months before his death would dwell on the Austrian cavalry's failure to support the grenadiers at Marengo. Their action that evening required 'closer analysis' ('es wäre interessant hierueber näheres zu erfahren').[10]

One of the Austrian accounts underlined this general incomprehension over the behaviour of the Austrian cavalry that day: 'No one in the main column could understand the flight of the cavalry. The main Austrian formations, broken by the cavalry fleeing through it, began also to give way.'[11]

Certainly, as Kaim attempted to deploy some infantry, the fleeing cavalry spread only panic and disorder. At one stage it looked as if the entire Austrian central column would be annihilated by the pursuing French. Fortunately for the Austrians, six battalions of fresh grenadiers under Weidenfeld were advancing towards the Austrian centre from Marengo. Their action demonstrated that, ably led, these new elite formations of grenadier battalions could perform wonders when grouped in larger tactical units.

Deploying as if on the parade ground, Weidenfeld's battalions gave a text-book demonstration of a disciplined rearguard action, forming square to repulse Murat's cavalry while allowing the fleeing central column to find its way back to the Austrian bridgehead. There a captured French officer observed the chaos and confusion: 'I have witnessed some defeats in the course of my military career but I never saw anything like this.' In the stampede this officer was thrown nearly 500 paces.[12]

But despite this panic, the Austrians were not annihilated. Napoleon – or rather, Kellerman and Desaix – had won a great victory but they had not crushed the Austrians. French losses were one in four while Austrian losses were one in five. The Austrian losses still amounted to nearly 6,000 wounded and 963 dead. Though General Hadik died of his wounds, none of the other dead officers was of higher rank than captain. The fourteen officer fatalities were unusually low and hinted at the Austrian army's officer corps having deteriorated in the 1790s.

But the First Consul had got all that he needed: a brilliant success and all the glory with which to ensure the continuation of his rule. Napoleon understandably named his favourite horse Marengo (at Marengo he had been mounted on another favoured steed Styria), and legend insists that his preferred dish was *poulet à la Marengo*. Melas cannot be faulted, save for giving up command too early. His troops had on the whole fought well for more than nine hours and his tactical disposition was inspired. He had 25 per cent superiority over his opponents when the battle opened. As one historian has noted: 'It is hard to ask much more from any commander's strategy.'[13]

At first Melas could not believe what he was told but the abrupt change in fortune brought him rapidly to his senses and the following day he sued for peace at Alessandria, where Napoleon put the seal on the Austrian surrender of Lombardy and all her strong points in Piedmont. The 'secondary' theatre had after all furnished a decisive victory.

The details of the battle that reached Vienna caused consternation and anger. Radetzky later recalled that Melas possessed a 'head which was better than his feet'. Irrespective of how good his head was, Vienna demanded it on a plate. Together with the hapless Zach, Melas was dismissed. The Austrian forces in Italy were placed under the command of Bellegarde.

The armistice of Alessandria was only a punctuation mark. During the next few months Austria's army displayed that admirable tenacity which characterised Habsburg forces throughout their struggles with Napoleon and made them his most implacable foe on the Continent. Under Bellegarde, the army in Italy was reinforced to 120,000 men while the forces on the Danube were built up to a nominal and impressive 280,000 men. These were to deal with Moreau, who, with some 100,000 men, was encamped around Munich. Vienna found Napoleon's peace terms unacceptable and was resolved to continue the war. The strategy involved remaining on the defensive in Italy while attacking Moreau in Bavaria. The Alessandria armistice was a vital breathing space.

Meanwhile enjoying the laurels of Marengo, Napoleon could now afford to give even Moreau orders. He no longer suggested but instructed Moreau to advance on Vienna along the traditional invasion route of the Danube. Macdonald would cover his right flank while Augereau on the Main would protect his left.

But for Moreau to achieve this, he had first to cross the river Inn where the Archduke John, nominally in command of the Austrian army there, enjoyed a strong defensive position. The Archduke John was another of the talented sons of Leopold who had to contend with a far less imaginative brother as Emperor. Unfortunately for the army, unlike the Archduke Charles, the inexperienced 18-year-old John's gifts did not lie in the military sphere.

Intrigues around the archdukes: the Archduke John

Kray's army that had faced Moreau had been beaten in a number of inconclusive actions and this was enough for the Emperor Francis and Thugut to request that Kray relinquish command. The obvious candidate for his replacement, the Archduke Charles, dropped out on the grounds that the Emperor, who had earlier resisted calls to place him in command, might be perceived as bowing to something as vulgar as popular pressure. Thugut warned that the appointment of Charles would only underline the mistaken earlier decision not to appoint him. Such were the convoluted thought processes of the court.

Baron Thugut, with ever an eye to the practicalities of the situation if they gave him the chance to ingratiate himself with his master, encouraged these thoughts with his own observation that the Archduke Charles would 'only demand reinforcements' which, as they were not available, 'would only force him to push for peace'.[14] Thugut knew well how to pander to the Emperor's suspicions and jealousies of his brother. Charles, increasingly frustrated by his attempts at military reform running into the sands, took himself off to Prague, pleading one of his recurring attacks of epilepsy. Charles saw no point in Austria's armies fighting a war in their present unmodernised condition. He counselled peace and a policy of playing for time to allow Austria to build up her strength.

This eminently wise policy was anathema to Thugut, who was prepared to gamble everything on a conflict with France à l'outrance. Thugut's own position after Marengo was becoming precarious. His grasp of foreign affairs would pass to Cobenzl, a protégé of Kaunitz who favoured the old Kaunitz policy of seeking an agreement with France, even a Revolutionary France. These tensions proved disastrous not only for Thugut, who was forced to resign in September, but also for Austria. Cobenzl's Francophile policies would not save him from a similar fate and he was dismissed shortly after Austerlitz in 1805.

Thanks to these petty intrigues, the army found itself in the curious position of not having a titular commander by the end of August 1800. What was needed, Thugut suggested, was a twin-track solution: two commanders. The first should be a de facto commander of enormous experience and proven courage; the second should be an enthusiastic archduke, not too difficult to handle, who would add the aura of the Imperial House to the cause.

For the first candidate Thugut strongly recommended Feldzeugmeister Franz Freiherr von Lauer, a senior officer in the Engineers corps with a long experience of fortification design but little direct exposure to the challenges of command on the battlefield. Lauer had served under Wurmser in the First Coalition War and had been with him when Mantua fell. As a gifted specialist he had even won the coveted Order of Maria Theresa but his service record described him as lacking finesse and possessing a raw and aggressive temperament, which was married to 'extreme self-regard'. He was also described as lacking that most important of military qualities: decisiveness. If these weaknesses were not enough, another report noticed that his soldiers held him in low esteem. All these personality defects paled into insignificance compared to his loyalty to Thugut, and Lauer's impeccable connections: his sister was a lady-in-waiting to the influential Queen of Naples.

Thus, as is so often the case despite the apparent triumph of egalitarianism, connections triumphed over ability. To add lustre to this uninspired choice, the Emperor Francis knew there would need to be a figurehead to raise morale after the armies' earlier defeats, and it could not be himself because the risk of defeat had to be kept at arm's length from the throne.

But who was to be this hapless archduke: the scapegoat for any failure Francis's army might incur? Francis first approached Archduke Ferdinand, brother of the Empress Ludovika, but Ferdinand wisely refused, having had long experience of court intrigue. Francis then suggested the role might suit the Archduke Josef, who pleaded Hungarian constitutional commitments. One by one, Thugut ticked the archdukes off his list until he reached John. It would after all only be a question of 'appearances' (*Schein*). The 'real' command would lie with Lauer.

John was certainly a talented young man and, like his military brother Charles, he was to develop outstanding intellectual gifts but at this stage he was only 18 and had not even completed his basic military training. He had just about mastered how to sit correctly on a horse but his hours were still spent being shouted at on the drill square.

John only realised that he was destined for the army on the Danube at the beginning of September. Unsurprisingly, he was shocked. His astonishment would no doubt have been even greater had he known that he was to be given 'command'. That detail was still kept secret from him and he fondly imagined he might serve as some unimportant adjutant.

These thoughts were confirmed when John received his orders to join Charles at the front. It is worth noting as another symptom of Habsburg methods in dealings with each other that the Archduke John did not possess even a uniform, or for that matter much more than the odd shirt. Materially and mentally he was unprepared for what was coming. It was winter but luckily his aunt, the Queen of Naples, hearing that her nephew was off to war, sent him some beautiful Neapolitan shirts of exquisite wool and cotton.

Joining the Emperor the two brothers rode together for some days until they reached the Bavarian pilgrimage village of Altötting. Not by a single phrase did the Emperor let slip or imply that he had plans for his brother. It was only two days later that the Emperor summoned John to his presence and gave him a letter outlining his 'command'. John was dumbstruck but knew where his duty lay. The Kaiser explained painstakingly that the 'command' was really about raising the morale of the troops and that the real power of executive command would rest with Lauer. John would obey Lauer to the letter and not question or withhold his signature from any of Lauer's orders, which would be published as if they hailed from the Archduke. All communication with the Emperor was to run directly and exclusively through Lauer.[15]

In this way Francis was ensuring that should disaster befall his forces not an iota of criticism would fall on him. The Archduke would act as a form of covering fire; a dazzling decoy for the opprobrium that might otherwise have attached itself to the Emperor. And if things went well, then Lauer could always be praised to ensure it did not all go to the young Archduke's head. Moreover, it would be good to have another archduke competent in military affairs to prevent excessive prestige passing to the Archduke Charles. There are few more revealing episodes than this to illustrate the Habsburgs' internecine rivalries and the callousness with which members of the family could be sacrificed to the 'greater good'.

Lauer's plans were not entirely without merit but their weaknesses soon became apparent. He first decided to abandon the very strong position his forces enjoyed along the Inn and push Moreau back on to the Bavarian Alps. This operation had barely got under way when Lauer changed his mind and decided to give up outflanking Moreau and to attack frontally, despite the fact that Moreau was now digging into a good defensive position near the forest of Hohenlinden.

The Archduke John meanwhile, young, sensitive and insecure and, full of doubts over the ambiguity of his role, had sought the advice of his talented brother Charles. But Charles knew better than to interfere with his elder brother's plans and simply offered John the following counsel: 'However difficult and tough your situation is, you must not flinch from it. Remember that the really great man reveals himself when, despite the crisis he finds himself in, he remains always calm and collected' ('in keiner Gelegenheit aus der Fassung kommt').[16]

A few days later, Charles sent some strategic recommendations to John concerning the lie of the land in the Bavarian theatre. But in a confidential letter, which for once did not pass through Lauer's hands, Charles was at pains to stress that he could not help his younger brother and that his own isolation at court now meant that his advice would always be questioned. 'Do what you wish with my suggestions but it may be best not to make any use of my letter. It is my desire to serve but not to appear.'

Lauer was convinced that the strong defensive position he had enjoyed on the Inn could now be sacrificed in favour of a more aggressive policy. The Austrians had used the succession of truces which had been declared during the autumn months to reorganise and replenish their forces: volunteer units from Tyrol, insurrection levies from Hungary, an assortment of light troops, all made their way to join Lauer.

Disaster at Hohenlinden

The weather had turned to snow and sleet, making it increasingly difficult for the Austrian scouts to judge either the strength of their opponents or their precise dispositions. This contributed significantly to the slow speed at which Lauer advanced, and it allowed Moreau to dig in for a strong defensive battle. Unfortunately, in this vacuum of intelligence Lauer's chief of staff Franz Weyrother believed the situation to be much more favourable for attack than in reality it was. He ordered a swift march to crush Moreau's right flank but this march soon degenerated into bottlenecks and delays. Lauer and Weyrother now changed plan and favoured a march along a new route towards Munich.

The first contact was on the Austrian left flank at Ampfing. The Austrians here had overwhelming superiority but the redoubtable Ney commanded the French and he conducted an exceptionally stubborn defence. Nevertheless, the numbers the Austrians brought to bear forced the French back. The Austrian offensive had been a success although the Austrians incurred nearly twice as many casualties as the French.

Four Austrian columns advanced on Hohenlinden, which lay astride the Munich road. It was heavily forested, which meant that communications would be impaired, and the onset of more snow and sleet did nothing to help. Moreau conceived a plan of particular elegance. He surrendered the high points of the forest to give the impression he was falling back while luring the Austrian column under Kolowrat into a trap. As they debouched from the woods and approached Hohenlinden, a strong flanking force led by Decaen and Richepance would take the Austrians by surprise.

As the Austrian advance guard emerged from the woods it quickly overwhelmed the French. Two grenadier battalions of the Sebottendorf regiment under General-Major Spannochi attacked their opponents with a bayonet charge and drove them back. Supported by three Bavarian battalions, the grenadiers advanced steadily until a strong French counter-attack drove them back to the treeline. Attacked by cavalry, the grenadiers formed square and repulsed three charges by a hundred chasseurs. Though it had been Moreau's strategy to lure the Austrians, he was surprised at the ease with which they advanced: one by one the hamlets around Hohenlinden fell to the Austrians. A battalion of the Gemmingen regiment stormed Forstern while another battalion, this time of the Branchainville regiment, captured the village of Tarding. Spurred on by their commander Prince Schwarzenberg, another battalion, the old Walloon regiment of Murray, swept into Kronacker, the key to the French left wing.

But on the French right wing the forward elements of Richepence's division had had better luck against the Austrians under Riesch and Kolowrat. They outmanoeuvred Kolowrat's forces. Riesch's troops took so long to reach the battlefield that Richepence was able to move his forces between the two columns with devastating consequences for Kolowrat. Suddenly Kolowrat, already engaged to his front and flank, faced an attack from his rear.

News of Richepence's movements quickly reached Weyrother, who rode swiftly in the direction of the fighting to see for himself what was happening. A storm of artillery greeted him, throwing him from his horse and depriving Lauer of his chief of staff at the critical moment in the battle. Three regiments of Bavarians who held this sector of the front cracked under the pressure of four infantry charges and fled. (The high ratio of Bavarian prisoners to casualties has been interpreted as suggesting the Bavarians' heart was not in the struggle.) As Kolowrat's regiments on the Austrian right flank were gradually surrounded by Decaen and Grouchy, the situation on the Austrian rear and right flank became critical.

Meanwhile at Kronacker, Schwarzenberg became aware that all was not well with the rest of the Austrian forces. He received an order to withdraw. Suddenly, a lull in the fighting occurred. As the smoke parted, a French officer appeared with a white flag, the traditional method for the victor or vanquished to parley, and called on the Austrians to surrender. Schwarzenberg replied by ordering his artillery to redouble their rate of fire. But the Austrians were falling apart, caught in a tactical noose which Moreau was relentlessly tightening.

Fortunately for the Austrians, it being December, darkness fell over the battlefield by five o'clock and under the cloak of this natural camouflage Schwarzenberg found a path through the woods to extricate what was left of his men. The battle was over. Hohenlinden was as complete a victory for the French as any general could have wished. Moreau, with none of the dash or energy of Napoleon, had won a decisive victory. In Napoleonic style he had destroyed his opponents' army far more convincingly than even Napoleon had done at Marengo. For the loss in dead and wounded of fewer than 3,000 men, Moreau had inflicted more than 12,000 casualties, including prisoners of the Austrians and their Bavarian allies. The loss of 50 Austrian guns, a number unheard of since the Seven Years War, was a disaster of particular humiliation. The utter failure of the Austrians to coordinate their attacks was dubbed by a Bavarian general present as 'ignorance and ineptitude'.[17]

During the orgy of blame that engulfed Vienna in the aftermath of the disaster of Hohenlinden, little attention was paid to the fundamental flaws in the Austrian strategy. The Archduke Charles with his keen strategic sense noted that the battle had been lost by 'fragmentation' of the Austrian forces which, divided into columns beset by poor communications, invited defeat. But no one listened to the Archduke Charles. Unfortunately, Weyrother, after surviving Hohenlinden, would live to devise another over-complicated allied battle plan, this time near the Moravian village of Austerlitz. In the meantime, the Archduke Charles was summoned back to take command of the shattered remains of the army and pick up the pieces.

The Archduke Charles returns

Agreeing in his own words to 'willingly sacrifice myself for the interests of the state',[18] Charles replaced his brother and Lauer on 17 December with full Imperial authority to command. The sight which greeted him was beyond his experience and as he reported to his brother, the Emperor, dispiriting. Less than half the army that had fought at Hohenlinden was still intact and what remained looked more like an 'Asiatic horde than a disciplined European army'.[19]

An armistice was a priority for the army though Thugut opposed it, still favouring a 'war to the knife'. Charles noted: 'if Moreau refuses to sign we are lost'.[20] Fortunately Moreau had his own concerns, notably the Austrian citadels threatening his lines of communication, which he had had to bypass. Accordingly, the next day an armistice was signed at Steyr in Upper Austria.

While the Archduke Charles took over the remnants of the Austrian army north of the Alps, Melas was succeeded south of the Alps by Bellegarde. To his credit, Melas did everything to ensure the transition was as smooth as possible. Preliminaries were signed at Treviso in late January. A few weeks later a Neapolitan force under the 'unfortunate' Mack, an Austrian general of whom we shall hear more, was wiped out. Much of Italy was again under French control and the Second Coalition against France had collapsed. Constrained by her pledge to London not to make peace until February, Vienna prevaricated until the formal peace was signed on 9 February at Lunéville. Blamed for all the disasters that had befallen Austrian arms, Thugut was sacked.

The Austrian diplomats who convened at Lunéville were led by Cobenzl and faced an unhappy task. After Marengo, Napoleon would have been satisfied with a frontier on the Mincio for his satellite Cisalpine Republic. After Hohenlinden he would accept nothing less than the Adige much further east. The Treaty of Lunéville confirmed Archduke Charles's warning that Austria would pay a high price for going to war in such an ill-prepared way. The treaty terms were of a harshness unknown in earlier Habsburg history. France cemented her claim to the left bank of the Rhine, and Austria had to accept the German principalities' 'mediatisation' as well as recognising the 'independence' of the Ligurian, Cisalpine and Batavian republics which, together with Switzerland, were now firmly within Napoleon's sphere of influence. Such a state of affairs could not represent the status quo for the Habsburgs. The humiliating terms of Lunéville meant that Vienna would immediately prepare for the next war against Napoleon.

The four years of peace were not wasted by Vienna. A series of reforms helped the army rebuild morale and ensured that the mistakes of the Second Coalition War were not repeated. Principal among these was the central issue of command. The Archduke Charles was not only given a command but he was placed in charge of the deliberations of the Aulic Council. But in a repeat of the previous campaigns' errors of judgement, the Archduke was not to be present at the principal theatre of the coming conflict. Instead of realising that Marengo had been Napoleon's choice of ground for unusual reasons and that he would have preferred to fight on the road to Vienna, the Austrians continued to believe that northern Italy would be the principal theatre of operations in the coming war. The Archduke was therefore given a command in that theatre.

To be fair, the Archduke Charles only had himself to blame for this assessment. On 3 March 1804, he had submitted a memorandum detailing how the French were unlikely to want to march all the way across Swabia and Bavaria and would therefore, in the event of hostilities, almost certainly seek a resolution in northern Italy where their lines of communication were far more cohesive. Moreover, the Archduke argued, in the Italian theatre there would be a tempting opportunity for the French to drive the Austrians back on to the Alps beyond Trieste. A victorious French army could menace Vienna via Styria as it had done in the closing phase of the First Coalition War.[21]

Ulm and the unfortunate Mack

Thus was the scene set for depriving the Austrians of the one general who might have averted the multiple disasters that would fall upon their armies in the months of 1805. Because Charles argued so forcefully that 'the Adige must therefore be considered the first and most preferable theatre of war',[22] it was only logical that the Archduke should take command of the 90,000-strong army in Italy, supported by his brother, the now not so inexperienced Archduke John in the Tyrol.

The Austrian forces north of the Alps were to coordinate their activities with the Russians, who numbered some 50,000 men under General Kutuzov. The 70,000 Austrian troops allotted to this theatre of operations were to be commanded by Mack. Charles instructed him to take special care to avoid confronting the French without the support of his Russian allies.

Mack, whose leadership in Italy in 1801 had not prevented the destruction of the pro-Austrian Neapolitan army, was a man whose imagination far outstripped his abilities. His qualities are hard to assess. He was a protégé of Lacy in the War of the Bavarian Succession and took part in the storming of Belgrade. His temperament appears to have been highly strung, and a fierce argument with Loudon after that campaign almost resulted in a court-martial.

In the campaigns in the Austrian Netherlands, Mack earned the praise of the Archduke Charles but the two men fundamentally disagreed on Austria's strategy. Mack always favoured a more aggressive approach to the French. A severe head injury during one of the earlier campaigns had made him difficult to deal with and his Neapolitan troops were said to have contemplated doing away with him on many occasions during the disastrous campaign of 1801. Tolstoy has left us a very brief portrait of the 'unfortunate Mack' in *War and Peace*. It is not flattering.

Mack argued forcefully that the Austrians should push forward without waiting for the Russians and occupy Bavaria and its resources. When asked whether there was not a danger that his forces would be caught by a larger French army, he dismissed such warnings with the phrase : 'All anxiety on this front is unfounded'. There was not 'the slightest chance' of the French intervening before the Russians arrived.[23]

Mack drove his army into Bavaria, where the Elector carefully welcomed the Habsburg forces but made sure that his own troops were withdrawn to the valley of the Upper Main where eventually they would side with the French. It was one of many Bavarian moves that displayed traditional anti-Austrian proclivities. By the beginning of October 45,000 Austrian troops were strung along the 150-mile-long front between the Inn and Ulm. The supply train barely kept up with Mack's progress and his artillery lagged far behind. But Mack was convinced his dispositions would confront the French as they attempted to break out of the Black Forest. Another Austrian force under Jellačić was approaching from the direction of the Tyrol, and a small but significant body of troops under Kienmayer, positioned to the rear of Mack's force, would establish contact with General Kutuzov's Russians.

It is hard to know whether Mack's plans might have worked against an eighteenth-century opponent but Napoleon was arguably at the height of his powers as a continental strategist and he now moved to strike quickly and effectively against his principal continental foe. Contrary to the Archduke Charles's supposition, Napoleon intended to strike the mortal blow at Vienna from north of the Alps. While Masséna was sent with 50,000 troops to face the Austrians in Italy, Napoleon marched his men to the Rhine, which they reached in twenty-nine days.

More than 75,000 infantry, 30,000 cavalry and 400 guns then marched from the Rhine to the Danube. One by one the German princes offered to help Napoleon. Since Napoleon's coronation as Emperor of France the previous year, the German princes, or *Reichfürsten*, had increasingly orientated themselves towards Paris. Already in 1803, the Reichdeputationshauptschluss (the conclusion of the Reich deputation) had come to a decision in Regensburg that undermined Emperor Francis's prerogatives. The 'Holy Roman Empire of the German Nation' over which Francis II was supposedly emperor had become nothing more than a polite fiction. Napoleon's ambitions had illustrated vividly the shell of a concept which, its centuries-old history notwithstanding, could not survive the combination of French military might and revolutionary ideas. He had mediatised the German princes, altering the political map of their lands. In Vienna, the Emperor and court had seen the direction the wind was taking and already had begun to take steps to adjust to the new realities.

The historic title of Holy Roman Emperor was becoming utterly meaningless and needed to be converted into something altogether more in keeping with the zeitgeist. Thus on 14 August 1804 barely two months after Napoleon had crowned himself Emperor of France, Francis II of the Holy Roman Empire became Emperor Francis I, Kaiser Franz I, of Austria.

Kaiser von Oesterreich

The new title of 'Emperor of Austria' was an invention. Francis was not interested in an 'Empire of the Austrians'. The Empire was that of the Casa d'Austria (House of Austria) but in taking the double-headed eagle of the Holy Roman Empire to be the flag of what was now called the Austrian Empire, the Emperor was not sacrificing an iota of Imperial continuity. At the same time, the new concept gave emphasis to his 'crown lands': a slightly more cohesive and durable ship in which to sail in these stormy times than the loose grouping of unreliable and spineless German *Reichfürste*. His two brothers, Charles and John would exploit the opportunity to capitalise on Napoleon's ambitions for Germany by stirring the pot of German nationalism and pushing Vienna towards leadership of the German 'nation'. But in 1805, such ideas were barely moving and Kaiser Franz was certainly not fighting for 'Germany's honour' as Mack's forces gathered around Ulm. Mack's army was to fight as it had always fought: for the dynasty.

By the second week of October, Napoleon was at the Danube. A short and sharp encounter at Wertingen between Murat's cavalry and a force of 5,000 Austrians under Auffenberg revealed a demoralised and passive Habsburg army virtually unchanged since the disaster at Hohenlinden. This was a portent of things to come. Mack became obsessed with Ulm as 'the key to half Germany' and imagined that his forces were not only superior in numbers to the French but also in possession of all the topographical advantages. Ulm would be an offensive base for launching powerful actions against the French. Because the Russians would never have consented to serve under someone as lowly born as Mack, the Emperor Francis had appointed another archduke, the Archduke Ferdinand as titular head of Mack's army.

The relationship between these two men left much to be desired. Mack and the Archduke Ferdinand did not cooperate even along the lines of the Archduke John and Lauer four years earlier, and the subordinate generals began to sense the tension between the two men. Mack, clearly insecure and over-challenged, confused activity with progress. Half-baked schemes to advance one unit here or there were quickly abandoned to be replaced with other schemes that were never fully carried out. All the while his opponent gathered his strength to pounce.

On 11 October the approaching Russian army was estimated to be nearly 200 miles away, or at least more than two weeks' march distant. Napoleon realised that Mack, by concentrating his forces around Ulm, had actually made the job of defeating his opponents piecemeal much easier. At the same time, at Austrian headquarters, the grim reality of Mack's position was becoming clearer by the hour. His scouts reported French units everywhere. Napoleon spurred his troops on, noting that but for Mack's forces he and his army 'would be in London now, avenging six centuries of outrage'.[24]

On the same day at Albeck, a large force of Austrians, led by Mack, probing for indications of French deployment and for possible routes of a breakout, came into contact with the 5,000-strong division of General Dupont. In the ensuing action Mack managed to drive the isolated French back but he did not follow this up, perhaps because he was slightly wounded in the engagement. The victorious Austrian force simply returned to Ulm.

Schwarzenberg's breakout. Ulm's surrender

There the Archduke Ferdinand, increasingly exasperated by Mack, secretly planned with Prince Schwarzenberg a nocturnal breakout to the north with the 6,000 cavalry. These rode out of Ulm at midnight on 14 October hotly pursued by French dragoons but by two o'clock they had made good their getaway. The following day Mack attempted a further breakout but was checked by Marshal Ney at the Battle of Elchingen where the Austrians were forced to fall back to Ulm in driving rain.

Two days later, a staff officer of Napoleon, Ségur, reached Ulm and at three in the morning asked Mack to surrender. Mack played for time and agreed to surrender on the 25th if the Russians had not arrived. But the morale of the Austrians was beyond repair. A storm on the 18th caused the Danube to burst its banks and carry away much of the Austrian camp as well as the unburied corpses that had turned Ulm into a 'pestilential latrine'.[25]

A day later Napoleon summoned Mack to Elchingen. In return for a written declaration that the Russian army was still impossibly far away, the Austrian agreed to surrender his army and the city, 'the Queen of the Danube' to the French the following day. As the rain ceased, the sun came out to reveal a long column of Austrian soldiers winding out of Ulm. On the small hill overlooking the city a party of seventeen Austrian generals resplendent in their white tunics and scarlet breeches looked hesitantly at Napoleon. A French officer asked one of the Austrians to have the kindness to point out which of their number was their commander. The Austrian replied: 'Moi monsieur: l'homme devant vous. Je suis le malheureux Mack en personne.' When presenting his sword to Napoleon, the Frenchman savoured the moment and returned it with the words: 'I return the general's sword and ask him to pass on my best wishes to his Emperor'.[26]

Francis was less obliging. On his return to Vienna, Mack was court-martialled, stripped of his rank and decorations, including the Maria Theresa Order, and then sentenced to a two-year spell in prison. The Habsburg ire was understandable. Mack had lost 51 battalions of infantry, 18 squadrons of cavalry and 60 guns. The Archduke Ferdinand reached Bohemia with barely 2,000 cavalry and the Austrian forces under Jellačić advancing from the Tyrol, unsupported and outnumbered, were forced to surrender on 14 November. The road to Vienna now lay wide open and an army of 75,000 Austrian troops, fully equipped to guard its approaches, no longer existed.

Marshal Kutuzov's Russian soldiers were still several days' march away but the forces they had hoped to link up with had literally vanished into thin air. Kutuzov had achieved prodigious feats of human endurance in marching his army from distant Galicia to the Danube valley. Thousands of stragglers had had to be abandoned and the footwear of most of those who had reached Austria was sorely in need of repair. By the time Kutuzov reached Braunau on 27 October, rumours of the disaster at Ulm were beginning to circulate.

The plight of Kutuzov now merged with the plight of defenceless Vienna. While Napoleon detached significant forces to guard the Alps and prevent the forces of the Archduke Charles marching to the relief of the Imperial capital, he manoeuvred the bulk of his army to cross Bavaria to find and annihilate the Russians.

Kutuzov, who had linked up with some Austrian remnants, abandoned Braunau and withdrew to a tighter line of defence 60 miles east on the banks of the river Enns. On the last day of October a firefight broke out between a large French force and some Austrians supported by Russian light troops at Traun. The allies conducted a disciplined withdrawal. As Kutuzov retreated along the Danube, he paused at Amstetten. While a French force under Mortier was dispatched to the north bank of the Danube at Linz to find the Russians, Kutuzov was reinforced by another Russian column, which had marched from the Turkish frontier.

The Russian scouts reported Mortier's position and, with the help of an able Austrian staff officer called Schmidt, Kutuzov drew up plans to defeat Mortier under the ruins of Durnstein castle so beloved of legend as the place where Richard the Lionheart was rescued by the minstrel Blondel. The skirmish was short but sharp: the gifted Schmidt was one of the fatalities but after a fierce fight the French withdrew to the south bank under the cover of darkness.

Lannes seizes the Wiener Donaubrücke

Napoleon immediately drew up plans to bring more of his army over the Danube to the north side and so prevent the Russians from linking up with any Austrians positioned around Vienna. The key to this strategy was to be the seizure of the Wiener Donaubrücke, a series of very fragile structures which carried the main road across the river to the north of Vienna.

Though the bridge was primed for destruction and guarded by the Austrians, the French generals simply walked across and announced to the astonished Austrians that, as an armistice had been declared, there was simply no point in any more blood being spilt. It struck one Austrian officer that all was not well when he saw the French grenadiers marching in step across the bridge but Marshal Lannes assured him his men were simply briskly marching 'to keep warm' in the cold temperatures.

The Austrian commander at the Donaubrücke had been retired for fifteen years. Count Auersperg was certainly not in the first flush of youthful energy. But as a later historian has pointed out, Auersperg's failure to defend the bridge denotes a failure 'of the will and intellect, if not downright imbecility'.[27] Even the French could not believe it. But Lannes was after all a Gascon.

The passage of Lannes over the Danube not only threatened Vienna, it severely compromised Kutuzov. Moreover, if Vienna were lost, Austrian troops coming up from south of the Alps would face a formidable obstacle in their path before they could link up with their Russian allies.

Kutuzov moved as rapidly as he could to get his army out of harm's way and withdrew north while his colleague, Bagration, threw up a screen at Schöngrabern, which Murat mistook for the entire Russian army. He sent an envoy to Kutuzov offering an armistice 'now there was peace between France and Austria'. Bagration was not taken in by the lie and Kutuzov paid the French back in their own coin by sending two staff officers to discuss terms and drag the talks out for 24 hours while Kutuzov got his army safely away. When Napoleon heard of the 'armistice' he was incandescent and sent a swingeing note to Murat who, when he received it, began to wake up to the fact that the Russians in front of him were not as numerous as he had first thought. By the time Murat attacked it was almost dark and the Russians detonated Schöngrabern to create a formidable obstacle to any pursuit. Covered by a regiment of Jaeger, Bagration confused the French sufficiently for Kutuzov to pass safely into Moravia by the following morning. By the time Napoleon reached Znaim to settle things with Murat his mood had blackened, not least because he had just been given an account of the Battle of Trafalgar.

Kutuzov continued to Brünn (today Brno in Moravia) where, joined by a strong Austrian force under Liechtenstein, he managed to bring his forces up to a formidable 80,000 men. Moreover, further reinforcements were on their way. Ten thousand elite troops of the Russian Imperial Guard were at Olmütz (Olomouc) in northern Moravia, having marched all the way from St Petersburg. More troops were marching from Poland and nearly 10,000 Austrians were assembled under the Archduke Ferdinand in Bohemia.

Above all, the Archduke Charles had managed to bring his army out of Italy in brilliant style, suddenly turning and attacking his pursuers. Meanwhile in Moravia, Napoleon was greeted with great warmth by the local population, famous for the beauty of their womenfolk, their native charm and wit. The Moravians found the French an altogether more agreeable occupying force after the Russians. But the French army was not in brilliant shape. Exhausted by its forced marches and far away from home, it needed a swift victory. If it were to retain its cohesion it would be as well to fight the decisive battle as soon as possible.

The Pratzen heights: Austerlitz

Between Brünn and Olmütz, where the allies were concentrating, Napoleon carefully reconnoitred the landscape and found, a few miles outside Brünn, the Pratzen plateau. He felt sure this would be where his troops would fight a great battle.

At Olmütz meanwhile, Kutuzov was greeted by both the Russian and Austrian Emperors. It was immediately apparent that the Tsar was *primus inter pares* and in command. The Austrian contingent was relatively small and undistinguished. The Habsburg Emperor felt it was beneath his dignity to oppose the will of the Tsar. The only Austrian to retain any influence over the military decisions was the ill-starred Austrian Chief of Staff, Weyrother, who had taken the place of the able Schmidt, killed by a musket ball at Dürnstein.

Unlike Schmidt, Weyrother lacked a firm grip on reality and, as we have already seen, had contributed significantly to the fiasco at Hohenlinden. The wiser counsels – Bagration, Kutuzov, Miloradovič and Dokhturov – favoured playing for time and if necessary wintering in the Carpathians to await re-inforcements, including the Archduke Charles, as well as the imminent decla-ration of war by the Prussians on the French.

But Tsar Alexander favoured a more dramatic response and Weyrother fell into line with typical Austrian *Anpassungsfähigkeit* (ability to fit in) and urged an advance on Brünn where the allies could menace Napoleon's right flank and send him retreating through the trackless mountains above Krems far to the west.

Weyrother divided the 89,000 troops at the allies' disposal into five columns but resolved to keep each column in close communication with the others, perhaps having learnt the dangers of excessive fragmentation at Hohenlinden. The Austrian contingent, 25,000 men including 3,000 cavalry, was commanded initially by Kolowrat but was transferred to Prince Liechtenstein. By the time battle was engaged, it had dwindled to twenty and a half battalions and forty-five squadrons of cavalry, amounting to 15,700 men.

From the beginning the allied deployment was plagued by inconsistency and woolly thinking on the part of the Austrian staff under Weyrother. Weyrother had planned to menace Napoleon's right flank but, by the time the allied army began to concentrate, it was heavily configured against the French left flank. The need to correct this error took 48 hours partly because Weyrother had only the haziest idea as to where Napoleon's right flank was.

In any event the Pratzen heights were to be critical to both sides' thinking. For Weyrother and the Russians it was the key to the French right. For Napoleon it would be the bait to lure the Russians into a battle of annihilation. Austerlitz, as Napoleon told his marshals on the eve of the battle, was not to be 'just an ordinary battle. . . . I prefer to abandon the ground to them and draw back my right. If they then dare to descend from the heights to take me in my flank, they will surely be beaten without hope of recovery.'[28]

To persuade the ranks of green-coated Russians to descend the heights an elaborate and theatrical 'retreat' by Murat's cavalry was staged. By mid afternoon, the Russians indeed began to descend and Napoleon had a leisurely dinner of *Grenadiermarsch* (fried potatoes, noodles and onions), confident that his trap was about to be sprung. At dawn, he issued further instructions and the village of Tellnitz was cleared of a squadron of Austrian chevauxlegers. A thick fog concealed the movements of Napoleon's army from the Russians on the heights. As the visitor to the battlefield can see today, the roads at the foot of the hill would be invisible from the heights in bad weather and Napoleon planned to take full advantage of his opponent's 'blindness'.

For his part, Weyrother did not discern the subtlety of his opponent's thinking. An allied officer, Langeron described how the Austrian 'came in with an immense map showing the area of Brünn and Austerlitz in the greatest precision and detail'. (The Austrian military cartographic institute set up by Maria Theresa was renowned for its maps.) As Langeron noted: 'Weyrother read his dispositions to us in a loud voice and with a boastful manner which betrayed smug self-satisfaction.' His audience of Russian generals was scarcely any better mentally prepared. Kutuzov had been drinking heavily for some days and was dozing half asleep in his chair. He and the other officers showed little interest in what the Austrian said.[29]

Weyrother proposed a left flanking movement spearheaded by the Austrian contingent with a powerful mixed column under Kienmayer, who would force the lower Goldbach stream with five battalions supported by twenty squadrons of cavalry. Two strong Russian columns would then cross the Goldbach and begin a decisive attack on the French right. All the reports, concluded Weyrother, suggested the French were weary and suffering from poor morale, especially their cavalry. As Weyrother pointed out, the Austrian army knew every inch of the terrain as they had conducted exercises there in 1804. It is still subject to debate to what extent the Russians understood what the Austrian was proposing. As Weyrother's orders were written in German, some time was needed to translate them into Russian.

Unsurprisingly, the execution of Weyrother's plan left a lot to be desired. While Kienmayer's battalions of barely 3,000 men, drawn from far from undistinguished regiments, was soon engaged, the Russian columns collided with each other. Liechtenstein's cavalry milled about aimlessly without orders until the Prince ploughed a route through the Russian infantry to reach the point where he assumed he was supposed to be. As the Russian columns became mixed up with each other, Weyrother watched from a hill, his face increasingly anxious. He felt he could hear the French below, but neither he nor anyone else on the hill could see them.

Meanwhile below, Kienmayer's Szekler infantry was bravely storming the village of Tellnitz only to be cut down by well dug in French voltigeurs. Five times they stormed across the Goldbach only to be driven back. Eventually the elite 7th Jaeger reinforced them and drove the French out. But Kienmayer's skirmish was a sideshow. A strong French force advanced under the cover of the mist on to the Pratzen heights to emerge in what Napoleon would later refer to as the golden sun of Austerlitz.

Towards nine in the morning a fierce battle developed along most of the front. As the French retook part of Tellnitz they began fanning out. An Austrian regiment of Hessen-Homburg hussars under Oberst Mohr charged them with devastating effect and Kienmayer was able to reoccupy the village. Mohr mistook the French 108th regiment for Bavarians, whom the hussars hated; few Frenchmen escaped.

The hapless French survivors of the 108th attempted to flee to the north only to come under murderous fire from their own side, a French light infantry regiment. Tellnitz was now safely in Austrian hands and two regiments of Austrian cavalry passed through it to take up attacking positions to the west. Further to the east, the village of Sokolnitz was engulfed in flames as Russian artillery bombarded it at close range. An hour later Sokolnitz had been occupied by the Russians, who had engaged the best part of 5,000 men to clear the village of a single regiment. However, the arrival of two French brigades sent the Russians back into the north-western corner of the village from where they repeatedly failed to drive the French out. Some 33,000 Russian and Austrian troops were now bogged down, attempting to put the Goldbach and its villages well behind them.

Meanwhile on the Pratzen heights, the French under Ste-Hilaire and Vandamme had collided with the fourth Austro-Russian column delayed by the usual deployment problems, the chief of which was Liechtenstein's improvised passage through their ranks. The surprise and shock of seeing the French, who seemed to appear from the fog below, galvanised the senior Russian officers. Suddenly the allied position had become immensely perilous as the rear of their three most advanced columns was about to be threatened by the unexpected appearance of the French on the heights. With commendable speed the fourth allied column recognised the danger and deployed, splitting into two. At the same time, the second allied column, which still had not reached the plain of the Goldbach, halted and, seeing what was happening on the heights behind them, reversed front and marched back up the heights against the right flank of Ste-Hilaire's breakthrough.

Major Frierenberger's guns

Meanwhile from the east a mass of unidentified regiments was advancing towards Ste-Hilaire. In the mist it was difficult to make out who they were. As they approached an officer called out from 300 yards in barely audible French: 'Don't shoot. We are Bavarians.' At first the Frenchman appeared satisfied by this but an enterprising officer as a precaution reordered his line to fire on the newly arrived troops if they proved hostile. As he climbed forward to reconnoitre at close range, he recognised the white Austrian uniforms. Although at first the troops appeared rather unpromising – the French account noted a number of invalids – the brigade which had emerged under General Rottermund contained 3,000 men, recognisable by their orange facings, of the elite Salzburg 'House' regiment, tough mountain fighters who with their Styrian counterparts would become some of the most highly decorated units in the Austrian army. Supported by a Russian brigade, the Austrians stormed the heights at the point of the bayonet. Weyrother watching from nearby had his horse shot from beneath him. But the French held on to the Pratzenberg, counter-attacking with the bayonet and slaughtering the wounded. Slowly the Russians fell back. Langeron's attempts to reinforce them from the plain below ran into a withering crossfire. At the little hamlet that is now called Stare Vinohrady, the Salzburgers fought stubbornly until attacked by two and a half brigades from three sides, but the allied fourth column on the Pratzen had ceased to exist. As the French poured in their fire from every side, the allies began to break into disorder.

Further to the north, attempts by Hohenlohe to deploy cavalry floundered on the clay and vines of Stare Vinohrady. Time and again the allied cavalry counter-attacks were poorly coordinated. The Austrian artillery showed its traditional professionalism when a Major Frierenberger arrived with a battery of 12 guns from Olmütz.

These guns from Olmütz reached Rausnitz at the moment when fugitives came pouring back to confirm the frightful news of the various disasters experienced by the army. The commander, although he had no real covering force, positioned the battery on the most advantageous site on some high ground to the right of Welloschowitz. The army he faced was a victorious one. Undaunted, the Austrian battery opened up in its turn against the main battery of the French and their leading troops. The Austrians fired their guns with such skill that they compelled the French to pull back their batteries in a matter of minutes. Some of the French pieces were silenced and the advance of the whole French left wing ground to a halt.

The gallant Austrian artillery major had not only enabled Bagration's units to escape total destruction, he had successfully blocked the road to Hungary. Frierenberger's actions were but a glimpse of success in an otherwise grim landscape. In an epic cavalry engagement the Russian Chevalier Garde, resplendent in dazzling white uniforms, had been annihilated by Napoleon's Guard cavalry, putting paid to the Russian reserve's attempts to retake the Pratzen heights. With the heights secured, Napoleon attacked the rear of the first three allied columns as they battled along the Goldbach below. A giant pincer movement was about to destroy a good third of the allied army. At Tellnitz, the Austro-Russian force which had been in non-stop action for nearly eight hours began to organise a fighting withdrawal. It had screened the retreat of the remnants of two Russian columns and it was high time to fall back. The Austrian cavalry formed the rearguard and the O'Reilly Chevauxlegers, perhaps the finest light horse the Habsburgs possessed, repeatedly charged the pursuing French cavalry and deployed a battery of horse artillery to good effect, keeping at bay an entire division of dragoons under General Boye. Napoleon, having seen this, was furious at the Austrian cavalry's superior quality. He ordered a hapless aide-de-camp to go and 'tell that general of my dragoons that he is no f— good'.[30]

'A battle has been fought . . .'

Kienmayer had conducted a model withdrawal without losing a single gun. But as the sun shone through the mist nothing could disguise the scale of the defeat. The Austrians and Russians now rallied on the road to Hungary. Though reinforcements were arriving, notably Merveldt, it was clear to both Emperors that this coalition war was over. Francis with his characteristic detachment sent a message to his wife saying simply, 'A battle has been fought . . . It has not turned out well.'

Francis knew it was time to see what terms he could secure from the French Emperor. Liechtenstein was sent to arrange the preliminaries, and at two in the afternoon on 4 December, a carriage escorted by a squadron of lancers and a squadron of hussars came into sight on the road to Hungary. The Austrian cavalry halted 200 paces behind while the carriage continued, stopping only where Napoleon was waiting in front of a hastily prepared fire. The door of the carriage opened and out stepped, immaculate in white and red beneath an enormous greatcoat, the Austrian Emperor. With all the breeding of his House he gazed impassively as Napoleon made to embrace him. Not by a flicker did he betray for a second his emotions. The Frenchman may have crowned himself an Emperor but in every inch of his demeanour the Austrian Kaiser demonstrated that, galling though the aftermath of a lost battle might be, the Habsburgs were above such petty humiliations. Prince Liechtenstein attempted to break the ice but it was Francis himself who thawed the atmosphere with a few polite superficialities designed to put the Corsican upstart at his ease. Eyewitnesses noted Francis's solemn bearing. Though only 36 years old, Francis appeared a generation older, his hat balanced on the back of his head, carrying a stick and incapable of the slightest spontaneous movement, so it seemed to the French.

The chill in the air soon dissipated, and within twenty minutes the sounds of laughter could be heard. Francis had won an armistice for himself and it would take effect within 24 hours. The hard-pressed Russian and Austrian troops could withdraw unmolested.

Austrian dead numbered about 600, considerably less than those of their Russian allies, many of whom appeared to have lost their lives as wounded men bayoneted by the French towards the end of the battle. Another 1,700 Austrians ended up as prisoners but, on the whole, the army's discipline had held throughout the day, in contrast to their Russian allies.

But Weyrother's planning had proved another example of disastrous Austrian staff-work. Once again allied columns, as at Hohenlinden, had been too far apart to offer each other practical support. Once again, as the battle developed in a way different from Weyrother's calculations, Austrian staff-work had proved incapable of adapting. The Russian generals lost each other in an orgy of blame but on the whole the collective Austrian view appears to have taken its cue from the Kaiser's low-key response. The Austrian units had fought well, in some cases exceptionally well, but the battle itself had 'not gone very well'.

The diplomatic consequences were to prove demanding for the Habsburg Emperor and his empire. Venetia, Friuli, Dalmatia and Istria went to the arriviste 'Kingdom' of Italy, while Tyrol and the Vorarlberg were handed over to the detested Bavarians. The spineless leaders of the German states were rewarded for their craven behaviour and elevated to such portentous titles as Grand Duke or, in the case of Bavaria and Württemberg, King. Kaiser Franz lost more than 2.5 million of his subjects and his family's traditional hegemony in Germany and Italy. It was not in the nature of the House of Austria to regard these calamities as anything more than a temporary setback. In four years the sword would be taken up again and this time at the head of the Austrian army there would be one of the outstanding soldiers of the age.

CHAPTER 10

Shattering the Myth

ASPERN AND ESSLING

The army had fought well but it had been out-generalled. After Ulm and Austerlitz, it was clear to the dynasty that two things were needed to offer the chance of success in any future struggle against Napoleon. First the Archduke Charles must be put in charge; and then the army had to be given time to train to adapt to modern warfare.

The Peace of Pressburg signed on Boxing Day 1805 did not impose a Carthaginian settlement on Vienna – that was almost to come in four years' time – but the conditions were certainly onerous. As usual the Emperor Francis coolly summed it up in a letter to Tsar Alexander. The treaty, he wrote, 'turned out to be capitulation before an enemy who pressed home his advantages to the full'.[1] With that detachment and low-key logic which marked so many of Francis's utterances, the Kaiser dispassionately concluded: 'I have been forced to abandon part of my provinces so that I may preserve the rest.' Amputation always signified life for the dynasty.

The 'part' that had to be sacrificed was significant: Venetia, Friuli, Dalmatia and Istria were all either rich agricultural lands or strategically important, although none of them formed part of the hereditary crown lands. The ceding of the Tyrol to Bavaria was another matter. The proud and tough men (and women) of the Tyrolean valleys spoke their own dialect and were fiercely contemptuous of outsiders. They only needed to hear a Bavarian accent for their hackles to rise. Heavy-handed Bavarian rule fuelled the embers of national revolt. The surrender of Lindau and the surviving Habsburg possessions close to Breisgau confirmed the anti-Habsburg arrangements in Germany.

These arrangements meant establishing the tapestry of German mini-states as dependencies of France. Baden and Württemberg had already been rewarded for their support of the Napoleonic cause. On 16 July 1806, the Napoleonic protectorate of the 'Rheinbund' confirmed the allegiance of sixteen princes of southern and western Germany who were now obliged, in the event of hostilities, to supply 65,000 soldiers to serve France. Amid great celebrations these little German princes, mediatised and much reduced, declared their wish to be forever separated from the German Empire. The Holy Roman Empire, which had been a Habsburg prerogative, had become an empty shell; its prestige diminished, its utility dismantled. Faced with the choice of the crown of Charlemagne or the guns of Napoleon, the leaders of these Lilliputian states had embraced collaboration.

Five days later, Emperor Francis laid aside the sacred regalia of the Holy Roman Empire and the magnificent crown of Charlemagne and never wore them again. Two years earlier, prompted by the defection of the German princes, the Emperor had been crowned Emperor of Austria. From now on the old Austrian crown lands were to be the engine of Habsburg power and, because many of the inhabitants were German-speaking, the dynasty saw clearly the need to ignite the flames of German nationhood, to 'fight fire with fire'.

With the tenacity of purpose which characterised Austria throughout this period, the Emperor supported this policy with a new programme of military reform. The keystone of this reform was, at last, the elevation of the Archduke Charles. Putting aside the petty intrigues and jealousies of the court, Francis appointed his brother 'Generalissimus', supreme commander, as well as President of the Aulic Council.

With his usual energy, Charles immersed himself in turning the Austrian army into a modern force, capable of holding its own against the French. This was no easy task. After Austerlitz, Napoleon stood at the zenith of his powers. He was a warlord who seemingly had never known defeat. Charles worked away at his reforms: new units of reserves, new tactics and drills, new formations and more cost-effective uniforms. Napoleon continued to wage war. A year after Austerlitz, the Prussians were wiped out in a single afternoon on the fields of Jena and Auerstädt. For once Napoleon was not exaggerating when, in his dispatch of 16 November 1806, he noted: 'Of the Saxon-Prussian army we have found nothing left. All of 145,000 men have been either killed or wounded or taken prisoner. The King, Queen, General Kalkreuth and 10 or 12 officers are all that have escaped.'[2]

The Archdukes create a Landwehr and a Reserve

The experience of the Napoleonic Levée en masse and the scale of the armies now waging war had left the Archduke Charles in no doubt that the Imperial forces needed to be recalibrated to incorporate a flexible and reliable reserve drawn from a wider base. The creation of the Landwehr (militia) and Reserveanstalt (reserve depot) went a long way to achieving this, providing a source of manpower that could release regular soldiers for the front line once hostilities broke out. Charles did not expect too much of the Landwehr at first, convinced as he was that Napoleon's army could only be defeated by highly trained regular troops. It was left to his brother the Archduke John, whose travels around Alpine Austria had left him impressed by the calibre and patriotism of the local population, to pursue the Landwehr idea to its logical conclusion. A shattered Prussia and a demoralised mediatised constellation of princes created a vacuum that could only be filled by Austria. The Archduke John knew well how to exploit this and Charles was happy to let his brother get to work on the new reserve.

It helped that the news of Prussia's annihilation at Jena encouraged many German writers to place their hopes for liberation not in Berlin but in Vienna. Thus the great Prussian writer Heinrich Kleist (1777–1811) turned his creative talents to praising the Archduke Charles while his Austrian contemporary Heinrich Collin (1771–1811), whose *Coriolan* inspired Beethoven, composed a poem with a refrain that became the hymn of the newly established Landwehr:

Auf, ihr Völker, bildet Heere!
An die Grenzen fort zur Wehre!

(Awake you peoples: form your armies!
To the frontiers: grab your weaponry!)

To Collin's cries were added those of the younger Ludwig Uhland: 'Awake powerful Austria!' and Ernst Moritz Arndt: 'Awake Friends! Franz is our Emperor not Bonaparte!' and finally, striking a note of almost Prussian vengefulness, Max von Schenkendorf: 'German Kaiser! German Kaiser! Come to Avenge! Come to Save!' ('Komm zu rächen! komm zu retten!'). These sentiments were not entirely welcome to Emperor Francis, who was always suspicious of populism. When told that someone at his court was a patriot, he waspishly and famously enquired: 'But is he a patriot for me?' a phrase later transposed and immortalised by John Osborne's 1966 play of the same name.[3]

The Archduke John was so engaged with the Landwehr that he devoted most of the winter of 1808 to the organisation of the force and its training. Typical of the Archduke John's devotion to the new unit was his insistence that orders and training were inescapably bound up with the idea of a 'comprehensive defence of the land' (*umfassenden Landesverteidigung*). Uniforms and weapons had to reflect local traditions. John fought many battles with the rigid

Austrian military hierarchy to ensure that the militia were not forced to adopt weapons that were alien to them or drill that was adapted for more formal manoeuvres.

As John noted: 'The utter concept of this method of waging war rests on movement and speed, cunning and courage, calm in critical moments: this is what we must encourage.'[4] The officers were urged to speak frequently with their men and involve themselves even with their domestic issues (*häuslichen Angelegenheiten*). At all times the officers of the Landwehr must demonstrate their 'support and paternal comfort'. To help encourage these instincts of solidarity among the other inhabitants of the crown lands, the songs of Collin were translated into Polish, Czech, Slovene and Hungarian.

While John worked ceaselessly on perfecting the Landwehr into a credible force, instilled with a *Befreiungshoffnungsrausch* (the intoxicating hope of liberty), Charles worked away at the regular forces in an attempt to raise not only morale and discipline but initiative and prestige.

The period of service in the regular army was reformed. Instead of a life-long commitment to 'the colours', service was now limited to men between the ages of 18 and 40. Fourteen years was the envisaged length of service in the artillery arm; twelve years in the cavalry and ten years in the infantry. Recruitment was by ballot and the prescribed term of service could, on expiry, be extended for a further six years through agreeing a 'Kapitulation'. (This automatically offered a bonus and the right to marry while in service.)

A newly organised regular Reserve consisted of those who were eligible for military service but were superfluous to standing military requirements. Members of the Reserve were required to train each year but they retained their jobs and were not required to change location. During their annual training they would be paid for their military service as if they were regulars.

In addition to its permanent establishment, each Austrian line regiment came to have two Reserve battalions, members of which had to train for four weeks in their first year of service and three weeks in their second. By 1808, this 'sedentary army' had reached a strength of 60,000 men.

To ensure that the manpower once available to the Habsburgs in the German provinces of the Holy Roman Empire was not entirely lost through the supineness of their rulers, 'Confinenwerbung' (Frontier recruitment) replaced the old 'Reichswerbung' (Imperial recruitment). This enabled German volunteers to join the Austrian service.

The Archduke John's Landwehr complemented this Reserve perfectly. Charged with the defence of the 'Habsburg soil' and including in its remit all men capable of bearing arms, not just those between 18 and 45, it drew on the experiences of the American War of Independence. For the first time in

Habsburg history, the Landwehr developed the concept of a nation in arms. Uniforms were to be worn over civilian clothes and the individual companies that made up the Landwehr were divided between localities. The Landwehr enjoyed a strong local flavour not dissimilar to the Yeomanry regiments of the British Army, which had been raised a few years earlier (without the particular social structures of the English rural population which were perhaps only echoed by the feudal arrangements of the Hungarian lands).

Four Landwehr companies comprised a Landwehr battalion, which usually trained every Sunday. Each month, training in larger formations took place. In the event of one of the Imperial frontiers being threatened, the Landwehr would muster and take an oath of loyalty in front of the local commanding general of the area. As the Landwehr recruited locally, many middle-class professionals were automatically drawn to its commissioned and non-commissioned officer ranks. Those who had never wished to bear arms – teachers, professors, doctors and lawyers – were turned by the Archduke John into patriotic and well-drilled defenders of the dynasty. Only in Galicia and the Bukowina was the Landwehr not introduced, because the local population was still considered politically unreliable, due to the painful partition of Poland some fifteen years earlier. Elsewhere, the Landwehr slowly became a regular feature of the Imperial military landscape and would rise to the occasion in 1809 with singular heroism, bearing out John's faith in the middle class he so greatly preferred to the aristocracy, whom he viewed as lethargic and gripped by a 'longing for distraction' (*Zerstreuungssucht*).

The creation of the Landwehr and its elevation to a well-trained force was an ambitious project which could not easily be perfected in the few years of peace between Austerlitz and the next round of hostilities. John was given the rank of Landwehrinspektor for Inner Austria (Styria, Carinthia and Carniola). He immediately set about imbuing the troops there with his ideals of a democratic defence of the regions along Spanish lines. From the summer of 1808, the uprisings of the Spanish militia and their successes had illuminated the Austrian military horizon like flashes of inspired lightning. But discipline in these newly formed units was still far from rock solid at home by the time hostilities began. Petrie notes how some units of the Landwehr had staged bayonet attacks against their officers and how two regiments refused to march at all.[5]

As the news of these formations spread, Napoleon began to realise that Austria planned to challenge him yet again. In 1808 he had accepted assurances from Vienna that the Landwehr was not an aggressive force but in January 1809, while at Valladolid, he decided to leave Marshal Soult to pursue the defeated British from Corunna. By returning to Paris Napoleon hoped to discover in more detail the significance of the disquieting rumours reaching him from Vienna.

As the fateful year of 1809 began, war became increasingly certain. In March, the Archduke Charles hastily ordered the establishment of volunteer battalions. Thousands flocked to the Habsburg colours. In Bohemia alone, 6,000 men rushed to join the newly formed Legion Erzherzog Karl. In Vienna, six battalions of volunteers were recruited, mostly from among middle-class professionals. They would put up a formidable fight against some of Napoleon's best troops.

Perhaps most important of all, the Archduke adopted a 'corps' system of army organisation which would be a key factor in the improved Austrian performance in the campaigns of 1809.

Mobility increased: The new Jaeger Corps and artillery reform

These developments were complemented by a strengthening of the Empire's light infantry capabilities. In 1804 a 'Jaegerregiment' had been established from the different light infantry formations that had fought since the First Coalition War. This had been increased to become a 'Jaeger Korps', inspiring the Archduke Charles to establish eight full battalions of Jaeger by 1808. Crack elite troops drawn from the Alpine valleys and forests, these were soldiers noted for their strong mental and physical qualities, but their elevation reflected other political considerations.

The proven quality of Austrian Alpine troops had led to the Tyrolean 'Landmiliz' being established from the remnants of the century-old Tyrolean 'Verteidigungsmiliz' or defence militia. Though Tyrol was now nominally part of Bavaria, the Tyroleans secretly organised themselves with little encouragement into a formidable irregular force of some 20,000 insurgents ready to strike as soon as Vienna gave the word. The incorporation of all these Alpine units into the coming campaign imparted something new to the army the Archduke Charles was creating: these forces would be the Habsburgs' first ever *Volksheer* (People's army).

These developments were only part of the process of bringing the Imperial forces into the new century. They were accompanied by equally significant reforms in drill and tactics. Artillery was reorganised into a distinct and wholly independent tactical unit. The Archduke abolished the old reliance on tactical lines of batteries supporting infantry in favour of more mobile formations, drawing on the experience of Napoleon's more inventive use of artillery. The brigade artillery was divided into batteries of eight guns while horse-artillery batteries would comprise smaller, more agile units of four guns and two howitzers, The so-called static artillery (*Positionsbatterien*) would be made up of four heavy guns and four howitzers. Garrison artillery was divided into fourteen districts to reduce the century-old exclusive dependence on Bohemia.

The Archduke John was appointed commandant of engineers and, in the short time available, he established a strong line of defensive forts along the French model. One of these, Komorn on the Danube, was fortified under Chasteler and would serve Austria well in the coming campaign.

Similar reforms awaited the infantry. Although the grenadier battalions were still denied regimental status, they were now formally grouped on a permanent basis into a 'Grenadier Korps', which was to serve as a tactical reserve directly under the command of the FZM or FM of any campaign (*Feldzeugmeister* or *Feldmarschall*).

In addition to the Grenadier Korps, the infantry now comprised 63 line regiments, one Jaeger regiment of eight battalions and 17 Grenz regiments (including the Czaikistenbattalion: boat crews on the Banat Military Frontier). Each regiment comprised five battalions, each of these made up of four companies. Cavalry was divided into eight Cuirassier, six Dragoon, six Chevauxleger, 12 Hussar and three Lancer regiments, each of eight squadrons. This gave a slight preponderance to light over heavy shock cavalry and again emphasised the need for greater mobility in the arm.

The new 'Generalgeniedirektor', the Archduke John, reorganised the structure of the Engineer corps, which was commanded by 145 officers, of whom nine were of general rank to reflect the corps's importance. A Mineurkorps and Pontonier battalion (sappers) of six companies were also placed under Archduke John's control.

Overhaul of staff and the Hofkriegsrat: New tactics: the Mass

After the fiasco of Weyrother's staff work at Austerlitz, the Archduke Charles ordered a total overhaul of the Austrian staff system. The *Generalquartiermeisterstab* (General Quartermaster Staff) was organised into a logistics staff comprising one general, 24 staff and 36 senior officers. Military transport was divided into divisions based on the regional capitals.

No less important was the overhaul of the venerable Aulic Council or Hofkriegsrat whose lack of support Charles had so often experienced in the previous five years. This institution was now split into four subdivisions with responsibility for: (1) military affairs; (2) political-economic issues; (3) artillery and engineering issues; and (4) judicial and legal matters. (Subdivisions 1 and 2 were the critical parts of the Council because they dealt with the issues of uniforms, training, recruitment and equipment.)

Charles was formally placed above the Council so that the chain of command was entirely unambiguous. At the same time the forces of the Empire were divided into corps formations which, in 1808, were assigned to the individual crown lands. Each corps had its own internal organisational structure, General Staff, artillery commander and quartermaster so that in the event of hostilities it could operate completely independently of any other military unit.

Changes were introduced to enable weapons drill to become simpler. On 1 September 1807, the new Reglement for infantry was introduced. Besides simplifying certain parts of musket drill, it reinforced marksmanship skills significantly. Every infantryman in the Austrian army now had to hit a certain number of targets, shooting from a distance of 300 paces, if he was to continue to serve. Fire discipline and formation drill were also strongly emphasised in training. A new quick-pace drill (120 paces a minute) was introduced to speed up movement and reactions. At the same time more complicated drills such as firing while marching in oblique formation, a relic of the Frederician wars, were dropped.

In their place came some of the Archduke's own ideas of tactical formation, which his military theorising had evolved after careful study of Napoleonic techniques. Notable among these was the 'Mass', a formation that drew infantry into flexible lines, capable of withstanding (even in theory on occasions charging!) cavalry and column attack. The 'Mass' in its novel use of company front and support lines became a hallmark of the 1809 Austrian infantry tactics and generally served them well.

The 1806–7 regulations also humanised discipline: 'All forms of maltreatment and heavy-handedness in the drilling of a soldier are firmly forbidden. Brutality is usually the evidence of some lack of knowledge and destroys that self-respect which must be at the very heart of a soldier.'[6]

To save money, the expensive classical helmet that virtually every unit of the Austrian army wore was to be replaced by a cheaper black felt shako. By 1809, not all of the Hungarian infantry regiments had been equipped with these, so Austria went to war against Napoleon more or less attired as she had been at Austerlitz, though with an army which had digested many useful lessons in the art of war.

In the whirlwind of reforms, the Archduke Charles left no stone unturned: new cadet companies were established in Olmütz and Graz while the Wiener Neustadt Academy was reorganised to lengthen the time of study to eight years. Everywhere the Archduke did his utmost to ensure that, when it came to the next measuring of swords with Napoleon, the Austrians would be in better shape. It was a desperate race against time.

Another two years, perhaps even another eighteen months, and most of these reforms would certainly have borne fruit. However, fate dictated that Austria would wage war once again against the Archduke's wishes and before she was ready. But that the campaign of 1809 was fought with such glory for Austrian arms is entirely due to the Archduke Charles. Europe stood at Napoleon's feet; only the insurgency in parts of Spain and the refusal of London to treat prevented him dominating the entire Continent. With Prussia vanquished and Russia pacified, Austria was under no illusions that she stood alone. Neither England nor Spain could offer her a single soldier or gun. Prussia, broken and dismembered, with her armies ruined, could barely offer moral support, and when some officers urged support for the Austrians, their spineless and weak King would have none of it. England, her treasury at a low ebb, offered diversions but none of these came to pass until long after the campaign on the Danube was over.

'Defence of the Fatherland'

The war party in Vienna – which included the Emperor's 22-year-old third wife, Maria Ludovika (who had been forced to flee her home in northern Italy), Metternich and Count Stadion – noted that Napoleon was in Spain, and that almost 200,000 French troops stood near the Danube. If not now, when? John gradually came over to the war party, as did Charles, reluctantly but dutifully following the consensus of his House. On 6 April 1809, Charles issued a rousing proclamation: 'The defence of the Fatherland calls us to new deeds. . . .'

With that genial duplicity which had long been a hallmark of diplomacy, Metternich, the Austrian Ambassador, remained in Paris, lulling Napoleon with soothing words into a false sense of security. The French Emperor believed that Vienna would never declare war with her Ambassador still *in situ*. It was only on 16 April that Napoleon cautiously ordered a concentration of his forces on the Danube. But communications between Paris and his commander there, Berthier, were complicated by bad weather, which affected the Napoleonic telegraph system because it relied on clear visibility throughout the seven-and-a-half-mile gaps that separated any two telegraph posts.

The Archduke Charles, by advancing along the Danube, hoped to launch a surprise attack against the French in Bavaria. The Archduke preferred first the north bank of the river in the hope of raising Prussian and other German support but he had overestimated the enfeebled Prussian capacity for recovery. When this failed to materialise, he moved most of his forces to the southern side of the river in a time-consuming manoeuvre. The Archduke John was to watch the Alps and march into northern Italy where it was hoped he could tie down as many French troops as possible. Another Austrian force would operate in Poland to observe Prince Poniatowski and his forces, which were loyal to Napoleon.

First clashes in Bavaria: Landshut and Eckmühl

At Landshut one of the Archduke's Corps (V) attacked a strong force of Bavarians, driving it from the town, before turning to attack an isolated French force under Davout occupying Regensburg. Unfortunately, the Archduke had discovered too late that Davout was unsupported. He could have been crushed 24 hours earlier, but Napoleon had now arrived. With his arrival, the uncoordinated and disparate French forces began to take on some cohesion. But even Napoleon misread what was happening. He did not realise until it was almost too late that Davout was facing most of the Archduke's army.

As soon as he saw his mistake, his legendary skills of improvisation took hold immediately. Davout was supported by the bulk of Napoleon's forces and a concerted effort was made to break the Austrian left, which was sheltering behind a battery of guns. Prince Rosenberg and his staff of IV Korps watched for two hours while 22 Austrian battalions held out against overwhelming numbers until 68 French battalions attacked them on three sides. As Napoleon committed his cavalry, Rosenberg's retreat degenerated into a rout. Repeatedly he had asked Charles for reinforcements but repeatedly Charles had advised him to extricate himself as best he 'thought fit'. The Archduke had no intention of sacrificing fresh troops on ground not of his own choosing.

Nevertheless, seeing panic taking hold among Rosenberg's men, Charles immediately deployed a Cuirassier brigade and his Grenadier Reserve under Rohan to stem the tide. The Austrian cavalry slowed the French advance, forcing the infantry to form squares, but Rohan's grenadiers with the exception of two battalions broke under the tide of IV Korps's demoralised remnants. IV Korps was facing annihilation as a heavy mass of French cuirassiers approached to finish off its survivors.

It was 7 p.m. and the rising moon illuminated a dramatic scene.[7] Six thousand French cuirassiers in two lines supported by their Württemberg and Bavarian auxiliaries advanced towards two much thinner lines of Austrian cuirassiers supported on their flanks by some squadrons of hussars. The tired French horsemen trotted forward while the Austrians with the gradient in their favour galloped towards them, about to break into a charge. As there were five French regiments against just two Austrian, this fight could only last a few moments and the Austrians were soon riding as fast as they could back to their lines. Two battalions of Austrian grenadiers appeared and formed square but were cut to pieces by St Sulpice's Cuirassiers. The Archduke Charles himself escaped only with the greatest of difficulty. Exhaustion on the part of the French, and darkness, rescued the Austrians from annihilation. Charles however could take some consolation from the fact that he had husbanded his forces and he had not even committed 33,000 of his troops.

Thus ended the Battle of Eckmühl; unsatisfactory for Napoleon, who had not deployed his characteristic ruthlessness to inflict a 'second Jena' and highly unsatisfactory for the Archduke Charles, who had seen his elite units fail to rise to the occasion, though they had bought him the time necessary to effect an escape from the clutches of his foe.

In fact Charles's position at this stage was stronger than it appeared. Eckmühl was a rearguard action fought by Rosenberg against a greatly superior enemy attacking him from the west, south and east. Two Austrian Korps, I and II, were far from demoralised and the Generalissimus still had his lines of communication with Vienna, though these now ran through Bohemia. True, II and IV Korps had been defeated and had retired in poor shape, but they had not been completely crushed. On the morning of 23 April Charles wrote to his brother, the Emperor, advising him to leave Schärding where he was awaiting results and not rely on the Archduke to be able to save either him or Vienna.

While Napoleon paused, Charles got most of his army across the Danube, leaving a small force to withstand the siege that was inevitable the following day when the French invested Regensburg. It was here that Napoleon received his only known wound in twenty years of making war, when a spent cannon-ball hit his foot. Napoleon's failure to pursue Charles has been attributed by the renowned French military historian General H. Bonnal to his dwindling grasp of the strategic imperative to destroy his opponents. His Bavarian campaign involved his forces in three battles in as many days but each time Charles was able to withdraw in reasonable order. As the Austrians had lost two-thirds of their artillery the question rightly arises as to what might have happened had the French cavalry pursued them 'epée dans les reins'. But Napoleon later admitted to Wimpfen that he never imagined the defeated Austrians would rise like a phoenix from the ashes within weeks.[8]

Napoleon bombards Vienna

The road to Vienna lay open and a direct march on Vienna seemed very tempting. Above all, Napoleon could not imagine that the Austrian forces might have improved since he had last routed them four years earlier. This underestimation of his foe was to cost Napoleon dearly.

It fell to Hiller's Korps to slow down the French advance on Vienna. At Neumarkt he inflicted a bloody nose on the French pursuit but later his movements became less energetic. By 2 May, the Emperor Francis had been at Linz and ordered Hiller to make a stand along the Traun river with his right wing holding Ebelsberg. Choosing a strong and defensible position exploiting the unfordable nature of the Traun, Hiller deployed half of his brigades as a rearguard and positioned his artillery on the heights above, from where they could sweep the river's floodplain with fire.

As the French arrived, Schustekh and Radetzky's troops covered the last withdrawal of the bulk of the Austrian troops, eventually being forced to withdraw at the point of the bayonet. The town of Ebelsberg was also cleared by the French after fierce fighting with the new Austrian Landwehr.

Hiller failed to take advantage of the French fragility while they were cut off from reinforcements with the bridges burning behind them. Instead he ordered a retreat. Entire regiments and batteries that had done nothing, 200 yards from the town, now simply about-faced and marched away. For this act of extravagant feebleness, Hiller was later denounced by one of the campaign's Austrian historians as utterly 'unworthy of the rank of general'.[9] Hiller would blame the conflicting orders he had received from Charles and the Emperor. Charles blamed the entire fiasco on Hiller. A few hours later, the two men were reunited at Krems, further up the Danube. By all accounts it was a far from cordial encounter.

The news of Charles's setbacks reached John in Italy and the Austrian forces occupying Warsaw. The need to break off these actions in the secondary theatres and support the main action along the Danube had become urgent. The Archduke John's 40,000 men had inflicted a defeat on Napoleon's son-in-law, Eugene de Beauharnais, at Sacile on the Venetian plain. But John gave up his ideas of pursuing his foe and began a fighting withdrawal over the Alps to support his brother. As the news of Charles's defeats reached Poland, the Austrians broke off their occupation of Warsaw. In Tyrol, the news of the Archduke Charles's struggle ignited the tinderbox. A tough group of assorted innkeepers and priests, including Andreas Hofer, Pater (Father) Haspinger, Martin Teimer, and their lieutenants Straub and Speckbacher, led the Tyrolese in a true *Volksaufstand* (popular uprising) against the detested Bavarians and hurled them out of the land of the red eagle.

In Vienna, the Stadt-Kommandant, Count O'Reilly, prepared his very modest dispositions as well as he could. The Irishman O'Reilly had joined Maria Theresa's army as a boy of 14, rising to high rank, partly thanks to his marriage to a Countess Sporck. The Archduke Maximilian, nominally in charge of the Austrian forces in the capital, ordered Hiller to march to support him from Krems but Hiller was under strict orders from Charles to rejoin the main army in Bohemia. Notwithstanding his rather strained relationship with the Archduke, not being a natural courtier, Hiller obeyed Charles's orders unhesitatingly.

Having resisted for a few hours, Vienna capitulated after a terrifying bombardment set houses ablaze in the old town. The Austrian writer Franz Grillparzer, patrolling the bastions, took refuge in a cellar where he found himself sitting next to Beethoven, who was also taking shelter from the bombardment. By 12 May, Napoleon entered the city as conqueror and master. By the 13th he was in the Imperial apartments in Schönbrunn. In disguise and accompanied by his faithful personal security chief, Schulmeister, he set off to explore the city, noting warily the Francophobia of its inhabitants. As he walked along the ramparts which had withstood the Siege of the Turks, Napoleon could enjoy and marvel that here he, the Emperor of the French, was in the capital of the heirs to the Caesars. But for all the satisfaction this clearly afforded him, his main task still lay ahead. Across the Danube stood the Archduke Charles with 130,000 troops. Unlike in 1805, Napoleon had entered Vienna before crushing his opponents. He had not secured any of the Danube crossings, and this was to have bitter consequences.

Lannes attempts to cross the Danube at Nussdorf

The attempt to secure a crossing at Nussdorf was entrusted to Lannes, Napoleon's favourite marshal who had taken the bridge at Hollabrunn by subterfuge four years earlier. In the intervening years, he had distinguished himself in Spain where, to the astonishment of his staff, he had advanced initially alone with a ladder over his shoulder to scale the ramparts of Saragossa. Lannes was the epitome of the dashing marshal of Napoleonic stamp who had risen through the ranks.

The Nussdorf bridge was held by two battalions of the newly formed Vienna and Lower Austria Landwehr. Clearly recognisable in their pike-grey uniforms with red facings, they were gradually being reinforced by regular troops, notably the Kerpen infantry regiment (later infantry regiment Nr 49). These volunteer units were not expected to put up much resistance. But as Ste-Hilaire's division sent an advance party of voltigeurs across the existing bridge, they were met by such a hail of fire that they were forced to take shelter on a small island in the river. Repeated attempts to secure the other side of the bridge failed. When Napoleon himself arrived to see what was holding things up, he sent a larger force of some 800 men at the charge, over the bridge, only to see them all beaten back by murderous fire along a very small front. As the

French closed, the Austrians threw them back using bayonet and sword with a violence that quite surprised the observing French officers.

Napoleon brought up artillery but this proved singularly ineffective. A further assault on the bridge brought no result other than the surrender of 900 French soldiers driven to seek shelter on the far side of the island. The Wiener Freiwillige (Volunteers) had earned their laurels in spectacular form. More importantly, being denied access to the other bank of the Danube at Nussdorf, the French could only cross the Danube further downriver, in the far more difficult terrain of the swampy Au landscape around the Lobau. It is no exaggeration to say that the great Austrian victory which was about to be played out at Aspern was made possible only by the steadfast courage of the Vienna Volunteers that day at Nussdorf.

Faced with the difficulties at Nussdorf, Napoleon focused on the construction of a bridge at Kaiser Ebersdorf. The modern-day rerouting of the Danube, accomplished by the great Viennese architect Otto Wagner at the turn of the twentieth century, gives the modern visitor little insight into the flow of the Danube in Napoleon's time, but the former Imperial hunting preserve of the Lobau still conveys an idea of the natural obstacles Napoleon faced in constructing his crossing here. His engineers had chosen to build a bridge which would have to run the 825 yards to the Lobau island over a sandbank, then the small island known as the Schneidergrund, then over another small island. Once the Lobau was reached with its myriad streams and forests, a further bridge had to be built, so that another branch of the Danube could be forded, this time 180 yards wide. Given the tendency for melted snow from the mountains to flow into the tributaries of the Danube in May after a few days of sun, thus raising its level dramatically, the construction of a bridge at this point was a challenging undertaking.

Fireships and mirrors: Napoleon struggles in the Lobau

There were human elements to add to the natural obstacles. Sudden flashes of sunlight glinting on the 'Wiener Hausberg', the Bisamberg, betrayed one of these threats to Napoleon's bridge construction. From the summit of the Bisamberg, an Austrian observation post deployed telescopes and signalling equipment to coordinate the actions of teams of engineers under Staff Captain Magdeburg further upstream. From their left bank base, Am Spitz, the engineers studied the currents of the great river very carefully, then began sending down floating trees, fireships and so-called water mills, formidable floating wheels as well as an array of other floating detritus which crashed into the construction of the French bridge with devastating effect.

The Archduke Charles gathered his forces on the left bank. These excluded III Korps under Kolowrat which was attempting, without much success, to harass a French force under Bernadotte around Linz. Critics of the Archduke Charles have questioned his failure to occupy and deny the Lobau island to Napoleon but the Archduke was conscious of the inferiority of his soldiers in the terrain of the Lobau.[10]

For his troops, the best chance of success was a conventional battlefield. Because the training of the last two years had been designed to equip them for precisely such a confrontation, the few Austrian troops stationed on the Lobau were quickly withdrawn after some desultory skirmishing.

Recently returned from Spain, the cavalry commander Lasalle joined Napoleon. He was keen to get the bulk of his horse over the bridge but at 5 p.m. on 19 May, a fireship crashed into the bridge, putting it out of action before less than half of his cavalry was over. Given that the bridge had been completed a mere five hours earlier, the effects of the Austrian operation directed from the Bisamberg heights were pivotal.

The Austrian observatory had communicated the progress of the bridge at Ebersdorf to Charles by semaphore telegraph. It was clear that the moment of decision was soon to arrive and Charles was determined to seize the initiative. Issuing orders to prepare for battle, the Archduke now gave a short Napoleonic oration of his own. In its sentiments it reforged the century-old indissoluble bond between the dynasty and its armed forces begun in 1619:

> Tomorrow or the following day there will be a great battle! The result of it will in all probability decide the fate of the monarchy and of the freedom of every one of you. Between eternal disgrace and undying fame there is no middle way .... this decisive battle will be waged under the eyes of our Kaiser and of the enslaved inhabitants of our capital who look for their liberation in the bravery of the army.

As Napoleon's army made its progress piecemeal across the river and the rest of his cavalry crossed in the course of the night, a secure bridgehead was constructed and Napoleon attempted to discover whether the Austrians, who were now assembling in front of him, were anything more than the rearguard of '8,000' that Lannes believed them to be. The Austrian cavalry screen gave nothing away, and the French cavalry commander Bessières, relying on reports of his scouts, said there was 'nothing within miles'. Only two able generals, Masséna and Mouton begged to differ.

As the river rose, Napoleon rode anxiously upwards towards Aspern, the village that was the key to his left, only to find Austrian hussars blocking his way beyond the line between Aspern and Essling, the village that was the key to his right. Between these two villages, which were to become the anvils of the coming battle, there was barely a mile of open ground. The villages were equidistant from the bridge and both had strong defensive features. Aspern had a walled cemetery and church while on the fringes of Essling stood a massive three-storey granary. But Napoleon was not expecting an attack, so he gave no orders for these two villages to be occupied in strength or fortified. By 1 p.m. on 21 May, Napoleon had safely transferred three divisions of infantry and two divisions of cavalry. As another fireship crashed into the bridge, Napoleon cursed the fate which had left him at the mercy of the Danube and Austrian obstacles but he appears not to have reckoned with an imminent Austrian attack. Indeed, according to Pelet, he was minded to withdraw back on to the Lobau, leaving only a strong force to hold the bridgehead.[11]

The struggle for Aspern

Napoleon was thus greatly perturbed to become aware of Hiller's advance guard (Nordmann's four battalions and eight squadrons) advancing on Aspern, driving in the weak French outposts shortly after 2 p.m. As Nordmann's battalions attempted to enter Aspern, a hastily erected defence by a single battalion of Molitor's infantry stood their ground. Supported by another battalion, they gradually drove off the rather half-hearted Austrian attack. A second attack was now made with the advance guard of I Korps (Bellegarde) but though this gained a toehold in the village it was easily driven off by French reinforcements from four regiments, which began pouring into the village from all sides. A third attack in the face of these reinforcements failed even more miserably, not least as it limited itself to probing the village only from the west and south-west.

By 5 p.m., seeing the failure of his attacks, the Archduke decided with no regard for his personal safety to ride over to Bellegarde's men and personally exhort them to take Aspern in a *Generalsturm*. After positioning VI Korps on the south-west, I Korps on the west and II Korps on the north, he led the attack himself at the head of the men of VI Korps.

This fourth attack, involving more than twenty battalions, brought the Austrians deep into the village, driving Molitor's outnumbered and exhausted defenders out of the church and the cemetery. Every house became a miniature fortress as the fight degenerated into fierce hand-to-hand combat in which every possible weapon – from ploughshares to buckets – was used. By 6 p.m. most of the village was in Austrian hands and a spirited counter-attack by St-Cyr failed to make any impression.

While the struggle for Aspern raged, Napoleon ordered his cavalry, some 7,000 horsemen, to attack the Austrian infantry of II Korps (Hohenzollern) and their artillery, which was bombarding the last French defenders of Aspern very effectively. The Austrian infantry was drawn up in 'Masses', the formation that the Archduke Charles had evolved for his infantry. The battalion 'Mass' involved an infantry battalion's companies forming a series of three lines each of company strength with wide gaps between the lines. As the French cavalry trotted towards the Austrian infantry, these companies closed the gaps and levelled their muskets with parade-ground precision at their officers' command. At 300 paces the French halted while their commander, Marulaz, ordered an aide to call on the Austrians to surrender:

> 'Lay down your arms,' cried the French officer only to be met with some shots and the cry in broad Viennese Meidling dialect of 'Get them your-self!' ('Heults eich selber!')[12]

The few shots fired were enough to convince the French that this 'generous' offer had been spurned and they cantered forward, waving their curved sabres wildly and shouting. The first three lines of Austrian infantry levelled their muskets and waited until, at 15 paces, their officers, distinguishable by their dark coats and drawn swords, gave the command: 'Feuer!' At that range, the rolling company volleys were devastating and half the French horsemen fell. Reinforced by d'Espagne's Cuirassiers, the remnants of Marulaz's charge turned to attack the flanks of the infantry but were driven off by an energetic Austrian cavalry counter-attack in which the O'Reilly Chevauxlegers, despite their lack of armour, distinguished themselves again, cutting down the brave d'Espagne as he tried to reorder his squadrons.

The granary at Essling

Meanwhile at the village of Essling, the Austrian columns under Rosenberg had finally arrived at 6 p.m. after a long march from their starting position. They immediately went into action against the single division of Boudet which, with the redoubtable Lannes, defended Essling. With great care, Lannes had used the afternoon to construct a strong defence of Essling, in particular ensuring the formidable granary was well supplied with ammunition for the imminent struggle.

Around 6 p.m. d'Espagne's Cuirassiers, hot from their repulse in the centre, were now ordered to attack Rosenberg's men, which they did. But once again they were driven off when the infantry deployed swiftly into 'Masses'. This manoeuvre slowed down Rosenberg's assault on Essling, so he now deployed his artillery, which set most of the village on fire. Three attempts by his infantry to storm the village failed, and the huge granary on its eastern perimeter proved impregnable though held by only a few companies of French marksmen.

The Austrian attacks continued until about 11 p.m. but were so badly coordinated that Lannes was able to move his beleaguered defenders to each crisis point as it developed, thus denying the Austrians anything but the briefest of tenures in Essling's 'Long Garden'. As night came, Rosenberg fell back in good order from Essling. More French cavalry had arrived over the newly repaired bridge but they too were unable to make any impression on the Austrian infantry, who had discovered a rock-like steadiness under fire that had eluded them in so many earlier campaigns.

The Archduke Charles had reason to be satisfied with the day's performance. Though aware that he had engaged only part of Napoleon's army, he had seen his infantry and cavalry perform well against the greatest army of the world under the most gifted military leader in history. As the French bridge began to function again, Charles ordered the renewal of floating fireships against it. He also deployed his Grenadier Reserve to Breitenlee. At first light, the morning would certainly bring a renewal of the attack.

The French pipped Charles to the post. Beginning at 3 a.m., they moved their reinforcements into Aspern. Taken by surprise by so early an assault, the Austrians fell back in confusion, leaving only the Aspern church and cemetery, which had been fortified by them in the night, in Habsburg hands. By 7 a.m. the Austrians had been driven out even from there, and the entire village was once again under French control.

At Essling another attack by Rosenberg had been beaten off by Lannes. With his two flanks now secure, it was time for Napoleon to take advantage of the apparent weakness of the Austrian centre and drive a wedge between the two wings, crushing the Archduke's forces into the dust. This ambitious task was originally planned for Davout, but because Davout was not ready it was given to Lannes, the most impetuous of all Napoleon's marshals and the only one to whom Napoleon extended his very rare gift of almost unqualified friendship.

Lannes led three divisions at the Archduke's centre but the ground he covered was swept by more than 200 Austrian guns which poured case and canister into the slow-moving French infantry, destroying most of the French guns in the process. The French advanced in compact formation, a comment on the deterioration in quality of Napoleon's troops, but this only made them even more vulnerable as the Austrian artillery cut huge swathes through their ranks.

Despite all this, Lannes's troops began to close with the Austrians, who started to panic as the Frenchmen came closer and closer. A spirited French cavalry attack caused two regiments of Hungarian 'Insurrectio' (Volunteer) cavalry to flee. As the Frenchmen closed in on Infantry Regiment Nr 15 'Zach', one of its battalions wavered and was sent to the second line immediately. Under cover of the French cavalry attack, Lannes had brought up some of his remaining artillery pieces and they began to fire at close range into what was left of Infantry Regiment Nr 15. Half the battalion fled in wild disorder, leaving only 200 men with fixed bayonets grouped around the colours and a handful of officers calmly awaiting their fate. For the Austrians the crisis of the battle had arrived. Their centre was about to cave in.

The Archduke Charles holds the line

Fortunately, the Archduke rose again to the occasion. With the reckless disregard for his own personal safety that so marked him as a field commander, Charles galloped off to the colours, his horse rearing, and pointing with his arm at the enemy he screamed at his troops to hold the line. This astonishing performance immediately rallied the regiment's fleeing soldiers and the remnants of the 'Zach' held firm. Many accounts have the Archduke seizing the colours.[13] Immortalised in paintings and the great equestrian statue by Fernkorn, which stands to this day opposite the Hofburg, the scene has been much embroidered. Such was Charles's innate modesty, he always denied seizing the colours, usually with the self-deprecating observation: 'Me carry such a heavy weight? . . . hardly!'

In any event, irrespective of whether he seized the colours of the beleaguered Zach regiment or not, his very appearance stabilised the situation. The example of the dynasty's warlord had a galvanising effect on the troops. The French who had come under relentless fire in turn began to waver. Ste-Hilaire, their leader, had been struck down by Austrian grapeshot. As the Archduke galloped across to bring up his Grenadier Reserve the French advance came to a standstill.

Napoleon, seeing his attack on the Austrian centre faltering, committed Bessières's Cuirassiers, but they had barely passed through the recovering Austrian infantry when they were hit by an Austrian cavalry counter-attack, again spearheaded by the O'Reilly Chevauxlegers, and they fell back in disorder. Lannes, surveying his decimated forces, asked Napoleon for reinforcements but Davout's Corps was still on the wrong side of the bridge, which had been smashed again in two places by another convoy of Austrian fireships. This time, the Austrian pyrotechnics carried off not only the bridge but also an entire company of engineers.

By 9.30 p.m., the French effort to break the Austrian centre was over. There were no more forces with which to renew the attempt and, as the Austrian infantry advanced, it became apparent to Napoleon that he was facing disaster with incalculable consequences for his army. How was he to get them back across the broken bridge to the safety of the Lobau?

Meanwhile at Aspern and Essling the battles continued with murderous intensity. At Aspern, Austrian artillery reduced what was left of the village to rubble before a vigorous attack led by the Splenyi infantry regiment supported by a battalion of the Benjowsky regiment proceeded to eject the weary French defenders at bayonet point. Back and forth the two armies fought. Just as the Austrians seized control, a fierce counter-attack once again drove them into the western corner of the village. At Essling, four battalions of Austrian grena-diers managed to achieve what the previous day twenty-five battalions of line infantry had failed to do. Led by d'Aspre, the grenadiers fell on Essling with such violence that the French were almost driven out of their impregnable granary. As the village seemed to be lost and the granary about to surrender, two battalions of the Young Guard appeared with the *pas de charge* beating on their drums. They recovered the situation enough to allow the French to disengage from the village and to withdraw towards the bridge where the Old Guard, Napoleon's last reserve, stood ready to cover the retreat once the bridge had been repaired.

An hour later the rubble of Aspern fell to the Austrians. Only the granary at Essling continued to hold out. At one point the Archduke had to order his grenadiers to desist from storming the granary so heavy were their casualties. One battalion was reduced to forty-six men in barely fifty minutes. Elsewhere in the village, the French fire notably slackened. Both armies were exhausted: they had been in action virtually without break for 24 hours.

Napoleon falls back

A spirited French rearguard action by cavalry and infantry failed to make any real impression on the Austrian Fröhlich infantry regiment which, drawn up in masses, easily beat off the attack. The action had bought time for the bridge to be repaired. The Archduke left it to his 200-gun battery to 'encourage' the French retreat rather than expose his weary troops to more slaughter. The French were retreating and they had been soundly defeated. The people of Vienna who had come out of the Imperial capital to watch the battle cheered on the French defeat, until Nansouty's Cuirassiers, unable to cross the bridge, venting their anger drew their sabres and forced the civilians back to the city, where the news of Napoleon's defeat spread like wildfire.

Later, strategists criticised the Archduke harshly for not falling on the French rearguards and driving them into the Danube. But Charles, ever aware of the responsibility of keeping the army intact to fight another day, sought a good moment to negotiate. Like most Austrian officers he would have agreed with that anonymous Austrian cavalry ensign during the Seven Years War who said, 'In combat it is a question of driving away the unrighteous enemy, not of exterminating the human race.'[14]

The battered French, falling back on the Lobau, took stock of what had happened. More than 21,000 of them lay dead or dying, including Napoleon's favourite marshal, Lannes, wounded by a cannonball which had shattered both his knees. Austrian casualties were almost as high. In addition they had lost one colour and six guns. Though the battle had not annihilated the French army, it was an undisputed defeat. The blow to Napoleon's prestige was immense, encouraging as it did every one of his enemies. Charles had reason to hope that the long-awaited British diversionary expedition would now take place, accompanied by a general uprising in Germany and Russia's desertion of the French alliance. Napoleon's own bulletins attempted to disguise the defeat but those who survived with him knew otherwise. As Napoleon would later say to his brother-in-law Murat: 'You did not see the Austrians at Aspern? Well you have seen nothing! Absolutely nothing!'[15]

As an apocalyptic thunderstorm now descended on the weary French troops, shivering and sheltering in the Lobau, Napoleon ignored advice to negotiate with the Austrians and applied all his energy to avenging his defeat as soon as possible. But first he lay down to rest, and it is said he slept for 36 hours without break.[16]

The operations of the Archduke John

What meanwhile had become of the army of the Archduke John on the southern side of the Alps? John it may be recalled had been tasked with observing French forces in Italy and cooperating with the uprising led by Andreas Hofer in Tyrol.

On 13 April John was at Udine, where he directed the operations that caught the French rearguard at Pordenone, and then defeated Eugene's forces at Sacile, inflicting 5,000 casualties. As the uprising in Tyrol gathered momentum, Eugene's forces appeared about to be crushed by a pincer move-ment executed by the Tyrolese and the Archduke John. But the news from Regensburg proved Eugene's salvation and John was hurrying back towards Austria via the Brenta, inflicting one last defeat on the French at Caldiero, when Eugene attacked him.

But as he withdrew, John dispersed his forces very widely to guard the frontiers. As part of his forces under Jellačić moved back via Laibach (Ljubljana) to Graz, he himself moved on to Klagenfurt and prepared to march towards Salzburg. Both Eugene and John were far from gifted military commanders. We have already acquainted ourselves with John's first efforts. Fortunately for him, he faced only Napoleon's stepson, to whom the French Emperor had written: 'I am sorry to see you have no notion what war is or how to carry it out.'[17]

The movements of these two different forces were generally unremarkable. Only at Graz did the presence of a Styrian garrison under Major Hacker stubbornly resist the French. The great fortifications of Graz were no stranger to the French. They had been besieged without success in 1805 when Napoleon had visited the picturesque city on the Mur briefly, punning wittily at the time: 'Ville de Grâce sur les rives de l'amour'.

Four years later, Graz became the fulcrum for an altogether more vivid series of conflicts. As the Archduke John fell back on Hungary, Broussier's division occupied Graz and began shelling the garrison from the Vorstadt. Hacker's garrison, which consisted of barely 900 men, resisted eight attempts by more than 3,000 infantry to take the fortress by storm. Each time Hacker's men drove the French back with losses. The few guns at Hacker's disposal lobbed cannonballs into the French positions on the other side of the river Mur.*

The struggle for the citadel of Graz assumed ever more dramatic proportions. As it was impossible to storm, the French prepared to starve the garrison out but an Austrian relief force under Gyulai, made up mostly of Croatian and other Grenzer, managed to break through and resupply the citadel. Gyulai's advance guard drove Broussier out of Graz but a few days later, on the evening of 25 June, hostilities flared up again. Two divisions under General Marmont approached Graz unaware that Broussier's men had retreated. After a difficult action in Dalmatia against Austrian irregulars, they had been ordered to march to the Danube to reinforce their Emperor after the defeat at Aspern.

The two divisions, which had spent the last three years on garrison duty in the barren rocks of Dalmatia, were 'crack' troops; 'the best corps in my army', noted Napoleon. They were undiluted by the weaker recruits of the recent three years. The 84th Ligne formed Marmont's advance guard. Pushing into Graz from the south, it was surprised to find the St Leonhard church and

---

* One of these can still be seen today lodged in the facade of the fine Biedermeier house to the left of the Kepler bridge.

cemetery with its high walls occupied by a company of Austrian infantry. Colonel Gambin advanced two of his companies but they were driven off.

Taking advantage of night, the French scaled the walls and surprised the defenders. Gambin locked his prisoners into the church and set about strengthening the churchyard's defences. His scouts brought the alarming news that the city was full of Austrian troops and that a large number were in fact advancing towards them from the main square less than half a mile away. Gambin had barely 1,200 men and two cannons to hold his perimeter. By daybreak the first of many assaults by several thousand Austrians began. Each one was beaten back, but on two occasions the Austrians penetrated the cemetery and, on one of these, were even able to release the prisoners in the church.

Gambin's men had no hope of surviving the night, so they broke out after dusk. For this heroic defence, which cost the 84th a quarter of their strength, Napoleon would award them the right to bear on their eagles the motto: 'Un contre X'. Austrian casualties were in excess of 500. (The cemetery today still recalls this struggle in the statue of the Madonna at its entrance whose heart is pierced by a French sabre. It is perhaps appropriate that two of Austria's greatest martial sons, Tegetthoff and Benedek, are buried here.)

When Marmont's main force met up with Gambin they stormed back into Graz bayoneting every prisoner and wounded Austrian they could find in a brutal assault. Mercifully for the inhabitants, Marmont was under strict orders not to tarry in Graz but make haste to Napoleon. His divisions executed a series of brilliant forced marches, which brought them rapidly over the eastern Alps towards Vienna.

The Battle of Raab

As these events unfolded in Styria, the Archduke John was confronting a numerically and qualitatively superior force under Eugene near the Hungarian fortress of Raab. Despite the mixed quality of some of the Archduke's forces, the Austrians occupied a formidable defensive position. Guarding their rear was the great citadel of Raab while their centre was powerfully strengthened by the stone farm of Kis-Megyer. John's right was anchored on the Raab river. The Austrians simply had to hold their position as Eugene spent his forces attempting to dislodge them.

Inevitably the stone farm, key to the Austrian centre, became the scene of the most violent attacks. Twelve hundred Austrian grenadiers, the cream of General Colloredo's command, withstood five assaults before requiring reinforcements by Kleinmeyer's Grenadier brigade and the Alvinczi infantry regiment. These drove off two French divisions, causing widespread panic in the rear of Eugene's lines. But while the French infantry was in headlong retreat, their cavalry charged the Austrian left flank's cavalry who were mostly Hungarian light cavalry raised by 'Insurrectio' and of questionable quality. These were completely routed and were about to be massacred when they were saved by two regular Hungarian hussar regiments (EZH Josef and EZH Ott). They held up the French at the cost of 200 casualties.

Inspired by their cavalry's success, the French infantry with their Italian regiments renewed their assault on the farmhouse. The Lecchi Italian Guard pushed the Austrian grenadiers out of the farmhouse and, with cavalry threatening to encircle his left, John felt compelled to withdraw. In five hours the Austrians had lost the control of the south bank of the Lower Danube and Napoleon's urgently needed reinforcements could now proceed to Vienna unharassed.

No greater contrast to Marmont's energy could be seen than the sluggish withdrawal of the Archduke John towards his brother. John had suffered around 5,000 casualties at Raab but his army had withdrawn more or less intact. After leaving units to reinforce the garrison at Raab, he moved slowly towards Pressburg with 15,000 men. He seemed deaf to his brother's request to make haste towards Vienna where Napoleon was taking meticulous care to prepare for another reckoning with his most implacable foe.

CHAPTER 11

Clash of Titans

WAGRAM

Aspern and Essling had given Napoleon a great shock. An army he had come to underestimate had proven capable of inflicting a substantial defeat on the Grande Armée. The Archduke Charles had tried out his new reformed war machine and it had been effective. Against any other general the Austrian army would undoubtedly gain the day, but against the greatest soldier of the time it would have its work cut out, as the following weeks would demonstrate.

The Battle of Wagram, one of the epic encounters to unfold on the stage of the Napoleonic Wars, was remarkable on many counts. With more than 300,000 men deployed it was, in 1809, the largest battle ever to have been fought in history. Moreover, like Aspern, it raged for the best part of two days and, as in that battle, all three arms of the Habsburg army fought superbly, making it a much closer contest than Napoleon ever expected.

Chastened by the logistical failures of his preparations at Aspern, Napoleon was determined never to repeat the circumstances that had led to his first defeat. On waking after his long sleep, he meticulously planned the construction of new bridges across the Danube, called up reinforcements from all over Europe, north and south of the Alps and, above all, kept his opponents guessing as to when and where he would fight the next great battle. The check at Aspern had proved salutary. This time nothing would be left to chance.

Napoleon builds up his advantage

For the Archduke Charles all these developments eroded the advantages he had held at Aspern. First and foremost, in contrast to that battle, he was now going to have to fight the next at a numerical disadvantage. By 4 July, Napoleon had almost 188,000 troops at his disposal while the Archduke possessed barely

135,000. Petrie notes that the Archduke in theory also had an additional 13,000 under the Archduke John, another 7,500 (V Korps) under Reuss and 1,800 men of III Korps detached on the Bisamberg but none of these units saw any action in the battle.[1]

To replenish the losses of Aspern, fresh troops, mainly Landwehr units, were rushed to the Archduke. At Wagram, Charles would face Napoleon's forces with 31 out of his 175 battalions, nearly a sixth of his army, composed of the relatively new Landwehr regiments.

To add to the Archduke's difficulties, the actual choice of battlefield lay with Napoleon. Right up until the French concentration on 4 July, the Archduke was in two minds as to where he would fight his battle. His staff favoured driving the French back into the Danube as they attempted to cross from the Lobau but the Archduke was aware from his observatory on the Bisamberg that Napoleon had reorganised his artillery, whose performance had been so weak at Aspern. A considerable French battery was now stationed on the Lobau. If the Austrians were to drive the French back as they crossed the Danube, they would have to do so under a merciless bombardment. The Archduke, conscious of his numerical inferiority, favoured a defensive position behind the little stream known as the Russbach. This was barely two and a half feet deep or more than three yards broad at its widest but behind it the ground rose slightly and in front of it were several villages which could be fortified to menace the French frontal assaults.

Further in front were the ruins of Aspern and Essling, which could also be used as positions to harass the French advance. Charles occupied this site with units of Nordmann's Advance Guard. It is worth recalling that, a year earlier, the Austrian High Command had war-gamed a battle closer to the Danube. Many officers who had participated in that exercise gave up with reluctance the idea of contesting the French crossing over the Danube. The placing of Nordmann's Advance Guard so far ahead of the Archduke's centre was a compromise which later events would challenge.

All in all, Charles's front stretched for some twelve miles from Bisamberg across to Obersiebenbrunn. On his left where, if all turned out well, he would eventually be reinforced by the Archduke John's 13,000 troops coming from Hungary, the village of Markgrafneusiedl formed a powerful obstacle. On the right, the Austrian position hinged on the two villages, Süssenbrunn and Breitenlee, while the key to the Austrian centre was the hamlet of Aderklaa and behind it Deutsch-Wagram. Of course Charles wanted to defeat Napoleon, but he was at a disadvantage in numbers, and supplies had had to come all the way from Moravia and Bohemia rather than nearby Vienna. As so often in Habsburg military history, his first priorities would be to preserve the army for future operations to defend his House and to support any future negotiations. To risk a repeat of the catastrophic Prussian defeat at Jena was not an option because, in this case, it would most likely see the Habsburg Empire erased from the map. For this reason, too, Charles settled on the choice of a strong defensive position well back from the river. He was realistic enough to realise that the dice were not loaded in favour of an Austrian victory. But the morale of his army was high and under their Generalissimus they knew they could deny Napoleon an easy victory.

When the French crossed the Danube, Charles ordered his artillery to open up. Earlier attempts at disruption by Austrian fireboats had proved fruitless because of countermeasures taken upstream by the French. But even though much of the French army was over the Danube by noon on 5 July, Charles at first did not expect Napoleon to fight that day. Rather, he assumed that the French army would need the day to bring themselves into position. The Imperial Guard had still not arrived by 3 p.m. and Bernadotte, an especially truculent marshal, had only reached his place in the line by 2 p.m.

At 5.30 p.m. the previous day, Charles had written to his brother John to tell him that he had no intention of fighting close to the Danube and that John should march towards Markgrafneusiedl. This strongly suggested that Charles was not expecting to fight on the 5th. But four hours later, a second letter to his other brother, the Emperor, suggested that Charles thought a general attack was imminent.[2]

Napoleon advances

Napoleon ordered a general advance at 2 p.m. Two hours earlier he had sent light cavalry to worry the Austrian outposts. Under orders, some Austrian units, under Liechtenstein's command, had begun to fall back. Nordmann's advance guard soon evacuated the Aspern/Essling line after losing most of their artillery. As the two armies finally made contact along the entire front, the Archduke's forces were drawn up in an L-shaped formation, the hinge of which rested on Aderklaa. Wimpffen, Charles's chief of staff, saw this as two pincers to crush the French, a scheme which Charles sought to abandon as the battle developed, only to realise that his staff could not deliver a rearrangement of his entire lines now that battle had begun.

The Austrian right was formed by VI Korps under Klenau, and III Korps under Kolowrat. Charles's centre was made up of I Korps (Bellegarde) and II Korps (Hohenzollern). To his left, arguably the weakest part of his position was Nordmann's Advance Guard and Rosenberg's IV Korps with Radetzky commanding the Advance Guard Division. The Grenadier Reserve

(17 battalions) was under the command of Liechtenstein. At the personal disposal of the Archduke Charles at all times, it stood behind the hinge of the Austrian position.

Against this strong position, Napoleon ordered Masséna against the Austrian right and Davout against the left where he was convinced the day would be decided. This thinking had unintended consequences for the French. Napoleon's dispositions that day left the centre of his position to arguably the weakest formations: the Army of Italy under Eugene and the Saxon troops under Bernadotte, a marshal who had married an earlier lover of Napoleon and who was erratic as a commander. The Army of Italy, while distinguishing itself at the Battle of Raab, was not up to the quality of Napoleon's best French regiments. The Saxon infantry (unlike their renowned cavalry) were even less reliable. Easily demoralised, they also bore the distinct disadvantage – in a battle where the enemy almost universally wore white – of wearing white uniforms themselves; and, of course, speaking German. This was to cause confusion on many occasions in the course of the battle, with deadly consequences for the unfortunate Saxons. Given the German 'Vaterland' propaganda that had been whipped up by the Austrians in the last few weeks, they might perhaps be excused their rather half-hearted efforts. The Austrians were not immune either to such considerations: on the second day of Wagram, grim harbinger of things to come a century later, a squadron of the Schwarzenberg Uhlans, Poles recruited from Galicia, feebly surrendered to their kinsmen serving in the Polish cavalry of the Imperial Guard.[3]

Bernadotte's Saxon cavalry were among the finest in Europe. As they advanced on Aderklaa, they successfully attacked the motionless Austrian cuirassiers of Roussel's brigade. (Roussel, like Nordmann and d'Aspre and several other Austrian officers, was a French émigré.)

The Austrian Jaeger and Vincent Chevauxleger

Bernadotte faced 90,000 Austrian troops, and the Austrian right wing alone comprised 50,000 troops. Austrian reinforcements in the form of Lederer's Cuirassiers drove off the Saxons easily. As Bernadotte's line began to stall opposite the village of Baumersdorf, a line of Austrian Jaeger rose up from the folds in the ground to pour a withering fire into the Army of Italy.

Behind the Jaeger stood the 68 guns of Hohenzollern's Korps (II) and his infantry drawn up in battalion 'masses'. As the Jaeger withdrew to the village of Baumersdorf, Hohenzollern sent 1,500 men of the 8th Jaeger battalion under General Hardegg and the 2nd battalion of the Archduke Charles Legion (a volunteer unit) to stiffen the village defences. The Army of Italy began to slow down. Oudinot, one of Napoleon's more capable generals, whose forces were the link between Davout and the Army of Italy, fed in his best troops, including the 'terrible' 57th regiment of the line, perhaps the most prestigious line regiment in the entire Napoleonic army.

The 'terrible' 57th stormed into Baumersdorf but the Austrian Jaeger could not be budged. Mostly recruited from the Alps or the hills of northern Bohemia, the defenders were physically some of the strongest soldiers in the Habsburg army and more than a match for the 'terrible' 57th who, for the first time in their regimental history, fell back in disorder. After regrouping and reinforced by an entire division, they stormed back up to Baumersdorf again. Despite the assault by more than 7,000 veteran French troops, the Austrians clung on tenaciously to every building. Once again, and with impeccable timing, the Archduke Charles turned up just as this onslaught began to make the Austrians waver. Placing himself at the head of the Vincent Chevauxlegers, Charles drew his sword and urged the light cavalry forward. When they appeared to hesitate, Charles galloped up to them and roughly shouted at them in Viennese dialect: 'It is clear to see that you gentlemen (*die Herrnschaften*) are no longer (*san nix mehr*) the Latour dragoons!'*

Their honour impugned, the light horse shouted back, '*Doch! Doch!* We are!' and charged straight back into the fray with more effect. Elsewhere along the line the Colloredo and Zach regiments held on with renewed energy. As had happened at Aspern and Essling, the Archduke's presence had stabilised the situation. Hohenzollern, placing himself at the head of some cavalry, charged the French, driving them well back over the Russbach. By 8 p.m. Oudinot's troops were in full retreat, silhouetted by the setting sun. Oudinot, the strongest link in the chain of attack, had suffered 5,000 casualties. The forces under Eugene and Bernadotte had fared even worse.

The Archduke rallies his troops again

Bernadotte had sent Dupas's brigade, a scratch force of Saxons and French units, to attack Bellegarde's centre between Baumersdorf and Wagram. As they crossed the Russbach, the Austrian skirmishers opened up from every conceivable fold in the ground. But this time the French, undaunted, moved forward and captured the Austrian gun line and sent the Austrian first line of infantry reeling back towards the Austrian second line, which began to waver, facing an attack from the French cavalry as well.

---

* A reference to the great charge of the Seven Years War at the Battle of Kunersdorf in which the Vincent regiment had taken part as the Latour dragoons.[4]

At this moment, yet again with his legendary timing, the Archduke Charles appeared. Placing himself at the head of the Erbach infantry regiment, he rallied his troops and pushed back Dupas's brigade. As Dupas fell back, his men noted with relief that support was arriving on his right. Through the din and smoke they could make out those two stalwarts, Macdonald and Lamarque leading seven battalions of the Army of Italy. The men of Bellegarde's infantry showed signs of wavering but fortunately for the Austrians their artillery began pouring canister and shot into the French ranks with such violence that, coupled with the Archduke rallying the infantry into a counter-attack, the French broke. A charge by Hohenzollern's Chevauxleger sent them tumbling back across the Marchfeld, seized by panic. 'It was useless to rally the men,' Macdonald later wrote: 'The men were carried away crossing the stream in the utmost confusion.'[5]

The Army of Italy had suffered 2,000 casualties. With their rout, Dupas's men finally broke and ran for their lives pursued by the Vincent Chevauxlegers and the Hesse-Homburg Hussars. As the sun set, the flames of the straw around Baumersdorf, ignited by artillery fire, illuminated the entire scene so that even Napoleon, who was watching with mounting concern from afar, could be in no doubt as to what was happening.

It was not yet over. Bernadotte's IX Corps ordered to take Wagram failed to make any impression on the defenders. The Austrian Reuss-Plauen regiment drove the Saxons back in house-to-house fighting. In panic, the retreating Saxons and the French fired upon each other as the gathering gloom disguised the differences in the Austrian and Saxon uniforms. Their rout which reduced their numbers by half could be made out in the twilight. On the Austrian left, Davout had been repulsed without the withdrawal turning to rout. The French cavalry had simply failed to penetrate Nostitz's four regiments and the fight there had never really developed beyond an artillery duel. Everywhere else the French Emperor had seen his men disastrously defeated. Only darkness brought the promise of some respite.

It is a sign of Napoleon's genius that, having witnessed the scenes of disorder that had overtaken even some of his best regiments, he remained utterly unperturbed and confident that the morrow would bring about the Austrians' destruction. He had failed to make a quick breakthrough but the morning would bring the long-awaited victory. Of that he was sure. But of one thing he was not sure and this gnawed away at him as night fell: what would the Archduke Charles do next? Berthier, his chief of staff, sent his trusted aide Lejeune to scout the Austrian positions and ascertain whether Charles planned to offer battle. Moving south towards Neusiedel around midnight, he saw troops massing for attack, and he hurried back to warn Napoleon, but the line of Austrian vedettes was impassable and Lejeune's priceless intelligence was wasted.

The Archduke seizes the initiative

Charles could contemplate the day's events with some satisfaction. His troops had fought well and had supported each other on several occasions without needing to be ordered to do so. He had not wished to fight along the lines of the 'pincers' tactics but the fact was that the disposition of his army had been well adjusted to see off the French assault. If the Archduke John could arrive in time, victory indeed might be possible, but Charles was not to know that his last message urging John to make all haste had been delayed by a terrible storm the previous night.

With or without John, Charles resolved, most audaciously for a Habsburg commander, to seize the initiative and launch an early attack on the French. Towards midnight he issued his orders for the battle to continue. At 4 a.m., shortly before dawn broke, a concerted attack would be made across his entire front, which would advance across the Russbach.

These orders, issued as they were shortly before midnight, did not reach the various Korps commanders until after 1 a.m. The staff machine of the Austrian command was unused to working so feverishly in the early hours of the morning. While some Korps, notably Rosenberg's, got into position ready for the 4 a.m. start, others which had far greater ground to travel, notably Klenau's on the Archduke's right but also Kolowrat beyond him, were simply not ready by that hour.

Irrespective of this and indeed oblivious to the asymmetry of the deployment, Rosenberg's advance guard led by Radetzky crashed into Davout's position shortly after 4.30 a.m. in front of the Austrian right flank, just as the French were preparing for an assault on Markgrafneusiedl. The Austrians, with colours aloft and bands playing, marched into Glinzendorf and Grosshofen achieving near-total surprise. Napoleon, hearing the sounds of battle to his right, immediately assumed that Archduke John had arrived. Swiftly he detached a division of cuirassiers, together with horse artillery and the Guard, to support Davout.

In the first light, Charles could see from his vantage point at Wagram that the expected attacks by his right-wing corps had simply not materialised, and that Rosenberg was isolated and in danger of being wiped out by superior French forces undistracted by the other Austrian Korps commanders Klenau or Kolowrat. These two Korps would need another hour at least before getting into position and, by that time, Rosenberg's Korps unsupported would simply have been annihilated.

Radetzky's fighting withdrawal

Reluctantly Charles gave the order shortly after 5 a.m. for Rosenberg to retire. Radetzky was to cover the retreat and in his *Memoirs* Radetzky noted that he had found nothing more difficult in his entire military career than to break off this action which had made such progress. He suddenly had to organise a fighting withdrawal to preserve the main body of Rosenberg's fighting force. The price was high: while it took Radetzky barely twenty-five minutes to effect the withdrawal, it cost him 1,000 casualties.[6]

For all its poor coordination with the rest of the Archduke's army, the attack had severely disordered Davout's arrangements. The marshal told Napoleon that he would need at least two hours before he could replenish his ammunition. In his hastily improvised counter-attack on Rosenberg, Davout had used up a prodigious amount of ordnance. Though it was not the Austrian intention, Rosenberg had delivered, albeit at some price, a highly effective spoiling attack, distracting Napoleon from the main assault against the Austrian centre. Moreover, to deliver the French attack effectively, Davout would need to resupply his infantry and artillery. Seeing that, apart from this, Davout had matters well in hand, Napoleon returned to his centre and ordered them to attack once they saw Davout's gunline advance past the square tower of Neusiedl to their right. Napoleon had had a nasty early morning shock, but he had got over it.

Bellegarde's Korps had another unpleasant surprise for Napoleon. As the Austrians had advanced towards Aderklaa shortly before 4 a.m. they had fully expected it to be well defended by Bernadotte's men, whom they had seen occupying the village the day before. Great was their astonishment and delight when their skirmishers approached the village and instead of the usual close-quarters firefight they were expecting they found the village virtually deserted save for a few score Saxon wounded. Stutterheim commanding Bellegarde's advance guard could not at first believe his luck. He immediately occupied the village with three battalions and energetically began turning it into a miniature fortress.

Had Bellegarde advanced more daringly at this moment he might have taken advantage of the fact that Napoleon had shifted his reserves to deal with the emergency on his right caused by Rosenberg and that in front of him stood only some much-shaken Saxon infantry. But such a display of energetic individual initiative was still not the Austrian way and indeed Charles had, as always, no wish to take risks that could endanger his plans. Aderklaa in Austrian hands without a single casualty was in any case a magnificent turn of events. The village was the key to the Austrian centre and its possession had disturbing implications for the French. While in French hands it was a dagger pointed at the heart of the Austrian centre, in Austrian hands it meant that no French advance against the Austrian centre could be made without the certainty of serious flank fire. Bernadotte's withdrawal, ostensibly on account of his men needing to rest 'further away from the front line', was a tactical error of giant proportions. There are conflicting reports as to why Bernadotte surrendered Aderklaa. The Austrians saw the Saxons evacuating the village shortly before dawn; 'no doubt under Bernadotte's orders', according to Loraine Petrie. Another source reports that the Saxon detachment left to defend the village had engaged in looting and fled as soon as they heard the Austrians coming.[7]

The destruction of Bernadotte

Bernadotte had clearly decided to contest the Austrians further behind Aderklaa but his new gunline was caught in a murderous crossfire from Aderklaa, Wagram and the Austrian batteries gathered behind the Russbach. As dawn broke, these rapidly disabled 16 of the 25-gun Saxon battery. Trying to make good his earlier mistake, Bernadotte committed his remaining infantry in an attack against Aderklaa but in the three hours given to him, Stutterheim had worked hard to make sure every house had loopholes for muskets and that the village perimeter was formidably defended. Shortly after 7 a.m, the first Saxon counter-attack went in, supported by the remnants of the French line infantry in Dupas's division. It broke up almost immediately on contact as a withering fire was poured into it from two sides. The infantry broke badly and the French joined the panic wholeheartedly.

Napoleon, dumbfounded at this new emergency, and seeing instantly the terrible implications, rode like fury to Masséna and ordered him to 'slaughter those rogues'. Masséna, who was engaged on the Austrian right, immediately detached some of his best French line regiments and some Hessian units. Undaunted by the battalion of Austrian Jaeger that now rose in front of them from a ditch 100 paces in front of Breitenlee, the French remorselessly continued their advance towards Stutterheim's men. These fought like lions but the sheer force of Masséna's numbers began to tell and the 2,000 men of Stutterheim's command started to run out of ammunition. This caused panic in the first line of Bellegarde's infantry stationed behind the village. When they began to flee towards Wagram, the first line of the Archduke's centre began to collapse.

As at Aspern, the wisdom of battalion 'Masses' was again proved. As the first line dissolved, the second line fixed bayonets and advanced through them ten paces. The Archduke himself, again seeing the crisis, rode up to them to give a few words of encouragement, which rallied the soldiers of the first line. With a swiftness of comprehension, he then galloped off to his Grenadier Reserve, which was approaching from the right. Merville's Grenadiers cheered their Generalissimus not least because he had ordered a liberal distribution of brandy that morning. Charles now ordered three battalions to attach themselves to Stutterheim and recapture the village. Faced with the grenadiers enfilading them to their left and the rolling company volleys of Bellegarde's front line which cut the French down as they passed the village, the attackers paused and fled, abandoning one of their eagles and many other trophies.*

An enterprising young Austrian subaltern of the Argenteau regiment promptly carried the eagle away. As the French retreated, a sharp-eyed voltigeur saw an attractive target in a dazzling white unform, mounted on a grey horse, and took aim. Fortunately, the bullet only hit the Archduke's shoulder and, though painful, the injury was not serious. The length of the range alone had saved him.

The Austrian commanders Merville and Stutterheim were less fortunate. Together with several grenadier field officers, they were wounded seriously and obliged to retire. The struggle for Aderklaa was not over. The Austrians drove out the Hessians and their artillery routed the Saxons again, but with Stutterheim carried from the field and Charles himself recovering, the task of holding the line in Aderklaa was given to the young Archduke Ludwig. This younger brother of Charles found himself the fulcrum of the entire battle.

The next attack was not long in coming. This time three strong columns of Molitor's infantry, supported by two 12-gun batteries, advanced purposefully on the village. The guns unlimbered and poured a hail of shot into the ramparts and walls of the village perimeter. When Liechtenstein's cavalry charged them, Molitor's men formed square and drove them off. Having seen his men running pell-mell from the direction of Aderklaa shortly after 10 a.m., Napoleon rode from one end of the French line to the other, encouraging them. Meeting Masséna, who had fallen from his horse a few days before the battle and was directing operations from his carriage, the French Emperor, notwithstanding the huge barrage of canister and shot flying around him, climbed into the carriage and asked: 'So my friend what about this rumpus here?' Masséna replied, 'As you see, Sire. It is not my fault.' To which Napoleon answered: 'I know that all too well. It's that braggart Bernadotte!'[8]

---

* For the 24th Legère, sad to relate, it was their second time: they had lost an eagle at Austerlitz four years earlier.

The crisis on Napoleon's left wing

Liechtenstein's cavalry had more luck against Lasalle's light cavalry, which had impetuously attempted to capture an Austrian battery. Molitor's men fought furiously for every house and wall in Aderklaa, a virtual repeat of the events at Essling and Aspern seven weeks before. This time, under their young Archduke, the Austrians fought no less tenaciously. After an hour-long struggle, Molitor's men fell back in confusion. It was perhaps at this juncture that Napoleon was heard to utter the remark: 'War was never like this. No trophies, no captured guns.'[9]

For the French there was yet more bad news to come. Since shortly after dawn a 'glittering line of bayonets' had been moving across the billiard table of green that is the Marchfeld east of the Bisamberg, the right hinge of the Austrian position. This was III and VI Korps, whose delay had so compromised Radetzky several hours earlier. With the French attack faltering, Napoleon's left wing was now in imminent danger of collapse. VI Korps was already driving in the French outposts at Aspern. Its cavalry, emerging from Raasdorf where Napoleon had but a few hours earlier had his headquarters, took the French gunners by complete surprise. Meanwhile, the Austrian III Korps had extended itself to link up with the Grenadier Reserve. Archduke Charles's right had advanced to threaten Napoleon's left and centre from the rear with two fresh Korps. Astonishingly, despite his significant inferiority in numbers, the Archduke Charles seemed poised to defeat his opponent. His troops had outfought their enemies all along the line and his right wing, having captured all Boudet's artillery at Aspern, was now threatening Napoleon's rear and his bridges back to the Lobau. Against any other general alive at that time the Archduke would have prevailed and won the battle without doubt. Unfortunately, on this day, his adversary was Napoleon.

With his usual rapidity of thought, Napoleon took in at a glance the disaster now threatening to sweep him away. Once again he rose to the occasion brilliantly, as only he could. He needed to buy time and he suspected that the Austrians would not exploit their advantage with too much haste. He first sent in his cuirassiers in three great lines to slow down Kolowrat (III Korps) just where that Korps hinged with the Grenadier Reserve. The Austrian infantry, especially the grenadiers, had learnt at Aspern that they had nothing to fear, even from some of the most formidable heavy cavalry in Europe. Steady as a rock, the grenadiers delivered a withering fire at the thousands of breast-plated cavalry. Within fifteen minutes, they felled one horseman in three. Bessières's horse was shot from beneath him. Half his regimental colonels fell dead or wounded, but the cuirassiers together with the Guard cavalry kept coming, and by their incessant charging, they brought the advancing Austrian infantry who could not abandon their squares to a standstill.

Screened by the sacrifice of his cavalry, Napoleon now moved Masséna rapidly to meet the emergency on the French left and rear. To achieve this, Masséna would have to make a flank march of the utmost vulnerability right across the front of the Austrian III Korps, leaving a large gap in the French centre that would need to be filled. Napoleon decided to plug this with his Imperial Guard reserve, drawn up behind a huge arc of some 100 guns. Luckily for Masséna's flank march, the Austrian advance of VI Korps under Klenau was running out of steam. As one analyst of the battle observed: 'In the moment of victory, the enterprise of the Austrians failed.'[10]

While this drama was unfolding, on the Austrian left, at Markgrafneusiedl, the Austrian defenders hung on, clinging to the tower for all they were worth and successfully repulsing cavalry and infantry alike. Nordmann who commanded the Austrian Advance Guard fell, mortally wounded, as did the dashing Hungarian Hussar commander, Vécsey. Four other Austrian generals were wounded as the fighting deteriorated into a desperate defence against ever increasing French assailants. As the Austrians formed a fresh line in the rear, the Archduke Charles arrived in person bringing reinforcements, including five infantry battalions and two cavalry regiments, courtesy of Hohenzollern's Korps (II). Gathering other cavalry units, Charles tried to mount a 40-squadron-strong attack on the French infantry but the attack was mismanaged. The units attacked piecemeal and were repulsed.

The Austrians annihilate Macdonald's square

By sheer force of numbers, the French advanced and, as Napoleon was brought the news that the smoke of the French line had advanced beyond the village, Markgrafneusiedl, he turned to his centre to deliver the long-awaited *coup de grâce*. This honour was to fall to Macdonald, at that time only a general but, by all accounts, a flamboyant character with eccentric habits. He had drawn up his men between the Imperial Guard reserve and the great battery in a vast square of extraordinary formation. In front there were eight battalions deployed one behind the other. Thirteen battalions made up the flanks and nine the rear, a lumbering juggernaut of about 8,000 men. As this tremendous column moved slowly towards the Austrian Grenadier Reserve and Kolowrat's infantry, the Austrian first line fell back but soon redeployed along the flanks of the French, from where they began to pour in such a hail of fire, assisted by artillery, that within twenty minutes the tightly compacted formations in

Macdonald's square had virtually ceased to exist as a fighting unit. It had suffered over 3,000 casualties. Most accounts give the survivors of Macdonald's square at under 1,500.

As Macdonald's shattered column began to disintegrate, Napoleon supported him with the Young Guard, leaving Napoleon with only the Old Guard and Marmont's fresh division as a reserve. But Macdonald's sacrifice had bought time and Charles now recognised that, as his brother John had failed to materialise, Napoleon's superiority of numbers would make this battle unwinnable. Radetzky later recalled in his dictated memoirs that, at this stage, with the fall of Markgrafneusiedl on the Austrian left and the halt of Klenau's Korps, the battle was lost and that the question of John's arrival at that moment was irrelevant. With his characteristic tact and flair for diplomacy, Radetzky does not mention whether the Archduke John's arrival three hours earlier might have been decisive. By 4 p.m, the battle was decided and Charles ordered a staged withdrawal. There was no French pursuit. Indicative of their exhaustion was how jittery they felt two hours later when the Archduke John's first scouts arrived, causing panic in the French ranks.[11]

John's delay has been much criticised but he had received conflicting orders and his men had marched 26 miles since 1 a.m., a solid achievement for any army. The French rested uneasily and worried that they would have to fight a third battle because their opponents had retired in good order and their army had not been crushed. Wagram taught Napoleon a hard lesson about the fighting quality of the Austrians, which he had so long despised and underestimated. Later, when any officer disparaged the martial spirit of the Habsburg armies, he would cut them short with the icy observation: 'It is clear you were not with me at Wagram.'[12]

CHAPTER 12

From Znaim to Leipzig

Wagram, often described as Napoleon's last great victory, left a bitter aftertaste. For the Austrian army, the defeat had been anything but traumatic. In many instances they had fought even better than at Aspern and Essling, proving that they had raised their abilities considerably since the days of Ulm and Austerlitz.

The 'great victory' was in fact undecided.[1] The French were too exhausted to offer immediate pursuit and the Austrians had captured more trophies and standards than the French. Most important of all, the Austrians had retreated with their army intact. True to his House and his cause, the Archduke had fought carefully so that his army could, *in extremis*, fight another day (though he hoped not soon because his men were exhausted after their two-day ordeal).

Nonetheless, he prepared to mount a strong rearguard action at Znaim in Moravia. To that end he drew up his reserve in a solid semicircle around the small Moravian town. The first priority for the Generalissimus was to get his men to safety along the Iglau road into the Bohemian fastnesses as soon as his supply wagons had cleared the roads. As the French began to advance, they found it impossible to make any progress against the grenadiers of V Korps, who repulsed one attack after another. An Austrian bayonet charge was put in with such violence that they drove the French off the bridge in front of Znaim, almost capturing Masséna and his staff. Hundreds of French and their Baden German allies were taken prisoners at this rout.

A little later, as the French cuirassiers rode to their infantry's assistance, the Austrians were driven back across the bridge into the town. Had it not been for the timely and energetic intervention of the volunteer Vienna battalion, the main gate would have been captured.

Thus were matters poised when, between 6 and 7 p.m., two courageous officers, the French Marbot and the Austrian d'Aspré, representing both armies passed along the lines crying out 'Cease Fire! Peace!' Both men were fired upon and wounded while carrying out these duties. Later, Napoleon was often criticised for losing this opportunity to crush his Austrian foe once and for all, but he had little choice. His army was in no state to organise a sustained vigorous pursuit into the heartlands of Moravia and Bohemia.

The Archduke concludes an armistice

To the chagrin of his brother the Emperor, who wanted to fight on, Charles concluded an armistice with Napoleon on 12 July and then resigned his command. The army could have fought on but Napoleon's position was growing stronger every day. Charles knew the temper of his troops. They had achieved wonders but Austria's greatest general was determined not to risk the destruction of his army. Though peace negotiations would drag on until October, the Fifth Coalition War was over. In the process of their discussions, Napoleon, for whom the rearrangement of crowns and monarchies was but a bagatelle, hinted again at supporting Charles in deposing his brother but if he thought the Archduke open to such temptations he had misread his man. Charles was first and foremost a Habsburg. His role as warlord was inconceivable except in the service of the dynasty and that meant supporting, not rivalling, his brother however great their disagreements. If he disagreed with his brother he could resign; he would not pursue the avenues of ephemeral power offered by a parvenu upstart who styled himself 'Emperor' of France. Napoleon was disappointed, as he always was when his more gifted military opponents spurned political power. Many years later he would write in exile of how baffled he was by the Duke of Wellington's reluctance to become King of England.

But if Napoleon had imagined that securing peace with the Habsburgs was the end of the growing resentment towards his redrawing the map of Central Europe, he was to be mistaken. Austria's defiance and the performance of her army had ignited the spark of Austrian German nationalism and given an example. In Tyrol the embers of rebellion had been fanned by the news of Aspern and Essling. Andreas Hofer, a simple Tyrolean patriot, supported by most of the civilian population, fought on. They ejected the detested Bavarian army from the Tyrol once again. But under the armistice agreed at Znaim, Austrian regular forces were ordered to withdraw from the Tyrol. Napoleon hurried reinforcements there to break the popular spirit that had risen from these valleys. But this spirit after Wagram was not confined to the backwoodsmen of the Tyrol. On 12 October, while the French Emperor was inspecting the Guard at Schönbrunn, an event occurred that would trouble him almost as much as had his military campaigning against the Archduke Charles.

The Vienna attempt on Napoleon's life

As the Emperor watched his famous Old Guard parade, a handsome young man approached in a top hat bearing the French Revolutionary cockade. As he drew near, asking to see the French Emperor for whom he was 'bearing a gift', he caught the attention of Napoleon's ever-vigilant aides. This was just as well as the young man's gift was a knife, which he suddenly brandished before being seized by Napoleon's adjutant, General Rapp. The adjutant has left us with the word-for-word account of what happened next.

The 17-year-old would-be assassin, Friedrich Staps, was the son of a Lutheran pastor in Naumburg. A pale and sensitive-looking young man, he seemed an unlikely murderer and Napoleon insisted on interrogating him personally, using Rapp, who was from Alsace, as an interpreter.[2]

The conversation is worthy of recording because it shows how Austrian military defiance of Napoleon had lit a spark that spread across all of Germany, well beyond the Habsburg Catholic heartlands. It also reflects the French Emperor's neurosis and unease at the threat this seemingly defenceless young man posed:

'What did you want to do with your knife?'

'I wanted to kill you.'

'You are out of your mind, young man. Are you a member of the Illuminati?'

'I am not out of my mind and I do not know what the Illuminati are.'

'Have I done anything against you?'

'Me and all other Germans!'

'What would you do if I pardoned you?'

'I should simply try to kill you again.'

At this Napoleon, according to Rapp, fell uneasily silent.[3] Staps would later be tried and shot in great secrecy and his family sworn to silence. Only with the publication of Rapp's memoirs in 1828 did the parents realise that their son had died a hero in the cause of a nascent German nationalism that the titanic struggle of Austrian arms at Wagram had inspired.

The Tyrolean uprising and the 'betrayal' of Hofer

Meanwhile in Tyrol, the 'Volkskrieg' continued. In August, notwithstanding the withdrawal of the regular Austrian troops, the Tyrolese ambushed and routed a joint Franco-Saxon force in the Eisackschlucht, the notorious *Sachsenklemme* (Saxon trap) near Brixen. A few days later, again armed with a mixture of weapons and exploiting the natural advantages of the terrain, the Tyrolese followed up their victory with another successful assault on the Franco-Saxon forces around the Pontlatzer bridge. On 13 August at Berg Isel near Innsbruck the Tyroleans drove the French out of Tyrol. The resistance of the Tyrolese was partly inspired by the Archduke John, who was personally known to their leaders. Moreover, Emperor Francis had earlier given his word that he would never permit Tyrol to be separated from his possessions.[4] The Archduke John continued to send words of encouragement to Innsbruck. But in this he faced resistance from the Emperor's wife, Maria Ludovika, for whom, as a Bourbon, the very word 'rebellion' had sinister overtones. In a letter of this time, she questioned John's actions.

> Lieber Johann! With what right can we encourage the Tyroleans to disloy-alty against their legal sovereign who is the King of Bavaria? We ceded him these lands by treaty, permanently renouncing our right to these lands.[5]

But in the euphoria following the victory at Aspern, the Emperor had ignored his wife's misgivings and had issued the following proclamation at Wolkersdorf which was to have fateful consequences for his loyal Tyrolean subjects:

> In the confidence of God and the justness of my cause I declare that my loyal county of Tyrol including Vorarlberg will never be divided from the body of the Imperial state and that I shall not sign any peace treaty which specifies the dissolution of this tie to my monarchy. . . .

To his credit the Archduke John realised that these words were a hostage to fortune because they encouraged the Tyroleans to make the utmost sacrifice in circumstances no Habsburg emperor controlled. Although John worked hard to prevent the proclamation being published in Tyrol, the news of the Imperial declaration soon reached Innsbruck, stirring up the population to further acts of revolt. By the autumn these were indeed empty words of encouragement. Austria as a defeated state could offer Hofer precious little moral support and even that came to an abrupt halt on 12 October as the patriotic and energetic minister, Count Stadion, a well-known opponent of Napoleon, resigned and was replaced by the more subtle and calculating Metternich, hitherto Imperial Ambassador to Paris. The 'Handbillet' of Emperor Francis was now quickly forgotten in Vienna. Metternich – fighting to preserve something, anything of Habsburg dignity – was not minded to allow a few thousand Tyrolean peasants to upset a settlement with Napoleon which alone could prevent Austria's erasure from the cabinet of powers.

But two days later, on 14 October 1809, the harsh terms of the Peace of Schönbrunn were signed and with it the Habsburgs ceased to be a great power. Salzburg, Berchtesgaden, the area of the Inn, Northern Tyrol, and Vorarlberg all went to Bavaria while Southern Tyrol was given to the 'Kingdom' of Italy. Western Galicia including Cracow went to the Grand Duchy of Warsaw while East Galicia and Tarnopol were granted to Russia. The beautiful lands of Friuli, modern day Slovenia, Dalmatia, Trieste and Istria were reorganised into the romantic-sounding 'Provinces of Illyria' under French military and civilian administration. In addition 85 million francs of reparations and a strict limit on the number of soldiers bearing the Habsburg uniform were imposed. Vienna was no longer capital of a great empire though Metternich, thanks to the strong performance of Austrian arms at Wagram, had negotiated the dynasty's survival.

Tyrol stood alone, and as the Archduke John pleaded with his brother he was cut short by the Empress, who reminded him that the House of Austria had signed the Treaty of Schönbrunn and it was not (unlike for example the Prussian Royal House) the family tradition to break its solemn treaty pledges. Against the concentrated advance of several French columns, the Tyrolese tried their best but there was never any doubt as to the outcome of the fifth and final battle of Berg Isel once the French had recovered from their operations along the Danube and could move reinforcements west.

The Tyrol suffered the revenge of the French and their detested Bavarian allies in silence, broken only by the screams of the civilian population to whom the occupiers showed no mercy. Strict martial law was imposed and the insurgency's leaders went into hiding as a police terror worthy of a totalitarian regime descended. A few weeks later Hofer was betrayed and taken to Mantua to be executed. By all accounts the sturdy, pious innkeeper refused both blindfold and the chance to kneel, shouting at the firing squad to aim for his heart and pledging loyalty to the House of Austria, which had lifted not a finger to save him. His last letter from Mantua to the Archduke John would haunt the Habsburg to his dying days. It simply read:

My heart like all Tyrol sees in you, Imperial and Royal Highness, its father and awaits its fate. As I have told my brothers in arms, the House of Austria will never abandon us; so in the thunder of the guns rise brothers merrily secure in our noble religion and the gentle sceptre of the House of Austria!

Hofer's death gave Tyrol a martyr to freedom that has endured to this day.[6]

The new Habsburg 'alliance': the 'Observation' Corps

Like the Tyrol, the rest of the Habsburg domains resembled a ruined and ravaged land. Cut off from access to the sea, virtually bankrupt and with an army that was drastically reduced, nominally to fewer than 100,000, Austria's very existence appeared to be in question. Metternich, with that elasticity of mind which was to mark him out as the premier diplomat of his day and famously the 'Coachman of Europe' (Der Kutscher Europas) realised that there was only one possible way in which he could preserve the Habsburg dynasty: Vienna would have to form an alliance with Napoleon.

Eighteen days before Hofer's execution, Emperor Francis, who had had such difficulty in retaining his composure when Napoleon had greeted him impertinently after Austerlitz as 'Cher Cousin', now had to accede to the far greater humiliation of marrying off his daughter Marie Louise to the Corsican usurper. At the marriage ceremony on 17 March 1810, in a moment of acute irony, the Archduke Charles had to stand in for the absent bridegroom. Truly in his indifference to such reversals could Francis say that his House was above humiliation.

It was clear to Metternich that the Habsburgs' reversion to their traditional use of marriage as statecraft had enabled him to gain some time for his master. His next challenge was to keep Austria out of the now imminent dispute between Napoleon and Russia. In this he was spectacularly successful because although Napoleon demanded a corps, Metternich managed to ensure that this force simply went to guard Napoleon's lines of communication and that (to the Russians' relief) it would remain anchored on Austrian rather than Russian territory in Galicia.

This 'Observation', later Auxiliary, Corps consisted of 3 Jaeger, 3 Grenz regiments, 12 battalions of line infantry, 4 battalions of grenadiers, 18 Chevauxleger and 16 Cuirassier squadrons – a significant force but one not destined to play any part in the great struggle ahead.

No Austrian units took part in the major battles of the forthcoming campaign although they were briefly present at the Battle of Gorodeczno. As the Grande Armée floundered in the snow, the support corps commanded by Prince Schwarzenberg was ordered back to Vienna where, with Prussia's entry into the war against Napoleon, it could recover and prepare for events moving inexorably in Vienna's favour. Prussia had taken more than five years to begin to recover from her defeat at Jena but her belated return to the struggle offered Vienna diplomatic options. Metternich well knew that the role of the 'armed intermediary' in the coming conflict would play very much to his strengths. As the French expedition to Moscow floundered, Metternich watched carefully and waited. Prussia, Sweden and England all began preparing for a new coalition war but for Austria the time was still not ripe.

When Napoleon erupted into Germany in early 1813 with a new army of conscripts to replace his losses in Russia, he showed that, as ever, he was a formidable strategist in adversity. The enfeebled Prussian army put up a poor show at Grossgoerschen (Lützen) while a Russo-Prussian force was routed at Bautzen. While these dramatic events played out in Germany, Metternich quietly assembled the Austrian forces in Bohemia and continued to await events. As the Prussians were forced to give up the strategic Oder line and the Silesian city of Breslau, the Austrian forces stood at Napoleon's flank. An armistice offered Napoleon and his adversaries a brief respite.

Once again Metternich offered a 'golden bridge' to peace. In a famously stormy meeting with Napoleon in Dresden, he argued the merits of accommodation with Prussia and Russia but discreetly left Austria out of this equation. Napoleon reacted, hurling his hat across the room and accusing Metternich of not knowing how to 'die for France'. Metternich responded by quietly opening the shutters so that the 'soldiers below' could hear how 'they should all die for France'.[7]

Prince Schwarzenberg: the new Generalissimus

As a renewal of hostilities appeared imminent, Metternich thought the moment right to switch sides and give up his 'neutrality', which he promptly did, waiting, characteristically, until the last possible moment, 10 August, 1813. Yet again this man's strategic genius was on display. Having seen Austria almost wiped off the face of the map of Europe in 1809, Metternich realised that only a massive coalition of *continental* powers – England was a military irrelevance – could help achieve his ends. Despite the limitations on Austria's peacetime strength imposed by the Treaty of Schönbrunn, the military had slowly and carefully built up its numbers. Napoleon now faced 280,000 Austrians and a further 80,000 being called up as a reserve. Given that Austria had fought – with an interruption of barely five years – unceasing war against France since 1792 this was quite an achievement.

It had suited both the Archduke Charles and his brother, the Emperor, that a new commander-in-chief be found. The new command was to be taken by a reliable aristocrat by the name of Schwarzenberg. Karl Philipp, Prince of Schwarzenberg, the new commander of the Imperial and Royal Armies was born in Vienna in 1771, a member of one of the Bohemian aristocratic families who owed their rise to the great redistribution of wealth in the early years of the seventeenth century overseen by Ferdinand II. He had joined the Imperial Army young and had taken part in the ill-starred Turkish campaigns of the Emperor Joseph II. By 1794 he had distinguished himself so considerably in the campaigns against the French Republic that he was promoted to Colonel and received the following glowing recommendation from the then army commandant, Prince Coburg: 'While all my generals and field officers cannot do much, the example of Prince Schwarzenberg is exemplary. He knows what he wants and gives his orders well.'[8]

As we have seen, it was Schwarzenberg who, together with the Archduke Ferdinand, saved the honour of General Mack's besieged army by staging a large cavalry breakout fighting their way to Eger. In 1809, as Ambassador to the Russian court, he had showed some diplomatic flair even though efforts to persuade the Russians to join the Austrians that year proved fruitless. Later, as Ambassador to Paris, he worked hard to support Metternich's policy of keeping Austria out of the 1812 campaign against Russia. Later, in 1813, he spent much time in Napoleon's presence. He was brave and capable but had none of the intellectual brilliance and almost reckless disregard for personal safety of the Archduke Charles.

Nevertheless, Prince Schwarzenberg is rightly counted a member of the pantheon of Austrian military commanders. Perhaps his best talent was to see this quality in others. This made him a formidable adversary; he always surrounded himself with excellent officers. On his appointment as commander-in-chief of the allied armies his first move was to secure Radetzky as his quartermaster general and chief of staff.

He had already sounded Radetzky out a few months earlier on his appointment to Paris, convinced that war was imminent. As the armed mediation of Austria gradually became armed belligerence, Radetzky began to draw up plans for the coming coalition campaign. As Metternich played for time, the gradual mobilisation of the Imperial and Royal Army gathered momentum.

Radetzky's staff-work at Leipzig

Radetzky did not let his commander down. He set about rewriting and re-organising the entire allied advance for the autumn of 1813. His role in executing the final plan was critical. At Dresden, on 27 August, an allied force, including a strong Austrian contingent, was heavily defeated, losing 25,000 men. The allied cavalry and artillery were poorly deployed, with none of the tactical instincts which had characterised the Archduke Charles's dispositions four years earlier. The Habsburg forces grumbled that this would never have happened under their old Generalissimus. The French on the other hand were deployed with their leader's usual tactical flair. Moreover, Napoleon showed an energy that had not been seen since Austerlitz. As the allies retreated, Napoleon pursued them with four large columns. But at Kulm the Russian rearguard halted and inflicted a blistering check to the French pursuit under General Vandamme. Vandamme might have escaped with some of his forces intact had not the Prussians under Kleist suddenly appeared, barring his withdrawal and finally avenging Jena in a crushing attack.

Further French defeats were to follow against the newly rejuvenated Prussian army. Oudinot and Marmont were both sent reeling while Ney was heavily defeated at Dennewitz by Bernadotte, the incompetent bungler of Wagram who had switched sides following his adoption by the Swedish royal family. Napoleon, who had been determined to take Berlin and menace the Russians around Danzig to induce them to leave Bohemia, had to think up a new strategy. He remained confident of beating the forces now arrayed against him in the north: 'this cloud of Cossacks and bad Landwehr'.[9]

But as Schwarzenberg advanced with 60,000 Austrians along the right bank of the Elbe, Napoleon's right flank was becoming vulnerable. Less than a fortnight later, Napoleon began concentrating his forces around Leipzig where he awaited the advance of a vast allied force. The long campaign of 1813 was now drawing to its inexorable climax. The forces arrayed against each other were enormous but Napoleon was heavily outnumbered. Against a coalition army that would exceed 365,000 men (of which barely a quarter were Austrian) at its height, the French and their German allies fielded barely 195,000 men. Radetzky argued forcefully that, as hostilities began, Napoleon was only 10,000 men weaker than his opponents, and that the Austrians had good reason to fear that the weight of the French attack would fall on their sector of the front.

Against this disparity in forces, even Napoleon would have his work cut out. It was the brilliance of Radetzky's staff-work which ensured that the weakness of the different individual sections of the coalition was masked by their excellent coordination. There was even a British rocket contingent commanded by Captain Brogue. On 16 October, Schwarzenberg formally began hostilities, sending a strong Russian force under Barclay de Tolly against the French southern flank. By mid-morning this attack, supported by Wittgenstein's corps and other Russian units, had petered out. Napoleon counter-attacked vigorously, regaining all the ground he had yielded to the Russians earlier.

At the same time, the Prussians under Blücher launched a strong attack against Napoleon's northern position. Although 54,000 Prussians advanced against Marmont's few divisions entrenched around Mockern, Marmont held his ground despite being outnumbered two to one. By the end of the first day, the battle had had no decisive outcome. Although the French had successfully beaten off their numerically superior opponents, they had failed to crush either force. As more and more allied troops responded to Radetzky's careful staff-work and were fed into the battle, the position of the French defenders became increasingly precarious. It was at this moment that under cover of darkness Napoleon should have organised his withdrawal but some strange ('inexplicable', as Radetzky later called it) obstinacy on his part persuaded him to hold on.[10]

The following day was calm, with both sides reorganising their units. Within the Leipzig perimeter Napoleon was busy reordering his troops, using his most reliable units in positions that would reinforce the weakest parts of his defence. While this occurred, the allies began to deploy their reinforcements of some 150,000 men, so the following day could see a single concentric attack on all fronts. Once again Radetzky worked tirelessly to ensure that the coordination problems which had so often bedevilled the allies were resolved as seamlessly as possible. This achievement was all the more remarkable given the large personalities with which he was faced, especially among the Russian generalship, let alone the likes of Blücher and Gneisenau among the Prussians. (It may have helped that Gneisenau had an Austrian title.)

Despite the extraordinary heroism displayed by the outnumbered defenders, the outcome of the battle could never really be in doubt. As the concentric attacks hammered away at the French positions, the first to crack were the two Saxon brigades, demoralised by the recently invented Congreve rockets, which were effective against the defenders of Sellerhausen, a mile and a half from the city centre.*

At this critical moment in the battle, the Saxons chose to abandon their French allies, and marched off to the enemy to the amazement of the nearby French cavalry, who at first cheered them on, thinking they were about to attack the Prussians. Despite this loss of some 4,000 troops, the French fought on. On the Austrian sector of the front, Klenau issued from Zweinanundorf to

---

* One of the ironies of the battle was that, with the rocket battery's commander, Captain Brogue, killed earlier, it was commanded by a youthful subaltern, Fox-Strangways, who was decorated by the Tsar subsequently for his efforts with the Order of St Anne. He was wearing its star forty years later during the Crimean War at the Battle of Inkerman, where he was the first British officer to be killed by the Russians.

attack the ramparts of Stoetteritz only to be repulsed by a furious French counter-attack.

The French reserves were becoming exhausted so, at 5 p.m., Napoleon ordered a general retreat over mined bridges in an attempt to save something of his army. As the Austrian contingent, led by Colloredo, prepared to storm Leipzig, Napoleon was relieved if not surprised that his opponents made no attempt to cut off his line of retreat. In true Austrian style, Schwarzenberg had left a modest opening. He, like the Archduke Charles, saw no merit in fighting a war to the last subaltern. Napoleon's forces escaped, although their casualties had been a staggering 75,000.[11]

For the Austrians, the smallest of the three main contingents, casualties were 15,000. The Russians and Prussians who had borne the brunt of the battle suffered close to 40,000. But the French had not been eliminated as a military force, as Wrede's Bavarian contingent discovered a few days later when, with unerring instinct, Napoleon wiped out this force at Hanau. Driven from Germany, Napoleon would now embark on the campaign that perhaps illustrated his genius more than any other: the Defence of France.

As Napoleon demonstrated with his back to the wall at Bar and Brienne and elsewhere, his brilliance of manoeuvre remained unequalled. But, as at Leipzig, the sheer force of numbers would eventually tell. Schwarzenberg, in true Austrian style, was always reluctant to risk his army even when he commanded vastly superior forces. This was particularly the case when facing Napoleon commanding. Radetzky devised much of the so-called 'Trachenberg Plan' whereby the allies agreed to avoid where possible confronting Napoleon in person. Instead they would attempt to wear down his subordinates successively through superiority in numbers.

Under Schwarzenberg's leadership the Austrian troops fought less well than under the Archduke Charles, and seemed to be in danger of reverting to their old ways. Thus, at Arcis-sur-Aube, 80,000 Austrians faced 28,000 relatively raw French conscripts but were so cautiously deployed that the French held out until dark before making good their retreat and destroying the bridge. In the course of the action they had inflicted far more casualties on the Austrians than they had incurred but neither time nor numbers were on the French Emperor's side.

With the fall of Paris, the Austrians basked in the glory of their triumph more than any of their allies. Their soldiers had posed an opposition whose pedigree and longevity, as demonstrated on the battlefields of Europe, were unrivalled. Entering Paris – dazzlingly attired in white and blue, equipped with their recently issued taller bearskins with large Biedermeier cockades in the Imperial yellow and black colours – the Hungarian grenadiers swiftly became the subject of countless watercolours and drawings. They became the embodiment of the Habsburg army's valour and traditions, and an exotic addition to Parisian life.[12]

These achievements were not confined to the artists' canvas. When the Prussian general Gneisenau threatened to form an alliance with Russia to claim Saxony, even going as far as to speculate on bringing Napoleon back from Elba to provoke a civil war in France to distract the British, Schwarzenberg threatened Habsburg mobilisation against 'diese Preussische Baggage'.* The Prussians stood down.

1. Ferdinand II (1578–1637), scourge of Protestants and devotee of the Jesuits. In the background the Prague castle window from which his representatives were defenestrated, provoking the Thirty Years War.

2. Albrecht Wenzel Eusebius Wallenstein (1583–1634), 'Soldier under Saturn' revolutionised the logistics of waging war. His failure to comprehend the imperative of unhesitating loyalty to his Habsburg master proved fatal.

3. Infantry from the era of Wallenstein up to the beginning of Maria Theresa's reign, 1600–1740. The musketeer (third from left) represents a typical soldier defending Vienna during the Siege of 1683.

4. Prince Eugene of Savoy (1663–1736). One of the greatest commanders in European history, his prompt action at Blenheim saved Marlborough's centre from imminent collapse while his victory at Zenta over the Ottomans laid the foundation of the Austrian Habsburgs' expansion into eastern Europe.

5. The Great Empress: Maria Theresa (1717–1780). Her reforms have endured in many instances for centuries and she established the Austrian army as one of the most formidable in Europe and more than capable of holding its own against Frederick of Prussia.

6. The products of Theresian and Josephinian military reforms were seen as the 'finest cavalry in the world'. Austrian dragoons, cuirassiers, chevauxleger and lancers (1760–1800).

Erzherzog Carl
Generalissimus
von der Östereich. Armee.

7. The Archduke Charles (1771–1847), the most formidable of Napoleon's opponents and the outstanding Habsburg of his generation. His victory over Napoleon at Aspern electrified Europe. Later when French officers disparaged the Austrians' fighting qualities, Napoleon cut them short with the remark : 'if you did not see the Austrians at Aspern, you have not seen anything!'

8. As a result of rising costs during the Napoleonic Wars, the imposing crested helmet which the infantry had donned earlier in the century was replaced by a bell-top shako. This headdress however failed to be widely distributed until after the dramatic 1809 campaign had concluded.

9. A detail of the battle of Aspern in Wienerzinn. Austrian flat tin soldiers were originally manufactured during Maria Theresa's reign to illustrate her victorious campaigns against Prussia and were used for educational purposes in military academies and cadet schools. These figures date from the 1920s and were made by the Vienna firm of Scheibert. They are painstakingly based on contemporary accounts and engravings of the battle.

10. The humbling of Napoleon: General Koller's coat and hat in which Napoleon sought to take refuge so as to avoid an angry French mob on the 25 April 1814. The Austrian general happily obliged at the Inn of La Calade. Disguised as an Austrian general Napoleon was then able to proceed across France unmolested.

11. Grenadiers of the Vienna 'House' regiment Hoch und Deutschmeister I.R. Nr 4 mounting guard in the Hofburg in 1820. The officer on the right is wearing the traditional top-coat which distinguished officers from other ranks. His pose suggests Enlightenment credentials.

12. Austrian infantry from the end of the Seven Years War to 1840. Grenadier bearskins became progressively more lavish during the final flowering of the Biedermeier era which followed the end of the Napoleonic wars. Together with two colours of button metal, more than 46 different facing colours indicated the identity of each regiment.

13. Prague's magnificent monument to Joseph Wenzel Radetzky (1766–1858) shows him carried by his soldiers atop a vast shield fashioned from Italian artillery captured during his 1848 campaign. The monument is expected to be restored to its original site beneath Prague's castle in 2018.

14. Alfred Fürst von Windischgrätz (1787–1862) led the forces which crushed the revolutions in Prague and Vienna in 1848. In Prague he witnessed his wife shot dead by a young insurgent and this experience undoubtedly hardened his attitude towards the rebels. He was instrumental in bringing Franz-Josef to the throne.

15. 'An Emperor we can show the soldiers' in Windischgrätz's phrase. Franz-Josef I (1830–1916) ruled for 68 years. From his first day to his last this Kaiser was rarely seen out of his uniform, as this postcard commemorating his 60th Jubilee in 1908 illustrates.

16. Ludwig Karl Wilhelm von Gablenz (1814–1874) commanded the Austrians successfully in the challenging campaign against the Danes in 1864. His aggressive quick instincts and love of frontal bayonet attacks shocked his more cautious Prussian colleagues.

17. Ludwig von Benedek (1804–1881). The ill-fated commander of the Austrian Nordarmee was supposed to represent the new breed of meritocratic general. Following his staunch defence of San Martino in 1859 he was widely seen as the best officer to lead the Austrians against the Prussians although he himself realised he was not up to the task. His defeat at Königgrätz was to prove disastrous for Austria and Europe.

18. Admiral Wilhelm von Tegetthoff (1827–1871) standing on the deck of his flagship SMS *Erzherzog Ferdinand Max* a few seconds before it rammed the Italian *Re d'Italia*. The dazzling performance of the Austrian navy at the Battle of Lissa in 1866 consolidated public support for the Imperial and Royal Navy.

19. k. (u.) k. military music. Infantry bands played a vital role in campaigns and the famous Radetzky March was played during murderous infantry assaults both at Oeversee and Königgrätz. The corpus of Austrian military music is one of the richest in the world.

20. Sentry-duty inspection. This sketch captures well the discipline and smartness of mounting guard. All three infantry soldiers have attached a sprig of oak leaves to their headdress, the traditional *Feldzeichen* of Habsburg troops.

21. The Austrian naval detachment's contribution to the defence of the European Legations during the Boxer rebellion in 1900 was widely celebrated in the Habsburg domains. These Viennese toy soldiers were first made by the firm of Wollner and stimulated renewed public interest in Austria-Hungary's navy. Details including the Maxim gun were carefully drawn from contemporary accounts.

22. 1914 Hungarian hussars. Despite their red breeches and richly elaborate headdress, the elan and horsemanship of the Habsburg hussar regiments continued to be admired even by their opponents. Within six months of the First World War breaking out they would be largely reorganised as infantry.

23. Stephen Tisza (1861–1918), Prime Minister of Hungary and the man Franz-Josef called 'the most powerful politician of my reign since the days of Prince Schwarzenberg'. An avowed enemy of Franz Ferdinand he enjoyed Franz-Josef's trust to the very end.

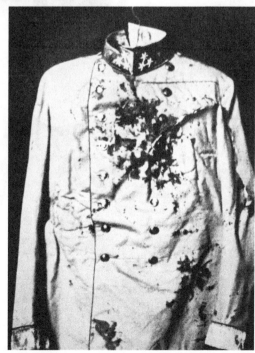

24. Archduke Franz Ferdinand, the Inspector General of the Army's tunic following his assassination in Sarajevo on the 28 June 1914. The doctors could not at first identify where the bullet had entered the archduke's uniform hence the cuts in the cloth.

25. Feldmarshallleutnant Hermann Kusmanek von Burgneustädten (1860–1934) commanded the garrison at the vast fortress of Przemyśl. He organised a valiant but ultimately hopeless defence and was forced to surrender the fortress early in 1915.

26. (Below) Austria-Hungary's last Imperial couple: Charles and Zita visiting Gorizia on the Isonzo front and watched anxiously by the best defensive commander of the First World War, Swetozar Boroevič von Bojna whose father had been a staunch member of the old Military Frontier's Serbian orthodox community.

27. (Left) Linienschiffsleutnant Gottfried Banfield (1890–1986), 'the eagle of Trieste' and Austria-Hungary's most highly decorated air ace. Born the son of an Irish naval officer in the Austro-Hungarian service, the young Banfield epitomised the qualities of a multi-national officer corps.

28. Banfield with his observer-gunner Lt Strobl in the cockpit of his Lohner flying boat. By 1918, Banfield had flown more sorties in the defence of Trieste than any other pilot in the Austrian Naval Air Service.

29. Three centuries of Austrian artillery. Dressed in brown with red facings, the Austrian artillery following Prince Liechtenstein's reforms became a *corps d'élite* with a reputation for courage and efficiency second to none.

30. As members of a multinational and multi-confessional army the spiritual needs of the k. (u.) k. soldiers required chaplains from all the faiths of the Book. Here an Austro-Hungarian Muslim regimental chaplain stands arm-in-arm with his German Christian and Jewish colleagues in 1917.

CHAPTER 13

Biedermeier, Vormärz and Radetzky

The reputation of Austrian arms was at its zenith. Its armies and even its staff-work had improved out of all recognition. Indeed, Napoleon conceded that the Austrian army had proved his most implacable foe.

The army inflicts a final humiliation on Napoleon

As Napoleon was escorted to the south of France to his exile on Elba, he was accompanied by four representatives of the allied powers. Of these utterly forgettable individuals, the Austrian General Koller, of whom no one had heard before (or after), was destined to be the instrument of one final cosmetic triumph over the Habsburgs' bitterest and most dangerous opponent. As the carriage carrying the abdicating French Emperor approached Aix-en-Provence, it was surrounded by angry crowds, jeering and shouting at the man who had once raised France to immortal glory but whose fallen star now brought out the worst instincts of the Provençal peasantry. Men who had barely a few months earlier pledged their lives for their Emperor struggled to tear him apart. Only the cavalry escort of Austrian uhlans managed to keep the mob away from the carriage. Twice the aggressive crowds appeared to overwhelm the squadron in attendance, only to be beaten back by the Uhlans who lowered their lances while their officers fired warning shots from their pistols. During one of these occasions, Napoleon resplendent in his uniform of Colonel of the Imperial Guard leant over to General Koller and quietly asked if the Austrian might do him the honour of lending him his white uniform to avoid 'any unpleasantness'.

At a nearby inn the disguise was applied and, to Napoleon's and his commissioners' relief, the mob were taken in by this primitive ruse and allowed the carriage to continue its journey unmolested until a reinforced escort arrived. Koller's uniform was preserved by the Habsburg military for posterity, a small symbol of the final humiliation inflicted on the greatest man of his time by his most implacable enemy. (For many years one of the most fascinating exhibits of the Heeresgeschichtlichesmuseum, it has not survived the recent modernisation programme of the museum, though a postcard illustrating the uniform, until recently for sale, is now, somewhat eccentrically, on display in a glass cabinet.)

While the Austrians had occupied Paris and brought their prisoner to the coast, the last remnants of the French occupation were expelled from Dalmatia and northern Italy, allowing Tyrol and Vorarlberg the opportunity of liberation from their hated Bavarian masters as well. On 2 and 3 May 1815, Murat, whose hold on his Neapolitan throne was tenuous and possible only because he had abandoned Napoleon, was defeated by the Austrians at Tolentino. All Italy, including Sicily, fell under Austrian influence. Though Napoleon re-emerged like a *deus ex machina* in the spring of 1815 and the Austrians sent another army to join the British and Prussians, it fell to the tenacity and skill of Wellington, with Prussian help, to defeat Napoleon once and for all on the gently sloping fields of Waterloo. Meanwhile, under Metternich's guidance, the Congress of Vienna had set about rewarding the victors and turning the clock back to the *status quo ante* where possible.

For the army the long peace of the 1830s allowed uniforms to become even more reflective of prestige. The Austrian army, in common with the British army at this time, adopted the new fashion of ever higher collars and head-dresses, although it never became ornate. Meanwhile, on the political level, the 'Holy alliance' between Russia, Austria and Prussia, established by Metternich, kept the peace of Europe. It tried to extinguish any 'progressive' legacy of the shattering events of the last two decades. The wily 'Coachman of Europe' kept the Pax Austriaca through a series of repressive measures. The lodges and other symbols of the eighteenth-century Josephinian Enlightenment were banned.*

Metternich's system imposes general conscription

For the military, the restoration of the old order had implications. Metternich's policies and the expansion of empire would require an efficient and obedient army as well as an ubiquitous secret police. It was, therefore, a time to reorganise. Under the terms of the new 'general conscription' (*Allgemeine*

---

* They would remain illegal in the Austrian part of the Empire until 1918, though thanks to a looser drawing of the Freedom of Assembly law of 1867 in the Hungarian part of the Empire, they flourished in nineteenth-century Budapest and along the Austro-Hungarian frontier, affording Austrian Freemasons the support of the so-called frontier lodges (*Confinenlogen*).[1]

Konscription) of 1815, Tyrol was included in the Imperial schedules for the first time, and was expected to contribute a Jaeger regiment in which active service would be for eight years with six further years in the reserve. This conscription was extended to the newly recovered Lombardy/Venetian territories. The Tyrolean Jaeger regiment raised under the command of Colonel Fenner von Fenneberg almost immediately saw action against Murat and took part in the subsequent triumphant occupation of Naples.

No longer working under the pressure of wartime conditions, bureaucrats and others tinkered with the regulations, sometimes with unfortunate results. By 1821, the consolidation of measures in the conscription regulations saw the final dismantling of most of the recruitment innovations brought in by the Archduke Charles. There were now numerous categories of people exempt from service, including clerics, all doctors of law and medicine, most government officials, teachers and artisans. This left a rather modest group of 'arme Teufels' (poor devils) available for recruitment. This number could be supplemented by village and town authorities banishing individuals to military service on account of their general undesirability. This flew in the face of Josephinian ideals: the men were prone to desert, especially if their regiments were on the move through the picturesque forests of Carinthia and the mountain passes of Carniola (latter-day Styria and Slovenia).

The peacetime establishment remained considerable. It was set at 400,000, of whom 50,000 were cavalry and 25,000 artillery. (5,400 technical corps and 4,000 transport personnel made up the remainder, along with 315,000 infantry.) The troops were distributed around the Empire into twelve garrisons, reflecting the far-flung nature of the 'modern' Habsburg Empire. They included the following cities at the heart of the realms: Vienna, Prague, Graz, Brünn (Brno) and Ofen (Budapest); and on the periphery, Agram (Zagreb), Hermannstadt (Sibiu), Zara (Zadar), Verona, Peterwardein (Petrovaraszdin), Temesvar (Timişoara) and Lemberg (Lvov). These twelve garrison cities (with the exception of Verona) would become uniquely attached to the Imperial army until the Empire collapsed in 1918. Today, the remains of their fortifications, their municipal parks with bandstands and cafes are the only legacy that remains. The ambience of the music, social conventions and elegant uniforms has been captured by writers within Austria and beyond.[2]

Certain legacies of the Napoleonic era continued to make themselves felt amidst all this administrative zeal. Commissions, which could still be purchased, remained an important source of income for the Regimental Inhaber (proprietary colonel). This practice proved resilient in even the most meritocratic regiments. Radetzky tried to stamp it out when he took over the army in Italy in 1836, but even his energy could not eradicate the system.

The 'Regimentsagenten'

Another curious survival was the role of the so-called 'Regimentsagenten'. There were three of these regimental 'agents', all of whom lived in Vienna. Between them, they conducted throughout the entire army the day-to-day business of provisioning, supplying and organising all non-military business, from delicate requests to marry from junior officers to demands for transfer to other units. History has told us little about Franz Dempsiter, Dr Alois Spitzer and Heinrich Mayer, but to these three enterprising men and their little empires of assistants the smooth running of the army in peacetime owed nearly everything. The scope of their activities appeared virtually limitless but no less vast was their actual division of labour. Thus while Dr Spitzer was responsible for the affairs of no fewer than 36 regiments of infantry and cavalry, the formidable Herr Dempsiter looked after the affairs of a staggering 57 regiments.

To give an indication of the scale of these men's activities it is useful perhaps to bear in mind the peripatetic nature of all infantry and cavalry postings, which along Metternich's expressly desired lines involved an elaborate choreography designed to prevent any regiment becoming too familiar with the local population. As the genie of nationalism released during the Napoleonic Wars continued to grow, it became an unspoken rule that regiments should not be stationed for very long in their areas of recruitment; for example, Italian troops should be posted to non-Italian provinces and Czech regiments to parts of the Empire remote from Bohemia. This required a game of military musical chairs which kept Messrs Dempsiter, Spitzer and Mayer fully employed for a generation. One example – the movements of the Vienna 'Haus' regiment, the famous Hoch und Deutschmeister Infanterie Regiment Nr 4 – will illustrate the scale of the logistical demands.

In 1815, the regiment was stationed in Milan. In 1816, it came back to Lower Austria and was in the town of St Pölten. In 1820, it was posted to Bergamo and in 1822, Naples. Three years later it was at Capua before being stationed in Klagenfurt in 1829. Linz, Graz, Verona followed before it finally returned to Vienna for the first time in twenty years, in 1840. Not that this was the end of its peregrinations. In 1846, it was posted to Tarnow and then, in 1847, Lemberg.

The policy of preventing fraternisation between soldiers and the population of the area in which they were recruited was to be vindicated vividly in 1848. As that year of revolutions approached, the army was generally under-employed. In 1821, a relatively small force under Frimont put down a rebellion in Naples. Another unit occupied Turin when the monarchy there was threatened, but apart from the odd disturbance in the satellite duchies of Modena and Parma ten years later, Europe was largely at peace.

Beneath this icy calm of the Metternich system, tension was rising. The absolutism that reigned behind the homely facade of Biedermeier comforts was increasingly questioned by a new generation. The 'rational' government which had briefly under Napoleon given Europeans a taste of new things and new ways could not be expunged from the collective consciousness of the Continent. Rebellion in France in 1830 brought some of the old revolutionary ideas to the fore again.

Vormärz

Two years before the 1848 eruption, tremors could be felt in Italy, and in Galicia where a revolt of the nobility was put down vigorously by the prompt action of an energetic young officer called Benedek. His less energetic contemporary, General Collin, further to the west, panicked and surrendered the city of Cracow to the insurgents, who promptly declared a national republic. But these events only illuminated the sky like flashes of lightning before the storm; they gave no inkling of what was to happen in Vienna two years later. The build-up to the revolutions of 1848 is known as Vormärz (pre-March) and describes the accumulation of perceived injustices and frictions which are ever the prelude to a popular uprising. As time passed, the innate conservatism of the system left it increasingly vulnerable to new challenges.

In Vienna, events finally came to a head on 13 March 1848. Students, the potential leadership of any revolt, armed themselves and began issuing a list of demands. These included press freedom, the abolition of serfdom, and, above all, the removal of the detested Chancellor Metternich who had come to personify cynicism, reaction and absolutism.

In the War Ministry, the minister, Latour, comprehended only too well the scale of the seismic challenge he now faced. He ordered a detachment of artillery guarded by a detachment of 'pioneers' along the Herrengasse. These were greeted with a hail of stones and, as the pioneers panicked and shot back, five civilians were killed. In the nearby Arsenal, Latour was surrounded by a violent mob. Under pressure, he was organising a plan to entrain two grenadier battalions to Hungary, from where there was more news of unrest. While one of these, the 'Ferrari' battalion, made up almost exclusively of Italians, marched off unmolested by the crowds, another, the 'Richter' battalion, found its way from its barracks in the Gumpendorferstrasse barred by a large mob.

The 'Richter' battalion, like all grenadier formations, was made up of composite units. However, the demonstrating students soon realised that this battalion consisted of exclusively German-speaking regiments drawn from IR 14, 49 and 59, three Alpine regiments recruited from Lower Austria, Upper Austria and Salzburg. United by a common language, the grenadiers and the students began to fraternise, the latter offering the former beer and wine until discipline was restored by their officers, who cleared a way with the help of a cavalry escort for the battalion to march to the Nordbahnhof two miles to the east.

As the regiment neared the station, they saw that a huge crowd had sealed all the approaches to the Nordbahnhof. To avoid bloodshed, the order was given to march to Floridsdorf along the Danube and entrain there but the same mob followed and sealed off the grenadiers' access to that station.

Latour over-reacts

When the news of these events reached Latour, the minister over-reacted and sent two squadrons of cavalry, some artillery and the entire infantry regiment 'Herzog von Nassau' (Nr 15) to drive the mob from the Floridsdorf station and the Tabor bridge, which they had closed to the grenadiers. This mixed force was commanded by Hugo von Bredy, a distinguished officer from a long line of Irishmen who had served the Habsburgs for generations. By the time they arrived, the grenadiers had completely lost discipline and were fraternising with the students. Incensed by this lack of military spirit, Bredy began to deploy his artillery, only to see the mob begin to cart his guns off. As this was happening, the officer ordered his infantry to open fire. The volley that crashed out killed a score of people but was returned with interest by the armed students, who fired into the densely packed infantry, inflicting more than a hundred casualties. Bredy went down with a bullet through his head and the colonel of the Nassau regiment fell from his horse in the hail of firing. The 'Richter' Grenadiers rushed to throw in their lot with the mob and from that moment their 800-strong force became the backbone of the rebellion in Vienna. They fought with enormous courage and heroism but their example was not followed in the rest of Austria. Spectacular and significant as their defection from the Imperial House was, they were the only Austrian military unit throughout the entire crisis of 1848 to mutiny. Every other unit of the Austrian army remained loyal to the dynasty.

The Hungarian crisis and the new Emperor Ferdinand

In Hungary, the situation was different. There, the crisis began to take the form of a nationalist uprising compromising the Hungarian elements of the army and, unsurprisingly, witnessing the almost wholesale defection of the Hussar regiments to the revolutionary cause.

To deal with this emergency, the Habsburg forces were woefully ill prepared. The only units that had trained for war and could be mobilised swiftly were the troops stationed in northern Italy, numbering barely 73,000 men.[3] Of these, 20,000 were Italian and could not be considered reliable while Venice rose up first. The King of Sardinia then declared war on the Habsburgs in an attempt to revive an Italian kingdom in the lands which Metternich had dismissed as 'purely a geographical expression'. Italy, the Sardinian King hoped, would unite the peninsula and drive the Austrians out 'by herself' ('Italia fara da se').

As it happened, all these fierce tremors which shook virtually every corner of the Empire occurred at a time when the throne was occupied by a melancholy half-wit known affectionately as 'Ferdinand der Gute' (Ferdinand the kindly) whose mental and physical attributes were wholly unequal to the challenges which now faced the dynasty. Ferdinand could be perceptive and bitingly witty but his deficiencies, possibly the result of his parents being first cousins, outweighed any mental consistency and robustness that might have enabled him to rule effectively.

When Francis I died in 1835, the temptation to pass the succession to one of his gifted brothers, the Archduke John or the Archduke Charles, had been squashed in favour of strict adherence to the principle of legitimacy. Both Metternich and Francis were convinced that any deviation from that principle would lead inevitably to an English style of monarchy which 'finds itself in a false position since the revolution of 1688'. The Austrian monarchy was a monarchy de jure resting on legitimacy while in Vienna's eyes the British monarchy was a monarchy de facto attempting to reconcile monarchical right with popular sovereignty.[4]

Despite the mental weakness of Franz's son Ferdinand, Metternich supported his accession, perhaps also convinced that this young man, perceived by the Archduke John as 'wholly incapable of decisive action', would allow Metternich to run the affairs of state with the minimum of interference. Indeed, Metternich proceeded to personify the system that now governed most of Central and Eastern Europe far more than the Emperor.

Ferdinand's reign witnessed huge encroachments by the 'apparatus of the state', with police informers and surveillance reaching levels that would be achieved in Central Europe only in totalitarian states a century later. It was a tribute to the popularity of the half-wit Emperor's predecessor that this unhappy state of affairs lasted thirteen years before there was an explosion. As the Archduke Albert wrote of Ferdinand's reign, 'It could not have lasted a year had not his predecessor enjoyed an unimpeachable position.'[5]

The 'tyranny' that was reported to have descended on the Empire was much exaggerated by liberal opinion, especially in England. The remarkable memoirs of *The Times* correspondent of the day, Charles Pridham, describe vividly how the machinery of a police state was mobilised to watch and monitor his every move as he attempted to get to Hungary to cover events there. From Vienna to Trieste he was treated to every conceivable measure of surveillance and official delay, worthy indeed of the wiles of the Eastern European communists in their dealings with correspondents a hundred and forty years later. But for the help of the British Consul in Trieste, who certainly defied the instructions of his Ambassador in Vienna, the supine and 'pragmatic' Ponsonby, he would almost certainly never have made it into Hungary at all.[6]

But though a price was eventually placed on his head by the infamously severe General Haynau, Pridham suffered no physical violence and it was somehow typical of the Metternich era that, despite the furious cries of journalists and writers against the reign of censorship and confiscation, none was ever imprisoned or physically attacked for attempting to subvert the rules. There were no 'show trials'. No records of torture during the Metternich period, of individuals disappearing or of incarceration without due process of law, exist.

Because the revolutionary events of 1848 affected the structure of the army directly, they also threatened the existence of the dynasty. Conditions in Vienna and Budapest suggested strongly that the fiction of the Emperor Ferdinand's reign be abandoned. The generals who were loyal to the dynasty awaited orders from Vienna but from the Emperor there came nothing. When Ferdinand went for a carriage ride, against the advice of his courtiers, and saw the angry Viennese crowd jeering, he mistook it for innocent emotional excess. 'Ma Liebe Wärner! Schauens die oan! So a Stuam!' ('My darling Viennese! Just look at them. How excited they get'), he observed in broad Viennese dialect, utterly unperturbed.[7] On another occasion when following a riot a stray cow found its way into the Hofburg courtyards, he looked down from a window languidly commenting to his horrified aides: 'That must be the first stupid cow to get into this palace without the help of any nepotism' ('ohne Protection').[8]

W.I.R. : Radetzky

Fortunately for the dynasty, the moment brought forth the men. Three distinguished soldiers emerged who, keeping their nerve, would ensure the survival of the House of Austria. When the Emperor said *Wir* (We), cynics joked that each letter stood for one of his generals. Chief among these was a man in his 83rd year whom we have already encountered on the battlefields of Europe a generation earlier: Field Marshal Johann Josef Wenzel, Count Radetzky von Radec. As we have observed, there was nothing in Radetzky's career to suggest that he would for a moment either surrender or give up the struggle for the Habsburgs. His greatest support was his popularity among his soldiers but also – and this is rarely referred to – among the Italian peasantry. These saw him as a guardian against the pretensions of their Italian aristocratic landlords and the intellectual musings of the Milanese middle classes whose ambitions carried no weight among the simple 'contadini'; a class division repeated throughout the monarchy.

Documents found recently in the USA indicate that Radetzky was not the simple reactionary that he is sometimes painted. As a young man he had embraced the Enlightenment ideals of the Josephinian era and had been one of the first young officers of the Imperial army to join a Masonic lodge.[9]

A strong conviction that progress was to be welcomed never left Radetzky. His support for those less fortunate than himself assisted many military careers, notably Benedek's. At the same time his human frailties endeared him to his Italian soldiers who knew the rumours (perfectly true) of his many illegitimate children and of his long, passionate and affectionate affair with his Italian housekeeper, Giudita Meregalli, who was equally devoted to him. Such a lifestyle was expensive and it was Radetzky's tragedy to be married to a wife who sought refuge from her husband's many infidelities in the relentless pursuit of material and costly luxuries. In 1798, he had married the rather stiff Friulan Countess Strassoldo. In eighteen years she had dutifully borne him eight children and, from 1805, two-thirds of every florin Radetzky earned were sent straight to Gorizia for his wife and family's needs, 4,000 out of 6,000 florins, according to one letter from Radetzky to his favourite daughter, Friederike Wenckheim.[10] In 1816, the General only staved off bankruptcy by pledging his debtors half of his future income. Even when he was made a Field Marshal in 1836, the financial worries did not cease.

In addition to his eight children with Countess Strassoldo, only two of whom would outlive him, the general had commitments with his Italian Signora Meregalli. She was a voluptuous, capable woman whose simplicity, warmth and charm were all any soldier could wish for. Milanese history has embroidered her character with many details but all the contemporary sources are agreed that she was a formidable cook. She had 'conquered' the old general with, among other gifts, her ravishing culinary skills, not least her *gnocchi di zucca* and *cotoletta alla Milanese*, a dish later exported to Vienna where it became the ubiquitous Wiener Schnitzel.

She too bore him eight children, five sons and three daughters, all of whom Radetzky recognised as his own and whom he supported financially.[11] Nor was the soldier's relationship with Signora Meregalli limited to domestic issues. When he was away from Lombardy he wrote regularly about the political situation in Europe generally. These letters show that he did not for a moment underestimate his Italian cook's intelligence. In one, he noted that it would be just his luck to be posted to Bohemia when it was his real wish 'with all his heart' to return to Italy. He deplored London's continual support for Italian revolution, writing to his daughter Friederike: 'As long as England does not stop to lead the campaign to destroy Europe, there will not be any peace.'[12]

For Radetzky, Signora Meregalli was also a vital source of information on what the Italians were thinking. Her connections with the leaders of the Lombard rebels have never been proven, though they are alluded to in Italian texts. In any event, as Radetzky's letters of March 1848 show, he knew the explosion was coming; that Piedmont was rearming and that all the warning signs were there. These warnings he conscientiously passed on to Vienna but his superiors filed them unread, being distracted by events nearer to home.

The Italians needed little encouragement to rise up. The Milanese intellectuals, excited by Piedmontese and British propaganda, seized weapons and began to menace the garrison. Confronted by an armed uprising, Radetzky knew he had to move swiftly. After five days of attacks he brought his forces out of Milan. The Imperial troops marched out of the city on a wet and windy night. The cannons roared and the clatter of rifle fire filled the night, illuminated as it was by the flames of the burning buildings. As Radetzky's advance guard punched a hole through the thin revolutionary forces holding the Porta Romana, the troops marched along the Lodi road past the motionless figure of their commander, who was watching with his small staff on horseback in the torrential rain of a thunderstorm. The rain poured off his hat and coat and, though drenched to the skin, the Field Marshal, motionless and calm, watched his men. Finally when almost the last soldiers had passed, Radetzky was heard to say 'Wir kehren wieder' ('We'll be back') before riding off into the rainy night.

As Radetzky retired into the formidable 'Quadrilateral' of fortresses: Verona, Mantua, Legnano and Peschiera, the only good news seemed to come from Tyrol, where the aged priest and veteran of 1809 Haspinger and the grandsons of Andreas Hofer had marched towards Mantua to avenge their grandfather's death. Haspinger's beard was now no longer red but silver white.

The fortifications Radetzky found on regaining the Quadrilateral were in a parlous state. In Verona some outworks were held only by three or four men. In Peschiera there was a garrison of fewer than 41 men, of whom 17 were officially classed as invalids. But the old Marshal was undeterred. From here he tore up the Italian peace overtures and made preparations to destroy his opponents. He had trained his troops over the previous years and he knew their quality. As early as 1833, he had written a paper for the Archduke John on the possibilities of defensive campaigning with Verona rather than the Mincio river as the key to his strategy. The experienced soldier knew every inch of the territory and he had fought many campaigns against far more deadly foes.

W.I.R.: Windischgrätz and Jellačić

While Radetzky prepared his counter-offensive, two other Habsburg generals moved to support the throne. The first of these was Prince Windischgrätz, a general very much of the reactionary school with a heavy, brutal face while the second was, perhaps, the most romantic of all Austrian generals of the mid-nineteenth century, the Croat, Josef Jellačić von Buzim. Together with Radetzky, the three made up with the initials of their surnames the Imperial and Royal WIR (the I and J were interchangeable). If the Kaiser used the royal We (*Wir*), he meant Windischgrätz, Jellačić, Radetzky – his three generals.

It was Windischgrätz who subdued Prague and then came back to deal with Vienna. The experience in Prague had hardened him even more. A few yards from the famous 'Powder Tower', he had seen his wife shot by the mob before his eyes. This tragedy persuaded him to suggest yet more radical steps. It was clear to Windischgrätz that the existing Kaiser was simply not up to the challenges of the moment. Metternich had fled Vienna. But Vienna was not Berlin; Austria was no Prussia where the army could take over. It existed to serve the dynasty, not to replace it.

'We need a Kaiser we can show the soldiers,' Windischgrätz told his brother-in-law Prince Felix Schwarzenberg, nephew of the victor of Leipzig in 1813. The obvious candidate was the young Archduke Franz-Josef, barely turned 18 and known as the 'Flower of the Habsburgs'. The boy was manly, a keen equestrian and a splendid-looking officer. But before the abdication of Ferdinand could even be thought of in practical terms, a number of Habsburg family members would need to be persuaded, and this would take time.

The situation in Vienna certainly called for desperate measures. In October, the Imperial family had to move to Olmütz for the second time. The mob had stormed the Arsenal and, in an act worthy of the worst excesses of the French Revolution, had hacked the hapless Latour to death, stringing up his body from a nearby lamp-post, still alive. In March, Metternich, the erstwhile 'Coachman of Europe' had already made his discreet exit from Vienna and politics hidden in a laundry basket.

Meanwhile the Hungarian rebellion was in full cry. The Hungarians wanted a constitution and demanded that all Habsburg troops stationed on Hungarian territory should swear allegiance to the Constitution rather than the Habsburg monarch. To make matters even more complex, the Hungarian troops were scattered throughout the realm. Of the twelve Hussar regiments only six were on Hungarian soil. Many were with Radetzky, and the last thing he needed was their marching off to defend their constitution. While he permitted some Hussar officers to return, the majority of the troops opted to remain. His troops, including several regiments made up of Italians, were loyal.

Determined to seize the opportunity presented by the rather indifferent quality of the Piedmontese troops ranged against him, Radetzky was thunderstruck by a request from Ferdinand, now in Innsbruck, to make peace with the Italians. Radetzky urged the young Prince Schwarzenberg to travel to the Imperial court immediately to have the decision rescinded.

Radetzky had often contemplated the action he now faced and had made the following manoeuvre the basis of many earlier exercises. As he recalled: 'An enemy army from the west pursues a much weaker Austrian Army across the Mincio and occupies the heights of Sommacampagna but the Austrian army retires on Verona and there reinforced resumes the offensive.'[13] This plan became reality for Radetzky.

On 28 April, 30,000 Piedmontese troops attacked 6,000 Austrians at Pastrengo and were swiftly beaten back in a short, sharp and defensive action, which would set the trend for the following weeks.

On 6 May the Piedmontese attacked again with a numerical superiority of 3:1 at Santa Lucia where the 10th Jaeger battalion under Colonel Karl von Kopal, together with a battalion of the Erzherzog Sigismund infantry regiment, mostly made up of Italians, took up a strong defensive position. Two companies of the Jaeger defended the cemetery, where the fighting raged for hours. The two battalions held off and defeated three Piedmontese brigades in an action which showed that, in the hands of the right officers, Italian troops loyal to the Habsburgs were a formidable instrument against their confrères. However, it did not all go Radetzky's way. Three weeks later the Austrian Tuscan division was defeated at Curtatone, and Peschiera, still weakly held, fell to the Piedmontese.

Custozza

Things looked up for the Austrians as Vicenza and the hills of Monte Berico were captured after a sharp action on the slopes beneath Palladio's Villa Rotunda in which Italian troops were again routed. Once more the Jaeger proved adept at fighting in the hilly terrain though their brave colonel Kopal fell at the head of his troops early on.

Reinforced by Haynau, the Austrians outfought the Piedmontese army with relatively little difficulty. On 24 July, in blistering heat, the two armies met near Custozza. Radetzky's energetic chief of staff, Hess, organised swift forced marches intended to swing the entire Austrian army on to the Italian centre. From Verona, Haynau dispatched reinforcements on his own initiative. The cautious leadership of the Piedmontese cost them the campaign, and Charles Albert, the 'traitor of Sardinia' as Radetzky called him, rapidly sued for peace. The Austrian losses were less than 1,200 of whom 70 were officers though the number of wounded, nearly 4,000, was very high, reflecting the unhealthy climate of northern Italy in late July which turned many injuries septic.

This significant Austrian victory raised morale: Radetzky was given the Commander's Cross of the Maria Theresa Order. Even so, events in Italy had no effect whatsoever on the mortal struggle at the Empire's centre. There, the confusion and conflicts of the numerous ties of clashing loyalties continued to sow disarray throughout the army.

One example gives a flavour of this. In the summer of 1848, a Polish Lancer regiment commanded by a 'German' Austrian, Blomberg, was stationed in the Banat, a Hungarian territory where a mixed population of Romanians, Serbs, Hungarians and Germans all lived relatively peacefully. An uprising against the rebel Hungarians by Serbs led by an officer who proclaimed his allegiance to the 'Kaiser' was met by an order from Blomberg's superiors to crush the revolt in the name of the 'König'. Emperor (Kaiser) and King (König) were, of course, the same person and when the Serbian officer reminded Blomberg of this he promptly took his Polish regiment away. This unfortunately left the German population of the Banat, who had expressed their loyalty to the Hungarians, to the tender mercies of the Serbs, who proceeded in the best traditions of the Frontier to burn them out. Blomberg wrote to the War Ministry begging to be taken away from this 'intolerably divided land'. (The Germans eventually were rescued by a detachment under a different Serbian officer!) It adds little coherence to this picture if it is explained that the Polish general involved here (a former Austrian officer) was later exiled (Bem), the colonel in charge of the Serbs later became a general (Mayerhofer) and the Hungarian commandant of Serbian extraction (Damjanović) was later executed.[14]

Croatia to the rescue

For Jellačić in Croatia things appeared a little less confusing but even he had to put up with some remarkable twists and turns. Summoned to the Emperor

Ferdinand in Innsbruck he gave a speech which silenced his (mostly Hungarian) critics, beginning with the words: 'My mission is to save the Empire' and ending, 'You gentlemen may survive the end of the Empire but I . . . I cannot.'[15] The privileges Jellačić demanded for the Croats were granted and his appointment as Ban (Viceroy) confirmed. But barely was he on his way back to Zagreb when Ferdinand granted an audience to Count Batthyány, the most brilliant of the Hungarian magnates, who persuaded him to sign an order rescinding Jellačić's appointment as Ban and dissolving the Croatian Sabor, or parliament. For Batthyány, Croatia was Hungarian territory to be ruled with a rod of iron from Budapest.

This news reached Jellačič just as he arrived at Zagreb and would have dismayed a lesser man but Jellačić simply ignored the orders (like Radetsky) and mobilised the troops of the Military Frontier and his Croats to march into Hungary, which he promptly did on 11 September. In his speech on becoming Ban he deployed his full powers of rhetoric and his conviction that to serve God and to serve Kaiser were inextricable bonds imposing responsibility on him as an officer and Croat. The speech is notable for his pledge to the Virgin Mary that he would never become a member of any secret society.

Jellačić in addition to being a skilled officer was an inspiring poet. In his orders and speeches to his men the imagery of Croatia as the rampart of Christian civilisation features strongly. A generation earlier, Napoleon's general Marmont had admired the military qualities of the Croats observing: 'Ante murale Europae contra immanissimum nominis christiani hostem'(the men who in the name of Christ stand in front of the walls of Europe against the countless hordes). As Marmont had then continued: 'The regime of military Croatia is a masterpiece in all ways honed by the incessant beating back of Moslem hordes since 1389 in which everything holds together in this system in which to command or to obey is the exclusive sphere of its conception. Devoted to service and loyal to the state they [the Croats] would move to Austria immediately if threatened by any change.'[16]

Marmont had been above all impressed by the legal procedures on the Military Frontier where every company of soldiers had its own tribunal consisting of two NCOs, the company commander and two privates, which was responsible for discipline and judged all disputes. All property on the frontier was owned by the crown and occupied in trust by the families of the district and could be surrendered instantly in the event of a family dying out or some dishonour falling upon them.

With Jellačić's entry into Hungary, the oath the Croats had taken to defend the Pragmatic Sanction in 1712 as loyal Hungarian subjects with special rights and privileges was violently ruptured. The Hungarian government, led by their

Finance Minister Kossuth, immediately ordered the Austrian Major-General Franz Ottinger (in the name of the King!) to drive Jellačić out, but Ottinger was unwilling to attack a general he knew well and whom he regarded as a brother in arms. The 'brotherhood of arms' was, in Jellačić's words, and no doubt Ottinger would have agreed, 'Greater than any race or creed'. To this element, Jellačić added the divine, writing in July to his mother as he prepared the invasion of Hungary: 'The goodness of God is eternal and the ways of His Providence unfathomable.' Now as Ban, Jellačić approached and Ottinger withdrew his outposts along the frontier before going over with his troops to the Ban. A second general sent by Kossuth also joined Jellačić.

With another officer, János Móga, a major-general of Hungarian extraction, supported by a battalion of the recently established 'National' Army or Honvéd, the uprising had better results, and Jellačić's troops, short on cavalry, were halted outside Budapest at the end of the month after a brief but sharp action at Pákozd.

Both sides now deployed artillery, which in both cases were batteries of the 5th Prague Artillery regiment and were manned on both sides by Czechs. As the Czechs on the Hungarian side were better shots than their colleagues from the same regiment on Jellačić's side, the Hungarian Revolution could proceed apace.[17] The renewed outbreak of violence at the beginning of October in Vienna came to the Hungarians' aid, distracting the Habsburg commanders.

Windischgrätz promoted: the counter-revolution triumphs

The Vienna revolution of October 1848, with its murder of Latour and departure of the Imperial family to Olmütz, was a turning point. On 16 October, Windischgrätz received unrestricted powers. The Emperor Ferdinand wrote: 'I give the Prince full powers to restore peace to my domains by his own judgement as swiftly as possible.'[18]

Windischgrätz needed no further encouragement, though he was also appointed Field Marshal. He linked up with Jellačić and, transporting his troops by train from Bohemia, he first sealed Vienna off with 70 battalions before storming the capital. There was never any doubt as to how this battle would end even though the rebels, the National Guard and the armed student groups fought bravely under their officers. Commanded by the Napoleonic veteran and former Austrian officer General Bem, the Viennese had barely 70 pieces of artillery. Although a 'Mobile Guard' of two battalions proved effective, Windischgrätz possessed all the trump cards.

After a week of bitter fighting, the city surrendered. But just then, news of an approaching Hungarian relief force was received by the rebels and the ceasefire was broken by the defenders. This Hungarian force was quickly seen off at Schwechat by Jellačić, and after another two days of bitter fighting, the Black and Gold flag of the Imperial House once again adorned St Stephen's Cathedral.

Windischgrätz had lost more than 12,000 men. The defenders had sustained 3,000 casualties. Bem and two former Austrian officers, Ernst Haug and Daniel Fenner von Fenneberg escaped, but another, Messenhauser, was court-martialled and, notwithstanding many direct pleas to the Emperor for clemency, was shot on Windischgrätz's express orders. Messenhauser, a former officer of the elite Deutschmeister regiment, himself gave the firing squad the order to fire.

With Vienna recovered and Jellačić's colourful troops stationed in the Vorstadt, the full might of the Imperial forces could now turn on Kossuth's Hungary. In Hungary the great orator and patriot, Lajos Kossuth, a fiery hothead of limitless vanity, had hoped to find a compromise with the Habsburgs, but it soon became apparent to him that room for compromise did not exist. In Vienna, an official proclamation was issued denouncing all officers fighting on the Hungarian side. Henceforth they were declared traitors. (As Deàk points out, this did not prevent many of them being welcomed with open arms when they deserted Kossuth over the following months.) In response the Hungarian parliament entrusted the command of the Hungarian forces along the Austrian frontier to a former k.k. (Imperial. Royal) Lieutenant, Artúr Görgey.

Hungary and Venice hold out: the new Emperor Franz-Josef

As the troubled year of 1848 came to a close, Hungary and Venice continued to hold out against the forces of the 'counter-revolution'. But the dynasty was recovering the initiative. In December, after some delicate negotiations among the members of the Imperial House, Ferdinand had been persuaded to abdicate in favour of the 'Flower of the Habsburgs', Franz-Josef. Windischgrätz and his brother-in-law Prince Schwarzenberg, who was appointed all-powerful 'Minister President', now finally had an Emperor they 'could show the soldiers'. Franz-Josef had all the relevant qualities: he was young, handsome and always in uniform. He was a trained officer and good horseman. Barely 18, he was learning, as that other beleaguered monarch, Pope Pius IX was learning in Rome, that the time of granting constitutions and other liberal concessions was over.

Kossuth continued to drum up support within Hungary and by the early weeks of 1849 had at his disposal a 'National' Army of nearly 200,000 men.

This formidable force, which comprised many of the best Hussar and light cavalry regiments of the Habsburg army, drove Windischgrätz and Jellačić's troops out of Budapest and cleared most of western Hungary of the Imperial Army. The Hungarian rebels needed seventeen days to take Buda, which was defended heroically by its *Kaisertreu* garrison. By May all Imperial troops had been driven out of Hungary and Transylvania by General Bem's Magyars.

In Italy, meanwhile, the King of Piedmont, Charles Albert, under pressure politically to avenge his defeat at Custozza, sent a young officer by the name of Cadorna to Radetzky's camp to announce in person the end of the existing ceasefire. Cadorna later recalled what happened:

> The old Austrian marshal received me with his customary warmth and friendship and when I told him we would be breaking off the truce, he walked to his ante-room where some officers were gathered and told them the news. To my consternation they broke out into cheers and cries of joy and began putting oak-leaves onto their shakoes and field caps.[19]

Radetzky's order that evening to his troops was terse: 'Forward! Soldiers! The Solution is Turin!'

The Austrian executed a brilliant flank march which threatened the Piedmontese rear beyond Magenta. Within five days, the Piedmontese were facing defeat as they realised they were threatened from two fronts. At Vigevano and Mortara, Colonel Benedek, sword in hand, led a single regiment (Nr 53) with fixed bayonets against an entire Piedmontese brigade, taking both points as darkness fell after vicious street fighting in Mortara. Benedek in the darkness shouted to the numerically superior Italians that they were surrounded and they believed him.

Two days later, the Piedmontese were decisively defeated at Novara, losing nearly 6,000 men. Of these barely 150 were officers, suggesting a lack of leadership and bravery so unlike the courage of the ordinary Italian soldiers. Only a spirited charge by some Italian cavalry saved any semblance of dignity on behalf of the Piedmontese. Their King wisely abdicated that evening in favour of his son Vittorio Emanuele. This triumph was tarnished by Haynau's mopping-up operations, in particular his capture of Brescia. His severe reprisals, in which women and teenagers were flogged, did much to alienate liberal opinion throughout Europe. Radetzky had noted that 'like a razor' Haynau needed 'to be sheathed quickly'. It cast Austria in a more despotic light than hitherto, even at the height of the Metternich regime. When, later, General Haynau, by then in his seventies, visited a brewery in Southwark the draymen famously threw him into a barrel of ale, thus occasioning a heated exchange between the mildly amused Palmerston and an outraged Queen Victoria who believed British hospitality had been compromised.[20]

But as the summer of 1849 wore on, Hungary had become the last outpost of rebellion. The heroic defence of Venice by Manin finally ended thanks to the first combined land, see and air operation in the history of warfare. Manin had defended the city for so long thanks to the incompetence of the Austrian governor who had surrendered the Arsenal without firing a shot a year earlier. But fatigue, disease and hunger accomplished what the Austrian artillery bombardment from the mainland failed to achieve.

In May 1849, faced with the risk that the Hungarian Republic would hold out indefinitely, Franz-Josef took the dramatic step of seeking help from Russia. In an unprecedented act of rebellion, Kossuth had formally 'dethroned' the Habsburgs from the pulpit of the Reformed Church in Debrecen.

Franz-Josef's decision, coming on the heels of another spectacular victory by Radetzky over the Piedmontese at Novara, would haunt his reign. The Hungarians would never forgive or forget this act. The Russians would also never lose their belief that the Austrian Emperor was indebted to them for the retention of his throne. As late as 1914, the Imperial Russian Foreign Minister, Sazonov, would argue that the Austrian Emperor was only able to sit on his throne on account of Russia's soldiers.

Franz-Josef asks for Russian help in crushing Hungary

In time, the Austrian army could probably have subdued the Hungarians without any help. But Franz-Josef was in a hurry and by the autumn 360,000 soldiers, including a Russian contingent of 20,000, closed in on the 150,000 Honvéd troops bottled up in the south-eastern corner of Hungary. Györgey, commander of the main Hungarian army, surrendered in August. It would not be until October that the last Magyar redoubt fell, but the rebellion was over.

The Austrian revenge was swift. Once again Haynau's name appears as the harbinger of brutality. He ejected all the Hungarian wounded from the hospitals in Budapest to make room for his own men. Meanwhile 498 former Habsburg officers, including 24 generals, were court-martialled. Of these 40 were hanged and the majority of the others given long sentences of incarceration. Thousands of civilians also found themselves imprisoned.[21] The rebellion had 'infected' nearly 10 per cent of all officers, though only with Kossuth's deposition of the 'unfaithful' Habsburgs in Debrecen in 1849 was their loyalty unequivocally no longer to the dynasty. Of these barely 15 per cent were German and less than 4 per cent were Poles.

Haynau's excesses gave his enemies in the Austrian high command and political elite the ammunition they needed to engineer his removal and he was dismissed in 1850. The memory of the executed officers, the so-called 'blood of Arad', would plague Austro-Hungarian relations for decades. The complexities of the relationship left deep scars on the young Emperor, Franz-Josef, who would make a good working relationship with the Magyars one of the keystones of his life's work. He recognised that many of the Hungarian rebels were loyal to his House. General Ernö Kiss for example wrote on the day before his execution: 'I served Hungary only to help Austria.'[22]

Perhaps the officers also felt loyalty to their regiments, which were often the closest many of these men might have had to a home and identity in a multinational empire. The 1848–49 war was a serious moment for all concerned. By the time it was over, the Hungarian uprising had cost 100,000 lives. Tens of thousands more had died in Italy. Once again, despite the confusion and challenges, the army had largely managed to remain true to the compact sealed by the events of June 1619. It had again saved the dynasty. The leadership qualities of men such as Jellačić and Radetzky, together with some 9,000 career officers, proved the lifeline of the Habsburgs.

CHAPTER 14

From Magenta and Solferino to the Düppel and Oeversee

Thanks to Radetzky, Jellačić and Windischgrätz, the army had survived the trauma of 1848–49. The terrible effects of nationalism had not begun to eat away at the fabric of the army's ethos or organisation. But the new Emperor Franz-Josef realised quickly that his power rested on his army and he never for a moment during his long reign neglected the well-being of his forces. From 1850 the army's prestige and the reputation of its great generals were promoted to reinforce the cohesion the young Emperor believed was essential to the maintenance of his army's ability to defend his House.

The victories of Custozza and Novara stabilised the Habsburg monarchy's position in northern Italy but the situation remained volatile. Radetzky was feted throughout the Empire and was made a knight of the Order of the Golden Fleece, the 'House' order of the Habsburgs. His financial problems continued partly because of the extravagance of his wife. It did not help that, of his legitimate children, five sons had entered the army where their low salaries made each of them, in the phrase of the time, 'as poor as a staff officer'.

Radetzky and the Heldenberg

Fortunately for Radetzky, a friend and admirer by the name of Josef Gottfried Pargfrieder, a successful industrialist, bailed the Marshal out so that in theory Radetzky could devote his last years to his mistress and his lovely summer chateau under the great horse chestnuts that stand across the park from the opera in Laibach (Ljubljana). Pargfrieder is one of the more eccentric figures encountered in Habsburg military history. He was convinced that he was the illegitimate son of Joseph II, a claim which the Emperor Francis never denied, though there is no evidence to suggest that he confirmed it either. Pargfrieder's epitaph alluded to it, albeit in a rather oblique way.*

Pargfrieder had made money in the trading of various metals. A devoted Freemason who admired Radetzky, who himself had become a Freemason as a young officer in the heady days of the Josephinian Enlightenment, Pargfrieder was the perfect guardian angel to ride to the rescue of the financially embattled Marshal.

Pargfrieder hit upon a way in which he could combine his business interests in metal and his desire to commemorate the great marshal. If the marshal would grant permission for his body after his death to be the centrepiece of a huge scheme of military commemoration, a 'Heldenberg' (mountain of heroes), Pargfrieder would help pay off the soldier's debts. This novel scheme took on ever more ambitious dimensions. Pargfrieder set about persuading other senior officers to contribute their corpses at the end of their lives to this grandiose project. Eventually there would be hundreds of busts set up in avenues around the project's centrepiece, Radetzky's tomb. Manufactured of tin, a material much in vogue, these busts would weather the test of time; an eternal monument to Austrian soldiery, a kind of Habsburg warriors' Valhalla.

Work began on the project with great enthusiasm in 1852 but by the time of Radetzky's death in 1859 the site was only partly completed. With the great soldier's death, Pargfrieder found it difficult to raise the money to complete the project. There was however enough money for the magnificent Radetzky crypt with its imposing Biedermeier script warning that 'just because we are sleeping it does not mean we are dead!'

The Heldenberg project could almost act as a metaphor for the state of the Habsburg army in the late 1850s. The aftermath of 1849 appeared to show a Habsburg Empire at the summit of its military prowess but underneath lay hubris and complacency. Here was an army still capable of intimidating Prussia in 1850 by mobilising 450,000 men under Radetzky and forcing Berlin to sign the humiliating 'Punctation' of Olmütz whereby Prussia's attempts to reorganise northern Germany under Prussian hegemony were comprehensively checked. Here was an army that still appeared to hold the Italian peninsula in its vice-like grip. Yet, on every front, factors were developing that, in less than twenty years, would conspire to prevent the Habsburg armies from saving the dynasty's position in either Italy or Germany.

* Pargfrieder's epitaph ran: K.I.S.I. P.F.V.F. which stood for: Kaiser Joseph's Sohn Joseph Pargfrieder Vivo Fecit

A new rifle and manual: cavalry and artillery reform

The factors were many and varied. The army in 1851 had received a new training manual, which for the first time addressed the question of open-order deployment and combat in broken terrain. This encouraged some if not much thinking about infantry tactics. These had not advanced since Napoleonic times. In 1855, the Lorenz rifle, an excellent muzzle-loading gun, was prescribed for the entire infantry. But while the manual might stress the importance of infantry firepower, parsimonious budgeting meant that the average infantryman had barely 60 shots a year to practise his marksmanship. Only Jaeger, whose marksmanship was traditionally a characteristic strength, were given an extra 25 shots a year. Although the manual had regulations to encourage the Jaeger in 'dispersed deployment', training in such formations was not considered a priority.

Unsurprisingly, following the events in Hungary in 1849, the Hussar regiments were considered ripe for complete reorganisation. To avoid any sense that they were being singled out, the entire cavalry arm was reformed. Notwithstanding their magnificent tradition as elite light horse, the Chevauxleger regiments were abolished in an act of unsentimental rationalisation. Officers and men were given the right to transfer to any cavalry regiment they wished; in practice most became dragoons. The light cavalry now consisted of 12 Hussar regiments and 12 Lancer regiments, each of six squadrons. The heavy cavalry – eight Dragoon and eight Cuirassier regiments – were each divided into eight squadrons. Training was intense and only horses of high quality were used. Heavy cavalry were encouraged to charge as shock troops. Light cavalry were tested especially in the art of forming complex formations during a charge. Far-seeing military men questioned the value of the cavalry arm as the nineteenth century progressed but the huge prestige of the arm (more than 70 per cent of its officers were drawn from the aristocracy) stifled radical reform.

These reforms were mirrored in the artillery, whose importance continued to gather momentum as the century progressed. In 1854, twelve regiments were established each with four 6-pounders, three 12-pounders and two-horsed batteries of eight guns each. Under the energetic leadership of Feldzeugmeister Vincent von Augustin the artillery officer corps was trained to high levels of mathematical expertise and the entire regiments, still recruited mostly from Bohemia, gained an *esprit de corps* which matched that of any elite unit in the army.

Similar reforms were imposed on the Pioneer Corps which was now organised into six battalions. The Engineers were also reorganised into twelve independent battalions of which one was a training battalion. Recruits needed two years in the training battalion before joining a field battalion. Each regiment consisted of four companies: three of sappers, one of mines detachments. The Engineer Staff consisted of eight generals, 26 colonels, 45 majors and 96 captains, a significant increase on earlier arrangements.

The arrival of the railways opened dramatic new possibilities, and a military railway office was set up with exclusive power to organise reinforcement transports and logistics. Also for the first time a Medical Corps of three battalions, stationed in Vienna, Budapest and Venice, was created. These medics were divided into companies, which would be attached to each army corps. The members of these *Sanitätsbattalions* were armed with rifles, bayonets and swords, there being at this time no Geneva Convention stipulating the rights of non-combatants on the battlefield.

The Armeeoberkommando replaces the Aulic Council

Finally the Hofkriegsrat, the nemesis of so many generals of initiative and energy in the Habsburg armies, was transformed into a new War Ministry. From 1851, the highest military authority was now the Army High Command (Armeeoberkommando). It reported to the supreme commander who was, of course, the Emperor. His Imperial Majesty's orders were conveyed by the Generaladjutantur, which was also responsible for relations with the War Ministry. A Chief of General Staff existed to advise the ministry, though he was not part of it and, at this stage, did not enjoy the sweeping powers he would later assume. These reforms were accompanied by an overhaul of military law and the abolition of running-the-gauntlet beatings and other forms of physical punishment.

The reforms were designed to bring Franz-Josef's army into an age coinciding with the first tremors of the Industrial Revolution. On paper, the 'new' Austrian army of the 1850s appeared a formidable force. In the field, the smallest operative unit was the brigade with its six battalions, including one jaeger and one grenadier battalion, accompanied by an artillery battery and various medical and logistics detachments. A cavalry brigade consisted of two heavy cavalry regiments and one light cavalry regiment with a horse-artillery battery. Two or three such brigades composed a division, and three of these divisions made up a Korps, which would thus comprise some 30,000 troops of which about 1,800 were cavalry. Each Korps would be equipped with 80 guns.

A series of diplomatic miscalculations soon weakened much of this work. With the death of the able Schwarzenberg in 1852, the 'strong men' of 1848 were no longer in the ascendant. The Crimean War, in which Austria played no part other than to occupy the Danube provinces of Moldavia and Wallachia, alienated Russia for three generations. It also prevented a rapprochement with France, now ruled by Napoleon III, Bonaparte's nephew: an adventurer in the boudoir as well as in the chancelleries of Europe. Although he lacked a scintilla of his famous uncle's brilliance, he was desperately ambitious, eager for prestige and for the recovery of France's active role on the Italian peninsula.

In 1857, Radetzky finally retired as governor of Lombardy and was replaced by Count Franz Gyulai, a Hungarian devoid of talent. When hostilities broke out two years later, Gyulai, aware of his military shortcomings, immediately asked to be relieved of his command.

Napoleon III's New Year 'bombshell'

No doubt factors other than the Austrian command in Lombardy lay behind French machinations, but following Radetzky's death in 1858, Napoleon III gave the Austrians warning of what was coming. At the New Year's Day reception for the diplomatic corps in the Tuileries in 1859, Napoleon approached the Austrian Ambassador, the rather stiff Baron Hübner, and after wishing him a Happy New Year nonchalantly added: 'I regret that our relations with you this year will not be as cordial as they were last year but please assure your Emperor that my regard for him remains undiminished.'

Thunderstruck, Hübner, one of the diplomats of the old school which the Metternich chancellery produced in great numbers, betrayed not by a flicker the faintest hint of what he was thinking and remained utterly impassive. He wished the Emperor a felicitous New Year. But he, and every other ambassador who overheard the exchange, was in no doubt: they had just witnessed an informal declaration of war.[1]

For three months the chancelleries of Europe made energetic diplomatic moves designed to avert a war. In London, where sympathy rested with the Italian Risorgimento, Queen Victoria offered one of her ambassadors as a mediator. Russia also offered to act as 'honest broker', but neither Vienna nor Paris appeared remotely interested. The marriage of Napoleon III's nephew to the daughter of the King of Sardinia, the Piedmontese Vittorio Emanuele, appeared to cement the Franco-Piedmont alliance.

As the year of 1859 wore on, Piedmont, under her Machiavellian political leader Camillo Cavour (1810–61), a stubborn but brilliant politician, set about goading Austria into declaring war. Cavour was conscious that France's offer to support the Italian cause with troops was unlikely to last for ever. Despite all these moves, as well as Hübner's clear warning, Austria did nothing to prepare for war. Volunteers from all over Italy flocked to Turin to join the Piedmontese regulars in the coming conflict. As the build-up of hostile troops continued, the leading Austrian generals, notably Gruenne, were against an ultimatum to Piedmont but, on 23 April, Franz-Josef was persuaded to send the Piedmontese a note demanding their immediate disarmament. As expected, this was rejected and war was declared. France immediately announced her intention to support Piedmont, honouring a secret alliance she had made with Cavour to wage war on Austria in return for Nice and Savoy.

Unfortunately, Gyulai's prompt offer of resignation was rejected by Gruenne, who dominated the military counsels (*Adjutantur*) of Franz-Josef. Gruenne favoured a defensive policy and overruled the advice of a gifted staff officer, Franz Kuhn, who proposed an aggressive strike against the Piedmontese followed by a strong defence of the Alpine passes through which much of the French army would march. But Kuhn was supported energetically by Hess, Radetzky's old chief of staff. The hapless Gyulai, who had no instinct for command, marched back and forth to the conflicting orders in torrential rain, exhausting his 107,000 troops before they had fired a shot. At Montebello, a stone's throw from Marengo, there was an indecisive skirmish in which the outnumbered Austrian units gave a good account of themselves, especially in the cemetery where the Styrian and Upper Austrian Jaeger infantry put up a heroic defence, virtually to the last man.[2] Another brief defensive skirmish a few days later at Palestro repeated the pattern of the earlier engagement. The French stormed the Austrian rearguard in overwhelming numbers. After a stubborn defence, unsupported by reinforcements, the Austrians fell back.

Inconclusive clash at Magenta

Finally, on 4 June, in blistering heat the main body of the Austrians collided with the French and Piedmontese at Magenta on the Ticino. Far from being a 'decisive French victory' as it is often described, the battle was evenly contested. The French Imperial Guard were nearly wiped out. By late afternoon, Napoleon III had actually given the order to retreat and had organised his artillery to cover what seemed to him would be an inevitable French withdrawal after Gablenz, an aggressive Saxon in the Austrian service, stormed the Ponte Nuovo putting the Zouaves and their general Cler to flight.

Cler was killed and even the Zouaves were no match for the Kaiserjaeger supported by Infantry Regiment Nr 54, made up largely of Moravians, who captured one of the French guns. Panicked by this action, the French Emperor hastily penned a report for the Paris newspapers noting that the French forces would 'reorganise' the following day.

At about the same time, three battalions of Infantry Regiment Nr 45 drove the French grenadiers from the west, headlong towards the fulcrum of the battle around the Ponte Nuovo. The Lombards in the Austrian regiment fought poorly, probably because they were fighting on their home ground against their supposed liberators. Disaffection also seemed to infect some of the Hungarian regiments. Ernst Wurmbrand came close to summarily executing his senior NCO.[3] Other Austrian regiments, made up of Venetians and Friulans, struggled bravely for several hours and by evening another counter-attack by the Austrians, including a Grenzer regiment, drove the exhausted French off their bridgehead, virtually forcing them into the river.

An attempt by the French general MacMahon to turn the Austrian flank floundered as four Austrian regular infantry regiments under Clam-Gallas pushed the French vanguard under Espinasse off the road. But in the wooded terrain, and with their backs to the wall, these French units made up of hardy Swiss in the 'Regiment Etrangère' gradually regained the initiative and began pushing a Hungarian regiment back towards Magenta. As the French brought up nearly 70 guns, modern and with rifled barrels, to blast their way through the barricaded streets of Magenta the Austrians finally fell back but even then they mounted a stubborn rearguard defence. As Espinasse entered the village, now engulfed in flames, his staff and aides were greeted by a hail of shot from the Austrian Jaeger. Within minutes ten bullets had hit his chief aide-de-camp. While his staff officers fell on all sides, an Austrian marksman shot the French general through the head as he dismounted from his horse.

Supported by freshly arrived Kaiserjaeger who had force-marched nearly twenty miles to the village, the Austrians withdrew in good order under the cover of darkness. The French Emperor slept fully clothed that night, expecting at any moment to flee. In the morning, he learnt that the Austrians had retreated east in three columns towards the shelter of the Quadrilateral, abandoning Lombardy. An over-enthusiastic attempt at pursuit was halted at Melegnano a few days later where the Austrian rearguard under Benedek inflicted more heavy casualties on the Zouaves, who lost a third of their number. Thereafter the Austrians moved eastwards undisturbed.

Though Magenta was inconclusive, dissatisfaction with the Austrian high command was palpable. Austrian losses had been high and the regiments made up of Lombards had not fought well. There was also dissatisfaction with some of the Hungarian regiments. In a policy aimed at sowing discontent among the Hungarian soldiers, the French had published earlier the details of the meeting between Napoleon III and Kossuth, the now-exiled Hungarian leader. Convinced, wrongly as it turned out, that Hungary was on the brink of revolt, Napoleon III had gone out of his way to disseminate propaganda implying that Hungary would be assisted by French arms after the liberation of Italy.

Schlick replaces Gyulai

Combined with the feelings of the majority of the local populace of Lombardy, these factors gave the Austrian army the sense that it was operating not in its patriotic heartlands but in occupied territory. The civilian population lost no opportunity to make it abundantly clear that they regarded the Austrians as an army of occupation, and this had a deleterious effect on their confrères in the army. The nationalist fissures in the army that had been visible in Radetzky's campaign of 1848 were widening. Without the sure touch of the great marshal in dealing with them, they were proving corrosive.

Meanwhile the young Franz-Josef showed his decisiveness by relieving Gyulai of his command, much to that officer's relief. Unfortunately, the young Emperor still did not resolve the ambivalence of the relations between the members of his staff. The Emperor assumed overall command, appointing as new commander of his Second Army the rather imposing one-eyed Schlick, another scion of an old family in Habsburg service since the days of Wallenstein. Schlick had lost his eye fighting against Napoleon at the tender age of 24, though this had in no way dented his reputation with the ladies. A contemporary photograph shows a heavyset face of rugged charm. But both he and his master continued to labour under a plethora of contradictory advice as the struggle between Gruenne and Hess continued, with terrible consequences for the Austrians over the next few days.

From this muddle emerged the decision to advance from the Quadrilateral and fight with the river Mincio at the Austrians' rear. The field they chose was well known to them. Dominated by the tower above the hill of Solferino, now called the 'Spia d'Italia', the Austrians had exercised here over many years on the flat ground to the south, the so-called Campo di Medole. Well might Benedek later claim that he knew almost every tree and hedge in the area.

The Austrian plan was hotly debated. It involved a large and slow envelopment of the French across the Campo di Medole. Hess criticised it immediately as being unwieldy and too slow. It would expose the Austrian centre to vigorous attack, but the pipe-smoking Gruenne, supported by General Ramming, persuaded the Emperor that Hess was being over-cautious.

The die was cast: while Schlick marched his troops off to take up position towards Solferino with Benedek at the northernmost point near San Martino, Wimpffen's First Army marched south towards the Campo to take up a position from where it could execute the envelopment. The Austrians displayed little skill in divining their opponents' intentions. As the Austrians took up position less than six miles away from their opponents on 23 July, they failed completely to comprehend that the French and their Piedmontese allies might actually attack them the following morning.

Solferino and San Martino

The French began moving at 2 a.m. to avoid the heat of the Italian sun. As it rose a couple of hours later, it revealed the Austrian dispositions with merciless clarity. Napoleon III possessed none of the military genius of his uncle but even he could see how thinly the Austrians were spread and how vulnerable was their centre where, by happy chance, his own army was now concentrating.

Nevertheless, the battle was to be no easy victory. All morning the French attacked the village of Solferino and were beaten back easily. The Piedmontese, attacking to the north, were defeated compehensively by Benedek, whose corps contained some of the most seasoned Austrian troops, notably the elite Salzburg 'House' regiment Nr 59.

Meanwhile, to the south, the vulnerable and extended Austrian position was attacked by a French division. For three hours, two battalions of jaeger and a battalion of regular infantry held out against a force nearly four times larger. The pressure could not be relieved. Franz-Josef, to the consternation of his immediate entourage, could not be found until 11 a.m. As he discussed the situation calmly with Hess, the orders that followed were ill-coordinated and piecemeal. By 2 p.m., a much stronger and reinforced French force stormed the Solferino redoubt, cleared it at the point of the bayonet and began to roll up the Austrian centre. The crisis of the battle had arrived and no one on the Austrian side appeared equal to it. It did not help that many units had had nothing to drink or eat for 48 hours in the blistering heat. One officer recalled how his men had been forced to drink the urine of their horses.[4]

The French artillery came into action with devastating effect but, as the Austrians began to fall back, a solitary Hussar regiment commanded by an enterprising Colonel Edelsheim charged the French infantry, cutting through it and sowing panic as far back as the depots, ambulances and stores. Edelsheim's charge, which was an astonishing achievement for a mere four squadrons, might have had some effect had he been supported by more cavalry. The neighbouring cavalry division was commanded by Mensdorff, scion of a Hungarian family usually famed for its *esprit d'escalier*, but on this occasion he refused to support Edelsheim's gallant charge. Edelsheim and his

Hungarian hussars were left to achieve what one contemporary described as 'a virtual repeat of Balaclava and the light brigade'.[5] Hopelessly unsupported, they had no choice but to fall back in much-diminished numbers. His charge showed that the Austrian horse was still the finest in Europe and throughout the battle no French cavalry came anywhere near emulating such heroic feats, but their action was a hint of the challenges the second half of the nineteenth century posed for the mounted arm.

To the north, at San Martino della Battaglia, Benedek demonstrated that the Habsburg armies could achieve great things under an energetic commander. Three Piedmontese divisions advanced in three large columns against Benedek's position south of San Martino. Despite a numerical superiority of 5,000 men, the Italians could make no headway against their opponent and by 9 a.m. Benedek had driven one Italian column four kilometres beyond where they had started. The other two columns fractured into brigades and attempted to take the steep hill of San Martino by storm. Twice the Salzburg 'House' regiment, resplendent in their 'canary orange' facings, drove them back at the point of the bayonet. A third attack came within 200 metres of the crest of the hill but was cut up by the sudden unmasking of a 30-gun battery. Firing at such close range, they virtually wiped out three Italian battalions in less than twenty minutes. Everywhere Benedek inspired his men, reportedly shouting out to his Salzburg troops after one successful bayonet charge that he would 'dearly love to kiss them all'.[6]

As the crisis at Solferino developed, Benedek was in rapid danger of being surrounded on three sides. Detaching a brigade including another elite regiment, the Graz 'House' regiment Nr 27, to form a left rearguard, Benedek continued to hold on. A thunderstorm of unusual intensity broke at 5 p.m. This gave him a breather. For three more hours, Benedek refused to budge, even after repeatedly receiving orders from Hess to retire. Reluctantly, Benedek organised a fighting retreat covered by his artillery. This stopped the Italians at almost point blank range from organising any pursuit. In any event the Italians were not up for anything energetic. A quarter of their forces were casualties, nearly 6,000 men compared to Benedek's 2,615.

Elsewhere on the battlefield the Austrian artillery had proved woefully inferior in range to the French rifled-bore cannon. The Austrian artillery was generally more accurate but it could not match the range of the French; one Austrian battery lost three guns in less than a minute to the French artillery. The long range of the French guns finally drove the Austrians out of the Solferino cemetery, the key to the Austrian centre.

Meanwhile to the south, the Austrian infantry fell back, showing its old professionalism by forming squares as the French cavalry approached. Their volleys decimated one leading Chasseur regiment, killing its colonel and ten officers, and after that the Austrians retired unmolested.

Franz-Josef resolves never to command an army in the field again

The orderly Austrian withdrawal could not disguise the scale of the defeat. It brought tears to the Emperor Franz-Josef's eyes to realise that his army, for all its bravery, had suffered that which it had avoided at Magenta: a truly decisive defeat. Nearly a fifth of his forces had vanished. Of his army of 160,000 more than 22,000 lay dead or dying on the battlefield, a loss so appalling that one Swiss observer, Henri Dumant, determined that day to establish the Red Cross.

There can be no doubt that more decisive and energetic strategic thinking would have narrowed the odds of Austria's defeat. Her troops nearly all fought with exceptional courage and, while their artillery was weak tactically, the infantry and cavalry gave a good account of themselves. Although the Austrian infantry may have lacked the elan of the French attacks with the bayonet, they proved tenacious in defence. Still, nothing could change the fact that, unlike ten years earlier, the white-coated Austrian troops were seen in Lombardy as a detested occupying force. That this 'infected' some units of the Austrian army made up of soldiers from Lombardy was inevitable but a close study of the campaign shows that Austria's defeat cannot be attributed to questions of nationality.

The Austrian army was quick to draw two important lessons from the campaign aside from the usual controversies that raged on strategy. Both would have profound consequences for the Austrian army in its future campaigns. One of these lessons would prove helpful, the other less so.

The artillery was convinced that it too needed modern rifled batteries, and a plan to re-equip the Austrian artillery was implemented rapidly. The infantry, impressed by the French attacks with the 'arme blanche', drew the less happy conclusion that bayonet charges, delivered with sufficient resolve, could carry a battle. The tough Alpine soldiers of Graz and Salzburg had showed time and again at San Martino that the bayonet charge was highly effective. The army ignored the third and arguably most important lesson: that the rapid increase in the intensity of firepower leads to a higher casualty rate.

Politically, Austria lost Lombardy (again) barely fifteen years after Radetzky had won his victories. The armistice at Villafranca which the two emperors signed confirmed Lombardy's transfer to France, which could then present that rich land to Vittorio Emanuele of Piedmont. Within six more years Austria's power on the peninsula would crumble in a series of uprisings that confirmed the trend of the Risorgimento and Italy's path towards nationhood. When Cavour died in 1861, his last words were 'Italia e a posto' ('Italy is all right').

The French mischievously insisted that all Hungarian prisoners of war be offered the chance to enlist in an anti-Austrian 'Legion' under the leadership of the exiled Kossuth. This proved unsuccessful. The desertion rate from this 'Legion' was higher even than in the Austrian army. Indeed, in the aftermath of Solferino, two of these volunteer Hungarian Hussar regiments offered their personal services to Franz-Josef as part of a general spontaneous outburst of loyalty to the dynasty.

Solferino ruled out any renewal of hostilities with France. Wisely, given the interests of the dynasty, Franz-Josef drew an obvious lesson. He would never command an army in the field again. He fired Gruenne and Gyulai and a dozen other officers. He encouraged his cousin the Archduke Albrecht, the son of the Archduke Charles, to take on greater military responsibility and promoted Benedek, a Protestant from the lowest grade of minor nobility, to Feldmarschallleutnant.

Benedek was given the command of the forces stationed in Hungary. Born in Hungary, albeit of a German family, and speaking good Hungarian, he was nevertheless not a Hungarian nationalist. As the officer commanding the one bright spot on the Solferino horizon, he naturally became something of a legend. The Viennese press saw in him a true meritocrat, by which they meant he had not enjoyed high birth. But Benedek's father, although not a count or prince, had been a military physician. His son owed every stage of his early military career to the 'protection' of his father's most illustrious patient, Radetzky. Characteristically, Radetzky had even arranged for the young Benedek to attend the Wiener Neustadt military academy, unprecedented for a Protestant at that time.

The Schleswig-Holstein campaign: General Gablenz

Almost before any of the lessons of Solferino could be digested, more pressing challenges arose to the north where, in the dual duchies of Schleswig and Holstein, the Habsburg armies would confront a new enemy: the Danes.

The story of the Schleswig-Holstein question was aptly summed up by Palmerston, who apparently said: 'The Schleswig-Holstein question is so complicated, ony three men in Europe have ever understood it. One was Prince Albert, who is dead. The second was a German professor who became mad. I am the third and I have forgotten all about it.'

Less than three years after Solferino, Austria, whose pre-eminence in Germany was resented by Prussia, confronted the dilemma of these duchies.

In essence the challenge was relatively straightforward. The duchies, whose population was overwhelmingly German in language and character, had attempted to sever their links with Denmark in 1848. Denmark had acquired them as a small legacy of their interference in German affairs in Wallenstein's day. The issue was complicated by the differences in legal and constitutional status of the two duchies and the fact that there were also some differences in their ethnic composition. Unsurprisingly, Denmark resisted a breakaway and moved to absorb the duchies totally. Because this technically breached the London Protocol of 1852, the German Diet in Frankfurt voted for intervention. In 1864, Austria agreed to cooperate with Prussia should the affairs of the duchies require intervention, and a corps under Gablenz was sent to Holstein to liaise with the Prussians.

Gablenz, whose reputation was made by driving the French out of Ponte Nuovo, was the son of a Saxon general. Born in 1814, Gablenz had been trained in the so-called military 'Knights' Academy in Dresden and had initially served in the Saxon army. But in 1833 he found his ambitions thwarted in Saxony and transferred to the Imperial Royal Army where he was appointed to Radetzky's staff. There he distinguished himself in the 1849 Hungarian campaign. Ten years later he demonstrated his exceptional capabilities at Magenta and Solferino, and was widely regarded as one of the most conscientious, decisive and able commanders in the Habsburg army. Above all, he was notable for his calmness, even under extreme pressure. His open and fair nature made him the object of considerable affection among his troops, though some complained that he was rather too partial to costly frontal assaults. After Benedek, he was the most popular soldier in the Habsburg army.

On 18 January 1864, as the Austrian corps marched off to Holstein, Franz-Josef dismissed the departing officers with the following words: 'I know that you will bring honour to our arms and that you will compete with the Prussian troops in your bravery and endurance'.[7]

The Austrian corps that was sent to Schleswig under Gablenz contained some of the finest infantry regiments in the Imperial army at that time. It consisted of four brigades. These included the so-called 'Black and Yellow' (*Schwarzgelb*) brigade under Count Nostitz, so called because it consisted of two infantry regiments which together made up the Imperial colours: 'Hessen', the 'House' regiment of Linz with black facings; and 'King of the Belgians' the elite 'House' regiment of Graz with yellow facings. In addition to these formations the expeditionary force included the Gondrecourt brigade, which distinguished itself earning the nickname 'the Iron Brigade'.

The conditions for the campaign were icy and bitter. The Danes fell back and, as the Austrians seized the villages of Over and Niederselk, the Danes were forced to retreat to Oeversee. Here they dug in, easily dispersing a Hussar regiment Gablenz had sent with one of his staff officers, Gründorf, to test their position. Gablenz's infantry had not yet arrived when Gründorf returned to report on the formidable strength of the Danish position. Gablenz's Chief of Staff advised against further action that day. The time was 3.30 in the afternoon.

Styrian success

But Gablenz was not a man to be so easily discouraged. Turning to Gründorf he asked which regiments were due to arrive. Gründorf told him that the Graz 'House' regiment and the Upper Styrian Jaegers were about to come up, where-upon Gablenz caught the young staff officer's eye and raised an inquisitive eyebrow. 'I think we should attack as soon as they arrive,' Gablenz insisted.[8] Half an hour later the two Styrian regiments arrived and attacked despite the sub-zero temperatures and a howling snowstorm. From the well-defended Sankelmarker wood a hail of bullets and artillery shot opened up. The Austrians, whose rifles had frozen, could not fire a shot, but the first bayonet charge went in and the Danish fire began to slacken. At the same time the Danish guns were silenced by Gablenz's artillery.

The Prussian officers attached to Gablenz's command watched with aston-ishment as the Styrians drove the Danes out of their strong positions at the point of the bayonet with their regimental band playing the 'Radetzky March' throughout, even in the snow and ice. Three counter-attacks by the Danes were beaten off. As a momentary lull in the storm allowed another counter-attack, Gablenz rode to the head of the Graz regiment's second battalion and with flags flying and bands playing led them with sword drawn at the Danes who were regrouping around the so-called 'Krug von Billschau'.

The music and Gablenz's cries of 'Kinder drauf, es muss sein!' ('Children get up there! It must succeed!'), mingled with the rapid fire of the Danes and wild cries of the Styrians, brought the 'Belgians' to the summit.*

Their regimental colonel, the Duke of Württemberg had his horse shot from beneath him and fell wounded, his sword broken. As the rifles' metal parts froze in the cold, the Styrians used the butts as clubs to beat back their opponents when their bayonets broke. Three bayonet attacks had been neces-sary to drive the Danes off their positions. After an hour the Danes fell back, streaming from the heights towards Flensburg. The temperature was just

---

* The honorary colonel of the Graz 'House' regiment traditionally for several generations was the King of the Belgians, hence their nickname: 'Die Belgier'.

below minus 22 degrees Celsius. As a cart carried off the 'Belgians'' wounded colonel, he dictated a note to his victorious troops which would become the treasured dispatch of this regiment for decades to come:

> Never have troops fought with such endurance and heroism as the regiment 'King of the Belgians'. I call to all soldiers who recognise in these countless examples of manly courage a noble heart that there are no better soldiers anywhere in the world than the knightly and good Styrians.[9]*

Prussians note the Austrian tactics at Oeversee

Having so far distinguished themselves only by their reluctance to risk casualties, the Prussians noted their ally's success. Barely two years later, some of these same Prussian officers would be fighting against the Austrians at Königgrätz, and would draw more practical lessons from this display of bravura. The victory at Oeversee cleared Schleswig of the enemy. A few days later, at Apenrade, the Austrians again proved the value of their storm tactics, and carried away their opponents at the point of the bayonet. Prussian blue, as Crankshaw noted, had still not 'arrived'.[10]

The Austrians could not disguise their losses, and when on 8 March Gablenz crossed the so-called *Koenigs-Au*, his *Anstoss-taktik* (frontal attack tactics) drove the Danes beyond Veile, but with fearful losses. As a Prussian observer noted: 'While our troops would not move forward without covering artillery fire, the Austrians sought no cover, always marching forward accompanied by their skirmishers who suffered terribly in the face of the Danes' well-dug-in defences. We were astonished at the bravery and élan of the Austrians but these charges with the "arme blanche" resulted in our losing quickly any superiority in numbers we might have enjoyed.'[11]

On 26 April, the Danish fortress at Fredericia surrendered to the Austrians, and with it all of Jutland. Meanwhile the Prussians had finally discovered their confidence and had stormed the Duppel heights so tenaciously held by the

---

* As a song in Styrian dialect of the 9th Jaeger dating from this memorable encounter noted:

In einer Stund' wars geschegn
Seind auch viel Leut schon g'legn
Belgianer, Jaeger durcheinand
Alle aus'm Steirerland!

(In an hour 'twas done
Lots of men lay already gone
Belgianer and Jaeger a myriad
All from the land of Styria)

Danes. The Peace of Vienna signed later on 30 October delivered the two duchies to Austria and Prussia.

These costly victories in Denmark underlined how the reforms mooted after Solferino needed further refinement. A rapid series of hierarchical changes was swiftly implemented. In October 1862, the Adjutant Korps and the Generalquartiermeisterstab had already been combined into a single General Staff. The monarchy was now divided into 80 military districts. Each of these districts possessed a regiment of four battalions each made up of six companies, totalling 4,090 men. The long-standing intimacy between the military district and the local 'House' regiment was reinforced by these arrangements.

But as so often, these administrative reforms were not accompanied by any radical change in tactics. The battalion remained the principal tactical unit and its deployment in 'Mass' was the dominant theme. Though some companies were trained to engage the enemy in open order, they were not encouraged to display initiative. They were expected to base their open-order formation on the requirements of the battalion as it advanced shoulder to shoulder against the enemy. The 'blank' weapon remained the principal armament to decide any engagement. Musketry was perceived as drawing out the conflict unnecessarily. The French example at Solferino remained, mistakenly, the tactic of choice. Resistance was to be overcome by entire brigades, if not larger formations, advancing with flags flying and bands playing. On the parade ground and exercise fields these tactics were perfected so that no onlooker could fail to be impressed. Oeversee was the proof. If the Austrian bayonet charge could triumph there, it must surely triumph anywhere.

In addition to these mistaken ideas, the military budget was almost halved between 1861 and 1865. The General Staff might have imagined it had 850,000 men with whom to hold down Venetia, intimidate Prussia and keep Hungary acquiescent but by 1865 the maximum number of troops available was less than 380,000. Company strength theoretically put at 146 was now only 54. Well might the war minister Feldmarschallleutnant Frank observe that 'the vital organs of the army are being amputated.'[12]

Bismarck, shrewd and observant, saw the effects of these constraints. At the same time his generals drew a lesson from the Danish campaign that although the Austrians were currently enjoying prestige and victories, they might be vulnerable in the event of new tactics and technology.

The 'needle' gun

These new tactics and technology were evolving in Prussia with the arrival of the 'needle' gun (so called on account of its needle-shaped firing-pin). The

Zündnadelgewehr was a breech-loading (*Hinterladergewehr*) bolt-action rifle which fired up to five times more rapidly than the (admittedly more accurate) Austrian Lorenz musket. Manufactured by Dreyse, it also allowed an infantryman to lie down and fire in the prone position. By 1866, the Prussians had had this weapon for nearly fifteen years, and their tactics had evolved accordingly.

The Austrian high command repeatedly rejected the Prussian *Zündnadelgewehr* throughout the 1850s and '60s. It was too expensive, required (another expense) additional training and, above all, implied looser-order tactics. These might affect the cohesion of the largely uneducated peasant infantry of the Habsburg troops.

There were other compelling reasons for the Austrians to reject the Dreyse weapon. When first trialled in the Austrian army in the 1850s it had proved unreliable: its gas seal was defective, sparks blasted into the face of the handler and its velocity at long range was much diminished. In addition, the firing-pins proved fragile, with potentially fatal consequences for the operator. At long range, observed one Austrian officer, it was 'scarcely more effective than a handful of pebbles'.[13]

Money lay at the heart of the decision to reject the breech-loading rifle, even as it overcame these technical deficiencies. The dwindling resources could not cope with any major radical innovation. This was felt keenly in all arms with the exception of the artillery, whose move to rifled barrels was prompted by the effectiveness of the rifled French guns at Solferino. But such investment in one arm came at a cost to another; even the cavalry was not immune from the prevailing obsession with budget costs: in 1865 there were 10,000 horsemen fewer than the active cavalry list suggested.

These financial limitations were not a problem for Prussia. As the 1860s progressed, the average Austrian infantryman had barely 20 rounds a year with which to practise. His Prussian counterpart had 100. Under their intellectually able General Staff chief, Helmuth von Moltke (1800–91), an intense training programme which encouraged initiative and marksmanship was introduced. The Prussian army began to make progress towards becoming once again the best infantry in Europe.

Ironically, the *esprit* and morale of the Imperial Austrian Army at this time had probably never been higher. Its *Kampfgeist* was overwhelming; its courage and experience formidable. The veterans of the Radetzky campaigns had forged a comradely unity that some historians of the army have argued was never to be repeated. The use of the intimate 'Du' rather than the formal 'Sie' had forged a brotherhood in arms among the officers that was unbreakable. In any potential conflict no neutral observer, including the veteran *Times* war corrrepondent Russell, believed the Prussians could be any match for the Austrians.

Bismarck's stratagem

Bismarck, Prussia's scheming Chancellor, saw matters differently. Joint Austro-Prussian administration of Schleswig-Holstein was a vehicle to provoke Franz-Josef into war and dislodge the Habsburgs not only from the Duchies but from any role in Germany. Proceeding with his usual methodical care, the German Chancellor first set about isolating the Austrians. Vague promises to France and Russia bought their acquiescence in Prussia's plans for dealing with Austria. In April 1866 he concluded an alliance with the newly crowned King of Italy, Vittorio Emanuele II. The terms, which obliged the Italians to attack Austria within 90 days of Prussia, completed Vienna's diplomatic isolation. In return Bismarck promised to use his best offices to secure the 'restoration' of Venetia. It would help the Prussian army hugely if Austria could be compelled to divide her forces to deal with the Italians.

In a cynical ploy Bismarck proposed abolishing the Confederation of German Princes and replacing it with an elected German parliament whose members did not represent Austria. This was a provocation to which Vienna replied by referring the question of the Duchies to the German diet. This violated the Convention of Gastein whereby the Duchies were designated as an exclusively Austro-Prussian affair. Such a war of nerves could not last for very much longer without an outbreak of hostilities. But even then the Prussian king, in awe of the Austrian army, could not be persuaded to declare war on the Habsburgs. A tense week followed. Both Austria and Prussia mobilised but the formal declaration of war would have to wait many more weeks. It was left to a Prussian officer, leading his troops towards an Austrian border post in northern Bohemia, to hand over a note to the Austrian border guard declaring that a state of war now existed between Prussia and Austria.

Thus did the two states enter the brief 'Six Weeks War': brief but immensely significant for European history. Under the terms of her treaty with Prussia, Italy mobilised to ensure that the Habsburgs would face a war on two fronts as Bismarck had planned: the Iron Chancellor was leaving nothing to chance, and not for moment did he underestimate his opponent.

CHAPTER 15

The Austro-Prussian War

KÖNIGGRÄTZ 1866

The Austrian army's failure to embrace new developments in infantry training and firepower was to cost it dearly in 1866. By contrast, its artillery took on the lessons learnt at Solferino and, by the time of the outbreak of war, it was the finest in Europe.

The Six Weeks War, culminating in the battle of Königgrätz,* remains one of the most decisive and fateful conflicts of the nineteenth century. The notion of a modern united Germany under Prussian leadership was born here. German hegemony in Europe, and the two terrible wars of the twentieth century fought to prevent it, could not have happened without Prussia's victory in 1866. From Königgrätz to Potsdam in 1945 runs a straight but unholy road. That road was laid in a few hours in the killing fields of the Swiep forest cradled between the folds of the seductively rolling landscape of northern Bohemia. The German writer Thomas Mann once remarked that Berlin was condemned always to be a city in waiting. The slaughter of Königgrätz and the defeat of Austria condemned Berlin to a far worse fate: she was to wait no longer to become the most dominant city in Europe.

Who were the men who acted as midwives to the birth of this fateful chain of events? They come together in as exotic a dramatis personae to walk across the stage of European military history as any we have encountered in our story so far. On the Prussian side there was the 'Iron Chancellor', Otto von Bismarck (1815–98). It was his political statecraft that first cajoled a reluctant Prussian monarch into war with Austria and then prevented his victory being ruined by that same monarch's demand for a Carthaginian peace. Heavy set in appearance, his ponderous bullying manner belied an agile mind and a withering

---

* Also known as Sadowa, after one of the villages where it was fought in northern Bohemia

sense of sarcasm that disarmed his slower-witted opponents. When once asked aggressively what he would do if a British army landed on the North Sea coast, Bismarck replied: 'Why . . . I would send a policeman to arrest it.' Though not a soldier by profession, he appears here dressed, somewhat implausibly, in the spiked helmet of a reserve militia officer.

As the perfect foil to all this bluster and pyrotechnics stood the second Prussian protagonist of that day, Helmuth von Moltke, Chief of the Prussian General Staff and, during this battle, directing operations with almost unfailing skill despite being in his 67th year. Where Bismarck was demonstrative, Moltke was self-effacing. The austere servant of the Prussian state was a focused soldier, living and breathing the *Geist* of the Prussian Enlightenment. Impassive, spare and unemotional, he never said anything that was not directly relevant to the matters in hand. Marrying an English girl late in life, he spent most of his time reading Goethe and Shakespeare; he had earlier translated nine volumes of Gibbon. It was Ludwig Benedek's bad fortune to be the officer 'on call' to confront these formidable characters and to be summoned to sacrifice himself for the Habsburg dynasty that particular year. A couple of years later it might have been the gifted Gablenz. A decade earlier it might even have been Radetzky.

The character of Ludwig Benedek

Benedek, Radetzky's protégé but the ultimate outsider in the Austrian military establishment, may have distinguished himself against the Italians at San Martino but he had none of his Prussian opponents' ruthlessness. Though held in great esteem by the rank and file, his meteoric rise had, as meteoric rises tend to, put a number of his contemporaries' noses out of joint. They resented the fact that this Protestant upstart's entry into the hitherto exclusively Catholic Theresian Military Academy had required a changing of the rules governing officer entry. Where were the generations of military service to the dynasty that gave such officers as Khevenhueller or Schwarzenberg such swagger? Benedek's waxed moustaches, slightly feminine frame and features, and his social awkwardness, all added up to the posturing of the arriviste. Benedek was all too painfully aware of these perceived shortcomings. To compensate for them he developed an almost exaggerated personal code of honour fuelled by unmistakable vanity. At the centre of this was the unwritten legacy of 1619: not for a moment did he ever forget that his duty as an officer was first and foremost to the dynasty.

From the point of view of the military historian, the 1866 campaign received at the time and in the run-up to the First World War, 'the golden era of staff studies', considerable attention. The use of railways to transport troops so efficiently was noted as innovative. Moltke's planned and effected conjunction of three armies was perceived as strategic skill bordering on genius. The initiative and training of the Prussian soldier were widely admired. Conversely, Austrian staff-work was criticised and the tactics of the Austrian infantry were seen as woefully unsuitable for modern warfare and the cause of enormous losses.

Leopold Amery, a school contemporary and later cabinet minister of Churchill in the Second World War, carefully studied the 1908 handbook on the 1866 campaign by J.H. Anderson, which was the set work for the staff examinations of that year. Amery's careful annotations underline the significance of the battle for military thinking a generation later.[1] In every military academy of note in Europe, the campaign was studied and analysed by the generation of officers who would lead their countries into the collective suicide of 1914. By far the most thoughtful treatise on the battle was by the French general Bonnal, whose penetrating analysis of the campaign remains to this day a masterly, impartial and dispassionate account of the conflict, devoid of either Moltke's 'hindsight' or the official Austrian account's enthusiasm for heaping blame on the hapless Feldzeugmeister Ludwig Benedek.[2]

The struggle for supremacy in Germany

The efficiency of the Prussian army notwithstanding, the war could never have happened without Bismarck's determination and realpolitik. He organised the break with Austria and the alliance with Italy to force the Habsburgs to wage war on two fronts. It speaks volumes for Bismarck's way of proceeding that, barely six weeks before hostilities began, he more or less proposed a partition of Germany between Prussia and Austria along north/south lines. The authors of this proposal were the two Gablenz brothers from Saxony, one the Austrian general, the other a member of the Prussian parliament. It was characteristic of Bismarck's methods that it did not trouble him in the slightest that such an arrangement would mean deserting Italy, with whom he had just formed an alliance.

Bismarck knew that his career as Prussia's leading politician was at stake. Equally, he was indifferent to popular hostility towards his policies. In Silesia, Catholic priests everywhere denounced the Prussian war against Austria, and Archbishop Melchers of Cologne wrote to the Prussian King condemning the 'civil war' in strong terms. Reservists in the Rhineland could only be persuaded to entrain by their officers at sword point.

On hearing the Bismarck/Gablenz proposal in Vienna, Kaiser Franz-Josef keenly observed on 24 May: 'It is to be regretted these proposals were not made earlier; presumably Count Bismarck had some deep purpose in making acceptable proposals only when their acceptance was no longer possible.'[3] The Gablenz plans fell at the fence of the Austrian Emperor's sense of honour. He felt he could not desert his Saxon and other German allies by committing a breach of faith with states with which he had just entered into an alliance.

But this sense of honour was misplaced. Moltke realised that these German allies of Austria were but 'an enemy in embryo' and that a decisive victory over Austria would in his phrase 'paralyse all other enemies'.[4] For Austria, it was also clear from the beginning that the decisive front would be to the north and that the campaign of the Northern Army (Nordarmee) would most likely be more demanding than that against Italy. Italy had asked Berlin for the Veneto in return for the alliance. Sensing this, Austria had already taken the decision in secret to surrender Venice and the Veneto to Napoleon III on the understanding that Napoleon would give it to Italy so as to allow Vienna to be free of any commitments in the south should events become critical with Prussia. At first Austria hoped for compensation for the surrender of Venice in the recovery, after a successful campaign, of Silesia, but as the war wore on this proved little more than a pious hope and, as events rapidly developed, the surrender of the 'Serenissima' to Italy with no compensation became inevitable.

As far as the Habsburg Emperor and his court were concerned, the war against Italy was politically irrelevant. The Habsburg armies were defending the prestige of the monarchy but not its territory. The Archduke Albert and his 130,000 troops were simply heading south to defend Austria's honour.

Benedek is chosen to lead the Nordarmee

Given the more serious nature of the looming conflict to the north the choice of Austrian commander in that theatre was fraught with political and dynastic considerations. The Archduke Albert, the son of the Archduke Charles, was a capable soldier and was the obvious choice of field marshal for a campaign against Italy where the Austrians enjoyed not only notable superiority in morale but also the happy circumstance that there was nothing to lose.[5]

This was clearly not the case with the campaign against Prussia. Austria's prestige, influence and rights in Germany would be lost irrevocably should her armies fail against Prussia. Such a defeat would be accompanied by considerable acrimony and public dissatisfaction. It was therefore out of the question to place a member of the Imperial House in the delicate position of *Feldherr*. Franz-Josef had learnt from Solferino the political risks of commanding an army that failed to rise to the occasion, and his obligations to his House precluded any member of his family enjoying operational command in the Nordarmee.

Thus the choice fell on the unwilling FZM Ludwig Benedek, the hero of San Martino, the 'meritocratic' professional officer who appeared to herald a new era in the upper echelons of the Habsburg army where aristocratic preference seemed again capable of yielding to ability and skill.

No one saw the pitfalls of the command in the north more clearly than the Feldmarschall himself. Twice Benedek asked his Emperor not to give him command of the Nordarmee. He longed for the Italian front where, as he pointed out to Franz-Josef, he knew 'every tree and bush' of the landscape.

These arguments told, and at first it seemed Benedek would get his way. After the council of war at the end of May, Benedek was about to set off for Verona but he was interrupted while still in bed and summoned to the Emperor's adjutant-general, who told him that it had been decided 'on account of public opinion' to appoint him to the command in the north after all. If any other commander was appointed and was then defeated the 'Emperor would have no choice but to abdicate'. As an argument calculated to brook no opposition, it swayed Benedek. Yet again a Habsburg was demonstrating that the army's first duty lay with its sovereign and the dynasty. Benedek duly obeyed, finding little consolation that the Emperor, as a 'sign of his confidence', was attaching the mentally feeble Archduke Ernst, a true product of centuries of inbreeding, to his staff as a corps commander.

It should not be thought from these considerations that morale was low in the Nordarmee or that opinion either private or public imagined a Prussian victory. Quite the opposite was the case. No less an authority than *The Times* of London believed an Austrian victory inevitable. 'The finest cavalry I have ever in my life seen,' wrote Russell, *The Times'* former Crimean War correspondent. Certainly in cavalry and artillery the Habsburg forces were as formidable as ever, while her infantry had showed the world two years earlier in Denmark that it lacked neither courage nor élan.[6]

Russell's assessment overlooked those peculiar weaknesses of the Austrian command system, notably complexity and duplication of functions: factors all too familiar to the Prussian officers who had observed the Austrian efforts in Denmark. The prevalence of aristocratic officers serving as corps commanders under the meritocratic Benedek also underlined a caste friction that would play a role at critical moments in the campaign.

Moltke's initial dispositions

There can be no doubt that the common view of seamless Prussian efficiency and serial Austrian incompetence, found in much of the literature covering the compaign up to this day, is flawed.[7]

Had the Austrians been commanded by Gablenz or a more aggressive figure it is not to be excluded that Prussia would have been 'infallibly ruined', in Bonnal's phrase, because Moltke's initial dispositions were far from perfect, as the perceptive French general had noticed. By 10 June 1866, three Prussian armies were spread out along a front of 156 miles before their opponent's intentions had remotely manifested themselves. Attempting to guard against a Saxon incursion against Berlin or Breslau, Moltke had placed his forces in a most precarious position, which would have proved fatal had the Austrians been fired with Napoleonic imagination and drive. As previous chapters have shown, tradition demanded of the Habsburg army that it should give highest priority to the protection of the dynasty. To this end, all hazardous risks and gambles were excluded as a matter of course.

Nevertheless it was not entirely to be ignored that the three Prussian armies, strung out so inopportunely, might not have been taken advantage of. No doubt it must have been with some relief that Moltke received an exact copy of the Austrian Order of Battle on 11 June, courtesy of the 'Cavalry of St George' (a polite euphemism for a spy).

This showed the Austrian concentration planned around Olmütz in northern Moravia and Moltke quickly reorganised his armies to guard against a threat to Silesia in a new plan which he later termed 'excellent'. This increased the ground between I and II Prussian Armies by a distance of eight marches. One might concur with Bonnal, who noted that 'the epithet excellent, applied to this plan by the Prussian, is a matter between Moltke and his conscience'.[8]

It was only by a stroke of luck and Moltke's own willpower that the evil effects of this deployment were later mitigated by more intelligence, this time communicating the Austrian decision to move the army corps from Olmütz to Bohemia. Between the Prussians and Bohemia lay the formidable mountain passes of the Riesengebirge, which had to be crossed by the Prussian II Army. It was Benedek's plan to oppose these slowly converging Prussian armies by taking up a position on interior lines around the Gitchin plateau, but first the Prussian II Army would have to be slowed down as it moved into the defiles of Silesia. To this end Benedek detached a couple of corps to occupy the exit points, and to hold the line of the nearby Iser with the Saxon army under Prince Albert.

At Trutnov (Trautenau) and Nachod the advance elements of the Prussian II Army under Bonin and Steinmetz found the Austrians ready for them as they debouched from the passes.

Gablenz at Trautenau

Resting in the town of Trutnov, the advance units of the Prussian I Corps suddenly found themselves attacked by Mondel's light infantry brigade, which opened fire on the startled Prussians from the heights. The Prussians had barely stacked their rifles and drums when the Austrian Jaeger poured in a fierce fire. Only by sheer force of numbers did the Prussians manage to drive the Austrians from the heights. In the small church on the hill above the town, a regiment of Austrian Poles fought virtually to the last man pew by pew before surrendering. The Prussians, having driven Mondel's men off the hill commanding Trutnov, found an Austrian battery of 40 guns carefully arranged on the heights two miles further back. These opened up a merciless barrage to support the Austrian counter-attack, which was carried out with great élan by two brigades with fixed bayonets, led by Grivičič and Wimpffen. Although these Austrians dislodged the Prussians, the cost was enormous. The Prussian needle gun favoured the defenders and two of Grivičič's regiments were utterly destroyed in the attack. Grivičič would later recall: 'Losses exceeded the worst I had experienced in three previous wars.'[9] Overall, Gablenz suffered 5,000 casualties against barely 1,200 Prussians. Nearly 200 of his officers had been killed against barely 60 of the enemy.

Despite this asymmetry in firepower, General Adolf von Bonin, the commander of the Prussian I Corps, dimly realised that he was facing the most energetic general in the Austrian army. He ordered his men to withdraw. As Bonin fell back in some confusion, he paid a high price for his failure to move the bulk of his forces across the Aupa river to support his advance guard. At the official inquiry into his actions during the war, one of his subordinates noted: 'We can't all be heroes.'[10] This withdrawal threatened Moltke's entire strategy because Bonin's force had been designated to cover the passage of the Prussian Guard Corps and II Army headquarters as they advanced.

Gablenz's achievement was all the more remarkable given that his troops had been on the march for nine consecutive days in dusty, dry conditions with little food. His X Corps had marched thirty miles to Trutnov from Josephstadt in less than 28 hours and had gone straight into action. But the victory of Trautenau, as the Austrians called it, could not disguise the overwhelming superiority of the Prussian infantry's firepower. Because Gablenz was under strict instructions not to cross the Prussian frontier, he could not follow up the victory in any way even if he had had the support to do so. It is significant that Gablenz's success was the result of the only flank attack the Austrians performed during the entire campaign, and that he eschewed the frontal shock tactics that had proved so costly in the Schleswig-Holstein campaign.

Benedek's chief of operations, Gideon Krismanič, had detached only two battalions to cover Gablenz. It was one of many errors the learned but over-cerebral Krismanič committed in the campaign. Krismanič, a scholar of the Seven Years War and a notable pedant, insisted on seeing everything in terms of the wars of Maria Theresa. He managed to overawe Benedek with his learning; another symptom of Benedek's lack of confidence at these times. Gablenz well knew that a renewed assault by Bonin the next day would be difficult to hold, not least because the Prussians were pouring through the mountains at the nearby pass of Nachod where the Prussian general Steinmetz had secured an important victory for his corps. There, the Austrian commander, Ramming, had deployed too far back to prevent the Prussian advance guard erupting from the defiles and deploying rapidly.

The action at nearby Nachod once again underlined the immense superiority in firepower of the Prussians. Six battalions of Prussian infantry had to face attacks from two Austrian brigades under Ramming, a reasonably competent Austrian general. Because these attacks were so sporadic and were carried out without the flanking possibilities which had helped Gablenz, the Prussians had no difficulty fighting them off. In contrast to Trutnov, the Prussians benefited from making effective use of their artillery because of the weak Austrian deployment.

The Austrians fall back and Benedek loses his nerve

After six hours of various disjointed Austrian attacks, the Prussians pushed them back towards Skalice (Skalitz) in utter confusion. Hundreds of troops surrendered and nearly 4,000 men had been wounded or killed. The chaos and confusion of this encounter (once again the Prussians had suffered disproportionately fewer casualties: barely 1,500) had a devastating effect on Austrian morale. Entire regiments had been almost wiped out and so quick were the survivors to become demoralised that over 2,000 men had surrendered immediately. The disintegration of several units, notably a Slovak battalion cut down in the long grass by pursuing Prussian infantry, was hastened by the Prussians resorting to *Schnellfeuer*.

Yet it need not have been thus. Gablenz had shown that, when they were aggressively led, the Austrians could defeat the Prussians. Indeed, Bonnal argues that had Ramming been successful at Nachod, it is likely the campaign would have played out entirely in Austria's favour because the Prussian II Army would not have been able to join the Prussian I Army. They would then have faced Benedek significantly outnumbered.

As it was, Ramming's failure to deploy his artillery and to mount his attacks vigorously accelerated the collapse in morale that Benedek's army and leadership found almost impossible to shake off. As if to complete the discomfort of the Austrians on the 28th, the Prussian Guard bumped into Gablenz's rearguard as it withdrew from Trutnov on Königinhof. In less than an hour they annihilated the remains of Grivičič's brigade near the village of Soor (name of ill omen: site of a great victory by Frederick II). Well might Leopold Amery annotate his copy of Anderson's study with the words: 'The events of 28th June had knocked the stuffing out of Benedek'.[11]

On the 29th the Austrian commander, Clam-Gallas, together with the Saxon army, attempted to engage the Prussian I Army at Jičín. They had only begun when the order to 'avoid any serious confrontation' was received and, unreinforced, they fell back in considerable disorder. Clam-Gallas, a general who dined better than he fought, was seen mounting his horse at a critical moment only to slide across the saddle and fall off the other side.

These orders illustrated all too well that Benedek had lost his nerve. His initial plan of operating along interior lines and defeating each Prussian army in turn had been shattered. Drawing unrealistically on the campaigns of Maria Theresa, Krismanič hastily composed a new position for Benedek but this proved impracticable, envisaging as it did an exposed position along the Elbe. The junction of two Prussian armies was by now more or less inevitable and on the 30th Benedek drew up a third plan, less ambitious, involving a retirement towards a defensive position on Königgrätz (Hradec Králové).

At about the same time, Benedek's opposite number, Moltke, the Prussian King and Bismarck entrained from Berlin to head for the front. The austere general had been highly dissatisfied with the command and control system afforded him by the modern telegraph system. Because the Austrians pulled down the telegraph poles as they retreated, several orders of Moltke had taken as long as three days to reach the relevant commander. By the time of Moltke's arrival in Bohemia on 1 June this situation had been remedied because the Prussian headquarters was moved to Jičín, well positioned for directing operations in northern Bohemia.

After the events of the previous five days, Benedek was plunged into the deepest gloom. The reports of the casualties and the rapid fire of the Prussian infantry underlined the impotence and helplessness of an army that allowed its opponents to fire five times more rapidly than its own infantry. Without fighting a set battle, Benedek had lost 30,000 men and on all sides the roads were a chaos of retreating units. A debacle on a truly terrifying scale was threatening. Benedek was a sufficiently intelligent soldier to realise that a new kind of warfare had arrived since his glory days at San Martino, seven years earlier, and that his infantry were completely unprepared for it.

Benedek's telegram

In this atmosphere, the Emperor's adjutant, Colonel Beck arrived and the two men drafted a desperate telegram to Vienna. It simply read:

> Your Majesty most urgently requested to make peace at any price. Catastrophe inevitable.
> Signed, Benedek

Beck saw Benedek's dilemma very clearly and he supported the telegram with one of his own to Crenneville, another Imperial adjutant in Vienna. This read:

> Armistice of peace imperative because withdrawal scarcely possible. My heart is breaking but I must report the truth.[12]

As can be imagined, the text of Benedek's telegram caused consternation in Vienna, buoyed up meanwhile by the news of the Archduke Albert's victory over the Italians at Custozza (see Chapter 16). The idea that peace should be made without a battle was anathema to the Emperor and he telegraphed back immediately:

> Impossible to conclude a peace. I order – if unavoidable, retreat in best order. Has there been a battle? [Note: the last sentence was added with the Emperor's approval by an adjutant.][13]

These documents underline the inevitable dangers when a commander-in-chief is remote from the front. The terseness of Benedek's correspondence strongly suggests an imminent emotional and mental breakdown while Franz-Josef is clearly bewildered and unprepared for bad news.

By the time the contents of Beck's telegram had become more widely known at court, the long-awaited battle had indeed taken place. At first Moltke thought Benedek was going to anchor his army between the two great Austrian fortresses of northern Bohemia, Josephstadt (Josefov) and Königgrätz (Hradec Králové) and his orders on 2 July reflect this. But perhaps stung by the telegraphic reply of the Emperor and aware that his men needed to rest, Benedek now began to develop yet another plan, this time to position himself around the plateau of Chlum and fight a defensive battle.

Moltke improvises and Benedek resolves to fight

When intelligence of the change in Austrian plans reached Moltke, he rapidly set about cancelling his earlier orders. In particular, he dispatched the following note to the Crown Prince and II Army:

> Your Royal Highness will be good enough at once to take the necessary steps to march to the assistance of the I Army with all your forces moving against the right flank of the enemy .... The orders sent from here this afternoon had a different object. They are now to be considered cancelled. Signed Von Moltke.[14]

Moltke's orders show that he feared an Austrian offensive, notwithstanding the rather unaggressive showing of the Imperial army a week earlier, and his objective was to deny Benedek the advantage of movement, pinning the Austrians down while II Army marched to take them in the flank by the early afternoon.

That Benedek was alive to this and took careful preparations to fight a battle from a strong defensive position is shown by his dispositions on 2 and 3 July. These illustrate that he had pulled himself together and was now thinking in a practical way at last. Moltke might not have known precisely where the Austrian army was around Chlum, but Benedek's artillery commanders seemed to know exactly where the Prussian I Army would be crossing the Bistritz stream. The common assumption that Benedek had no plan is not borne out by events on the ground.[15]

Working feverishly through the afternoon and evening of 2 July, the Austrian artillery took up a strong defensive arc around the village of Chlum and synchronised their batteries to fire down carefully marked lines which stretched from the village to where the Prussians would advance. This energetic and highly effective activity, which took several hours to complete, contradicts notions that the Austrians were not prepared to fight or were confused over the direction from which the Prussians would come.

The Austrian artillery was equipped with precision guns with rifled barrels. If the infantry had been starved of funds, the artillery arm of the Imperial Royal Army was now absolutely up-to-date. It would demonstrate the following day that it had both the finest and some of the most courageous artillery in the world. Moreover, Benedek was not only preparing to fight a strong defence, he was planning to inflict a serious check on the Prussian armies. To guard against any incursion of the Prussian II Army on his right flank, he placed two entire corps behind Chlum to form a barrier to any advance from that quarter. This would buy him time to inflict the bloodiest of noses on the Prussian I Army. Like every careful commander, Benedek also drew up a coherent plan for withdrawal. Through Beck, he had asked the Emperor for permission to dismiss Krizmanič. His new chief of staff, Alfred Henikstein, had only arrived on the morning of the battle, so most of these plans can be attributed to Benedek himself. Both his cavalry and artillery knew exactly where they were to erect a new defensive arc in the event of a withdrawal, to allow the infantry to withdraw to the fortress of Königgrätz. Benedek had roused himself from his gloom and, freed from Krismanič, now appeared to have pulled himself together.

Confident that the army would now fight from a strong position, and with morale unquestionably raised by the appearance of their Feldzeugmeister riding among them, the Austrians may have slept more peacefully than at any time in the war. By taking up his position on the hallowed ground of Maria Theresa's battles against Prussia, Benedek, for all his earlier vacillation, was simply expressing the traditions of the Imperial House. As Friedjung has written:

> Ferdinand II encompassed by rebels, Maria Theresa in conflict with all the armies of the Continent, Francis in his ceaseless wars against Napoleon: all had put their fortunes to the test on the battlefield however unfavourable the circumstances. Austria's position in Europe did not rest so much on great victories as on her defensive strength. Never did she abandon a position without a struggle as Prussia had learnt at Olmütz a few years earlier or Russia would at the Congress of Berlin a few years later.[16]

In the Prussian camp the orders for the I Army to begin its concentration were carried out as a thick mist, accompanied by rain, heralded the dawn. The 7th Division under Fransecky, a tough and resourceful Prussian from Hesse, was at Cerekwitz close to the Austrian centre. As the 6th Division under Horn drove in the Austrian outposts around the village of Sadowa, Fransecky's men advanced to the sound of the guns and occupied the hamlet of Benatek. By 8 a.m., there was firing all along the line and the Prussian King watching from the nearby hill of Dub gave the order for his armies to advance. Four minutes later the batteries of the Austrian artillery opened up and the entire line of the Prussian advance ground to a halt. The hail of shell that now rained down upon the Prussian I Army was accurate and terrible in the extreme. Entire companies were blown to bits as they struggled to cross the Bistritz. Only Fransecky's division completed its deployment across the river. Elsewhere the Prussian offensive came to a halt (described disingenuously in the official Prussian history of the campaign as the 5th and 6th Divisions being 'held in continual readiness'). The main body of the Prussian forces was pinned down with not the slightest possibility of moving to the attack.[17]

Fransecky's occupation of the Swiepwald

There now occurred on the Prussian left one of those modest tactical moments whose consequences are utterly disproportionate to the initial intention. Displaying the initiative and aggressive spirit which characterised the Prussian army throughout this campaign, Fransecky's 7th Division moved four battalions out of the village of Benatek into the nearby Swiep (Maslowed) wood.

This wood, nearly a mile long and about 1,200 yards wide, is today one of the most extraordinary battlefields to be found anywhere in Europe. Every corner and recess is filled with monuments to the thousands slaughtered within its leafy and seemingly tranquil ravines and dells. Its eerie stillness and silence provoke reflection, even among those unfamiliar with the details of what occurred there.

Fransecky's battalions, exposed as they were rather forward of the rest of the Prussian line, moved into the northern edge of the wood around 8.30 a.m., driving in the Austrian outposts which had been most carelessly positioned by 4th Corps commanded by Prince Festetics. As so often happens, the offensive swiftly became a desperate struggle on the defensive as the Austrian 4th Corps reacted like a hornets' nest. Together with 2nd Corps under Count Thun, 4th Corps had been positioned on Benedek's right to watch for the arrival of the Prussian Crown Prince's army and to hold up his progress while Benedek inflicted a drubbing on the Prussian forces pinned down along the Bistritz. Suddenly provoked by Fransecky's bold occupation of the wood, these two corps, nearly a quarter of Benedek's entire strength, formed up to drive the Prussians out at the point of the bayonet in defiance of Benedek's tactical instructions to avoid frontal attacks, and in disobedience of their orders to guard the Austrian right flank.

Attacking only in brigade strength, the Austrians yet again fed their troops into the battle in piecemeal fashion. Whereas a general attack on the wood would have been successful by sheer weight of numbers, the Austrian 4th Corps commander Mollinary (who had replaced Festetics after he was wounded) committed only one brigade at a time. As the Prussians took up a strong position in the interior of the wood, the Austrian Jaeger were cut to pieces before they came anywhere near their enemy.

Fransecky had been rather impetuous. He had committed a foolish and highly risky manoeuvre which threatened the flank of the Prussian army and, had it been any other army, almost certainly would have compromised Moltke's entire strategy. The projection of a single infantry brigade, unsupported by artillery or indeed any other forces, against two hostile corps would certainly not have been in Moltke's book of warfare.

Mollinary's insubordination

Mollinary realised the Prussian error and made haste to make them pay but in committing so many troops he exposed Benedek's flank. By 9.30 a.m., one Prussian brigade was fighting for its life against an entire Austrian corps. Every company Fransecky had was in action. From a high point in the wood from where his horse was shot from beneath him, the Prussian general was unable to direct the battle, so thick was the smoke from the firing. The noise was deafening: the cries of the soldiers, guttural Prussian commands and anguished Slavic curses made it difficult to think. But Fransecky knew that a retreat to the open ground behind the forest would see his forces slaughtered by the Austrians in a matter of minutes. There was no option other than to hold on for dear life, even if it was against odds of nearly ten to one.

Benedek from his postion on the hilltop at Chlum watched the massed ranks of Mollinary's troops marching towards the wood around 10 a.m. and was horrified. He immediately dispatched an aide-de-camp to order Mollinary to break off the action and return to the Chlum–Nedelist line. This order, which reached Mollinary fifty minutes later, was deliberately disobeyed. By 11 a.m. a second corps (2nd Corps) had joined the attack again in defiance of orders.

Elsewhere the battle was going entirely to Benedek's plan. Austrian artillery was inflicting havoc on the Prussian army, neutralising their infantry's superiority in weapons. The Prussians, pinned down, had no choice but to sit out the destructive barrage until reinforcements arrived from the east. Stoic and impassive, they waited as with every shell that landed dozens of their comrades were swept away.

Mollinary's disobedience was later justified by the heat of battle and his perception that the Prussians in the wood were about to be annihilated. In fact it is more than likely that Mollinary was hoping to win his Maria Theresa Order by attacking like Gablenz at Oeversee, frontally with the bayonet. It has to be said he was almost successful. By 11.15 a.m., the Prussian centre in the wood was breaking and nearly a third of Fransecky's command lay dead or dying on the fringes of the wood.

The Prussian 7th Division was paying a high price for exposing itself so far forward of the rest of the Prussian line. From a tactical point of view Mollinary was clearly taking advantage of his opponent's injudicious deployment. But his attempt to eject the Prussians from the Swiepwald and turn the Prussian flank in uncoordinated attacks was so costly and so slow that any potential advantage was lost. Moreover, moving his corps out of position had opened up a massive hole on the Austrian right flank.

On receiving Benedek's order around 11 a.m. Mollinary had hastily composed a report explaining that the fight in the wood was 'going well'. When Benedek received this forty minutes later he exploded with rage and sent a second, more imperative command to Mollinary to break off the action but Mollinary once again chose to disobey, convinced he had the entire Prussian left wing rather than just a single brigade.

Count Thun and his 2nd Corps proved more compliant with Benedek's orders but Mollinary still remained disobedient and rode off to argue the case for renewing the assault on the wood. But time, that critical factor in all battles, was running out for the Austrians. It would be nearly two hours before a humbled Mollinary, after a stormy encounter with his commander-in-chief, returned to set in train the redeployment he should have begun hours earlier. By then the damage was done. It was too late.

Arrival of the Prussian Guard

By this time the Prussian Crown Prince's advance guard in the form of the 1st Guard Division had appeared on the heights of Hořenowes above the Swiep wood after a prodigious forced march. Thun's 2nd and Mollinary's 4th Corps would now have to retire across the front of these new arrivals, a manoeuvre whose difficulty cannot be overstated. Mollinary's refusal to obey his commander-in-chief's orders during the vital two hours of the late morning is the single most important tactical factor leading to the Austrian debacle that day.

From the heights of Chlum-Lipa at midday, Benedek had been contemplating sending in his reserve to crush the Prussian centre, which was still pinned down along the Bistritz. In a famous incident recounted in Bismarck's memoirs, it was at about this time that the King of Prussia, Moltke and Bismarck, dressed rather incongruously in the uniform of a Landwehr captain, appeared on the Roskos hill to take stock of the battle. Almost immediately the Austrian gunners spotted them and within two minutes their nearest battery had opened up, bracketing the group in their first salvo and carrying away most of the King's uhlan escort in their second.

As they hurriedly took cover behind the hill, a rather shaken Bismarck asked Moltke if he still really thought the battle was going well. Unconvinced by Moltke's low-key confidence, and noticing that the Prussian general had run out of cigars, he offered him one of his last remaining two. One was a cheap Virginia while the other was a prize Havana. The stiff and austere Moltke savoured each very slowly and then, after much deliberation, chose the better of the two. From that moment Bismarck realised the battle was won; Moltke was not given to indulgence. He would never have selected the better of the two if he thought for a moment the Prussians were going to lose. 'Your Majesty,' Moltke replied a little later to a more direct enquiry from the King, 'today you will win not just the battle but the entire campaign'.[18]

Moltke was confident that the Crown Prince had responded to his amended orders to march with all vigour and haste towards the heights of Hořenowes, dominated then by two great lime trees. (These are still extant but sadly no longer a striking landmark, owing to the planting of a wood around them after the battle.) Shortly after 12.30 p.m., just as it began to look as though one Prussian army was facing annihilation at the hands of the Austrian artillery, the Prussian Guard took the village of Hořenowes at a rush, easily driving the startled Austrian gunners off the heights.

An hour later, they had driven the Austrians out of Maslowed village, and the Prussian cavalry began to engage the manoeuvring Austrian corps of Thun as it sought finally to redeploy along its original lines. The cavalry made no impression on the Austrian infantry, which formed square to repulse them but, as the Austrians were manoeuvring out of this formation, the Prussian Guard fell upon them. The Prussians were no longer deterred by the Austrian batteries, which had protected 2nd and 4th Corps initially but had now been driven off the Maslowed–Lochenitz ridge. The artillery of 4th Corps, some hundred guns, continued to pound the Prussian Guard at Maslowed from a new position hastily set up 3,500 yards away.

The critical moment of the battle had now arrived. Fortunately for the Prussians, a young general, Hiller von Gärtringen, had the whole of the Prussian 1st Guard Division in hand at Hořenowes and saw how close the Austrian centre was. On his own initiative, he formed a plan to attack Chlum some 4,800 yards to the south-west. Chlum was the key to Benedek's centre, dominated by the tower of the church, which now clearly rose ahead of Gärtringen.

Ordering his own batteries to draw the fire of the Austrian 4th Corps guns upon themselves, the Prussian hastily assembled two brigades. Pointing at the church tower, Hiller drew his sword and led them at the run towards Chlum. Two battalions of skirmishers raced ahead of them and quickly routed the single Austrian battalion, which was posted on the edge of Chlum village. As the skirmishers reached the village, putting the astonished Austrians to flight, Gärtringen brought up the rest of his men.

'Plauschens net so dumm!'

About the same time, Benedek noticed the first line of the Prussian army opposite him beginning to waver. Now was the moment to attack with the reserve and annihilate the Prussians before him, but just as he was about to give the order to throw in his reserves, a bloodstained adjutant rode up from the village of Chlum, barely 200 yards behind him. The adjutant saluted and shouted: 'The Prussians are in Chlum'. Benedek turned ashen white. He replied sharply in Viennese dialect: 'Plauschens net so dumm!' ('Don't chatter so foolishly'), but the officer simply replied: 'It is really so.'[19]

About to commit his reserves to his front, Benedek reacted swiftly. Turning his mount and followed by his bewildered staff, he galloped the 200 yards back towards the church at Chlum. A hail of bullets greeted him, some of them so-called friendly fire, decimating his staff and furnishing proof of the new situation. Benedek ordered his reserve under Ramming to about-face and storm the village: 'Chlum must be retaken.'

On the Chlum-Lipa heights the massed batteries of the Austrians, which had been hammering the Prussian army for hours, suddenly found their teams of gunners falling to a hail of infantry fire as the thin Austrian screen at their rear fell back in disorder. Shot at from all sides, the gunners' positions were untenable and the order to withdraw was given.

At this moment of chaos, the Austrian artillery rose to the occasion heroically once again. A battery of horse artillery under Captain Groeben (Nr 7/ VIII) saw the need to cover the withdrawal of the artillery. His battery stopped firing to its front, turned round 180 degrees, rode up to within 200 paces of the nearest Prussians, then unlimbered and poured case shot into them. For eight minutes the battery kept firing as one by one every gunner began to be picked off by the Prussian infantry. After ordering ten salvoes, Captain Groeben fell with a bullet through the head. The rest of the crews and the horses fell until only one gun continued to fire. But after three more minutes, gun Nr VI under Lieutenant Merkel and one wounded gunner by the name of Schunk managed to limber up and, with two surviving but wounded horses, ride out of harm's way. As the Prussians advanced across the intervening 200 yards they eventually found a pile of brown-uniformed bodies and abandoned guns. The battery of the 'dead' had twenty minutes earlier consisted of 53 men and three officers. In less than twelve minutes 54 of them lay dead along with 68 horses. Apart from Lieutenant Merkel and artillerist Schunk, both wounded, Nr 7 battery/ VIII had ceased to exist.[20]

But Groeben's sacrifice had not been in vain and many of the Austrian guns were saved. As Ramming's corps marched through Chlum with bands playing, flags flying and bayonets lowered, a fierce fight broke out between the 1st Guard Division and the Deutschmeister regiment in Rosberic. In a desperate and violent attack, the Deutschmeister finally ejected the now exhausted Prussian Guard from the village at 4 p.m., buying further time for Benedek to organise his withdrawal and for the batteries to fall back to the agreed point to lay down a new arc of fire. It was at this moment that Hiller von Gärtringen, the architect of the bold Prussian initiative to take Chlum, was killed by an artillery shell which landed on the open ground south of Chlum. He fell in the midst of his triumph without having seen its full glory.

At 5 p.m. a Prussian counter-attack with three fresh battalions took place and the Deutschmeister began to fall back under the usual hail of fire from the Prussian needle guns. Their attempts to advance were beaten back in a veritable hurricane of bullets.

Even at this moment the famous bitter-sweet Viennese sense of humour asserted itself among the men of the Vienna 'House' regiment. As they advanced with their bayonets and standards, an NCO was heard to steady his men:

> 'Vorwärts Leutn! Alle fallen wir nicht, und wann . . . bleiben wir trotzdem liegen? Denn sama eh a feiner G'sellschaft.'[21] ('Forward, boys. We won't all fall and what if we do? Well, we're a rather fine society.')

Benedek commits his cavalry

By this time Benedek knew his army was facing annihilation if he did not retreat. In this phase of the battle Benedek again displayed all his courage and coolness under fire. His withdrawal from the battlefield followed his prearranged plans like clockwork. The pincers of Moltke's converging armies began to close around the hapless Austrians, but the Austrian artillery and cavalry reserve played their parts to perfection, denying Moltke the crushing victory his skilful strategic planning surely owed him. As the afternoon wore on, the Austrian artillery formed a new line of fire on the Stösser–Freihofen–Ziegelschlag line and brought the advance of the Prussian I Army to a halt covering the approaches to Königgrätz. While the Prussian squadrons probed, it was the turn of the Austrian cavalry to play its part in holding up any Prussian 'pursuit'. In fact such a 'pursuit' was slow and laborious and, as Bonnal points out, does not merit the name.[22]

As the first shells began to burst in the rear of the Austrian infantry retreating towards the bridges over the Elbe, Benedek galloped over to Prince Holstein, commander of the Austrian Reserve Cavalry. No less an authority than *The Times* correspondent and veteran of the Crimean War, W.H. Russell had described the Austrian cavalry in his earlier dispatches as 'the finest horse I ever did see': no modest compliment from a man who had reported the Charge of the Light Brigade. The 'finest horse' were about to prove the veracity of Russell's words.[23]

Holstein, in pike blue general's uniform complete with cocked hat and ostrich feathers, was sitting impassively on his horse in front of 5,000 stationary cavalry. As if sniffing the air for signs of bad weather, he was watching the horizon. Benedek quickly shouted: 'Attack! Immediately attack!' ('Angreifen! Sofort Angreifen!') The Prince silently saluted, drew his sword, and, without looking round, pointed his blade and galloped forward to lead an attack which would amount to one of the largest cavalry actions in history. Behind him his officers took their cue; trumpets sounded as thousands of Austrian and Hungarian sabres flashed under the lowering sun. The ground began to reverberate to the sound of hooves galloping across the fields. Eyewitnesses noted the cries of hurrah just before the Austrian cavalry crashed into their opponents. For one young subaltern, Wurmbrand, exhausted by hunger and thirst and about to be wounded in several places by Prussian lances, the sight of his general in a cocked hat leading the charge was the most inspiring image of the entire battle.[24]

Holstein's charge heralded three large cavalry actions that now took place. The first occurred near Rosberitz around 4 p.m. between the Prussian 3rd Light Cavalry Brigade and the Austrian 1st Reserve Division. Though the Prussians were reinforced by two more regiments, the Austrian horse drove their opponents headlong back to the Prussian lines, buying a useful twenty-five minutes to allow Benedek's infantry to conduct its fighting withdrawal. Holstein's men were better mounted than their Prussian opponents and had been immobile for most of the day; they needed no encouragement to bring the fight to the enemy. Helmets and heads were dented, tunics ripped and horses mutilated in less than twenty minutes of furious hand-to-hand fighting.

The second, slightly smaller, engagement occurred towards 4.30 p.m. at nearby Stresetice (Strezetitz) a large area of giant fields that seem, even today, made for a decisive cavalry battle. Once again the Austrian horse, a Cuirassier brigade, proved superior to the Prussian dragoons who were only rescued from certain destruction by the timely arrival of a regiment of Prussian uhlans. This inconclusive encounter once again bought a vital half-hour for the retreating Austrians. The uhlans were beaten off, but not before the young Wurmbrand received seven wounds from their lances. The last two thrusts had dismounted him. As he struggled to his feet and turned to look for his horse he saw about a thousand Austrian horsemen charging towards him to drive off the Prussians behind him.[25]

A third even more dramatic encounter took place near Problus between the Prussian Garde-Dragoner and the Austrian Alexander Lancers around the same time. Involving elite formations, it was more bitterly contested. The Austrian lancers penetrated almost as far as the King's entourage, and had the pleasure of hearing the cry 'Save the King!' and a dozen panic-stricken courtiers draw their (in this context utterly useless) court swords. Only the prompt arrival of Prussian infantry and artillery turned the engagement in the Prussians' favour and forced the Austrians to retire. The Austrian Cuirassier regiment Nr 8 rode to the lancers' rescue, only to be so severely handled by the Prussian infantry that it lost 380 out of 580 men and 23 out of 28 officers.

Once again the advance of the Prussian I Army had been checked, though it continued to make some progress until the Austrian artillery, deployed in a new defensive arc, brought it to a complete halt a few minutes later, allowing Benedek's 3rd and 10th Corps to draw off unmolested by about 6 p.m. Although the Austrian cavalry had been deployed only briefly, it had proved its historical superiority over the Prussian horse.

As a Prussian cavalry officer who witnessed all this noted: 'The Austrian cavalry performed, with the greatest success, one of the most difficult tactical manoeuvres mounted troops can ever attempt: they brought the entire fighting line of the advancing Prussian army to a halt and its moral effect was more significant than its material.'[26] Thanks to their action, Königgrätz would be neither Sedan nor Cannae.

Benedek absorbs the blame

Covered by their superb artillery, the Austrians continued to retreat in good order, the final rounds being fired from their batteries at 9 p.m. in the gathering darkness. Earlier there had been terrible scenes of panic as the first retreating units approached the fortress of Königgrätz under the impression that the Prussian horse were just behind them. The confusion was compounded by the fortress commandant ordering the flooding of the castle's moats and defensive earthworks, with the result that hundreds drowned in the ensuing chaos until gradually it dawned on the men that there was no Prussian pursuit.

Benedek's men were exhausted and demoralised; his army had partly ceased to exist. The Prussian army, though elated, was not in great shape either and certainly was incapable of carrying out any pursuit. As the road to Poysdorf in Austria poignantly still shows in its sombre black obelisks, cholera was also about to take hold of the Prussian army. While the King, all of his earlier anxiety and caution now forgotten, urged with his generals an advance on Vienna, Bismarck was aware that the Archduke Albrecht was coming up from Italy with 100,000 victorious troops after his dazzling victory against numerically superior Italian forces. In any event, it was never Bismarck's plan to humiliate Austria and impose a Carthaginian peace on his great rival. Prussia needed a future ally and for Austria not to be entirely alienated. As Benedek retreated to Olmütz, the Prussians occupied Prague while the Archduke Albert was elevated to commander-in-chief and arrived with 50,000 troops by train from Venice in Vienna on 10 July. His plans for a fighting defence came to naught. On 21 July at Nikolsburg (Mikulov) the Austrians signed an armistice.

Benedek's dreams and career were over. His troops still adored him but the aristocratic officer clique – taking its cue from the Emperor and court to find a scapegoat and aided by a well coordinated press campaign – joined in the general denunciation. The very papers that had sung Benedek's praises a few weeks earlier now called for his head.

In this moment of misfortune, Benedek showed his strength of character. He absorbed all the blame although others were no less culpable. At his court-martial he cut a noble figure, striding across the courtyard of the Wiener Neustadt academy watched silently from the windows above by the young cadets. He refused to implicate anyone or blame anyone. It was entirely his fault. He had been in command and he must take the responsibility. His logic was faultless and expressed fully what the great Austrian historian Ritter von Srbik would refer to as the 'old spirit' of the army, 'uncontaminated by any material or personal ambitions and invested by an all-encompassing sense of duty and honour'.[27]

To shift blame to others might imply criticism of the dynasty and that was clearly unacceptable for any officer, let alone one of Benedek's stamp. His career had existed to serve the dynasty, and serve the dynasty he would do until his dying breath. To his credit, Franz-Josef ordered the court-martial proceedings to be discontinued.

When Benedek's wife, weary of the abuse heaped upon her husband, defended him publicly and criticised the Emperor, he threatened to divorce her if she did not immediately desist. Withdrawing to his modest villa on the Elisabethstrasse in Graz, he led a life of blameless retirement, refusing ever to discuss the campaign. When, in November 1866, the Archduke Albert visited him, there occurred an exchange which appears to have sealed the General's lips for ever. After the Archduke left, Benedek burned all his medals and decorations. The compact between soldier and dynasty which was sealed in June 1619 certainly knew no more poignant exponent of its unwritten code than the tragic Benedek. He had always placed service to the Emperor above all considerations. But even his sacrifice left a bitter taste. Shortly before he died in 1881, he expressly instructed that he should not be buried, as military convention usually dictated, in his uniform. It was a gallant officer's silent but eloquent reply to his sovereign.[28]

CHAPTER 16

Victories in the South

CUSTOZZA AND LISSA 1866

The debacle of the Austrian Nordarmee was all the more distressing because it came hard on the heels of spectacular successes in the south. Overshadowed by events in Bohemia, the campaigns in Italy showed that the Habsburg forces were capable of impressive results, even though they served no strategic purpose.

Vittorio Emanuele declares war

Less than two weeks before Königgrätz, Vittorio Emanuele had declared war on Austria in accordance with his alliance with Prussia. Unlike in Bohemia, the formalities had been observed and the Italian monarch had dispatched an aide with a formal declaration of war to the Austrian headquarters in Verona where the Archduke Albert had taken up residence.

As we have seen, Albert was fighting solely for his House's honour. The decision to cede Venetia to Napoleon III, who would in turn give it to Italy, had already been taken in Vienna. In this way Austria hoped to be free of a two-front war, should events in Bohemia take a turn for the worse. Albert, stiff, conservative and much less imaginative than his father, the great Archduke Charles, was nevertheless a capable soldier. While his troops could never feel the same affection and warmth for him that they felt for Benedek, they knew that under his consistent leadership they could not fail to beat their Italian foes.

The commander of the Italian forces, Marmora did not inspire much confidence. At 62, he was a veteran of Piedmontese defeats at the hands of Radetzky and Benedek in 1848 and 1859, and should have known better. But he was, like many Italian senior commanders, first and foremost a supreme egotist, and he listened to advice sparingly. He convinced himself that the Archduke would remain behind the Adige and not even the urgent advice of Moltke's personal liaison officer Theodor Berhardi could dissuade Marmora from pursuing a flawed strategy that invited brutal retribution from any opponent imbued with the slightest aggressive spirit.

The Southern Army of the Habsburgs was made up of many fine regiments. The Archduke commanded barely 75,000 troops against a foe of 200,000 equipped with more than twice the amount of artillery he could muster. As his orders to his army upon declaration of war noted, this disparity in numbers was not at all intimidating: 'Soldiers!' he exhorted them. 'Never forget how often this enemy has run away from you!'[1]

Ably advised by his chief of staff, General John, the Archduke Albrecht waited for Marmora's army to cross the Mincio. Albrecht hoped to disrupt Marmora's army so as to render it incapable of uniting with another Italian army advancing from the south under Cialdini. To keep Marmora in check while holding Cialdini under observation required some forced marches across the northern Italian plains in scorching heat. Neck scarves and a proliferation of sun-protective materials punctuated the white tunics of Albrecht's infantry, while his cavalry abandoned their heavy costume and headdress to adopt lighter blouses and, in the case of his lancers, soft caps. By the time the morning of the 24th dawned, the Imperial Royal Army had divested itself of all its Alpine kit and had come to resemble increasingly a lightly armed skirmishing force which, but for the absence of the colour of khaki, might have been recognisable on the North West Frontier a generation later.

Risking serious disruption had he been faced by a more energetic opponent, the Archduke wheeled his forces west to occupy the high ground around Villafranca. His V corps under Rodičhad conducted the most punishing night march to Sona but neither Italian skirmishers nor cavalry patrols disturbed their deployment on the hills around Custozza. To the surprise of the Austrians, these hills had not been seized by the Italians. Only around the high ground east of Vallegio did the Italians blunder into the Austrians at 6 a.m. As Marmora rode up to the small eminence of Monte Croce shortly after dawn, he was staggered to see an entire Austrian corps (Hartung IX) moving towards him in three columns less than two miles away. The Italians were about to be swept back to their Mincio crossings in great style. With improvisation, Marmora hastily assembled a defence, ordering two divisions to march up to Villafranca where Albert's wing was lightly defended by an Austrian division under Ludwig Pulz. As this deployment began, the quixotic opportunities which war affords the alert and energetic mind came into play.

Rodakowski sees a chance

Pulz was under strict orders to 'maintain only contact' with the Italian III Corps under Della Rocca. He was therefore mildly surprised to see four squadrons of his lancers, mostly Poles from Galicia under their colonel Rodakowski, line up in formation, lower their lances as their colonel drew his sword and gallop towards the Italian infantry in the early morning light. Pulz had expected the horsemen to be on a reconnaissance. With the feathers in their caps catching the sun and the pennants of their lances fluttering in the wind, the lancers' charge threw up a huge cloud of dust.

As Rodakowski galloped forward, he was joined by seven more squadrons of lancers, which had been assigned to watch the Verona road. This breakdown in discipline was at first interpreted as a sophisticated feint. Pulz explained to a puzzled staff officer watching the scene unfold that, despite Edelsheim's heroic charge at Solferino, there was no real precedent in the Austrian army for the charge of a single light cavalry brigade towards two infantry divisions supported by artillery and twenty squadrons of heavy cavalry.

Pulz, looking on, heard artillery and infantry volley fire open up in response to Rodakowski's charge and felt compelled to support his horsemen, so he advanced with what was left of his cavalry.[2] Another 300 horsemen thundered off. As an impetuous cavalry commander, Rodakowski had engaged the Italian infantry at their weakest point, the gap between the two divisions, and had succeeded in disrupting some of the Italians. But the majority of the Italian infantry had seen the threat in good time and had formed square. With withering volley fire they had easily repulsed the attack, which cost Rodakowski half his command. As the lancers wheeled around it looked as if they were facing the same fate that had overtaken Edelsheim at Solferino and Lord Cardigan at Balaclava, twelve years earlier.

Some, perhaps no more than a troop, of Rodakowski's lancers had penetrated beyond the infantry. Their appearance, however brief, had a stupendous effect on the excitable Italian troops milling around the supply wagons to the rear of Della Rocca's troops. The Italians, promptly fearing being ridden down by enemy horse, excitedly took to their heels. The panic gathered momentum and infected even the Italian reinforcements marching up to support Della Rocca. Suddenly a horde of riderless horses and fleeing Italian infantry began to charge back towards the Mincio, where they imagined safety awaited them. By 9 a.m., the bridge at Goito was a mass of fugitives screaming that the 'Tedeschi' (Germans) were coming to slaughter them.[3]

The front line of Della Rocca's troops held firm but the Polish charge had a demoralising effect on them and they dared not advance for fear of an Austrian counter-attack, even though this sector of the Austrian line was thinly held and could not have withstood a vigorous push by the two Italian divisions.

Rodakowski's charge, as brilliant (and indeed more effective) as that of the Light Brigade at Balaclava, was a poor start to the battle for the Italians. Albert's rather thin left wing was the Achilles heel of the Austrian deployment that day and could have proved the beginning of severe problems for the Austrians had it been correctly evaluated and exploited by the Italians, something Rodakowski's 500 men had rendered impossible.

Elsewhere the battle, though less dramatic, was also not developing as the Italians had planned. On the Austrian right, an Italian division under Cerale was caught in the flank by an Austrian infantry brigade under Eugen Piret containing several 'crack' grenadier battalions and some skirmishing Croats well concealed in the woods on the Italians' other flank. Within minutes the Italians were fleeing again back to the Mincio, offering only stubborn resistance at the village of Oliosi where repeated attacks by the Austrian grenadiers were repulsed with heavy loss for nearly an hour.

The Austrian *Stosstaktik*, so disastrous in the Swiepwald two weeks later, proved more successful against the Italians, though almost as costly. Sirtori's division fell back under the pressure of the Austrian bayonet charges but inflicted heavy casualties on Bauer's brigade (660 of Bauer's men fell in less than fifteen minutes as they advanced).

Nowhere this day did the Austrian frontal attacks prove as expensive as at Monte Croce, where two Austrian brigades from IX Corps (Hartung) were virtually annihilated as they attempted to dislodge well dug-in Italian infantry under Brignone. More than 2,500 Austrians were lost in these poorly executed and coordinated attacks, which fizzled out owing to lack of reinforcements.

By 10 a.m. the crisis of the battle had arrived for the Austrians. Everywhere along their line they had failed to seize any strategically important ground and their numbers were dwindling. A concerted push by the Italians, who were fighting well, would unmask the deficiencies of the Archduke's command and his weakness in numbers, with potentially catastrophic results for the Habsburg army.

The Italians break

After nearly three and a half hours of intense fighting, the Austrians had shown aggressive spirit and it was this which finally demoralised the Italians. Despite their strong defence of Monte Croce, Brignone's troops began to panic because the Austrians simply kept re-forming into new lines, advancing again: white-coated troops with bands playing and bayonets lowered. Riding 'to safety', on Marmora's advice, the Italian King instantly saw his troops' weakness and tried to reinforce them, but to no avail. The Brignone line broke after the fourth assault by the Austrians and the sight of the tall Hungarian grenadiers advancing put even their rearmost lines to flight.

As Marmora rode to try to rally Brignone's men, he noticed that the nearby heights of Custozza also appeared to be occupied by white-coated troops. These were the soldiers of Böck's brigade, Romanians, often decried as unreliable but advancing in good discipline. The Italian reinforcements came up, and an Austrian brigade under Scudier, which had advanced up the heights of Custozza, panicked and withdrew rapidly (an act for which their commanding officer Anton Scudier would be court-martialled after the war).

Scudier's precipitate withdrawal opened a small but dangerous gap in the Austrian centre, which could have been exploited with serious consequences had not Rodič's corps stormed the Monte Vento and Santa Lucia heights. There, the Austrians discovered evidence of Italian atrocities committed against some captured Jaeger troops, two of whom had been stripped naked and beaten to death before being hanged with leather from their uniforms.[4]

Rodič's men, notably Piret's brigade supported later by Moering, neutralised the effects of Scudier's withdrawal. Custozza became a fragile *point d'appui* for the Italians. Flanked on either side by Austrians, they withdrew at around 3 p.m. Panic, the greatest enemy of the Italian army that day, took hold across Marmora's front. Sensing his moment, the Archduke now ordered a grand envelopment but, as Pulz rode towards Villafranca, he found thousands of Italians laying down their arms without a fight as Della Rocca began withdrawing. Everywhere the Italians were breaking, with the exception of the few brave men who had filled the gap vacated by Scudier – and they were about to be ejected by three Austrian brigades. Only the valiant Granatieri di Sardegna saved Italian honour that day, withdrawing in perfect order around 5 p.m. The battle ended after the Austrians brought up a couple of batteries to blow to bits any remaining Italian defenders of Custozza who lingered.

As the Archduke Albert surveyed the scene from the heights he saw a vast shattered Italian army in headlong retreat. Later historians and some of his own officers have severely censured him for not ordering an aggressive pursuit but this was not the Habsburg tradition, as we have seen. Albert, like his father before him, knew that the dynasty could never afford to take the risk. Those who criticise Albert for 'timidity' miss the point. This was not how the Habsburgs waged war, especially, in Albert's phrase a 'defensive war'.[5]

Victory was really concerned with honour and could only be tactical because Venetia had already been surrendered to all intents and purposes. Moreover, to effect a crushing pursuit Albert would have needed fresh troops.

The Austrian casualties were high. Nearly 9,000 Austrian dead and wounded, including some 400 officers, lay scattered around the battlefield.[6]

Many of the survivors had been in action without interruption for more than 18 hours. Without exception they had fought bravely against an opponent who enjoyed significant numerical superiority. (In the event the absence of the Italian Cialdini's corps somewhat evened the numbers out.) In the blistering heat of those June days on the north Italian plain, many of Albert's troops were utterly exhausted. Some had died of heatstroke; many others were dehydrated and ill. V Corps under Rodič was the only force capable of conducting a pursuit, but to what end? One Italian army was crushed; it did not need to be destroyed. Moreover, like his father, Albert had a realistic view of his strategic gifts and knew that he was no Napoleon.

Albert at this stage was aware that he might need to fight another battle against the Italians but the Archduke was confident that his army would not let him down. While some of his officers might grumble that he had not delivered the *coup de grâce* to Italian military pretensions, morale was high. The formidable fortresses of the Quadrilateral remained a massive projection of Austrian power in northern Italy and Albert aimed to lure the Italians towards them one more time, to fight another battle at Custozza if necessary.

But the Italian spirit was broken at Custozza. Attempts by Garibaldi's redshirted volunteers to advance towards Trento were easily seen off by a few companies of Kaiserjaeger, even more formidable defending their homeland than they were on the conventional battlefield. As at San Martino seven years earlier, a surprising number of these Tyroleans bore Italian names. Brought up in the lush Alpine valleys around Bozen and Meran and nurtured by the simple Catholic piety of those regions, they regarded the godless Garibaldi and his followers as the personification of the 'Antichrist', and they fought furiously against them.

Bismarck had set great store on the opening of yet another front against the Austrians. The news of Custozza, while received bleakly in Berlin, stirred Prussian pressure on Italy to initiate new hostilities against the Austrians along the Dalmatian coast.

Operations in Dalmatia: Enter the Austrian navy

Here was an opportunity for the young state of Italy to test its proudest acquisition: its brand new ironclad fleet purchased from Britain, France and America. This even included an ironclad turret ship, the *Affondatore*. Although the Imperial Austrian Navy possessed some armoured cruisers, many of its ships were wooden and considerably inferior in armament. Morale was undoubtedly high in the relatively recently formed Italian navy as it moved into Austrian waters to threaten the former Venetian territories of western Dalmatia.

The nearest of these was Lissa (Vis), a strategically important island which had witnessed several Royal Naval engagements in the Napoleonic Wars (there is still a monument to 'Captain Hoste's action' on the island). On the morning of 20 July, the Italian fleet under the command of Admiral Persano arrived with a view to disembarking marines to seize control of the island, which was lightly defended. Persano was under intense political pressure to make an aggressive gesture.

A few hours earlier, the commander of the Austrian fleet, Admiral Wilhelm Tegetthoff, had been searching in vain for the Italian fleet. After scouting around Ancona, he approached the island of Vis as part of a final sweep of the Adriatic before returning north towards Pola, the Imperial Navy's second (after Venice) most important base in Istria. Tegetthoff, the son of an Austrian army colonel whose family had roots in Westphalia, had joined the Habsburg navy and had studied at the Austrian naval school in Venice.

It was Joseph II who had established the familiar red–white–red naval ensign for the Austrian gunboats of the Danube, but it would be another ten years before the Archduke Charles, in his capacity as inspector-general of the Austrian forces, established a school in Vienna for naval cadets.

The development of a modern Austrian navy of any real credibility only really began with the decision of the Vienna Congress to award Venice to Austria in 1815. Even then, the Imperial Royal Navy, or 'Austrian-Venetian' navy as it was also known, was a picturesque rather than formidable instrument, starved of funds. When Tegetthoff went to Venice to study at the Arsenal in the 1840s, he was part of a group of relatively impoverished officers who could only look with envy at the French and British warships which came to visit the Serenissima. Indeed, the Royal Navy was one reason why the Austrians spent as little as they did on their navy. No one in Vienna wanted to risk 'complications' with their age-old ally, England. This did not mean that Austrian naval ships could not on occasion support their English allies. When Muhammad Ali Pasha attempted to establish with French support a personal empire in Egypt, Austrian warships cooperated with the Royal Navy in crushing the revolt. An Austrian landing party led by the Archduke Friederich was so successful that it brought the Habsburg flag to the castle of Acre for the first time since the Crusades. They also brought the exploits of Austrian sailors to a wider audience.

The year 1848 focused Austrian naval minds even more vividly. The Venice uprising under Manin not only caused the capture of many valuable weapons from the Arsenal, it also resulted in the rebels' seizure of the Habsburg fleet.

This was to have profound consequences for the future of the Austrian navy. Despite the recovery of Venice, it was decided to establish the navy further east at Pola in Istria, and to reorganise the force with the help of foreign officers, notably Danish and German. The Venetian element remained strong among the crews but it was increasingly diluted with Dalmatian and Istrian Italians, as well as Croats from the Quarnero. By 1853, SMS *Husar* could even boast the privilege of possessing a crew made up entirely of Hungarians and Croats. German became the official language of command although, as in Imperial army regiments, officers tended to have a good knowledge of at least two other languages, notably Italian (Venetian dialect) and Croat. As gunnery became more sophisticated, Czechs, the Empire's natural artillerists, were also recruited. By 1914 there would be more than 2,000 Czech officers in the Imperial Navy, most serving in the gunnery commands.[7]

This reorganisation created a new breed of Imperial officer, rather rougher than his land equivalent, more careless in dress, less obviously formal in manner but highly practical and utterly confident. For such men personal courage was everything and the hard experience of the treacherous Adriatic invested them with strong prejudices. The wind was always more reliable than steam, an axe or cudgel preferable to a sword, and home was always 'the elements'.[8]

Franz-Josef's brother, Ferdinand Max, better known as Maximilian, the ill-fated Emperor of Mexico, is credited with the modernisation of the Habsburg navy. Before unwisely accepting Napoleon III's offer of a throne in Mexico, Maximilian worked hard to bring a semblance of enlightened government to Lombardy and to overhaul the Imperial Navy. Maximilian was an intellectual and a liberal, revered in certain Italian circles, where his governorship of Lombardy had been praised for its sensitivity towards Italian irredentist feelings. In 1854, Franz-Josef, keen to occupy such a popular rival, gave Maximilian command of the navy with a view to its systematic modernisation.

The Austrian engineer, Josef Ressel – inventor of the ship's propeller, and credited with inaugurating the era of steam on the seas – was encouraged to design a new generation of warships, the first of which, *Radetzky*, was constructed at a British shipyard in 1854. Three years later, one of the new Austrian steamships, *Novara*, was dispatched by Maximilian on a journey around the world. The red–white–red ensign began to be seen in the harbours of the Mediterranean and beyond.

When the *Novara* began its journey from Trieste on 30 April 1857, Maximilian watched, unaware that in less than five years it would take him to Mexico and the dubious empire from which he would return in a coffin (again transported by the *Novara*). The only redeeming feature of the entire Mexican adventure was that, with the exception of a lavishly uniformed honour guard and some Austrian volunteers, no formal elements of the Imperial and Royal Army participated in this tragedy in which a Habsburg had to rely on feeble and irresolute French bayonets to carry out Napoleon III's *folie de grandeur*.[9]

By the time the *Novara* returned from its epic journey two years later, the Imperial Royal Navy was on a firm footing but in the short war of 1859 it had been confined to its harbours by aggressive French patrolling in the Adriatic. Although the Austrian navy lacked Nelsonian spirit in 1859, it continued to make progress on a technical level. Mines and torpedoes were both largely Austrian inventions, the latter under the auspices of Robert Whitehead, who had established a factory at Fiume where he developed the weapon. (It would not be until the 1870s that the Austrian navy got its first torpedo boat.)

Naval officers were keen to rid the navy of its appearance as an appendage of the Imperial Army, and the best way they could demonstrate its independence was by adopting a more offensive role. Right up to his day of departure for Mexico, Archduke Maximilian encouraged the navy. His patronage alone secured the Austrian navy the funds required for modernisation.

Admiral Tegetthoff

In the person of Wilhelm Tegetthoff, the Archduke found a worthy protégé to lead these developments. Taciturn, unyielding and not known for his spirit of compromise, Tegetthoff was a man of immense humanity with liberal instincts. He spoke German and French as well as the Venetian dialect. He demanded much from his sailors but was venerated by them on account of his fairness and decisiveness. He cared deeply for his men, like his contemporary, Benedek.

With two frigates, supported by a Prussian gunboat, he attacked a vastly superior Danish fleet which was blockading Hamburg harbour in 1864. His ships suffered immensely in the battle, but his discipline and tenacity eventually forced the Danes to raise the blockade. As the 1860s wore on, Tegetthoff studied the events of the American Civil War in which ironclad ships played a significant role.[10]

Reports of the American Civil War that reached Europe made it clear that the era of the wooden warship was drawing to a close. Already in 1861, the first armoured warship had entered Imperial Austrian service in the shape of *Drachen* (Dragon), aptly named, given its heavy armament. This was the first of seven to be completed by 1866. Other lessons too were digested from the conflict across the Atlantic. It was reported that anchor chains were effective in the absence of plate armour and, most significantly of all, given what was to come in the Adriatic, there were vivid reports of the effectiveness of ramming and the offensive 'Damn the torpedoes! Full steam ahead' school of naval warfare, personified by the American admiral Farragut's famous order to his fleet at the Battle of Mobile Bay in 1864.[11]

Action at Lissa

We left Tegetthoff fast approaching the Italian fleet off the island of Lissa. By this stage in July, the Archduke Albert was all too aware of the need to minimise unnecessary risks, following the news of Königgrätz. Unmoved, Tegetthoff turned a Nelsonian blind eye to instructions from Vienna to avoid 'placing the entire fleet at risk'.[12]

For years he had lectured his fellow officers that a fleet did not exist to rot in a moment of crisis in some harbour, and he was now determined to demonstrate the veracity of this philosophy. What followed has been studied and applauded in every naval academy in the world and certainly made naval history.

The Italian fleet that was deployed in line to the north of the island of Vis presented an impressive force. No fewer than 12 ironclad ships and 17 other warships faced Tegetthoff's 18 ships, of which only seven were armoured. Adopting the classic arrowhead formation of attack, the Austrians bore down on the Italians, who appeared to be taken completely by surprise. The weather had helped the Austrians steal up on their opponents under a thin sea mist.

If the weather was on the Austrian side, the Italian reputation for logistical inefficiency was to prove all too richly deserved. The Italian commander, the 60-year-old Admiral Persano, had just decided to transfer his flag from the flagship *Re d'Italia* to the turreted ironclad *Affondatore* and was in the process of so doing when Tegetthoff's first line, led by his flagship *Erzherzog Ferdinand Max*, appeared out of the mist. In the excitement Persano made haste to make it to the *Affondatore* but the news that he had transferred his flag was not transmitted to the rest of the Italian fleet.

The Italian ships' captains anxiously scanned the *Re d'Italia* for signals that would instruct them what to do, now that the Austrians had appeared. But they looked in vain at the *Re d'Italia*, while Persano's increasingly frenetic signalling from *Affondatore* was ignored. Another note of tactical dissonance was sounded by the curious reluctance of several Italian ships under Admiral Albini, which had 'detached' from the main line, to play any part in the imminent clash. (Albini was perceived to have had some histrionic exchanges earlier that day.)[13]

Tegetthoff's bold attack on the stationary line still afforded the Italian fleet the chance to 'cross the Austrian T'.* As Tegetthoff approached, a storm of shot hit the *Erzherzog Ferdinand Max*. A famous painting by Romako captures the atmosphere vividly as Tegetthoff standing on the bridge of his smoke-laden and damaged ship continued to bear down on his enemy. It is entirely characteristic of the man that just before battle was joined Tegetthoff had signalled: 'Must be victory at Lissa' but that the only word that had been transmitted clearly before the fog of battle descended was 'Must' ('Muss Sieg von Lissa werden'). It was enough.[14]

Tegetthoff saw a gap open up in the Italian line around the Italian flagship and adjusted his course slightly. 'Ram and sink the enemy!' he is supposed to have cried in Venetian dialect and then in German, just before his bow collided with the *Palestro* seeking to cover the *Re d'Italia*. *Palestro* disengaged and Tegetthoff, now steaming at nearly 12 knots, turned to starboard to engage the former Italian flagship on whose deck, trying to capture the scene for eternity, was the gifted Venetian painter Ippolito Caffi. The *Erzherzog Ferdinand Max* crashed into the *Re d'Italia*, gouging a huge hole out of the Italian flagship. As the once-proud flagship sank in less than two minutes, Tegetthoff's crew shouted thunderously: 'Viva San Marco!', the ancient Venetian battle-cry.

Tegetthoff now turned his attention to finishing off *Palestro* and rammed her again while pouring shot into her at close range. The two ships disengaged and *Palestro* blew up shortly after 2.30 p.m. Elsewhere, ships collided with each other in a tremendous melee in which, time and again, fortune and skilful seamanship favoured the Austrians. The *Kaiser* rammed the *Re di Portogallo* with such force that the entire Austrian masthead was embedded in the deck of the Italian ship, which rapidly disengaged and fled. *Affondatore* was about to ram the *Kaiser* but also broke off the engagement.

The wooden second line of Tegetthoff's attack was no less successful despite the disparity in armour with the Italians. The Austrian *Novara* suffered 47 direct hits but limped on to attack and drive off two Italian ships. The heavily armoured Italian *Ancona* passed between it and the *Archduke Ferdinand Max* and fired a broadside at Tegetthoff's ship, which certainly would have rendered her at the very least immobile had the Italian gunners not forgotten to load the shot.

---

* Crossing the enemy's T refers to the naval manoeuvre whereby a fleet sails across the line of the approaching enemy allowing each of its ships to fire a broadside in turn at the approaching fleet.

After two hours, the Italians broke off the action. Persano at first claimed a great victory, an act of blatant deception for which he was rightly court-martialled later. Tegetthoff had more than proved his point and, while utterly irrelevant at any strategic level by this stage, the victory at Lissa gave the Austrian navy the morale boost to its traditions for the rest of its existence.

Moreover, its independence was now assured. Already in 1865, a naval section had been established in the War Ministry. This was now expanded, and its autonomy was eventually given concrete form in a new Imperial and Royal Navy office in a separate building behind the Danube canal, adorned with the ceramic coats of arms of all the Empire's naval possessions.

From 1872, the final link with the Imperial and Royal Army was broken when the Austrian marine infantry corps was abolished. From now on, the navy would deploy only armed sailors on its decks and, for naval landing parties, members of the so-called Imperial and Royal 'Matrosenkorps'. As we shall see later, though it was clear that Austria remained principally a 'land' empire, her naval forces began to expand slowly. It would be another twenty-one years before she received her first turret ship. Even ten years after Lissa, the eight new ships of the Imperial and Royal Navy were wooden frigates of the old style.

But by the turn of the century, under the patronage of another archduke, Franz Ferdinand, a bold modernisation programme was introduced. In 1897 the first armoured cruisers were laid down. Ten years later, the first Austrian dread-noughts, designed by Siegfried Popper, would be built incorporating some of the most modern features to be found in any navy in the world at that time (see Chapter 20). Arguably, none of this would have been possible without Tegetthoff's establishment of a distinct naval ethos of courage, boldness and aggression, embodying the traditions of greater navies with far longer pedigrees.

PART 3

IMPERIAL AND ROYAL

CHAPTER 17

k. (u.) k.

THE 'NEW ARMY' AND THE BOSNIAN INSURGENCY

'Casca il mondo'

Admiral Tegetthoff and the Archduke Albert's victories in the south could not disguise the defeat further north. Königgrätz had ended Austrian influence in Germany at a stroke. Prussia was now the strongest German-speaking state, a late emerging power that was about to alter the balance of power in Europe completely. 'Casca il mondo!' ('The world has fallen'), cried the Cardinal Secretary of State in Rome, as well he might, when he was brought the news. Pius IX put it more bluntly. 'Austria', he declared, had become a 'second-rate oriental power'. The centuries-old presence of the Habsburgs in Germany was at an end, and her presence in Italy had been stripped back to the minimum consonant with protecting the great harbour of Trieste and covering the approaches to the eastern Alps.

Luckily for the Habsburgs, General Moering, the Austrian officer given the task of negotiating the new frontier delineation, persuaded the Italians to agree the salients around Cortina d'Ampezzo, a favourite winter resort for the Viennese *Beamtenschaft*. He was also successful in insisting that Italy take on the Veneto's share of the Austrian state debt. In addition to all the important strategic highpoints and access routes to Cortina, eight priceless Tintorettos and Veroneses made their way to the Kunsthistorisches Museum in Vienna. In return, Vienna recognised the 'Kingdom of Italy'.

In Vienna the news of the Prussian victory was received with a less apoca-lyptic judgement than that of the Vatican. At first, the Viennese continued to celebrate the masked ball season in the Prater without interruption. The controversy over Benedek gathered momentum as the liberal press, totally misreading Benedek's deeply conservative character, proceeded to use him as a stick with which to beat the establishment. The defeat's consequences were perceived by the emerging *Bürgertum* and prosperous professional upper-middle classes as exclusively the problem of the 'upper classes', in particular the aristocratic officer caste. Otherwise, a palpable sense of prosperity and confidence, symbolised by the newly constructed Ringstrasse – and which the term 'Gründerzeit' came to symbolise – appeared unchecked by the debacle at Königgrätz.

Such indifference was not possible in the army. Defeat at the hands of the Prussians was traumatic, worse than anything Napoleon had inflicted on the Habsburg forces. It required a radical reorganisation of the monarchy's political and military arrangements. It was not within Bismarck's power to destroy the monarchy and it was always his intention simply to push the Habsburgs out of Germany, thus realising the so-called 'small-German solution' to the question of Germany. Bismarck resolutely pursued the path of compromise. In this he was implacably opposed by the Prussian King. In stark contrast to his initial reticence, the King had now swung to the other extreme and was bent on revenge.

Realistically, Bismarck had little choice. French sabre-rattling and, more significantly, cholera in the ranks of his army, helped him persuade Prussia to sheath her sword. But he kept the pressure on Vienna. In 1866, Bismarck for the first, and perhaps last, time showed just how revolutionary he could be. He had linked arms over a sea of Austrian troubles with the subversive Italians, he had encouraged radicals in Bohemia to revolt against the Habsburgs and, most ruthlessly and cynically of all, he had intimated to Hungary Prussian support for Hungarian independence, even bankrolling a rebel general by name of Klapka to form an anti-Habsburg legion. Hungarian prisoners of war were encouraged by the Prussians to join Klapka's growing band in an attempt to disrupt the Habsburgs even more.

The Hungarian compromise (Ausgleich)

To meet these threats, Vienna had already opened discussions with Budapest some weeks before the war. The talks were accelerated. Ironically, the travails of the Imperial and Royal House played a role in creating agreement. Franz-Josef had evacuated his wife and children to Buda as the cholera-ridden Prussian army lumbered slowly across the Bohemian frontier. The Empress Sissy, whose affection for the Hungarian cause was no secret, did much to create an atmosphere favourable to compromise. When Franz-Josef met the Magyar politician Deák he was impressed by the Hungarian's loyal opening words: 'Hungary would ask for no more after Königgrätz than she had asked before and it is the Hungarians' wish to be loyal to their King.'[1]

Despite these sentiments, the talks almost stalled on the thorny issue of the status of Hungarian regiments. The Hungarian statesmen, Deák, and later Andrassy, sought nothing less than full sovereignty and independence for Hungarian regiments that would swear loyalty not to the Emperor but exclusively to the King, one of the demands of 1848: a fine point of protocol given that both Emperor and King were the same person, but one that meant much to the proud Hungarians. The magnates were prepared to contribute troops to a common defence structure but they were vehemently opposed to the continuation of the common army. In their view, the national 'Honvéd' army of 1848 was to be resurrected, though in a form at peace with the Habsburgs. Such an army would have Hungarian as the exclusive language of command. Unsurprisingly, these demands were unacceptable to the Emperor Franz-Josef. Yet partly thanks to the Empress, and with goodwill and flexibility, a remarkable 'Compromise' emerged which defused these tensions.

Henceforth the army was to consist of three autonomous organisations reflecting the constitutional background of the country. Formal military power would reside in the 'common army' which would be designated k. (u.) k. (Imperial *and* Royal), rather than simply k.k. The k.k. designation survived only in the k.k. Landwehr, a territorial force limited to the German-speaking regions of the Empire. The addition of a simple letter gave the Hungarians a sense of equality where they had earlier perceived the slight of subordination. The new title was not formally confirmed until 1889 but, from 1867, Hungarian regiments could swear their allegiance to the King of Hungary rather than the Austrian Emperor. In return for this concession, the Magyars agreed that German remained the language of command (*Kommandosprache*) throughout the army. The Hungarian territorial equivalent of the k.k. Landwehr was designated Honvéd (Magyar király Honvédség). The Honvéd was allowed to use Hungarian as its everyday service language (*Dienstsprache*). The Croatian Landwehr (Hrvatsko Domobrantsvo) all spoke Croatian or Serbian in their everyday activities.*

Other non-German-speaking regiments, depending on their provenance, would have a so-called *Regimentsprache*, or regimental language in addition to these two languages of command and service. For example, a Hungarian regiment made up largely of Romanians would require officers conversant in at least three languages: German, Magyar and Romanian. The far-reaching constitutional arrangements of the 'Ausgleich' (Compromise) heralded the end of the Austrian Empire and the beginning of the dual monarchy,

---

* The modern (1918–91) union of Serbo-Croat as one language was not officially recognised in the monarchy.

Austria-Hungary. This possessed a system of government whereby both the Hungarian and Austrian parts of the monarchy had separate parliaments and cabinets as well as separate constitutions. In theory the army could become the victim of internal politics. In practice the rights of the monarch with regard to foreign policy and military matters acted as a strong counterbalance to civilian oversight.[2] Although foreign and military affairs were subject to a structure which had no time limit, financial affairs with regard to the two parts of the Dual Monarchy were subject to renegotiation every ten years, something which would be a cause of future disequilibrium. Nevertheless, the 'Ausgleich' was a tremendous achievement. It provided the foundations for nearly fifty years of stability and peace within the Empire, creating the political and constitutional institutions that guided the Empire into the next century and allowing the prosperity and development that saw the great flowering of intellectual, scientific and artistic activity which marked Vienna in the run up to the First World War.

Difficulties and tensions between Buda and Vienna would remain but Franz-Josef never forgot his wife's love of the Magyars, and the Magyars never forgot that their King had loved their Queen. On a more practical level, the working relationship that emerged remained a constant for both sides.

It would be Franz-Josef's later heir, Franz Ferdinand's open determination to embark on profound political steps to change these fundamentals of the relationship between the dynasty and Hungary which made him in Franz-Josef's eyes a dangerous if not mortal threat to the survival of the Empire.

The end of 'Austrian white'

These far-reaching constitutional and political changes of the 'Ausgleich' were accompanied on the tactical military level by radical developments. The symbol of the Habsburg army for centuries, the white tunic, vanished along with the white cloaks of the heavy cavalry and lancers. From 1867, white remained only as the 'Gala' uniform of the generals. What Joseph II had tried to achieve without success over a decade occurred in an afternoon, thanks to the marksmanship of the Prussian infantry. The generals alone, and only during a 'levée' or other official celebration, would continue to wear white, a tradition long abandoned by the other 'Catholic' nations, France and Spain. After nearly two hundred years it was a colour that no longer had any place on the battlefield.

The white was replaced with a dark (but not Prussian) blue tunic and, for hot weather, the blue blouse which the Austrian lancers had pioneered in the Italian campaigns. The choice of blue reflected to some extent that recurring theme in European history whereby the uniform of the victors is often the inspiration for the new uniform of the vanquished; as if military dress in some way imparts a mystical tactical superiority as well as visual brilliance.

The new Austrian uniform took on several features derived from lessons learnt during recent campaigning in the field, especially with regard to comfort and pockets. It was single-breasted and lighter than its predecessor. Hungarian distinctions on hose and sleeve were retained, including the 'Bear's paw' cuff. Rank distinctions remained unchanged. Officers continued to be recognised instantly by their gold sash or, if they were wearing a sword, its port-epée knot. An off-duty field cap of black cloth common to all ranks from emperor to post boy was introduced, and would remain in use up to and even during the First Republic in the 1930s. The use by all ranks of an identical headdress was unique and progressive. It symbolised the army as a family or brotherhood in arms.

At first it was decided to reduce facing colours to three or four but regard for regimental traditions ensured the survival of that pride of the Imperial and Royal infantry right up to 1918: the many-hued *Farbkastel* (box of colours). Some 28 different nuances of red, blue and grey with such exotic names as *ponceaurot, karmesinrot* and *aschgrau* (literally: 'vibrant pumice red', 'carmine red' and 'ash grey') were to be used along with the famous regional regimental distinctions such as sulphur yellow, imperial yellow (Graz), rose pink (Trieste), black (Linz), chocolate (Carinthia), canary-orange (Salzburg), etc.

Other features appeared to owe rather less to modern lessons of warfare. The use of bright scarlet, *krapprot* breeches had previously been the prerogative of only some Lancer regiments. It now became ubiquitous for all Dragoon and Lancer regiments. The introduction of this vivid colour owed much to the melancholy circumstance whereby the untimely death of the Archduke Max as Emperor of Mexico had rendered all the red material made up for his volunteer regiments surplus to requirements. The Moravian cloth factory that had received the order had wisely asked for a guarantee that all the material made would be bought. This the Austrian Finance Ministry optimistically agreed to. The slack was taken up, literally, by the Austrian cavalry.[3]

The Austrian volunteer corps in Mexico for whom all this material had been destined had comprised 6,545 men in 1865. These had been recruited from former soldiers of the Imperial Army, with preference given to those under 40. Many of the officers were aristocrats seeking to escape debts and other affairs within Europe. A typical example was Johann Carl Khevenhueller, who promptly chalked up more debts, several duels and the usual romantic entanglements though he proved himself a dashing and brave leader of the still legendary 'Red Hussars'. As a photograph taken as he assumed his command shows, this Khevenhueller was a worthy heir to the swashbuckling general of Maria Theresa who had conquered Prague. The Mexico debacle deprived him and many others of the chance of a new life away from their family responsibilities back in Austria. By 1867 these men would have no further use for scarlet breeches.[4]

Reorganisation of the cavalry, conscription and a new rifle

The introduction of scarlet was only one of many changes which now affected the 'new' Austro-Hungarian cavalry. The abolition of Cuirassier regiments, already agreed before the 1866 war, was confirmed and they became dragoons. The Cavalry arm continued to dream of another great mounted encounter along the lines of Stresetice for another two generations but in reality, although they did not yet realise it, their role as a critical force of the Habsburg army had finally drawn to an end. Nonetheless, they continued to enjoy their traditional social and equipment prerogatives. Photographs of their early twentieth-century manoeuvres betray an anachronistic quality which in the age of the motor car appears to have had no obvious effect on the high reputation they continued to enjoy.

Inspired by the Prussian model, other changes were introduced, notably in organisation. The ten corps were reorganised into 22 divisions along Prussian lines with a single independent light cavalry division and a single heavy cavalry division. Otherwise the divisions were mixed. A typical division, for example, was made up of forty infantry, four 'Grenz' and nine cavalry regiments.

The breech-loading rifle and that other Prussian strength, universal conscription, were also reintroduced. The new Austrian rifle, made by Werndl, a single-shot breech-loader with a hinged breech block was rightly judged to be durable and one of the best designed in Europe. Conscription reflected not only admiration of the Prussian model but the new Prussian philosophy that if one wished to 'democratise the state one must militarise the people'. Königgrätz, one of the largest battles in history, had underlined the growing links in the state between tactics, armaments and industrialisation. The Austrian lieutenant Gustav Ratzenhofer, a military theorist and sociologist much influenced by developments in Prussia, noted a few years later in 1875: 'The summoning up of all resources to defend the state has become the unavoidable necessity of every politician and the duty of every patriot.'[5]

Conscription and the abolition of the right to buy exemption from conscription became acceptable even to the emerging bourgeoisie, among whom doubts about the rationale for military priorities were beginning to develop. The new Dual Monarchy, Austria-Hungary, could never become a second Prussia but the constitutional transformation, accompanied by the strong economic boom of the *Gründerzeit*, brought about military reform more rapidly than might have occurred otherwise.

Conscription had important consequences for the Habsburgs' army. What had been in old Austria a professional army of predominantly, though not exclusively, 'German' stamp was now to become an even more multinational *Volksheer* (people's army). In Hungary, on the other hand, the privileges the Hungarians had won with regard to their 'Honvéd' were but the first step in the transformation of that unit into a linguistically cohesive entity. By 1914 the 'Honvéd' whose language of command was Hungarian, would comprise 32 infantry regiments, 10 cavalry (Hussar) and 8 field artillery regiments as well as a mounted artillery unit.

The Hungarians were not content to stop at the creation of a Magyar reserve. Many remembered the fierce fighting they had had to endure in 1848–49 at the hands of the Kaisertreu Croats and Serbs of the Military Frontier. The abolition of the Military Frontier and its age-old privileges was added to the demands of the magnates. This multinational anachronism, which had given such steadfast service to the Habsburgs over the centuries, finally fell victim to the inexorable advance of the territorial and national principle.

In 1871, the 'Waradiner', 'Peterwardeiner' and 'Otocaner' were incorporated as Line infantry regiments. A new Hussar regiment was made out of the Jaczygier and Kumanier light horse, and the other frontier troops were incorporated into existing light units. Their officers – Boroevič, Poppovič, Maroičič, Grivičič, Petrovič, Preradovič, Trešcec, Strizič – all rose to prestigious rank seemingly impervious to the pernicious nationalism which was slowly but inexorably making them a tragic anachronism.

The introduction of the new 'conscript' army brought the army recruitment structures into parts of the Empire which had never regularly supplied soldiers for the army. The arrival of the military authorities in 1869 to select conscripts from remote parts of southern Dalmatia resulted in one village, Krivosije, erupting into a full-blown uprising which needed 18 infantry battalions with artillery support to quell. The uprising also revolved around the right to carry weapons, a *sine qua non* of existence for men in the borderlands of Dalmatia, Montenegro and Albania right up to modern times.

This Dalmatian uprising, and the surprising difficulty with which it was eventually suppressed, was a straw in the wind. The rebels won their right to carry arms, and the Austrian military began to see in the barren landscape of the Dinaric mountains a new and challenging field for their activities requiring very different skills from those associated with conventional European war, just as in the Turkish wars of old.

With the role of the dynasty limited in its traditional German and Italian zones of influence, it is hardly surprising that the Dual Monarchy looked increasingly towards the Balkan peninsula to defend its influence. But here she came up against the interests of Russia. Fortunately, at that time and for some years to come, England, under Disraeli, remained suspicious of Russian expansion and was therefore willing to support Austria in the Balkans.

In 1875, there was a bloody revolt against Ottoman rule in Hercegovina, a picturesque province linked by the Ivan saddle and the Narenta valley to Bosnia. Even a century later, and barely half a day's railway journey from the sophistication of Central Europe, both provinces retain characteristics of the Near East. The white limestone dolines of Hercegovina and the high-altitude lush valleys of Bosnia exact a fascination for the traveller arriving from Zagreb. The Adriatic coast might boast the glories of the Venetian Renaissance but these interior lands had been neglected by the humanist and enlightenment influences of European civilisation. A provincial strain of Ottoman culture was predominant and was to remain so.

The revolt in 1875 was watched closely by the Austrian authorities in nearby Dalmatia. Initially, the governor of Dalmatia, Baron Rodič, received instructions from Vienna to abstain from intervention and maintain calm. Even so, the advocacy for involvement was growing and, on 29 January, at a sitting of the Crown Council, the possibility of a full-blown occupation of Bosnia and Hercegovina was openly discussed.[6] Russia tentatively agreed to Vienna occupying Bosnia and Hercegovina in return for Austrian neutrality elsewhere.

While it was agreed that a military occupation was at this time and for the foreseeable future not feasible, the Crown Council decided to prepare public opinion for such an eventual move. In addition, intelligence-gathering operations along the frontier were stepped up. Two months later in March, an *Observationkorps* was established and orders given to prepare various scenarios for an occupation. On 13 November 1876 the Emperor had chaired a strategy meeting with four generals and the Archduke Albrecht to discuss the final occupation plan. By the spring of 1878, the military scenarios had been exhaustively prepared. The arrival of more than 100,000 Bosnian refugees added to the pressure for action.

Philippovič's instructions to occupy Bosnia

As the decision to deploy was taken, Feldzeugmeister Josef Freiherr von Philippovič received instructions which were enlightened: 'One of the first and most important tasks which the occupation will create is the preservation of property and the protection of personal security as well as the total impartiality in dealing with the different nationalities and confessions.' (The instructions went on to make clear that the greatest threat to an Austrian occupation would come from the Serbian orthodox population.)[7]

Vienna was keen to act in concert with Russia. As the military preparations gathered momentum, her diplomacy went into overdrive. Russia was offered generous terms with regard to Bulgaria. A secret treaty was arrived at whereby Austria pledged neutrality in the event of Russian expansion into Bulgaria in return for Bosnia-Hercegovina. The attraction of these territories for the Austrian Emperor reflected many illusions. Most persuasive of these was that these new territories would somehow compensate for the loss of Lombardy and Venetia. Another illusion was that they could be gained and sustained in a bloodless *coup de main*. Most dangerous of all was that it would in some way bring stability to the region. The Vienna statesmen did not see that the lure of the Balkans led inevitably and inexorably towards a conflict with Russia.

After initial setbacks in the Russo-Turkish War of 1877–78, the Russians made a clean sweep of the Turks and advanced towards Constantinople. Andrássy, Franz-Josef's foreign minister, skilfully avoided Austria becoming involved. But, as the Turks fell back in disarray, Serbia, Montenegro and Romania were now all declared independent. Under the terms of the Treaty of San Stefano, Russia demanded a 'Big Bulgaria', still nominally under Turkish suzerainty but open to Russian influence. Suddenly the entire Balkan peninsula was recast as a playground for competing Austro-Russian rivalries in which the Russian weapons of Pan-Slavism and 'Mother Russia' were set in motion with gusto.

Andrássy felt the Russians had tricked him and he was right. Like all Habsburgs, Franz-Josef took a dim view of public servants who placed the dynasty in an unhappy situation, and was moved to sack him. But in the end it was an initiative by Disraeli, the English Prime Minister, that preserved Andrássy. Disraeli's idea for a conference in Berlin and his subsequent negotiations there are rightly considered his finest political achievement. With Bismarck in the chair as 'honest broker', the Treaty of San Stefano was undone. Russia was humiliated but Austria, strongly supported by Disraeli, got the right to occupy the two provinces of Bosnia and Hercegovina. The territories were to remain under Turkish suzerainty but were to be administered by Austria-Hungary. It was a novel idea for the time and typical of Disraeli's subtle intellect.[8] The implementation of such a plan was fraught with challenges, although Andrássy boasted that the provinces could be swiftly occupied by 'two infantry companies and a military band'.[9]

The move towards occupation of the two provinces was not popular. The Hungarians bitterly resented any increase in the Slav population of the Empire. Even the generals were sceptical about the demands the two new and difficult provinces would make on their resources. They knew better than Andrássy the martial qualities of the inhabitants of these provinces. But the Emperor was more sanguine. Confiding to the diplomat Hübner, he said: 'I know very well that this step is highly unpopular with us not only in Hungary but also here, but public opinion is in error: the gain of this territory is a necessity; for otherwise Dalmatia will be lost.'[10]

Thus was the stage set for the newly reformed Imperial and Royal Army to engage in a limited, but most challenging excursion into mountain warfare. The German military attaché to Vienna, Colonel Keller, travelling along the frontier a few months earlier, had written, 'If the Austrians believe they can occupy Bosnia just to the strains of a military band they will be disappointed.'[11] The expeditionary force was commanded by Philippovič, an able soldier with long roots in the old Military Frontier. A tough Croat with some Serbian ancestry, he had first seen service with Jellačić in 1848 and then fought bravely at Solferino. He was a wise choice for the occupation as both the territory and its peoples were a known quantity to him. But even he was surprised at the ferocity of the resistance his troops now encountered. Both the Serbian orthodox population and the majority Muslim inhabitants offered pockets of tenacious opposition. Belgrade, starting its meteoric rise as the most dynamic Balkan state, inspired the Serbs, even though many of these bandit leaders had just months before been in contact with Philippovič to offer their support to the Austrians 'for our empire'.

The Austrian invasion

The Austrian General Staff believed that the Ottomans, in compliance with the Treaty of Berlin, had ordered the withdrawal of their troops. They were therefore confident that four infantry divisions, totalling 75,000 men, would more than suffice for the occupation of both provinces.

The invasion began on 29 July 1878 and almost immediately encountered violent obstacles. Three Austro-Hungarian columns, the 7th Division under the Duke of Württemberg, the 6th Division under FML (Feldmarschall-Leutnant) Tegetthoff and the 20th Division under Count Szapáry crossed into Bosnia over the river Save while a fourth column pushed up from Dalmatia.

The first surprise the Austrians encountered was that regular Turkish units were still present in the provinces and were putting up bitter resistance, in breach of the Congress of Berlin's terms. Some 80,000 of them were under instructions from the local Turkish military command in Bosnia, acting apparently on orders from the 'Porte' to slow down the Austrians in the hope of extracting diplomatic concessions. On 1 July, Philippovič's forces reached Banja Luka where some 3,000 Turkish regulars, supported by various skirmishers supplied by the local population, held up his troops for several hours. It took two Austrian mountain brigades of elite troops to clear them out of the town. A week later and even more stiff opposition was encountered at Jajce where, on 7 August, some 6,000 rebels and Turkish regulars ambushed the Austro-Hungarian column and were beaten off only with the greatest of difficulty.

The next unpleasant surprise was the reaction of the civilian population. In addition to the Ottoman regular troops, the Bosnian Muslims now rose up under various chieftains, notably dervish Hadje Loja, a local clan leader. Hadje's blood-chilling notoriety soon spread as far away as Vienna where tales of his cruelty to wounded Imperial and Royal soldiers caused sensational headlines. An enterprising Viennese baker with a macabre sense of humour bestowed the ultimate Viennese compliment on this figure of terror by inventing a new dark roll in his honour, which in time came to be known as a 'Bosniaken'.

Loja's insurgents fought with all the methods of rebellion at their disposal. Guerrillas ambushed the Austrian supply lines and regularly massacred patrols. No Austrians were ever taken prisoner. Muslim women poured burning oil out of windows on to troops unfortunate enough to be marching below as they entered their villages. Smaller Austrian outposts were attacked under cover of darkness with fire and sword. The *Stosstaktik* of 1866, already consigned to the archives in the light of experience at Königgrätz, were of no use in this environment. The army had adapted, and their Werndl rifles were much more helpful, but partisan warfare on this scale had not been encountered for nearly a century. Austro-Hungarian casualties mounted rapidly. The main Austrian column under Tegetthoff reached Derventa within a few days of crossing the Bosnian frontier but had to fight fierce engagements at Doboj and Maglaj. At Žepče, a force of 7,000 insurgents attacked the second column on 7 August. It took almost another two weeks of uninterrupted fighting for the column to reach Sarajevo. Count Szapáry's forces, the third column, were deployed in the direction of Tuzla but were so roughly handled by the insurgents that it took them months to reach their objective, and then only after significant reinforcements arrived.

All this slowed down the advance considerably and Philippovič began to see the ominous prospect of having to fight his way out through the valleys of the Narenta in the winter if something more radical was not done soon. In response to these difficulties, Philippovič requested reinforcements, and a further four divisions, a cavalry brigade and a logistics battalion were mobilised. The troops stationed in Dalmatia were reinforced at the same time.

By the beginning of September 1878, more than 154,000 infantry, 4,490 cavalry and 292 artillery pieces were deployed: a colossal force, the equivalent of nearly four full army corps for what was still described in Vienna as a 'little local insurgency'. The Imperial and Royal War Ministry statistics gave only a hint of the real casualty figures. Official statistics referred to 198 fatalities. In reality the deaths by the end of the campaign exceeded 3,300, with nearly 7,000 wounded and more than 110,000 suffering from various illnesses brought on by a combination of poor sanitary conditions, the scorching climate and inhospitable terrain.[12]

Moreover, the fighting was not only tough and bloody, it was accompanied by appalling atrocities in the worst traditions of the eighteenth-century Military Frontier. Bodies were mutilated by rebels. Women and children seen as collaborating with the Austrians were murdered in broad daylight. Unsurprisingly, this in turn led to increasing brutality on the part of the occupiers, although the locals soon realised that, compared to the reprisals of the Ottoman troops, the Austrians and Hungarians were mere novices in the arts of Balkan cruelty.

Austria seizes the Sandžak and Sarajevo

By September the campaign began to make swifter progress. An Austro-Hungarian column seized the strategically important Sandžak where the Austrians had been granted garrison rights by the Treaty of Berlin. The column went on to capture Priboj and Prijepolje, which were stormed by the second week in September.

To the south, Philippovič's 'southern' army advanced more slowly. At Čitluk and Ljubuški it encountered some 12,000 Turkish regulars. After putting up a spirited defence, these eventually retreated to the coast where ships awaited their embarkation for Ottoman ports.

The fighting for Sarajevo in late August illustrated well the characteristics of the struggle and the difficulties that were encountered. On 19 August towards 5 a.m., taking advantage of the thick fog which enveloped the town, a strong Austrian force approached from the direction of Radova to the north. At the same time, another unit crept stealthily towards the castle, which was protected by a three-metre-high wall on its northern flank. Suddenly the fog lifted and the attackers found themselves horribly exposed. By late morning, a full battle was under way with an entire Austrian brigade pinned down by artillery fire. As more guns came into action the entire advance ground to a halt. Oberst Lemaič, who commanded the brigade that had advanced furthest, suddenly found himself under a hail of fire from Winchester, Martini-Henry and Snyder rifles. These began to take a frightful toll of his Hungarian units, who found themselves in a firefight of such intensity that after about forty minutes, they began to run out of ammunition.[13]

Only a spirited bayonet charge in the best tradition of 1866 prevented the Austro-Hungarian position from being overrun by the insurgents who, noticing the slackening Austrian fire, had crept to within fifty yards of Lemaič's men. The cry of 'Hurrah!' and 'Zivio Austria!' from the Croats accompanied the charge which drove the Bosnians back to the Broška stream. But with no ammunition the Austrians could not exploit this until reinforcements arrived.

While the insurgents withdrew into the castle, Lemaič brought up nine fresh companies to storm the position. But at 300 paces, a fire of such ferocity poured from every loophole, parapet and rampart that the attack was brought to a standstill. The insurgents' artillery continued to rain shells down upon Lemaič's men, who were unsupported by any Austro-Hungarian artillery because it was still making its way across the rough terrain from Radova several miles away. With no artillery there was not the remotest chance of a frontal attack succeeding. Lemaič's brigade was paralysed. By midday the entire Austrian attack had ground to a halt.

A second column under General Müller was advancing from the west. By 9 a.m. it had seized the Sarajevo cemetery and so-called Kosarsko Hill without a struggle. From here the Austrian mountain artillery batteries finally came into play but the range (two miles) was too far for these light-calibre guns to make much impact. The insurgents counter-attacked Kosarsko Hill. The Graz House regiment Nr 27 only succeeded in driving their opponents from every garden and building beyond the hill after a fierce hand-to-hand struggle lasting more than two hours. While this fight ensued, Müller's force was also incapable of any progress.

A third force under FML Tegetthoff was under even greater strain. After a desperate fight along the Miljačka river, the Austrians forced the insurgents back towards the Sarajevo citadel but the insurgents held on tenaciously, making use of the walls and fortifications. Tegetthoff's men were also hope-lessly pinned down. After seven hours of fighting, three Austro-Hungarian columns, made up of some of the finest troops in the Imperial and Royal Army, were still struggling to make any progress against a supposedly 'rabble' force.

By midday, 52 guns arrived. They were placed in a rough semicircle to the north-east of the town near Pašino Brdo and were deployed against the castle and the northern and western suburbs of Sarajevo. As a half-battalion advanced, the guns loaded with shrapnel supported the attack effectively. Two companies of the Hungarian regiment Nr 52 fixed bayonets and charged and reached the outer wall of the western suburbs. Supported by the regiment's third battalion, they proceeded to clear the streets in bitter house-to-house fighting. Barricades were erected across every little street by the insurgents and from every house there poured a destructive fire as the Imperial troops inched forward. Even after the Austro-Hungarians had advanced a few yards, hidden marksmen opened fire from behind them.

Progress was slow. It took the tough young Hungarian men in Infantry regiment Nr 38 two hours to advance 500 metres. As the troops reached the outskirts of the Muslim quarters, men literally sprang from the roofs brandishing knives and daggers. No quarter was either asked or given in these gruesome encounters. Every insurgent had to be killed for any advance to make progress. This was especially the case when some Austrians approached the Cekricia Mosque in the heart of the Muslim district. Five attempts to storm this building failed. Only when the Styrians of the 27th arrived did the mosque finally fall. As a section of the 27th moved into the Serbian quarter, a hail of bullets fell on them from the minaret of the mosque. Even as they took the 'Konak', the Turkish governor's palace, shots rang out from behind them. In every part of the city, even as flames engulfed the wooden houses, no weakening in the enemy's will to resist could be discerned.

Meanwhile to the north, where the battle had begun, Oberst Lemaič remained pinned down unable to move forward despite the dramatic events to the west and south of the city. It would be another six hours before the castle fell. In nearly twelve hours of uninterrupted fighting, more than 14,000 Austro-Hungarian troops had fought against nearly 6,000 insurgents. The Austrians had sustained over 3,000 casualties, while half the insurgents lay dead or dying on the streets of the town. It was a day after the Emperor's birthday. By 5 p.m. the Imperial flag flew from the castle and the cries of 'Hurrah!' rang round every street. The surviving insurgents, pursued by a few companies of infantry, fled towards Pale. The band of the 46th regiment struck up the Haydn anthem 'Gott erhalte' and its solemn chords filled the corpse-strewn streets while a small audience of women and children gazed on in bemusement.[14]

A new era for Bosnia-Hercegovina: Benjamin Kállay

The Imperial and Royal Army succeeded in bringing Central Europe and the modern age closer to remote and almost forgotten lands. The great Balkan writer Ivo Andrič has left this picture of the encounter between the army of a great civilisation and a society still medieval in its outlook.

The only troops they had seen had been the badly dressed, poorly paid Ottomans or even worse the violent ill-disciplined Bosnian militia. The 'Power and Order' of an Imperial force, triumphant, glittering and self-confident; such an army staggered their senses. Behind the smart helmets and dazzling uniforms of the parading hussars, in fact expressed by every polished button was the almost unimaginable power, order and prosperity of another world.[15]

The prosperity of another world was not long in coming. The Imperial and Royal administration of Bosnia-Hercegovina, 'with the command of the All-Highest', was initiated on 29 October 1878. It heralded the beginning of what commentators throughout Europe characterised correctly as a 'model administration'.[16]

To this end a 'Bosnian Commission' responsible to the Joint Ministerial Cabinet was established to administer the provinces jointly in the name of both parts of the Dual Monarchy. This was another indication of the serious-ness with which the Emperor regarded the great compromise with Budapest. Until 1882, the Bosnian Commission was under the guidance of 'Sektionschef' J. Szlávy, a well-meaning but unimaginative bureacrat. On 4 July 1882, Szlávy was replaced by Benjamin Kállay (1839–1903), a Hungarian who was a gifted linguist and a Balkan specialist of immense talent. It was Kállay who laid the foundations of one of the most enlightened administrations in modern history. Already in 1877, Kállay had submitted a paper on the proposed annexation of the two provinces and how the administration could best be organised.

Kállay's understanding of the region was based on a sincere attempt to improve the conditions of the peoples who inhabited it. He was above all devoted to the idea that Bosnians should develop a sense of identity inde-pendent of Serbs or Croats. Kállay saw the need for infrastructure as the key to establishing this identity. Roads and railways constructed mostly by k. (u.) k. military engineers began to make the most remote areas accessible. No one who has travelled on the railway from Sarajevo to Mostar, even in recent times, can fail to admire the breathtaking gradients, tunnels, elliptical curves and dramatic defiles, the astonishing feats of engineering that the Austrians brought to this isolated Arcadian landscape.

Parallel with these infrastructural achievements came cultural progress on a grand scale. Museums, theatres and imposing buildings in the styles of the Ringstrasse arose throughout the province. And, as three hundred years earlier in Graz, the Jesuits were again brought in to establish an education system for an indigenous, well-educated elite who would, in time, assume a leading role in the provinces' government and administration. The writer Ivo Andrić was taught to read and write by them. Progress over barely twenty years was astonishing, giving the lie to the widely held view that persists even to this day that the Habsburg Empire lacked dynamism in the late nineteenth century. Austria's spectacular investment in the region, still vibrantly visible more than a century later, belies the conventional narrative of a Habsburg monarchy 'ripe for detruction'.[17]

The issue of creating Bosnian military units was at first controversial. A 'Jaeger' battalion, established in 1879, proved so successful that universal conscription in the provinces was introduced in 1881, despite a vociferous diplomatic protest on the part of the 'Porte', which rightly regarded it as a breach of the letter if not the spirit of the Treaty of Berlin agreements.

Certainly it was a diplomatic challenge to explain how subjects of the Ottoman Empire (as the Bosnians legally were at this time) could swear an oath to the Austrian Emperor on taking up their military service. Vienna dealt with the issue in a traditional manner. It simply refused to acknowledge the Ottoman protests.[18]

Die Bosniaken kommen

In this way, by 1885, strongly supported by Kállay, four Bosnian-Hercegovinian infantry companies had grown into four full-size battalions which were committed to serving as an integral part of the army. As such they were also eligible for service to defend any part of the Dual Monarchy's territory. Each battalion was established in a different part of the two provinces, the four depots being Sarajevo, Tuzla, Banja Luka and Mostar. Each battalion was trained by experienced NCOs from elite Austrian mountain regiments, who were expected to hand their duties over as soon as practicable to promising recruits. Two imams were given the rank of regimental chaplain and the duty of tending to the souls of the soldiers.

In 1886, the introduction of a repeating rifle for the first time increased the firepower of these soldiers significantly. The new rifle had an 11mm calibre (in contrast to the 8mm calibre of the existing rifle) and a range of 2,000 metres. It was especially suitable for mountain warfare because it was light and easy to use.

By 1895, when they were granted regimental bands, each Bosnian regiment was in status and organisation virtually identical to pre-existing infantry regiments of the line. Their uniform was to be strikingly different. It was pike blue with 'Alizarin' red facings. Trousers were to the knee, cut in Balkan style with gaiters and marked by two brightly polished buttons on the calf; the entire ensemble was set off with a *krapprot* fez with a blue (later black) tassel. Any thought that these troops were only picturesque was dispelled by their demeanour and physique. In some companies the average height was well over 6 feet 2 inches. With their muscular frames and finely chiselled faces burnt brown by the harsh Balkan sun there could be no doubting that here was an elite unit in the making.

With the appointment of the Styrian musician and composer Eduard Wagnes (1863–1936) as bandmaster of the second Bosnian infantry regiment, the 'Bosancen' struck musical gold. Wagnes began composing marches including several masterpieces that today form part of the repertoire.[19] Wagnes not only conducted and rehearsed his musicians every day, but immortalised these troops in his celebrated march 'Die Bosniaken kommen', which soon grew so popular that it became de facto the regimental march of all four Bosnian infantry regiments and the Bosnian 'Field Jaeger'. What Beethoven had done in composing a regimental march for the Hoch und Deutschmeister, Wagnes showed he could do a century later for his Bosnians. The string orchestra of the Bosnians played at garrison balls from Sarajevo to Graz.

The 'Field Jaeger', raised in 1903 from single companies detached from each infantry regiment, soon proved a fearless addition to the regular infantry. They were attired in a uniform similar to the Kaiserjaeger except that the ubiquitous fez was retained and the Tyrolean eagle was replaced as a badge by the Imperial double-headed eagle.

The Bosniaken were not always given an easy ride in the Empire. The 2nd Bosnian regiment was stationed in Graz where it often came up against the pan-German prejudices of the local population, who were known to jeer at first and even jostle the soldiers when they marched to the city's Stadtpark to perform. In Vienna, the 1st Bosnian regiment was better received and became a much-loved attraction, fascinating children and adults alike with their appearance. Marching through the Hofburg to the strains of Wagnes's march, they soon became a regular element of any state visit, impressing especially Emperor Wilhelm II of Germany, not otherwise renowned for his high regard for the Imperial Austrian army or indeed Islamised Slavs.

In addition to these units, an extensive gendarmerie patrolled the frontiers of the two provinces. These units were involved in week-long duties in the inhospitable terrain of the mountains stretching across Montenegro and Albania. By the time the Austrian Foreign Minister, Baron Aehrenthal, had pulled off his dramatic coup of formally annexing the two provinces in 1908, the provinces were flourishing. Never before, and certainly never since, have these two regions enjoyed such benign and supportive rule. Within a generation, Kállay's administration had brought these lands out of Ottoman poverty into the modern prosperity of the early twentieth century.

Aehrenthal's annexation in 1908, though at first adhered to by the hapless Russian Foreign Minister Iszvolsky, was soon bitterly resented once the minister realised the force of Pan-Slav sentiments at home. The self-appointed patron of the Slavic world was too weak in 1908 to resist Aehrenthal's forward diplomacy. The recent Russo-Japanese War had sapped her strength. But she was determined on revenge. The annexation of the two provinces, perhaps more than anything else, set Austria-Hungary and Russia on a collision path. Aehrenthal's diplomatic success, the incorporation of these provinces fully into the Habsburg monarchy, was to be a pyrrhic victory.

CHAPTER 18

Towards a Twentieth-century Navy
THE SIEGE AT PEKIN

With the exception of the deployment of two artillery batteries to Palestine in 1916 to support the Turks against the British in Gaza, the army of the Dual Monarchy never served in an overseas colonial environment. However, the nineteenth-century expansion of the Habsburg navy ensured that landing parties, made up of armed sailors rather than marine infantry, were not unheard of. The events in China around the turn of the century appeared to confirm the wisdom of strengthening the embryonic navy.

The Boxers and the Austrian Legation Guard detachment

The great siege of the eleven Western legations in the summer of 1900 had many causes. Chief among them was Western greed, which saw a declining Chinese Empire as rich pickings for colonial expansion. In particular the activities of the Protestant missionaries in the region were deeply resented by the Chinese authorities and population. The growth of a patriotic secret society, the infamous 'Boxers' (righteous society of fists) dedicated to the protection of Chinese values in the face of all this Western influence was the catalyst for the conflict and the attempts to storm the legations.

These were protected by detachments from eight nations and, while the siege lasted, news of these events in distant Peking came to dominate the headlines of the European newspapers. The Austrian role in the siege was modest. Thanks to the quality of the personalities involved we have excellent detailed accounts of the action. The recent publication of private memoirs in Vienna offer a belated but valuable counter-view to the conventional narrative which is much influenced by *The Times* correspondent Dr G.E. Morrison. His account has dominated most Western descriptions of the siege.

Yet Morrison's correspondence was prejudiced with regard to the Austrians. One Austrian officer who was serving there, Lieutenant Commander, later Captain, von Winterhalder, branded it a 'Kabinettstuck' (display cabinet) of 'tendentious opinions'.[1] Given the tremendous prestige of The Times in the twentieth century, many later writers such as Peter Fleming have tended to accept Morrison's account without probing further.[2]

The Austrian contingent consisted of only thirty sailors from the Austrian cruiser Zenta. The commander of that vessel, Captain Thomann von Montalmar, together with Linienschiffsleutnant (Lieutenant Commander) Theodor von Winterhalder, had responded to a telegram from the Imperial and Royal Austro-Hungarian legation on 2 June urgently demanding 'immediate consultations'. Quite what was in the Austrian legation staff's mind is unclear. The security situation was deteriorating, as were relations with the official Chinese government. There were increasing numbers of attacks on Chinese Christians. Both Winterhalder and Thomann expected to return to their ship after their discussions. Consequently, they were both in civilian clothes and had left their uniforms in their ship. They were not on holiday or sightseeing as Morrison later wrote.

Accompanying Thomann and Winterhalder was a unit of thirty sailors, two midshipmen and two other officers, the senior of whom, Linienschiffsleutnant Josef Kollar, commanded the detachment, which was also equipped with a Maxim gun. This was a precautionary deployment. Kollar's men were expected to remain behind in Peking while Thomann returned with Winterhalder to decide whether further reinforcements were necessary. The Austrian detachment was a small but significant contribution to the 420 men who arrived between 1 and 3 June to protect the legations in response to anxious telegrams.[3]

The modest size of the Austrian detachment was the result of the Imperial and Royal Foreign Ministry prohibiting Thomann from exceeding the size of the legation Guard detachment dispatched in 1898. That had consisted also of just thirty men. The Austro-Hungarian diplomatists fussed over the implications of dispatching a larger force. In an era where a response to any political event was carefully calibrated, Vienna saw no reason to raise the temperature.

A few weeks later the remaining crew of the Zenta played a prominent part in the storming of the Taku forts, the key to securing any route to the interior, but by that time hostilities had begun in earnest. Nearly 160 of these 'Matrosen', half the cruiser's entire crew, led the first wave of the assault against the well-defended Chinese positions, supported by some German sailors. The red–white–red Austrian battle ensign was the first Western standard to be erected on the towers as the battle ended; an auspicious opening for the largely Croat sailors of the *Zenta* armed with their efficient Mannlicher rifles.

That the Habsburg battle ensign should have been the first Western standard to be raised in the conflict was somewhat ironic, given that Habsburg policy at that time coincided more closely with the best interests of Peking than the policies of the other European states. By 1895, most of China's outlying territories had been amputated, a disastrous war with Japan only serving to encourage the other states' avarice. When two German missionaries were murdered in 1897, Germany seized the city of Tsingtsao along with mining concessions in Shantung as indemnity. In this unseemly scramble for spheres of interest, only one European nation remained aloof, uninterested in any partition of Chinese territory to its own advantage, and that was Austria-Hungary.

The Dual Monarchy's interest in and knowledge of China predated that of all her rivals. It was a Styrian Jesuit priest who first brought reports of conditions on that vast continent to a larger European audience. While Ferdinand II struggled to harness the force of the Society of Jesus to ensure his dynasty's triumph in Graz, the capital of Inner Austria, Wilhelm Herdtrich was born in the same city, in 1625. A brilliant pupil worthy of the Keplerian traditions of his home town, Herdtrich later joined the Society and made his way across the Chinese interior to introduce the intellectual and spiritual gifts of his order to the mandarins. Herdtrich, who was appointed court mathematician to the Chinese Emperor Kangxi, wrote works on Confucian philosophy that remain authoritative classics to this day.[4]

More than two hundred years later, Imperial Austria's relations with China remained ambivalent. On the one hand, European 'Abendland' (Western) solidarity dictated support for what *The Times* called 'the great experiment' of Europe's relationship with China. On the other hand, the Dual Monarchy regarded events in China with intellectual detachment. Perhaps there was a subconscious affinity between two fading empires of byzantine complexity.

After 1879, Germany was an ally of the Dual Monarchy and, though it was purely a 'defensive' alliance, it in theory encouraged naval cooperation. Adventures on the high seas were an opportunity for the Imperial and Royal Navy to gain more experience in exotic waters beyond the Adriatic.

Arthur von Rosthorn

Austria's ambivalence comes through strongly in the writings of Arthur von Rosthorn, the Imperial and Royal Legation's First Secretary and acting chargé d'affaires in Peking. Rosthorn was of Anglo-Austrian extraction and was certainly one of the most perceptive westerners in Peking during the siege. Born in 1862, he had studied at the universities of Vienna and Oxford, was fluent in Chinese and had been awarded a doctorate by the University of Leipzig. In the absence of his minister, Baron Czikann, the senior Austrian diplomat, who was on vacation, Rosthorn was in charge of the legation.

Writing a few weeks after the siege, Rosthorn noted that the xenophobia of the Chinese was unsurprising, 'given that in the 60 years with which China had come into regular contact with the West, she had experienced only damage and humiliation.'[5]

'We Europeans do not imagine that the Chinese are capable of the patriotic feelings we have. That is a great mistake.' For Rosthorn, the Boxers were an understandable and logical consequence of European avarice and greed. 'If I had been born Chinese, I too would have become a Boxer,' he wrote, criticising the Western missionaries with their 'cult of intolerance' and contrasting it negatively with the simple indifference to Christianity most Chinese demonstrated before the Boxers set the tone of resistance to all things foreign.

These views inevitably came into conflict with those of more 'colonially minded' members of the diplomatic community, in particular Sir Claude Macdonald, the British Minister and a tough Scot who had served in the Highland Light Infantry. Relations between the Austrians and the British Legation were to become strained as the Boxer Rebellion gathered momentum.

The Austrian sailors installed themselves in three upper rooms in the legation, and then hoisted one of the *Zenta*'s battle ensigns on to the roof. After setting up the Maxim gun on a block of wood opposite the main entrance to the compound, eight sailors under one of the midshipmen were detached to guard the nearby Belgian legation, eight minutes' walk away.

The following day (4 June) Thomann and Winterhalder, their 'conversations' with Rosthorn completed, prepared to take the train back to Tientsin but in the meantime the Boxers had occupied two stations and interrupted the line. No trains were running. Rosthorn and Thomann agreed to send a telegram requesting reinforcements, in this case in the form of a 70-strong detachment. The telegram was received by Guido Kottowitz von Kortschak, the startled First Officer of the *Zenta*, who had been expecting news of Thomann's return. This was the first cry for help to reach the outside world because all the other legations took 48 hours to consult their governments first, by which time the rail and telegram link was well and truly broken.

The Austrian sailors drew a perimeter around the legation's 12-foot wall, expelling the Chinese 'sentries' who were outside every legation as an Imperial Chinese 'courtesy' but were useless as a barrier between the growing hostile elements and the legation. A handsome young Austrian midshipman, by name of Boyneburg, set about erecting wire between posts and organising various mantraps. The Rosthorns' tennis net was utilised to cover part of the perimeter, and whilst these precautions at first caused much humour as several members of the legation fell into Boyneburg's mantraps, the news that one of the local staff of the Japanese legation had been caught and beheaded near the railway station reminded everyone that serious challenges lay ahead.

On the evening of the 13th, after storming and burning the American mission chapel, a huge crowd appeared in front of the Austrian legation shouting terrifying cries of '*Sha! Sha!*' ('Kill! Kill!'). Winterhalder positioned on the roof with five sailors ordered volley fire and the crowd, which was 150 metres distant, after the third volley fell silent and dispersed. The Maxim gun had not been fired but the effect of the Mannlicher rifles was comforting.

Two English ladies, Miss Dudgeon and Mrs Mears, arrived from the office of Sir Robert Hart, the senior European customs official, to seek shelter with the Austrians. Hart, an old China hand, felt the Austrian legation to be the safest place for them. That night all the religious mission stations were attacked and at the Tung Tang Catholic cathedral Father Garrigue met a martyr's death on the steps of his altar. Around 2 a.m. the Boxers renewed their attack on the Austrian legation but a burst of fire from the Maxim gun sent them scuttling back. To the dismay of the Austrians when dawn came, instead of the mass of dead bodies they hoped to find there was only the wreckage of a few torches and the odd trace of blood. The Boxer casualties had been dragged away under the cover of darkness to preserve the myth of invincibility.

The siege begins

Thus began the rebellion. The Austrians could congratulate themselves on surviving the first attacks but they soon lost themselves in a technical debate over the elevation of the Maxim. They would later learn that the original elevation had been deadly accurate and that the Boxers had that evening suffered scores of casualties.

Three days later, a flare to the north abruptly announced an attack on the Belgian legation and Winterhalder with a dozen sailors with bayonets fixed took off at the trot to be joined by a French patrol, although these men soon broke away, apparently incensed at Winterhalder's high-handed manner. Fortunately, by the time Winterhalder arrived at the Belgian compound, order had been restored: young Boyneburg had let the Boxers advance to fifty paces and had then, with his eight-man-strong detachment, poured three volleys into the Boxers with such devastating effect that they had too little time to collect their dead.

Once again the Maxim was in action and a ricochet struck the electricity wires, plunging the legations into darkness, to the fury of the German Minister von Ketteler who proceeded to give the unamused Austrian sailors an unnecessary lesson in ballistics. While the Croat sailors, who understood very little German, looked on, one of the midshipmen respectfully pointed out to the German that a ricochet was usually indifferent to elevation.

The siege now settled into a routine. The Austrian legation was much in demand for its seemingly endless supplies of beer, sandwiches and Styrian mineral water. Other than the Italians, who had fired the first shots on the night of the 13th, only the Austrians had been more or less continuously in action. Some stampeding horses had roused the American and British defenders to their weapons but the Boxers appeared to have withdrawn to focus their attention on the Chinese Christians. As the hot days of mid-June continued, the Austrians engaged in some aggressive patrolling, especially towards the Boxer temples where, in one day, they killed forty-eight Boxers and discovered a huge hoard of silver. Unfortunately for the Austrian sailors, the Japanese got their wagons to the temple first and the silver had disappeared by the time the sailors returned.

After 16 June, the attacks on the periphery renewed momentum. One evening, the Belgian Minister appeared with some of his staff to ask Rosthorn if they could evacuate to the Austrian legation permanently. Rosthorn was reluctant to countenance this and led them back with some more Austrian sailors to the Belgian legation, where they found a Boxer attack in full swing. Rosthorn's arrival beat off the attack but it was agreed that the outlying location of the Belgians made their position untenable. Belgian papers were transferred to the Austrian legation safe. On 18 June, the Belgian legation was evacuated on the specific request of the Minister, Monsieur Joostens.

Two days later, the murder of the German Minister, von Ketteler, as he was carried in a sedan chair to the Foreign Ministry, puffing his cigar, confirmed that the crisis was far from resolution. Ketteler, a slightly overbearing figure, had assumed his diplomatic status would confer protection enough and had eschewed offers of an armed escort. It was an expensive miscalculation and he seemed genuinely surprised when his murderers' blades cut him down.

Von Rosthorn's wife, Paula, noted that while von Ketteler's death depressed the diplomats, Midshipman Boyneburg and the Austrian sailors greeted the news of the atrocity with almost childlike enthusiasm as it meant that 'things were finally hotting up' (*endlich losgehen*). Reluctantly Thomann concluded that in the event of a proper organised attack with firearms, the Austrian legation would be attacked on three sides, making it impossible to defend.

On 20 June, the decision to withdraw to the French legation was taken. Thomann and Rosthorn packed up their possessions and began burning all sensitive documents and ciphers. After a final dinner, the Austrian flag was lowered and the Rosthorns, with the naval escort, bid the house which had been 'a part of our homeland' a sad farewell. As the shots began to whistle around the legation, the Rosthorns scrambled through the nearby Customs House. From there, with the help of a ladder, they made it on to the roof, which overlooked part of the French legation. Jumping eight feet down into the French garden, they found themselves reunited with their sailors and officers, most of whom had been dispatched there earlier.

The French Minister, Monsieur Pichon was adamant that Frau Rosthorn should evacuate to the spacious British legation where most of the European women were gathered along with 400 other Europeans. Frau Rosthorn was filled with admiration for how the English had organised these diverse groups of refugees into an ordered and disciplined civilian population. Each task, whether the sewing of curtains or organisation of supplies, was allotted to a particular group. Children and babies were also accommodated in this multinational camp. An evening or two later, Frau Rosthorn watched her old home go up in flames as the Austro-Hungarian legation was torched by the Chinese. A lot of shotgun cartridges, property of the absent minister, Baron Czikann who was keen on his flighting duck, detonated in an explosion of blue smoke. Rosthorn and Thomann had had no time to bring the ammunition with them.

Captain Thomann's 'command'

It had been agreed among the legations that Captain Thomann, as the senior officer present, would take overall command. On this evening, a panic sparked by the Americans caused Thomann to order a withdrawal from the outer perimeter. Although this too had been agreed earlier, it proved unnecessary and the Americans returned to their positions. Hard words were spoken and Thomann was relieved of his command de facto via a note circulated by the British Minister, Sir Claude Macdonald, and signed by the French and the Russian ministers.

The note, in some ways an eerie premonition of the European line-up in 1914, sought to vest overall command in the person of the British Minister. To achieve this, Thomann was slandered and then libelled as a coward. Thomann had merely acted as had been agreed when the jittery Americans abandoned their part of the perimeter. Unfortunately, Morrison's accusations of incompetence and cowardice stuck. They have remained a recurring theme of later descriptions of the siege in the English language. Morrison ignored Thomann's later behaviour which would give the lie to all this.

In any event, the British démarche was not recognised by either the German military attaché Count Soden or even the commander of the French naval contingent, Lieutenant D'Arcy, notwithstanding the fact that the French Minister Pichon had signed it! Neither the Japanese nor the Belgians, let alone the Austrians, accepted it. Yet Morrison's account implies that all the legations seamlessly agreed to Sir Claude taking command.

In fact the consequence of this naked British grab for power was that Macdonald's orders were often ignored, not least because he was unaware of conditions beyond the confines of his own perimeter. Macdonald's endeavours to get the legation guards to 'concentrate' in the British legation were seen by the Austrians as an ambitious attempt by the British 'to pretend that they alone saved the legations'.[6]

While Macdonald gathered as much material and manpower as he could within his own compound, he failed to realise that as long as the other legations continued to man their defences they would act as a kind of 'buffer' for his own legation. In this way the British legation continued to enjoy a charmed life remote from the pressure building up elsewhere along the legations' line of defence.

At this stage the Austrians were still making use of the British facilities and Frau Rosthorn continued to help in the infirmary hurriedly erected by Dr Poole. But one afternoon, nursing a wounded Russian soldier who was bleeding profusely, she fainted. After recovering, she made her way back to the French legation and asked to remain with her husband, subject to all the officers present agreeing, which they did.

Frau Rosthorn's Molotov cocktails

In Frau Rosthorn's words, the French legation was 'significantly more interesting'. Its exposed position, compared to that of the British legation, became immediately apparent when a grenade exploded above her bedroom on her first night. Fortunately, as Boyneburg pointed out, mealtimes were relatively quiet because the Chinese took their 'Chow Chow' very seriously. Horsemeat, pulses and asparagus together with truffles seemed to be the garrison's regular fare, and Monsieur Pichon supplemented the food with some Bordeaux from his own family estates in Pauillac.

As the Chinese began to mine the walls of the French legation on 29 June, the Austrians, including both Rosthorns, made 'bombs' of straw and petrol loaded into empty bottles. These early versions of Molotov cocktails proved effective but also dangerous to the defenders. When the Chinese discovered the source of this plague of incendiaries, they began firing and hurling stones at Frau Rosthorn. One of the bottles landed on a petrol can, setting fire to an entire box of these projectiles: exploding into flame, they engulfed Frau Rosthorn. As she fell to the ground, only the prompt intervention of the Croatian sailors who jumped on her flaming body prevented serious burns. The Croats had jumped with such enthusiasm that, she later wrote, she felt they had 'broken every bone in her back'.[7] Frau Rosthorn's conduct as the only female combatant was worthy of the highest praise though later she simply said that she remained with her husband on the front line because she 'felt he could never come to any real harm if I were close to him', a characteristic Austrian female trait, shared in more tragic circumstances fourteen years later by the Duchess of Hohenberg in Sarajevo.

On the same evening, the increased intensity of the fighting was exemplified when Boyneburg was shot in the head at close range. Thanks to the 'Trepanation' performed by Dr Velde, the Belgian legation physician, he began to recover rapidly, though he would die a year later from the effects of this wound.

A relatively secure footpath between two walls ran between the French and British legations. Frau Rosthorn used this daily to visit her wounded compatriots, in particular Boyneburg. Even though it was the least exposed of the legations, the British compound resembled a fortress: trenches had been dug; more than 40,000 sandbags filled and earthworks thrown up. These bristling defences also extended to the mental state of the British Minister, who became obsessed with the idea that the Austrians were organising opposition to his tenuous role as 'commander-in-chief'. Arthur Rosthorn, whose intellectual contempt for Macdonald was thinly disguised, soon found himself the object of increasing hostility on the part of the Minister. The formal break came over the rather modest matter of the Austrian naval detachment's spades.

These had been stored at the British legation, where they had been put to good use. When Arthur Rosthorn came to reclaim them, Macdonald pretended to know nothing about them. The same pantomime was played out when, a few minutes later, Rosthorn claimed the 60 days' worth of rice supplies of the Austrian naval detachment. A furious row ensued, culminating in Macdonald losing his cool and suddenly shouting at Frau Rosthorn who was with her husband that she 'should clean up immediately the mess she leaves on my floors! Immediately!'[8]

Macdonald was clearly feeling rather highly strung that afternoon but Arthur Rosthorn's response can be imagined. For about a minute it looked as if the two men were about to resort to the kind of violence hitherto reserved for the Boxers. But Macdonald stiffly backed down: 'I did not mean your wife to clean it up herself; one of her servants could oblige ...'. The break between the Austrian and British legations was total and Arthur Rosthorn swore never to set foot in the British legation again, even if it might save his life.

More and more bullets fell around the French legation where most of the Austrian naval detachment was now positioned. Arthur Rosthorn was wounded in the eye but Frau Rosthorn fortunately had her personal small bottle of cocaine, which relieved the pain. Captain Thomann however was not so lucky. As he stood discussing with the French commander D'Arcy how to help Rosthorn, a grenade exploded in front of him, killing him instantly. Throughout his time during the siege, notwithstanding the controversy over his early behaviour, Thomann had conducted himself heroically, constantly moving to the thick of the fighting. His burial in the French legation garden three hours later was conducted by an Italian priest under a hail of bullets. All present felt they had lost a brave comrade. The Austrian sailors had lost three of their officers as well as suffering a score of other casualties but, because they were Croats and only their NCOs spoke any German, it was difficult to keep track.

On 14 July, Bastille Day, the Austrians and French broke open the last bottles of champagne. The day began peacefully but as the afternoon wore on the unmistakable sounds of dissonant trombones announced another attack. This time a huge mine was exploded under the French legation, throwing Arthur Rosthorn into the air and burying him under several feet of earth. He later recalled that for nearly two minutes he had assumed in the utter darkness that he was dead until a second mine exploded, throwing him into the air once again and releasing him from this premature grave. At the same time, at the nearby German legation, 200 Chinese had penetrated the tennis court where a dozen German sailors fixed bayonets and, with much shouting of 'Hurrah', drove the panic-stricken Chinese out without even firing a shot.

The following morning, Frau Rosthorn was invited by the acting German Minister to make her quarters in the German legation, where she was pleasantly surprised by the 'calm and order' that prevailed. 'We could almost forget that we were at war.'[9] Flowers were brought to the table and every bullet hole or piece of shell splinter was tidied up as soon as possible and all traces of the dust removed, 'so that one could almost imagine the bullet or grenade simply had not exploded in the German legation'. There was even fresh water and starched linen. Her reaction typified the German–Austrian relationship and the Austrians' admiration for German order: another portent of things to come.

The relief of the legations boosts the k. (u.) k. navy

By 17 July a kind of armistice appeared to reign and a curious exchange of messages between the ministers and the Chinese was initiated. A few days later telegram links with the outside world were restored and Rosthorn received the news that two Austrian warships were on their way under Admiral Montecuccoli to relieve the legations. The Austrian sailors threw their caps into the air when Rosthorn read the telegram to them. It looked as if the Austrian contingents might be the first to arrive. One young officer in the relief force on board SMS *Kaiserin und Königin Maria Theresia* was Georg von Trapp, the only k. (u.) k. officer to have been immortalised by Hollywood.

When the 20,000-strong relief force finally arrived on 17 August, the Austrian contingent consisted of 27 sailors under the command of Midshipman Lechanowsky. They had marched for the last nine days across much difficult terrain. Barely a footnote in the story of the Habsburg armed forces, the significance of the Imperial and Royal naval presence in Peking during the summer of 1900 exceeded all expectations with regard to encouraging domestic public support for the Habsburg navy. The successful defence of the legations coupled with the publicity given to the international relief column generated much excitement back in Vienna. Toy soldiers were manufactured depicting the Austrian navy's heroic defence, complete with Maxim gun and, condescendingly, fleeing Boxers. It became the height of fashion to dress children in naval uniforms, a tradition continued to this day by the Vienna Boys' Choir.[10]

Two years later, the elevation of the heir apparent, Franz Ferdinand to the rank of admiral injected new impetus into the activities of the navy. A comprehensive and ambitious programme of naval expansion was initiated, first under Admiral Spaun and then Admiral Montecuccoli. The Boxer Rebellion harnessed the public's support for this programme as well, complementing the Archduke's own enthusiasm, born of his own 'World tour' in 1892–93 as a young man on board the light cruiser *Kaiserin Elisabeth*.

The Habsburg navy ships: the dreadnought *Viribus Unitis*

In the last twenty years of its existence the Imperial and Royal Navy 'flew the flag' on more than 85 so-called 'Missionsreisen' of which 34 were to Eastern Asia. Notwithstanding huge arguments over financing and budgets, the navy underwent significant modernisation. The determination to be the leading naval power of the Adriatic in the face of rising Italian competition became a strategic imperative. To the relatively modest 'Monarch' class of capital ships were added the 'Habsburg', 'Radetzky' and 'Erzherzog Karl' classes, which enjoyed significantly increased armour and gunnery.

The 'Monarch' class, like the older 'Aspern' and 'Kaiserin und Königin Maria Theresia' which had seen service in China, were light cruisers with crews of barely 450. They had been designed with coastal duties along the Adriatic in mind though they were to be used not only as far afield as China, but as supports for civilian evacuation during the Spanish-American War off Cuba, and during the Crete crisis of 1897–98 as well.

The 'Radetzky' and 'Habsburg' classes took the navy to another level. At 8,232, tons the 'Habsburg' represented a significant increase in size and were the first battleships which could be considered truly 'ocean-going'. This ambitious naval programme fell victim to the annual feuding over naval budgets between the Austrian and Hungarian parliaments. The Hungarians saw little value to the Hungarian taxpayer in supporting a programme of ship construction which took place in Trieste, a key city of the Austrian part of the Empire. Admiral Spaun resorted to many wiles to get his naval estimates approved but in 1904 the ever-fractious politicians successfully moved a reduction in the naval budget of 50 per cent, and Spaun resigned. Spaun's replacement, Rudolf Montecuccoli, renewed the struggle with the politicians. Supported by the Archduke Franz Ferdinand, he succeeded in winning approval for the next class, the 'Radetzky', which resembled the British 'King Edward VII' class, having a main armament of four 30.5cm guns laid out in twin turrets. When the 'Radetzky' turned up at the Coronation Naval Review at Spithead in 1911 it was praised for its sharp lines and very comfortable officers' quarters. With a crew of nearly 900 officers and men it demonstrated how far the Imperial and Royal Navy had come in less than a dozen years.

The later 'Tegetthoff' class of 'Dreadnoughts' (all big-gun ships, named after HMS *Dreadnought* launched in 1906, the first ship to enjoy uniform battery armament) were designed by the renowned ship's architect Siegfried Popper. Popper had been born in Prague in 1848. Overseeing in the late 1860s the construction of more modest Austrian warships at the Armstrong works in Newcastle, he became friends with the chief naval architect of the British Royal Navy, Sir William White, who was much impressed by Popper's brilliance and superior calculative ability. Popper's friendship with White meant that he was kept fully abreast of English innovations in the projected 'Dreadnought' class. His own 'Tegettfhoff'-class 'Dreadnoughts' would come to be considered some of the most impressive warships of their class anywhere in the world and famously were the first ships ever to have been constructed with triple 30.5cm-gun turrets.[11]

Once again, infighting among the politicians led to skilful ruses to secure funding on the part of the navy. Montecuccoli had announced on 20 February

1909 that Austria would be building a new generation of battleship, of nearly 19,000 tons displacement, to head off Italy's proposed construction of a 'Dreadnought' rival. When the politicians balked at the expenditure, Montecuccoli persuaded both the Triestine shipyard and the Skoda armaments factory to begin work on construction at their own risk while the Admiral whipped up a public relations campaign involving virtually every powerful figure in the Empire from the Emperor downwards.

Construction was approved on credit and the politicians left to rubber-stamp the process when their bickering died down. When the STT shipyard in Trieste voiced objections, Montecuccoli literally drew out of his pocket a personal cheque written on his account for 32 million crowns (about £12 million in today's money). Work began on the first two ships: the *Viribus Unitis* and the *Tegetthoff*. The Hungarians eventually agreed to support the programme on condition that one ship was given a Hungarian name, the *Szent István* (St Stephen, Hungary's patron saint) and constructed in the Hungarian port of Fiume (Rijeka).[12]

The *Viribus Unitis*, commissioned in 1912, contained many features that were innovative in the design of battleships, notably with regard to its radio-telegraphy systems. A particularly interesting feature of the design was the main armament of twelve 30.5cm guns, carried in four triple turrets, arranged in two superimposed pairs fore and aft on the centre line. Like all Austrian mountings, these were electrically driven and could elevate to 20 degrees, firing a 450 kilogram shell capable of penetrating 47cm of armour up to three miles away. Popper's design weaknesses, sadly only too soon to reveal themselves, were confined to the retention of the 'mine bottom' whose space between hull and bulkhead would in the event of a torpedo hit be too small for the resultant expanding gases.

As the great crisis of 1914 approached, the Dual Monarchy could take some comfort in the fact that it possessed a significant naval force, greater in tonnage than its Italian rival. In addition, a naval air arm began to take form from 1910. It would prove itself more than equal to the challenges ahead. The heir to the Imperial throne, Archduke Franz Ferdinand expressed some satisfaction in the way his personal interests had prevailed with the development of the fleet. But in the army, the situation was less happy. A number of crises came to focus the Archduke's attention on shortcomings and weaknesses. Coupled with wider strategic disagreements, the relationship between *Thronfolger* (heir) and General Staff would be stretched to breaking point.

CHAPTER 19

The Evidenzbüro and Colonel Redl.

THE k. (u.) k. ARMY ON THE EVE OF CATASTROPHE

The rivalry between Russia and Austria-Hungary over the Balkans brought with it an increase in military intelligence activity as the nineteenth century drew to a close. What had been the preserve of a few staff officers of the Generalquartierstab (Quartermaster general staff; after 1865 Generalstab), rapidly increased in scope and numbers. As in other important areas of her armed forces, Austria's military intelligence capabilities were intrinsically bound up with the sensitivities of the dynasty.

Habsburg military intelligence: the Evidenzbüro

As early as 1801, intelligence 'offices' had been established along the Military Frontier and a budget of more than 100,000 gulden was sanctioned for their activities in 1812.[1] As Radetzky pointed out, the results of these activities were 'pitiful'. It fell to Feldmarschallleutnant Hess to create the first 'Intelligence Section' in 1843. Hess had experienced at first hand some of the poor intelligence of the Austrians during the coalition wars.

In 1850, this section was incorporated into the 'All-Highest Imperial Royal Central Operations Chancery' and on 22 December that year it was transformed into an autonomous body reporting to the Staff. The new section was given the name Evidenzbüro. It was to be commanded by Major Kalik, whose discretion and linguistic skills were widely perceived as making him the obvious choice for the new office. Its peacetime activities were limited to gathering information on the size and formation of foreign armies. In the war archives of Vienna there is an extensive example of an early effort in this direction, namely a remarkably detailed report on the state and condition of the British army.

Kalik led the new organisation for fifteen years. In addition to some 2,000 gulden in ducats and silver florins for 'special purposes', Kalik was to receive 'support' from the Austrian diplomats abroad. In practice, this meant the establishment of a military attaché in the legations and embassies of the monarchy. This support was erratic. For example, in 1859, as relations deteriorated with France, Colonel Johann von Loewenthal arrived in Paris to assess the French military structure. But his running of agents did not begin until 13 May, barely a fortnight before hostilities. From the start, his agents were divided into paid agents and so-called 'V' *Vertrauen* (confidence) men. These were Austrian patriots working abroad prepared to provide information without material reward.

In 1866, these efforts were more successful during the war with Prussia. So effective were they that the Prussian movements towards Bohemia were all communicated well in advance to the Austrians. Unfortunately, some of the 'Cavalry of St George', were also in the pay of the Prussians.

In 1871, on the retirement of Kalik, by now a major-general, a new officer, Colonel von Hoffinger took over the Evidenzbüro. Hoffinger focused his resources on Italy. With the introduction of conscription, he also devoted his activities to the increasingly important issue of mobilisation times. Because these depended on railway timetables, the Austrian General Staff began to examine in great detail the organisation and efficiency of these routes. Here the work of the attaché was critical. He would make up to twenty journeys a year to compile with extravagant exactitude the distances and timings of the most important rail routes available to a potential enemy. Often, windfalls came their way after long service. For example a copy of the complete Italian mobilisation plans reached Vienna via a veteran attaché in St Petersburg. The military men were assisted by a new generation of diplomats, graduates of the Imperial and Royal Oriental Academy, who began to fill the growing number of consular posts. Some of these would become significant figures in the later foreign policy of the Empire, for example Baron Burian who as Consul in Moscow had to be restrained from pursuing too aggressive a line in intelligence gathering. Another highly effective consul in this regard was the Vice-Consul in Warsaw, Julius Pinter, from 1883 to 1885 staff officer in the Evidenzbüro.[2]

But as this activity increased, other nations also began to invest in their intelligence apparatus. In the 1870s, military espionage in Austrian Poland (Galicia-Lodemeria) became ever more important. A consequence of this activity was the establishment of a counter-espionage organisation for the first time in Imperial military structures. This proved highly effective, not least because the Russians had yet to develop their offensive intelligence-gathering capacity to a high level. A few years later, after 1895, the Russians overhauled their entire intelligence-gathering system, and the balance changed.

A consequence of the development of Russia's military intelligence activities against the monarchy was the increased cooperation between the Evidenzbüro and its German equivalent, the Imperial German Kundschaftdienst. This was illustrated vividly in 1889 when a Russian spy, Wenzel Marek, stole the plans for the great Austrian Galician fortress of Przemyśl. Unaware of the degree of cooperation between the two organisations, he allowed himself to be tricked on to German soil where he was promptly arrested and handed over to the Austrians before he could dispose of the plans to the Russians.

Marek's capture brought an instant Russian response. They rounded up 29 suspected Austrian agents, who were later executed. The Emperor Franz-Josef, who followed the activities of his Evidenzbüro carefully, noted on the documents detailing all this: 'The families of these people must be cared for as it is important that such dangerous and self-sacrificing duties do not go unrewarded.'[3] The arrest a little later by the Tsar's police of the Russian colonel Grimm, who was working for the Germans, brought equally negative consequences for Austrian military espionage activities because Grimm had revealed the close relationship between the Austrians and the Germans in matters of shared intelligence.

The tempo of activity against Russia was stepped up. Two officers from the Austrian General Staff were sent each year to Kazan to learn Russian, a circumstance which horrified the Russian War minister Wannowski, who noted when asked by the Austrian Ambassador whether more officers could be sent: 'You ask that we should give Austria the weapons with which to destroy us!'[4] Under Desiderius Kolossváry de Kolossvár, and later Artur Giesl von Gieslingen, activities were stepped up, not only against Russia but also against Belgrade, where the spectacular murder of the King and Queen by a group of army officers in 1903 had transferred the crown of that country from the pro-Austrian Obrenovič dynasty to the increasingly pro-Russian Karadjordjević.[5]

Artur Giesl von Gieslingen was the elder brother of Vladimir Giesl von Gieslingen who had attained high rank in the army and was minister in Belgrade in 1914. Artur Giesl enjoyed the particular confidence of the Emperor, being one of the first to find the dead bodies of Crown Prince Rudolf and his mistress. The murder of the Crown Prince by agents in collusion with powerful circles in France around Georges Clemenceau (1841–1929) has never been substantiated but this plausible version of events remained submerged in the carefully constructed myth of the Mayerling suicide until the late Empress Zita revealed some tantalising details of a very different interpretation of those events on her return to Austria in 1982 to the writer Erich Feigl.[6]

A web of agents and consulates began to cover Serbia in the closing years of the 1890s. As the new century dawned, more targets emerged. In 1902, the Italian intelligence machinery which had been directed against France for many years started to orientate itself more aggressively towards the Dual Monarchy. Irredentist propaganda was stepped up in Trieste and Trento, ably supported by the Italian Consul in the Austrian harbour city, Galli.[7]

Italian officers started visiting Austrian border areas with increasing frequency, and some were even detained briefly. From 1900 until 1907, a spate of spy trials fascinated the Viennese public, a sure sign that tensions were increasing between the powers within a Europe that still seemed outwardly so calm. Then as today, the intensity of the intelligence activities was a weathervane for the political climate. The Chief of the General Staff Conrad's response was to advocate war. In a fierce inter-departmental row with Aehrenthal, Conrad lost out. The Emperor and the Archduke Franz Ferdinand both backed peace and Conrad was dismissed in 1911. He was replaced by the utterly unknown General Blasius Schemua, a Slovene. But the crisis of the Balkan wars appeared to confirm the dangers the monarchy faced and Aehrenthal's death in 1912 paved the way for Conrad's return. His reappointment undoubtedly strengthened the war party.

By spring 1913, the political temperature was rising fast. The idea that the First World War broke like a thunderstorm in a bright blue undisturbed sky has become a popular myth, especially in Britain. Statesmen in every European country and indeed in the United States knew that war was imminent and that it would be on a hitherto unprecedented scale. Few indeed could foresee its duration, but that it was coming could not be doubted. In the highly charged twentieth-century debate on war guilt, all countries had a vested interest in playing down their foreknowledge of terrible events, but the facts as reported by the Evidenzbüro disprove this particular strain of myopia. As Robert Graves pointed out in his brilliant autobiography, *Goodbye to All That*, even British generals toured the public schools officer training corps in 1912 predicting a war with Germany within eighteen months.

Balkan tensions

The two Balkan wars illuminated the landscape like forks of lightning before the storm. By 1913, no one in public affairs could honestly pretend that peace lay ahead. The Ambassadors' Conference in London had avoided the conflagration partly by the creation of an independent Albanian state but elsewhere the signs were unmistakable. The Austrian military intelligence posts noted these signs: the vast increase in defensive works constructed along the Italian side of the Austrian frontier in the Dolomites; the dramatic extension of Italian railways. The military attaché in Belgrade, Major Otto Gellinek, noted that every Serbian officer expected to invade Bosnia as soon as Franz-Josef died. A report from a Romanian diplomat landed in the Evidenzbüro's Vienna headquarters on 6 May 1913. It disclosed the view that some circles in Serbia wished to involve Russia in a 'great European war' that would dismember the Habsburg Empire's Slav provinces.

The Serbian minister, Pasič, during his visit to St Petersburg five months earlier, had requested artillery and other weapons for the 'imminent war', promising the Russians that he would 'tie down at least one Austrian division'. These moves were known elsewhere in Europe and the contrast between the facade of normality and the undercurrents of intrigue tested both the dynasty and its senior officers. On the surface the only visible problem was that Oberleutnant Neustadl, a young reconnaissance officer, had disappeared along the Albanian–Serbian frontier a few weeks earlier and was feared, correctly as it turned out, to be dead.

Others in Vienna were also under no illusions. Stefan Zweig recalled bumping into Bertha von Suttner, the Nobel Peace Prize winner, on the streets of Vienna in early 1914, and her terrifying expression as she warned him that war was imminent and that the 'entire apparatus' of armaments was being 'relentlessly cranked up'. 'People do not realise what is going on!' she had almost screamed at him.[8]

Across the Alps in Rome, Pope Pius X saw very clearly that Europe would be engulfed in a terrible war. In 1913, he warned a stunned, departing Brazilian Ambassador that 'a terrible European war would come before 1914 was out'.[9] Pius X reckoned with the consequences for Vienna. His Cardinal Secretary of State, Merry del Val concluded an historic concordat with Serbia 'under great time pressure' less than a week before the Archduke Franz Ferdinand's assassination in 1914. The Vatican, impeccably connected with German and Austrian military circles, appears to have known of the impending explosion in the Balkans and to have been convinced that the dice would roll in Serbia's favour. Two years earlier, the Pontiff had told a startled Princess Zita that her husband not Franz Ferdinand would be Austria's next Emperor.

In England, even Sir Edward Grey was aware of what might be coming. At the Foreign Office his chief adviser, Arthur Nicolson, *primus inter pares* among the Germanophobe diplomats, had warned as early as 1909 that Britain would have to 'play the same role' with regard to Germany as she had with regard to Napoleonic France a century earlier, and Spain two hundred years before that.[10]

Even if Grey had disagreed with Nicolson, there were at least half a dozen senior diplomats with whom he was in regular contact who fully supported this thesis.[11]

These men held important positions and included: Eyre Crowe, Goschen, Bertie, Cartwright and Hardinge. Many of them owed their status and career advancement to their royal connections with the no less Germanophobe Edward VII. The Austrian military attaché in London could only observe with increasing concern the deterioration in Anglo-German relations. By the beginning of 1914, Grey was sufficiently convinced of imminent hostilities to be embroiled in talks between the Royal Navy and the Imperial Russian fleet aimed at cooperation in the Baltic against Berlin. These compromising discussions were leaked to the press by a German spy and caused the normally unflappable and upright Foreign Secretary to resort to some uncharacteristic evasion at Parliamentary Questions.[12]

In Germany the sense of ineluctable showdown was even more intense. The German General Staff were fixated on the planned extension of the Russian railway system but England loomed large in Berlin, where Edward VII's encirclement policies were perceived as a mortal threat. Edward had even asked Franz-Josef at Ischl to consider breaking off his alliance with Germany and Italy. In return, Edward pledged that the Royal Navy would bombard Ostia should Italy try anything. It was an offer Franz-Josef could not accept. He was, he pointed out, a loyal ally and 'a German prince'.[13]

The newly appointed German Ambassador to London, Lichnowsky, reported back on his first meeting with the War Minister Haldane. Haldane, who had studied at Göttingen, was considered to be a Germanophile. But even he noted that 'England could not tolerate Germany's becoming the dominant Power on the Continent and uniting it under her leadership'. England would therefore 'always side with France in a European war'. When he heard this, the German Kaiser exploded in rage and called an immediate 'war council'.[14]

Notwithstanding that it was a Sunday, army and naval leaders were summoned to discuss Lichnowsky's report. Haldane's statement was a 'desirable clarification of the situation for the benefit of those who had felt sure of England'. The German Kaiser insisted that the German fleet would 'naturally prepare itself for the war against England' with 'immediate submarine warfare against English troop transports in the Scheldt or around Dunkirk'. At this conference it is interesting to note Moltke's comment that 'war was unavoidable and the sooner the better'. Only Tirpitz counselled postponement until the Kiel Canal was completed. Though no friend of England, Tirpitz was certainly not an Anglophobe; he had, after all, sent his daughter to be educated at Cheltenham Ladies' College. The delay was to be exploited to 'prepare the press' for the coming war against Russia.[15]

In Russia equally hostile thoughts prevailed. In February 1914 an historic joint army and navy planning meeting was held at St Petersburg chaired by the Russian Foreign Minister, Sazonov. The inevitability of a European war was discussed, not for the first time. A few weeks earlier, the Tsar had told the British Ambassador that 'The disintegration of the Austrian Empire is merely a question of time.'[16] St Petersburg had already ascertained whether the Austrians could be beaten and the Austrian Evidenzbüro had unwittingly played a critical role.

Major Wyndham's hint

One morning in the early February of 1909, a young Russian Guards officer called on the Austrian military attaché in St Petersburg, Major Lelio Spannocchi. The Russian offered his 'services' to the Austrian, in particular the details of the Russian fortifications around Warsaw where his uncle was in charge of the fortress construction department. The astonished Spannocchi was speechless. Fearing the visitor to be an agent provocateur, he offered the officer an innocuous address and asked him to leave, without shaking hands.[17]

As it happened, later that day Spannocchi was having tea with the British military attaché, Major Guy Wyndham. Wyndham was a veteran of the Boer War, well connected, married to a Cornwallis-West and together they represented, in Spannocchi's words, 'an utterly delightful couple who allowed me to get to know and treasure the fine ways of English domesticity'.[18]

When Spannocchi recounted the story, expressing his revulsion towards so blatant an act of treason (Franz-Josef had expressly forbidden his military attachés to engage in any running of agents), Wyndham quietly observed: 'You know, Spannocchi, you should not be so proud or surprised. These things happen; I understand the Russians have a very highly placed source somewhere in your General Staff who gives them everything they want.'[19]

Major Wyndham did not elaborate but if he had hoped his indiscretion to pass as a throwaway remark, he was to be disappointed. Wyndham's motivation for this indiscretion has long fascinated writers. Markus believes Wyndham did not get along with his Ambassador, Arthur Nicolson, who passionately advocated Russian interests. Wyndham as a veteran of the Boer War may simply have remembered the generous Habsburg support for the British cause in that conflict, in contrast to Germany.[20]

So seriously did Spannocchi take the hint that a few days later in Vienna, on leave, he confided the details of the conversation to the recently appointed Head of the Evidenzbüro, Colonel Eugen Hordlicka.

Hordlicka had replaced Artur Giesl von Gieslingen as Evidenzbüro chief and was keen to stamp his authority on the organisation. But on hearing Spannocchi out, Hordlicka was unimpressed: 'I insist, Major that you do not destabilise us with such idle gossip (*Tartarenmeldungen*). Imagine the consequences for the entire General Staff if the Emperor were to hear such a thing. This kind of news can only be presented when one has firm evidence in the hand.'21

The ensuing row between the two officers must have shaken the walls of the Evidenzbüro chief's office. Spannocchi, unamused that such reliable intelligence should instantly be discarded, drew himself up to his full height and reminded Hordlicka that as military attaché he was not answerable to the Evidenzbüro but directly to the Minister of War. 'If you do not wish to give any weight to my judgement, I shall descend to the floor below this office and present this information to the Minister personally and recommend the immediate surveillance of the General Staff.'

At this Hordlicka gave way, urging Spannocchi not to be so rash. The Evidenzbüro would investigate the accusation. He, personally, would not directly involve himself but his deputy would take all the details and compile a report. At this moment the deputy was summoned and a short plump officer in the green and black velvet uniform of the General Staff shuffled into the office.

'Have you met Colonel Redl?' Hordlicka asked Spannocchi. 'You can tell him everything you know. He is our best military counter-espionage expert.' A few minutes later safely ensconced in Redl's office Spannocchi told the officer about Wyndham's news. As Spannocchi later recalled: 'Redl turned bright red and looked at a chest of drawers saying that all my reports had been received and carefully filed; an utter irrelevance!'22

But Count Spannocchi was far from suspecting this colonel whose reputation was still in the ascendant. Redl told Spannocchi to 'keep the information to himself' while he discreetly 'investigated'. A few days later, on his return to St Petersburg, Spannocchi found he suddenly had to deal with many reports which were critical of his activities. A curious conspiracy now engulfed him and within six months he was tersely informed that he was recalled to his regiment. When he queried this, Spannocchi was told that someone of his junior rank was not appropriate for the military representation to such an important country as Russia. A general or, at the very least, a full colonel would replace him.

From the beginning, Spannocchi realised he had offended some powerful elements in the military by his behaviour, but not for a moment did he suspect Redl. Rather, he felt the 'humourless' Hordlicka with 'his unattractive sounding name' was to blame. Here was another case of the social tensions that infected the armed services. In this instance the friction between a headstrong cavalry count whose ancestors had fought at Hohenlinden and the cautious and bureaucratic military intelligence officer with the ugly name was sharper than usual.

In such a dispute, the Emperor could be relied upon to take the side of Spannocchi and, to Redl's great discomfort, Kaiser Franz-Josef refused to sign the order recalling Spannocchi. Fortunately for Redl, at this very moment the Russian military attaché in Vienna, Colonel Mitrofan Martchenko, was caught engaging in espionage and asked to leave. With a ruthlessness no doubt stemming from concern for his own skin, Redl now proceeded to involve Spannocchi in this scandal indirectly. Aware that the Russians would now be hypersensitive to any intelligence activities of the Austrian embassy in the wake of Martchenko's recall, Redl arranged for Spannocchi to be instructed to find 'concrete proof' concerning conscription estimates. The 'official' figures needed to be 'confirmed'.

Spannocchi arranged to meet a journalist, a Baltic German aristocratic adventurer by the name of Ungern-Sternberg. At their meeting Sternberg asked for 200 roubles and Spannocchi, under the surveillance of the Russian secret police, was now compromised by a simple and well-known entrapment device when Sternberg simply wrote in his notebook the words, 'Received from Graf Spannocchi : 200 Roubles'. When the police seized Sternberg, the career of the Austrian military attaché in Russia was over and the Count was asked to leave. Well might Spannocchi have asked how it was that the Russian authorities came to focus on Sternberg precisely at this time.

It would be two years before Spannocchi knew the answer. In the meantime, Colonel Redl was promoted and transferred to Prague. Films, plays and books have done little to clarify the career of Colonel Redl. Only one thing is clear: in the run-up to 1914, he supplied the Russian military high command with every possible detail concerning Austria's Order of Battle against Russia and possibly even Serbia. The latter was of particular interest to British military intelligence which, from 1909, spent considerable sums of money attempting to discover its details.[23] This fabulous trove of intelligence treasure gave the Russian army a clear advantage from the beginning of hostilities in 1914, despite subsequent modifications to the Austrian plans.

Redl's betrayal

Redl's significance lies in the fact that armed with his knowledge, the Russians saw the Habsburg armies for what they were: relatively poorly equipped, increasingly riven by national tensions and wholly unprepared to fight a major modern war, in particular against two foes.

A list of the plans betrayed to the Russians (and the French and Italians) is damning enough. The list presented to the members of the Austrian Reichsrat in 1913 still makes for staggering reading:

1. complete Order of Battle for the Imperial and Royal Army inclusive of all details of all garrison strengths in the event of the outbreak of war;

2. overview of all ammunition depots along the Russian frontier;

3. details of armaments deployed in all fortifications along the Russian frontier, including Przemyśl;

4. General Staff observations concerning the manoeuvres of 1909, in particular the quality of certain regiments and equipment;

5. full and extensive details concerning Austro-Hungarian mobilisation plans against Russia, Serbia and Italy.

In addition to these documents, Austrian spies in Russia, existing and potential, were swiftly unmasked, with Redl's help, and executed (notable among them the young Russian officer who had volunteered to work for Spannocchi).

How had such dramatic espionage come to be possible? Redl's career had been meteoric. Born in Lemberg, in 1864, the son of a minor railway official and one of seven children, he demonstrated his abilities while at the Moravian cadet school near Brünn at Karthaus. In 1892, he finished his training with glowing reports, becoming one of only twenty-five officer cadets granted entry to the prestigious Kriegschule, or staff academy, which educated fledgling staff officers. By this time, the staff officers were beginning to enjoy the same prestige and intellectual eminence as that which invested the German Great General Staff in the aftermath of Königgrätz. A gift for languages and good equestrian skills were basic requirements for those who would be entitled to wear the smart green uniform with black velvet facings, which was the staff officers' unique privilege. Redl had both these qualities; he was another testament to the social mobility that existed in the Habsburg monarchy.

A medical report dated 1891 noted syphilis, but the form with which Redl was infected at that time was not considered life-threatening. In fact the doctors were mistaken. The syphilis affected the officer's heart, and by 1913 he was a seriously ill man unlikely to live much longer.

But at this stage he was highly regarded and his upbringing in Lemberg had given him a facility for Slav languages which the staff academy soon put to good use. In particular, the Chief of the General Staff, Beck, became a powerful supporter of the young officer. Redl would later become one of the two officers sent each year to Kazan to study Russian. The presence of these officers on

Russian territory was well known to the Russian authorities and clearly Redl would have been watched carefully during his time there. With his flair for intelligence, it was inevitable that he would be attached to the Evidenzbüro.

It was not until 1901 that Redl was recruited to spy for the Russians by a shadowy figure of the Okhrana simply called Herr Pratt. Pratt, like so many Russian spies, was a Balt who spoke perfect German. He became a valuable agent for the Russians in Vienna. His mission was to recruit long-term agents in the Austrian military. Whether he, as some sources suggest, blackmailed Redl over an affair with a brother officer or whether the Austrian volunteered his services remains debatable. The latest research leans towards the latter. In any event, the Russians found they had a prize agent at the heart of the enemy. When Redl was transferred as chief of staff to the VIII Army Corps in Prague in 1912, the Russians had struck gold. Mobilisation plans, orders of battle, the entire paperwork of the army's intentions were carefully photographed and passed on. In no other country in Europe, barely a year before 1914, was so much valuable military intelligence betrayed. Knowing full well that war was imminent, the Russians stepped up their demands. The Prague Chief of Staff did not disappoint.

In return, he received thousands of crowns, which enabled him to enjoy the lifestyle which was the preserve of wealthy aristocratic cavalry officers. Redl was not one of those of whom it could be said he was 'as poor as a staff officer'. But he was not well, and he must have sensed that he would not live a great deal longer. The money and lifestyle had accelerated his decline and, as happens with many agents, he grew careless and complacent. At the beginning of April 1913, a letter, postmarked Berlin, arrived at a Poste Restante address in a Vienna post office. After the six-week time limit for collection had expired it was returned to the Berlin post authorities who, with dedicated Prussian thoroughness, opened the envelope to discover who the sender was.

Inside were 6,000 crowns in banknotes and two addresses, one in Geneva and the other in Paris. Both were known to Prussian officials as being associated with foreign agents. Major Walter Nicolai, the newly appointed head of the German military intelligence service, immediately informed his counterparts in the Evidenzbüro of his findings. Because it was clear that the spy must be in Vienna or at least visiting the Austrian capital, great pains were taken to set a trap should he or she come to collect the envelope. The original envelope had been tampered with, so an identical one was procured and given to the Germans to post.

On 25 May just as the Austrians had almost given up on identifying the spy, a man in civilian dress appeared and picked up the envelope along with two others which had arrived, addressed to 'Nikon Nizetas'. Three Vienna detectives had followed the man to the Stefansplatz where they had lost him because he had got into a motorised taxi and driven off, a rather rare event in 1913.

Colonel Redl's arrest and liquidation

The detectives noted the number of the car and awaited its return, then questioned the driver who arrived ten minutes later: he said that his passenger had asked to be driven to the Hotel Klomser. Inside the car was the case of a penknife with which the passenger had clearly opened the letters. The detectives set off for the Hotel Klomser, where they asked a startled receptionist which guest had just arrived by taxi. The answer came 'The Chief of the General Staff of the Prague Corps, Colonel Redl'. Now it was the turn of the detectives to appear surprised, and just as they had convinced themselves they had made a mistake, Redl appeared. One of the quick-minded men offered him the penknife case asking if the Colonel had lost it. He answered that he had and with that all doubt was removed.

Two of the detectives watched the entrances while the third telephoned Regierungsrat Gayer in the police department who, horrified at the report, picked up the phone to a Major Ronge in the Evidenzbüro who had been monitoring the case. Ronge recalled: 'I was silent for two minutes. Could the former member of our Evidenzbüro, the witness at so many key espionage trials really be a traitor?'[24] Ronge moved swiftly. First the Chief of the General Staff Conrad von Hötzendorf was informed as he was dining at the Grand Hotel on the Ring. Conrad was astonished but with his legendary absence of imagination he saw the case typically in superficial housekeeping terms. He made it clear to Ronge that Redl was not to be alive by dawn.

Ronge, accompanied by some other officers, headed for the Hotel Klomser to await Redl's return. But when they entered his room they found that he was in his nightshirt and attempting to take his life with a cord. Redl appeared a broken man. He insisted that he speak alone with Ronge. While the other officers waited in a nearby room Redl confessed to Ronge how he had spied for foreign states throughout 1910 and 1911 but he did not mention anything about the Austrian mobilisation plans, focusing more on technical details to do with reservists. He had no accomplices because, as Ronge noted, he had been 'in this business long enough to know that accomplices are the beginning of the end for a good spy'. Finally 'Redl asked for a revolver.'[25]

At this point Ronge was joined by another officer, Colonel Urbanski. Ronge had asked Redl if he had his own pistol. When Redl replied in the negative and asked again 'most humbly' for a revolver, there occurred yet another of those quintessential Austrian scenes where tragedy and comedy become mordantly juxtaposed. None of the officers present had their service automatics with them. No self-respecting k. (u.) k. officer ever carried one in Vienna. Ronge now set off across Vienna to catch a tram to the War Ministry on the Stubenring to find a recent issue Browning automatic in one of the ministry safes. In the meantime the condemned man wrote a letter to the commandant of the Prague Corps, his former colleague from the Evidenzbüro, Giesl, and another letter to Giesl's brother Vladimir, the Austro-Hungarian Minister in Belgrade. The contents of this letter have not come down to us but they cannot have been without relevance to the events of the following year in Belgrade. The time now was shortly before 1 a.m. The nearby Cafe Central was closing as Ronge returned with the Browning automatic. The Vienna night became silent, but the young Count Alphy Clary wandering back home after a jolly night out could not fail to notice the officers standing silently and seemingly aimlessly around the hotel.[26]

Ronge returned within an hour, placed the pistol on the table in Redl's room and walked out of the hotel. At 5 a.m., barely twelve hours after the fateful letter had been collected from the Vienna post office, a shot rang out and a police official waiting in the reception area rushed upstairs and checked the room. He found the door open and Colonel Redl dead on the floor. He had shot himself through the mouth. Outside perhaps the officers stiffened, clicked heels and saluted, then walked silently off into the night.

It became impossible to hush up the death of so senior and significant an officer of the General Staff. Too many people were involved for the secret to be kept watertight, and the means deployed to deal with Redl's treachery were controversial. The Archduke Franz Ferdinand in particular was outraged at what had happened. Not only was his strict Catholic upbringing revolted by the encouragement to suicide, but he questioned why the chance to interrogate Redl more fully about the details of his betrayal was lost. It became yet another bone of contention between him and Conrad.

The Archduke's criticisms ran into the sand of the monarch's military cabinet and when, in early January 1914, Franz-Josef fastened the prestigious Order of Leopold on the tunic of Colonel Urbanski, the matter was considered closed. Even so, a week later, the personal effects of the traitor were auctioned in Prague and a camera containing a film was bought by a schoolboy and developed. To his surprise it contained a copy of an order from the heir to the throne to the Prague Corps commander. When he showed this to an enterprising young reporter by the name of Egon Erwin Kisch, the journalist realised he had a scoop. The news reignited the scandal.[27]

This latest piece of Austrian *Schlamperei* (bungling) turned Franz Ferdinand apoplectic and, on 19 January, he telegraphed the War Minister stating that he was expecting those responsible to be punished for this indiscretion. The analysis of Redl's perceived damage to the military plans of the monarchy continued behind closed doors. There can be no doubt that Redl's betrayal inflicted immense injury on the monarchy's military security and reputation, but neither the destruction of the monarchy nor its initial defeats in 1914 can be attributed to him.

Arguably his most substantial military betrayal, the mobilisation and offensive plans in the event of war with Russia, were partly neutralised. A new plan was drawn up which changed the positioning of the right flank of the northern army so that it no longer concentrated behind the San and Dneister. The Russian general Danilow would later write that, on mobilising, the Austrians were not where he expected them to be.[28] This did not help the Austrians.

Indeed, even Redl's own VIII Corps, where he was chief of staff, would be switched to the Serbian front as opposed to the Russian front when hostilities broke out. The Soviet general and professor of war A. Swetchin, who served in the Imperial Russian High Command in 1914, later wrote that although they had 'hit the jackpot' with the plans Redl betrayed, 'in the event the changes the Austrian High Command made to the plans in 1914 made the documents more confusing than helpful'.[29] This has the ring of disinformation about it and Russia's swift mobilisation and the excellent performance of her troops belie this comment. Russia had already mobilised some units as early as February 1914.[30]

On the political level, Redl's information gave the Russian army confidence. Although it was strongly denied at the time by the internal investigation led by Freiherr von Georgi, it would seem that some information concerning Germany was also betrayed. It should also be noted that Redl was not only working for the Russians. Both the Italians and French were supplying him with money and in the case of France it must be asked what interest they could have had in military intelligence concerning an army that was to be deployed almost exclusively on the eastern or southern fronts.[31]

We may never know whether the famous 'Schlieffen Plan' of the German General Staff, which contributed directly to Britain's entry into the war in 1914, reached London and Paris via Redl. Winston Churchill in his memoirs strongly hints that the Schlieffen Plan was in the hands of the Entente long before hostilities began.[32]

Consequences of the Redl affair

Irrespective of the extent of the betrayal, the Redl affair ignited the national and social rivalries which were coming to affect the army with each year that passed. The *Budapest*, a Hungarian daily, wrote on 3 June 1914: 'The Redl affair cannot be seen as a private matter. Redl is not a single person but a system in which ... an absence of patriotism in this unhappy Monarchy is considered the highest form of military virtue.... The Austro-Hungarian soldier does not possess a Fatherland.'[33] A glimpse at the table from the Austrian *Military Yearbook* for 1910 shows how rich the tapestry of different nationalities in the armed forces was on the eve of the First World War.[34]

Social tensions also found an outlet in the Redl affair. Inspired by the Archduke Franz Ferdinand whose views were conservative, a new outbreak of the old nineteenth-century debate on the social origins of the Imperial and Royal officer class arose. Inevitably it was suggested that Redl's betrayal had stemmed from his 'plebeian origins'. For those officers whose advancement had stemmed from ability, or courage on the battlefield, Redl threatened to discredit the high regard with which the non-aristocratic officer corps was held.

This nervousness inevitably affected the public security apparatus. On the same day that the *Budapest* article appeared, all provincial cities of the monarchy were instructed to establish a counter-intelligence bureau under the control of the Vienna police bureau. As the tensions between nationalities grew, one group, which had played an increasingly important part in the Imperial and Royal Army, felt itself threatened by the growth of German nationalism and shrill anti-Semitism: the Jews.

As a consequence of the introduction of compulsory universal military service in 1868, the numbers of Jewish recruits into the Imperial and Royal Army had risen steadily. In 1872, the number of Jewish soldiers was estimated as 12,471. By 1902, this number had risen to nearly 60,000.[35]

In certain areas such as the medical corps and the administrative branches of the army, the Jews were well represented, but it would be a mistake to imagine that they were not also present in line regiments, where the number of Jews was slightly higher than average. Their linguistic abilities and their knowledge of the 'Kommandosprache' of the army made them especially in demand as NCOs. In 1886 out of 38 candidates for the rank of NCO in the 5th Corps Artillery regiment 26 were Jewish. It is clear from these figures that in the Imperial and Royal Army there was far less anti-Semitism than in any other army in Europe at that time, and there were no formal restrictions regarding the entry of Jews into the army 'be it as officers or as enlisted men'.[36]

This enlightened attitude also contrasted favourably with some civilian walks of life. In 1910, Moritz Frühling, himself a Jew, wrote: 'It is to the honour of the Austrian Military Administration that among all other departments it is the only one which shows a truly modern and liberal attitude towards the Jewish citizens.'[37]

Kaiser Franz-Josef regarded the German nationalists with suspicion and was profoundly disturbed by the anti-Semitic rhetoric both of Georg von Schönerer and of Karl Lueger, the Mayor of Vienna who used anti-Semitism as a political tool. Lueger, on being elected mayor, was not granted an audience with the Emperor for nearly a year. When Franz-Josef finally consented to see him, he received him standing and instead of the usual banal formula of congratulations gave the surprised Lueger a lecture on the evils of anti-Semitism. A crestfallen Lueger, asked afterwards how the Emperor had received him, told his astonished audience that the Emperor had said: 'Ich will ka Judenhetz in Wien! Lass meine Juden in Ruh' ('I do not want Jew-baiting in Vienna. Leave my Jews in peace').[38]

Arthur Schnitzler recalled in his memoirs that Lueger was not in his view a 'convinced' anti-Semite. He was a frequent guest in many Jewish homes in Vienna, the Schnitzlers' included. He used anti-Semitism ruthlessly as a political weapon to win votes.[39] With regard to the Jews in the army, Franz-Josef was even more supportive. Anti-Semitism revolted him especially in this context, given the bravery shown by Jews on the battlefields of 1878. The Emperor was heard to observe in the late 1880s: 'More than 30,000 Jewish soldiers serve in my army. Many a smaller European state might be glad to have as many soldiers in its army altogether.'[40]

In the army, incidents of anti-Semitism were rare, and many Jewish officers confirmed that even officers with Pan-German attitudes seldom displayed anti-Semitic bias on duty. In one infamous incident, the Archduke Friedrich blocked the promotion of a Jewish officer in the cavalry which was part of his 5th Corps command. These were isolated events. On the whole the Imperial and Royal officer well understood that his duty placed him above the petty nationalist issues of the day. As in 1619, his allegiance was not to any particular nationality or confession but to the dynasty.

The Ehren Codex and the duel

This sense of a 'higher loyalty' was nowhere more apparent than in the honour code of the army, known as the 'Ehren Codex'. The ultimate instrument of enforcement was not just the military tribunal but the duel. In the late 1890s, although Jews were still denied the so-called 'Satisfaktionsfähigkeit' (the capability to fight a duel) at universities, in the army they were considered as capable of satisfaction as any other officer.

There are many recorded instances of this. In some cases duels had to be fought if both contestants were to retain their commissions. In the elite Dragoon regiment Nr 2 for example, one officer cadet insulted a Jewish officer without granting him 'satisfaction' because he considered a Jew unworthy of a duel – an attitude shared by many students' fraternities at this time. When Feldmarshallleutnant Wilhelm Gradl, the commander of the Vienna Cavalry Division, heard of this, he personally addressed the cadets, emphasised that a Jewish cadet was to be respected as much as any non-Jewish one and ordered that the duel take place within 24 hours. In the event, the duel sent both men to hospital for a few days and the matter was then forgotten.[41] The duel involving a Jewish officer was immortalised in both Schnitzler's *Leutnant Gustl* and Joseph Roth's *Radetzkymarsch*.[42] On another occasion, the Emperor himself intervened in a dispute concerning whether a Jewish officer was eligible for membership of the Jockey Club.

By 1914 nearly 18 per cent of all reserve officers were Jews, drawn from the universities where, by the turn of the century, nearly 21 per cent of students were Jews. They regarded the tunic that hung for most of the year in their wardrobe as the ultimate symbol of their acceptance in the land of their birth. In many areas of life in the Empire, the more extreme forms of anti-Semitism simply did not prevail. The proportion of Jewish officers in the Hungarian Honvéd was even higher. Such numbers contrasted starkly with the numbers of Jewish officer cadets in other European armies, notably that of Prussia, which rejected some 30,000 Jews for the officer corps over a comparable six-year period. The appalling 'Dreyfus affair', which so demoralised the French military, could never have happened anywhere in the Imperial and Royal Army. When the First World War broke out, the first Austrian soldier to die for the Imperial colours would be a Jew by the name of Dukatenzähler.[43]

But, even in June 1914, thoughts of such a conflict were still speculative. We shall probably never know how many believed the trigger would come on the Feast of St Vitus, 28 June 1914 in Sarajevo. Two weeks before the Archduke set off with his wife for Sarajevo the Evidenzbüro received a new chief, Colonel Oskar Hranilović-Czvetassin. He was about to become extremely busy.

CHAPTER 20

The Military Road to Sarajevo

The details of the assassination of the Archduke Franz Ferdinand continue to excite historians. Yet few focus on the peculiar coincidence that so many of the protagonists were wearing the uniform of k. (u.) k. officers. The perspective the Austro-Hungarian army throws on these melancholy events is illuminating. The unfortunate Archduke was a high-ranking military official as well as heir to the throne. Franz Ferdinand would not have been in Sarajevo had he not been attending manoeuvres in his capacity as inspector-general of the army. The invitation and the timing of the manoeuvres had been determined by the General Staff. His host was another high-ranking officer, Oskar Potiorek, and the Archduke's security was in his hands. At two critical moments in the coming days another officer, Erik von Merizzi, Potiorek's ADC would play a significant and unfortunate cameo role.

The Archduke's itinerary

A scrap of paper is perhaps a strange trigger for an examination of the cataclysm of June 1914. Yet no matter how much is written about the events in Sarajevo on 28 June, no matter how many gruesome exhibits of those sombre events are put on display, it is this apparently harmless document that is the most unnerving. Notwithstanding its refined layout and typeface, the printed itinerary of the Archduke Franz Ferdinand's visit to Sarajevo is particularly sinister, and perhaps as much to blame as anything for starting the First World War. Between the sections marked 10.30 a.m. and 11.30 a.m., the details of the Heir Apparent's route to Sarajevo refer twice to the seemingly harmless 'Appel-Kai'. The Appel-Kai or Quay was a relatively short road running along the Miljačka river between the town hall of Sarajevo and the railway station.

As it was bounded on one side by the river it afforded a potential assassin an unrestricted view of his intended victim. By mentioning this road and the timings so precisely, the official itinerary gave, intentionally or unintentionally, all the information any assassin would need as to where in the city he should place himself that morning for a guaranteed opportunity to shoot the Archduke. This simple piece of paper is not so much a timetable as an open invitation to murder; an archducal death warrant, on Imperial military stationery.

The visit was part of a larger programme organised by the army. With soldierly thoroughness, details of the distribution list of the itinerary were kept. Of the 187 copies that were printed, 27 were sent to the military governor of Bosnia-Hercegovina, 35 were sent to various other ministries and a further eight were distributed to each of two corps headquarters (III and XV) of the Imperial and Royal Army. The remaining 117 were sent to Sarajevo in the spring of 1914.[1] Around the middle of March, one of these had found its way onto the desk of the duty officer of Serbian Military Intelligence at the very moment when the crisis in relations between the Serbian military and the Serbian government was entering a new and difficult phase. The Serbian government, led by Nikola Pasič, a pro-Russian politician, was trying to cut the wings of the Serbian military or at least dramatically reduce its influence over policy.[2]

There was nothing unusual in inviting Franz Ferdinand, in his new role as army inspector-general, to attend manoeuvres in Bosnia. But the invitation has to be seen against the backdrop of the deteriorating relationship between the Archduke and his Chief of Staff, Conrad von Hötzendorf. The idea had first been bruited in late October 1913, shortly after Conrad had had a blazing row with Franz Ferdinand and had tendered his resignation. The row had been simmering for some months and was partly triggered by Conrad's repeated insistence that the Habsburg army prepare for an imminent war with Serbia and Russia. When the Archduke at manoeuvres had ordered the deployment of some troops without consulting Conrad, harsh words were exchanged. The Archduke even solemnly threatened Conrad that if he persisted in his course of thinking he 'would end up like Wallenstein'.[3]

Colonel Bardolff, the head of Franz Ferdinand's military chancery, later recalled how a few months earlier, in February 1913, he had attempted to advance Conrad's recommendations for a war with Serbia and Russia, only to be cut short by the Archduke:

I had barely finished speaking when Franz Ferdinand, in the presence of his wife, exploded with emotion. 'Conrad's idea is madness! A war with Russia will be the end of us. If we attack Serbia, Russia will support her and we shall have a war with Russia. Should the Russian Tsar and the Austrian Emperor push each other off their thrones in order to open the road for revolution? Tell Conrad that I reject completely any further suggestions in this direction' ('*weitere Vorstellungen in dieser Richtung entschieden ablehne*').[4]

Bardolff recalled the exchange: 'It was a scene that has remained with me for the rest of my life.'

These views of the Archduke did not go unnoticed in Berlin, where they caused increasing concern in military circles that were planning for a war against Russia. The Archduke was appointed Inspector of the Army, a post which carried more weight than it had in the days of the Archduke Albrecht. In war, Franz Ferdinand could be expected to exercise presumptive supreme command.[5] No less a general than von Schlieffen expressed his concern at the Archduke's Russophile sentiments. 'Your Heir to the throne is very friendly towards the Russians indeed' ('Ihr Thronfolger ist wohl sehr russenfreundlich') von Schlieffen announced grimly one day to a startled Austrian military attaché, Count Joseph Stürgkh.[6]

Six months later the arguments had been revisited with even more passion. Conrad wrote to his mistress Gina Reininghaus that he felt 'immense relief' to have resigned from a position that was 'unworkable'. But a few days later, a personal apology and plea by the Archduke persuaded Conrad to stay on. The two men seemingly agreed to differ on the question of military action against Serbia. A month later, the invitation to attend manoeuvres was formally extended by Conrad's long-time colleague, the military governor of the two provinces, Feldmarschallleutnant Oskar Potiorek, after consultations with Conrad.

Oskar Potiorek

Potiorek was a neurotic, secretive bachelor with repressed homosexual procliv-ities. He had been the runner-up for the post of Chief of the General Staff in 1906 when Conrad had been appointed with the Archduke's backing. Diligent, hard-working and devoted to the service, he took the news of Conrad's appointment badly. His failure to get the top job made him even more mis-anthropic, choleric and misogynistic. He eventually accepted the Bosnia post as a prestigious consolation prize, though even the Emperor wondered whether someone who was so obviously a misogynist (*Weibfeind*) was suitable for such a sensitive post.

The idea of tacking on to the Archduke's military programme a 'civil' visit to Sarajevo came from Potiorek. It would give his 'frontier' posting a huge injection of publicity. The idea appealed also to the Archduke. It offered him an opportunity to familiarise himself further with the provinces, accompanied by his wife. The stifling protocol of the Habsburg capital constantly dictated an inferior position to the Archduke's wife on account of her not being considered *ebenbürtig* (of equal birth-status).

Countess Sophie Chotek's old and illustrious Bohemian family did not belong to one of those families recognised by the Habsburg house laws as being worthy of marital union with the Imperial house. Franz Ferdinand had had to acknowledge his wife's unsuitability as consort of a future Habsburg Emperor. He was compelled to contract a morganatic marriage in which neither his wife nor his children would be eligible for any of the rights or privileges normally granted to the Habsburg family. And even though Franz-Josef had elevated the Countess to the unusual (in the Habsburg domains) rank of Duchess in 1909, she still had to trail behind the youngest archduchesses, far from her husband at all court functions. These restrictions were imposed with iron rigidity by the court chamberlain, Prince Montenuovo. He was himself the offspring of a morganatic marriage of the Neubergs and therefore especially sensitive to any departure from protocol. Such rules were a constant thorn in the flesh of the Archduke. Nevertheless, the thesis that he went to Sarajevo simply to 'show his wife off' is an exaggeration.[7] The Duchess of Hohenberg was with her husband on 28 June in Sarajevo for one reason only: she feared for his safety and felt he would be in less danger if she were at his side.[8]

These fears were well founded. Despite the model administration given to Bosnia and Hercegovina after their occupation in 1878, the two provinces were open to destabilisation by neighbouring Serbia. When, in 1903, the pro-Austrian Serbian ruling dynasty, the Obrenovičs, were murdered in a putsch by Serbian officers, the pro-Russian Karadjordjević family were installed. The Karadjordjevićs were far more robust in pursuing a policy of 'Greater Serbian' expansion and closer ties with Russia. Following the defeat of Russia in the 1904–5 Russo-Japanese War, Tsarist attentions moved from Asia back to the Balkans, and a steady process of encouraging the Slav nations of the peninsula to roll back both Ottoman and Habsburg influence began in earnest.

Austro-Russian rivalry in the Balkans

Thanks to the Anglo-Russian convention negotiated by Britain's Foreign Secretary, Sir Edward Grey, in 1907, London found itself increasingly in support of Russian interests in the region. Egged on by a Russophile Ambassador, Arthur Nicolson, in St Petersburg from 1906 to 1910, the British

Foreign Office increasingly saw the Balkans through Russian eyes. During the annexation of Bosnia-Hercegovina crisis of 1908–9, Sir Edward Grey supported the Russian point of view wholeheartedly. The crisis outraged public opinion in Russia but as it came so soon after her defeat at the hands of the Japanese, the Tsar's armies were in no position to react firmly. In addition, the mediocre Russian Foreign Minister, Izvolsky, had been comprehensively outmanoeuvred by his Austrian counterpart, Aehrenthal. Russia, Serbia and Grey had to back down. To rub salt into the wounds, Aehrenthal extracted from Serbia a formal pledge to 'abandon the attitude of protest and opposition' towards the annexation, and to place her relations with Bosnia-Hercegovina on a 'basis of good-neighbourliness'.[9]

In a move that illustrated his ruthless diplomatic style, Aehrenthal released documents to the press proving that Russia had connived in the annexation proposal for many months, and that Izvolsky had offered to support Austria's annexation in return for Vienna lobbying to open the Straits to the Black Sea to Russian warships. Izvolsky was made to appear inept and naive, a humiliation he never forgave. In 1914, during the July crisis, he encouraged, as Russian Ambassador to Paris, the coming conflict with Austria, calling it 'my war'.[10]

Aehrenthal's diplomatic brilliance earned him elevation to the high nobility when the Emperor created him a count in recognition of his services. But his 'victory' was pyrrhic. Serbia, Russia, London and Paris reinforced their determination to avoid a similar diplomatic defeat at the hands of the Ballplatz (the seat of the Austrian Foreign Ministry) in the future. Another unhappy consequence of the crisis was the establishment of closer military ties between the Austro-Hungarian Empire and Germany. Regular staff talks between Conrad on the Austrian side and Moltke on the German side were initiated although, according to Bardolff, these amounted to little more than an annual conversation on the establishment of a joint automobile corps. But any lingering resentment among older Austrian officers towards Berlin disappeared when Conrad took over the post of Chief of the General Staff in 1906. One of his first acts was to shelve the War Plan D. R. (Deutsches Reich).[11]

Russia had concluded a military alliance with France in 1894. In the aftermath of the Annexation Crisis, French capital was encouraged to penetrate Serbia. By January1912, Prince Lajos Windischgrätz, sent by the Evidenzbüro on a delicate reconnaissance mission to Belgrade, noted that the latest fortification artillery was of Creusot manufacture and that most of the gun crews were French artillery officers in mufti.[12]

In October 1912, a Balkan League, led by Serbia and strongly supported by Russian diplomacy and Bulgaria, attacked the remaining Ottoman forces in the peninsula. Assisted by Montenegro and Greece, it hurled the Turks from their last remaining strongpoints, including parts of Albania. Conrad, much of whose spare time was spent dreaming of his affair with Gina Reininghaus, a married woman, predicted a 'long struggle in which the Turks would prove victorious'. It was the first of a number of calamitous predictions on the part of the Austrian Staff chief. If love was blind, Conrad was, in an admittedly tight field, the most myopic military commander of his time. He continued to see the Balkan wars in the light of the Austro-Prussian or Franco-Prussian engagements rather than the more recent and relevant Boer War and Russo-Japanese War.[13] By the time the war ended Metternich's dictum had come to pass: the sick man of Europe was 'no longer on the Bosporus but on the Danube'.

The Balkan League had been financed and partly organised by the energetic and formidable Baron Nicholas Hartwig. Hartwig, as Russian Minister in Belgrade from 1909, had worked tirelessly to undermine the Dual Monarchy and promote Pan-Slavism under Russian patronage. Now in the wake of the First Balkan War, the anti-Ottoman allies fell out and hostilities began again. Thanks to Hartwig's support, Serbia emerged victorious. Conrad's assessment had been that 'Bulgaria would easily hold its own' but once again this proved unrealistic. Hartwig's work had reaped fruit. A Serbia double in size and population existed, pointing a geographical, ethnic and political dagger at the heart of Austria-Hungary's South Slav possessions. As Hartwig noted, 'it is now the turn of Austria'.[14]

The Archduke's military experiences: the challenge of Hungary

As early as 1913, Aehrenthal's successor at the Ballplatz, Count Leopold Berchtold, had written that an armed conflict with Serbia was inevitable. In modern parlance, 'containment' of the Serbian problem had evidently failed.[15] Thus the Archduke knew that a visit to Sarajevo posed risks. There are many reports that he was also aware that there would be an attempt to kill him.[16]

The Archduke had so many enemies, it was hardly surprising he believed they were out to eliminate him. The *Neue Freie Presse*, the leading liberal paper of Vienna, had described him with typical Viennese irony as a 'true man of the sixteenth century' ('Un vero uomo del cinquecento'). The phrase was not intended to be flattering. It implied a primitive late medieval Catholic fanaticism that the Archduke undoubtedly possessed. But these Austrian criticisms were mild in comparison to barbs hurled at the Archduke from Budapest where the Hungarian magnates saw in his imminent accession to the throne a direct challenge to Magyar authority. The Archduke made no secret of his intentions to unravel the 'Ausgleich' (Compromise) of 1867 concluded by Franz-Josef. Franz Ferdinand hated the Hungarians. He was, in Czernin's phrase, 'a good hater'.[17] Unwittingly, the army had played an important role in nurturing this particular hatred.

As a young cavalry subaltern, the Archduke had been assigned to a Hussar regiment against his wishes. Franz-Josef had hoped this would give his nephew a happy introduction to the Magyar nobility. The regiment was supposed to be one of the 'German' Hussar regiments which recruited from outside Hungary. But even this one was inevitably dominated by Magyar officers so that the *Dienstsprache* and *Regimentsprache* tended to be Hungarian.

Franz Ferdinand was furious that no one wanted to speak German to him. He refused to speak Hungarian and this excluded him from the intimate cama- raderie of his brother officers. He wrote a long memorandum to the then Chief of the General Staff, Beck, which even today reads like an emotionally charged indictment. It expressed all the Archduke's wounded sense of *amour propre* that an army whose 'language of command is German' should 'tolerate amongst its officers the exclusive use of another language'.

From 1909, the Archduke's military office began developing plans for 'dealing' with the Hungarians once Franz Ferdinand ascended to the throne. The so-called 'Nachlass/Thronwechsel' (Legacy/Transition) documents reveal that Franz Ferdinand was prepared to provoke a constitutional crisis and if necessary resort to 'extreme measures' to bring the Hungarians to heel.[18]

The Archduke believed in 'liberating' the Croats and Romanians from Hungarian rule. His strategy for dealing with the truculent Magyars when he inherited the throne was very simple: he would not allow himself to be crowned King of Hungary until the Hungarian constitution had been amended to allow universal suffrage. Universal suffrage would completely transform the situation, as the Magyars were a racial minority in their own kingdom. Feudal Magyar supremacy would be broken. The 'Nachlass' documents show that Franz Ferdinand was prepared for an armed conflict with the Hungarians. 'All concessions to the Hungarians made over the years' concerning the use of their language in the military field were to be revoked.[19] The long-standing conven- tion that Hungarian officers were only posted to Hungarian regiments was to be annulled by order of the War Ministry. By the beginning of April 1914 a plan had been drawn up to move non-Magyar units into the Hungarian part of the Empire.[20] These schemes aimed at the total deconstruction of the building blocks of the Dual Monarchy established with such difficulty over decades by Franz-Josef. The Emperor knew better than anyone the dangers in attacking the use of the Hungarian language in his Magyar regiments. Had not this very issue threatened to derail the great Compromise of 1867?

The Emperor's illness

In the spring of 1914 the Archduke's plans might have been discounted had the Emperor been younger or in better health, but at the beginning of May the Emperor fell seriously ill with a near-fatal attack of bronchitis. The court began preparing for the inevitable and the Archduke's train was put on standby. Suddenly it seemed as if Franz Ferdinand could be Emperor by the end of the month. The scare lasted only two weeks and the Emperor recovered, but it had focused minds.

Towards the end of May 1914, another encounter underlined the fragility of the situation. The Archduchess (later Empress) Zita recalled how she and her husband, Franz Ferdinand's nephew and the future Emperor Charles, were alone with Franz Ferdinand after supper at the Belvedere. Suddenly Franz Ferdinand turned to Charles and said: 'I have something to say but I must say it quickly as I don't want your aunt to hear anything of this. I know I shall soon be murdered! In this desk are papers which concern you. When it happens take them. They are for you.'[21] Franz Ferdinand himself had stated – and few sentences uttered by a Habsburg ring more true or prophetic than these – that the Habsburg crown was indeed a 'a martyr's crown', and 'only those born to inherit it should aspire to it'.[22]

June 1914 progressed and the tension began to mount over the Archduke's projected plans for the Hungarian elements in the army. Hungary's Prime Minister, the hard, ascetic, Calvinist Stephen (István) Tisza, was convinced of Hungary's privileges in the world. In 1912, Tisza had brilliantly manipulated the Hungarian parliament to approve the military estimates. It was a feat of considerable political dexterity which brought him the unqualified support of Franz-Josef. The old Emperor who had come to dread the Hungarian parliament's ten-yearly fight over military estimates was impressed. Tisza was the toughest politician he had encountered since the formidable Prince Schwarzenberg of his youth.

The Archduke and Tisza

A major problem was Franz Ferdinand's refusal to meet Tisza. This was an extraordinary state of affairs and it did not augur well for the future of the Empire that its next sovereign was unable to talk to its premier statesman. Even the German Kaiser tried in vain to persuade the Archduke at Miramar castle near Trieste in March 1914 that he 'must' talk to the Hungarian minister. Franz Ferdinand remained intransigent. Berlin watched, increasingly frustrated and concerned. The German Foreign Minister Gottlieb von Jagow observed that the future integrity of Austria-Hungary, Germany's sole reliable ally, under Franz Ferdinand 'could not be assured as long as the Archduke refused to work out some modus vivendi with Tisza'.[23]

Tisza, the man who would dance alone for four hours without pause to the accompaniment of a solitary violinist, was also a man of deep passions. He was fully acquainted with the Archduke's views on him and Hungary. He knew from several sources that the Archduke planned a kind of *coup d'état* against Hungary on his succession. 'If Franz Ferdinand as Emperor Franz II uses the army against me,' he warned, 'I will start a national revolution against him and the last word will be mine.'[24]

It is a sign of how alarming this stand-off was seen in Berlin that the German Kaiser, after failing at Miramar, asked the Austrian Ambassador to ask Prince Windischgrätz to arrange a discreet meeting between the two antagonists. It was Tisza's turn to be unyielding. He refused, citing the need for the 'formal permission' of the Emperor before such talks could be held. Eventually in early June, much to Berlin's relief, Count Andrássy, a close collaborator of Tisza, was prevailed upon to begin exploratory talks with the Archduke. These made no progress because the Archduke refused 'flatly' to discuss the Magyar point of view either with regard to the army or the constitution.[25]

The bitter dispute between the Archduke and Tisza over 'reform' of the Hungarian army units and Magyar privileges was played out against a backdrop of increasing financial instability. The two Balkan wars and their attendant crises had required repeated and expensive Austro-Hungarian mobilisations. These had resulted in dramatically increased military expenditure, which could not be sustained. The army budgets had a sudden and deleterious effect on the Habsburg economy which, until 1912, had been booming. Stocks fell abruptly, public debt soared and Austria's plans for economic penetration of Serbia and other parts of the Balkans ground to a halt. Two-thirds of the Empire's sovereign debt in 1914 were acquired between 1912 and 1913.[26]

Berlin's divergence from Austria-Hungary over Serbia

The slack was taken up by Berlin. Railways in Bosnia, the key to the provinces' modernisation, were no longer to be financed by the Austrian Bodenkreditanstalt, the protégé bank of the Archduke Franz Ferdinand, but by the German Dresdner Bank, the economic arm of the German High Command. Along with the other members of the ' 4 Great Ds' – the Diskoconto, Deutsche and Darmstädter – Dresdner began to penetrate the strategic land routes to the east. Franz Ferdinand's Bodenkreditanstalt found itself increasingly squeezed out of the south-east European picture.[27]

The conclusion of the Second Balkan War showed Berlin that Serbia was the key player in the region. From that moment onwards, Berlin's attitude towards Serbia diverged from Vienna's substantially. On the financial and military level Austrian sensitivities in the Balkans were ignored. The divergence of approach placed increasing strain on Austro-German relations. Berchtold complained bitterly to Tschirsky, the German Ambassador in Vienna, that for all the help Germany was in recognising the mortal threat Serbia posed to the Habsburg monarchy, 'we might as well belong to the other grouping'.[28]

In early 1913, the German General Staff and the Deutsche Bank frustrated Berchtold's attempts to carve out a sphere of influence in southern Anatolia. As if to underline further the fragility of the Austro-German relationship, Franz Ferdinand was furious that Conrad was received so warmly by the German High Command during the manoeuvres of the Imperial German army in September 1913. The Germans had hoped the Archduke would attend these exercises but tensions between Vienna and Berlin caused the Archduke ostentatiously to turn down the invitation. Undaunted, Berlin had invited Conrad without first consulting the Archduke, treading further on his sensibilities. The Balkans, Serbia and even the Dual Monarchy were becoming simply part of a larger mosaic of German *Weltpolitik*.[29]

Franz Ferdinand saw the trend clearly and was dismayed. Despite his strong personal affection for the German Kaiser, he saw Berlin treading on Austrian prerogatives at every corner, particularly in the military and economic spheres. He was all too familiar with the reports of the Austrian Minister in Cetinje, Wladimir Giesl who was engaged in one fierce argument after another with his German counterpart, von Eckardt. Von Eckhardt strove to undermine Giesl at every turn in the Montenegrin capital. The pattern of German encroachment would be repeated when Giesl arrived to take up his position in Belgrade on 5 December 1913.[30] By the beginning of 1914, Serbia's largest trading partner was Germany. As so often happens, the flag followed the trade. Significant informal military exchanges with Serbia were promoted, assisted by the Serbian Minister in Berlin, Miloš Bogičević, who had impeccable German family connections and would later defect to Germany after war broke out.[31]

Bogičević's career brought him very close to senior German officers, and his subsequent defection to Germany during the war, and later unexplained death, pose the question as to whether he was working for German military circles all along. Through Bogičević, visiting Serbian officers were brought into contact with many high-ranking officers within the German Kaiser's entourage. The efficiency, aggressive thinking and technological progress of the German military impressed these Serbian officers who dreamt of a dominant role in Serbian society akin to that enjoyed by the Prussian military caste in Germany.

Colonel 'Apis'

One Serbian officer was especially interested in the German military. He visited Germany three times between 1905 and 1913, spending several months there in the spring of 1913. His name was Dragutin Dmitrievič, though he was more commonly known by his nickname 'Apis'. He was a founder member and leader of the Serbian secret society, Unity or Death (Ujedinjenje ili Smrt), also known as 'The Black Hand'.[32]

'Apis' shared many qualities with Potiorek, the Austrian military governor of Bosnia. He was secretive, a repressed homosexual as well as an unambiguous admirer of the German military. Major Dmitrievič's secret society with its quasi-Masonic initiation ritual of oath, dagger and candle had organised the assassination of the Obrenovič King and Queen. Dmitrievič in fact had received three bullets in the attack on the Obrenovičs' palace. Although he had recovered from his wounds, the bullets had never been removed. If there were those in Berlin who wished to develop links with a Serbian 'strongman', then 'Apis' was their man. By 1913, he was a handshake away from the German Kaiser.

That 'Apis' was cultivating the Germans is indicated by the fact that they offered him financial support for his political struggle with the leader of the Serbian Radical party, Nikola Pasič. Pasič was determined to limit the influence of the army, especially in the newly conquered territories of Macedonia or 'New Serbia'. The Germans even offered 'Apis' a printing press and other equipment to help his campaign. Increasingly Berlin sought to develop more intimate military links. By March 1914, Belgrade was rife with rumours of a military coup. It is hard to suppress the speculation that 'Apis' was keen to cement German support by removing the Archduke, who was a thorn in Germany's strategic plans. Berlin's pro-Serb policies could be relied upon to rein in any extreme measures on the part of Vienna, many of whose leading circles would see the assassination of the Archduke as a blessing.[33]

Major Gellinek's reports

The dispatches of Major Otto Gellinek, Imperial and Royal military attaché in Belgrade in 1914, illuminate much of this developing German–Serb military relationship. Gellinek's reports are a model of the military attaché's craft.

Well-informed, discreet and detached, they offer a unique insight into the state of the Black Hand and the Serbian military in the years before 1914 and Germany's own anti-Habsburg agenda in the Balkans.[34]

Gellinek was under no illusions as to the influence of the Black Hand. He dubbed its members the 'unanswerable praetorians' and noted that the Society offered 'strong protection' to its members and caused 'serious problems' for the country's politicians. One of the officers of the Black Hand regularly carried a part of murdered Queen Draga in his briefcase and escaped all attempts by the political class to bring him to heel after another murder scandal. Such was the Black Hand's political influence, he emerged with a royal pardon and golden courage medal.[35] In all political, economic and strategic questions, 'the officer corps were a key factor', Gellinek observed in a revealing report on the tensions between the Serbian military and the government of Pasič, penned in May 1914.[36]

Throughout the first six months of 1914, the German legation in Belgrade courted the Serbian officers of the Black Hand as a counterweight to Pasič and his Russian adviser Hartwig. On 24 March, Gellinek noted that a retired German major in the pay of the German armaments firm Krupp had agreed that two members of the Black Hand, Colonels Bojović and Stajević, could visit Essen to see the firing ranges as a prelude to the purchase of nine batteries of howitzers. That Germany might be supplying modern artillery to Serbia at a time when Serbia was so openly hostile to Austria-Hungary was startling. The weapons could only be for use against Germany's 'ally', Austria-Hungary. But there was worse news to come. The issue of Krupp armaments had first been raised in 1905 and then later in 1907. On both occasions Pasič had vetoed the contracts.[37]

When a clearly surprised Major Gellinek asked his German counterpart, Major Fürstenberg, where the Serbs could get the money for such a purchase he was astonished to hear from Fürstenberg: 'Germany is ready to open lines of credit to Belgrade to cover all costs.'[38] To rub salt into the wound, Fürstenberg pointed out that Herr Kosegarten of the Deutsche Waffenfabrik would also be in Belgrade that month to offer 300,000 rifles, 'at a cost of 85 francs per rifle and bayonet'. The sinister intimacy between German military circles and the Black Hand could not enjoy more conclusive proof.

By May 1914, the negotiations were accelerated, not least because, as the German legation pointed out to Gellinek, Serbia's acquisition of the 'new territories' had caused inflation and a financial crisis which was 'impoverishing Serbia'.[39] Clearly the economic situation of Serbia was ripe for German exploitation. The mention of the new territories was significant. They had become the bone of contention between Pasič and the Black Hand, who could not agree on whether the civil or military leadership should take priority in the recently acquired region. Eager to offer support for the military party in this area, the German legation began to focus its best brains on the territories. News of this German interest reached the Quirinal in Rome, still nominally a German ally in late May. (Leaked to the Vatican, it quickly spurred Pope Pius X to hasten negotiations for a concordat with Belgrade. The Cardinal Secretary of State saw clearly where Germany's interference with domestic Serbian politics was leading.)[40]

Throughout the late spring of 1914, the German legation sent one of its most able diplomats, Dietrich von Scharfenberg, on a prolonged tour of 'New Serbia' to assess its potential for economic dependency on Berlin. Scharfenberg's report noted the 'lively trade with Germany' and the 'care needed' to develop these 'good ties'. Not once did Scharfenberg refer to any tensions between Serbia and Germany's ally, Austria-Hungary. 'As a courtesy', Gellinek was allowed to peruse the German report.[41] The report's conclusion was simple: Serbia could benefit enormously from German capital. The acquisitions of the Balkan wars had impoverished the country. The new territories offered Berlin a once in a generation opportunity. Gellinek's dispatch reached the Archduke Franz Ferdinand through his Military Chancery and made disquieting reading.

These strong ties between the German and Serbian military survived even the July crisis. On 21 July, three weeks after the assassination, Gellinek accompanied his newly arrived German counterpart to present his credentials to the Serbian defence ministry. It was noticeable that, while his German colleague was immediately escorted into the Chief of the General Staff's office for drinks, Gellinek was told to remain outside cooling his heels with only the murals depicting the 'redemption of Bosnia' and its return to Serbia to keep him company. 'I found these tasteless and disgusting in the light of what had happened in Sarajevo three weeks earlier,' Gellinek wrote emotionally, an unusual departure for him. It is hard not to imagine that the normally reserved Gellinek was moved to this language by the frustration that Austria's ally was *persona gratissima* in Belgrade.[42] Even when, a week later, the Austrians declared war on Serbia, after breaking off diplomatic relations, the Germans refused to hand over the formal Austro-Hungarian declaration of war on their ally's behalf. Right up to the end, some German circles hoped to preserve the fruits of Germany's burgeoning special relationship with Serbia.

They were not the only ones to enjoy an ambivalent relationship with the Serbs. Some months earlier, a line of communication had been opened up between 'Apis' and Tisza. It has been suggested that two Serbian businessmen,

Dada and Djorcić had even arranged for the two men to meet early in 1914.[43] Like the Germans, Tisza saw Serbia as a useful ally, a country which could provide a focus for the aspirations of the Croats and Serbs within the Empire. The fewer Slavs in the Habsburg lands, the better for Hungary. Tisza would have sympathised with German policy. If Serbia could be persuaded to orientate herself away from Russia and towards Germany, that was good news for Hungary. Tisza was always against war with Serbia even after the Archduke's assassination.[44]

By the middle of June 1914, The Archduke's imminent accession to the throne stood in the way of powerful interests: Stephen Tisza and his desire to preserve Magyar privilege; the desire in German military circles to launch a preventive war against Russia; the wish of his own General Staff chief to launch a war against Serbia. None of these projects could be secured with the Archduke alive. The question arises as to whether 'Apis' organised Franz Ferdinand's murder to ingratiate himself with his new-found supporters among the German military, relying on a promise from Tisza that the Dual Monarchy would not go to war against Serbia in the event of an assassination.[45]

Germany plans for Austria-Hungary's break-up

There were other issues at stake, too. Germany's agenda for the region had implications for the entire future of the Dual Monarchy. Berchtold's myopia was all the more remarkable given that by early 1914 one German establishment figure after another had, in a contemporary's phrase, expressed themselves 'with the indecent frankness with which a younger member of a family prepares for the demise of the older relative'.[46]

Every German scheme for economic expansion before 1914 implied the economic and subsequent political absorption of Austria, and the domination of her subject lands by Germany. As early as 1903, Professor Lagarde could state that 'from the German Foreign Ministry point of view, the Germanisation of Austria is a vital question'. In 1913 Dr von Winterstetten, an influential figure in Munich wrote: 'We have lent millions of our citizens to the Austrian joint stock company as an investment in order to cement her amalgamation into the Reich.'[47] In his book *Grossdeutschland*, Richard Tannenberg offered to 'occupy the territories around Prague and Laibach so that no German student can be ever be insulted again'. In the German Reichstag, Dr Eduard Hasse spoke in favour of Trieste becoming 'a German port' and the Austrian littoral serving as 'a basis for German power'. Paul de Lagarde put the issue more bluntly: Germany without Austria was not '*lebensfähig*' (capable of life).[48] Such thoughts chimed with Wickham Steed's dispatches from Trieste, which increasingly highlighted the threat to the Austrian Lloyd and other Austrian commercial firms from German banking interests.[49]

Franz Ferdinand was aware of these sentiments and if Czernin, and Eisenmenger, his personal physician, are to be believed, he found them deeply insulting. Such ideas explicitly cast a shadow over his own plans to reinvigorate the Empire. It is clear just from these few quotes that, for many Germans, Franz Ferdinand's policies were a direct threat not only to Magyar hegemony but also to the ambitions of German financiers, soldiers and statesmen. His removal would be far more in the interests of Germany or Hungary than of Serbia. Indeed, the death of Franz Ferdinand removed the most formidable obstacle to the realisation of German plans.[50] As 1914 developed, the German agenda began to affect Serbian internal politics. The journal *Pijemont*, the public voice of the military party, made no secret of its belief that 'War with Austria-Hungary was imminent', but it began criticising Russia and its influence in the Balkans. It called for Serbia to play a role independent of Russia, and openly accused the Russian minister Hartwig of pulling Pasič's strings and being 'the real government' of Serbia. Here was a propaganda move to prepare the ground for German penetration.

The printing presses for *Pijemont* were supplied and paid for by German 'well-wishers'. Dedijer quotes the evidence that German 'Freemasons' had supplied the presses for the editor, Jovanovič Čup, a well-known Serbian Freemason. Tempting though it might be to revisit the secret society conspiracy theory it should be borne in mind that the Archduke had no more staunch supporter and loyal friend than the Duke of Portland who, by his own admission, was one of England's most prominent Freemasons.[51] Notwithstanding this fact, no less a person than the great 'Queen of the Malissari', the expert on Albania, Edith Durham, consistently advanced the thesis of involvement by members of the Grand Orient Lodge in the assassination of the Archduke.[52]

One week before the Archduke entrained for Trieste from where the dreadnought *Viribus Unitis* would take him to the Dalmatian coast and on to Sarajevo, the German Kaiser made one final attempt to persuade the Archduke to come to terms with Tisza. At Konopište in Bohemia, the Archduke's estate, a German delegation, including Admiral Tirpitz and the German Emperor, held what was to be the final round of power talks before the 'catastrophe'. The Konopište talks have been described as little more than an opportunity to admire the castle's renowned roses, the German Admiral being a well-known horticulturist.[53] This theory simply does not stand up to close scrutiny.[54] Fortunately, Count Berchtold was received the following day and committed to paper his exchanges with the Archduke. These concerned foreign policy and therefore can be assumed to sum up the Archduke's thoughts in the immediate hours following the German Kaiser's visit. They prove that the questions of Hungary and Russia were uppermost in the Archduke's mind. Berchtold noted that the Archduke pushed strongly for 'a rapprochement with St Petersburg'.[55] Such a view was hardly calculated to endear Franz Ferdinand to those in Germany's military who believed an imminent conflict with Russia was necessary because of the forthcoming modernisation of the Russian railway system.

The Austrian Foreign Ministry documents show that the difficulties with Tisza featured prominently in this last encounter at Konopište.[56] When again the German Kaiser implored the Archduke to meet Tisza, Franz Ferdinand retorted that 'Hungary is maintained in medieval conditions by a tiny oligarchy. ... Every Magyar works against Austria and the Monarchy as a whole. ... Tisza is dictator in Hungary and wants to be in Austria.'[57] The Empire's domestic environment was proving as critical to events as the international horizon.[58]

Franz Ferdinand's desire for better relations with Russia faced resistance in St Petersburg as well as Berlin. A year earlier, as we have seen, the Tsar had told the British Ambassador, Buchanan, that 'the disintegration of the Austrian Empire was merely a question of time'.[59] An article a few weeks later in the Russian *Novoje Vremya* openly discussed the 'impending collapse' of the Habsburg Empire.

In late February 1914, a special military and naval conference chaired by Sazonov in St Petersburg discussed the 'imminent European War'. One month earlier, Sazonov had even suggested to the Tsar the idea of 'provoking a European war' in order to seize Constantinople. In March, the German Ambassador to Russia, Pourtales, informed Berlin that 'the desire to settle once and for all accounts with Austria-Hungary is widespread'.[60]

Despite these developments, Franz Ferdinand was determined to push his idea of a revival of the Dreikaiserbund, bringing an improved relationship with Russia. The more perceptive of the outside powers watched on and stepped up their own precautions. A day after the Konopište meeting, the Vatican signed its first concordat with Serbia. It had been drafted and agreed, as noted earlier, under 'immense time pressure'. Belgrade's minister from Paris had signed it on behalf of Serbia.

The Archduke travels to the manoeuvres

The following day, the Archduke boarded the late evening train from Vienna's Southern Railway station for Trieste. The electric lighting failed in his carriage. 'What do you say about the lighting? Just like a graveyard,' the Archduke mordantly quipped. It was to be the first of many similar events that would later be invested with the quality of 'portents'. (These included the gypsy who on being asked to tell the Archduke's fortune had suddenly recoiled in horror and said that he would be responsible for unleashing a terrible war.)[61]

Shortly before the Archduke's departure from the Vienna Southern Railway station, Serbia's Minister in Vienna Joca Jovanović warned the civilian governor of Bosnia, Bilinski, who was also joint finance minister, to reconsider the Archduke's visit. The Serbian government had received information to the effect that the Archduke's life was in danger. Pašić had picked up on the intelligence that certain individuals were being smuggled across the Serbian–Austrian border with weapons to assassinate the Archduke. Jovanović offered no details and this rather vague warning went no further.

Bilinski later claimed that he was unaware of a civil programme attached to the Imperial couple's visit to the military manoeuvres. This claim is invalidated by the distribution list of the Imperial couple's itinerary, 35 copies of which, as we have seen, were sent to various ministries including Bilinski's.

In Sarajevo, the military governor Potiorek put the finishing touches to the preparations for the imminent visit.[62] Though fluent in Slovene, like so many inhabitants of the Carinthian valleys towards the Drave, Potiorek was a man convinced of the superiority of 'German' culture. When later he was appointed to Sarajevo, the local Croat newspaper acutely noted that he was 'of Slovene origins but his inclinations should make him a German' ('Seinem Empfinden nach soll er ein Deutscher sein').[63]

Potiorek admired Prussian discipline. The Archduke had passed him over for the top job in the army partly out of suspicion of Potiorek's Pan-German sympathies.[64] In June 1900, commenting on the anniversary of the Battle of Königgrätz, Potiorek had said 'that battle could never have been won. Absolutely not. We lost that battle years before it took place. Lost with our internal and external politics. Lost with our government, our industry, our schools. In short lost with everything that is called Austria.'[65] A photograph of him with the German Kaiser on board a ship, taken a few years earlier, shows the Austrian full of deference and military respect.

Potiorek's posting to Sarajevo had not been without its critics. The Emperor wondered whether Potiorek would not 'be perhaps too sharp' ('vielleicht zu scharf').[66] But Franz-Josef saw some merit in giving him, the son of a modest Carinthian official, a chance to demonstrate his skills in a difficult area.

In his new role Potiorek proved a controversial military administrator. His inability to delegate, and his failure to share his thoughts with senior officers, provoked much criticism. Each evening, Potiorek would lock himself up in the 'Konak', the governor's Jugendstil villa, working on his papers till late into the night. His activities remained a mystery to all his subordinates though they acknowledged that he was well informed about local conditions.

The only man allowed to penetrate this carapace was a young ADC by the name of Erik von Merizzi. Merizzi was the son of one of Potiorek's closest comrades from the time when he had served in Laibach (Ljubljana). To the dismay and resentment of his staff, Potiorek treated Merizzi with special favour. The two men indeed were virtually inseparable. The younger Merizzi was amusing, arrogant and irreverent; the perfect foil to the earnest, spartan general. A snapshot of them with the Archduke during manoeuvres reveals their characters all too clearly: an earnest Archduke attempts to focus Potiorek, perhaps distracted by Merizzi's uninhibited humour.

As he knew he held a position of particular favour, Merizzi did not hesitate to behave in a way that demonstrated to his fellow officers his exalted position. They complained bitterly of Merizzi's complacent and high-handed manner. So widespread was the resentment it made its way far enough up the line to become a topic of conversation between the Archduke and a member of his military chancery, Colonel Bolfras. It is not clear whether the relationship between Potiorek and his Flügeladjutant was homosexual or not. Clearly it was 'unusual' and, for Franz Ferdinand, a man of devout Catholic views, it was 'unnatural'. He ordered his Military Chancery to 'put an end to this business of the Flügeladjutant'.[67]

The manoeuvres were prepared throughout the month of May. Both the Archduke and his wife arrived on schedule at Bad Ilidže and, from the 26th to the 27th, the Archduke attended the manoeuvres. Conrad, who had also watched the exercises, excused himself from dinner on the 27th and returned to Karlovac. His relationship with the Archduke had unmistakably cooled. Conrad had failed to attend Mass on a Sunday while in the company of the Archduke, an infuriating solecism in Franz Ferdinand's book. Conrad's passionate affair with a married woman, Gina Reininghaus, was also disapproved of by the Archduke. Moreover, was not Conrad becoming too susceptible to German flattery? The other staff officers looked on silently, pretending not to notice the hostility. There were even rumours that the Archduke was about to ask for Conrad's resignation.

Over dinner in Bad Ilidže on the evening of the 27th, the Archduke debated at length whether he should make the trip to Sarajevo the following morning. Several officers in his suite cautioned against the visit, recommending that he leave out Sarajevo and return in the morning to Mostar where the *Viribus Unitis* was waiting to take the royal couple back to Trieste. After all, the manoeuvres had been a great success; why not head back home? The Duchess had already visited the Sarajevo sights the previous day while her husband was in the field. The city dignitaries could hardly complain that they had been ignored.

As the Archduke showed that he was persuaded to cut short his trip, one young officer strongly protested. It was Merizzi. The young major, the cynosure of Potiorek's eye perhaps realised that cancellation of the trip would be a great blow to the pride of his protector. So vigorously did Merizzi argue that a premature departure of the Archduke would be interpreted as an 'insult' to the loyal Bosnian population (as well as, by implication, to the Military Governor), the Archduke diffidently agreed to proceed with the programme.[68]

No one pointed out that the following day, 28 June, was the 'Vidov Dan', the 'Day of the Black Birds', the anniversary of the battle when the flower of Serbian chivalry had been wiped out by the Turks in 1389 on the famous Field of Ravens in Kosovo. It was an anniversary so seared into the collective memory of the Serb nation that the visit of an Austrian archduke on such a day was an obvious provocation.

Between them Merizzi and Potiorek, two men whose relationship was bound by ties the Archduke found 'disquieting', had ensured that the Imperial couple would be in Sarajevo on the morning of the 28th. Between them these two, unwittingly perhaps, would contribute almost as much to the death of the Archduke and his wife as the Black Hand assassination squad. Meanwhile Colonel 'Apis' and his organisation had arranged that no fewer than six armed assassins would be in the Bosnian capital that morning. Thanks to the printed programme, reprinted in the local press the day before, the assassins all knew where to stand: the Appel Quay would offer the best chances.

Potiorek's series of judgements

Potiorek assisted the macabre chain of events that day in another way. It was his decision not to deploy troops from the nearby garrison in rows two deep, as had occurred when the Emperor had visited Sarajevo a few years earlier. The troops were 'tired' after the manoeuvres and, Potiorek felt they were superfluous. Security was thus left in the hands of some 150 policemen who were spread throughout the city very thinly. It later emerged that one policeman obligingly pointed out to a conspirator the car in which the Archduke was travelling.

As the seven-vehicle cavalcade made its way along the Appel Quay, a young conspirator by the name of Ciganovič knocked the detonator off the bomb he was carrying and hurled it at the Archduke's car, an open-topped Gräf & Stift Bois de Boulogne six-seater phaeton. The car, which belonged to Count Harrach and was driven by his chauffeur, swerved as the projectile fell through the air and bounced off the rear hood of the car to land spluttering in the gutter before exploding just as the fourth car passed by.

Twenty members of the crowd were slightly injured and a minute splinter lodged itself in Merizzi's finger. The ADC had been travelling just behind the

Archduke's car. It was 10.30 a.m. The Mayor of Sarajevo, who had imagined the bomb to be but a salvo of artillery greeting the Archduke, had driven on to the Town Hall. When the Imperial couple arrived a few minutes later, he launched into his speech as if nothing had happened. The Archduke listened for about fifty seconds and then cut him short, bristling with rage. 'Herr Bürgermeister! We come to visit Sarajevo and a bomb is hurled at us! That is outrageous! Now get on with your speech.'

After the speeches, a Major Hoeger suggested calling the 250 troops stationed in the town to line the Archduke's route but Potiorek again overruled this suggestion. Potiorek suggested to the Archduke that they should visit the wounded Merizzi in the hospital and then drive on to Ilidže. Most sources indicate that this was the Archduke's suggestion. Jeřabek has shown that it was in fact Potiorek's inspiration, despite the fact that the news had already reached him that Merizzi had suffered no harm requiring extended hospitalisation.[69] When Baron Morsey suggested such a visit might be dangerous, Potiorek snapped at him: 'Do you think Sarajevo is full of assassins?'

Merizzi had suffered a minute splinter in his finger and his condition was not worthy of the remotest attention and yet the 'Flügeladjutant' was now to be the reason why the Archduke and his wife returned to the Appel Quay. The Archduke asked his secretary to ask his wife to return to Bad Ilidže in a separate vehicle but Sophie, true to form, refused to leave her husband's side when there might be the slightest danger. She continued to imagine that her presence could in some way protect him. Potiorek would ride behind the Archduke in the same car.

Potiorek's instructions that the convoy should head for the hospital were issued in the presence of the Mayor, Fehim Curčič, who travelled in the first car of the convoy. But he had a limited amount of German. Either for that reason, or because he did not imagine his driver needed to be told, he failed to inform his chauffeur that the new route involved them continuing along the Appel Quay rather than turning off into Franz-Josef Street.

As the convoy of cars set off, Potiorek jokingly remarked to the Archduke that he took this route 'every day wondering whether on account of some assassin it would be his last'. On hearing this, the Imperial couple laughed, the Archduke saying that 'it was superfluous to do anything other than trust in God'.[70]

'Also doch noch einmal'

This was to be the last conversation the Imperial couple had. A minute later Potiorek saw that the Mayor's car in front of him had followed the old route and was turning off the Appel Quay. Potiorek standing up in his cocked hat shouted at the driver of the Imperial car not to follow the car into the side street. But the driver had to stop the car and reverse and as the vehicle came to a halt, a young man who had waited along the Appel Quay all morning with a Browning pistol found himself less than two feet away from his intended victim. Two shots rang out and Potiorek saw to his amazement a young man thrown to the floor by the crowd and the drawn sabre of a nearby gendarme flash in the sunlight as it came down on the assassin. Potiorek later recalled: 'At first I felt not the slightest nervousness but relief. The Imperial couple opposite me were sitting completely calmly. I thought I heard the Archduke say: "Well. After all, another go" ("Also doch noch einmal").' The bullets had, like the bomb earlier, missed their target, or so the Feldmarschallleutnant thought.[71]

Ordering the car to to cross the bridge to the apparent safety of the Konak, Potiorek noticed that the sudden movement of the car caused the Duchess to sink lower into her seat but still he imagined that she had fainted. It would be another few minutes before the astounded governor realised as he tried to make the Duchess comfortable that the Archduke's mouth was full of blood, though his cocked hat was still firmly on his head. On reaching the Konak, both Archduke and Duchess were carried upstairs. The Duchess was laid on Potiorek's bed and the Archduke on the chaise-longue in Potiorek's study.

It would be another twenty minutes before various doctors from the garrison and the Imperial suite arrived to declare that the couple were dead. The bullet had entered the Archduke's neck but despite heavy bleeding the uniform had not given the wound away until the doctors struggled to cut the tunic open. The Duchess had been shot in the stomach and had not bled at all. Only the opening of her dress revealed the bullet hole. Gavrilo Princip, a young Bosnian Serb, trained and armed by the Black Hand, had fired the opening shots in what was to become the most terrible war in European history. He would later testify that the second shot was aimed at Potiorek but hit the Duchess. (The sequence of shots is not agreed on: according to some authors it was the second shot that hit the Archduke.)

Amidst the chaos and confusion that reigned in the Konak, Potiorek moved calmly and swiftly to fulfil his duties. He drafted three telegrams: one to the Emperor's private office at Bad Ischl addressed to Count Paar, one to Conrad who had just arrived at Karlovac, and one to the Minister of War.

CHAPTER 21

The Army and the July Crisis

Many accounts of the July crisis, like those of the assassination, ignore the role of the Habsburg army. Yet the entire diplomatic process cannot be understood without reference to the army and the Austro-Hungarian General Staff. The army exerted tremendous influence over policy and pace. Just as the assassination would have been impossible had not Franz Ferdinand been invited in a military capacity to the manoeuvres in Bosnia, so too was the response of the diplomats in Vienna contingent on military imperatives, in particular the issue of the army assisting the summer harvest and the War Plan 'B' (Balkan) for the invasion of Serbia and War Plan 'R' for dealing with Russia. Austrian policy fluctuated in speed and content as it engaged with these realities.

Potiorek's three telegrams were received in different ways. For the aged Emperor enjoying the splendid Alpine air in his summer villa in Ischl, the news was communicated to him by Count Paar. This elderly retainer had over the years brought his master some devastating messages: the shocking news of his wife's murder by an Italian anarchist, and his son and heir Rudolf's tragic death at Mayerling. True to training and character, Paar walked slowly along the long, dark corridor in the Kaiservilla, which was hung with the antlers of countless slaughtered stags, and knocked on the door of the Emperor's study. He announced his 'dutiful and obedient' presence and silently handed over the 'latest news' from Bosnia. Potiorek's telegram was brief, punctiliously correct from the point of view of protocol, and to the point:

> Deeply regret to report that His Imperial Highness and the Duchess of
> Hohenberg were both assassinated here today.

The Emperor received the news impassively, got up from his desk and according to one well-known account fatalistically said: 'The Lord God has achieved a higher order than I managed.' The violation of the dynasty's laws by the morganatic marriage of Franz Ferdinand had also offended God? The Emperor's failed attempts to rein in his heir's plans had been achieved by fate? Later, members of his family would dispute this account.[1]

For the War Minister Krobatin and the Chief of the General Staff, Conrad, the telegrams came, as they did for all the 'war party', as long overdue acts of vindication.[2] Here was a classic *casus foederis*. Here was the opportunity to settle accounts once and for all with the 'terrorist' state that was the Empire's southern neighbour. In February 1914, Conrad had asked Moltke: 'What are we waiting for?' As early as their first joint staff talks of 1909, Conrad had envisaged German military support for Austrian action against Serbia. Conrad was constantly advocating war. A few weeks after his outburst to Moltke he had urged war to the German Ambassador in Vienna, Tschirsky, this time against Russia. The diplomat had replied truthfully, 'two important people are against such a thing: your Archduke Franz Ferdinand and my Kaiser Wilhelm.'[3]

Franz Ferdinand's views in this case were entirely in accord with those of the Emperor, who eagerly devoted the last years of his reign to the maintenance of peace. Only the Emperor had the power to declare war. Unlike the German Kaiser, Franz-Josef had no 'entourage' or military and industrialist cliques which manipulated the throne. He stood aloof and Olympian above all party and politics. As he had remarked to the visiting American statesman Theodore Roosevelt a couple of years earlier, he, Franz-Josef, was the last of the 'old order of monarchs'. He had added: 'You see in me the representative of an idea which no longer exists anywhere else in Europe.'[4]

Having digested the implications of the telegram, the Emperor made preparations to return to Vienna and on 30 June was back in his summer palace at Schönbrunn on the outskirts of Vienna, where he prepared to receive his Foreign Minister, Count Berchtold. In the intervening 24 hours, the Emperor had clearly received a detailed account of the assassination from his own staff and military cabinet. Berchtold recalled in his diaries that he found the Emperor 'extremely well informed' concerning the details of the assassination as he listened impassively to Berchtold, who insisted that it was now the moment for the monarchy not to show any 'weakness' but a time to embark on 'a clear programme' against Serbia.[5]

Franz-Josef's caution

The Emperor agreed that the affair concerned the 'prestige' of his Empire but he appears implicitly to have counselled caution. He agreed with Berchtold that it was necessary to await the conclusion of the investigation into the assassination. Above all, the Kaiser counselled Berchtold to speak to Tisza. The invitation to consult Tisza, whose views on projected hostilities with Serbia and indeed the late Archduke were known to the Emperor, was a tactic to slow things down and take the heat out of the crisis. At this stage the Emperor, whose reign had taught him the incalculable dangers of war, appears to have been opposed to hostilities. Berchtold, so often accused wrongly of being a warmonger, was convinced that there would have to be a military reckoning with Serbia. But on this day he took his cue from his Emperor and appears to have maintained an open mind as to the timing of such action. He had just completed a paper on Balkan policy, which strongly recommended a 'forward' policy in the Balkans led by more assertive diplomacy with regard to Serbia, but he had not proposed any military action.[6]

Franz-Josef knew how resolutely opposed to war with Serbia Tisza was. The suggestion that Berchtold speak first to Tisza was in the Habsburg courtly world of hints and nuance as close to an unambivalent message to Berchtold at this stage of the crisis as the Emperor felt he could advance. To say anything more cautious would have offended the memory of the murdered heir. To say anything less cautious would risk complications in a rapidly moving situation. The Emperor had experienced many crises in his life. He realised that the assassinations were a provocation increasing a momentum which might become unstoppable. He was gently testing the brakes. Nothing demonstrated better the 84-year-old monarch's grip on affairs and commitment to peace than this first meeting with Berchtold.[7]

The Foreign Minister's meeting with Tisza went along lines that no doubt Franz-Josef had predicted. Berchtold had to content himself with Tisza's strong support for a 'tough diplomatic offensive' but 'no question' of war. The moment was not yet right, Tisza remarked. Far better to wait until Vienna had the support of other Balkan states. In a letter to the Emperor, Tisza noted that it was vital 'to make use of the recent outrage to destroy' the German Kaiser's 'prejudiced pro-Serbian attitude'.[8] Tisza's opposition appeared immediately to draw the venom from the gathering lust for war. The Austro-Hungarian Ambassador in Berlin, the 73-year-old Count Szögeny, one of the many Hungarians in the upper echelons of the Foreign Ministry, expressed to Prince Bülow what Tisza and the rest of the Hungarian magnates must have thought: the assassination was a 'dispensation of providence' which at a stroke removed the 'threat of civil war' within the monarchy.[9]

The fact that it had put the Empire at the risk of extinction through a much greater war escaped the Ambassador though it was probably not lost on Bülow, who had always believed that Austria's future lay with her 'incorporation into the German Reich'. He would later write: 'May the future grant the German Austrian race its way back again with Germany as its mother. . . .'[10]

The army pushes for war

The army and the General Staff responded more predictably. War appeared the only credible response to the assassination. The military prestige of a great empire was at stake. Anything less than an armed response would validate the views of those in Germany and elsewhere who had written off the monarchy as paralysed and incapable of action. Younger men in the services far removed from the dynamic of statecraft intuitively came to the same conclusion. The young naval Lieutenant Banfield, coming to the end of a tour of duty at the fledgling airfield at Wiener Neustadt, recalled many years later how he and his brother officers, receiving the news, fell silent until one said, reflecting the views of them all: 'This means war.'[11]

Meanwhile police investigations continued in Sarajevo. It was not long before the links between the conspirators and Belgrade began to emerge. The name of the Serbian Major Vojin Tankosič was mentioned and this caused a flurry of telegrams to the Austrian military attaché in Belgrade, Major Gellinek. In response, Gellinek pointed the finger at Tankosič's friend and superior, Colonel 'Apis' as being 'close to the heart' of the conspiracy, but this information mysteriously never seems to have left the War Ministry.[12] It is hard to suppress the thought that the name of 'Apis', linked as it was with the German military, was kept out of the investigation for a reason. For an Austria which would need Berlin's support it was best not to allude to anything that could highlight the links between military circles in Berlin and Belgrade. These links, described in detail by Gellinek's reports only a month earlier, had entered a new phase of intimacy but now they were about to become an embarrassment for all concerned and needed to be suppressed.

At this initial stage in the crisis, German diplomacy pursued a pacific course. Tschirsky's first dispatches on the assassination prove that he counselled caution, in keeping with Berlin's 'unhelpful' policy a year earlier, which had so exasperated Berchtold that he had sent an ultimatum to Montenegro in October 1913 to get them to withdraw from Albanian territory without even consulting Berlin.

At Tschirsky's first meeting with the Emperor after the assassination, neither man mentioned the assassination of the Archduke. Tschirsky later noted he had wished to proffer condolences but the All-Highest gave him no opening. This was curious. It implies that the Emperor (for the diplomat would have had to wait to take his lead from him) was keen to move on to practicalities, in particular whether Berlin was ready to change tack and become more supportive of Vienna vis-à-vis Serbia. The Emperor was again sending a hint. By not referring once to his nephew's murder, he was conveying a silent accusation. He was uninterested in German condolences because even if there had been no German complicity in the assassination (and of that he could not be sure) Germany's military and financial encouragement of Serbia had created the conditions for such outrages against the monarchy. His silence fitted perfectly with Tisza's advice to 'make use of the recent outrages' to persuade the German Kaiser to give up his 'prejudiced pro-Serbian attitude'.[13]

In his later conversation with Berchtold, Tschirsky maintained his detachment. He stated that 'it was all very well' for Austria to plan a final settling of accounts with Serbia, but Germany would 'only intervene' if the Austrians had 'a concrete plan of action' that must make it 'clear how far one wants to go'. This rather half-hearted response reflected the German Ambassador's instructions. Two days later, the State Secretary for Foreign Affairs, Zimmerman (deputising for his chief Jagow who was on his honeymoon), spoke to the Imperial and Royal Ambassador in Berlin, Szögeny, in precisely the same way.

Zimmerman urged 'great prudence' on Szögeny and advised against making 'humiliating demands'. Szögeny in any event was cautious. He was the oldest serving diplomat in the Austrian service and at 73 was looking forward to retirement. Like most Hungarians he had greeted the news of the assassination with 'undisguised relief'.[14] But the military in Berlin and Vienna were set on another course and in the first of several fluctuations of policy by all the protagonists of the July crisis, Berlin began to move away from earlier resistance to conflict. The first outward sign of this change was the German Kaiser's response to the advice of his own diplomats.

His marginalia scribbled on the side of Tschirsky's dispatch illuminate the German ruler's mood. 'Who authorised Tschirsky to say this?' Tschirsky was to 'stop speaking this nonsense' immediately. It was 'now or never'.[15]

Hoyos meets Naumann

A meeting in Vienna between Berchtold's chef du cabinet, Count Hoyos, and the German publicist, Victor Naumann, expressed this new mood. Naumann enjoyed the confidence of the German military, and was well connected with German nationalist organisations in Vienna. On 1 July he visited Hoyos, who wrote a memorandum recording the discussion.[16]

The memorandum quoted Naumann as saying that, 'now when Kaiser Wilhelm is horrified at the Sarajevo murder, if spoken to in the right way he will give us all the assurances ... and this time go to the length of war. ...'.[17] Naumann continued in this vein, reassuring Hoyos that he, Naumann, 'would see' that the German press resolutely fell into line behind Austria's strong policy of action. 'Public opinion in Germany will stand by the Austrian ally.'[18]

At about the same time as Naumann was winding Hoyos up in Vienna, Potiorek had begun sending a series of telegrams containing, in modern parlance, 'sexed-up' evidence exaggerating the domestic problems in Bosnia and Hercegovina in an attempt to justify 'action'. A convinced member of the war party even before the assassination, Potiorek now 'advocated a blatant variation of save the domestic situation by attacking a foreign enemy'.[19] Such distortions illustrated how the balance of Imperial opinion still favoured peace. Potiorek like Conrad realised that their Emperor was the most formidable obstacle to war. Both men worked hard to distort the realities of the situation on the ground and to cast developments in terms of the Empire's prestige in order to win him round.

The Austrian 'war party' really only existed among the military and a handful of diplomats. More ammunition was needed if the momentum was to pass to their side. German support would provide this if Berlin could be persuaded to give up her policy towards Belgrade. As this remained 'unclear', the decision was taken to bypass Tschirsky (and the aged Hungarian Szögeny) and garner support for military intervention from Berlin directly. Berchtold, strongly supported in senior Austrian military circles, took the unusual step of sending a diplomatic mission led by Hoyos directly to Berlin.[20]

Hoyos personified the younger generation of Austrian diplomats, who were nearly all products of the Theresianum, where they had been imbued with a mission to 'stop the rot' of Habsburg decline. By 1914, these men in influential positions included Counts Forgách, Hoyos and Szapáry, and Baron Musulin. They are often lumped together with Berchtold as the 'war party', but none of them, other than Forgách, was determined on war at this stage.[21] Berchtold's wife two weeks later would leave on a pilgrimage to France and Hoyos had married a French woman who had just given birth, a few weeks earlier, to his son. Hoyos's mother was a Whitehead and he was therefore half English. He planned, most reluctantly, to send his wife and newborn child to France in the event of hostilities but understandably hoped these could be avoided. The Austrian Minister in Belgrade, General Wladimir Giesl von Gieslingen recalled that, as late as 7 July, his meetings with Berchtold and Tisza strongly suggested that war was not the preferred policy. Tisza had angrily told him: 'If the Emperor wants to make war, he must find a new Prime Minister.'[22]

Tisza, however, was not consulted over Hoyos's mission. Hoyos was instructed to convey to the German Emperor a personal message from

Franz-Josef and a memorandum outlining an analysis suggesting that a final reckoning with Serbia was inevitable. As Tschirsky had urged Berchtold to formulate a 'concrete' plan of action, this memorandum aimed to provide just that. Hoyos, unlike Szögeny, was blessed with impeccable connections with Germany: his sister had married a Bismarck. He was seen as being far more 'persuasive' in Berlin than the Hungarian, who might be open to interference from his fellow Magyar Tisza. Hoyos arrived in Berlin on 5 July and delivered his letter. In it, Franz-Josef stressed the danger of Russian policy and declared that the plot had been hatched in Belgrade. While he avoided using the word 'war', there was little doubt that he favoured action because he stressed that the 'band of conspirators' could not go unpunished.

Although the German Kaiser insisted to Hoyos that he would need to consult his chancellor Bethmann-Hollweg, he was confident that Germany would support Austria-Hungary. All initial caution had been abandoned. German military and industrial circles around Naumann had clearly been active. The German Kaiser insisted that it was vital for Vienna to take advantage of the favourable situation and move swiftly. Later that same day, the German Kaiser spoke to Bethmann in the following terms. It was Germany's 'vital interest' which required the 'preservation of Austria intact . . . the sooner Austria moves the better'. These themes were repeated an hour later when Wilhelm met several important military leaders. It was agreed that the following day, 6 July, Zimmerman and Bethmann would tell Hoyos that 'the time had come' and that Germany fully endorsed Austrian action. The so-called 'blank cheque' had been given. As the minutes of the meetings show, it was given in full awareness that an Austrian move against Serbia would lead to 'complications' with Russia.[23]

The following day Zimmerman urged Hoyos 'to go to war without diplomatic delays'. Bethmann repeated the message that 'reprisals were amply justified' and required 'immediate action'. But although Germany had offered its unconditional support, no decision had been taken in Vienna to go to war.

Tisza isolated: Conrad addresses the Joint Council of Ministers

When Hoyos returned from his mission on the 7th, the Joint Council of Ministers met to discuss Hoyos' message from Berlin.[24] Opening the meeting, Tisza was clearly irritated that Hoyos had gone to Berlin at all. He made his displeasure known by referring to the mission as 'regrettable'. There was, he noted, 'no imperative reason to go to war with Serbia'. He would 'never agree to a surprise attack on Serbia', such 'as regrettably has been discussed in Berlin by Count Hoyos'.[25] Nor was it 'for Germany' to decide 'how and when' Austria was to proceed against Serbia. A 'diplomatic success' against Serbia was far more desirable than hostilities.

Berchtold responded that 'diplomatic successes against Serbia only temporarily enhanced the prestige of the monarchy while intensifying the strain of relations with Belgrade'. The others present, including Bilinski, supported Berchtold. The minutes show clearly that Tisza was isolated in his views. Minuting the Hungarian's objections, Berchtold moved swiftly on to the next item on the agenda, the question of formulating demands to be complied with by Belgrade.

Tisza felt the ground moving beneath him because Berchtold, emboldened by Hoyos's mission, had clearly edged closer to the war party and had skilfully initiated discussion of an ultimatum. The minutes of the meeting show how Tisza tried to claw back lost ground. The word 'war' was replaced at his insistence with 'energetic action' and the phrase 'present demands to make war certain' was crossed out and replaced, again at Tisza's request, with 'demands must be made to make their rejection probable'.[26] Tisza stipulated two further delaying points: first that the 'Note' must be 'very carefully thought out', and second that 'it be submitted' to the Hungarian Prime Minister (i.e. himself) 'before dispatch'. Furthermore the note was not to contain 'terms that would clearly betray our intention to make impossible demands'.[27]

The minutes of this meeting underlined how policy had been shifting since the first days after the assassination: Tisza, the strong man of Austro-Hungarian politics, was not only increasingly isolated, he had implicitly agreed, albeit reluctantly, to a policy aiming at the elimination of Serbia as a factor in Balkan power politics. Tisza might advise or be consulted on the implementation, but he could no longer prevent it. Tisza's confidence that he could still master events must have taken a knock at this meeting. The council moved on to its next topic: the 'options and implications of war with Russia'.

For these discussions, the Chief of Staff, Conrad, was invited to join the council. Because the discussions were 'confidential', no minutes were kept, barring the mention for the record that they had taken place. Conrad at this stage remained of the view that his punitive campaign against Serbia would be the priority, and that it would be vital to secure the river crossings around Belgrade before Serbian counter-measures were deployed. He insisted he favoured energetic action but, on 7 July, it was not only Tisza who favoured delay. The issue of the annual harvest presented itself. The harvest on which the Empire would live for the next year was still being gathered with the help of the army. As Conrad had always realised, many of his troops would not be back in their barracks until the last week of July. To recall them would sound the alarm.

Berchtold, increasingly deferring to Conrad, supported this delay. He had been apprised of the visit of the French Premier, Poincaré, to Russia later that month. It would be a hostage to fortune to deliver a démarche to Serbia while the Russians and French were in so intimate an embrace. It would not do for them both to plot against Austria's latest move over the clink of champagne glasses. Berchtold set 23 July for the delivery of the note: the day the French party were to leave Russia. In the meantime he urged Conrad and others to go on holiday so as 'not to demonstrate that anything might be amiss'.[28]

Not all voices were clamouring for war. As the decisions of 7 July were discussed, some news of what was afoot leaked out. Five days later, on the 13th Count Lützow, the half-English former Imperial and Royal Ambassador to Rome, called on Berchtold and Count Forgách at the Ballplatz. Thanks to the cohesiveness of Viennese society, Lützow had picked up that a series of stiff demands of Belgrade was being formulated, and he was keen to ventilate his concern. By 12 July, the mood in Vienna had clearly hardened.

On being received warmly by Berchtold, he said he had heard that a strong note was being prepared but he believed that if the demands were unreasonable Serbia would reject them. 'The idea of a local war was a pure mental aberration' ('Lokaliserung ist ein reines Hirngespenst').[29] Lützow grimly warned Berchtold that, with Serbia's rejection of the demands, a world war would ensue and 'with that you are putting the survival of the entire Monarchy at risk' (auf eine karte). As Lützow recalled, 'Berchtold fell silent at these words and did not respond.'[30]

Lützow warns London of the military option

As an experienced colleague, Lützow understood the significance of Berchtold's silence. Later the same day discussing the risks with another senior colleague he was appalled to hear him say: 'Why worry? The worst that can happen to us is that we might lose Galicia.' Alarmed, Lützow took the unusual step of inviting the British Ambassador, Maurice de Bunsen, to lunch two days later, on the 15th, leaving the startled Englishman in no doubt that the situation was 'serious' and that 'a kind of indictment' was being framed against Serbia. This indictment would require 'unconditional acceptance within a short time-limit', otherwise force would be used. 'Austria was in no mood to parley.' The military option was being readied.

As was no doubt intended by Lützow, Bunsen immediately on the 15th telegraphed this information to London though he discreetly did not reveal the identity of his informant. Indiscreetly, the Foreign Office in London responded the next day, demanding the source's name. Even when Bunsen complied with this, London's reaction remained aloof, dilatory and recklessly relaxed. Nicolson, the Permanent Under-Secretary, in one of the more crass of his annotations minuted that he 'doubted' Austria would resort to action.[31] Nicolson appeared to have forgotten that Austria had mobilised twice the previous year and, as recently as October 1913, had sent a successful ultimatum to the Montenegrins.

Nicolson, who really should have known better, did nothing to inform his chief Grey that matters were really serious. More than a week before the final Austrian Note was delivered, and indeed even before it was receiving its final draft at the hands of Musulin, London had all the information it needed to see that Vienna meant to impose on the Serbs an 'ultimatum' with a time limit, after which force would be deployed. It would be pleasant to record that Nicolson and other Germanophobes in the Foreign Office simply ignored this vital piece of information. Unfortunately, the evidence points to Nicolson having told the Russian and Serbian envoys the significance of the intelligence from Vienna while suppressing its importance at home. It was hardly the first or indeed the last time that a piece of information entrusted to a diplomat would end up in precisely the wrong place. Rarely has such valuable diplomatic intelligence from so faultless a source at such an important time been so ill-used. Grey would only hear about the 'ultimatum' a week later; the British Cabinet only after it had been delivered. If London had wished to exercise some restraint on Vienna, here was the moment. Like many other moments in the July crisis, it came and it passed.[32]

Lützow's 'calculated indiscretion' and the quality of the intelligence he had just handed London was all the more extraordinary given that at this very moment Berchtold was going to considerable lengths to shield his intentions, even from his German allies. There was to be no leakage. The excellent Imperial and Royal Military Deciphering Service had broken the Italian ciphers and were horrified to see the Empire's intentions conveyed to Italian diplomats en poste in two 'enemy' capitals thanks to German diplomatic gossip. In fact, Berchtold need not have worried. It was too late: Nicolson was responsible for ensuring that the contents of de Bunsen's illuminating report was conveyed to the Serbian minister via the Russians.[33]

Meanwhile the Austrian military authorities continued with their investigations in Sarajevo in an attempt to find conclusive proof of official Serbian complicity. Despite the interrogation of the conspirators, including Gavrilo Princip who had fired the shots that had killed the Imperial couple, this link proved elusive. When the German Kaiser had told his Ambassador in London, Lichnowsky, that the 'spiritual instigators' of the assassination were to be found in 'the political and military circles of Belgrade', he could not have based that information on anything that had come from Vienna. By the end of the first week in July, Potiorek's military investigators were still flailing around trying to find a shred of evidence that could link the crime to 'political and military circles in Belgrade'.

On 10 July, in a sign of impatience with the slow pace of events, Berchtold, again taking his cue from the military, dispatched Sektionchef Wiesner to Sarajevo with a time limit of 48 hours to wire back evidence of Serbian complicity. The hapless Wiesner, a conscientious and honest official, such as the Habsburg Empire produced in their thousands, struggled to find anything that could link the crime with Belgrade. The investigating judge in Sarajevo, another honest official, despite massive pressure from Potiorek put the cause of the assassination squarely down to the absence of any meaningful security. 'All the evidence,' Wiesner telegraphed on the 13th, pointed 'away' from official Serbian connivance in the crime.[34]

This setback did not deter Berchtold who, at this stage of the crisis, appears to have been much influenced by his 'Young Turks' at the Ballplatz, notably Forgách, and the German Ambassador Tschirsky. Tschirsky in particular, reprimanded by Kaiser Wilhelm for advocating prudence in the initial days of the crisis, was now busy making up for lost time. Having shifted his position radically, he began constantly to badger Berchtold into extreme measures.

Conrad's mobilisation plans delay the 'grand indictment'

Berchtold's plans for a 'grand indictment' were not hindered by the absence of relevant evidence in Sarajevo. Baron Musulin was entrusted with attempting a suitable draft of the Austrian démarche which could be discussed at the Council of Joint Ministers on 19 July. On the 14th, Tisza and Berchtold had agreed that no démarche should be delivered to Serbia before the departure of the French Premier from Russia, which turned out to be on the 23rd.

In accordance with Berchtold's extravagant security precautions, the council meeting of 19 July was held at the Foreign Minister's private residence, with all participants arriving in 'unofficial' vehicles. Musulin had prepared the draft of the note, which Berchtold proceeded to edit, sharpening up some of the demands. For example point 6, calling on Belgrade to 'open a judicial inquiry against those implicated in the plot', became 'to allow the agents of the Imperial and Royal police to proceed . . . to search for accomplices of the plot who are on Serbian territory'.

Once again it was left to Tisza to resist but, in the face of the unanimity of his colleagues, he was reduced to insisting that he would veto the decision to send the note 'if one inch of Serbian territory will be annexed by us'.[35] A letter sent by Forgách to Merey, the k. (u.) k. ambassador in Rome strongly implies that although Austria would take no part in a division of the spoils, Serbia would be partitioned among her neighbours.[36]

Tisza insisted that on the outbreak of hostilities a memorandum was to be sent to the major powers underlining the Empire's determination not to annex any Serbian territory 'beyond strategically necessary frontier rectifications'. This reference to 'strategically necessary frontier rectifications' was a concession to Conrad. Conrad, who had suggested marching into Italy and occupying the Quadrilateral as well as urging everyone to war against Serbia only a few years earlier, continued to live up to his reputation as a 'military giant' who was a 'political pygmy'. At this meeting, he was overheard muttering to Krobatin, the War Minister, that 'during the Balkan Wars the Powers had talked about the *status quo ante* but afterwards nobody bothered about it again.'[37]

Conrad's lack of realism with regard to political affairs was matched by his colleagues' lack of understanding of the realities of the Imperial and Royal Army. They relied entirely on Conrad for their understanding of war. At no time during this meeting did Conrad share the information that the Imperial and Royal Army could not be ready to take any action against Serbia until the middle of August. Nor did he disclose that his annual staff conversations with Moltke had been limited to meaningless generalities. Conrad fondly imagined that Germany would unequivocally offer their army as 'Rückdeckung', guarding his back while he proceeded to hurl the bulk of his forces against Serbia. Berchtold imagined that the continuing German enthusiasm for a quick and resolute action was all the support he needed. The German Kaiser had noted in the marginalia of a telegram dated 10 July: 'It is taking a very long time!'

But Conrad had barely understood the realities of his own army's mobilisation plans let alone those of his ally. As at the beginning of every major war in every country, the long years of prosperous peace had failed to produce either ability or imagination at the top of the military tree. Miscalculation and a poor grip on reality marked the decision-making process of the upper echelons of the Imperial and Royal Army. In any event Conrad was not about to counsel delay ahead of a declaration of war he had spent his entire career advocating.

In Berlin, an unfortunate weakness in the chain of command of the diplomatic process became apparent. While the German Emperor and military circles were urging Vienna to get a move on, the Foreign Minister Jagow, softened up by a heady combination of domestic bliss (he had just returned from his honeymoon) and some unsettling telegrams, began to panic. He started dictating cables reflecting how 'we anxiously desire the localisation

of the conflict' lest the 'intervention of the Powers bring incalculable conse-
quences'. Unfortunately, this warning was drowned in the determination of the
German Ambassador in Vienna, Tschirsky, to spur Berchtold on to war.
Tschirsky made no effort to communicate Jagow's mollifying words to Vienna.

The Austrian Note

Jagow would have to wait until the 22nd, less than 24 hours before the Austrian
démarche was to be delivered in Belgrade, to receive from the Austrian
Ambassador in Berlin, Szögeny, the text of the Austrian Note. Although Jagow
wrote later that he found the text 'pretty stiff and going beyond its purpose',
Berlin made no attempt to change or tone down its contents. Vienna would no
doubt have resisted any attempts at dilution. Musulin had polished the note
'like a gemstone'. It was intended to be severe but not to exclude all possibility
of Serbian compliance.

There is some evidence that other German diplomats had attempted to
offer useful advice to Serbia earlier. On 30 June, Zimmerman had urged Serbia
to open a judicial inquiry into the assassinations. On 8 July, the new German
military attaché had arrived in Belgrade and presented his credentials, a sign
that relations between Belgrade and Germany were not at this stage especially
strained. Even as late as 20 July, Pasič would ask Germany for its good offices
to influence Vienna 'towards conciliation'. When the note was finally presented,
the German legation in Belgrade refused to believe Serbia could accept it.
At the same time they did not believe that its partial rejection would lead to
war. The warm glow that had marked Germano-Serb relations only a few days
earlier took time to dim.

On 24 July, the German minister bumped into a Serbian politician in
Belgrade and said: 'You cannot accept it.' In Paris, the German ambassador
Schoen urged the Serbs to ask for 'further clarification'. Even when Austria
eventually declared war, her ally, who had urged her into this step, now refused
to 'pass on' the declaration of war as requested by Vienna in the absence of the
Austrian minister, who had left Belgrade three days earlier. A new German
narrative was already emerging. Prince Bülow expressed it perfectly when he
later wrote: 'Austria's German ally on behalf of and through the instrumentality
of the Habsburg monarch had allowed itself to become involved in the most
terrible of all wars'.[38]

On 18 July, the acting British Minister in Belgrade, Crackenthorpe, an
avowed Serbophile, telegrammed that the 'Serbian government was certain
that restraint will be exercised on Austria from Berlin'. 'Crackers', as he was
known, had not covered himself in glory in his reporting. Earlier he had

systematically suppressed his consuls' reports of Serbian atrocities in the Balkans. These reports eventually reached London via Constantinople, the headquarters of the Levant Consular Service, where they were automatically copied and forwarded, much to Crackenthorpe's chagrin.[39]

Hartwig, the Russian Minister in Belgrade, had urged extreme caution on the Serbs, a position favoured also by Sazonov in St Petersburg. When Hartwig had heard the news of the assassination, he had said: 'For heaven's sake let us hope it is not a Serb who has pulled the trigger.' Hartwig realised how fragile Prime Minister Pašić's and indeed Serbia's position was in July 1914. Given the vast resources of the Habsburg Empire, Serbia could not hope to win a war against Austria in the long run.

On the evening of 10 July, Hartwig visited the Austrian Minister Wladimir Giesl who as a former professional officer for many years was the recipient of the last letter the Russian spy Colonel Redl wrote before committing suicide. Despite being political rivals, Giesl and Hartwig were on good terms. Hartwig always reminded him that he loved Vienna ('*Nur in Wien kann man leben*').[40] Giesl, who had earlier been minister in the Montenegrin capital, had come to respect Russian diplomacy. His greatest problems in Cetinje had been with his German colleague who had constantly worked against Austrian policy.[41] Giesl had just that morning returned to Belgrade after consultations in Vienna. The Russian was keen to clear up false rumours that he had 'celebrated' the Archduke's death and incorrect reports that he had refused to fly the legation flag at half-mast. After their conversation, Giesl was convinced that Hartwig had not been privy to the plot, though he suspected the office of the Russian military attaché, Artamonov.[42]

Hartwig believed that the Yugoslav Crown Prince Alexander was a 'passive tool in the hands of the military party', the rivals of Pašić. Hartwig had just left the crown prince at dinner and was expected back to give him a briefing the same evening. Unfortunately, barely had the minister smoked two of his Russian cigarettes and spoken these words than he suffered a seizure and died of a massive heart attack. Hartwig had been about to go to Bad Nauheim for his annual cure where, in previous years, he had lost significant weight. He had had a long history of heart disease and his sudden death – despite rumours that he had been 'poisoned' by the 'Borgia like Giesl'– surprised no one who knew him except his daughter Ludmilla. She insisted on retrieving the contents of the Austrian diplomat's ashtray containing the remains of Hartwig's last two cigarettes. Giesl would later write that, 'Had Hartwig been alive, he would have forced unconditional acceptance of the Austrian Note on the Serbs and the world war would not have broken out'.[43] Hartwig's death removed another one of the key factors for peace in the Balkans at that moment. Only Hartwig might have been in a position to resist the pressure of Pan-Slav circles in St Petersburg, which were in no mood to compromise.

The Austrian Note was finalised ten days later on 20 July. It was truly a 'grand indictment'. Musulin had done his work well as far as the drafting was concerned.[44] On the following day Berchtold travelled to Ischl where Kaiser Franz-Josef accepted the judgement of his ministers and assented to the note's delivery. Tisza had been 'bought off' with the promise that there would be no annexation of Serbian territory.

In the meantime, Berchtold had heard from Count Szapáry in St Petersburg that Poincaré had stressed to him that 'Serbia had friends', words which Szapáry, who was certainly not a warmonger, interpreted as 'significant'. The Austrian Note was immediately characterised on its distribution to the Entente Powers as an 'ultimatum', though this was not true technically. It was explicitly not an ultimatum but a 'démarche with a time limit', as Berchtold pedantically telegrammed to his embassies. The time limit was 48 hours. After reminding Belgrade of its previous undertakings to live in a spirit of good-neighbourliness, the note pointed to Serbia's repeated breaches of good faith, culminating in the assassination.

It went on to make ten demands. These ranged from closing down the propaganda patriotic society, Narodna Obrana, to arresting Serbs implicated in the Sarajevo crime and, more forcefully, insisting that Austrian officials should be allowed on to Serbian territory to investigate the conspiracy to murder the Archduke.

For all the note's eloquence as a diplomatic document, and through no fault of Musulin, the Austrians had botched the investigation. It had focused on Narodna Obrana to the exclusion of the secret society of the Black Hand (Liberty or Death: *Ujedinjenje ili Smrt*). This was both a legal and political error. Gellinek's dispatches from Belgrade pointing to the complicity of the Black Hand had not been forwarded from the War Ministry, nor had several penetrating earlier dispatches concerning the organisation's infiltration of Serbian political society.

Thus the note lost the chance to bring to international attention the links between the regicides of 1903 and the murder of 1914. Ironically, this omission made its acceptance by Serbia slightly easier. Though Pašič regarded the Black Hand as his mortal political enemy, he was aware that he had got wind of the plot and its connection with 'Apis' and the Black Hand. He could not plausibly plead ignorance of the plot if that organisation was named, given that its tentacles stretched powerfully into Serbian official life. Pašič had good reason to fear investigations into 'Apis's' secret society: his own son was a member.

By not mentioning the Black Hand, the note lost an opportunity to line up all the monarchs of Europe in a display of monarchical solidarity against an avowedly terrorist organisation. Throughout the July crisis, Berchtold and his advisers failed to play the strong cards they held and were constantly on the wrong side of international 'perception', hence Berchtold's frustration at his note being called an 'ultimatum'.

Berchtold's accompanying instructions to Giesl limited the envoy's actions considerably and gave no room for the Austrian Minister in Belgrade to be flexible. Only 'unconditional acceptance' on the part of Belgrade could avoid a rupture. Giesl was not to be drawn into discussion of any of the points. According to Giesl, most of his colleagues at the Ballplatz assumed the Serbs would accept the note unreservedly.[45]

The note's 48-hour time limit was not wasted by the Serbs even though Pasič was campaigning and was about to visit Salonika 'incognito' for a few days.[46] An urgent telegram stopped Pasič's train, and the Prime Minister returned to Belgrade at 5 a.m. He immediately sought the advice of the Entente legations but these were poorly staffed at this moment of crisis: Hartwig was dead; Artamanov, the Russian military attaché was on holiday in Switzerland. At the British legation, the minister was also on holiday and the legation was in the care of the Serbophile Crackenthorpe. At the French legation, whence not a single telegram had been dispatched since 4 July, the new minister Boppe had arrived in Belgrade barely an hour before Pasič.

The consensus in the advice of these men, as far as we can tell, appears to have been to avoid armed conflict by accepting unconditionally the Austrian demands, and a first draft was drawn up doing precisely that. As late as 12.30 p.m. on the afternoon of the 25th, Crackenthorpe was wiring Grey that the 'ten points' of the Austrian note 'are accepted without reserve'.[47] Yet by the morning of the 25th, a huge change had occurred, overtaking Crackenthorpe's dispatch.

Serbia mobilises: the dazzling Serbian reply

Already, twelve hours earlier, the decision to mobilise Serbian forces had been taken. By 2 a.m. on the morning of the 25th, the Belgrade field horse-drawn artillery began limbering up and was seen by one Serb minister riding out of the city as he returned to his apartment shortly after 2.30 a.m. The Serbian political and military leadership assumed that, as in the days of Joseph II and Prince Eugene, Belgrade would be seized after a brief struggle. Had Colonel 'Apis' acquired the Austro-Hungarian mobilisation plan, the Serbian leadership could have relaxed. It would be weeks before the Imperial and Royal

Army would be ready to advance into Serbian territory and then, in accordance with the strategic premise of defending Bosnia and Hercegovina, the advance would come from elsewhere.

Despite Redl's betrayal of the Austro-Hungarian Order of Battle, there was the widespread illusion in London, Paris and St Petersburg of imminent and ongoing Austrian military 'operations' against Serbia. This was to be a key misconception in the closing days of the July crisis; not least because nowhere was it believed more passionately than in the 'dream and reality' capital of the world, Vienna. The somnolent fantasy of Robert Musil's 'Kakania' was now evident in the decision-making process in Vienna. Within a few days, Musil's sleepy world would give way to Karl Kraus's *Last Days of Mankind*, the most biting satire of a war ever penned.

Historians are agreed that the early Serb mobilisation was connected with telegrams that reached Belgrade from St Petersburg, promising fulsome support. A telegram from the Tsar reached Prince Alexander pledging help. Eyewitnesses tell of the crown prince going on the night of the 24th to the Belgrade officers' club and reading out a message from the Tsar promising military support.[48]

The telegrams sent to Belgrade from Russia that day left Belgrade in no doubt that they would not be alone. Thus it came about that, from having agreed to accept more or less unreservedly the demands of the Austrian démarche, Pasič moved towards a more sophisticated approach.

It has proved impossible to tell the extent to which the next draft Serbian reply was written with Russian and even French help. There is no documentary evidence to suggest the involvement of either. Yet the Serbian reply remains to this day one of the most brilliant examples of diplomatic draftsmanship ever undertaken and, while forgotten in most surveys of the July crisis, it repays close analysis. In the words of Baron Musulin, who had drafted the Austrian Note, it was 'the most dazzling specimen of diplomatic skill I have ever witnessed'.[49]

Its brilliance lay in the simple fact that the reply simulated compliance while eluding commitment to fulfilling Vienna's demands in any meaningful way. It is a tribute to its quality that even a hundred years later authoritative accounts of the July crisis refer to the Serbs accepting 'all but one point of the Austrian ultimatum'.[50] But a careful perusal of the Serbian reply shows it did no such thing. It rejected outright point 6. It only partially accepted points 1, 2 and 3 and offered a wholly unsatisfactory if not downright dishonest reply to point 8. It was evasive on points 4, 5 and 9. Yet all this was clothed in such conciliatory language, it fooled many a diplomat.[51] More significantly, it fooled not only Sir Edward Grey, but also the German Kaiser who, on reading it, exclaimed: 'A masterful response for only 48 hours ... and with it all need for war disappears. Giesl could have saved himself the railfare and remained in Belgrade.'[52]

The Serbian reply's astonishing success was all the more remarkable given that halfway through typing the penultimate draft with the clock ticking during the afternoon of the 25th, the Serbian typist in the smoke-filled room of Pašić's office broke the machine, which happened to be the only typewriter in the building. It was decided to write the entire reply out in longhand in heliographic ink. The final version was notable for its crossing-outs and blots of ink. Scruffy and improvised and delivered literally minutes before the time limit expired, it was a truly Balkan effort in format and delivery. Yet in content it was masterly.

Giesl waded through the document. Despite the lack of clarity on the page, due to some of the ink having smudged, he quickly saw its contradictions. By the time he had reached the end of it five minutes later, he knew that he had no choice but to leave Belgrade in accordance with his instructions. The time was two minutes to six, and the train he was instructed by Berchtold to catch should the Serbian reply prove unsatisfactory left the Belgrade railway station at 6.30 p.m.

Giesl had in any event been apprised some hours earlier that the Serbian reply would only accept those points which were compatible with 'her honour and dignity'. A Serbian minister, Janković, had called in on the legation to ask Giesl a 'personal favour'. In return he had told Giesl that the Austrian Note was going to be rejected in part. This confirmed earlier reports that the mood of those around Pašić was hardening. On receiving this intelligence and the news that Serbia had mobilised, Giesl promptly telegrammed Berchtold that acceptance of the note was unlikely and proceeded to burn his ciphers in the legation garden.

He and his wife had packed that night, and the Austro-Hungarian diplomats were all gathered with one suitcase per person. The legation archive had already been sent to Semlin, on 12 July. The German legation had been briefed and Giesl's staff readied for departure. Cars waited outside the legation to make the journey to the railway station, some ten minutes away. By 5 p.m., Giesl was in a 'dark suit'. He was entitled to wear a full general's uniform and, had he been the warmonger the Serbs later accused him of being, he would no doubt have worn it.

At Pašić's office, no one could agree as to who should deliver the reply. Once again the train times were a factor. Most of Pašić's closest associates were preparing to evacuate Belgrade and wanted to catch the 6 p.m. train to Niš where the government and the diplomatic corps were planning to reassemble. Pašić pocketed the envelope and went down the stairs slowly to where a car awaited him to take him to the Austrian legation. As Prime Minister, Pašič could count on the railway officials holding up any train he might be about to catch if he were delayed. At 5.55 p.m. Pašič handed the envelope to Giesl, and the two men politely exchanged courtesies. Then the Serbian premier left to be followed, less than fifteen minutes later, by the Austrian Minister and the legation staff. Although Giesl had told only his German counterpart of the likelihood of his departure, most of the diplomatic corps were at the main railway station to see him off. Also on the platform were many Serbian officers, some of whom, according to eye-witnesses, mischievously called out 'Au revoir a Budapeste!'

Ten minutes after the train departed, it steamed into Semlin, the Austro-Hungarian border post where it halted for Giesl to go to the stationmaster's office and receive a telephone call from Tisza. The Hungarian Premier who had done so much to delay hostilities simply asked 'Did it have to be?' ('Musste es denn sein?') to which Giesl replied simply 'Yes' ('Ja') and returned to the train which was due to arrive at Budapest the following morning, when the conversation could no doubt be continued before he entrained for Vienna.[53]

The news of the rupture of diplomatic relations reached the Emperor who noted, as he had when he agreed for the note to be sent, that it 'did not necessarily mean war'. There was still time for Serbia to fall into step with the demands of the note. But in its brilliance, the Serbian reply had stolen all chance of an Austrian diplomatic victory. As Musulin recalled, while he and Berchtold and the others sat dumbfounded in the Ballplatz discussing it, 'there was the grim realisation that we had achieved nothing with the note and we were back where we started'.[54]

Franz-Josef orders mobilisation: the affair at Temes-Kubin

As a cautionary measure, the Emperor had ordered the partial mobilisation of two-fifths of the monarchy's forces. This was set to begin three days later after the Sunday holiday. As Krobatin, the War Minister, took the order at Ischl, he turned at the door to the Emperor's study with questioning eyes. Franz-Josef was looking at him with a pained expression Krobatin had rarely seen before. The Emperor simply said: 'Go now. I cannot do anything else' ('Ich kann nicht anders').[55] At this stage, no instructions were issued for troops stationed in Galicia along the Russia frontier.

To forestall any diplomatic pressure to negotiate on the terms of the note, Berchtold now pressed for a formal declaration of war against Serbia. In this he was no doubt assisted by a telegram which has since disappeared but whose contents we know because it is cited in many other documents. The telegram from Headquarters 4th Corps Budapest, dated 27 July, referred to events taking place on 26 July:

> 4th Corps Headquarters reports Serbian units on board Danube steamship opened fire on our troops at Temes-Kubin. Engagement developed into large skirmish. Numbers of dead and wounded unknown.[56]

Though this telegram has disappeared it was cited in an interview Berchtold had with Franz-Josef just before the Emperor assented to a declaration of war on the 28th. In a message to Romania's King Carol the same day, Franz-Josef stated that he was forced to declare war on Serbia 'after Serbia, without even declaring war, had provoked a skirmish'. This was political dynamite because, if Vienna could demonstrate that Austria-Hungary had been attacked, the defensive clauses of the Triple Alliance to which Romania (secretly) and Italy (formally) subscribed could be deemed to have been activated.

On the 28th, Berchtold used the report of the 'skirmish at Temes-Kubin' to justify instructions to his ambassadors to reject attempts at mediation on the part of the Entente powers. Thus Mensdorff in London was told to inform Sir Edward Grey that attempts at mediation were too late, 'as yesterday on the Serbian side they fired on our frontier troops'.[57]

So keen was Berchtold to exploit this news, he even wrote the engagement into the Emperor's speech justifying the declaration of war. But to its credit, plagued by *Schlamperei* and incompetence though it was, the Habsburg monarchy still contained men of integrity. The next day, Berchtold realised that he had at the very least been manipulated. Following requests from various departments for details of the 'skirmish', the following telegram was found from Oberstleutnant Baumgartner of the 14th Infantry brigade (and this one has not disappeared). It was dated the 26th and reported that 'This afternoon troops of the 14th infantry brigade briefly opened fire on a Serbian steamer at Temes-Kubin. The steamer halted and was searched before being permitted to continue its journey'.[58] There was no mention of a 'large skirmish' or 'numbers of dead and wounded'. The era of Karl Kraus had arrived. Such distortions of the truth as that conveyed in the earlier telegram would provide ample material for his writings.

We do not know when Berchtold received the details of what really had transpired at Temes-Kubin. It is to his credit that he immediately struck out the phrases referring to the attack from the declaration of war document he had been drafting. He later told the Emperor that he had decided to remove *('eliminieren')* the reference on the 'grounds of further information', demonstrating that the events at Temes-Kubin were not of a scale to justify inclusion in so important a document.

With good reason, Franz-Josef was unamused. According to Conrad, Franz-Josef had stated on 5 July that if Germany supported Vienna he would say yes to war. On 25 July, when diplomatic relations were broken off, he stated that 'diplomatic rupture does not mean war'. He repeated this two days later when he met Giesl.[59] The Emperor strove to maintain peace, only sacrificing it when it proved impossible to maintain it consonant with his personal sense of his Empire's honour.

Colonel Seelinger of the Emperor's press bureau believed that Franz-Josef had refused to sign the declaration of war until Berchtold had read out a telegram describing a 'border incident'. Albertini quotes Seelinger's story from an article in the New York Times, dated 20 August 1924. As the momentum of events built up, the Emperor found that those who were most keen on war continued to cut corners.[60]

Conrad orders Voivode Putnik's arrest

Another indication that people were beginning to let standards slip was the decision taken by Conrad to arrest the Commander-in-Chief (Voivode) of the Serbian army, General Putnik, who had been taking the waters at Bad Gleichenberg in Styria. Putnik had tried to return to Serbia on the 25th, the day of the expiry of the time limit on the Austrian Note. Tisza, apprised by Conrad that he was passing through Budapest, asked the Foreign Ministry if he might be detained. The Foreign Ministry had not replied by the time the policemen swooped. When the Foreign Ministry reply eventually arrived, it pointed out tersely that 'no state of war' existed between the two states to justify such behaviour.

When he heard of these events, the Emperor was again unimpressed, and personally ordered the General's 'immediate' release and return to Serbia in a special railway carriage under the Emperor's protection. Seizing enemy commanders before hostilities had started was not how the Habsburg monarchy had ever conducted war. The Emperor astutely did not criticise his Chief of General Staff directly at this important moment, but he circulated a terse note to his War Minister, Krobatin, which was unmistakable in its implied reprimand of Conrad. Observing that, 'irrespective of who ordered this', he totally disapproved of this step. The Emperor went on to say that he expected his senior generals 'to behave with swiftness and independence but not at the expense of tact and at all times with discretion'. (Conrad justified his behaviour by referring to Imperial citizens stranded in Serbia who might be taken hostage. Like most of Conrad's appreciations, this one also lacked any foundation in reality.)[61] A further example also demonstrated the Emperor's determination to wage war honourably. A few weeks later, with the Empire now at war against Belgium and England, the War Ministry on Conrad's insistence advised that it was time to change the titles of those regiments which mentioned the name of an Entente sovereign, such as the famous Infantry regiment Nr 27 King of the Belgians, the Hussar regiment Nr 12 King Edward VII King of England, Emperor of India etc. Franz-Josef testily replied that he found such changes 'unnecessary', and ordered the names to remain.

Conrad's weak judgement was not limited to superficial details. With the declaration of war firmly pocketed, the Austrian commander finally announced that there was no question of any quick action against Belgrade. It would take at least two weeks to attack Serbia. Conrad was preparing a Daun-like uncoiling of Austrian soldiery advancing from the interior of the threatened Bosnian provinces, and he asked for 14 days to make his preparations. In the event, this was too optimistic.

In what was another of his unrealistic assessments, Conrad also told Berchtold to tell the Emperor on 31 July that he 'was confident that he could induce Italy not only to fulfil her allied obligations against France, but also place troops at our disposal for use in Galicia'.[62]

Russia announces mobilisation

Between them, Conrad and Berchtold had finally got the Emperor to sign their country's death warrant. As Russia began to mobilise publicly on the 31st (she had been privately mobilising for some time before that day, at least as early as the second week in July),[63] last-minute frantic attempts by Germany to get the Austrians to go into reverse withered.

Bethmann-Hollweg, the German Chancellor, had urged the Austrians to compromise. The famous 'Halt in Belgrade' option, so favoured by Grey, failed to take into account that Conrad's Plan 'B' (Balkan) for hostilities against Serbia did not involve the traditional occupation of Belgrade but a well-prepared offensive from Bosnia. Even if the Vienna statesmen had accepted Grey's 'Halt in Belgrade' proposal, Conrad's military plans would have prevented its execution.

In any event, the mobilisation of Russia swiftly banished mediation. On the 31st, the Austrian military attaché in Berlin, Oberstleutnant Bienerth, was summoned to Moltke and found him 'extremely agitated as I had never seen him before'.[64] Moltke had just been at the Foreign Ministry where another reverse of gears was in full swing to head off a conflagration that would bring England into the war against Germany, a danger recognised somewhat belatedly.

Moltke told Bienerth that it was time for Austria to mobilise 'at once against Russia' and that such a development would provide Germany with the *casus foederis* to become involved. A telegram urging action was now dispatched to Vienna. When this telegram reached Berchtold, another from Bethmann arrived at the same time demanding, in the name of the German Kaiser, the taking up of the latest mediation offer extended from London. For a few seconds Berchtold looked unblinkingly at the two telegrams before his Viennese training took over and he observed boredly: 'How strange. Can someone perhaps tell me: who is actually organising things these days in Berlin?' ('Wer führt Regie heutzutag in Berlin?')[65]

As Berchtold's lofty response implied, it was too late anyway. Mediation at this stage was unacceptable to Vienna because it would have involved a climb-down on the part of the monarchy and a great loss of prestige. Russia's mobili-sation plans rendered all thought of mediation irrelevant. Developments in Russia brought new challenges for the military. Conrad had always argued that he would need to know by the fifth day of mobilisation if Russia was to be hostile if the deployments for Plan 'B' (Balkan) were not to prevent some part of the deployment for Plan 'R' (Russia). Conrad does not appear to have thought through what the political effect would be on Germany once Russia mobilised, triggering her alliance with France. He had assumed that Germany would provide some cover against Russia but he was not prepared for the imperatives of the Schlieffen Plan, with its call for a sudden thrust westwards, virtually denuding Germany's Eastern front.

Berlin urges Conrad to 'forget Serbia'

To be fair to Conrad, the Germans were also operating in a new dimension. On 31 July, Moltke had telegraphed Conrad: 'Compel Italy to do her duty as an ally through compensations', a plea for the Empire to surrender the Trentino and Trieste, something unacceptable to anyone in Vienna. It was a disturbing sign of what was to come. As in peace, so in war, Germany's own agenda was taking over with scant regard for the interests of Vienna.

A few days later Kaiser Wilhelm telegraphed Franz-Josef with the message:

> I am prepared in fulfilment of my obligations as an ally to go to war against Russia and France immediately.

There were no alliance obligations demanding such action. Neither Russia nor France had attacked the monarchy. The message continued:

> In this hard struggle it is of the greatest importance that Austria directs her chief force against Russia and does not split it by a simultaneous offensive against Serbia. In this grave struggle Serbia plays a quite subordinate role requiring only defensive measures.[66]

There is no description of Franz-Josef's reaction to this telegram but his response might be imagined. No document of 1914 underlines more clearly that Germany's military circles had always regarded Austria-Hungary's military as a pawn in a larger game. Austria had gone to war to liquidate Serbia as a factor in Balkan politics. For that reason she had asked Germany to guard her back against Russia. A few days later she was being asked to throw her entire weight into a struggle against Russia and forget about her plans to attack Serbia.

Conrad's lack of imagination could not have prepared him or the Habsburg army for such a turn of events. Even so, he drafted a telegram to Moltke in which he observed: 'We asked for our back to be guarded while we liquidated Serbia and you have brought upon us the *Weltkrieg*!' (For understandable reasons, the telegram was never sent, and Glaise Horstenau suppressed it in his huge work on the Austrian military archives.)[67]

But it was Count Lützow who surely had been right on 13 July. A local war against Serbia was pure fantasy. The *Weltkrieg* which would inevitably follow from 'unreasonable demands against Serbia' would set at mortal risk the Empire's existence.

CHAPTER 22

Austria-Hungary's Last War

1914

Austria-Hungary's army entered the Great War unprepared for a major conflict. Her troops had not fired a shot in anger for more than a generation. The lessons her opponents had digested – the British during the Boer War, the Serbs during the Balkan wars, the Russians during the recent Russo-Japanese War – had all been ignored by Vienna. The only Austrian officer present during the Boer War, Major Robert Trimmel had sent reports warning of the advances in camouflage and tactics the British had had to adopt but his reports were dismissed as 'irrelevant'. Austria-Hungary would never fight 'a colonial war', was the General Staff's lofty retort. A lack of imagination pervaded the highest levels of command. When, in 1906, Franz-Josef was shown a modern Austrian prototype of an armoured car, he watched, mounted on his horse, with bemusement. 'Such a thing,' he said, 'would never be of any military value.'[1]

If this mentality was not enough, all the relevant Austro-Hungarian war plans, as we have seen, had been sold to the Entente. Political and nationalist rivalries threatened to weaken the cohesion of the armed forces. Examining these, the Allies could be forgiven for imagining that the Habsburg armies would rapidly disintegrate under prolonged pressure. This was not to prove the case, but well might the future German liaison officer with the Austrian General Staff General Cramon note: 'The Austrian military was adequate to wage a campaign against Serbia but inadequately prepared for any war against a major European power.'[2] Although the military budget had risen from 262 million crowns in 1895 to 306 million crowns in 1906, Austria was still spending proportionately less on her forces than any other European power. The Habsburg Empire was the least militarised state in Europe.

On the outbreak of hostilities, the army had evolved into a predominantly infantry arm: 700 out of every 1,000 soldiers were infantry. For every 1,000 officers, 791 were German-Austrians, 97 were Hungarians, 47 were Czechs, 23 Poles and 22 Croats or Serbs. The rest were English, Italian, Belgian, Slovene, Ruthene and Albanian.[3] The predominance of the German language shows that the army, though multinational and multi-confessional, was never multicultural in a modern sense. Conrad since 1906 had enjoyed greater powers than his predecessors as Generalstabchef. His remit had been extended to cover Landwehr and Honvédség forces as well as the Common Army but his staff lagged behind their German counterparts in organisation, dynamism and ethos.[4]

When the German military machine mobilised, Conrad felt the demands of his ally all too acutely, as indeed did many other Austrian generals. It had never been Austria-Hungary's intention to go to war with either France or England but the realities of the alliance system soon outstripped the wishful thinking of the Emperor and indeed his Ambassador in London, Count Mensdorff, a cousin of Edward VII. Mensdorff felt almost as English as he did Austrian or Hungarian. As the formal declaration of war was delivered, he remarked: 'What a supreme irony and injustice, that I, perhaps the most "Anglophile" of Austrian Ambassadors, should be responsible for handing over the first declaration of war to be presented in the history of our two Empires' century-old relations.'[5]

Mensdorff was not alone in feeling keenly the pressure of events on old ties and bonds. Count Lützow, who had warned Berchtold of the dangers ahead, had an English mother and was one of many Austrian aristocrats who found their links with England suddenly broken. Alphy Clary summed up the feelings of many when he recalled that the loss of the pleasures of English society at Marienbad and elsewhere would 'impoverish' many an Austrian.[6]

Even Franz-Josef who for years, much to the irritation of the Archduke Franz Ferdinand, had kept all his personal cash reserves at the Bank of England, felt the effects. Fortunately the tacit agreement among sovereigns to honour mutual financial obligations took priority over Foreign Office bureaucracy. Pressure from that direction to hasten a declaration of war against Austria-Hungary encountered, much to Eyre Crowe's consternation, resistance at the highest level. The week-long delay in London in declaring war against Austria-Hungary allowed the Bank of England discreetly to honour its obligations to the Habsburg monarch and repatriate all his cash reserves.[7]

Rudolf von Slatin, better known as Slatin Pasha, who had been adviser to General Gordon at Khartoum, was a general in the British army despite his being an Austrian subject. In his homeland he held the rank of Lieutenant in the Imperial and Royal Reserve. Though considered 'indispensable' by the British Sirdar of Egypt, he was reluctantly allowed to depart for his native

Vienna where he felt his duty lay. 'I have the privilege to hold the rank of General in the British Army but in this moment of crisis for my country I must return and support them,' he explained to his British officer friends who vowed to welcome him again after the war.[8]

The British Royal Navy escorted Mensdorff to Trieste. Grey and his entire office had personally waved farewell to him at Victoria station. The Royal Navy hoisted one welcoming friendly signal after another to the distraught Ambassador. At the same time, Franz-Josef sent a telegram to the British officers' mess of the King's Dragoon Guards of which he was honorary colonel, noting that he deeply regretted that 'his regiment and his country were at war'. In the event of any member of the regiment being captured he had given instructions that they were to be 'treated as his personal guest' until the cessation of hostilities.[9] The regiment was unfortunately not permitted by the British War Office to reciprocate and in 1915 the men were ordered to remove their Habsburg eagle badges from their caps and collars.[10]

The imperatives of war came more and more to overshadow chivalrous gestures. Clausewitz erred when he said that war was the continuation of diplomacy by other means. For a start, those who run wars are not the diplomatists. In Vienna, as in Berlin and London, the diplomats began to leave the table of decision-making. Gradually their places were taken by hard men in uniforms whose first priority was the safety of their men. The diplomatists in Vienna knew this reality well. Berchtold told his colleagues that he intended to don a cavalry uniform in an attempt to do something 'useful'. When, in August, Conrad called on the Foreign Ministry to bid 'farewell' before he entrained to the front, he found not a single diplomat in the building, even though he had given notice that he would be 'dropping in' en route for the Nordbahnhof. To his disgust, the Ballplatz was utterly deserted. Neither Berchtold nor any of his cabinet was to be found. They had all left some hours before to dine near the Strudelhof. 'These monocle-heroes', Conrad wrote bitterly to his mistress Gina Reininghaus, were 'thinking only of entertainments when hostilities have already commenced'.[11] In fact, the diplomatists knew better than Conrad that their jobs were over for the foreseeable future.

Austria-Hungary supplies the German army with artillery batteries

In response to a German request for artillery support on the Western front, Conrad offered two batteries of the formidable Austrian Skoda 30.5cm howitzers. For the German Schlieffen Plan to work, the Belgian and French forts which stood between the German army and Paris had to be reduced as swiftly as possible and the German artillery was simply not up to the task, Krupp notwithstanding. They needed the Austrian guns that were on the Galician front and the Italian frontier, in Cracow and Gorizia respectively. These and their crews were entrained on 12 and 13 August, arriving in time for use against Namur on the 20th, where they soon proved their worth.[12] They were also devastatingly effective in reducing Antwerp. Those who have visited the small museum near Ypres at a sinister hill known as 'The Dump' (Hill 60) will have seen contemporary photographs of the guns and their Austrian crews riding to war along the Western front. The German artillery could never have punched a hole through the so-called 'impregnable' line of Belgian fortresses without the help of these weapons, even though their withdrawal from the Galician front came at a price.[13]

The detachment of the howitzer batteries to the German army's Western front was perhaps the only troop movement that went in accord with Conrad's plan. Elsewhere, pressure to move the majority of his troops to Galicia in accordance with Plan 'R' caused some awkward moments with the military 'technicians', who had now taken over the organisation of the Imperial and Royal Railway Authority. Conrad had initially agreed with his chief railway adviser, Colonel Straub, that the day of general mobilisation should be 30 July, and that the so-called 'B-Staffel', comprising the three armies of Conrad's strategic reserve, would entrain for Bosnia that day. To coordinate the timetables, no train on the Austro-Hungarian networks was permitted to travel faster than the slowest train on a branch narrow-gauge line. Maximum speed never exceeded 18km per hour, roughly the speed of a bicycle, and considerably slower than the average of 30km per hour maintained by the German railways.

Within 24 hours, and under growing pressure from Berlin, Conrad had changed his mind, deciding to focus on the 'main struggle' against Russia. A horrified Straub listened as Conrad insisted that 'B-Staffel' be rerouted north to Galicia. Straub insisted it was too late to effect such a change. Better to wait for the 'B-Staffel' to reach the Serbian frontier and then redirect it northwards. Thousands of troops would thus arrive on the Balkan front after hours of travelling without food or drink, only to be ordered again to their trains to begin the long journey back north.[14]

On the same day that Conrad vouchsafed the German High Command his howitzer batteries, the appointment of Potiorek as commander of the Austro-Hungarian forces on the Serbian front was confirmed. Potiorek had been formally exonerated by the Emperor for any *Schlamperei* before and during the Archduke's visit to Sarajevo, and he was now seething with determination to inflict some sharp move on Serbia. His obvious personal failings were ignored in the interests of morale and the war effort.

Initial success in Galicia

Above both Potiorek and Conrad, as the nominal *de jure* if not de facto commander, was the Archduke Friedrich, son of the Archduke Albrecht, the victor of Custozza in 1866. But his, as in earlier campaigns, was a figurehead role. Conrad was the overall commander of strategy.

The forces on the move now were vast. Never before in the history of European warfare had such large bodies of men and horses been deployed. In the course of August 1914, the Imperial and Royal Army mobilised 1.5 million men, one million horses and 200,000 tons of equipment. The transport of all this materiel took weeks. The 37 infantry divisions assembled in Galicia slowly; several would arrive at the beginning of September. Until 28 August, Conrad had only 31 divisions in the area rather than the 40 he had originally hoped for. (Three had been subtracted for service on the Balkan front and two others would not arrive before 4 September. The other four had simply not materialised.)[15]

Despite overwhelming intelligence pointing to the preponderance of Russian forces, Conrad encouraged the III Army under Brudermann to advance towards Lemberg where his four corps would encounter seven Russian corps, an army twice their size. Had Brudermann taken up a strong defensive position it is possible that he would have lured the Russians into a trap. But Conrad repeatedly urged him to wage 'an active defensive'.

Conrad's orders need to be seen in context. He required support on his flank for his attack with I and IV Armies to the north. Here, in Conrad's phrase, there was 'a happy beginning'. The Austrians took the eastern flank of the Russian IV Army first and then attacked the western flank, capturing thousands of prisoners and 28 guns. Conrad sensed success and, emboldened by the rout of the Russians, sent his cavalry forward on 25 August. As the Russians fell back towards Lublin, Conrad advanced, outrunning his supply lines. On 27 August,[16] an entire Austro-Hungarian cavalry division encountered a screen of Cossacks. No doubt filled with tales of the late afternoon at Königgrätz, they lowered their lances and drew their sabres to canter towards the stationary Russian horsemen. As they were less than a hundred yards away, the Russian horseman parted like the waves to reveal their support infantry complete with machine guns. The cavalry engagement at Jaroslavice taught the Imperial and Royal cavalry a deadly lesson. If the Austrian infantry had not arrived on the scene to support their withdrawal, the 4th Cavalry Division would have ceased to exist.

The decade-old dreams of an elite force were shattered in an afternoon. Among the hundreds of wounded abandoned for dead was the painter Oskar

Kokoschka, who had joined the smart Dragoon regiment Nr 15 (Erzherzog Joseph), with the financial assistance of his friend the architect Adolf Loos. Loos volunteered for military service and designed his own practical and American-style uniform. He was sceptical of an Austrian victory because the Entente troops had better-designed clothes and were more practically attired in puttees which were, in Loos's view, far more effective against trench foot. Kokoschka later recalled:

> I made a wonderful target in my light blue tunic, with white facings, red breeches and gilt helmet .... it was a uniform which stood out only too well. As I rode out I felt spied upon by an unseen enemy deep in the hidden recesses of the dark foliage of the forest.[17]

Like Loos, Conrad focused on superficialities. He wrote later that the fault of the cavalry could be traced entirely to their officers and 'the utterly impractical uniform and training'. Yet it had been Conrad who, as army chief, had failed to overcome cavalry resistance to more practical uniforms and, more importantly, to ensure that they were equipped with modern weapons, notably machine guns. The battle had broken many cavalry myths, and the mounted regiments reacted accordingly. As Botho Coreth, another young cavalry officer from the 4th Dragoon regiment who experienced Conrad's 'happy beginning', noted in his memoirs: 'From now on, cavalry regiments divided their troops into a mounted half and an infantry half'.[18]

Near Zamość, between Cracow and Przemyśl, there was better news for the Austrians because a single corps (Nr 14) attacked a disorganised Russian division and captured thousands of prisoners and more than 60 guns. The Battle of Komarów was a bright interlude and almost heralded the encirclement of an entire Russian army (V). But the Austrians did not 'act with Prussian resolution' and in any event the Russians saw the danger and swiftly withdrew. Even so, the Austrians had captured 20,000 prisoners and 100 guns by the end of August.

Russian recovery

Unfortunately this encounter could not disguise less happy events further east where Conrad's encouragement to III Army to advance had provoked a collision between 91 Austrian battalions with 300 guns, and 192 Russian battalions with 685 guns. The consequences of this asymmetry of firepower were almost inevitable. Brudermann, in the van of the Austro-Hungarian III Army, lost two-thirds of his eight divisions and only extricated his troops with the greatest of difficulty. Conrad refused to believe that his forces in the sector were facing such large hostile forces and reordered the attack. The result was that on 30 August, there was another encounter with the loss of 20,000 men and 70 guns. Conrad wrote to his mistress, Gina, that it was 'the most terrible day of his life'.[19] Even here Conrad was mistaken, for there was worse to come: Lemberg fell a few days later and Conrad's son was killed in action.

Napoleon had found out at Austerlitz that Russian infantry could recover far more quickly than its western counterparts. By 9 September, Russian forces were threatening Conrad's western communications with the German army. Conrad appealed to the Germans for help. Although Germany had fought brilliantly and had crushed the Russians at Tannenberg a few weeks earlier, there was no question of reinforcements for Conrad. 'He surely cannot ask any more of VIII Army than it has already achieved,' the German Kaiser minuted against the Austrian's request.[20]

Conrad's generalship had proved disastrous. Nearly half the Austro-Hungarian forces in Galicia – 400,000 men – had been lost. Over 100,000 of these had been taken prisoner. The Chief of the General Staff had been calling non-stop for war for almost six years. Now he had had his first taste of it, he had overseen the destruction of nearly a third of the Empire's armies in less than six weeks.

It might have been some consolation for Conrad had the Habsburg Empire held its own on the Balkan front but there matters were proving equally challenging. In an admittedly competitive field, Potiorek ran Conrad a close second for military incompetence in 1914.

Potiorek crosses the Drina

On 12 August, Potiorek wrote in his diary that 'My war has today begun'. At midday the same day he had sent a telegram to the Military Chancery of His Majesty (MKSM) announcing portentously that 'my regiment at 7:00 a.m. crossed the Lower Drina without significant resistance and occupied Serbian territory!' A sceptical Kaiser Franz-Josef queried in neat pencil and Viennese patois: 'Only *one* battalion?' ('Wohl nur 1 Baon?'). Potiorek's 'Aufmarsch' plans had been delayed by a lack of bridging materials. When these finally arrived, the Austro-Hungarian V Army began to cross the Drina in force, only to encounter stiff Serbian resistance.[21]

Potiorek was perfectly aware that II Army was destined for Galicia but he was determined to make full use of its temporary presence on the Balkan front. While the Army High Command (AOK) under Conrad sent II Army orders to prepare to entrain for Galicia, Potiorek ordered it to cross the Save and to begin occupying Serbian territory. Supported by the Danube flotilla, II Army seized Šabac, and this was perceived immediately by the Serbs as a feint. It thus encountered less resistance as the Serbs moved their forces across their front with 'sleepwalker's certainty' to deal with Potiorek's 'battalion'.[22] The Serbs recognised that the main Habsburg attack would come from the Austrian V and VI Armies and arranged their dispositions accordingly. Two Serbian divisions would hit the Austrian V Army in the flank as it advanced up the Jadar valley. But the Serbian commander General Putnik wanted only to draw the Austrians to the Cer plain, south-east of Lješnica, where he hoped the decisive action could be fought.

Into this trap stumbled the Austro-Hungarian 21st Light Infantry Division under General Przyborski, an officer who even before the war had not enjoyed a dazzling reputation. As the son-in-law of the earlier war minister Schönaich, he was perceived as a 'Ringstrasse general' (i.e. fit only to promenade).

Przyborski was one of many generals, including Conrad, for whom war was a completely novel experience. This was the case for most armies in 1914, but not for the Serbs. The experience of two Balkan conflicts in the previous two years had taught them much. They knew how to deploy and withdraw swiftly and how to ambush. The 21st Light Infantry Division was almost wiped out in a few hours. Przyborski was retired. The 29th Light Infantry Division fared little better at Šabac and found itself firing on its own troops as the Serbs withdrew silently and rapidly before them. In a report that Karl Kraus could have penned for his great satire, *The Last Days of Mankind*, the official bulletin read: 'Decisive victory of our troops against powerful enemy forces.' In fact the 29th had retired in total disorder towards Šabac.[23]

Perhaps buoyed by his own propaganda, Potiorek ordered V Army to occupy the Kolubara heights on 16 August. This proved challenging because the Serbs, far from being 'brushed off with a dishcloth', as Potiorek had predicted, were showing increasing aggression day by day. On the 17th, Serbian cavalry virtually annihilated the survivors of the 21st Light Infantry. What was left of the Division was withdrawn for '*Retablierung*' (re-establishment) in the hope that reorganisation might bring at least two brigades back into action at a future date.

Although a half-hearted Serbian attack on Šabac a day later was beaten off with ease, the combination of Potiorek's incompetence and Serbian pressure had ensured that II Army, which Conrad had hoped to deploy in Galicia, was fully committed to Potiorek's campaign. Poor Austrian supplies, inadequate provision of food and difficult terrain were creating problems. Conrad and Potiorek's complicated plan of invading Serbia from Bosnia rather than via Belgrade and the flatlands of the Voivodina had led Austrian troops into much

more challenging terrain. The Serbs were operating along interior lines, skilfully breaking the communications between the three armies they faced. The
weather in mid-August was ferociously hot, and the Serbs knew how to
camouflage themselves in these conditions.

As the situation deteriorated, Potiorek wired Conrad, asking for permission to engage all of II Army. From the recesses of the great fortress of
Przemyśl on the Galician front, hundreds of miles away from the Serbian
front, Conrad exploded in rage. But on 21 August, Potiorek persuaded the
Head of the Emperor's Military Chancery to sign an order granting Potiorek
full autonomy in the Balkans. From now on Conrad lost even the minimum
of control over events on the southern front. Potiorek proceeded without
having to refer his commands to Przemyśl. Conrad angrily telegraphed
Vienna that 'Potiorek possesses more than enough forces to deal with any
Serbian attack'.[24] But the Emperor wrote to his Chief of General Staff on 23
August that 'a reduction of forces on the Balkan front is not appropriate'
('zweckmässig').

The V Army, over-extended and unsupported, fell back in the face of stiff
Serbian defences making every use of the local terrain. The VI Army fared no
better. Informed by Hungarian officers about what was going on, Tisza penned
a swift critique of a campaign that was 'ill-prepared with remote columns and
frontal attacks put in without artillery preparation against well-constructed
defensive positions'. Fortunately for Potiorek, the Serbs, too exhausted by their
fighting, could not harass the Austrian withdrawal.

As Potiorek's troops withdrew, they took their frustration out on the
civilian population in the most appalling manner, reminiscent of the worst
excesses of the Pandours. The summary execution of civilians, including
women, on the grounds of aiding the enemy, destroyed the army's reputation
for fair dealing in a matter of hours. Reports of these atrocities gave the
Entente an enormous propaganda victory. Once again the old Emperor had to
intervene to stop these departures from acceptable behaviour, warning that
such actions were bound to 'alienate civilians from the monarchy'.[25]

Austro-Hungarian setbacks on all fronts

The indifferent performance of the Imperial and Royal troops against seasoned
Serbian regulars was accompanied by histrionics among some of the senior
officers. Count Zedtwitz refused to cover the withdrawal towards Šabac with
his division. In response, General Tersztyansky observed that such a
commander lacked both 'the character and determination to deal with critical
situations', and called for Zedtwitz to be court-martialled for 'timidity' in the

face of the enemy. It did not come to that. Zedtwitz was dismissed from his command that same afternoon.[26]

Zedtwitz's successor, Zanantoni, was keen to avoid the mistakes of his predecessor and offered his division as 'ready to hold Šabac on a point of honour'. Tersztyansky now committed an entire corps (IV) to cross the Save and support Zanantoni but as they crossed the river on the 23rd, the confusion began. The IV Corps had been standing by to entrain for Galicia and the news that they were to be deployed on the firing line against the Serbs came as a surprise. Determined to do their duty, they crossed with all the precision of peacetime manoeuvres only to be fired upon by well dug-in Serbs. As the Austrians attempted to form up, they came under a withering crossfire and were cut to pieces. Within twenty minutes they were hurtling back in panic, seeking shelter in Šabac. Tersztyansky ordered the evacuation of Šabac that night. This was achieved just in time, a day before Serbian artillery destroyed the Austrian bridgehead.

By the beginning of September, the Austro-Hungarian operations had come to a disastrous impasse on both fronts. The news that a Montenegrin incursion into Bosnia had been successfully beaten back could not detract from the disasters of the opening weeks. Not only had the 'decisive result' proved elusive in both campaigns, the Imperial and Royal Army had shown that it was unprepared for hostilities. The long peace since 1878 had eroded the fighting ability of the army, as peacetime soldiering tends to do. Parades and exercises that, as even Conrad observed, were 'little more than a children's theatre', had ill equipped the Imperial and Royal Army for war.[27] The Serbs on the other hand had learnt many useful lessons in the two recent Balkan wars and the Russians had discovered the benefits of camouflage, thanks to the Russo-Japanese War less than ten years earlier. The Habsburg army had had no such education. Above all, its command and control systems, traditionally the weakness of the Habsburg military, continued to demonstrate certain shortcomings.

At sea in the Adriatic, there had been more setbacks. On 16 August, the venerable light cruiser *Zenta*, whose sailors, fourteen years earlier, had fought alongside the British and French against the Chinese, was sunk by a 40-strong Anglo-French battle group close to the Bay of Cattaro. The Anglo-French flotilla consisted of 13 battleships, including three dreadnoughts, as well as five cruisers and 20 destroyers. Against these odds, the *Zenta* stood absolutely no chance but she fought bravely for nearly two hours to allow her accompanying destroyer *Ulan* to make good the chance of escape. This heroic action, the Battle of Antivari, cost the lives of most of *Zenta*'s crew. The Entente navy had hoped to provoke the Imperial and Royal Navy to sortie out to defend the *Zenta* but, when this failed to happen, the Anglo-French fleet had no choice but to retire to Malta. Neither the French nor the Royal navies had sufficient logistics support to remain in the Adriatic for very long.

These setbacks suggested that observers who had predicted the Habsburg monarchy would suffer an early collapse would be proved right. They were to be disappointed. Similar setbacks to those of August 1914 had happened before. Had not Maria Theresa faced a debacle in 1740? Had not Kaiser Franz experienced disasters at the hands of Napoleon? Franz-Josef had implied all this when he said to Conrad before his departure with the staff for Przemyśl: 'I know it will be very hard for us but I intend to do my duty'. Habsburg military tradition had rarely enjoyed initial success. There was no reason for it to be different in 1914.[28]

With time, the Habsburgs would find the right men to lead their armies with distinction, and they would learn from their mistakes, as they always had done. They knew from bitter experience that things would most likely get far worse before they improved.

As the autumn rains set in on both fronts, the problems of the Imperial and Royal Army multiplied. The poor performance of the V Army on the Balkan front and the loss of Šabac brought Potiorek's offensive to a standstill. In Galicia, the loss of the III Army meant that only German assistance could stabilise the situation.

Potiorek planned to advance with the VI Army against Valjevo, preempting a Serbian attack. The Serbs aimed to divide the VI and V Armies by a strike at Janja. The demoralised remnants of the unfortunate 21st Light Infantry Division were reorganised under martial law and while the commander of the V Army, Frank, was 'rather depressed', he allowed himself to be persuaded by Potiorek that he could contribute some forces to a renewed offensive. But Frank was right to be depressed. The V Army was close to collapse and its mountain artillery were virtually useless against the higher-calibre French field artillery of the Serbs. As Major Gellinek, whose reports as military attaché in Belgrade on the Black Hand had been ignored during the July crisis, and who was now serving on Potiorek's staff observed, 'The effect of our mountain artillery was nil.'[29]

On 6 September, while Potiorek was waiting for the rain to stop so that he could organise his new attack, the Serbs, indifferent to the bad weather, began attacking various points along the Save river. For the Serbs, the first failed offensive of the Austrians had revealed their opponents' inferiority. This opened up many opportunities to support Russia by drawing off as many Austrian troops as possible from the Galician front.

The battle-hardened 29th Imperial and Royal Infantry Division fought a successful defensive action over the next two days in which they inflicted on the Serbian 'Timok' Division more than 5,500 casualties. Further along the front, however, the Austrian attacks ran into problems; an attempt by Potiorek's XIII Corps to cross the Drina was defeated with heavy casualties. The unfortunate remnants of the 21st Light Infantry Division once again came under artillery fire, which soon demoralised them, and amid the chaos of sinking pontoon bridges, they broke yet again. In one day the V Army had lost more than 4,400 men, though casualties among the VI Army amounted to barely 700. Potiorek, in the best traditions of better-known generals in Flanders, was indifferent to these figures and brusquely ordered the V Army to 'attempt to cross the Drina as many times as possible until it succeeds'. The result was yet more casualties in return for no progress.

Serbia invades Hungary

Meanwhile a day later, on 10 September, Serbian forces occupied Hungarian territory for the first time, crossing over into the lightly defended Banat and forcing the evacuation of Semlin. This caused consternation in Budapest and Vienna where the Military Chancery of the Emperor demanded immediate 'clarification' from Potiorek. Potiorek's explanation that the Serb forces around Semlin were insignificant was not a message calculated to impress. A day later, nine battalions, including Landsturm units, were dispatched to eject the invaders on Vienna's orders.

Although the Serbian offensive into the Hungarian territory of Syrmia had run out of steam, Potiorek had to abandon the line of the Drina between Foča and Višegrad. The ill-fated 21st Light Infantry Division were so demoralised (more than 150 men had self-inflicted wounds to escape action) that Potiorek put them again under strict martial law on grounds of cowardice. The division had suffered a further 2,000 casualties on 16 September.

Better luck followed the 29th Division, which crossed the Save on the 16th and advanced on Jarak. Potiorek now ordered the VI Army to support and dig in. But the key to Potiorek's offensive calculations and the widening of the bridgehead were the 33 infantry battalions of General Alfred Krauss, and these had become literally bogged down in a swamp. Unsupported, and under increasing fire, the VI Army had no choice but to withdraw. Around the Jagodnja peaks a fierce hand-to-hand struggle ensued in which the Austrians were forced to cede the peaks three times before finally holding them, albeit at a cost of another 2,000 casualties. The Potiorek offensive had settled down to a stalemate.

But such a static situation could not last long. The Serbs were constantly reinforced and the Austrians began to run low on ammunition. An urgent telegram to the Imperial Military Chancery asking for more ammunition, especially howitzer shells, received the reply on 26 September that most ammunition dumps in the Empire were already exhausted and that only the daily production of ammunition could be forwarded to the fronts. Potiorek had to get whatever shells he could from the distant Sarajevo garrison. He had wasted much ammunition by continuing to order almost suicidal attacks. One, by the VIII Corps, had been beaten back with such heavy casualties that Marterer in the Emperor's Military Chancery scribbled next to the report: 'Who ordered this senselessness?'[30]

As reserve battalions appeared to replace the losses, many of the new, inexperienced soldiers fled at the first sound of fire. Potiorek soon realised that the only way to make any use of these young recruits was to incorporate them into the front line battalions to fill the gaps of the fallen in the hope that the *esprit* of the experienced units rubbed off on the raw youths joining them. As usual with Potiorek, orders to enforce the strictest of discipline were issued to prevent any outbreaks of 'timidity'. The offensive capability of Potiorek's army was fast disappearing. The V Army was in no condition to undertake any offensive action and the VI Army was rapidly heading the same way. Nevertheless it was now that Potiorek displayed for the first and last time some of the skills that had made his reputation in the first place.

Potoriek clears the Serbs out of Bosnia

In an action that to this day is considered an exemplary piece of 'movement warfare', Potiorek dispatched and coordinated several elements of the VI Army to clear the Serbs out of southern Bosnia. The operation lasted barely ten days but was executed with tactical brilliance and achieved the lasting effect of keeping the Serbs out of Bosnia for the rest of the war. The three-day battle between 18 and 21 October around the Romanja planina saw Potiorek skilfully surround a Serbian army on three sides and then drive it back across the Drina.

This operation, which cost the Serbian 'Uzice' army many thousands of casualties, was all the more remarkable because Potiorek's forces, notably the elite 8th Mountain Brigade, were significantly outnumbered by the Serbs. Unfortunately, heavy rain and the arrival of the first snows prevented the Austrians from following up their victory as vigorously as they might have done. A few weeks later, rumours that a Russian force of 35,000 men was approaching the Banat from the east renewed Potiorek's offensive plans. As October ended, the Serbian attacks were pressed with less vigour. On 1 November, Potiorek could reoccupy Šabac.

Unfortunately, a combination of Serbian artillery and pouring rain brought the preparations for a decisive attack to a halt. On 11 November, attempts to cross the Danube at Semendra led to confusion. Czech units had already shown signs of disaffection when camped in the Prater in Vienna at the beginning of hostilities. After two months of Potiorek's leadership, they now refused to advance. Martial law was imposed.[31]

By now the Serbs were already withdrawing. On 15 November, elements of the V Army reached the Kolubara heights and entered Valjevo where they took more than 8,000 prisoners, 42 artillery pieces and 31 machine guns. This 'victory' made Potiorek very popular in Hungary, where the perceived threat of Serbian invasion had brought back unhappy memories of 1849. Potiorek's *Glanzpunkt* came as Conrad's fortunes in Galicia were again at a low ebb.

There, the great fortress of Przemyśl was again invested by the Russians who, approaching Cracow, were threatening to erupt into northern Hungary. As Conrad's star sank, '*Bravo, Potiorek!*' became the phrase of the day in Vienna and Budapest, and the commander found himself suddenly declared an honorary citizen of Bleiburg, Banja Luka and Sarajevo. These modest baubles were to be Potiorek's final honours.

When Marterer arrived on a surprise visit from the Emperor on 16 November, he found everything 'in the best harmony'. Potiorek took the opportunity to outline his plans for the next steps: two days' rest and then the seizure of Belgrade, to be followed by a swing towards Kragujevac. Such an offensive would persuade a vacillating Bulgaria that Serbia was on its knees and hasten Sofia's adherence to the Triple Alliance.

Potiorek could not bring himself to allow his soldiers to do simply nothing for three days while they recovered. He insisted they establish themselves fully on the Kolubara heights during that time. Three days later, rain began to cause floods beyond the Kolubara. These problems were exacerbated by a brief sunny interlude, which caused the snow on the heights to melt. In these difficult conditions, illness began to overtake Potiorek's troops. They had had little warm food in days.

Moreover, the further Potiorek's troops advanced, the more difficult any reinforcement became. By the 22nd, the snow lay more than three feet deep in many places. In these conditions, shoes fell to bits, and General Appel telegrammed Potiorek demanding 'urgently' 60,000 replacement pairs. Men and horses had in some instances eaten nothing for nearly five days, and had had no bread for eight.

On 24 November, the Minister of War, Krobatin, appeared with an encouraging message from the Emperor for Potiorek. 'Whatever is said about you, you will not be replaced.' In return for this enigmatic and ambivalent message,

Krobatin was showered with requests for everything from uniform cloth to narrow-gauge railway parts. Despite the lack of equipment and food, Potiorek's troops cleared the Kolubara fastnesses of all Serb troops by the 28th, taking many prisoners. The V Army had reversed its run of bad luck. Four days later, and Imperial and Royal units entered an abandoned Belgrade. It had taken several months, but the city which had so often in the past fallen to the guns of the Habsburgs was in Austrian hands once again.

Unfortunately Potiorek drew the wrong conclusion from his peaceful occupation of the Serbian capital. He assumed it signified the collapse of the Serbian army. He forgot that from the moment Belgrade had mobilised on the night of 24/25 July, it had never been Serbia's intention to defend its capital.

As three 100-ton trains of equipment and supplies reached Valjevo, Potiorek could now consolidate his troops for the next stage. Though he had a high temperature from a cold on the 3rd, and retired to his bed for several hours, Potiorek's optimism knew no bounds, convinced as he was that Serbia's military power had been neutralised.

Serbia counter-attacks

The Serbs lost no time in disabusing the Austrians of their hopes. They had reorganised their forces under a gifted French-trained general, Misič.[32] On 3 December, Misič launched a counter-offensive. By early afternoon the following day, the Austrian XVI Corps was in full retreat. Misič had chosen his moment well, ensuring that the 300 tons of newly arrived materiel could not even be unloaded to reach the troops on the front line. Hungry, exhausted, shoeless and demoralised, Potiorek's 'army of beggars' fell back from all the territory they had just gained.

As the XVI and XV Corps withdrew under the hammer blows of Misič's attack, retreat began to turn to rout. After nearly a month of daily fighting, the V and VI Armies began to crumble swiftly; so quickly in fact that the Serbian vanguard lost contact with the fleeing Austrians. By the 7th, Valjevo was evacuated. The Serbs caught up with the Austrians on the night of the 9th, when a sharp rearguard action took place between the Serbian First Army and the Austro-Hungarian 29th Infantry Division. The fighting was exceptionally fierce. One Czech Infantry regiment (94) lost 53 officers and 800 men in six hours.

By 10 December, it was clear that disaster was overtaking both V and VI Armies. By the 11th, the Emperor was informed of these events by a mischievous telegram from Conrad, whose own personal fortunes had momentarily revived thanks to the positive outcome of the Battle of Limanowa. Franz-Josef was described as 'depressed and tired as if he had not slept'.[33] The same day, Potiorek crossed the river Save with his troops. He was never to return to Serbian territory again.

Potiorek received a terse telegram from the Emperor's military cabinet demanding 'an explanation'. The Viennese newspapers which had celebrated the 'Conquest of Belgrade' only a few days earlier now fell eerily silent. An official bulletin referred to 'planned redispositions of units' (*planmässiger Umgruppierung*). It was another euphemism lampooned by Karl Kraus.

Potoriek's dismissal

Potiorek had ordered Belgrade to be defended to the last man by V Army but by 13 December Conrad was telegraphing Potiorek to preserve the V Army at all costs. It would be needed on the undefended southern flank of the monarchy. The implication of Conrad's message was clear. Belgrade, or rather the small bridgehead at its foot, would have to be surrendered. On 15 December, Marterer was dispatched from Vienna by the Emperor to find out what was going on. 'You will not have anything happy to say on your return but at least one will know the truth,' Franz-Josef told him as he took his leave.[34]

Marterer's investigation was swift and merciless. After taking statements from most of the senior officers, he came to a terse conclusion: 'Potiorek's attitude is a crime . . . . if he appeared among his troops they would shoot him'.[35] On the 19th, on his return to Vienna, the young officer reported to the Emperor that, after all he had heard, 'in his view' Potiorek was responsible for the disaster. 'Then he must go' was Kaiser Franz-Josef's simple reply. Archduke Eugen with General Krauss as chief of staff would replace him. When the news was communicated to Potiorek, the defeated general confided to his diary that it came as 'a relief'. The debacle of the Austro-Hungarian campaign against Serbia invigorated the Entente forces, and there can be no doubt it severely compromised Austria's efforts against the Russians. As the German Kaiser Wilhelm observed: 'a few hundred thousand Serbs changed the course of history'.[36]

On the Eastern front, the Austrian collapse at the end of August had persuaded both Conrad and more importantly, Ludendorff, the German commander in the east, that without 'direct assistance' the Austro-Hungarian army in Galicia would not be able to hold its defensive positions through the winter. In late September a strong German force pushed forward from their railheads north of Cracow expecting to find a Russian flank to relieve the pressure on their ally. In fact the Russian army, under Ivanow, had already withdrawn from the San to the Vistula. When Conrad became aware of this he redoubled his efforts to recapture Lemberg.

The Austrian military intelligence apparatus functioned well to support Conrad in his reading of his opponents' intentions. Some Russian General Staff orders were captured. The language officer of the Evidenzbüro attached to Conrad's staff, Lieutenant Victor Marchesetti, was equipped with the monarchy's only mobile wireless interception vehicle, thanks to the generosity of a Viennese banker. This enabled Marchesetti to intercept many Russian signals and to break the Russian military ciphers.[37]

By November, Conrad had come up against a large Russian force opposite Ivangorod and was defeated as he attempted to execute a flank attack against superior forces. Outnumbered by 13 divisions to eight, Conrad lost 40,000 men. Conrad's second offensive in Galicia was over.

Rather than question his own leadership, Conrad criticised his German allies. He judged the German attack around Warsaw as a 'crude mistaken attack' ('groben Missangriff').[38] The Germans were unamused. They responded with a forceful recommendation to place the Austrian I Army under German leadership. Growing criticism of Austrian military leadership even persuaded the German Emperor to write to Kaiser Franz Josef suggesting that a 'joint command' of Ludendorff and the Archduke Friederich was the best way forward. This suggestion was keenly calculated. It had the merit of removing the senior Austrian operations officer while superficially safeguarding the Habsburg dynasty's interest.

The Emperor, the Austrian High Command and Conrad rejected such a ruthless power grab by Berlin. It was only the first of many attempts by Berlin to subordinate Austrian forces to German operational control and the pressure would gradually reach a level impossible to resist.

One chink of light illuminated the general picture of gloom and despair in Galicia. The Austrian III Army had fought well and its commander, a frontier Croat by the name of Swetozar Boroevič, was beginning to make a name for himself as a reliable and capable strategist. Boroevič was above all a realist capable of calculating risk in a way that eluded both Conrad and Potiorek. Although baptised into the Orthodox Church – his father was a prominent member of that community – Boroevič considered himself a Croat. He was the perfect exemplar of the old jumble of races and religions that had made up the old Military Frontier.

The struggle for Przemyśl

In addition to the casualty list and the criticism of his leadership, Conrad had to cope with new difficulties: cholera and other illnesses that infected his troops began to take their toll. As Conrad's army fell back behind the San, the strong fortress of Przemyśl with its garrison of 120,000 men was abandoned for a second time, though not before its munitions and resources had been raided by the retreating armies, who had unceremoniously dumped their wounded on the fortress's hospitals. When the Russians had approached the monarchy's most important fortress a month earlier and demanded its surrender, the brave fortress commandant, General Herman Kusmanek von Burgneustätten, had sent a response insisting that it was 'beneath his honour to offer the reply the shameful Russian request merited'. Kusmanek, a tough Saxon from Transylvania, was probably the most able fortress commander of the war. Though it had only lasted from 17 September to 10 October, the first siege had inflicted significant damage, which needed to be repaired as swiftly as possible. Work detachments filled in Russian trenches, strengthened wire and gun emplacements. Despite these steps, Kusmanek's fortress was now in a worse state than during the initial siege. Yet there could be no question of abandoning the fortress. Vienna and public opinion throughout the monarchy expected Przemyśl 'fest in unserer Hand' ('firmly in our grip', a phrase which led to one of Karl Kraus's more acerbic and brilliant scenes in his *Last Days of Mankind*).

The capture of a Russian dossier outlining a plan, whereby a fifth column of pro-Russian civilians would prepare the way for the Russian advance into Galicia, so excited Conrad that he asked the Emperor immediately to impose martial law on the civilian population of Galicia and investigate with the greatest vigour all those who might possibly be in league with the enemy. The effects of these intrusions on the loyal and suffering citizens of the Habsburgs in Galicia can be imagined. The Emperor, who had already in July 1914 told over-zealous officials to stop rounding up Serbs in Bosnia 'lest they all become the monarchy's enemy', knew full well what Conrad was demanding, but so great was the emergency in Galicia, the old Emperor felt he could not oppose measures, though he feared the evil effects of Conrad's policies. Nowhere was the 'spy fever' arguably more acute than in the fortress of Przemyśl itself. The Russians had used it as a post for gathering intelligence already during the Crimean War. After the great fortress was extended and modernised in the early 1870s, the first notable case of espionage was recorded in 1875, when a zealous post official discovered a plan of the fortress in a letter which had been returned undelivered.

By 1914, Conrad's neurosis about Russian spies became an obsession that would cost the lives of many innocent people.[39] The civilian population of the city was divided bitterly between Poles and Ruthenes (Ukrainians) who competed for exclusive advantage at every turn. Between them, numbering almost a third of the population by 1914, were the Jews. By the middle of

September much of the civilian population had been evacuated, and this continued after the first siege was relieved on 10 October. Przemyśl was more than just a city fortress. It was a city surrounded by one of the most extensive series of fortifications ever built, stretching for more than thirty-six miles. Its core consisted of the inner redoubts constructed in the first half of the nineteenth century by the 'Austrian Vauban' Franz Freiherr von Scholl. They were six miles in circumference. Between 1861 and 1886, the various outer fortified lines for gun emplacements miles beyond the city walls had been added. These outer walls and their infrastructure of ammunition depots and accommodation were the work of Daniel Freiherr von Salis-Soglio, a Swiss engineer in the Austrian service. Salis-Soglio created a series of forts along a perimeter which stretched for miles, using steel and concrete to create a line of defences which in length and depth was truly remarkable. The visitor to Przemyśl today is restricted by the sensitivity of the modern Polish–Ukrainian border from appreciating the extent of the fortress miles to the east of the city. During the closing years of the Cold War this frontier between Poland and the Soviet Union was a much calmer and quieter place, and visitors could spend many afternoons picking their way through the almost Piranesian ruins whose brickwork lay ignored by all, save for the occasional uninterested Soviet sentry.

Salis-Soglio's work was strengthened by his successor Moriz, Ritter von Brunner. Both Brunner and Salis-Soglio's efforts were commemorated by the rare distinction that their names were given to two of the outer perimeter forts. Brunner armoured the gun positions and also the viewing platforms for the gunnery officers to observe their fire. He was responsible for a recognisably 'Austrian' school of fortification, much admired in other countries.[40] But although the fortress was modernised repeatedly, such were the rapid developments in siege technology that by 1914 Przemyśl was no longer considered modern, though it would demonstrate that its obsolescent defences were capable of withstanding assault.

The first siege had shown Kusmanek where the Russians would launch their major attacks. He had deployed his troops accordingly. The Russian commander, Dmitriew, had consistently underestimated the size of Kusmanek's garrison. More importantly, the Russians lacked siege artillery. Their infantry charges were unsupported, murderously repulsed by the fortress's guns. The Russians particularly feared the four 30.5cm howitzers, which proved as effective in defence as they had proved in Belgium in attack. Their 360 kilo shells were likened by the Russians to a metal plague.[41]

With the withdrawal of Conrad's forces in the night of 5 November, Przemyśl's second period of ordeal began. A survey on 11 November reported a garrison of 130,767 soldiers and 21,484 horses. In addition, there were 2,000

Russian prisoners and 30,000 civilians, 18,000 of whom were totally reliant on the military for food. The garrison strength was more or less identical to that during the earlier siege. A Landwehr and a pilots' company joined Kusmanek. The first siege had seen Austrian pilots, including the world record holder for long-distance flying, Captain Blaschke, flying post to and from the city, the first mechanised airmail service in history.

The Russians showed that they had learnt some lessons from the failure of the first siege. They sealed the perimeter, preventing the evacuation of various cholera hospitals. The able Kusmanek ordered aggressive patrolling and this kept the Russians on the defensive, reducing their infantry activities to a bare minimum. Instead, the Russians now concentrated on constructing a siege line opposite Kusmanek's fortified perimeter with shelters for their troops. For the first month, Kusmanek's tactics kept the initiative firmly with the Austrians. Time and again the garrison commandant ordered his patrols to provoke the Russians out of their passivity. Kusmanek was keen to disrupt his enemy's plans, constantly keeping them guessing in the hope that he would disorder their wider troop movements as well. On 14 November, Kusmanek ordered 15 battalions, a half-squadron of cavalry and eight batteries towards Tapin on the easternmost extremity of his perimeter.

The force was commanded by Kusmanek's most senior officer, Feldmarshallleutnant Arpád Tamásy, who achieved surprise with a break-through which so disrupted his enemy that Russian reinforcements destined to harass Conrad's retreating forces to the north had to be hurriedly rushed back to Przemyśl. Tamásy had achieved his purpose and retreated in perfect order to the safety of the perimeter.

Further breakouts brought in useful intelligence through prisoners, though the Russians had learnt well how to disguise their troop unit rotations from Kusmanek's prying eyes. Unfortunately, as November came to a close, a harsh winter began to undermine Kusmanek's activities along the exposed perimeter. His troops were not equipped with winter uniforms and a number of his sentries froze to death. At the beginning of December the Russians regained the initiative by adopting a much more aggressive tactic of probing along the perimeter for weaknesses, drawing away Kusmanek's reserves.

An intense suspicion, amounting to paranoia, that the Russians had broken Austrian signal codes brought a virtual radio blackout over Przemyśl so that Kusmanek had no idea how the campaign to his west was progressing and therefore what chance of relief Przemyśl enjoyed. The suspicion in this case was well placed; patrols learnt quickly from the peasantry that the Russians had told them to expect an Austrian breakout. The projected actions were cancelled and, with the frustration, there came another round of spy mania. It was even rumoured that Kusmanek deciphered his signals himself because he could not trust anyone.[42]

The Austro-Hungarian, and in this case it was mostly Hungarian, military leadership within the fortress continued to support the renewed offensive of the III Army. But poor coordination with the fortress artillery and increasing exhaustion as well as improved Russian counter-tactics made these moves more difficult. A typical sortie might result in 700 prisoners and therefore 700 extra mouths to feed. In addition the sortie might have cost 800 casualties.

As December wore on, the news of the success of Austrian arms at Limanowa-Lapanow raised spirits. It was the first piece of solid good news since the war had begun.

Conrad recovers

Facing almost certain replacement following his initial debacle in Galicia, Conrad had finally risen to the occasion. With the help of the XIV 'Innsbrucker Korps', an elite unit made up of Tyrol's finest and toughest men under FML Roth, the Austrians had surprised the rear of the Russian Third Army. The attack was put in with such ferocity that the Russian army was sent reeling back. Conrad supported Roth ably with a Hungarian Honvéd division and even a German reserve battalion. Reinforcements from the Austrian VI Corps completed the precariousness of the Russians' position. When a few days later they retreated, the reputation of Austro-Hungarian arms and Conrad's career had been saved.

The news of Limanowa-Lapanow stirred Kusmanek to plan a breakout to link up with what he hoped would be an imminent relief force. A ferocious attack on the Russian siege lines by 24 battalions and three and a half squadrons of cavalry on 15 December cleared the Russian trenches between the VI and III defensive areas, but a general deterioration in the overall Austrian position rendered the planned breakout meaningless. The Russians had counter-attacked the III Army less than twenty-five miles from the fortress and as the Austrians withdrew, Kusmanek had no choice but to bring his men back.

Christmas approached and the Russians stepped up their attacks, almost capturing some of the perimeter's artillery in one spirited attack in the early morning fog. At the same time Russian aircraft dropped thousands of leaflets imploring the local population to surrender. The leaflets noted that the Russian commander hoped to give the city as a present to the Tsar for Orthodox Christmas. This was wishful thinking but, on 22 December, Kusmanek lost 2,000 men holding a position in his IVth Bezirk (District),which had been threatened by a Russian occupation of one of the perimeter strongpoints. It would be several weeks before that part of his front became calmer. The IV Bezirk became the fulcrum of various attacks in the run-up to Christmas, though the defenders held the position without too much difficulty.

A Christmas ceasefire brought a traditional exchange of gifts along the front. The Russians left meat and bread while the Austrians offered schnapps and milk, more than they could spare, to give the impression that supplies were plentiful. A sign put up by the Russians opposite the VI Bezirk read:

> From our deepest hearts we wish all of you brave defenders of the fortress
> a peaceful and happy Christmas. Peace on earth and may God grant your
> wishes. That is the desire of the gunners of Imperial Russian Battery
> number 5 of the Xth Artillery Brigade.[43]

Unfortunately for Kusmanek, this respite would prove all too brief. The Army High Command once again needed a breakout to support III Army. Kusmanek ordered another sortie, this time losing 224 men. In any event, the Russians had long ceased to be worried by these excursions of Kusmanek.

The year 1915 would dawn with little hope for Kusmanek's garrison. After a failed breakout on 27 December with 20 battalions, Kusmanek ordered his troops to remain within the perimeter confine. The noose was tightening.

CHAPTER 23

1915–1916

BAYONETS IN THE DOLOMITES

The new year would prove to be even more challenging for the Imperial and Royal armed forces than 1914. The Empire's ability to recover from the disasters of 1914 on two fronts, and even face new threats, showed that it was still capable of waging war, albeit as the junior partner to the increasingly dominant German military machine. As well as a new front against its neighbour to the south, Italy, the year saw the decision to deploy two batteries with 813 gunners and 22 officers to Palestine to support the Ottoman effort against the British.[1]

The fall of Przemyśl encourages Italy

From the monarchy's point of view, the year was dominated by one event: the treachery of Italy. 'A betrayal of which history knows no parallel' was Franz-Josef's phrase before he declared war on his erstwhile ally. Italy's defection did not come as a surprise.

Even before hostilities began, Moltke had been writing to Conrad, urging him to cement Italy in her alliance by offering 'territorial concessions'. To the intense irritation of the Emperor and the Imperial and Royal Ambassador in Rome, Count Mérey, the German Ambassador in Rome hinted to the Italian government that Vienna was ready to make concessions in the Trentino, South Tyrol and even Trieste.

This behaviour by the German Ambassador gave rise to friction in relations between the two allies, which were rapidly mirrored in the tensions arising between the respective general and indeed naval staffs. Admiral Haus had been under much pressure from his German naval colleagues to adopt a more aggressive naval strategy in the Adriatic.[2] Moltke and Conrad's relationship had deteriorated with the Austrian emergency in Galicia.

Rome waited to see how the dice rolled in the fortunes of war. The Vatican was convinced that Italy should remain neutral and it exerted a powerful influence over Italian public opinion. When news of Przemyśl's imminent fall came through in March 1915, it seemed an opportune moment for Rome to explore the synergies of backing the Entente. In this sense the great fortress of Przemyśl, which had become increasingly insignificant from a tactical military point of view in 1915, had become a powerful barometer of Vienna's strategic fortunes.

The end of Kusmanek's trials at Przemyśl would not come swiftly. As the year began, the fortress commandant had taken some comfort from the dazzling success of the Imperial and Royal forces of Pflanzer-Baltin. Pflanzer, a Hungarian with gypsy blood, was a gifted officer. He had moved with great energy in the Bukovina where he had driven the Russians before him with the initiative and skill which would make him one of the most impressive commanding officers of the Imperial and Royal Army until the ceasefire of 1918.

But Pflanzer's actions offered no prospect of immediate relief, and by Kusmanek's own calculations, the fortress had only enough provisions to last until 18 February. In fact, by slaughtering 10,000 horses at the beginning of February, Kusmanek managed to win another month. He had begun 1915 with 127,811 men and 14,546 horses. The slaughter of these horses essentially immobilised his forces. It also led to some macabre humour. One joke ran: 'What is the difference between the Siege of Przemyśl and the Siege of Troy? At Troy the heroes were in the horse. At Przemyśl the horses were in the hero.'[3]

Some improvised sorties captured kraut and beetroot and, above all, potatoes, but Kusmanek's requirements soon outstripped these. Imposing general belt-tightening, he was confident that he could now hold the fortress until 23 March. Unfortunately, sickness and apathy were on the increase. At the beginning of December 1914, Kusmanek had registered his sick at 4,879. By March 1915 this had risen to 12,140 with a further 7,000 unfit for duty. These figures belie the suggestions of some observers that the siege did not take a toll on garrison life.[4]

On 26 January, a few Russian officers appeared to complain about the use of 'dum-dum' bullets by the Austro-Hungarian garrison. Kusmanek took advantage of the complaints to lodge some of his own criticisms concerning Russian ammunition, inviting the Russians to a lavish six-course lunch especially prepared on Kusmanek's orders to give the impression that there was no shortage of food in the city.[5] Given that some later accounts of the siege have referred to the Austro-Hungarian officers living 'in every luxury', it would seem that it was not only the Russians who were taken in by such ruses.[6]

Inevitably, as conditions deteriorated certain infantry regiments became disaffected. IR 35, made up of Ruthenes, was especially demoralised. There were more than 24,000 men in the fortress who were officially *dienstuntauglich* (incapable of duty). Meanwhile, the Russians had established an efficient perimeter railway and were containing the Austrian patrols far more effectively.

Following communication with III Army and the ArmeeOberKommando (AOK) in Teschen, Kusmanek was moved to make one final gesture of defiance. This time the breakout, set for 19 March, was to be nothing more than a *Himmelsfahrtkommando* (best translated as a 'forlorn hope' or 'suicide mission').

When the signal outlining Kusmanek's intentions for 19 March reached Vienna, the Emperor questioned whether such a 'sanguinary' action was really necessary. This was a point of view shared by most of the troops designated for the sortie. One British historian described what followed as a 'Burlesque'.[7] In fact it was painfully serious. The 23rd Honvéd Infantry Division lost more than 68 per cent of its complement in less than seven hours. Several other divisions lost more than a third of their men. Such was the price to be paid for 'honour'. The failed attack proved to the world that surrender was an honourable option. It was the only option. On 22 March Kusmanek wirelessed that he had destroyed all his ciphers and would shortly destroy all munitions and defences to render the fortress useless to the enemy before finally blowing up the radio mast.

A flight to safety by the last remaining planes brought one aircraft west but the flight path of the others was not helped by the decision to blow up the main fortress magazine thirty seconds after they had taken off. The explosion sent the planes reeling off course. Four balloons enjoyed a gentler ascent but easterly winds blew them back over the Russian lines. On 24 March Przemyśl surrendered. Nine generals, 93 staff officers, 7,500 field officers and 117,000 other ranks fell into Russian hands.

Though Przemyśl was no longer of any military significance, its capture posed a vast propaganda threat to Vienna, where the details of the siege had been passionately followed by soldiers and civilians alike. Karl Kraus caught this brilliantly in the following 'imaginary' exchange between a military press officer and a member of the General Staff keen to limit the negative publicity:

'Have you got the report ready on Przemyśl? . . . NO? You haven't woken up yet? . . . Yes such a good party . . . . Na come on otherwise you'll miss the next rave-up tonight . . . . main point is that the fortifications were nothing, just a load of obsolescent junk. Absolute crap . . . got it? What's that you say? Most modern armaments? Where did you get that idea from? Absolute crap; utterly useless for modern war [laughing].'[8]

Rome felt the moment propitious to engage with the Entente, who had for months been making mouth-watering gestures. The Italians proved themselves formidable negotiators. Their demands were exhaustive and for the British, notably Lloyd George and Sir Edward Grey, exhausting. Italian demands included all of Tyrol south of the Alps, the Trentino, Gorizia and Gradiska, Trieste and Istria. As an afterthought were added Dalmatia as far as the Narenta, control of the Straits of Otranto through Valona in Albania, various islands, and a solemn commitment on the part of the Entente not to conclude a separate peace or permit any mediation for peace on the part of the Vatican.

Enshrined as the secret Treaty of London 1915, this 'infamous' document, published by the Bolsheviks after they seized power, is an embarrassment to all the signatories except Italy which was simply grasping all it could in return for what would be the most sanguinary campaigns it had ever launched, against an enemy it had never yet once defeated on the battlefield.

Austro-German rivalry in Rome: the issue of the Trentino forces Berchtold to resign

As the talks continued, Italy maintained its conversations with Germany and Austria-Hungary in parallel. In early January, Germany had dispatched the formidable Prince Bülow to Rome. Bülow was a former Ambassador to Rome, married to an Italian noblewoman and a Knight of the Order of Annunziata, and therefore one of twelve elect permitted to call the Italian King their 'cousin'. Every year, Bülow wintered in Rome in the Villa Malta on the Pincio. In preparation for his arrival, the German-controlled Italian Banca Commerciale had opened an account into which Berlin remitted significant sums to ensure Bülow's eminent suitability for his task.

In Vienna, Prince Bülow's mission was regarded with mixed feelings. Berchtold had supported it and had even mentioned in private the possibility of ceding the Trentino. But the new Austrian Ambassador to Rome, Baron Macchio, was more careful and opted not to appear at the railway station to greet Prince Bülow on his arrival in Rome; the awaiting delegation was led by the Turkish Ambassador instead. Macchio was told to keep a sharp eye on Bülow's activities. It soon became evident that Bülow was offering the Italians much more than the Trentino. When it became widely known that even the Trentino had been dangled as bait for 'discussion', the ensuing furore cost Berchtold his job. He could finally exchange his silk hat for a dragoon helmet.

Tisza led the charges against him. The Magyar had already openly criticised Germany for not wanting to show 'the spiked helmet in the Alps' and safeguard Austria's rear, and he saw all too well that if the Trentino was to be surrendered, it would be a precedent for ceding Hungarian Transylvania to Romania. Furious with Berchtold, Tisza characteristically went straight to the Emperor on 10 January, a week after Bülow had arrived in Rome, and demanded the Foreign Minister's resignation. Berchtold's willingness to compromise on the Trentino had been fuelled by his obsession with crushing Serbia. By reaching an agreement with Italy, he thought Austria could deploy more troops to eliminate Serbia.

Franz-Josef offered the job of Foreign Minister to Tisza. The shrewd old Emperor knew that Tisza's acceptance would mean the subordination of Magyar to Imperial interests. But for precisely that reason, Tisza rejected the offer and installed instead his loyal henchman Baron Burian, rightly perceived by all as 'Tisza's tool'. He took over from Berchtold on 14 January.

This changing of the guard at the Ballplatz did not inhibit German pretensions. As the Serbian envoy in Athens observed at this time: 'Germany is shaping Austria-Hungary's future to fit carefully into her own plans.' The Trentino did not have a role in any master plan of German penetration of the east, unlike Serbia. Berlin could thus be utterly indifferent to its fate.

Bülow performed his work well. He had been shocked on his arrival by 'how we could have lost so much ground so quickly'.[9] He was particularly irritated to see the street stalls of Rome selling statues of the Madonna and Child in which the infant's fingers had been severed. Around the statues was the message 'Give us back our land severed by the barbarian Germans'. These were ascribed by Bülow to Belgian propaganda.

In an attempt to counter this, Bülow focused on the ruling few. His parties at the Villa Malta became more and more lavish. In the words of the British Ambassador, they were 'a barometric register of the rise and fall of our respective stock in official circles'.[10] As the duel by dinner invitations or the 'battle of the balls' continued in the Eternal City, Berlin kept up the pressure on Vienna. A delegation led by Count Wedel, scion of another Prussian family, arrived for an audience with the Emperor to plead for the cession of territory.

Indeed, so great was the pressure on Vienna from Berlin, there was even talk of a 'Silesian offer' which would compensate Vienna with Silesia in return for her surrendering territory in the south to Italy. The Vatican, the heir to the throne, the Archduke Charles, and Count Ledochowski, the Theresianum-educated General of the Jesuits, were all mobilised to advance this proposal. On 8 March, the joint ministers in the presence of the Emperor discussed surrendering the Trentino to Italy. But Kaiser Franz-Josef was adamant that no points along the Isonzo should be bargained away. Further concessions would bring the Italian frontier too close to Trieste, the great port of the Empire which had developed over three hundred years into one of the most prosperous and entrepreneurial cities in Europe.[11]

At Bülow's first meeting with Sonnino, the Italian Foreign Minister had mentioned Trieste as more or less at the top of his 'shopping list'. But this even affected Germany's interests. Berlin increasingly saw the future of the great Austrian port in terms of Germany's ambitions in the eastern Mediterranean. Bülow rapidly moved the conversation back to the Trentino.

But if the ceding of the Trentino was a matter of indifference for Berlin, it was also fraught with difficulty for Vienna on account of the Imperial and Royal Army. The Tyrolean Kaiserjaeger regiments of light infantry belonged to the elite formations of the army, and in Galicia they had demonstrated their courage and vigorous fighting qualities at every moment of the previous six months. Many of these were from the Trentino. Though they might have Italian names and speak Italian at home, there were few soldiers more loyal to the Emperor.

Franz-Josef had reservations concerning the effect on the morale of these soldiers in the event of their homes being ceded to the Kingdom of Italy. Few of them had affection for the kingdom's corrupt and inefficient ways. Conrad, who had always urged a preventive war on Italy, shared these views fully. He was expressing the 'army' viewpoint when he wrote to Burian, the new Foreign Minister, stating that it would be more sensible to make peace with Russia than keep Italy happy; far better to give Russia eastern Galicia than cede the Trentino to Italy. Galicia, the traditional recruiting ground of the Imperial and Royal Lancers, was from a purely military point of view an easier sacrifice. A few good cavalry regiments would be lost, but so would a large number of Ruthenes, many of whom had yet to prove their mettle in this war.

Understandable though these views were, they showed, yet again, Conrad's diplomatic naivety. By the end of March, with the fall of Przemyśl, Russia was in no mood to negotiate. Her armies had demonstrated repeatedly the inferiority of their Austro-Hungarian opponents. Conrad also suggested making peace with Serbia, forgetting that only a few weeks earlier he had demanded that the corpse of his arch-rival Aehrenthal be exhumed from its grave 'so that he can see where his peaceful policies towards Serbia have brought us'.[12]

Conrad made these pacific views known to his military colleagues in Berlin. The Prussian War Minister von Wild noted: 'I have alerted Falkenhayn to these signs of our ally's weakness .... we cannot put up with these half-baked ideas. There can be no excursions off the beaten track and tomorrow we shall make this clear to Conrad and shine a light which will fundamentally illuminate his dark-room of political fantasy.' (Wild wrote to his wife on 14 April: 'What do we care if Italy cuts part of the genitals off the dying camel which is Austria?')[13]

The Germans changed Conrad's mind, but he veered off in the direction of another utterly unrealistic fantasy: 'Of course after we have won the war, Austria will be so strengthened by victory as to be able to treat with Germany as an equal.'[14] Other Germans expressed themselves more moderately but urged Vienna to make concessions, which could 'always be returned by the victor in this war'. But it was too late. On 26 April, the Italians signed the Treaty of London and began concentrating their troops near the eastern Alps. In Vienna, rumours of this agreement began to circulate almost within hours of its signing, notably from their legation in Athens. Burian redoubled his efforts. In Rome, Macchio and Bülow together made the Italian government one final spectacular offer: all Tyrol south of the German language barrier, Gradiska, Valona and Free City status for Trieste, plus negotiations over the future status of Istria and Dalmatia.

Had the Austrians and Germans backed this offer up with substantial bribes to the King and leading politicians it might have kept Italy out of the war. As it was, the offer was leaked to the Italian press, which almost unanimously greeted it as 'generous'. The overwhelming majority of the Italian population were in favour of neutrality. This was also true in particular of the commercial middle classes. But the Entente had not wasted its time.

London deploys 'monetary magic'

In London, Alfred de Rothschild had offered to act as an intermediary between Imperiali, the Italian Ambassador, and Asquith, the British Prime Minister. Rothschild was one of many 'working most actively' in the British diplomat Rodd's phrase, 'in support of the Allies'. In this elaborate pre-game auction, Bülow, though possessed of significant funds, simply could not compete, and in any event he had bid low.

When it came to 'monetary magic', London still held the strongest cards, as it had done in Pitt's day. Imperiali later wrote to San Giuliano, the Italian Foreign Minister, describing how 'someone who works in the City had visited him with an offer of £20,000,000'.[15] This staggering sum, approaching in value well over a billion pounds today, was the price London placed on forcing Austria to open a new front.

The interventionist government of Salandra, which favoured war, had just resigned. In the ensuing vacuum, power moved to the monarch. The 'bid' was well calculated. Citing slightly implausibly the fear that his throne would be swept away if he appointed a pro-German government, the King refused to accept Salandra's resignation. Salandra's main rival was Giolitti, who might easily have formed a government of 'neutralists', but he did not wish to oppose the King's will. The King asked Giolitti to keep a low profile, even take a holiday for a week, and Giolitti, remarkably, obeyed. In this way the House of Savoy, with the support of the House of Rothschild, appeared to be the ultimate arbiter of Italy's fate in 1915. On 20 May, Italy publicly mobilised, although her troops had already been *in movimento* for many weeks.

On 23 May the declaration of war was handed to Baron Macchio. Rather weakly, it referred to 'The present and future threats to Italy's national aspirations'. This limp statement was met with Franz-Josef's famous proclamation referring to how 'the King of Italy has declared war on me; a breach of faith of which history knows no parallel'.[16] The Emperor referred to the great victories of his youth: Custozza, Novara and Lissa, all names which carried bitter memories for his new enemy. As realists, the Italians were more disturbed by the news just in from the Carpathians where, to widespread surprise, Conrad had finally pulled off something of a masterstroke.

Breakthrough at Görlitz

In early April Conrad had asked the Germans for four divisions. To Conrad's amazement, Falkenhayn responded with four corps, three times as many troops as he had requested. Conrad had drawn up a plan to force a decisive action in the east that would achieve more than just the relief of the embattled III Army. Though the forces to be deployed would be slightly more Austro-Hungarian than German, Conrad agreed to share command. Falkenhayn appointed Field Marshal August von Mackensen (1849–1945) as commander, supported by von Seeckt, then only a young but capable colonel, as chief of staff. The German 11th Army and the Imperial and Royal 4th Army were combined as separate units into a unified command system. The AOK had to agree all plans with Mackensen's staff.

Conrad's concept of a breakthrough at Gorlice (Görlitz) in the Carpathians was to be one of the war's most effective thrusts.[17] Conrad wanted the offensive to have a much more ambitious objective, at the very least the relief of Lemberg. But the Germans were more modest in their aims. It was important to demonstrate after the string of Austrian failures that the armies of the Central Powers were very far from beaten so that countries such as Romania, which were weighing their options, might think twice before joining the

Entente. A campaign which cleared central Galicia of Russian troops would be salutary.

If Conrad was the inspiration and strategic spirit behind the campaign, the Germans brought the tactical experience of the Western front. The offensive opened in Western front style with a four-hour bombardment of unprecedented intensity on the Eastern front. The Russians had prepared their first line of trenches but their second and third lines were not dug in and within an hour the bombardment had wiped out these lines. Unsupported, and suffering from the hail of ordnance, the Russians tried to fall back, only to be caught by yet more *Trommelfeuer*. The Russians estimated that 700,000 shells fell within three hours.

The casualties were enormous. In less than a day, the Russians lost 210,000 out of 250,000 men. Of these only 14,000 were taken prisoner. This far exceeded German expectations, and they immediately demanded reinforcements to exploit the Russian collapse. Everywhere the Russians fell back. Even the brilliant Russian general Brusilov's troops, which had penetrated deep into the Carpathians, were in danger of being outflanked and had to organise a rapid withdrawal towards Przemyśl. When they got there, hoping to make a stand, they suddenly realised that the Russian III Army on their right had virtually ceased to exist as a fighting entity. Brusilov's men continued their retreat.

By 3 June, Bavarian troops retook Przemyśl. They arrived less than six weeks after Kusmanek and his officers had been forced to surrender their swords. Mackensen telegrammed the Emperor Franz-Josef to 'place the fortress at Your Majesty's feet'.[18] The news of Przemyśl's recapture by Bavarians was greeted in Vienna with some ambivalence. Why had the k. (u.) k. army not retaken the fortress?

For the Italians, these setbacks for the Entente, though daunting, came too late for them to rethink their alignments. The news of the great Austro-German victory at Görlitz reached Rome just as the Italian King had decided, in the tradition of his ancestors, to take up arms against the hated Austriaci. Romania, geographically closer to the scene of conflict, improvised more skilfully, remaining loyal to its commitments to the Austro-Hungarian monarchy for a little longer.

From the beginning of the Italian declaration of war, it was clear that hostilities along this new 'third front' would have a markedly different character from the Empire's other two fronts. A Swiss military observer in Galicia commented a few weeks earlier: 'the only race the Imperial and Royal Army universally despise are the Italians. If it comes to war with the Italians, I fear it will be prosecuted with murderous enthusiasm.'[19]

The new Italian front

Thanks to the poor showing of the Italians in the war of 1866, the Austrians had been able to dictate the new frontier arrangements at the subsequent peace treaty, ensuring that most of the strategic salients and heights were firmly in Austrian hands. Even Trieste, barely seventy miles from Venice, had the Isonzo and the fortress of Gorizia (the 'Verdun' of Austria, as the Allied propagandists liked to call it), guarding its north-western approaches.

But Trieste's position was more vulnerable from the south-west. The Italians had established a strong airbase behind Grado, the Austrian resort, on the eastern edge of the lagoons. As the crow flew, that was barely ten miles from the Austrian harbour. The protection of Austrian airspace around Trieste immediately became an urgent priority. Young Geoffrey (later Gottfried and later still Goffredo) Banfield was charged with commanding Trieste's first naval air station. He later recalled the primitive state of the city's defences, which amounted to one machine gun hastily placed on the tower of the Lloyd arsenal.[20] As Venice was used by the Italians as a staging post for their logistics for the front, Banfield and his squadron were involved in several bombing raids on the city which he recalled would never have been necessary had Venice been declared by the Italians an 'open city'.[21]

Though the Evidenzbüro had been supplying Vienna with accurate information concerning Italy's military preparations and intentions, it was only two days before Italy's formal declaration of war that Conrad decided to move to the Austrian littoral two corps (XV and XVI) that had originally been destined for Serbia. This was to be the nucleus of a new reorganised V Army, to be commanded by FML Swetozar Boroević, whose skill and tenacity had been demonstrated in Galicia earlier that year.

Boroević's existing command, the much-battered III Army, was reorganised into a VII Corps, also destined for the Italian front and under the nominal command of the Archduke Eugen. In addition to these movements, two defensive forces were hastily established along the Carinthian and Tyrolean southern frontiers, the first under GdK (General der Kavallerie) Rohr, the second under GdK Dankl.

The Italian mobilisation had been slow and, for once, Austrian logistics delivered a formidable defensive force in a matter of days. Once Italy had announced its reneging on the obligations of the Triple Alliance, the Imperial and Royal Navy embarked immediately on a demonstration in force along the Adriatic coast. No one could accuse the navy of being unprepared.

By the beginning of March, most of the Imperial and Royal Navy's capital ships, spearheaded by the three dreadnoughts, *Viribus Unitis, Tegetthoff* and

Prinz Eugen under Admiral Haus, were at sea. This time there were no French or British ships to engage and the Italian navy wisely remained in its ports. A spectacular operation aimed at the maximum disruption of Italian logistics was launched while Italy continued to move units and equipment north.

One of the keys to these Italian troop movements was the port of Ancona, an important railhead and distribution centre. On the morning of 24 May, at 4.35 a.m. several hours after Rome issued its formal declaration of war to Baron Macchio, the inhabitants of Ancona were woken by explosions of deafening intensity. The three dreadnoughts opened up with their full complement of thirty-six 30.5cm guns with devastating effect. Within minutes the Italian coastal batteries and signal stations were completely destroyed.

Behind the dreadnoughts the six battleships of the 'Archduke' and 'Habsburg' class proceeded to fire on pre-assigned targets including the railway station, Italian army barracks and naval installations as well as most of the ships in the harbour. Thus within hours of Italy deciding to declare war on the Dual Monarchy, the Imperial and Royal Navy had demonstrated that it could strike at the very nerve centre of Italian military and naval planning. The raid on Ancona was in every way a success completely out of proportion to the damage inflicted, and illustrative of the careful planning of which the Habsburg war machine was capable.

As well as disrupting troop movements up and down the peninsula and seriously disordering the Italian mobilisation plans, the raid paralysed Italian naval planning for the rest of the war. The effect on morale was even more devastating. Captain Herbert Richmond, the British liaison officer with the Italian fleet at Taranto, wrote bitterly after the raid:

> The Italians have admitted that the Austrians have command of the sea in the Adriatic in spite of their inferior naval force and without fighting an action. They might as well sell their fleet and rake up their organs and monkeys again for, by heaven, that seems more their profession than sea fighting.[22]

Notwithstanding these disruptions and setbacks, the overall Italian commander, Luigi Cadorna, son of the general whose fate it had been to be vanquished by Radetzky a half century earlier, kept his nerve. He assembled three armies to threaten a wide front stretching from western Tyrol to the Julian Alps and the famous Laibach 'Gap', one of the principal invasion routes into Central Europe.

The attack of the Italian 4th Army at Toblach was beaten off easily, and the centre of gravity of the Italian army swiftly moved towards the Isonzo river. Despite superiority in numbers, the challenging terrain of the Carso made offensive activities difficult, and the front settled down along a line stretching from the Austrian littoral near Duino, where a few years earlier Rilke had composed his famous 'Elegies', to the summit of the Triglav mountains in the Julian Alps, towards Tolmein. This 64-km-long part of the overall 450-km-front was to become the scene of eleven bitterly fought defensive battles by the Austrians which would cost them and their Italian opponents nearly half a million casualties each. The twelfth battle, which saw the Italians on the defensive, was no less sanguinary and would be immortalised by the name of Caporetto.

First Battle of the Isonzo

Initially the entire front between the Ortler mountains and the Adriatic was held by 128 Austro-Hungarian battalions, many of which were nowhere near full strength and totalled 220,000 men. When the First Battle of the Isonzo erupted in July, Boroević possessed four battalions as a disposable reserve and only two of the invaluable 30.5cm howitzers. Cadorna on the other hand possessed more than a million men under arms and a huge superiority in artillery. Italy's new allies in London and Paris did their sums and felt confident of an imminent Italian breakthrough against an Imperial and Royal Army which, so far, had not distinguished itself consistently on any front.

The views of London and Paris were shared not only by the rest of the Entente. In April, Conrad felt compelled to warn that the breaking out of hostilities with Italy meant that 'the Italians would be in Vienna in 5 weeks'. Conrad noted ponderously that 'Given the huge numerical superiority of the Italians and their artillery we must count on our forts being swiftly demolished and the Italians quickly occupying our territory'. Fortunately for the Austrians, as was so often the case, Conrad's assessment was wrong.[23]

The relatively modest Austrian forces swiftly deployed from Galicia and the Balkans included some of the finest regiments in the Austro-Hungarian army. Though many of these had been significantly reduced by the campaigns in Galicia, they still enjoyed a formidable *esprit de corps*, and the losses had been made up by new reservists. Above all, they were fighting for their homeland. The four Tyrolean Landesschützen regiments knew every peak and valley of the Trentino. The Carinthian 'Khevenhueller' Infantry Regiment Nr 7 had grown up in the Karawanken ranges of the eastern Alps while the Salzburg 'Rainer' and Graz 'King of the Belgians' were equally at home in the Julian Alps a few valleys away from their home cities. Tough and experienced, they would prove themselves to be easily capable of holding off an enemy who outnumbered them never less than four to one. A German liaison officer noted that, in contrast to the 'Russian terror' in Galicia, these Imperial units seemed to harbour 'not the slightest Italian terror'.[24]

Conrad had hoped to get the Germans to commit troops to shore up the thin Austrian line but Berlin, still smarting from the failure of its expensive diplomatic charm offensive in Rome, was most reluctant. After much nagging by Conrad, Falkenhayn agreed to deploy a Bavarian brigade, to be given the designation 'Alpine Korps', but the presence of Bavarians immediately brought out all the traditional contempt of the Salzburg and Tyrolean troops for their 'Bayerische Hunden' comrades. Falkenhayn wrote a furious memo to Conrad reminding him that Austria's illustrious Alpine regiments could only now deploy on the Italian front on account of the earlier support they had received in Galicia from the Bavarians.

The Austro-German military relationship deteriorated further on 8 July, when the German Kaiser ordered that not a single German soldier was to cross the Italian frontier. This so irritated Franz-Josef that he ordered the immediate suspension of the use of the word 'Waffenbruderschaft' (Brotherhood of arms) in official communiqués. As the battle began, Conrad tried to orchestrate the Italian front from Teschen. His limited success meant that he could only look on as his outnumbered and unsupported army faced the full might of Cadorna's assault alone.

Fortunately for the Austrians, the Italians also had deficiencies of materiel. Machine guns were not as widespread as they were in the Imperial and Royal Army; and from the beginning the Austrian naval air stations at nearby Trieste and Pola provided air supremacy. The only hostile Italian bombers to penetrate regularly across the Austrian lines were so ineffective that the Austrians soon gave them Viennese nicknames such as 'Franzl' or 'Bombenschani'. Moreover, thanks to the carefully prepared network of Austrian military intelligence in Switzerland under the control of Colonel von Einem, a detailed appreciation of the Italian order of battle was available.

Cadorna's first proper assault on the Isonzo went in near Redipuglia not far from Trieste on 23 June, and was beaten back with 15,000 casualties. A second offensive two weeks later was equally unsuccessful. The third Isonzo battle showed that the Italians too were capable of improvising and developing; twenty-seven generals were subsequently relieved of their command. Marshal Joffre had visited Udine to inject some ginger into the stalled Italian offensive and had brought a new weapon which would have its debut in that battle: the short-range mortar (*Minenwerfer*); and the Italians used it to terrifying effect on the Gorizia bridgehead. The impact of such ordnance on the limestone landscape can be imagined. The rock splintered and at a time when metal helmets had not been issued the number of head wounds caused by the explosions rose dramatically. The dead and wounded soon poisoned the waters of the river and a crisis in the water supply threatened. By the end of the Second Battle of the Isonzo each side had already suffered in excess of 40,000 casualties. The murderous third battle, fought over two days in early November, added another 100,000 to the butcher's bill. Moreover, disease, notably cholera, stalked the killing fields. Asked how he was getting on by a visiting staff officer, Boroević, taciturn and serious, commented laconically that at least his losses were less than his troops had suffered in the Carpathians a year earlier.

Boroević's defence of the Isonzo

The Austrians soon learnt how to turn the landscape to their advantage, digging into the Carso (Karst) and fortifying the terrain with great ingenuity. Boroević's skill as a defensive commander began to manifest itself increasingly, much to the chagrin of his rivals, who found him altogether far too austere for their tastes. It is to Conrad's credit that at least in this military detail the General Staff Chief's judgement did not let him down. Conrad appreciated Boroević's qualities. Perhaps the southern Slav represented a warrior toughness that Conrad would have loved to possess himself. In any event, Conrad deflected much criticism from Boroević, and always defended him.

Conrad knew that Boroević's example filled the troops with confidence and optimism. Against superior odds, time and again, Austrian positions held out, frustrating Cadorna's plan to settle everything in one vast bayonet charge. As summer turned to autumn, the Alpine characteristics of the battlefield began to exert more influence over the logistics. The front crept ever upwards, encompassing nearly every peak below 4,000 metres. As the Italians built roads to enhance their logistics, the Austrians threw out more cable cars and narrow-gauge railways. When the first snow began to fall in early November, winter Alpine conditions began to prevail. The fourth Isonzo battle brought Cadorna little relief from the growing pressure his masters in Rome were feeling, not only from their allies but also from the domestic population alienated from a war costing so much blood and sacrifice for so elusive an end. Despite the deployment of Western front tactics and intense barrages, the 38 and a half Italian divisions still could make no impact on the 19 Austrian divisions, supported by one German division. The fifth Isonzo battle lasted until Christmas but with the exception of the deployment for the first time of Italian aerial bombers over Gorizia, there was very little to give the Entente any hint of progress. Like its predecessors, that battle ended in failure for the Italians. Like the Turks who were more than capable of holding down the British at Gallipoli, the Austrians had pinned down the Italians quite easily so far.

The only 'success' Italy's entry into the war had brought the Entente was the removal of many Austrian elite Alpine regimental troops from the Galician front. Had they been present during the aftermath of Conrad's victory at Görlitz, a Russian collapse might have been brought about a year earlier.

Görlitz had in any event led to the recapture of Lemberg and brought the Russians more or less to a full-blown retreat. News of this had almost panicked the Petrograd malcontents into bringing down the Tsar. In the euphoria that followed, plans were drawn up to take advantage of the successes on the Russian front by organising a strong Austro-German force to renew the offensive against Serbia as well as an Austrian offensive, the so-called 'Black and Gold' (*Schwarzgelb*: Habsburg colours) to drive the Russians back and secure Galicia once and for all.

But the crisis for Petrograd soon passed and a Russian counter-attack once again painfully illuminated the weaknesses in the Austrian Higher Command. The shortcomings were echoed by the indifferent showing of many units that found themselves shorn of their elite components, the Alpine troops who had been rushed back to deal with the Italian crisis. It did not help that they were facing, in General Brusilov, the most aggressive commander in the Russian army. Brusilow's counter-attack came out of marshy terrain from which no member of Conrad's staff expected an attack. The Austrian IV Army was so wearied after its previous energetic two months of marching and fighting, ever advancing and capturing towns, that it was unprepared for Brusilov's move. The Russian 8th Army swept the Austrians out of the town of Łuck, which was surrendered by General Roth after a feeble organisation of the town's bridgehead.

The Austrian Emergency in Russia

The poor performance of the Austrians did not go unnoticed by the Germans, who offered to replace Austrian units in the Balkans in preparation for the imminent attack on Serbia. As this would have resulted in the Balkans becoming a predominantly German sphere of operations, an eventuality of which Franz-Josef in particular did not approve, the offer was declined. The perilous condition of the Imperial and Royal IV Army meant German help in the form of two divisions could not be refused. The quid pro quo for this support on the Eastern front was a bitter one for Conrad to swallow: the IV Army would come under overall German command. Conrad's increasing difficulties with his German military colleagues were noted in Vienna. One officer Andrian sent Burian a report on 15 September 1915, discussing Conrad's 'bad mood over Falkenhayn'.[25] It was another straw in the wind of increasing Austrian military dependency on Germany.

But the 'Austrian Emergency'[26] in Russia had dramatically increased the numbers of Austrian casualties and prisoners. In addition, thousands of weapons fell intact into the Russians' hands, which meant they could equip an entire division with Austrian rifles and ammunition. Nevertheless by the end of October 1915, the Eastern front had settled down. Because the Russians were no longer capable of taking the offensive, the Austrians and Germans began freeing up the troops earmarked a few months earlier for dealing with Serbia.

The majority of these troops were German. The Imperial and Royal Army had lost 230,886 men in the failed 'Black and Gold' offensive. Of these, more than 100,000 were prisoners. Austrian forces on the Eastern front had been reduced from half a million to a quarter of a million. 'Black and Gold' had proved once and for all that Austria, in Falkenhayn's phrase, 'would never defeat Russia'.

It had also proved the shortcomings of Conrad's leadership and command structures. There was too much thoughtless attack and inadequate planning. The Russians had fought well. Their cavalry was far superior on their home marshy terrain than the parade-ground-equipped k. (u.) k. dragoons and lancers. Above all, as far as this front was concerned, the Habsburgs' war had become a German war, commanded by Germans.

Serbia eliminated

It was to be no different in Serbia in the spring of 1915. Germany, having seen Russia as the key to hostilities in 1914, had a change of heart one year into the war. Serbia now became a priority. Elimination of the Serbs would keep Romania in check, intimidate Greece and bring Bulgaria firmly and squarely into the ranks of the Central Powers. These aims, if realised, would also bring German influence to play along the principal land route to the east.

The German Kaiser had belittled the war with Serbia in August 1914. The hard men of the German military command had viewed Serbia rather differently, and they meant to ensure that it became a permanent German satellite. Conrad, as always politically behind the curve, was hoping for strong German reinforcements for the Isonzo. His earlier obsession, Serbia, had paled into insignificance compared to Italy. In fact, at this very moment, Conrad advised coming to terms with Serbia. But Falkenhayn had the bit between his teeth, not least because 'With this operation Austria-Hungary abdicates as a Great Power and the leadership comes into the hands of Germany.'[27] The irritating fly buzzing around German Staff Headquarters in the form of the pitiful Conrad would be swatted away for good with this operation.

On 6 September, a pact with military protocols was signed between Bulgaria and the Central Powers. A condition of the arrangements was that hostilities against Serbia would begin no later than within 30 days. Falkenhayn insisted that the Austro-German forces come under the command of Mackensen. Conrad was to enjoy a subordinate command of the Austro-Bulgarian force. He was unamused but had nothing to counter with apart from bitterly observing he thought the view from Berlin was that the 'Balkans were not worth the bones of a Pomeranian grenadier'.[28]

But Falkenhayn had read the situation correctly: twelve months of war had brought the Dual Monarchy to second division power status. The failure of the 'Black and Gold' offensive gave the Germans all the moral high ground they needed. Tisza also took advantage of the German headwinds, not for the first time, and pushed for a Hungarian, Kövess von Kövesshaza, to take command of the Imperial and Royal forces rather than Conrad's initial choice of Carl von Tersztyansky. This was just window-dressing. Mackensen was answerable to Falkenhayn, and Mackensen, now in his 67th year, certainly had no intention of consulting any Austrians.

Attacked on three fronts, the Serbs were defeated in less than five weeks, their forces having taken shelter in the northern interior of the country. The offensive began on 6 October and was over by 8 November. Mackensen had given the twentieth century its first taste of blitzkrieg. The Austrian III Army, stiffened with two German divisions, crossed the Drina on 6 October. Four days later the 'Prinz Eugen' March was ringing out from a captured Kalemegdan in Belgrade. The Serbs retreated to the south, where they were just in time for Bulgaria to declare war and attack them in the rear on the 14th. The Bulgarian move broke any communication the Serbs had with Salonika where some hastily dispatched French and British troops awaited.

Fortunately for the Serbs, the weather came to their rescue and the October rains slowed down the Germans even more effectively than it had Potiorek a year earlier. The Serbs began their epic retreat to the sea as the starving, exhausted remains of Putnik's army, harassed by Albanians, made their way to the Adriatic. Few of Putnik's men made it to safety. The elimination of Serbia as a factor in Balkan politics had been achieved. Two mountain batteries in Slovenia were freed up to be shipped from Trieste to Palestine, where they supported Turkish troops in two successful actions fought in Gaza against the British, who suffered severe casualties as a result of the Austrian guns.

Vienna looked on approvingly. Along all fronts the Imperial and Royal Army had fought with varying degrees of courage and it had avoided the disintegration its enemies had so long predicted. Even so, the Imperial and Royal Army had suffered catastrophic losses. Of the 'Old Army' there could no longer be any more than a hazy memory. By 1915, the Dual Monarchy had mobilised nearly 5.6 million men. A year later it had lost more than 56,000 officers and NCOs, and 2.5 million men. Proportionately, the Imperial and

Royal Army had suffered the highest casualty rate of any belligerent. The former career officer caste had been largely wiped out and the reserve officers who replaced them were from many walks of life and many professions. By 1916, 10 per cent of the new officer class was drawn from the universities and was Jewish. During the subsequent years until 1918, more than 300,000 Jews served in the Imperial and Royal Army.[29] But so strong was the ethos of the officer profession that these changes in no way affected either the cohesion of the officer class or the respect in which it was held by the rank and file. Anti-Semitism continued to be a very rare occurrence in Imperial and Royal military circles.

The survival of the Imperial and Royal Army had come at the price of increasing dependence on Germany and the issues of German command and Austro-Hungarian subordination would be thrown into ever sharper relief as 1916 progressed and a new Emperor, Charles, ascended the throne to don the 'martyr's crown'.

CHAPTER 24

1916–1918

THE END OF THE OLD ARMY

Conrad's optimism

1916 began on a confident note. Conrad, attending the meeting of ministers in Vienna on 7 January, displayed all his usual hubris and diplomatic naivety. No longer was there any more talk of a separate peace with Russia or a deal with Serbia or Italy. All these props had been cast away with the enthusiasm of a lame man miraculously brought to his feet.

Conrad was convinced that 1916 would bring, not just the end of the war, but a triumphant conclusion of hostilities together with the annexation of Serbia and even Montenegro. The Balkan back door had been secured. Only the Montenegrins were still defiant and Conrad told the ministers that the following day, 8 January 1916, had been agreed for a combined naval and military operation to wipe that little kingdom off the map.

Montenegro conquered

In a display of solidarity with Serbia and Russia, the Montenegrins declared war in 1914. Immediately they stepped up sending wireless information on the Imperial and Royal Navy dispositions in the bay of Cattaro. This spectacular series of fiords, the greatest natural defensive harbour in the Mediterranean, lay at the foot of the Montenegrin kingdom. Montenegrin batteries overlooked the Austrian facilities from the dramatic mountain of Lovćen, home to the tomb of the founder of Montenegro, the Poet-King Njegoš. Mount Lovćen was quickly fortified by the Montenegrins and a French military wireless station was established there, with another at Budva further along the coast.

The Austrian navy moved swiftly to shell these installations and reduce the fortifications that menaced them from above. During the autumn of 1914 two warships of the 'Monarch' class bombarded the Montenegrin positions but with little effect. A year later, in October 1915, they were joined by the cruisers *Kaiser Franz Joseph, Kaiser Karl VI, Aspern* and *Budapest* with *Panther* in attendance.[1]

The Austrian XIX Corps was given the task of ascending the mountain along a path which the former Austrian military attaché in Cetinje, the Montenegrin capital, had mapped out some months earlier. It was rumoured he had filled in the details over many evenings playing bridge with senior Montenegrin officers during the previous three years. To ensure that the attack was not held up by the Montenegrin batteries above, the Imperial and Royal Navy was asked to provide covering fire. This challenge fell to the *Budapest*, a woefully small and obsolescent cruiser armed with 24cm guns. The height of the target was too great for the elevation of her guns, but her captain was not to be defeated by such petty considerations. He hit upon the idea of flooding certain compartments of his ship and shifting coal so that the elevation of the guns could be extended a few degrees to hit the batteries perched above.

Feldmarschallleutnant Trollmann's corps found the support of the *Budapest* invaluable because it put down a barrage that allowed them to scale the towering height of the Lovčen in less than 30 hours. Once arrived at the summit, the Montenegrins fled, suing for unconditional surrender two weeks later. The operation had proved a textbook example of a combined military and naval assault.

It was with the greatest of difficulty that Conrad could be restrained from remonstrating with the Emperor over the decision not to annex Montenegro for 'military strategic reasons'. All the Austrians on the ministerial council had been in favour but Tisza, ever wary of an increase in the Slav population of the monarchy, had vetoed the proposal. Franz-Josef was equally sceptical as he felt some monarchical solidarity with King Nikola of Montenegro. (Reports had reached him that the Montenegrin King had fled his miniature palace in Cetinje only after placing a large portrait of Franz-Josef prominently in his study.)[2] Franz-Josef unquestioningly took Tisza's side once again.

Tisza for his part returned the compliment a little later. When the German nationalists became fired up in early 1915 with the ideas of the German writer Friedrich Naumann's *Mitteleuropa*, an influential book which implied greater political and economic union between Berlin and Vienna, Tisza skilfully assisted Franz-Josef in preventing the idea from gaining traction. The Hungarian publicly announced that such an arrangement could not be permitted without a renegotiation of the Hungarian 'Ausgleich' of 1867 occurring first.

Before 1914, Tisza had been happy to use the Germans to head off the threat that Franz Ferdinand posed to Hungary. Now he was able to see off Berlin when Hungarian interests were threatened again. This time the danger was a potential preponderance of Germans in a Berlin-dominated 'Mitteleuropa'. At every moment of challenge, Tisza fought like a tiger to defend Magyar interests.

For Franz-Josef, still smarting from the frictions of sharing overall responsibility for command with Falkenhayn, the challenge was even clearer. Falkenhayn himself had made no secret that he saw the future of the Habsburgs as akin to that of the Bavarian Wittelsbachs after 1866: that is, as subordination to the Hohenzollerns.[3] Von Bülow, demoralised by his failure to sell Austrian Tyrol in Rome, put the issue even more sharply: 'Even if Germany loses this war, she will nevertheless have won the struggle by annexing Austria.'[4]

Such developments could only take place literally over Franz-Josef's dead body. While he lived, the debate on 'Mitteleuropa' lost some of its momentum. The entire episode revealed again the Emperor's respect for Tisza as the most formidable and impressive politician of his empire. The two men cooperated highly effectively where they perceived their interests coincided.

The surrender of Montenegro completed the rosy picture which the beginning of 1916 offered the Empire internally and externally. If the war could have been ended somehow, there can be no doubt that Vienna and Budapest could have emerged with their possessions intact. But the dynamics of war have a habit of developing in unpredictable ways.

Neither Germany, bogged down in the bloodletting of the Western front, nor the Entente, still smarting from the setbacks of the Dardanelles and the uninspiring performance of the Italian army, was in any mood to parley. With the elimination of Serbia and Montenegro, Conrad, as usual blind to the realities of the situation, believed that the time was ripe for a decisive offensive to deal with Italy. But this would need German involvement. Throughout February, Falkenhayn focused far more on the imminent offensive on the Western front at Verdun than on any 'sideshow' of Conrad's. In any event, winter had closed down the Italian front far more effectively than any Habsburg army. Both the Italian Alpini mountain troops and the Habsburg Tyrolean units achieved wonders in the eastern Alps but, until spring melted the snows, there was not the slightest chance of decisive movement by either of the protagonists. Even the transport of artillery and supplies along this front challenged every participant.

Conrad's 'sideshow'

By the time Conrad's planned campaign was launched from the fastnesses of the South Tyrol it was May and the Italians had already prepared well for the coming attack. On 18 April, they had mined the summit of the Col di Lana in the Dolomites, just south-west of Cortina d'Ampezzo. The Italians had been tunnelling for weeks and had painstakingly placed more than 5,500 kilos of dynamite under the summit. When it detonated, the explosion buried most of the two companies of the Second Tyrolean Kaiserjaeger regiment stationed on the summit and initiated a phase of mining and counter-mining whose results can still be seen today in the tunnels and passages that survive in the Dolomites.

News of the explosion shocked Vienna, where it overshadowed news of far more significant losses on the Eastern front. Conrad's repeated refusal to base his command of the Italian front on any direct experience – he had not left Teschen once to acquaint himself with conditions in the Alps – began to be questioned in the highest quarters. He had already angered the normally placid heir to the throne, Archduke Charles, by refusing him a significant command, and now the nominal overall commander Archduke Eugen sent a sharp message asking if it was not now time for Conrad's personal presence in the Dolomites.

Conrad's response that he saw 'no reason' to travel south irritated the dynasty. Conrad made it clear that he preferred to discuss with the Emperor details of new uniforms that were being designed. When he sent his recommendations on uniforms, Franz-Josef refused to approve them. In typical Imperial style, he was sending an unequivocal message to his Chief of the General Staff that he was dissatisfied with his conduct.

Strategically, Conrad was right. The loss of the 2,462-metre peak did not help the Italians. A new defensive perimeter was established less than half a mile further back on the equally daunting Mount Sief. The exploded Dolomitic peak became the scene of many struggles over the coming months and was rightly named the 'blood mountain' by Italians and Austrians alike.

On 15 May, the Austro-Hungarian troops launched their Alpine offensive. A force of 157,000 advanced despite bitter winds, icy temperatures and more than 20cm of snow. The attack was preceded by an artillery barrage: this benefited from aerial observation correcting the fall of shot. The Imperial and Royal Navy anchored in the distant Adriatic were in support. They managed to score a direct hit on the Italian 34th Division Headquarters with their second salvo thanks to such aerial assistance.[5]

The future Emperor Charles's first command

Everywhere the Austrian advance was successful. The night before, the future Emperor, Charles, had given his first order as a corps commander (XX Corps).

It was a typical indication of his humanity. The Archduke summoned the senior officers under his command and ordered that 'unnecessary sacrifice of lives' in the advance would not be tolerated and that officers found guilty of wasting the lives of their troops on useless frontal attacks without reason would 'suffer consequences'.[6] This order expressed Charles's personal conviction that as the only future leader of the belligerent states to have had a professional military training he was under an almost sacred obligation to take decisions that would save rather than cost lives.

Charles also ordered the XX Corps to be given the soubriquet 'Edelweiss' Corps. In contrast to Conrad, he soon earned the respect and affection of his troops by visiting, much to the angst of his staff, forward positions all along the front. Once when his aide-de-camp vigorously protested, reminding the Archduke 'with all respect' that he was under orders from the Emperor not to put himself in any danger, Charles simply paused, thought for a moment and then smiled: 'Nevertheless I think we should continue.'[7]

The Italians fell back towards the Venetian plain, evacuating Asiago and Monte Melitta. Thanks to their extensive network of railways, reinforcements soon arrived. The Austrian advance was on the brink of falling upon the plains around the Po river but had overreached itself. After several weeks of uninterrupted fighting, the troops were exhausted. The Italian line held and the Austrian advantage began to ebb away. Hurriedly, the Austrians sought reinforcements from Boroević's nearby Isonzo army and even from as far away as Galicia on the eastern front, but the situation was deteriorating for the Austrians on both fronts. On the Isonzo front, Boroević was achieving miracles with his outnumbered forces, but he could not spare a single man or horse.

Brusilov's offensive

Meanwhile in Galicia, Brusilov had retaken the initiative and on 4 June, all too aware that the Italian war effort was apparently crumbling, he launched a sharp offensive against the Imperial and Royal IV Army. Hit by a fearful barrage, unprecedented in intensity on the Eastern front, the IV Army disintegrated in a matter of hours. The following day, Conrad sent a desperate plea for German help. Germany could spare little from the bloodletting of the Western front and the unhelpful reply came back that Conrad should withdraw troops from the Italian front to stiffen his forces in Galicia.

The hole that Brusilov had punched through the Austrian line was a staggering 74 kilometres deep and 20 kilometres broad. The Germans demanded the immediate dismissal of the rather lacklustre Archduke Joseph Ferdinand, the commander of IV Army. Conrad agreed and, for the first time in Habsburg military history, an archduke was removed from field command in the middle of a campaign.

But changing commanders – the new Feldzeugmeister was Tersztyansky – could not help; the Austrian predicament was too great. Moreover, Tersztyansky, whom Tisza had vetoed for the campaign against Serbia, was perhaps not the most suitable officer to command an army, half of whom were Hungarian Honvéd troops. As the emergency developed, it became increasingly irrelevant who commanded the Imperial and Royal IV Army. It had ceased to exist. Its Ruthenian regiments had laid down their weapons by the thousand. The Russians now threatened to wipe out the Imperial and Royal VII Army under Pflanzer-Baltin. Pflanzer's Ruthenian regiments also began to crumble and the reports of mass Ruthenian desertions outraged the Emperor. He dispatched Marterer to Teschen to find out what was happening. The news of Marterer's imminent arrival filled the Imperial and Royal General Staff with even more gloom. Marterer had organised Potiorek's dismissal. He had the reputation of being Franz-Josef's 'hatchet man'.

The 'Teschener Wirtschaft' (Teschen goings-on), as Marterer called the conditions around Conrad at Teschen, presented Marterer with a picture of chaos. Brusilov's offensive had caught the green-uniformed staff officers of Teschen completely unawares. No one had thought the Russians remotely capable of launching such an attack. Many senior officers had settled down to a spring routine of hunting and socialising. The most senior commanders at the front, even Pflanzer-Baltin, had invited their wives to join them. Others had even settled their entire families as though the Galician front line was some far-flung extension of the leafy Vienna suburbs of Hietzing. The fact that the families of senior officers were then evacuated in cars while the wounded lay dying in need of transport all around them provided Marterer with all the information he needed. Franz-Josef was faced with no choice but to leave the solution to Berlin. Conrad was summoned not to Vienna but to Berlin on 8 June for 'urgent' talks with Falkenhayn.

Falkenhayn gave Conrad such a blistering analysis of Austro-Hungarian military shortcomings that a junior Austrian staff officer sent with an urgent message to interrupt the conversation found Conrad 'with his head between his hands, blankly staring at the map', completely humiliated by the peremptory and harsh Prussian vowels of the German general.[8] Conrad would later recall that he would gladly go through 'his ears being boxed ten times' than repeat the 'conversation' of that day.[9] Falkenhayn had made it unmistakably clear that German military leadership was the only way forward. Alexander von Linsingen, a capable Prussian general would pull the Habsburg chestnuts out of the fire but, in return, Conrad would subordinate all movements of the

Imperial and Royal Army to German wishes. All Austro-Hungarian offensive operations in Italy were to be halted. There was to be an immediate transfer of Austrian reinforcements from that sector to Galicia.

Falkenhayn's anger was understandable. A breakthrough at Verdun or along the Somme and the long-awaited victory in the west was now, along with his reputation, jeopardised by the collapse and incompetence of his ally's IV Army. At least Conrad was spared the news of the fate of his VII Army. Two days later, Pflanzer-Baltin's forces were crushed near Czernowitz (Cernauti). With that army's disintegration vanished any semblance of Habsburg military autonomy on the Eastern front. Conrad was peremptorily informed that from now on von Seeckt would be serving as 'Senior Chief of Staff' VII Army. The Austrian staff chief, Zeynek, was sent on 'unlimited leave'. 'We are now without doubt entirely in the hands of the Germans,' a young Austrian staff officer wrote.[10]

Despite Conrad's protestations, Falkenhayn insisted that overall command of the Eastern Sector south of the Pripjet marshes be placed in Mackensen's hands. Having made this decision, Falkenhayn ignored Conrad completely for the rest of the war. The equation of power between Germany and the Dual Monarchy had taken on a new aspect, which inexorably was leading to the total subjugation of the monarchy to Berlin. Thanks to an accident of railway planning, a young Hungarian staff officer, Windischgrätz, found himself walking along the tracks during a delay in train schedules with no less a person than the German Kaiser. The German promised that after the war Europe would be dominated by Germany. With Franz-Josef's demise 'of course Austria-Hungary' would become a protectorate of her stronger ally. When the astonished Windischgrätz wrote a report of this exchange to Conrad, Conrad sent it back to him and told him to 'destroy all trace of the report' and 'speak of it to no one'.[11]

Romania enters the war

The news of the debacle on the Eastern front shocked the aged Emperor Franz-Josef. The facts were inescapable. Brusilov had inflicted more than 475,000 losses on the Austro-Hungarians, including 226,000 prisoners of war. Two Habsburg armies had ceased to exist, the IV partly through desertions, the VII through defeat. Seeing the poor showing of the Habsburg forces, Romania seized the moment to join the Entente and attack the open flank of Hungary, Transylvania. Events gave Franz-Josef no other option but to bow to this inevitable transfer of military power from Vienna to Berlin.

Falkenhayn, heeding the advice of the German Kaiser, offered the Dual Monarchy a piece of inspired window-dressing. The new 12th Army, which would take the field against Romania, would consist of Mackensen's 'Southern Army' and a newly organised k.(u.) k. VII Army. Falkenhayn suggested that the nominal overall commander could be the Archduke Charles, guided by von Seeckt who would be his chief of staff. This was a brilliant move on Berlin's part because it ensured that the prestige of the Habsburg heir to the throne, and therefore all the reinforcements Vienna could offer, would be harnessed to Mackensen's forces for the coming campaign. In the event of any difficulty, Charles would be supported by Vienna in every way to avoid the stigma of defeat attaching itself to the future Emperor.

These events all played out against the backdrop of a growing and wide-spread sense of Conrad's incompetence. Studying the reports of Marterer, Franz-Josef could only concur with the German liaison officer at the AOK in Teschen, General Cramon. Cramon was fed up with having to trail around the cafes of Teschen to find Conrad. Often, when the German liaison officer eventually tracked Conrad down, he found the Austrian ensconced in a corner of some cafe holding hands with his amour, Gina Reininghaus. Cramon had long written Conrad off as a 'Papierstrategist' who was 'on the verge of senility'. But, to the surprise of all his colleagues, Cramon resisted the idea of dismissing Conrad, on the grounds that it would render the Austro-Hungarian troops even more demoralised if they knew their top military commander had been sacked. In fact Conrad's fate had become subordinated to a much greater game in which Hindenburg and Ludendorff as well as Falkenhayn were to become involved.

'A great intrigue'

With his usual perspicacity, Franz-Josef realised: 'there is a great intrigue in play'. The 'intrigue' was whether the issue of an overall German joint command could be resisted for much longer. As Hindenburg brought Brusilov to a standstill, Cramon was instructed to remind the Imperial and Royal General Staff that 'once again' Austria-Hungary 'owed its survival solely and uniquely to the Germans'.[12]

A draft document proclaiming the German Emperor as commander-in-chief of the Austrian, German, Turkish and Bulgarian forces was drawn up with the date of 25 August. The young Habsburg heir, Charles, also noted the 'great intrigue' and forbade von Seeckt to communicate with Falkenhayn behind his back. Culturally like most Habsburgs, Charles harboured prejudices against the Germans. Similar views are still to be met today. But Charles, the professional soldier, knew that everything, including the lives of his troops, depended on the German military, and he was in no way minded to put the relationship with Berlin at risk.

On the same day that the German Kaiser was supposed to be declared overall commander, Conrad's adjutant, Count Herberstein and the Archduke Frederick had a joint audience with the Emperor. Afterwards, Franz-Josef dictated a typically ambivalent note:

> It is my will where possible to bring to fruition the thesis of the German Kaiser with regard to a unified high command. My military high command is allowed – after careful agreement with the German high command – to produce such suggestions to resolve this matter as are compatible with my sovereign dignity and the honour of my army and do not limit the hitherto unfettered freedom of action of my high command and my forces.[13]

The formulation was skilful: a clear attempt to win time – a consistent Habsburg trait. But with the Romanian declaration of war on 27 August, time was not in abundance. Franz-Josef realised that the future of his empire was at stake and therefore certain sacrifices were inevitable.

The army loses its independence. Berlin assumes overall control

On 7 September 1916, the overall command of all the Central Powers' armed forces was placed in the hands of the German Kaiser, whose decisions would be binding. Just over two years into the Habsburgs' last war, Austria-Hungary's military autonomy was at an end. The Generalstab had brought this woeful state of affairs to pass. In their consummate and consistent failure to see the reality of the threats to the existence of the Dual Monarchy, they had allowed the monarchy to become a satellite of a military-dominated Germany. Just as they had not wished to see that the trail from Sarajevo could be traced through Colonel 'Apis' to Berlin, so they had failed to realise that Germany's so-called 'blank cheque' was on the contrary filled out with extensive and painful conditions. It was an inevitable consequence that 28 June 1914 should lead to 7 September 1916. The executioner of the Dual Monarchy was to be found in Berlin rather than in Belgrade, St Petersburg or Paris.

Ludendorff, like Napoleon a century before him, saw the Habsburg monarchy in simplistic terms. It was a resource to be plundered. Its menfolk had to be mobilised and dispatched to the front and its women had to be unstintingly harnessed to munitions factories. The easy-going ways of the Habsburgs might not have been appropriate for modern war but the Habsburg Empire represented a pool of untapped material that Prussian efficiency could exploit to the full. The *Menschenmaterial* (human material) was *gut*. The military leadership at the highest levels needed to be swept away, along with civilian politicians who resisted German encroachment.

First among these was the Austrian Minister President, Count Stürgkh. *Ordnung* (order) would come to the monarchy through a purge of its old decrepit structures. Ludendorff's staff drew up a blueprint for incorporating the monarchy into the German Empire. They were running faster than the German Kaiser. Uninhibited by the slightest feeling of monarchical solidarity, the German generals openly asked why they should even wait for the old Emperor to pass away. Austria no longer possessed the military strength to resist. Her economy was entirely supported by billions of crowns in loans from German banks.

Meanwhile, three Romanian armies advanced towards Hungary. Inexperienced, and facing in Mackensen one of the most brilliant generals of the time, the Romanians stood little chance despite their superiority in numbers. A certain effete quality appeared to invest the officer corps. It was widely rumoured that, when hostilities broke out, the first order issued by the Romanian High Command was that only officers of field rank and above were permitted to wear rouge on the front.[14]

The Romanians quickly fell back in the face of German and Austrian attacks. The passes in Transylvania gave some respite but by 23 November, Austro-German, Bulgarian and Turkish troops were advancing towards Bucharest. The Romanian capital fell two weeks later. In barely twenty-five days of hostilities, the Romanians had been compelled to surrender. The Russians were forced to abandon all thoughts of a fresh offensive in Galicia. As the Romanian crisis developed, St Petersburg rushed 20 divisions to plug the gap that had suddenly opened on the Russian southern flank. Mackensen had once again demonstrated the new art of blitzkrieg. A year earlier, just before the Serbian campaign, Mackensen had been invited to Schönbrunn for dinner. Upright and immensely distinguished for his 67 years, he had made a fine impression on the aged Emperor. 'With men like that, you can never go wrong,' Franz-Josef had remarked to an aide afterwards.[15]

Decline of Franz-Josef

The Emperor was slowly fading and he would not live to hear the news of Mackensen's dazzling elimination of Romania from the ranks of his empire's enemies. Members of his Military Chancery already tacitly noticed that he fell asleep during meetings, though on waking Franz-Josef still demonstrated his old grasp of all the essentials of the situation.

One officer who visited him at this time to be decorated with the military Order of Merit was the young air ace Gottfried Banfield. Banfield found the old Emperor 'profoundly alert'. After the investiture, he was taken aside for an hour-long conversation in which the Emperor expressed great interest in the technical details of aerial warfare. Banfield, who would be decorated again with the Order of Maria Theresa a year later by the Emperor Charles, never forgot this encounter with the last monarch of the old school. 'It moved me more deeply than anything else I have ever experienced in my long life,' he recalled many years later. The young officer was especially touched by the Emperor's parting words, so typical of the old Habsburg: 'See, my dear Banfield, that you look after yourself and remain alive. Austria will need men like you after this war is over.'[16]

The young heir to the throne, Charles, having surprised his staff and the officers on the Russian and Italian fronts with his general contempt for danger, had transferred to Transylvania. The future Emperor had endeared himself to all who came into contact with him. He was tall, handsome, sensitive, disciplined, and above all humane. Anatole France, the Nobel Prize winning poet would later write: 'The only honest man to emerge during this entire war was Charles of Austria; but he was a saint and nobody listened to him.'[17]

Long before his beatification in the twenty-first century, the stories of Charles's compassion and modesty had circulated throughout the army. The staff officers he had overruled for trying to prevent him visiting front-line trenches; the weak and infirm who found their fleeting contact with him enriching in both the spiritual and the material sense. Many a young officer had been able to visit his family at Christmas because the Archduke volunteered to stand in for their duties. In the best tradition of the Habsburgs he was no great intellectual, but he was intelligent and reflective. He was under no illusions as to the challenges lying ahead. Perhaps his only fault was to believe in the best intentions of all with whom he came into contact. 'I have no enemies! Only temporary opponents' was a favourite saying. In this he was the opposite of his late uncle, Franz Ferdinand, who regarded men with the greatest of suspicion until they proved otherwise.

The Emperor Charles takes up the reins

This did not mean that the Archduke yielded automatically to the elder statesmen of the Empire. He would soon have sharp differences with Conrad and with Tisza, whom he regarded with considerable circumspection. Tisza was the only man capable of moving the Emperor *almost* to speaking badly of someone.[18]

Charles's life at the front was in any event drawing to a close. Just as the campaign against Romania was moving to a conclusion, news of his uncle's decline reached the Archduke near the beautiful Transylvanian hill town of Schässburg (Sighişoara). A few hours later, the Archduke entrained from the small station at Schässburg, leaving behind him the camaraderie and affection of a simpler life he would never know again.

Eighteen hours later he was in Vienna with his young wife Zita. The old Austrian Kaiser still managed to keep up appearances. When a bishop sent to bestow a papal blessing on the dying monarch was ushered into the Imperial apartments, he found to his surprise that the Emperor was not lying in bed barely able to speak, but standing upright in a corner of the room in his blue uniform. The following day when Charles and Zita came to visit, the Emperor immediately sprang up from his chair to greet Charles's wife. The Emperor spent more than an hour with them, no doubt imparting what wisdom he felt he could. But Charles, who had not seen him for some time, immediately noticed the Kaiser's decrepitude. On the following day, the 21st, Franz-Josef complained of 'still having so much to do, I cannot afford to be ill', and retired to his iron military bed.[19] Two hours later, a priest was summoned to administer the last rites, and three hours later, around nine, the Emperor was dead.

Franz-Josef had ruled for so long, sixty-eight years, that many simply could not imagine Austria or the Empire without him. The dynastic consciousness of the old Habsburgs had been married to the Josephinian concept of self-sacrificing devotion in the service of the state. He enshrined the dignity and duty of his role, combining the devotion of a faithful Catholic with the consciousness of his own Imperial majesty. Where these two came into conflict, he never hesitated to give precedence to the latter.

As one of his cavalry officers, the painter Oskar Kokoschka, later wrote:

The Habsburg Empire ruled by the old Emperor in the enlightened spirit of Joseph II was not an ideal state. But before the First World War, summary trials, witch hunts, torture, public executions, secret death sentences, concentration camps, deportations and dispossessions were unknown there; so were slave-labour – Austria had no colonies – and child labour. Antisemitism was a punishable offence (compare France or Russia).[20]

It was characteristic of Charles who, together with most of the court, was waiting outside Franz-Josef's bedroom, that the first person the new Emperor allowed to enter the deceased's apartment was the late Emperor's *Lebensgefährtin*, Katharina Schratt. Franz-Josef's companion quietly laid two white roses on his chest.[21] As the cries of 'Long Live the Emperor!' rang out along the corridors of Schönbrunn, the new 29-year-old monarch began to confront a task which could hardly have been accomplished by any of his ancestors. None of them had had to fight a war against England, France and Russia supported by a host of other minor states with a German ally increasingly determined to see Austria's future as a satellite of Berlin. Count Herberstein observed that 'the monarchy has never been in such a serious situation as it is now and it is precisely now we need a strong hand to sort the internal situation out'.[22]

The deteriorating internal political situation was self-evident. Dramatic shortages of foodstuffs and the arrival of thousands of wounded were bad enough. But just before Franz-Josef had died, the aged Kaiser had been brought the news of the assassination of his Prime Minister Stürgkh, an event he described as 'worse than a battle lost'. The old Emperor had simply recalled Ernest von Koeber, an earlier incumbent, and matters rumbled on as before. But the assassination had highlighted the rising tensions within the varied national framework of the non-Hungarian side of the Empire. Stürgkh's assassin had been the pacifist son of the well-known socialist Victor Adler, thus adding a political crisis to the gradual deterioration of civilian life.

CHAPTER 25

Finis Austriae?

The army welcomes the new Emperor

The new Emperor was inheriting an empire where anarchy and social disintegration were already in evidence. Miners and other workers began a series of strikes. Hunger stalked the streets of Vienna as the supplies of grain failed to make their way from Hungary. Other foodstuffs also became rare. In 1914, the Hungarian government had pledged to supply Austria with 30,000 pigs annually. By 1916, this number had shrunk to less than 8,000.

The arrival of thousands of orthodox Jewish refugees from Galicia, many of whom found they could organise themselves skilfully to manage the supply of foodstuffs coming from the east, provoked much resentment.[1] Charles could only try to comprehend the myriad problems descending about his head, and then delegate. As he was a professional soldier, the war was still his first priority and at this stage it occupied much of his daily thought. It was symptomatic of this that on ascending the throne he dispensed with the pomp of a coronation and travelled immediately down to the Italian front and then on to the General Staff headquarters in Teschen.

The army observed the arrival of a new monarch without missing a beat. On 24 November, all the military and naval personnel of the monarchy swore an oath to their new Emperor. The ceremony included all wounded soldiers in convalescent homes or hospitals throughout the Empire. A week later, the proclamation announcing the Emperor Charles's assumption of the supreme command was read throughout the monarchy. Alongside these formal acts, the new Emperor made it known informally that he regarded the domination of the German military in his Empire's affairs as unwelcome. By now, not only the supreme command of the combined armies lay with the German Kaiser.

Following their collapse during the Brusilov offensive, Austro-Hungarian units on the Eastern front were becoming increasingly integrated with German units, and were beginning to lose their separate identity.

The question of supreme command: Conrad's reassignment

Charles asked Conrad to communicate to Hindenburg that he wished the article of the agreement giving the German Emperor supreme command to be changed. The German Kaiser and Hindenburg were unamused. In any event Berlin was rapidly sliding towards military dictatorship. The German generals feared the dissolution of the Central Powers alliance if the Austrian request was granted. Bulgaria and Turkey would drop out, they warned. On 5 December, Charles travelled to Pless to meet the generals and the German Kaiser to discuss this. In a calculated expression of Imperial displeasure with the status quo, Charles did not appear in his host's German uniform, as custom dictated. Despite his honorary rank as a German field marshal, Charles and his suite were dressed in their Imperial and Royal uniforms. His train arrived thirty minutes late, another calculated snub.

The Germans did not notice, or at least pretended not to. The question of the German Kaiser's supreme command was resolved through compromise. Conrad, with whom Charles's relations had gradually deteriorated, was dismissed by the new Emperor, who assumed in theory 'full operational control' of the Imperial and Royal Armies. Conrad begged for retirement; Gina's charms beckoned, but the new Emperor told him to take charge of the western part of the Italian front.

The Germans shed no tears over Conrad's departure. They were in any event set on practical issues: increases in the Austrian output of armaments. The daily production of four million bullets was to be doubled. The annual production of 13,500 artillery pieces was also to be doubled. The subordination of the life of the Dual Monarchy to military requirements was what interested the German High Command. Charles might think he enjoyed 'supreme command' over his troops but, in practice, his empire, like his armed forces, was already dependent on Berlin. With the exception of those on the Italian front, his armies were no longer capable of autonomous action. Political infighting had rendered decisive government in Vienna and the other non-Hungarian parts of the monarchy virtually impossible. The recently appointed premier, Koeber, failed to form a convincing government in Vienna. Two days before Christmas Charles replaced him with Clam-Martinic.

The Germans took a step that underlined further their ally's fragility. For the first time since 1866, they set up a secret military intelligence network to spy on Vienna. The new Emperor, far from fitting into the German schemes for subordinating the Habsburg Empire into the German Reich as a kind of greater Bavaria, was showing disturbing signs of independent thought. From now on he and his wife Zita were to be watched, and their every movement or conversation reported to Berlin.[2]

Charles's coronation in Budapest

Charles astutely saw the need to support his programme and ideas by cementing the trust of his Magyar subjects. The day after Franz-Josef's death, Tisza had wasted no time in paying his respects and urging the new monarch to allow himself to be crowned in Budapest. It will be recalled how Franz Ferdinand was planning to delay his coronation until a reforming constitution was imposed on the Magyars. Tisza did not suspect Charles of harbouring similar powerful prejudices; Charles after all spoke good Hungarian. But the temptation to get Charles wedded to Hungary and publicly vowing in front of the Magyar chivalry to defend the four corners of Hungarian territory must have seemed an opportunity too useful to miss.

From Charles's point of view, he had no desire to imitate the perpetual guerrilla warfare his murdered uncle had waged against the Magyars. It was a chance for both him and his wife to harness the Hungarian sentiments to his reign during the war. Reform could come later. Despite his decision to avoid a costly coronation ceremony in Vienna, Charles accepted Tisza's offer and set the stage for one of the most extraordinary and never-to-be repeated pageants of the twentieth century.

On 30 December 1916, wearing the crown with the crooked cross of Mathias Corvinus and St Stephen which Maria Theresa had donned before him, he galloped on his horse up the coronation hill in front of the Mathias church in Budapest flashing his sword to defend the four corners of his kingdom. The hill had been built with soil laboriously taken from every corner of Hungary's far-flung lands. The stirrups and tack of his iron-grey horse were made of solid gold and Charles's sword was nearly a thousand years old, the personal sabre, it was reputed, of Attila the Hun. The moment so rich in symbolism and powerful national passion remains to this day an iconic image of Hungary. In 1988, even during Communist times, a black and white film of the Hungarian coronation was shown in Budapest to packed audiences. The film cleverly slowed down the footage to show the young Crown Prince Otto lifted slowly up from a carriage to view his father taking the oath. At that moment a profound silence fell over the cinema audience.

Charles was keen to demonstrate that he was not entirely in the hands of his Hungarian hosts and as soon as the ceremony was finished and the photographs taken, he hurried back with his wife and son Otto to Vienna. Swiftly changing into field uniform, he returned to Baden near Vienna where he had established his military headquarters.

Even if final victory remained elusive, the fall of Bucharest, combined with the stabilising of the Italian and Russian fronts, augured well for the new year of 1917. Charles was under no illusions. He saw more clearly than his generals that every day the war continued brought the collapse of his Empire nearer. The Hungarians might have shown that they could still live well in Budapest but Vienna and elsewhere in the Empire told a different story.

On 12 December, it had been agreed between Berlin and Vienna that they should 'fly a kite' to test Allied reactions to the possibility of negotiations. A note was published in the Vienna papers and was sent to the neutral powers, the USA, Switzerland and Spain, for forwarding to the Entente. In it was a suggestion that 'further bloodshed' in this 'defensive war' could be avoided by 'peace negotiations'. The conditions were 'Honour, Existence (*Dasein*) and the freedom of development of our peoples'. If the Entente was not prepared to enter into such talks, then the war would be prosecuted until the Central Powers brought it to a 'victorious conclusion'.[3]

The Entente rejects Habsburg peace feelers

The note was explicitly rejected on 5 January 1917 by the Allies, who quibbled with its formulations, especially the reference to the Central Powers fighting a 'defensive war', and took refuge in a sentence which promised little room for manoeuvre: 'No peace is possible without the restoration of injured rights and freedoms and the recognition of the principle of nationality. . . .'.[4] The mention of the 'principle of nationality' pointed a dagger at the heart of the Habsburg Empire. The destruction of the Habsburg Empire had become an implicit Allied war aim, despite the protestations of so many Allied statesmen later in the war, and of course after it, when the baleful effects of Allied policy in this direction were apparent to an even wider audience.

It had been implied by Grey as early as July 1914, in his exchange with Mensdorff shortly before the Austrian Note was delivered. Grey had obviously stressed the point sufficiently for it to enjoy an important place in the official record of the conversation:

> In the event of a war breaking out between four of the major powers, many things would be swept away.[5]

Mensdorff missed the point. With Berchtold and Berlin he preferred to focus on Grey's indiscreet reference to 'four' of the powers, which implied London remaining neutral.[6] Given that in 1914 the Hungarians, the Austrian Germans and the Czechs as well as Berlin were all predicting the collapse of the Habsburg Empire even without a war, Grey's warning in its context was unmistakable.

It was a sign of the new Emperor's ability to hope for the best that he now decided, in the face of this Entente brush-off, to entrust his wife's brother, Prince Sixtus, with a personal peace mission. The two men had known each other since childhood. In 1914, Prince Sixtus had followed his family tradition but owing to a French law prohibiting members of the former Royal (Bourbon) House from serving in the French army, he had enlisted in the Belgian army. Two of his brothers, Felix and René, served in the Austrian army. His contacts with the French elite were impeccable. In what was to be perhaps the last attempt at dynastic diplomacy in European history, Charles wrote to Sixtus outlining his wish for peace in the full knowledge that the letter might be disclosed to Poincaré, the French President, and the French Prime Minister Ribot. Charles's letter was a response to some early feelers towards a discussion of potential peace terms from Paris, which was reeling under the frequent mutinies which had broken out in the French army that spring.

On 17 April 1917, Ribot met Lloyd George, by now Prime Minister of Britain, to discuss the Austrian suggestion. But the Treaty of London, with its proposed concessions to Italy, meant that neither France nor London could act alone. Italy, halfway through the sanguinary series of battles of the Isonzo, was unlikely to cooperate. By agreeing to refer the matter to Rome, the Anglo-French politicians ensured that the Austrian initiative was doomed to failure. As the fortunes of war swung first one way and then the other, talk of peace faltered on the alternative triumph and despair of the Entente. When things were going badly for the Entente the thought of peace appeared to involve too many concessions. When things went a little better, the determination to fight to the bitter end reasserted itself.

In any event, many leading circles in the Entente had long settled on a war that could not end with German power on the Continent intact. As a later master of the art of diplomacy, Henry Kissinger wrote: British statesmen 'always judged Germany by her capabilities not her intentions' and it was German capabilities which needed to be arrested in the interest of a balance of power on the Continent which was favourable to London.[7]

Contrary to popular opinion, which was later influenced by German propaganda accusing the Habsburgs of seeking a 'separate' peace, Charles was not interested in anything other than a general peace. On 13 February 1917, he discussed the peace initiative with the German Kaiser who fully supported it, saying: 'Good. Proceed further with this. I concur' ('Gut mach weiter ich bin einverstanden'). Indeed, the idea of contacting Sixtus had first been mooted by Bethmann-Hollweg.[8]

Even if Bethmann-Hollweg and the German Kaiser were 'einverstanden', Charles's efforts were doomed, not least because of the subordination of the Habsburg military machine to Berlin. Not only was this subordination increasingly present on the ground, it was reflected in critical matters of strategy. For example in January 1917 Charles vigorously protested against the widening of the submarine campaign, predicting rightly that it would bring America into the war. When he remonstrated with the German High Command, he was told that the order had already been given and that it was too late for it to be rescinded.[9]

Charles opposes Lenin's insertion into Russia

Similarly, Charles was strongly opposed to the dispatch of Lenin from Switzerland to Russia to incite revolution against the Tsar. Although the Austrian Kaiser could ensure that Lenin was not allowed to pass through Habsburg territory, he could not prevent the Germans from organising Lenin's journey in the infamous *plombierten Zug* or sealed train to Russia. Once again, Charles was prescient. He knew what a communist revolution in Russia would mean for his own empire and he was appalled at the short-sightedness of a German High Command committed to neutralising Russia even at the price of introducing the Leninist 'bacillus' into a fragile monarchy like tsarist Russia.[10]

The military dictatorship that ran Germany in 1917 was not interested in peace, except one imposed by German victory. When Charles wrote to the German Emperor that 'We must make an end at any price by the late summer', he was expressing views that could not resonate with the German High Command. The German High Command was increasingly synonymous with the Imperial and Royal High Command. These men were indifferent to the threat of either nationalism or communism. They were fighting 'a war to the death against the Slavs'.[11] It meant nothing to Berlin that every tenth officer of Charles's army on the Isonzo was of Serbian origin.

The toppling of the Russian Tsar in 1917 did not of itself bring peace. At first the Kerensky government sought to honour its obligations to the Entente, but Russia was exhausted. The Russians might have resisted Bolshevism if there had been a real alternative, but there was none. Capitalism had collapsed and with it not only wages and management structures but industrial production as well. In the summer of 1917, virtually all of Russia went on strike. In these conditions, no Russian army could continue to wage war, so Petrograd sued for peace.

As Charles had predicted, the simple arguments of communism were now added to nationalism and hunger among his troops. In 1914, the early months of the war had demonstrated the fragility of several regiments, notably those made up of Czechs and Ruthenes. Infantry regiment Nr 36, made up of 95 per cent Czechs, had turned on its officers and deserted en masse on the Carpathian front. The regiment was disbanded, 'never to be raised again'. The House regiment of Prague, IR 28, was rumoured to have marched over to the Russian lines with bands playing and flags flying, a demonstratively anti-Czech piece of German propaganda, ungrounded in fact. Some elements of the regiment did desert and other elements were sufficiently demoralised to be disbanded but the fine performance of several companies on the Isonzo front ensured that IR 28, Prague's 'finest', was reconstituted and allowed to give a good account of itself in 1917. The performance of these Slav regiments continued to defy the expectations of the Entente, who never understood their loyalty to the dynasty.

Italian obstinacy frustrated all the peace efforts of Prince Sixtus even after Charles had expressed – ill-advisedly, perhaps – a willingness to intercede on France's behalf to recover Alsace-Lorraine. In his efforts Charles had even been prepared to contemplate compensation in colonial Africa for loss of the Trentino, an unprecedented thought for his House. Prince Sixtus had written to his brother-in-law pointing out the 'advantage' of such an exchange: 'A negro is better value than an irredentist'.[12]

The blame for the failure of these peace feelers cannot be laid solely at Italy's door. The momentum of war created its own dynamic and all the Austrian protagonists were swept along by it. Of no one was this more true than Charles's new Foreign Minister, Ottokar Czernin. Czernin had been minister in Bucharest and a controversial figure at the Ballplatz. In a letter written in early July 1914, Forgách had disparagingly referred to him as 'our unbelievable minister in Bucharest'.[13]

Czernin was at least not in the pocket of Tisza as his predecessor, Burian, had been. Like so many of his class of Bohemian aristocracy, Czernin's sympathies lay with the Pan-Germans of the Empire, the only German Austrians who in culture and aspiration were really Austrian Germans and looked to Berlin rather than Vienna for guidance. In addition, Czernin possessed an egoism that made him wish to play an altogether more dominant role in the affairs of the Empire than was the prerogative of the Foreign Minister. The combination of his personal defects and pro-German feelings would work against the interests of the monarchy. Czernin became increasingly convinced that Austria could only survive as part of Germany. Fortunately for the Imperial and Royal Army, these thoughts were not widespread along the Isonzo front where Austrian and Hungarian patriotism was prominently on display.

As 1917 progressed and Charles's peace feelers ran into the sands, the temptation to push for some kind of military solution to the stalemate reasserted itself on the Italian front. As winter came to an end, the tenth battle of the Isonzo began with a five-hour barrage by the Italians. This was followed by a furious assault on the Austrian hills around Gorizia. The Habsburg regiments, from Salzburg and Upper Austria, beat their attackers back easily. By 5 July, the Italians had lost 36,000 dead and more than 95,000 wounded. The tenth battle of the Isonzo was over.

A month and a half later, Cadorna, reinforced with much new equipment from the French, including heavy-calibre artillery, planned a new offensive, this time against the Austrian positions along the southern part of the Carso towards Trieste. By 4 September, the Italians had seized the heights of Monte Gabriele where a fierce fight erupted, sweeping Austrian wounded and medical facilities away. Shells exploded around the limestone landscape showering the air with deadly shards of rock. By 8 September, the Austro-Hungarian position was looking decidedly shaky but the only reinforcement available was the Linz 'House' regiment IR 14, which was recovering nearby from recent action along the Julian Alps. Though outnumbered, the Upper Austrians stabilised the front and drove the Italians back off most of the heights. The Austrian mountain artillery ensured that the Italian appetite for a further offensive remained subdued. Each side had suffered more than 100,000 casualties in the six weeks of fighting. For the Italians there was little consolation. In eleven murderous battles of the Isonzo over nearly two and a half years, they had covered barely a third of the distance to Trieste.

The Twelfth Battle of the Isonzo

The Austrians could only be partly satisfied with this state of affairs. Despite the sluggish Italian progress, it had become apparent to the Austro-Hungarian military command that their forces were coming under increasing threat. Another all-out assault would bring irresistible pressure to bear on the defenders. For this reason the idea of a grand Austro-German attack began to be discussed among senior Austrian officers.

A counter-offensive which could drive the Italians back at least as far as Cividale had been bruited many months before by Conrad but the plan had gathered dust. It was now hastily revived by General Arz, Boroević's chief of staff. Arz identified the basin between Tolmein (Tolmin) and Flitsch (Bovec) as the area for the offensive. He was convinced an attack would need some German stiffening and he therefore addressed a request for reinforcements to the German High Command.

The Germans were disposed to be cooperative. They dispatched General Krafft von Delmesingen, an experienced commander of mountain troops to reconnoitre the front and determine whether the Austrian plan was practicable. After several days, Krafft enthusiastically agreed and seven German divisions, made up of various Bavarian and Swabian units experienced in mountain warfare, together with artillery and mortars and reinforced aerial units were sent to the Slovene hills behind Flitsch. To this XIV Army were added seven Austrian divisions released from the now rapidly quiescent Eastern front even though the formal armistice would not be signed for many months.[14]

The problem of how to effect such a powerful concentration of forces along narrow roads and passes under the surveillance of the Italian air force without giving the imminent offensive away exercised the best brains of the Imperial and Royal Army. Much of the equipment and artillery had to be transported to positions well above 1,000 metres at the dead of night by lifts or on the backs of soldiers. Thousands of trains deposited tens of thousands of troops and an artillery park began to assume monstrous proportions. Strict secrecy was enforced. The soldiers were told nothing of the coming campaign and their anxiety was increased considerably when each was given ten postcards with the printed message 'I am well and happy' in the ten languages of the monarchy.

Strict precautions were also taken concerning wireless traffic though Italian intercepts revealed the recurrence of the word *Waffentreue* (loyalty in arms). This in fact was the code name for the operation and had been coined by Ludendorff. Many observers had also noted the presence of German regiments noisily celebrating in Graz about fifty miles away before heading to the railway station where dozens of German trains were steaming up.

In any event the Italians were well informed of what was coming. Three days before the offensive was planned to start, four Imperial and Royal officers, three Czechs and a Romanian, deserted to bring news of the impending attack to the Italians. Such individual cases of desertion were not infrequent though few were as lucky as these men. Strict countermeasures were in force to deal with deserters. A year earlier, Banfield in Trieste had machine-gunned from the air an infantry soldier attempting to desert to Grado in a boat.[15]

Cadorna, the Italian commander, immediately inspected the Italian front-line positions of his Second Army but judged them to be 'impregnable', at least until reinforcements were rushed up to hold them. It remains a mystery to this day why Cadorna did not act more vigorously on the information of the Austrian deserters. It is open to debate whether any steps Cadorna might have taken could have prevented what was about to take place. The Twelfth Battle of the Isonzo, more widely known after the name of the village at the foot of the basin, Kobarid (Caporetto), was to deploy tactics and weapons in an unprecedented way. As a result the battle has become an essential object of study for military academies around the world to this day.[16]

Chemical warfare

Chief of the innovations was to be the use of gas-shells fired in the opening barrage. The deployment of gas was, in comparison with all the armies of the Western front, rare in the Imperial and Royal Army. Its use had been banned by the Emperor Franz-Josef until almost the very end of his reign. Only after it was deployed by Italian troops did he reluctantly consent to its use by his own forces. By then other countries had deployed it extensively, though with mixed results.

Before the war, the French had developed various chemical agents for the gendarmerie to use when suppressing internal disturbances.[17] With the outbreak of war in 1914, the French deployed these chemical agents north of Supees in Flanders in late August but the effect fell far short of expectations. The use of chemical agents was a key topic in talks in London during the autumn of 1914 and it was noted that in the USA a certain Mr Hammond had patented an artillery shell loaded with prussic acid.[18] At the same time the German General Staff had held discussions with the large chemical firm at Leverkusen (today Bayer) to develop a poison gas schrapnel shell. This was deployed at Neuve Chapelle in October 1914, again with nugatory effect. Scientists and soldiers continued to develop the new weapon, encouraged not least by the increasing stalemate on the Western front.

By the summer of 1917, all the leading powers, with the exception of Austria-Hungary, had developed and used gas weapons regularly on the front. The French had released gas as well as phosphorus shells on 22 February 1916 at Verdun. A variant of these, chloropicrin, was used by the Russians in the late summer of 1916, while by July 1917 mustard gas was widely in use by the British, Germans and French.[19]

The three largest producers of poison gas were Germany, France and Britain. German production has been estimated at 69,090 cubic tons, French at 37,390 cubic tons, British at 25,400 cubic tons and Austro-Hungarian at 5,770 cubic tons. On the Italian front, gas had already been deployed on

13 December 1915 by the Italians. Its effects were noted by the Austrian High Command as 'tears, vomiting, and unconsciousness'.[20] On 24 February 1916, the Imperial and Royal 44th Landsturminfanterie division reported that the Italians had used 'gas bombs'. It had been this report that finally persuaded the aged Franz-Josef to withdraw his express prohibition of the use of gas weapons.

From the spring of 1916, Austria began producing 100 tons of gas per month, in various locations including the Skoda works in Pilsen and factories in Lower Austria and Aussig (Usti nad Labem) in southern Bohemia. An Austrian unit, the 62nd Sappeur-Spezial regiment, was created to handle these weapons. On 29 June 1916, a 'blown' attack was tried at Doberdo but proved to affect the Austrians adversely as well as the Italians. A later attack in the Assa gorge was equally unsuccessful. The new Austrian unit was transferred to the Eastern front where it cooperated with German chemical units before both German and Austrian gas personnel were transported back to the Isonzo for the coming offensive. The 62nd Sappeur regiment would be directly involved in the coming campaign and was ordered to deploy chemical agents in the opening stage of the battle.

Later criticism that the Emperor Charles had authorised the use of gas on the Italian front as some kind of personal commitment to this weapon was Entente propaganda. It is interesting to see how powerfully enduring the story has been. Nearly a hundred years later, it re-emerged in newspapers when the Vatican beatified the late Emperor. In fact, the decision to deploy gas for this campaign was a tactical one and therefore taken by the German general commanding, in this case von Below, after consultation with the commander of the German gas contingent, Major Pfeil. The Emperor Charles shouldered the responsibility as commander but he was not consulted on such tactical issues.

Though he had not been consulted, there can be little doubt that the Emperor Charles would have found the rationale behind deploying gas entirely convincing. He was the most militarily experienced of all the sovereigns of the First World War, and where his troops' safety was concerned, he was prepared to use such weapons.

He had the misgivings any soldier of the old school would have had. He had prohibited the Austrian air service from using phosphorus bombs, unlike their Italian counterparts who also deployed phosphorus bullets. (It took Banfield a month in hospital to recover from just one that had lodged in his back.) Charles had also, on the urging of his wife, the Empress Zita, ordered the Trieste naval air station to desist from bombing Venice for some six months between 11 November 1916 and 17 April 1917.[21] There were to be altogether

42 bombing raids on Venice, a major one on 14 August 1917 involved most of Banfield's flight from Trieste and damaged several artworks and churches. (The destruction of the Tiepolo frescoes of the Chiesa degli Scalzi, near the railway station occurred in 1915 and allowed the Italians, after the war, to reclaim as reparations the outstanding Tintoretto works from the Kunsthistorisches Museum ceded under the treaty of 1866.)

The arguments in favour of deploying gas at Karfreit were compelling. The Italian defences were formidable, as Cadorna had noted two days earlier. Italian artillery and machine guns covered the entire area of the Caporetto basin. They were positioned so skilfully that on the narrow entrance to the basin where the Austro-Hungarian troops would attack, conventional Austrian artillery was unable to silence them. If the Austrian part of the attack were to enjoy any chance of success, these defences would have to be neutralised as quickly and effectively as possible. The alternative was thousands of Austrian casualties as their advance was mown down with all the effectiveness massed machine guns had demonstrated on the Western front.

The Austrian sector: Flitsch and Tolmein

The Austrians had by far the most difficult part of the plan to execute, namely the advance along the ridges on either side of the basin. The prediction of heavy casualties was received soberly by the Austrian senior commanders from all sides. Major Pfeil's belief that, owing to the narrow confined basin, gas would prove far more effective than earlier gas attacks offered only slight consolation.

Along with the extensive and concentrated use of gas shells, a new tactic, that of the deep breakthrough, was planned. The German troops, which would follow the initial bombardment and punch a hole through the Italian positions further down the valley, would not wait for the Austrians on the peaks on either side to catch up. Instead they would push as far forward as possible sowing confusion and panic among the (hopefully) retreating Italians.

On the morning of 24 October, the Austro-German attack began. The initial bombardment was skilfully planned: first a barrage of shells loaded with prussic acid (Diphenylarsinchlorid: so-called *Blaukreuz*) was fired at the Italian command centres and artillery and machine-gun emplacements. This agent, while not deadly, could penetrate gas masks and caused coughing and sneezing, which forced the wearers of the masks to tear them off. A few minutes later, the second barrage delivered shells armed with phosphorus agents (so-called *Grünkreuz*) whose effects were far more deadly, causing a massive seizure of respiratory organs in minutes. This so-called *Buntschiessen* (coloured fire) proved particularly lethal. The effects of this bombardment were testified to by an Austrian officer, Fritz Weber, who a few hours later stumbled across entire companies of Italian troops motionless and dead whose gestures showed that they had not even had time to put on their ineffective gas masks.[22]

The Austro-German bombardment was halted for two hours at 4.30 a.m. before being resumed with conventional ordnance by every gun and mortar the Austrian and German artillery could muster. At 8 a.m. the infantry advanced along the entire Isonzo front from Duino in the south to Rombon in the north.

The effects were dramatic. The Austrians and the Germans reached the third Italian line by nightfall after taking tens of thousands of Italian prisoners. Throughout their advance, the Austrian mountain artillery, by now widely regarded as the finest in the world, supported their infantry's progress with accurate fire. By 30 October, the Austrians and their German allies had reached the Tagliamento, and fresh orders were received to cross and continue their advance beyond Friuli and deep into the Venetian plain. Especially noticeable among the Austrian advance units were the Bosnians. At Cornino, where a railway bridge had been blown by the retreating Italians, two companies of Bosnians from the 4th regiment of Bosnian-Hercegovinian infantry stormed across the ruins of the bridge, their fezzes and grenades striking fear into the Italian defenders. The Bosnians reconstructed a new bridgehead overnight, which they then defended against repeated counter-attacks for the next 48 hours. It was this action which persuaded Cadorna to rebuild his defensive line further back along the Piave.[23] Ernest Hemingway, in *A Farewell to Arms*, immortalised the confusion behind the Italian lines as *carabinieri* attempted to stem the tide of fleeing humanity by the ruthless expedient of arresting and summarily executing all the officers they found retreating.[24]

From the Italian perspective nothing appeared to be able to stem the attack. The Germans had shown themselves capable of bringing their command and control units remarkably far forward. The Austrian commanders were much slower in advancing and, bereft of wireless communications unlike their German colleagues, they were incapable of keeping up with their troops' advance guards. The result for the Austrians was that they were unable to control the situation as the Italians fled west, leaving behind them nearly a quarter of a million men as prisoners. Italian casualties eventually numbered 10,000 dead, though more than 293,000 would be taken prisoner.

As a later famous German officer, Rommel, who was a young company commander at the battle, wrote in his classic text on infantry tactics, the Italians surrendered to a single officer in their tens of thousands. All along the

Italian front they were in full retreat. Thousands flocked towards a single German officer, begging to surrender.

Along the Adriatic, naval units supported the attack. The Imperial and Royal Navy's *Wien* and *Budapest*, two of the 'Monarch' class battleships, dispatched a naval landing party to retake Grado on the edge of the lagoons. But the landing party encountered no Italian resistance; just an official civic welcome complete with a band playing the 'Kaiserhymne'.[25]

Seven French and six British divisions were rushed by rail and ship from France to northern Italy in accordance with plans already drawn up to support Italy in March. On 9 November, Carinthian troops reached the Piave and were fully prepared to cross the river when the German High Command ordered a two-week halt to offensive activity. There was no tactical reason for this because the German logistics had more than kept up with their units. Those Austrian units that had crossed the Piave were ordered back.

It has been suggested that the Germans were wary of knocking Italy out of the war completely. An Austria-Hungary relieved of the Italian front and freed from the Eastern front was not necessarily a reliable ally in Berlin's eyes. An armistice with Italy would reignite Austrian peace moves towards the Entente; this time with a stronger hand. A 'separate' peace would be even more likely under such conditions and this would leave Germany to fight on alone against the Entente.[26]

Such an attitude would have been entirely consistent with Germany's behaviour towards her ally both before and during the war. Vienna's circumstances were always subordinated to the interests of Berlin. In this case it suited Berlin for Italy to be humbled but not crushed, not least because the release of hundreds of thousands of Imperial troops would offer Vienna a defence against the German Plan 'O'. The infamous Plan 'O' had been drawn up by the German General Staff a year earlier. It envisaged a German military occupation of Bohemia and then the rest of Austria in the event of the Emperor Charles pulling his Empire out of the war in a separate peace.[27]

With Allied help, the Italian front stabilised in December 1917, and the internal pressures on Charles began to mount. The Twelfth Battle of the Isonzo was a pyrrhic victory. The new Italian commander, Diaz, was far more cautious than his predecessor, the luckless Cadorna, and he was happy to wait for internal centrifugal forces to weaken his opponents.

Political unrest in the monarchy

Already in May 1917, political unrest was gaining momentum throughout the Austrian half of the Empire. The first meeting of the Austrian Reichsrat since

1914 was held on 30 May and its mood was ugly. Instead of discussing concessions and autonomy, Count Clam-Martinic, an aristocrat of the old school
who was Charles's Prime Minister, struck entirely the wrong note in stressing
the need for loyalty to the new monarch. The Slavs had been radicalised
through a combination of hunger and insensitive regulations imposed by Pan-
German officials amidst a mood of increasing paranoia and German propaganda. The arrest of Karel Kramář, the leader of the Czech national party, for
'treason' had only poured fuel on the flames. Charles moved swiftly to release
Kramář and issue a general amnesty to political prisoners in 1917, but it was
too late; the alienation of the political classes of the Czechs, Poles and other
Slavs was inexorably leading to a call for greater autonomy.

Men who had seemed isolated figures attempting to spread sedition,
Kramář in Bohemia, Markov in Galicia or Trumbić in Croatia, had become
widely popular, an inevitable response to the greater German dominance of
the monarchy's affairs and the crass Berlin propaganda on the 'inferiority'
of the Slavs. The Czech National Council and the Yugoslav Council had
exploited the suppression of the Austrian parliament and filled the vacuum.
Charles did his best but Kramář promptly repaid his Emperor by declaring the
foundation of the 'State of Czechoslovakia'. The Poles, increasingly nervous of
the Berlin proposal to create an independent Ukraine, also went over to active
opposition. The news of these events had a deleterious effect on the army's Slav
regiments but, thanks to their officers, the men held together united by a
growing contempt for politicians of any hue.

The nationality arguments were no longer confined to the Habsburg lands.
Thomáš Masaryk, the leading Czech politician, did not share Palácký's famous
view that the peoples of Central Europe needed the Habsburg Empire to
protect them from Russia and Germany. He had long seen the impending
disintegration of the monarchy as desirable even though he had striven to
work within the confines of the existing monarchical structures in the years
before 1914. When he had tried to set up the Czech National Council in Paris
in 1916, he had received little support. His travels to Russia to organise
the Czechoslovak 'legions'– units of disaffected Czechs and Slovaks, mostly
prisoners of war – were considered equally irrelevant. But as Vienna fell under
the domination of Berlin and the Pan-German element in Austria, Czech
disaffection grew. The final catalyst was the Entente's vocal and open inclination towards the dismemberment of the Dual Monarchy, stimulated by the
American President's unhappy focus on the 'sacred' idea of self-determination.
By 9 August 1918, the Czechs and Slovaks would be termed in London 'an
allied nation'. The Habsburg Empire had almost ceased to be recognised by
its opponents.[28]

On the Venetian plain, the war continued. The arrival of British and French units stiffened the Italians, and the Austrians quickly realised they were up against a more stubborn enemy. It was not the first time that French and British personnel had been engaged against the Austrians. As Geoffrey Banfield recalled, by the time of Caporetto, 50 Imperial and Royal flying boats stationed in Trieste and Pola and other points along the Adriatic faced more than 150 hostile aircraft. Of these, 29 were French and 28 English.[29] Given this disparity, it is all the more remarkable that Banfield and his comrades denied the Entente undisputed access to Imperial airspace up to the very end of the war. (Banfield also successfully denied parts of the north-eastern Adriatic to the Royal Navy, notably disabling the British monitors *Earl of Peterborough* and *Sir Thomas Picton* on 24 May 1917.)

Conrad's reforms: deterioration of military supplies

As 1917 drew to a close, the army began to implement the so-called Conrad reforms. Drawn up by Conrad before his dismissal in March 1917, these mostly concerned the reorganisation of units. In addition to a renumbering of regiments of the line and the confirmation of cavalry as a dismounted arm, the main practical reform was the bringing up to strength of the machine-gun contingents per regiment. Each regiment was equipped with eight heavy machine guns, as well as trench mortars and, where appropriate, searchlights and electric fencing from one of the relatively new electrical engineering units.

Such technical details could not distract from the critical supply situation of the Austro-Hungarian troops. The provisions hoped for by the breakthrough into the Venetian plain had not materialised. On 17 February 1918, Boroević urgently telegrammed Conrad's successor, the Chief of General Staff, Arthur Arz von Straussenburg, noting that without the immediate delivery of supplies there would be a breakdown in discipline. The troops knew that following the so-called 'Bread Peace' with Russia of February 1918, huge supplies of food from the Ukraine were now heading west. They were also aware, according to Boroević, that the German troops were better supplied. 'My soldiers cannot put up with any experiments. They need to be fed if they are to live and fight.'[30]

Boroević's assessment was correct and no exaggeration. The spring of 1918 saw several mutinies across the entire Empire. Slovene troops refused to bear arms in Styria, Czechs in Bohemia, and Hungarians in Budapest also briefly refused to obey orders. In Pécs, a regiment composed mostly of Serbs from the old Military Frontier also revolted. Even some Bosnian recruits rebelled at Mostar along with some Slovaks stationed in a reserve battalion in nearby

Kragujevac. Less worrying was the rather mild-mannered mutiny among sailors in Cattaro, where the long months of enforced inactivity had sown increasing frustration. This was a strange event: the officers were politely confined to their quarters and the leader of the mutiny, a Czech gunnery officer, refused to remove the Imperial Ensign from the ship and replace it with the red flag.[31]

In every case the mutinies were put down with iron discipline and the mutineers severely dealt with. In several instances, the ringleaders, including the hapless Czech naval officer, were shot. By the summer, order had been restored, much to the surprise of the Entente propagandists who had of course been predicting the imminent collapse of the multinational army for years. Their hope that the Empire had been in a state of suspended dissolution was not borne out and they now resorted to even more ruthless measures to put pressure on the young Emperor.

Clemenceau's calculated indiscretion undermines the Austro-German alliance

In a gesture of mischievous defiance utterly in keeping with his deep long-standing hostility to the Habsburgs, the new President of France, Clemenceau, broke the pledges earlier French statesmen had given to keep the Prince Sixtus peace moves of earlier years secret, and published the correspondence. Czernin had made some poorly advised public jibes against Clemenceau. The French premier had repaid Czernin in his own coin. It was not the first time Clemenceau had demonstrated his antagonism towards the Habsburgs. His earlier relationship with Franz-Josef's heir, Crown Prince Rudolf, in 1889, and his attempt to persuade him into seizing power had proved fatal for Rudolf. When Rudolf refused, he was, according to Habsburg family account, murdered by a professional assassin at the hunting lodge of Mayerling.[32]

Clemenceau's decision to publish deeply compromised Charles. The Emperor moved swiftly to dismiss Czernin, who, in any event, was behaving more and more 'like a lunatic'. At one moment, on 13 April, the Emperor telephoned Gayer, Chief of Vienna police, and asked if Czernin could be arrested. In a masterly piece of bureaucratic logic testifying to Austria being a *Rechtstaat* (a state governed by the rule of law) even in the midst of war, Gayer replied diffidently. 'I am afraid we cannot arrest him, Your Majesty; not until he has done something illegal.'[33]

Letters from Charles, offering to intercede on behalf of France for the restoration of Alsace-Lorraine, went down very badly in Berlin. The German Ambassador in Vienna, Wedel, had been engaged in pro-German propaganda for some months. He did not lose a moment in smearing both the Emperor and his Bourbon-Parma wife. The political and military leadership in Berlin had its own prejudices confirmed. The total absorption of Austria-Hungary into the German Reich began to be more widely discussed.[34]

Charles was advised to explain himself in person at a meeting with the German Kaiser. Precisely one month after Clemenceau's calculated indiscretion, the two Emperors met at Spa with their staffs in attendance. The Germans wisely exploited the embarrassment to make a generous offer of seamless cooperation. This envisaged after the war the reduction of the Habsburg Empire to the status that Bavaria currently enjoyed within the German Reich. The 'offer' dovetailed neatly with Wedel's efforts in Vienna to deconstruct the Habsburgs' credibility among their own peoples.

Demonstrating the skills which had kept his House safe in perilous times, Charles accepted the deadly embrace but noted it could only be worked out in detail once the Central Powers were victorious. It was a classic Habsburg technique for dealing with unpleasant realities: the instruments of delay and prevarication under a veneer of charm and a semblance of subordination. How well Frederick II, Napoleon and later Bismarck had come to know and despise these 'qualities'. The German Kaiser no doubt thought he had finally clinched what had eluded the greatest warlords in history. But he had grasped at thin air, and what he imagined was a tangible body was, for Berlin's purposes, no more than a phantom.

While these diplomatic steps were played out on the Western front, the war continued in the south as the snows melted. Rumours that the Americans were planning to reinforce the Italians strengthened the arguments of those who favoured a push across the Venetian plain. But there were to be no German reinforcements and the state of Boroević's troops, following another harsh winter, was far from ideal for offensive action.

These considerations persuaded Boroević to urge the delay of any planned renewed offensive. Any offensive lacked the numerical superiority required for even a chance of success, and it envisaged a push along far too broad a front. As Boroević knew, his men were simply not ready for a great push against a foe who had exploited the last six months to strengthen their defensive positions. The river Piave, flooded by the spring melting of the ice on the Julian Alps, was also a formidable obstacle.

Failure of Boroević's final offensive

The original date for the offensive had been set for 10 June 1918, but Boroević requested a ten-day delay to feed up his troops. Unfortunately the message informing the Imperial and Royal Navy of the delay was not correctly understood, or it was ignored by the new Imperial Navy commander, Admiral Nikolaus von Horthy. Horthy had intended to coordinate with the land attack to plan a raid on the Otranto Barrage which had been laid by the Entente in 1915.

The barrage had proved singularly ineffective against Austrian submarines, which had escaped into the Mediterranean with ease to harass Allied shipping. Despite frequent raids, the barrage had nonetheless so far inhibited any breakout by the Imperial Navy's battleships. Horthy hoped to provoke a response that would bring the enemy's ships on to the guns of his four most powerful ships, the dreadnoughts of the 'Tegetthoff' class: *Viribus Unitis, Tegetthoff, Prinz Eugen* and *Szent István*. But shortly after setting sail, *Szent István* developed turbine trouble, which meant her speed had to be reduced to 12 knots.

In this rather vulnerable state, she was spotted by two light Italian MAS (Motoscafo Armato Silurante) torpedo boats. Each boat was armed with two torpedoes and a light machine gun. MAS 15 with a crew of eight under the command of Lieutenant Rizzo fired its two torpedoes, both of which hit *Szent István* amidships in the area of the bulkhead dividing the two boiler rooms. Poor riveting in the dreadnought's construction now proved fatal. She was soon listing 10 degrees to port with no power to operate pumps. The first and last Imperial and Royal battleship to be built at the Hungarian port Fiume rolled over two hours later with a loss of 89 men out of her complement of 1,094. With Tenente Rizzo and his eight-man crew at large in the Adriatic, the era of asymmetrical naval warfare had arrived.

The loss of the *Szent István* prompted Horthy, who had already placed his flag in *Viribus Unitis*, to call off the projected assault on the barrage immediately. The element of surprise had been lost. The Imperial and Royal Navy had put out to sea for the last time.

But if the failed attack on the Otranto Barrage was to be the navy's last sortie, the army fought on. Boroević's attack a few days later with 24 divisions came up against 27 well-dug-in Allied divisions and a torrential Piave river. Attempting to construct a bridge over the watercourse, the Austro-Hungarian pioneers came under such heavy fire that they were virtually wiped out. The historian Glaise Horstenau noted that the 'crossing of the Piave brought this corps' long and distinguished history to an end'.[35]

An attempt to deploy the 62nd 'Spezial' and launch a gas attack was called off on account of the rain, though some shells were fired, inflicting little more than the effects of tear gas under these conditions. Notwithstanding these setbacks, the predominantly Hungarian VI Army, under the command of their 'Hungarian' Archduke Joseph, made progress over the Piave and captured Montello. Boroević's men also crossed the river further south along the Piave delta. But this was not enough to break the Allies, and there were no reinforcements. The Germans were no longer present on the southern front. In fact on 19 June they were demanding that Boroevič send his six best divisions to join them in the coming 'decisive' battle on the Western front rather than waste them on a 'hopeless offensive'.[36] Boroevič expressed the situation with characteristic brevity when he met the Emperor on 20 June: 'reinforcements or retreat'.

Charles was quickly of the same mind and came to a logical conclusion: in the absence of reinforcements the chance of victory over Italy was lost and would not reappear soon. The Piave bridgeheads which had cost so many lives were surrendered, and the army was withdrawn to the left bank of the river. At 7.15 p.m. on 20 June, he ordered Boroevič's army to withdraw.

The withdrawal luckily coincided with the failure of the Allies to counterattack. For three days the Imperial and Royal troops could withdraw virtually unnoticed by their opponents. By the time the Italians opened up on the Austrian positions with their artillery, the positions had been abandoned.

For everyone in the Imperial and Royal Army, from the Kaiser downwards, the failed offensive was perceived as a defeat. Ironically, the Entente did not see it as a defeat. To their consternation, the Imperial and Royal Army was showing no signs of disintegration despite reports of mutiny, hunger, strikes and the eternal problem of the feuding nationalities. This 'defeated' army had attacked the armies of three nations with numerical inferiority, and had conducted a skilful withdrawal, inflicting heavy casualties and taking more than 40,000 prisoners. Such was not the behaviour of an army on the brink of collapse. Halfway through 1918, the Imperial and Royal Army appeared to be in rather better shape than any other army in Europe.

Pflanzer-Baltin's fighting withdrawal from Albania

To the south, further down the Adriatic in Albania, the Habsburg army would demonstrate that under inspired leadership it could still achieve great things. As French, Italian and Serb forces gathered to drive the Austrians out of Albania, the Austrian High Command reacted swiftly to the threat by dispatching one of their most experienced generals, Pflanzer-Baltin, to assume control. After an epic journey by air, sea and rail, Pflanzer-Baltin arrived in August. In a brilliant series of counter-attacks, he drove the French out of Fier and Berat. The Albanians were in any event sympathetic to the Austrians. Their future king, Ahmed Zogu, had so impressed the Austrian officers, he had been dispatched for 'training' to Vienna, where he had served as an aide-de-camp to Franz-Josef.

Pflanzer-Baltin consolidated his position, which only the surrender of Bulgaria towards the end of September made untenable. Undeterred, harassed by three armies to the east and blocked by the sea to the west, Pflanzer conducted a dazzling fighting withdrawal. Only the Germans were chagrined as he refused to fit his strategy in with Berlin's war aims and von Seeckt urged the Austrian High Command to replace him; a request that, happily, Vienna ignored. Pflanzer brought his entire army intact out of Albania. In this he was ably assisted by Austrian submarines, which disabled the leading elements of a British naval force dispatched to deny Pflanzer's army the possibility of evacuation by sea. The damage inflicted on HMS *Weymouth*, the leading British cruiser which lost its stern and a dozen sailors, so disorganised the Royal Navy that they withdrew, allowing Pflanzer's men to disembark safely. The disabling of HMS *Weymouth* brought a Maria Theresa Order (eventually) for the Austrian submarine's commander, Linienschiffsleutnant Hermann Rigele. He was the last Austrian to be awarded this illustrious distinction whose history had been so bound up with Habsburg arms.

Pflanzer's campaign was yet another example of the old army continuing to defy the expectations of its foes. Two Imperial and Royal divisions (106th and 39th Honvéd) were transported to help the German army on the Western front where their arrival in tattered uniforms and their lack of footwear inspired such pity in the German officers that they paid for them to be entirely reclothed out of their own stores. For all its material poverty, the Habsburg army was still a living, active historically evolved body upon which 'only the greatest storms could make any impression'.[37]

Despite the huge losses they had sustained, the traditions of the army and its loyalty to the dynasty remained intact. It continued to fight even as the Dual Monarchy began no longer to function politically. The Czechs and Slovaks had already been officially recognised by the British as 'an allied nation' in August 1918. Yet two months later, when the Allies launched their big offensive against Boroević on 24 October, his forces, which included several Czech regiments, fought heroically for four days. The Austrians were outnumbered three to one but they still managed to deny the Italian, French and British armies the strongpoints of Feltre and Fonzaso. As a staff officer later observed: 'The world had never before beheld a spectacle like this: an army fighting on behalf of a country that had ceased to exist.'[38] The Emperor, in this last great battle against hopeless odds, had addressed his troops in stirring words: 'All the peoples of the monarchy have found a common home in the army. For that reason it has been enabled to accomplish so much.'[39]

Charles seeks an armistice for his war-weary army

Charles was enough of a realist to recognise that the war was lost and, with it, his empire, unless he acted swiftly. Three weeks earlier on 4 October, after informing his German allies, he had addressed a note to President Wilson requesting an immediate armistice. An unhelpful reply, arriving a few weeks later, dwelt on 'the rights of the Czechoslovaks'.[40] The message underlined the fact that the Entente and the USA were only interested in coming to terms with the Habsburg monarchy once the Habsburg monarchy had ceased to exist.

Irrespective of the heroic fighting on the Italian front, this process was already under way. Where the Czechs led, the 'German' Austrians followed. On 21 October, the deputies of the German-speaking parts of the Empire met in Vienna to discuss a new structure: 'German' Austria. While they did this, Charles was in Hungary trying to cement the support of the Magyars who, with typical *sacro egoismo*, had ordered their troops to be withdrawn from the Italian front to defend the lands of St Stephen. The Honvéd regiments and Hungarian line regiments, which had distinguished themselves in their last battle, withdrew and the High Command moved several Alpine regiments to replace them. But one of these, from Salzburg, seeing its Hungarian comrades cheerfully marching back from the front, could not resist the temptation to follow suit. Such disaffection in an elite regiment became swiftly a harbinger of widespread unrest.

The Imperial and Royal Army finally began the process which the Allies had longed for but had in more than four years of fighting been unable to achieve. On 28 October, a Czech delegation met the governor of Bohemia, Count Max von Coudenhove off the train at the Franz-Josef station in Prague, and asked respectfully for his permission to proceed with the establishment of a Czechoslovak state. When Coudenhove agreed, they were delighted. True to bureaucratic form, they then with great formality and apology proceeded to arrest him.

When the South Slavs followed the Czechs in declaring their independence, the Hungarians also withdrew, notwithstanding the Emperor's attempts to persuade them otherwise. But it is significant that the disintegration of the army only began after the Empire had ceased to be a single state. By any definition, the army had performed its duty exemplarily. When the armistice was finally signed on 3 November, not a single Allied soldier stood anywhere on Imperial territory. That evening, an Italian boat, the *Audace*, gingerly landed a few sailors on the Molo San Carlo near a deserted Piazza Grande in Trieste to 'claim' the city.

Boroević's offer of support to Charles

It is a common misconception to imagine that the Habsburg army melted away. The Italians manipulated the time of the ceasefire they had agreed with the Austrians on 3 November. They then used this deceit to 'capture' 200,000 Imperial and Royal soldiers who had already laid down their arms at the so-called 'Battle' of Vittorio Veneto. Even then, they failed to neutralise Boroević's entire army. Some 80,000 soldiers now retired with Boroević to Carinthia and Tyrol in good order, ready to defend the crown lands against any incursions.

At the end of the first week of November 1918, Boroević telegraphed the Emperor twice to offer this force, which was well disciplined and contained many 'crack' regiments, to occupy Vienna and discharge its 'traditional obligations' to the dynasty.[41] Special trains were prepared, and a forward base at Wiener Neustadt was planned with reliable troops. Boroević confided to the Bishop of Klagenfurt that these troops 'could offer the Emperor the freedom of manoeuvre in his negotiations which he appears to have lost'. But then came the fateful sentence, born of an older respect for law and command: 'I can however only help him if he commands me to.' Boroević, like every Habsburg commander since 1619, could do nothing without the support of the dynasty.

Caught up in the chaos of November 1918, it is unclear whether Charles ever received Boroević's message. The sources are divided. We know enough about Charles's character to imagine that he would have done everything he could to avoid further bloodshed. Boroević was no Haynau, 'a razor to be used sparingly', in Radetzky's phrase, but the arrival of this determined taciturn Croat in Vienna at the head of an army could only have resulted in violence, and the Emperor was determined to avoid this.

On 11 November, a few days after Boroević's last telegram was sent, Charles issued the following declaration:

> I have not hesitated to restore constitutional life and I have opened up for the peoples the path of their development as independent states. Filled now as ever with unwavering devotion to all my peoples, I do not wish to oppose the free government with my own person. I recognise in advance whatever decisions German Austria may make about its future form. I renounce all participation in the affairs of state . . . . the happiness of my peoples has from the beginning been the object of my most ardent wishes. Only an inner peace can heal the wounds of this war.[42]

The last sentence, characteristic of the Emperor's sensibility and deeply held Christian beliefs, can be read as the formal reply to Boroević's telegrams. It is ironic that nearly three hundred years to the day after Ferdinand II had prayed for soldiers to deliver him from his difficulties in Vienna, the last Habsburg Emperor, whose simple prie-dieu was always close at hand, and who never took any significant decision without prayer, was convinced that his troops could not be part of any solution.

Charles must have been aware of his options but he put his duty as a sovereign even above his duty as a soldier. His proclamation of 11 November formally brought to a close the story of the Imperial and Royal Army. The compact sealed by Ferdinand II that fateful morning in June 1619, when Dampierre's dragoons rode to his rescue in the Hofburg, was broken. Without the dynasty to command them, no Habsburg army could exist.

CHAPTER 26

Aftermath

The dissolution of the monarchy and the decision by the Emperor Charles to withdraw from political life led to a dislocation of centuries-old structures which would traumatise Central Europe for most of the twentieth century. By granting the clamour for freedom all that it demanded, the last Habsburg Kaiser acted as a catalyst for the two great movements of twentieth-century European history: nationalism and socialism; two movements which would reach their zenith in the unhappy and tragic symbiosis twenty years later of National Socialism. Yet a sense of a different loyalty persisted. Engelbert Dollfuss, the Chancellor of Austria murdered by the Nazis, had nurtured an Austrian as opposed to a German patriotism. He had drawn on his experience in the war as a Tyrolean Kaiserschützen officer and had sought to remind Austrians of their homeland.

Even in the later dark days of the Anschluss, with the Gestapo watching every cultural activity, a performance of Grillparzer's *König Ottokar's Glück und Ende* (King Ottokar's Good Fortune and Death) in the German Volkstheater could bring forth a loud cheering demonstration in response to Ottokar von Horneck's great Act III monologue on Austria. The speech is a masterpiece of Austrian as opposed to German sentiment: 'Wo habt ihr dessengleichen schon gesehen?... Drum ist der Oesterreicher froh und frank/ Trägt seinen Fehl, trägt offen seine Freude/Beneidet nicht, lässt lieber sich beneiden' ('Where have you seen such to compare? Thus is the Austrian happy and honest. He carries his blemishes and openly his joy. He envies not, better envy him').[1]

For the officers and soldiers of the Imperial and Royal Army, the collapse of the old multinational empire placed a question mark over all their beliefs and careers. The dislocation of the first days of November 1918 was by no means felt by the rank and file exclusively. For the officers, the trauma was often more intense. Boroevič, the 'Lion of the Isonzo' offered his services to the new South Slav state of Yugoslavia but the offer was rejected. His possessions en route by train for Carinthia were pillaged in Ljubljana. The looters took all his clothes and his decorations (including his Maria Theresa Order). Other possessions he had left behind in Croatia were stolen and his property confiscated without compensation. When he was first presented to the Bishop of Klagenfurt in early November 1918, he could honestly say that his only possessions were his 'uniform and two handkerchiefs'.[2]

With his wife, he made his home in a small three-room apartment near Klagenfurt but they could not survive on a pension made worthless by the inflation that bedevilled the new republic of Austria. He was kept alive by modest sums in the gift of the Emperor (an echo of Franz-Josef subsidising the impoverished composer Bruckner towards the end of his life). When Boroevič died in 1920 at the age of 64, virtually penniless, the Emperor Charles paid out of his own pocket for a fine memorial to be erected in the Vienna Central Cemetery. Did Charles ever regret refusing Boroevič's offer of military support? In any event, this gesture of Charles dispelled the canard of 'legendary Habsburg ingratitude' towards the monarchy's commanders.

Early on a sun-swept November morning in 1918, the commander of the Trieste naval air station Gottfried Banfield waited quietly in his office for his Italian opponents to arrive. Eventually, a famous Italian air ace called Berezzi turned up to take over the base. On being presented to Banfield, the Italian stiffened and saluted: 'Banfield? What an honour. I am so sorry we have not met earlier.' To which Banfield answered evenly: 'Please don't regret it. I am afraid that if we had met earlier, one of us would be unlikely to be present here today.'[3]

Unfortunately for Banfield this was to be the last example of chivalry he would experience at Italian hands for the time being. Two days later he was arrested and thrown into solitary confinement from which only the intervention of the British and American consuls in Trieste released him. He was given 48 hours to leave Trieste for good. Like so many Austrian airmen, including such aces as Frank Linke Crawford (another officer with British connections), he was unemployable in the new republican Austria which was in the full phase of social and financial dislocation.

If there were limited prospects for the airmen, they were non-existent for the naval officers. On 31 October, the Emperor Charles had signed the order handing over the navy to the South Slav Council. That day, the red–white–red battle ensign, familiar in the Mediterranean since the days of Nelson, was struck for the last time. The Austrian, Czech, Polish, Hungarian and Italian officers all began making their way home. In the confused situation that followed, the Italians attached limpet mines to the *Viribus Unitis* in Pola harbour and the ensuing explosions sank her. The rest of the capital ships were distributed among the Entente powers, who broke them up.

In Austria the loss of an Imperial identity left wounds that have only really been lastingly healed in the twenty-first century. The short but sharp 'civil war' in Vienna in February 1934 illustrated perfectly how accurate were the departing Emperor Charles's fears of violent social dislocation should the army involve itself in politics. Even now an objective appreciation of such historical figures as Dollfuss, a proud Austrian patriot but an opponent of the demo-cratic process and socialism, murdered by the Nazis in 1934, remains highly sensitive for the Second Republic. The fierce divisions Austria faced in 1934 continue to defy a comfortable modern assessment.

Following the Anschluss in 1938, many former Imperial and Royal officers were incorporated into the German Wehrmacht. Two-hundred-and-twenty former Habsburg officers served as generals, including three who attained the rank of Generaloberst in the German Wehrmacht. Not all were Nazis. Admiral Canaris made it a point of honour that his military intelligence office in Vienna was staffed by what he referred to as 'patriotic Austrians not Austrian Nazis'. These were recruited by the Admiral's deputy, Lahousen-Vivremont, the 'epitome of a Habsburg officer'.[4]

On coming to power in Germany, Hitler made many attempts to meet Emperor Charles's son and heir, Otto von Habsburg, then a student in Germany. The young Habsburg was true to his House: he saw immediately that the Nazi Party was the antithesis of everything his family had ever stood for and refused to meet Hitler. His cousin Max Hohenberg, son of the Archduke murdered at Sarajevo, also refused to cooperate with the Nazis and was thrown into Dachau concentration camp.

Those officers who most openly embraced the ideals of the Nazi Party often came from German nationalist families and often, though not exclu-sively, from the German ethnic 'extremities' of the Empire. (For example Colonel-General Loehr, who masterminded the bombing of Belgrade for which he was executed after the war, was from the German minority on the fringes of the old Military Frontier at Severin.)[5]

Non-German officers followed the pull of their national origins. Nearly all the former Austrian officers of Polish origin joined the newly constituted Polish army under Pilsudski. Twenty years later, they were fighting against the Wehrmacht (e.g. Bór-Komorowski, the commander of the Warsaw Uprising). In a much-reduced Hungary, racial cohesion was assisted by the stripping out of the 'Kingdom' of all her Slav minorities. Some of the former Hungarian soldiers found a role for themselves in the new (still Royal) Honvéd, whose commander-in-chief was the former captain of the *Szent István*, Admiral Horthy.

Acting as 'Regent', Horthy betrayed the Emperor Charles twice in two failed attempts to re-establish the monarchy in Budapest.[6] A man without many royalist scruples, he was condemned in Vienna as a Regent without a King and an Admiral without a navy. Yet despite these defects, for as long as he could he resisted Hitler's demands to deliver the Jewish population of Budapest to the death camps. The fact that Budapest uniquely enjoyed a significant Jewish population, unlike Vienna and other Central European cities after the Second World War, can be in part attributed to him. Something perhaps of his Habsburg training had survived.

The officers and soldiers of Czech origins had perhaps the most challenging of fates. The state erected by Masaryk promised a kind of Central European Switzerland. In fact the Czechs were a minority in their new country and relentlessly discriminated against the former 'German' Austrians. Commonly referred to as 'Sudeten-Germans' by British and Nazi officials, these people felt themselves to be Germans. From the beginning, the Czech government regarded them as a three-million-strong fifth column. A purge of the officer class in the new Czechoslovak army was therefore inevitable. The old Wiener-Neustadt Academy trained officers were replaced by the 'Legionaries', men who had deserted the Habsburg cause on the Eastern front and had imbibed Russian ways. Only the cavalry and the military music retained recognisably Habsburg features.

In the Ukraine, the Austrian trained officers were quickly engaged as a kind of fulcrum for various attempts, all of them futile, to erect a nationalist entity capable of defying the influence of Moscow. Like many of their comrades in other countries, most of them were monarchists until the day of their death.

The same cannot perhaps be said of one group of former k. (u.) k. officers who would find distinguished service after the Second World War outside Europe in the Israel Defence Force. Rudolf Loew, Wolfgang von Weisl and Sigmund Edler von Friedmann all made brilliant careers later in life in the *Haganah*. One rose to be Deputy Chief of Staff. Another became Head of the Israeli Supreme Military Court. All recalled their early days as k. (u.) k. cadets with affection, though they readily admitted that that might seem strange at first glance. None of them recalled a single act of anti-Semitism against them during their time of service in the Imperial and Royal Army.[7]

The Emperor Charles died in 1922. Exiled with his family by the victorious powers following his second failed attempt to return to Hungary, he caught a chill while walking down from his damp house above Funchal on the island of Madeira. His son, Otto, kept the torch of Habsburg values alive intellectually and spiritually during the Second World War and for a half-century afterwards. His disdain for Nazi values and the false gods of nationalism remained with him until his death. He was fond of pointing out that although an Austrian by birth, Adolf Hitler had at least been rejected for military service in 1914 by the k. (u.) k. Army. The Bavarians had been less fussy.

With Gorbachev's ordering of the Soviet withdrawal from Central Europe in 1989, the heir to the Habsburg throne organised a bold picnic along the newly opened Iron Curtain. Since then intellectual life in the lands of the former Habsburg Empire has been freed to rediscover the centuries-old traditions of pre-Soviet and pre-1918 life.

Today, the Habsburg army is no more. The last person to have served in its forces died in Lemberg aged well over 100 in 2008. In literature, art and music something of its memory lives on. It certainly has the finest corpus of any army's military music, with contributions by Schubert, Beethoven and Strauss as well as Lehár, Ziehrer, Komzák and Wagnes. The obituary of the Imperial and Royal Army was penned by some of the greatest writers of the twentieth century. Joseph Roth, Arthur Schnitzler, Alexander Lernet-Holenia and Robert Musil have all immortalised the traditions, ethos and mores of the old army. In his great novel about the Trotta family, *Radetzkymarsch*, Roth gave the old army the literary equivalent of its last rites. The beautiful paintings of Alexander Pock and the drawings of Schönpflug offer a memorable visual accompaniment to Roth's theme.[8]

Nor can we forget the fact that the army received, post factum, some glorious cinematographic treatment, thanks to the American film industry being largely founded by Austrian and Hungarian exiles in the 1920s. The great Hollywood filmmaker Erich von Stroheim revivified its colourful pageants so effectively that one extra, himself a former k. (u.) k. officer, felt himself involuntarily stiffening and saluting when during a rehearsal the actor playing Franz-Josef strolled on to the set earlier than expected.

Many of the Central European intellectual and cultural elite of the twentieth century had served in the army. Some like Wittgenstein and Erwin Schrödinger, who had served as an artillery officer near Trieste in 1916, would revolutionise the way philosophy and science regarded the world through picture theory and quantum mechanics.[9] Others, like Fritz Kreisler, brought even greater pathos to their playing, having spent 'six weeks in the trenches'.[10] The founder of modern Viennese architecture, Adolf Loos donned the uniform of an infantry subaltern. The greatest expressionist poet of the German language, Rainer Maria Rilke, served as an officer in the military archives. Even Hanns Eisler, the 'enfant terrible' of Berlin music in the 1920s, fondly recalled his military service as a subaltern in a Muslim Bosnian infantry regiment.

Few who hear today the martial drum-rolls announcing the 'Radetzky March' to bring the annual Vienna New Year's Day concert to a close remember that this 'Marseillaise of Reaction', as Viennese liberals dubbed it, was played while Styrian infantry, with bayonets fixed, advanced under fire on the icy fastnesses of the Oeversee ramparts; or that it was blasted out to rally the decimated troops of the Hoch und Deutschmeister Regiment at Königgrätz. The Vienna Philharmonic still plays it with a military precision and crispness few other orchestras in the world can match. For them at least, it has a serious as well as a light-hearted dimension.

The contribution of the Imperial and Royal Army to the culture and history of Europe though significant was not of course its primary purpose. Its record as a fighting force, still disparaged and neglected, has been shown in these pages to be far from indifferent. Given that it always fought to defend first and foremost the dynasty rather than to annihilate its opponents it is remarkable that it won the majority of its campaigns.

Today, as the research of a new generation of military historians in Central Europe opens up access to this story to younger audiences, one can only marvel at the old generalisations about the poor fighting quality of the Imperial and Royal forces. After 1918, it was not for Lenin to glorify the epic of the San or the defence of Przemyśl; nor for the Czechs under Masaryk to probe beyond the humorous adventures of the Good Soldier Švejk. The great monument to Radetzky still gathers dust in a warehouse behind Prague castle and the pre-1914 story of Bohemia remains carefully mothballed. Those wide fields of abstraction known as 'nationalism' and 'self-determination' which were ignited nearly a hundred years ago by the fireworks of President Wilson still await comprehensive reappraisal but without doubt they are coming under scrutiny. The dynamic forces stirring throughout Europe as the twenty-first century gathers momentum are unlikely to allow the aspic which has formed around this story to remain intact for very much longer.

The problems of Central Europe, notably how to organise small entities of different nationalities so that they can enjoy the security and prosperity that the Imperial and Royal Army once guaranteed them, remain. The armed forces and the dynasty they served offered for many centuries a solution. Palacký predicted correctly that once the Habsburgs departed from Central Europe, the vacuum would be filled by German and Russian influence. As the countries of Central and Eastern Europe, the successor states, emerge from the twentieth century, and as Austria, no longer the *letzte Haltestelle* (last bus stop) before the Iron Curtain, rekindles her cultural and trade links with the Danube basin, this century-old story is undoubtedly set for vigorous assessment.

NOTES

Introduction

1. Quoted in Adam Wandruszka, *The House of Habsburg*, London, 1964, p. xv.
2. Quoted in Richard Bassett, *The Austrians*, London, 1988, p. 54 and Lord Frederick Hamilton, *The Vanished Pomps of Yesterday*, London, 1921, p. 51.
3. Edward Crankshaw, *The Habsburgs*, London, 1972, p. 66.
4. Quoted in Gabriele Matzner-Holzer, *Verfreundete Nachbarn*, Vienna, 2005, p. 68.
5. A.J.P. Taylor, *The Course of German History*, London, 1945, p. 218.
6. Quoted in Otto von Habsburg, *Zurück zur Mitte*, Vienna, 1991, p. 75.
7. M. Hartley, *The Man Who Saved Austria*, London, 1912, p. 62.
8. Lewis Namier, *Conflicts: Studies in Contemporary History*, London, 1942, p. 103.
9. A.J.P. Taylor, *The Habsburg Monarchy 1809–1918*, London, 1948, pp. 255, 263–73.
10. Norman Stone, *The Eastern Front*, London, 1977, p. 71. For this interpretation's more recent resilience see Geoffrey Wawro, *A Mad Catastrophe*, Austin, Texas, 2014, which quotes Sir Michael Howard referring to the 'truly lamentable performance' of the Habsburg armies.
11. See Wawro, op. cit.
12. See H.V. Patera (with Gottfried Pils), *Unter Oesterreichs Fahnen*, Vienna, 1960, p. 153 for the detailed list.
13. Edward Crankshaw, *The Fall of the House of Habsburg*, London, 1963, p. 462.
14. *The World Was Never the Same: 36 Events Which Shaped History*, Oklahoma City, 2011.
15. Wandruszka, op. cit.
16. Anthony Meredith, SJ, Sermon, 22 June 1994, Farm Street, London. Based on William Roper's *Life of Thomas More* (1553); the London,1932 edition, p. 70 gives a slightly different wording, leaving out Fisher. See also R.W. Chambers, *Thomas More*, London, 1938, pp. 287–90, 389–95.
17. Wandruszka, op. cit., p. 127. Also see Derek Beales, *A History of Joseph II*, Vol. II, Cambridge, 2009, p. 543.
18. Karl Eugen Czernin, *Die Sixtusaffaire*, Enzersfeld, 2004 (2nd reprint), p. 29.

Part 1 The Habsburg Connection

Chapter 1 The Kaiser's Cuirassiers: A Dynasty Saved

1. R.W. Seton-Watson, *History of the Czechs and Slovaks*, London, 1943, p. 99.
2. Karl-Eugen Czernin, *Die Einzig gerechte Sache*, Enzersfeld, 2013.
3. Wilhelm Lamormaini SJ, *Virtutes Ferdinand II Romanorum Imperatoris*, Graz, 1638. See also F. E. von Hurter-Ammann, *Geschichte Kaiser Ferdinands II und seiner Eltern bis zu dessen Krönung in Frankfurt*, Schaffhausen, 1850, for the relationship between Ferdinand and his confessor.
4. See R.J.W. Evans, *The Making of the Habsburg Monarchy*, Oxford, 1979, pp. 86–109
5. See Francis Watson, *Soldier under Saturn*, London, 1938, p. 51 *et seq.*
6. Ibid., p. 95
7. H.V. Patera, *Unter Oesterreichs Fahnen*, Vienna, 1960, p. 41.

8. Ibid., p. 46.
9. Peter H. Wilson, *Europe's Tragedy*, London, 2009, p. 302.
10. E. von Frauenholz, *Das Heereswesen in der Zeit der dreissigjaehrigen Krieges*. Munich, 1938, Vols 1–21, p. 105.
11. Josef Pekař, '*Bila hora': Prague 1922*, pp. 28–30 (see also in Jarozlav Meznik, *Josef Pekař a historicke myty: Pekarovske Studie*. Prague, 1995.
12. Evans, op. cit., p. 104.
13. Lamormaini SJ, op. cit., p. 10.
14. Wilson, op. cit., p. 400.
15. Ibid., p. 470.
16. Gottfried Hess, *Graf Pappenheim*, Leipzig, 1855.
17. Wilson, op. cit., p. 491.
18. Ibid., p. 535.
19. Evans, op. cit., chapter 10.
20. Benedictus Pereira, SJ, *De Magia de observatione somniorum et de divinatione astrologia*, Cologne, 1598.
21. Evans, op. cit., p. 348.
22. Ibid., p. 349.
23. Watson, op. cit., p. 188 *et seq.*
24. Heinrich Ritter von Srbik, *Wallenstein's Ende*, Vienna, 1920. For the role of Piccolomini see Golo Mann, *Wallenstein: Sein Leben erzaehlt*, Frankfurt, 1971, p.1087.
25. G. Lorenz, *Quellen zur Geschichte Wallensteins*, Vienna, 1987. See also H.F. Schwarz, *The Imperial Privy Council in the 17th Century*, Cambridge, Mass., 1943, p. 227 for a thumbnail sketch of Eggenberg.
26. Watson, op. cit., p. 404.
27. L.N. Tolstoy, *War and Peace*, Vol. 2, London, 1957, p. 717.
28. Rainer Maria Rilke, *Die Weise von Liebe und Tod des Cornets Christoph Rilke*, Leipzig, 1912.
29. Raimondo Montecuccoli, *Dell'arte militare*, Venice, 1657.
30. Johann Schefers, *Johann Graf von Sporck*, Delbruck, 1998; G.J. Rosenkranz, *Graf Johann Sporck*, Paderborn, 1954.
31. Patera, op. cit., p. 22.
32. For example Robert Fludde, *The Squesing of Pastor Foster's Sponge*, London, 1631.

Chapter 2 For God and Emperor: The Relief of Vienna

1. Rainer Maria Rilke, *Die Weise von Liebe und Tod des Cornets Christoph Rilke*, Leipzig, 1912.
2. Ibid., p. 5. See also Michael Hochedlinger, *Austria's Wars of Emergence: War, State and Society 1683–1797*, London, 2003.
3. John Stoye, *Siege of Vienna*, London, 2000.
4. Ibid., p. 103.
5. Ibid., p. 111.
6. See H. Tietze, *Die Juden Wiens*, 1928. M. Grünwald, *Geschichte der Juden in Wien 1625–1740*, Vienna, 1913. Also *1000 Jahre Oesterreichisches, Judentum*, catalogue, Vienna, 1982.
7. Wiener Stadt und Landarchiv HA 9009.
8. M. Grünwald, *Samuel Oppenheimer und sein Kreis*, Vienna, 1928. For Oppenheimer in the context of the private capital 'expertise and organisation' see David Parrott, *The Business of War*, Cambridge, 2012, p. 21.
9. Catalogue: *Die Türken vor Wien Kat.zur 82. Sonderaustellung des Historischen Museums der Stadt Wien*, Vienna, 1983, p. 79.
10. Ibid., p. 77.
11. K. Teply, *Die Einführung des Kaffees in Wien. Georg Franz Koltschitzky, Johannes Diodati, Isaak de Luca* (Forschungen und Beiträge zur Wiener Stadtgeschichte 6), Vienna, 1980.
12. *Die Türken vor Wien*, op. cit., p. 88.

Chapter 3 'The noble knight': Prince Eugen and the War of the Spanish Succession

1. H. Belloc, *Six British Battles*, London, 1931, p. 116.
2. G. Wheatcroft, *Enemy at the Gates*, London, 1997, chapter 11.
3. See Giovanni Badone, *Le Aquili e i Gigli, Una Storia mai scritta*, Milan, 1869.
4. Ibid.
5. George Macmunn, *Prince Eugene*, London, 1934, p. 99 *et seq.*
6. Belloc, op. cit., p. 116.
7. Ibid., p. 146.

8. Charles Spencer, *Blenheim: Battle for Europe*, London, 2005, p. 261.
9. Belloc, op. cit., p. 171.
10. Rudolf Ottenfeld, *Die Oesterreichische Armee 1700–1867*, Vienna, 1895, p. 13.
11. Frederick Kohlrausch, *A History of Germany*, London, 1844, p. 538.
12. Giovanni Badone op. cit., p. 34 *et seq.*
13. Ottenfeld, op. cit., p.14 and p. 56 *et seq.*
14. Ibid., pp. 57–59.
15. Ibid., p. 19.
16. Ibid., p. 45.
17. Wheatcroft, op. cit.
18. Ottenfeld quotes him verbatim: op. cit., p. 30 *et seq.*
19. William Coxe, *A History of the House of Austria*, Vol. III, London, 1888, p. 83.
20. See A. Randa, *Oesterreich in Uebersee*, Vienna, 1966, p. 55.
21. Adam Wandruszka, *The House of Habsburg*, London, 1964, p. 136.
22. Coxe, op. cit., Vol. III, p. 114.

Chapter 4 'Our Blood and Life': The Great Empress

1. William Coxe, *A History of the House of Austria*, Vol. III, London, 1888, p. 199.
2. Adm Wandruszka, *The House of Habsburg*, London, 1964, p. 141. Also Ludwig Jedlicka (ed.), *Maria Theresia in ihren Briefen und Statschriften*, Vienna, 1953.
3. The claim was based on the Elector being a son of Ferdinand I.
4. Coxe, op. cit., p. 242.
5. Ibid., p. 243
6. Reed Browning, *The War of the Austrian Succession*, London, 1993, p. 33.
7. Lord Macaulay, 'Essay on Frederick the Great', in *Life and Works*, London, 1897, Vol. VI, pp. 660–1, p. 141.
8. Wandruszka, op, cit., p. 141.
9. Lorraine Petrie, F., *Napoleon's Conquest of Prussia*, London, 1907, p. 21.
10. Christopher Duffy, *Sieben Jahre Krieg 1756–1763: die Armee Maria Theresias*, 2003, Vienna, p. 147.
11. Duncker, 'Actenstücke', quoted in Duffy, *Army*, op. cit., p. 151.
12. Ibid., p. 205.
13. Browning, op. cit.,p.103.
14. Duncker, in Duffy, *Army*, op. cit., p. 201.
15. A. Arneth, *Geschichte Maria Theresa*, Vienna, 1863, Vol. IV, p. 181.
16. Coxe, op. cit., p. 252.
17. Ibid., p. 255.
18. Robinson to Lord Harrington, 28 June 1741 quoted in Coxe, op. cit., Vol. III p. 268.
19. For Silva-Tarouca see Th. G. von Karajan, *Maria Theresa und Graf Emmanuel Sylva-Tarouca*, Vienna, 1856.
20. Ibid., p. 269
21. Koller quoted in original Latin ibid., p. 269. See the orginal text with Maria Theresa's handwritten Latin improvements, penned only minutes before the speech was delivered, in Vienna Haus Hof und Staatsarchiv. Ungarische Akten F427.
22. Jedlicka, op. cit., p. 44.
23. Gerald Schlag, *Unser Leben und Blut*, Vienna, 1998, p. 15.
24. See Andreas Gestrich, *Das Wiener Diarium in Sieben Jährigen Krieg*, Göttingen, 2006.
25. Rudolf Ottenfeld, *Die Oesterreichische Armee 1700–1867*, Vienna, 1895, p. 146.
26. Coxe, op. cit., p. 256.
27. Browning, op. cit., p. 278.
28. Andreas Thuerheim, FM Otto Abensperg und Traun, Vienna, 1877.
29. J.J. Khevenhueller-Metsch, *Aus der Zeit Maria Theresas 1742–1766*, Vienna, 1907, 4 vols, Vol. II, p. 72.
30. Coxe, op. cit., p. 283.
31. Ibid.
32. E.E. Morris, *The Early Hanoverians*, London, 1886, p. 127.
33. Duffy, *Army*, op. cit., p. 158.
34. Coxe, op. cit., p. 306.
35. Ibid.
36. Duffy, *Army*, op. cit., p. 158.
37. Ibid., p. 159.
38. Frederick to Prince Henry of Prussia, PCXVIII, quoted in *Politische Correspondenz Friedrich der Grosse*, ed. J.G. Droysen et al., Vols 1–43 Berlin 1879–1939 Vol. VI, p. 624 (hereafter PC followed by volume and page number).

39. Browning, op. cit., p. 295.
40. Ibid.
41. Ibid., p. 356.
42. Edward Crankshaw, *Maria Theresa*, London, 1969, p. 6 *et seq.*, the first full-length study in the English language of the Empress for more than half a century.

Chapter 5: Austria Resurgent: Theresian Military Reforms

1. Rudolf Ottenfeld, *Die Oesterreichische Armee von 1700 bis 1867*, Vienna, 1895, p. 78.
2. 1757 Artillerie Reglement.
3. Ottenfeld, op. cit., p. 78.
4. Jean Baptiste Gribeauval, *Réglement concernant les fonts e les constructions de l'artillerie en France*, 3 vols, 1764–92 Paris, Vol. 1, p. 122.
5. Ottenfeld, op. cit., p. 81
6. Ibid., pp. 78–89.
7. Ibid.
8. Vicomte de Mirabeau, *Système militaire de la Prusse*, Paris, 1788, p. 25.
9. J. Cognazzo, *Freymütiger Beytrag zur Geschichte der Oesterreichen Militärdienstes*, Frankfurt, 1799, p. 106.
10. Christopher Duffy, *The Army of Maria Theresa: the Armed Forces of Imperilal Austria 1740–1780*, London, 1977, p. 72.
11. Count Otto Podewils, *Friedrich der Grosse und Maria Theresa*, Berlin, 1937, p. 37.
12. Cognazzo, op. cit., pp. 143–4.
13. Introduction in *Regulament und Ordnung des gesammten Kaiserlich-Königlichen Fuss-Volcks*, 1749 I. i
14. Podewils, op. cit., p. 141.
15. Eszterhazy quoted in Ottenfeld, op. cit., p. 94.
16. Duffy, *Army*, op. cit., p. 21.
17. Wandruszka, op. cit., p. 141.
18. Andrew Bisset (ed.), *Memoirs and Papers of Sir Andrew Mitchell*, London, 1850, Vol. II, p. 35.
19. Duffy, *Army*, op. cit., p. 172.
20. Ibid.
21. Cognazzo quoted ibid., p. 177.
22. Ibid., p. 180.

Chapter 6 Mater Castrorum

1. Frederick to Wilhelmina 3 October 1757, PCXV, pp. 398–400.
2. Christopher Duffy, *The Army of Maria Theresa: The Armed Forces of Imperial Austria 1740–1780*, London, 1977, p. 181.
3. Frederick Kohlrausch, *A History of Germany*, London, 1844, p. 571.
4. Ibid.
5. Duffy, *Army*, op. cit., p. 186.
6. Archenholz quoted ibid., p. 188.
7. Franz A.J. Szabo, *Seven Years War in Europe*, Harlow, 2008, p. 151.
8. Ibid., p. 153.
9. Duffy, *Army*, op. cit., p. 189.
10. Frederick to Prince Henry, PCXVII, p. 217.
11. Szabo, op. cit., p. 190.
12. William Coxe, *A History of the House of Austria*, Vols I–III, London, 1853, p. 395.
13. Ibid., p. 392.
14. William Wraxall, *Memoirs of the Courts of Berlin, Dresden, Warsaw and Vienna, 1777–9*, London, 1800, p. 387.
15. Szabo, op. cit., p. 203.
16. Ibid., p. 204.
17. Vienna Kriegsarchiv: Kabinetschreiben, 24 July 1759.
18. Frederick to Prince Henry PCXVIII p. 627, no. 11,578.
19. Frederick to Prince Henry (with Henry's later comments), PCXVIII, 14 December 1759.
20. Ibid., Frederick to Fouqué, PC XIX, p. 432.
21. J. Archenholz, *Geschichte des Siebenjaehrigen Krieges in Deutschland*, Frankfurt, 1788, Vol. II, p. 42.
22. Andrew Bisset (ed.), *Memoirs and Papers of Sir Andrew Mitchell*, London, 1850, Vol. II, p 133.
23. Hildebrandt C., *Anekdoten aus dem Leben Friedrich der Grose*, 6 vols, Halberstadt, 1829, p. 36.
24. Frederick to D'Argens, 27 August 1760, PCXIX, p. 191, no. 146.

25. Kohlrausch op. cit., p. 592.
26. Archenholz, op. cit.,Vol. II, p. 106.
27. Szabo, op.cit. p. 322.
28. Relations de l'Armée Prussiene, 6 November PCXX pp. 52–5, No. 12,467.
29. Frederick to Finckenstein, 10 December 1761, PCXXI pp. 112–13, No. 13,332.
30. Frederick, instructions to General Werner, 13 April 1762, PCXXI, pp. 367–69, No. 13,608.
31. Duffy, *Army*, op. cit., p. 205.

Chapter 7 The Army and the Josephinian Enlightenment

1. Christopher Duffy, *The Army of Maria Theresa*, London, 1977, p. 214. Also J. Jobst, *Die Neustadter Burg und die k.u.k Theresianische Militärakademie*, Vienna, 1908, p. 274.
2. Crankshaw, *Maria Theresa*, London, 1969, p. 285. Also see Camillo Paganel, *Storia di Giuseppe II*, Milan, 1843, p. 82 *et seq.*
3. Crankshaw, op. cit., p. 29.
4. Paganel Camillo, *Storia di Giuseppe Secondo: Imperatore di Germania*, Milan, 1843, p. 117
5. Ibid., p. 143.
6. Michael Hochedlinger, *Austria's Wars of Emergence: War, State and Society in the Habsburg Monarchy 1683–1797*, London, 2003, p. 276.
7. See Derek Beales, *A History of Joseph II*, Vol. II, pp. 196–203, and Josef Karniel, *Die Toleranzpolitik Kaiser Josef II*, Gerlingen, 1986.
8. See Beales, op.cit., p. 543 *et seq.*
9. Ibid., p. 144.
10. Rudolf Ottenfeld, *Die Oesterreichische Armee von 1700 bis 1867*, Vienna, 1895, p. 187.
11. Quoted in T. Blanning, *Joseph II and Enlightened Despotism*, Harlow, 1994, p. 127.
12. J. C. Allmayer-Beck, *Das Heerwesen unter Josef II* (catalogue entry for the NÖ Landesaustellung: 'Kaiser Joseph II und seine Zeit'), Melk, 1980.
13. Lacy reglement quoted in Ottenfeld, op. cit., p. 169.
14. 'Despotismus gemildert durch schlamperei' see Victor Adler, op.cit., p. 43.
15. Ottenfeld, op. cit., p. 193.
16. Allmayer-Beck, op. cit., p. 46.
17. Ibid., p. 48.
18. Adam Wandruszka, *The House of Habsburg*, New York, 1964, p. 147.
19. Frederick Kohlrausch, *A History of Germany*, London, 1844, p. 610.
20. F.H Bauer, *Der Hinterlad Carabin System Crespi*, Vienna, 1977.
21. A. Dollecszek, *K. und K. Blanken und Handfeuer Waffen*, Vienna, 1894.
22. Paganel, op. cit., p. 120.
23. Nathaniel William Wraxall, *Memoirs of the Courts of Berlin, Dresclen, Warsaw and Vienna 1777–9*, London, 1800, p. 348.
24. Allmayer-Beck, op. cit., p. 49.
25. Ibid., p. 49.
26. Ibid., p. 50.
27. William Coxe, *A History of the House of Austria*, Vols I–III, London, 1853, p. 523.
28. Ibid., p. 528.

Part 2 Revolution and Reaction

Chapter 8 The Army and the French Revolution

1. Adam Wandruszka, *The House of Habsburg*, New York, 1964, p. 160.
2. Quoted in Rudolf Ottenfeld, *Die Oesterreichische Armee von 1700 bis 1867*, Vienna, 1895, p. 256.
3. Ibid.
4. Frederick Kohlrausch, *A History of Germany*, London, 1844, p. 304.
5. J.A.H. Guibert, *Essai générale de tactique*, Paris, 1773, pp. 122, 142 and plate XIV.
6. Napoleon's offer as always was 'imaginative'. It involved partitioning Austria and making the future König von Böhmen a Marshal of France.
7. Erzherzog (EZH) Carl, *Grundsäetze der Strategie*, Vienna, 1796.
8. Dietrichstein to Thugut, quoted in A. Vivenot, *Thugut, Clerfayt und Wurmser 1797*, Vienna, 1870.
9. Martin Boycott Brown, *The Road to Rivoli*, London, 2001, p. 237 *et seq.*
10. Ibid., p. 240,
11. Napoleon correspondence No. 257, Paris, 1859. Quoted in Boycott Brown, op. cit., p. 242.
12. A. Debidour, *Recueil des Actes du Directoire Executif*, 4 vols, Paris, 1910, p. 787.

13. Ibid. p. 787.
14. Karl A. Roider, *Baron Thugut and Austria's Response to the French Revolution*, Princeton, 1987, p. 387.
15. Thugut's origins and the various myths arising from them are well covered ibid., p. 6 *et seq.*
16. Vivenot, op. cit., p. 56 *et seq.*
17. A. Voykoswitch, *Castiglione*, Klagenfurt, 1997.
18. Boycott Brown, op. cit., p. 257.
19. Guglielmo Ferrero: *The Gamble: Bonaparte in Italy 1796-1797*, London, 1939, p. 208.
20. Ibid., p. 289.
21. Ibid., p. 281.

Chapter 9 From Marengo to Austerlitz: The Second and Third Coalition Wars

1. A. B. Rodger, *War of the Second Coalition*, Oxford, 1961, p. 162.
2. Graf Radetzky, *Der k.k. öesterreichische Feldmarshall Graf Radetzky: Eine biographische Skizze nach den eigenen Dictaten, etc.*, Stuttgart, 1858, p. 34.
3. Rodger, op. cit., p. 166.
4. Ibid., p. 234.
5. Radetzky, op. cit., p. 48.
6. Ibid., p. 51.
7. James Arnold, *Marengo and Hohenlinden*, London, 1999 p. 72.
8. Marshal A. Marmont, *Mémoires du Maréchal Marmont, duc de Raguse*, Vol. II, Paris, 1857, pp. 131-5.
9. Karl Mras, 'Geschichte des Feldzuges in Italien 1800', *Oesterreischische Militärische Zeitschrift*, V–IX, Vienna, 1822.
10. Radetzky, op. cit., p. 54.
11. Ibid., p. 54.
12. Arnold, op. cit., p.182.
13. Rodger, op. cit., p. 246.
14. Hans Magenschab, *Erzherhog Johann*, Graz, 1995, p. 111.
15. Ibid., p. 114.
16. Ibid., p. 115.
17. E. Picard, *La Campagne de* 1800 *en Allemagne*, Paris, 1907: Zweibrücken to Max Emmanuel, p. 375.
18. Arnold, op. cit., p. 256.
19. Ibid., p. 256.
20. Ibid., p. 257.
21. Christopher Duffy, *Austerlitz 1805*, London, 1977, p. 31.
22. Ibid., p. 32.
23. Oskar Regele, *FM Mack*, Vienna, 1968.
24. Thierry Lentz (ed.), *Correspondence de Napoleon Ier, publiée par ordre de L'Empreur Napoleon III*, Vols I–VII, Paris, 1858–1970, Vol. VI (9381), Paris, 1860.
25. Duffy, op. cit., p. 50.
26. Ibid., p. 50.
27. Ibid., p. 51.
28. Baron Ségur, *Memoires de Comte de Ségur*, Vols I–III, Vol. II, London, 1824, p. 451.
29. Comte Langeron, *Mémoires du Comte Langeron: Austerlitz, campagne de Russie et bataille de Berlin* Paris, 1895, pp. 289–360.
30. Duffy, op. cit., p. 146, quoting a member of Soult's staff: *Mémoires du Général Comte de Saint-Chamans*, Paris, 1896, p. 27.

Chapter 10 Shattering the Myth: Aspern and Essling

1. Christopher Duffy, *Austerlitz 1805*, London, 1977, p. 162.
2. F. Loraine Petrie, *Napoleon's Conquest of Prussia*, London, 1907, p. 301.
3. See Herman Bahr, *Wien*, 1912, p. 39.
4. Hans Magenschab, *Erzherzog Johann*, Graz, 2008, p. 183.
5. F. Loraine Petrie, *Napoleon and the Archduke Charles*, London, 1909, p. 27.
6. Rudolf Ottenfeld, *Die Oesterreichische Armee von 1700 bis 1867*, Vienna, 1895, p. 172.
7. Loraine Petrie, op. cit., p. 191.
8. H. Bonnal, *Landshut 1809*, Paris, 1888, p. 67. Also Loraine Petrie, op. cit., p. 28.
9. Binder von Krieglstein, *Der Krieg Oesterreichs gegen Napoleon 1809*, Berlin, 1906, p. 252.
10. Loraine Petrie, op cit., p. 268.
11. Ibid., p. 269.

12. Herbert V. Patera (with G. Pils), *Unter Oesterreichs Fahnen*, Vienna, 1960, p. 137. (In non-patois German: 'Holen sie euch selber'.)
13. Loraine Petrie, op. cit., p. 290.
14. KA *Schreiben eines Offiziers der Cavallerie*: Kriegswissenschaftliche Mémoire Kriege gegen Preussen, Vol. II, p. 24.
15. H.V. Patera, *Unter Oesterreichs Fahnen*, Vienna, 1960, p. 54.
16. Loraine Petrie, op cit, p. 278.
17. Ibid., p. 303.

Chapter 11 Clash of Titans: Wagram

1. F. Loraine Petrie, *Napoleon and the Archduke Charles*, London, 1909, p. 352.
2. Ibid., p. 354.
3. J. Arnold, *Armies on the Danube*, New York, 1995, p. 130.
4. Ibid., p. 133.
5. Ibid., p. 131.
6. Graf Radetzky, *Der K.K. Oesterichische Feldmarshall Graf Radetzky: eine biographische Skizze*, ed. Hellwand, Stuttgart, 1858, p. 82.
7. Loraine Petrie, op. cit., p. 361.
8. Ibid., p. 139.
9. Arnold, op. cit., p. 141.
10. Loraine Petrie, op. cit., p. 371.
11. Radetzky, op. cit., p. 84.
12. Quoted by Ian Castle in *Aspern & Wagram 1809*, London, 1994, p. 90. See also Gunther Rothenberg, *The Emperor's Last Victory*, London, 2004 and James Arnold's *Napoleon Conquers Austria: The 1809 Campaign for Vienna*, London, 1995, p. 200.

Chapter 12 From Znaim to Leipzig

1. David Chandler implies this by describing it as only 'ultimately decisive': *Dictionary of the Napoleonic Wars*, London, 1979, p. 476. Alan Sked sums it up well in *Radetzky: Imperial Victor and Military Genius*, London, 2011, p. 27. Also F. Loraine Petrie, *Napoleon and the Archduke Charles*, London, 1909, p. 406.
2. Oskar Marshall von Bieberstein (ed.), *Die Memoiren des generals Rapp, Adjutanten Napoleon I*, Leipzig, 1902, p. 25 *et seq.*
3. Ibid.
4. H.V. Patera, *Unter Oesterreichs Fahnen*, Vienna, 1960, p. 58.
5. Hans Magenschab, *Andreas Hofer*, Graz, 2002, p. 198.
6. Ibid., p. 202.
7. E. Gombrich, *A Little History of the World*, London, 2005.
8. Thiers, *Histoire de la Révolution Française*, Vol. XVI, Paris, 1827. See also Radetzky, *Eine biographische Skizzze*, op. cit., p. 169.
9. F. Loraine Petrie, *Napoleon's Last Campaign in Germany 1813*, London, 1912, p. 27 et seq.
10. Graf Radetzky, *Der K.K. Oesterreïchische Feldmarshall Graf Radetzky: eine biographische Skizze*, ed. Hellwand, Stuttgart, 1858, p. 223.
11. Ibid., p. 238 *et seq.*
12. Austrian headdress became so fashionable that the Duke of Beaufort on marrying his daughter to the Austrian Ambassador in 1844 opted to equip his entire regiment of Gloucestershire Yeomanry in ornate Austrian shakos complete with 'Austrian wave' pattern decoration and Biedermeier cockades. See W.Y. Carman, *Headdress of the British Army: Yeomanry*, London, 1970. (The last survivor of these exotic items is preserved in the Gieves & Hawkes shop in Savile Row.) The Grenadier bearskins became gradually taller as the wars progressed, reaching their apotheosis in the *Adjustierung* of 1814 which epitomised the grace and simplicity of the Biedermeier age. Today a faint echo of this elegance is the smaller but definitely Austrian pattern Grenadier bearskin (and indeed drill) of the Royal Guard in Denmark, daily on parade in Copenhagen.

Chapter 13 Biedermeier, Vormärz and Radetzky

1. Gunter K. Kodek, *Von der Alchemie bis zur Aufklväerung: Chronik der Freimaurerei in Oesterreich und den Habsburgischen Kronländer*, Vols I–IX, Vienna, 1998.
2. A.E. Haswell Miller, *Vanished Armies*, London, 2009.
3. István Deák, *Der k.(u) k. Offizier: 1848–1914*, Vienna, 1991, p. 14.
4. Metternich (Vienna, 30 June, 1821 to Eszterhazy, Weisungen Grossbritannien Fasc. 217. No I.

5. Adam Wandruszka, *The House of Habsburg*, London, 1964, p. 161. It is worth noting that Kaiser Franz's strict adherence to the principles of monarchical legitimacy made him increasingly sceptical of London which, Metternich advised him, found itself in 'a false position since the revolution of 1688'. See Paul W. Schroeder, *Metternich's Diplomacy at its Zenith 1820–1823*, Austin, Texas, 1962, p. 262.
6. Charles Pridham, *Kossuth and Magyar Land*, London, 1851.
7. Gerd Holler, *Gerechtigkeit für Ferdinand*, Vienna, 1986.
8. I am grateful to the late Professor Georg Eisler and to Herr Magister Reinhold Gayer for relating this anecdote.
9. See Otto Stradal, 'War Radetzky Freimaurer?' in *Der andere Radetzky*, Vienna, 1971. Also Ludwig Jedlicka, *Vom alten zum neuen Oesterreich*, St Pölten, 1975. Professor Broucek claims to have found Radetzky's membership file in America.
10. Jedlicka, op. cit., p. 20.
11. Letters discovered among the US documents contradict attempts to downplay Signora Meregalli's importance in Radetzky's life: for example references to her merely as 'a washerwoman'. See Alan Sked, *Radetzky: Imperial Victor and Military Genius*, London, 2011, p. 112.
12. Ibid., p. 29, letter dated 23 November 1853.
13. Graf Radetzky, *Der K.K. Oesterreichische Feldmarschall Graf Radetzky*, ed. Hellwand, Stuttgart, 1858, p. 99 *et seq.*
14. Deák, op. cit., p. 40 *et seq.*
15. M. Hartley, *The Man Who Saved Austria*, London, 1927, p. 73.
16. Ibid., p. 86.
17. Deák, op. cit., p. 50.
18. H.V. Patera, *Unter Oesterreichs Fahnen*, Vienna, 1960, p. 74.
19. Ibid., p. 83.
20. Haynau has recently made rather a comeback in the Heeresgeschichtlichesmuseum (HGM). A huge portrait of him now adorns one of the walls on the first floor. Surprisingly, there is no allusion to his notoriety or the vivid controversies which marked his career.
21. Deák, op. cit., p. 53.
22. Ibid., p. 54.

Chapter 14 From Magenta and Solferino to the Düppel and Oeversee

1. Philip Guedalla, *The Second Empire*, New York, 1922, p. 273. Also see Sir Horace Rumbold, *The Austrian Court in the Nineteenth Century*. London, 1909, p. 194.
2. W. Ritter von Gruendorf, *Memoiren eines Oesterreichischen Generalsäblers*, Stuttgart, 1913, p. 73.
3. Ernst Graf Wurmbrand, *Ein Leben für alt-Oesterreich*, Vienna, 1988, p. 205 *et seq.*
4. Ibid., p. 207.
5. Oskar Regele, *FZM Benedek und der Weg nach Königgrätz*, Vienna, 1960, p. 38.
6. H.V. Patera, *Unter Oesterreichs Fahnen*, Vienna, 1960, p. 91.
7. Gruendorf, op. cit., p. 205.
8. Patera, op. cit., p. 92.
9. Crankshaw, *Bismarck*, London, 1982, p. 46.
10. Patera, op. cit., p. 93.
11. Ibid., p. 96. Also István Deák, *Der k. (und) k. Offizier: 1848–1914*, Vienna, 1991, p. 66.
12. G. Wawro, *The Austro Prussian War: Austria's War with Prussia and Italy 1866*, Cambridge, 1996, p. 21.
13. W.H. Russell, 'The finest cavalry I have ever seen', *The Times*, 11 July 1866.

Chapter 15 The Austro-Prussian War: Königgrätz 1866

1. J.H.Anderson, Campaign of 1866, London, 1908 annotated by Leo Amery: author's collection.
2. H. Bonnal, *The Campaign of 1866*, London, 1904.
3. H. Friedjung, *Der Kampf um der Vorherrschaft in Deutschland 2 vols,* 1897–98 Stuttgart, Vol I, p. 174.
4. Kriegsgeschichtliche Abteilung des grossen Generalstabs, *Der Feldzug von 1866 in Deutschland,* Berlin, 1867, chapter 2.
5. See Heinrich Ritter von Srbik, *Erzherzog Albrecht, Benedek und der altoesterreichische Soldatengeist* in *Aus Oesterreichs Vergangenheit*, Salzburg, 1949
6. *The Times*, 6 June 1866.
7. G. Wawro, *The Austro-Prussian War: Austria's War with Prussia and Italy 1866*, Cambridge, 1996.
8. Bonnal, *Campaign* p. 39.
9. Grivičič: Kriegsarchiv Vienna, KA/AFA/1866 2296.

10. Wawro, op. cit., p. 148 quoting Lettow-Vorbeck.
11. Amery annotations to Anderson, *Campaign*, op. cit., p. 15.
12. Friedjung, op. cit., p. 228.
13. See ibid., p. 228.
14. Bonnal, *Campaign*, op.cit., p. 37.
15. Wawro, op. cit., p. 227.
16. Friedjung, op. cit., p. 229.
17. Bonnal, *Campaign,* op. cit., p. 160.
18. Friedjung, op. cit., p. 233.
19. A. Craig Gordon, *Königgrätz*, Vienna, 1966, p. 224. Also Ludwig Benedek, *Benedeks Nachgelassene Papiere*, Leipzig, 1901, p. 376; Frank Zimmer, *Bismarck's Kampf gegen Kaiser Franz Josef*, Graz, 1996, p. 121.
20. H.V. Patera, *Unter Oesterreichs Fahnen*, Vienna, 1960, p. 147.
21. Regimental History IR4: *Geschichte des k. u. k. Infanterieregiment No. 4,* Hoch und Deutschmeister, Vienna, 1879, 1908, p. 87. Also quoted in Patera, op. cit., p. 105.
22. Bonnal, *Campaign*, op. cit., p. 214.
23. *The Times*, 6 June 1866.
24. Bonnal, *Campaign*, op. cit., p. 231. Later authors have disputed the scale of this cavalry battle. See e.g. Wawro, op. cit., p. 268. But Wurmbrand's eyewitness account is compelling see Ernst Graf Wurmbrand, *Ein Leben für alt-Osterreich*, Vienna, 1988, p. 304.
25. Wurmbrand, op. cit., pp. 304-6.
26. Quoted in Patera, op. cit., p. 106.
27. Srbik, op. cit., p. 14.
28. Regele, *FZM* Benedek, op. cit., Vienna, 1960, p. 389.

Chapter 16 Victories in the South: Custozza and Lissa 1866

1. PRO FO 7/708, Nr 370: Vienna, 26 June Bloomfield-Clarendon.
2. Kriegsarchiv Vienna, KA/AFA 1866, 2395 6-218.
3. G. Wawro, *The Austro-Prussian War: Austria's War with Prussia and Italy 1866*, Cambridge, 1996, p. 106, quoting Lemoyne.
4. Ibid., p. 115.
5. Ibid., p. 116.
6. H.V. Patera, *Unter Oesterreichs Fahnen*, Vienna, 1960, p. 98. For the illiteracy of Military Frontier cammanders see Caesar Scomparini, *Der Berufsoffizier der Jetztzeit: Sein Wissen seine Thätigkeit und seine soziale Stellung*, Pressburg, 1890.
7. See permanent exhibition at the Czech Military Museum, Prague.
8. J.C. Allmayer-Beck *Die K. (u.) K.- Armee 1848–1914*, Vienna, 1974, p. 104.
9. Joan Haslip, *Mexican Adventurer*, London, 1971: Helmut Neuhold, *Oesterreichs Kriegshelden*, Graz, 2012, chapter 12.
10. One of his brothers was to become an American naval officer.
11. G. Scotti, *Lissa 1866*, Trieste, 2004, p. 86 *et seq.*
12. Allmayer-Beck, op. cit., p. 109.
13. Scotti, *Lissa 1866*, op. cit., p. 138.
14. Allmayer-Beck, op. cit., p. 112.

Part 3 Imperial and Royal

Chapter 17 k. (u.) k.: The 'new army' and the Bosnian Insurgency

1. Horace Rumbold, *The Austrian Court in the Nineteenth Century* , London, 1909, p. 117.
2. István Deák, *Der k. (u.) k. Offizier 1848-1918*, Vienna, 1991, p. 71.
3. J.C. Allmayer-Beck, *Die K. (u.) K.-Armee 1848-1914*, Vienna, 1974, p. 124. Also see H.V. Patera, *Unter Oesterreichs Fahnen*, Vienna, 1960, p. 196.
4. Helmut Neuhold, *Oesterreich's Kriegshelden*, Graz, 2012, p. 233.
5. Allmayer-Beck, op. cit., p. 126.
6. Ernest Bauer, *Zwischen Halbmond und Doppeladler*, Vienna, 1971, p. 45. See Also Regimental Histories: *Geschichte des k. u. k. Peterwardeiner Infanterie Regiment Nr. 70*, Peterwardein, 1898, pp. 98–145.
7. Bauer, op.cit., p. 45.
8. See William Flavell Moneypenny and George Earle Buckle, *Life of Disraeli*, London, 6 vols, 1910–1920, Vol. VI, pp. 250 and 372.
9. Deák, op. cit., p. 81.

10. Edward Crankshaw, *Fall of the House of Habsburg*, London, 1969, p. 174.
11. Bauer, op. cit., p. 50.
12. Deák, op. cit., p. 81.
13. Werner Schachinger, *Die Bosniaken kommen*, Graz, 1989, p. 12.
14. A fine obelisk in Graz, designed under the auspices of Freiherr Bouvier von Azula, commemorates the Styrian casualties.
15. Ivo Andrić, *Na Drini Ćuprija: Most na Drini*, Belgrade, 1945, pp. 102-3 (author's translation).
16. Rumbold, op. cit., p. 118.
17. See for example the following shining example from Geoffrey Wawro, *A Mad Catastrophe*, Austin, Texas, 2014. 'Austria-Hungary had been rotting from within for years, hollowed out by repression . . . and corruption', an imaginative view of Kállay's administration. In fact as Williamson has pointed out even between 1900 and 1913, Austria-Hungary's GNP rose by a staggering 42 per cent while the industrial workforce doubled. See S. Williamson, *Austria Hungary and the Origins of World War I*, London, 1991.
18. Bauer, op. cit., p. 130.
19. G. Pils (with G. Martin and Eugen Brixen), *Das war Oesterreichs Militärmusik*, Graz, 1982.

Chapter 18 Towards a Twentieth-Century Navy: The Siege at Pekin

1. Theodor Ritter von Winterhalder, *Kaempfe in China*, Vienna, 1902, p. 200 footnote.
2. Peter Fleming, *The Siege at Peking*, Oxford, 1984.
3. See Alexander Pechmann, *Peking 1900*, Vienna, 2001, p. 22. Frau von Rosthorn gives the number as 420.
4. Wilhelm Herdtrich S.J., *Principii Confucia Vita*, Graz, 1687.
5. Pechmann (ed.), op. cit., p. 12.
6. Ibid., quoting Rosthorn, p. 54.
7. Ibid., p. 57.
8. Ibid., p. 58 *et seq.*
9. Ibid.
10. Also see Wollner, *Zinnfiguren einst und jetzt*: Anniversary toy soldier catalogue, Vienna, 2012.
11. Popper was a gifted translator of Hebrew texts into German. He died after being knocked over by a tram in 1933. An honorary Doctor of the University of Vienna, he returned this honour in 1923 when that institution introduced a numerus clausus for Jewish students. See *Welt Untergang*, catalogue to the Jüdisches Museum Wien (JMW 1914 exhibition, Vienna, 2014, p. 224 (essay by Oliver Trulei). The late naval historian David Lyon considered the model of *Viribus Unitis* in Vienna to be the finest model of a twentieth-century warship ever made.
12. Paul J. Kemp, *The Austrian Navy*, London, 1991 p. 83.

Chapter 19 Colonel Redl.: The k. (u.) k. Army on the Eve of Catastrophe

1. Max Ronge, *Krieg und Industrie Spionage*, Vienna, 1930, p. 14.
2. Ibid., p. 19.
3. Ibid.
4. Ibid., p. 20
5. Bogičević maintains the Austrian Foreign Minister Goluchowski supported the assassination. See M. Bogičević, *Kriegsursachen*, Amsterdam, 1919, p. 16. Goluchowski's attempt to arrange a dynastic marriage with a German princess had been spurned by the Obrenovićs.
6. Erich Feigl, *Kaiser Karl*, Vienna, 1984, pp. 7-26. I interviewed Herr Feigl in 1983 exhaustively on this topic. He was most convincing in presenting the circumstantial evidence though Crown Prince Otto was understandably far more cautious in evaluating his mother's version of events (author interviews: 28 January 1983, Erich Feigl; 12 November 1983, EZH Dr Otto von Habsburg). See also Bertha Szeps, *My Life and History*, London, 1938.
7. Father of the later highly distinguished Ambassador to London in the 1990s, Paolo Galli.
8. Stefan Zweig, *Die Welt von Gestern*, Stockholm, 1944.
9. Merry del Val, *Memories of Pius X*, London, 1924, p. 19. Also H. Daniel-Rops, *History of the Church of Christ*, Vol. IX, *A Fight for God* .
10. Nicolson, 27 March 1909. See F.R. Bridge, *The Diplomacy of Austria Hungary and Great Britain*, London, 1979, pp. 17-18 Also A.F. Pribram, *Austria-Hungary and Great Britain 1908-1914*, Oxford, 1951, pp. 84-5 and 232.
11. See also Zara Steiner, *Decisions for War*, London, 1984.
12. See Joyce G. Williams, *Colonel House and Sir Edward Grey*, New York, 1984.
13. See Karl Tschuppik, *The Reign of Emperor Francis Joseph*, London, 1930, pp. 399-400.

14. J.C.G. Rohl, *Delusion or Design*, London,1973, p. 29. Fritz Fischer, *Griff nach der Weltmacht*, Düsseldorf, 1962, p. 236.

15. Ibid., p. 22.

16. Ibid.

17. Georg Markus, *Der Fall Redl*, Vienna, 1984, p. 129.

18. Ibid., p. 130.

19. Ibid., 131.

20. London only had one friend during the Boer War and that was Vienna where, Franz-Josef was fond of saying, to the consternation of German diplomats, 'Dans cette affaire, je suis totalement Anglais.' See Horace Rumbold, *The Austrian Court in the Nineteenth Century*, London, 1909, p. 358. Indeed Austro-Hungarian support for the British army in South Africa even extended to offering to supply the British with Czech siege artillery (and their crews). When Edward VII over-interpreted this and lobbied hard at Bad Ischl to detach Vienna from Berlin Franz-Josef felt compelled to remind him 'Ich bin ein Deutscher Fürst' (I am a German prince). See Oesterreichische Landmannshaft, *Oesterreichs Deutsches Bekenntnis*, Vienna, 1976.

21. Ibid.

22. Spannocchi, War Diaries, KA 1909 quoted in Markus, op.cit., p. 26.

23. Bogičević, op. cit., p. 25.

24. Ronge, op. cit., p. 91.

25. Ibid., p. 83.

26. Alfons Clary-Aldringen, *Geschichten eines alten Oesterreichers*, Vienna, 1984, p. 97.

27. Egon Erwin Kisch, *Der Rasende Reporter*, Prague, 1929.

28. Ronge, op. cit., p. 85.

29. Ibid., p. 86 disputed by Markus, op. cit., p. 244.

30. Bogičević, op. cit., p. 43.

31. Markus, op. cit., p. 246.

32. See Winston Churchill, *The World Crisis*, Vol. I, London, 1929, p. 202.

33. *Pesti Hírláp Budapest*, 3 June 1914. Quoted in Markus, op. cit., p. 247.

34. Deák illustrates this: *Der k. (u)k. Offizier: 1848-1914*, Vienna, 1991, p. 216. Between 1912 and 1914 the number of officers in the Evidenzbüro increased from 28 to 42.

35. Erwin. Schmidl, 'Juden in der k.und k. Armee', in *Studia Judaica*, Eisenstadt, 1989. Also Deák, op. cit., p. 207.

36. Schmidl, op. cit., p. 49, quoting communication from Imperial and Royal General Staff to Russian High Command, 1905.

37. Ibid., p. 123. See also Marcus Patka (ed.), *Weltuntergang: Jüdisches Leben und Sterben im Ersten Weltkrieg* (catalogue), Vienna, 2014.

38. The words are often directly attributed to Franz-Josef but in fact were Lueger's later characterisation (in Viennese dialect) of the Emperor's words to him. See Richard S. Geehre (ed.), *'I decide who is a Jew': The Papers of Dr Karl Lueger*. Washington, DC, 1982. For a recent biography of Lueger see John W. Boyer, *Karl Lueger: Christlichesozial Politik als Beruf*, Vienna, 2010.

39. Arthur Schnitzler, *Jugend in Wien*, Vienna, 1968, pp. 146-7.

40. Schmidl, op. cit.

41. Ibid., p. 76.

42. Josef Roth, *Radetzkymarsch*, Cologne, 1979.

43. Otto von Habsburg, *Züruck zur Mitte*, Vienna, 1991 p. 148. Also Schmidl, op. cit., p. 74 et seq. For the contrasting situation in the German army see Bülow, op. cit., pp. 401-2.

Chapter 20 The Military Road to Sarajevo

1. Gerd Holler, *Erzherzog Franz Ferdinand von Habsburg d'Este*, Vienna, 1991.

2. Vladimir Dedijer, *The Road to Sarajevo*, New York, 1966, p. 317.

3. See Gunther Rothenberg, *The Army of Franz-Josef*, West Lafayette 1998.

4. Carl Frh. von Bardolff, *Soldat in alten Oesterreich*, Jena, 1938, p. 177.

5. Rothenberg, op. cit., p. 153.

6. Joseph Graf Stürkgh in G. Eduard Ritter von Steinitz, *Erinnerungen an Franz Josef II*, Berlin, 1931, p. 269.

7. A.J.P. Taylor, *The First World War*, London, 1967, p. 17.

8. See Holler, op. cit.; also Gordon Brook-Shepherd, *Victims at Sarajevo*, London, 1984.

9. F.R. Bridge, *Great Britian and Austria-Hungary, 1906-1914: A diplomatic history*, London, 1972, p. 127; Luigi Albertini, *Le Origini della Guerra del 1914: le relazioni europee dal Congresso di Berlino all' attentato di Sarajevo* Vols 1–III, Milan, 1942–3.

10. F.R. Bridge, op. cit., p. 199.

552   NOTES to pp. 417-29

11. The Kriegsfall DR (Deutsches Reich) had been worked up long before Edward VII's visit to Franz-Josef in Ischl in 1908 when he had promised Royal Naval support for a bombardment of Rome from Ostia. The plans instigated by Beck were immediately abandoned by Conrad on his becoming Chief of the General Staff. See Bardolff, op. cit., p. 91.
12. Lajos Windischgraetz, *My Adventures and Misadventures*, London, 1965, p. 43.
13. See Conrad Franz von Hötzendorf, *Zum Studium der Taktik*, Vienna, 1912.
14. Hartwig quoted in S. McMeekin, *The Russian Origins of the First World War*, Cambridge, Mass., 2011, p. 53.
15. Hugo Hantsch, *Leopold Graf Berchtold*, Graz, 1963.
16. Dedijer, op. cit., p. 86.
17. Ottokar Czernin, *In the World War*, London, 1921.
18. Brook-Shepherd, op. cit., p. 289.
19. Ibid.
20. Dedijer, op. cit., p. 367.
21. R.B. conversation with Kaiserin Zita, 21 August 1982. Also Brook-Shepherd, op. cit., p. 235.
22. Adam Wandruszka, *The House of Habsburg*, New York, 1965, p. 175.
23. See O.H. Wedel, *Austro-German Diplomatic Relations 1908–1914*, Oxford, 1934.
24. Dedijer, op. cit., p. 127.
25. Windischgraetz, op. cit., p. 63.
26. Samuel Williamson, *Austria-Hungary and the Origins of the First World War*, New York, 1990, p. 158.
27. W.W Gottlieb, *Studies in Secret Diplomacy during the First World War* , London, 1957, p. 45.
28. Williamson, op.cit., p. 149.
29. Peter Broucek, *Kaiser Karl*, Vienna, 1997, p. 43 *et seq.*
30. Wladimir Giesl von Gieslingen, *Zwei Jahrzehnte im Nahen Orient: Aufzeichnungen des Generals der Kavallerie: Baron Wladimir Giesl*, ed. Eduard Ritter von Steinitz, Berlin, 1927.
31. Dedijer, op. cit., p. 421.
32. Ibid., p. 386.
33. That 'Apis' was horrified when Austria declared war on Serbia is attested by Bogičević, who recalled 'Apis' saying: 'Bože! Bože! sta ucismo?' ('My God! My God! what have we done?'). See Bogičević, op. cit., p. 16 *et seq.*
34. Kriegsarchiv, KA 1914, Praes 47/4/16–40.
35. Ibid., 18.I.1914
36. Ibid., 10.V.1914
37. Bogičević, op. cit., p. 14.
38. KA 1914 Praes 47/4/16-40. Gellinek, 24.III.1914.
39. Ibid.
40. Merry del Val, *Memories of Pius X*, London, 1924, p. 19. Also D.H. Rops, *A Fight for God*, New York, 1966, Vol. IX, p. 240.
41. KA Praes 47/4/16-40, Gellinek, op. cit., 25 May 1915.
42. KA Praes 47/4/16-40, ibid., 21 July 1914.
43. Dedijer, op. cit., p. 396.
44. Stoyadinovič, quoted Dedijer., p. 416.
45. Prince von Bülow, *Memoirs*, London, 1931, pp. 396–7, 'Keep a close eye on relations with Serbia'.
46. Gottlieb, op. cit., p. 260.
47. Ibid.
48. Rapp, *Grossdeutsch-Kleindeutsch*, Munich, 1922, p. 285.
49. Henry V. Wickham Steed, *The Habsburg Monarchy*, London, 1930, p. 109.
50. E. Lewin, *Germany's Road to the East*, London, 1916, p. 255 *et seq.*
51. Dedijer, op. cit., p. 416. Also Duke of Portland, *Men, Women and Things*, London, 1932. Clary copy inscribed by Portland to 'my dear Alphy': author's collection.
52. Edith Durham, *The Serajevo Crime*, London, 1925.
53. Brook-Shepherd, op. cit., p. 229.
54. Rohl, *Delusion or Design?* London, 1973.
55. Hantsch, op. cit., Vol. II, pp. 545–66.
56. *Die Grosse der Europeaischen Kabinette* Vol. XXXIX, p. 367. Quoted in Dedijer, op. cit.
57. Ibid. Also see Bülow, op. cit., pp. 397–9, on Franz Ferdinand's antagonism towards Berlin.
58. Robert Cooper, *The Breaking of Nations*, London,2003.
59. George Buchanan, *My Mission to Russia*, London, 1923.
60. McMeekin, op. cit., p. 33.
61. Czernin, op. cit., p. 74.
62. Rudolf Jeřabek, *Potiorek: General in Schatten von Sarajevo*, Graz, 1991, p. 27 *et seq.*

63. Ibid., p. 45.
64. Czernin, op. cit., p. 78.
65. Jeřábek, op, cit., p, 29
66. Ibid., p. 43.
67. Ibid., p. 45.
68. Ibid., p. 82. Also Brook-Shepherd, op. cit., p. 241.
69. Jeřábek, op. cit., p. 84 *et seq*. This significant revelation has not saved recent studies from repeating the canard that it was Franz Ferdinand's idea to visit the wounded officer: e.g. Wawro, *Mad Catastrophe*, p. 105; Christopher Clark, *Sleepwalkers*, London, 2013, etc.
70. Jeřábek, op. cit., p. 85.
71. Ibid., p. 86, quoting Potiorek's evidence.

Chapter 21 The Army and the July Crisis

1. Margutti, *Von alten Kaiser: Vienna 1922*. Also see Gordon Brook-Shepherd, *Victims at Sarajevo*, London, 1984, and author conversation KZ, 21 August 1982.
2. V. Dedijer, *The Road to Sarajevo*, New York, 1966, p. 87.
3. L. Albertini, *Le Origini della Guerra del 1914*, Milan, 1942–3, Vol. II, p. 9 *et seq*.
4. H. Wickham Steed, *The Habsburg Monarchy*, London, 1930, p. 212.
5. Berchtold papers quoted in Hantsch, *Leopold Graf Berchtold*, Graz, 1963, p. 85.
6. Ibid., p. 85.
7. See M. Rauchensteiner, *Tod des Doppeladlers*, Graz, 1993, revised edition 2014, for an opposing point of view on Franz-Josef's role.
8. See Emil Ludwig, *July 1914*, London, 1929, p. 36.
9. Albertini, op. cit., p. 137.
10. Von Bülow, *Memoirs*, London, 1931, p. 154.
11. Author (RB) conversation with Gottfried Banfield 28 January 1979.
12. Williamson, *Austria-Hungary and the Outbreak of the First World War*, London, 1991 p. 139. Also Barabara Jelavich, *What Austria Knew about the Black Hand*, Vienna, 1991, p. 136; Austrian History Year book, Vol. XXII, Minnesota, 1991.
13. Ludwig, op. cit., p. 36. See also Bülow, op. cit., p. 158, for Franz-Joseph's form on this tactic.
14. Oswald Wedel, *Austro German Diplomatic Relations 1908–1914*, Oxford, 1934.
15. Albertini, op. cit., p. 141 et seq.
16. Ibid., pp. 147–52. Also author's conversation count Jean-George Hoyos, 8 October 1984.
17. HHSA OE-V-VIII 9966.
18. Count Jean-George Hoyos about his father to the author, 18 May 1984, Schloss Hollabrunn, Lower Austria.
19. Williamson, op. cit., p. 193.
20. Steiner, *Decisions for War*, London, 1984, p. 36.
21. Stella Musulin (daughter-in-law), conversation with author, 6 May 1984; ditto Szapáry Lázló (son), 9 September 1983, Lower Austria.
22. Giesl von Gieslingen, *Zwei Jahrzehnte im Nahen Orient*, ed. von Steinitz, Berlin, 1927, p. 161 *et seq*.
23. Albertini, op. cit., pp. 151–5.
24. F. A. Hoyos, *Der Deutsch-Englische Gegensatz und sein Einfluss auf die Balkanpolitik Oesterreich Ungarns*, Berlin, 1922, p. 12 *et seq*.
25. Albertini, op. cit., pp. 167–73.
26. Ibid., p.177.
27. Ibid., pp. 170–1 and p. 177.
28. Conrad von Hötzendorf, *Private Aufzeichnungen*, Vienna, 1983, p. 44.
29. Count Heinrich Lützow, *In diplomatischen Dienst der k.u.k. Monarchie*, Vienna, 1971, p. 158.
30. Ibid.
31. Albertini, op. cit., p. 170, 'Diplomatic success would be sterile'.
32. Ibid., pp. 281–2
33. Ibid., p. 282. Albertini strongly implies via the Serbophile Crackenthorpe, acting nunister in Belgrade.
34. Dedijer, op. cit., p. 89.
35. Albertini, op. cit., p. 179.
36. Letter from Forgách to Mérey quoted in Hantsch, op. cit., Vol. II, p. 592. 'Was nach geschehen würde ist eine andene Frage'.
37. Ibid., p. 258.
38. Von Bülow, op. cit., p. 155.
39. *Plus ça change*: for London's robust pro-Serbian stance in the 1990s see Brendan Simms, *Unfinest Hour*, London, 1998.

40. Giesl, op. cit., p. 253. Giesl to Albertini, in Albertini, op. cit., pp.151-2. The facsimile of Giesl's original letter from Salzburg dated 18 August 1932 is inserted between pp. 151 and 152 of the original Italian edition cited here.
41. Giesl op. cit., p. 167 *et seq.* These considerations illuminate the fragility of the hypothesis of Austro-German harmony and *Brüderschaft* with regard to Serbia: see for example Christopher Clark, *The Sleepwalkers*, London, 2013, which ignores Giesl's writings altogether.
42. Ibid., pp. 376–7 for the facsimile of Giesl's second letter to Albertini.
43. Giesl, ibid., p. 260.
44. Musulin, *Das Haus am Ballplatz*, Munich, 1924, p. 222 *et seq.*
45. Giesl, op. cit., p. 256. Also Musulin, op. cit., p. 226.
46. Salonika's importance as a centre of Russian intelligence was well recognised in this period. See Leo Amery, quoted by Julian Amery in *Approach March*, London, 1977, p. 156 *et seq.* Author's conversation with JA, 11 November 1991.
47. Dedijer, op. cit.
48. Musulin, op. cit., p. 241. Also see A.E. Pribram, *Austria-Hungary and Great Britain 1908-1914*, Oxford, 1951, p. 238.
49. See for example, among the crop of 2013/14, Clark, Hastings, Wawro etc.
50. Albertini, op.cit., pp. 368–9 for facsimile text of handwritten Serbian reply complete with crossings out.
51. Albertini, op. cit., quoting Kaiser Wilhelm marginalia, p. 377 *et seq.*
52. Dedijer, op. cit., p. 387.
53. Musulin, op. cit., p. 244 for analysis of its contradictions. Also Albertini, op. cit., pp. 384–5.
54. Krobatin quoted in Steinitz (ed.), *Erinnerungen an Franz-Josef I*, Berlin, 1931, p. 325.
55. Rauchensteiner, op. cit., Graz, p. 92.
56. Albertini, op. cit., p. 455 et seq.
57. Ibid., p. 457.
58. Albertini, op.cit., pp 376–81, pp. 648–50, p. 462.
59. *New York Times*, 20 August 1924.
60. Conrad, *Private Aufzeichnungen*, Vienna, 1977, p. 386.
61. Albertini, op.cit., Vol. III, pp. 272–3.
62. Maurice Paleologue, *An Ambassador's Memoirs 1914-1917*, Paris, 1925, p. 29. Also McMeekin, *The Russian Origins of the First World War*, Cambridge, Mass, 2011, p. 27.
63. Albertini, Vol. II, op.cit., p. 668.
64. Ibid., p. 669.
65. HHSA OeVA Vo. III Nr 11125, p. 944.
66. Broucek conversation with author, 1 December 2012, Vienna. See Albertini op. cit., Vol. III, p. 501 *et seq.*
67. See Edmund Glaise-Horstenau (ed.), *Oesterreich-Ungarns letzte Krieg 1914-18*, Vienna, 1929.

Chapter 22 Austria-Hungary's Last War: 1914

1. See Marcus Patka (ed.), *Welt Untergang*, Catalogue of the exhibition, *Jüdisches Leben und Sterben im Ersten Weltkrieg*, Vienna, 2014. J.M.W. 'Weltuntergang' Catalogue op. cit., pp. 218–25 for the Jewish contribution to technical development of Austria-Hungary's armed forces. Also Peter Jung, *The Austro-Hungarian Forces in World War I (2)*, Botley, 2003, p. 24.
2. August von Cramon, *Unser Oesterreich-Ungarische Bundesgenosse im Weltkrieg*, Berlin, 1922, p. 20.
3. See Deák, *Der k.(u)k. Offiziers 1848-1914*, Vienna, 1991, pp. 219–21, and Rothenberg, *The Army of Francis Joseph*, West Lafayette, 1998, p. 127.
4. Rothenberg, op. cit., p. 125.
5. Bridge, op. cit., London, 1979, pp. 214–18. Also author's conversation with Tuschi Graf Mensdorff-Pouilly, 18 January 1983, Vienna.
6. Clary, *Geschichten eines alten Oesterreichkers*, Vienna, 1984, p. 108.
7. See Bardolff, *Soldat in alten Oesterreich*, Jena, 1938, p. 169 and Bridge, op. cit., pp. 217–18.
8. See G. Brook-Shepherd, *Between Two Flags*, London, 1972. Also Richard Hill, *Slatin Pasha*, Oxford, 1965, p. 118 *et seq.*
9. Letter preserved in the officers' mess of the Queen's Dragoon Guards at Wolfenbüttel. Seen by author 15 November 1989. Also see Regimental Journal of The 1st The Queen's Dragoon Guards, Vol. 1, no. 8, 1966. Michael Mann, *Regimental History of The 1st The Queen's Dragoon Guards*, London, 1993. There is a reference in the Sandhurst RMC journal of 1924 to an officer of the KDG who reported being badly treated when he was captured by the Austrians, precisely because he was wearing the Habsburg eagle on his cap badge! Such reports in 1915 may have hastened the War Ministry's decision to re-badge the regiment though at that stage of the war the scope for British and Austrian troops to be directly engaged in hostilities against each other was limited to Palestine.

10. See Mann, op. cit., p. 352.
11. Gina Reininghaus, *Mein Leben mit Conrad von Hötzendorf*, Leipzig, 1935, p. 59.
12. Rauchensteiner, *Tod des Deppeladiers*, Graz, 1997, p. 98.
13. C. Ortner, *Oesterreich Ungarn Artillerie*, Vienna, 2007, p. 37 *et seq.*
14. Norman Stone, *The Eastern Front*, London, 1974, p. 27. Also Rauchensteiner, op. cit., p. 116.
15. Stone, op. cit., p. 81.
16. Rauchensteiner, op. cit., p. 127 puts this on 20 August.
17. Oskar Kokoschka, *My Life*, London, 1971, p. 134.
18. Botho Coreth, *Aufwachsen im Spätherbst*, Vienna, 1976, p. 76.
19. Reininghaus, op. cit., p. 63.
20. Stone, op. cit., p. 90.
21. Jeřabek, *Potiorek: General im Schatten von Sarajevo*, Graz, 1991, p. 119.
22. Ibid.
23. Ibid., p. 121.
24. Rauchensteiner, op. cit., p. 134.
25. See Rauchensteiner, op. cit., pp. 128–31.
26. Jeřabek, op. cit., p. 128.
27. Reininghaus, op. cit., p. 82.
28. Quoted in Conrad, *Private Aufzeichnungen*, Vienna, 1977, p. 79.
29. Jeřabek, op. cit., p. 142.
30. Ibid., p. 154.
31. Mrs Anthony Monkton's grandmother's 1914 Vienna diaries (unpublished), London.
32. Živojin Mišič, *Une Lutte dure et permanente*, Belgrade, 1987.
33. Tschuppik, *The Reign of the Emperor Franz-Joseph*, London, 1930, p. 487 *et seq.*
34. Jeřabek, op. cit., p. 194.
35. Ibid., p. 196.
36. Mišič, op. cit., p. 47.
37. Ronge, op. cit., p. 110.
38. Rauchensteiner, op. cit., p. 167.
39. Franz Forstner, *Przemsýl, Oesterreich-Ungarns bedeutendste Festung*, Vienna, 1987, p.127. Also Ronge, op. cit., p. 102,
40. Ronge, *Krieg und Industrie Spionage*, Vienna, 1930, p. 88.
41. Forstner, op. cit., p. 180.
42. Ibid., p. 211.
43. Ibid., p. 220.

Chapter 23 1915–1916: Bayonets in the Dolomites

1. The deployment was partly for prestige reasons as Austria had long enjoyed a strong consular presence in Jerusalem and the unique privilege of its own postal service (k. (u.) k. Levant Post). A military band accompanied the immaculately uniformed batteries and drew large crowds wherever it went in Palestine. By 1914, 9,000 Jews from Austria-Hungary had emigrated to Jerusalem, making the Austrian Consul responsible for the safety of the highest number of Jews in the area. (See Patka, *Welt Untergang*, JMW, Vienna, 2014, pp. 110–25).
2. Rauchensteiner, *Tod des Doppeladlers*, Graz, 1997, p. 175.
3. Forstner, *Przemsyl: Oesterreich-Ungarns bedeutendste Festung*, Vienna, 1987, p. 214.
4. Stone, *The Eastern Front*, London, 1974, p. 114.
5. Forstner, op. cit., p. 220.
6. Stone, op. cit., p. 115.
7. Ibid., p. 115 *et seq.*
8. Karl Kraus, *Die letzten Tage der Menschheit*, Vol. I, Vienna, 1964, p. 211. Scene 16: Ein Generaalstäbler (erscheint und geht zum Telefon) – Servus also hast den Bericht über Przemysl fertig? – Noch nicht? Ah bist nicht ausgeschlafen –Geh schau dazu, sonst kommst wieder zum Mullatieren zu spät etc. . . .
9. Gottlieb, *Studies in Secret Diplomacy during the First World War*, London, 1957, p. 283.
10. Ibid., p. 285.
11. See Anna Millo, *L'elite del Potere*, Trieste, 1983.
12. Reininghaus, *Mein Leben nict Conrad von Hötzendorf*, Leipzig, 1935, p. 127.
13. Rauchensteiner, op. cit., p. 229.
14. Gottlieb, op. cit., p. 260.
15. Documenti Diplomatici (370, p. 203) quoted in Gottlieb, op. cit.,, p. 227.
16. Kriegserklaerung, 24 May 1915 (author's collection).

17. Stone devoted three sentences to this: see Stone, op. cit., p. 178. Rauchensteiner, op. cit., p. 212 *et seq.*
18. Rauchensteiner, op. cit., p. 283 et seq.
19. Ibid., quoting Colonel Bridler, p. 217.
20. Giorgio Voghera, *Gli Anni di Trieste*, Gorizia, 1994. Also Banfield, op. cit. p. 55.
21. Banfield to author 21 January 1979 and 5 April 1983.
22. Kemp, *The Austrian Navy*, London, 1991, p. 87.
23. Rauchensteiner, op. cit., p. 244.
24. Ibid., p. 245.
25. Ibid., p. 293.
26. Stone, op. cit., p. 122.
27. Falkenhayn quoted in Rauchensteiner, op. cit., p. 307.
28. Ibid., p. 307.
29. Schmidl, *Juden in der k. (u.) k. Armee 1788–1918*, Eisenstadt, 1989, p. 144.

Chapter 24 1916–1918: The End of the Old Army

1. Kemp, *The Austrian Navy*, London, 1991, p. 11.
2. Rauchensteiner, *Tod des Doppeladlers*, Graz, 1997, p. 318.
3. Ibid., p. 314.
4. Gabriele Matzner-Holzer, *Verfreundete Nachbarn*, Vienna, 2005, p. 68.
5. Rauchensteiner, op. cit., p. 338.
6. Peter Broucek, *Kaiser Karl I*, Vienna, 1997, pp. 386.
7. KZ to RB 1982.
8. Rauchensteiner, op. cit., p. 339 *et seq.*
9. Conrad, *Private Aufzeichnongen*, Vienna, 1977, p. 355.
10. Ibid., p. 357.
11. Windischgraetz, *My Adventures and Misadventures*, London, 1965, p. 143.
12. Rauchensteiner, op. cit., p. 359.
13. Ibid., p. 366.
14. Both Norman Stone and Anatole Lieven have amused me with this plausible anecdote over the decades. It has defied documentary confirmation from more conventional sources.
15. Josef Redlich, *Franz Josef*, London, 1926, p. 179.
16. Gottfried Banfield to author, 23 January 1979, Trieste.
17. Anatole France, *Correspondences*, Paris, 1924.
18. Herbert Vivian, *Life of the Emperor Charles*, London, 1929, p. 63.
19. Tschuppik, op cit., p. 494 et seq.
20. Kokoschka, *My Life*, London, 1971, p. 82.
21. Joan Haslip, *The Emperor and the Actress*, London, 1985, p. 270.
22. Herberstein quoted in Rauchensteiner, op. cit., p. 383.

Chapter 25 *Finis Austriae?*

1. Wolf von Schierbrand, *Austria-Hungary: The Polyglot Empire*, New York, 1917, p. 273.
2. Kaiserin Zita, conversation with RB, 21 August 1982, Schloss Waldstein. See also Bülow, op. cit., p. 153 for Berlin's point of view.
3. *Neue Freie Presse*, 12 December 1916.
4. Ibid., 5 January 1917.
5. Grey to de Bunsen, London, 23 July 1914 in quoted H.M.S.O., *War 1914: Punishing the Serbs*, London, 1999, p. 18.
6. Ibid., p. 14.
7. H. Kissinger, *Diplomacy*, London, 1992, pp. 294 and 810 *et seq.*
8. K.E. Czernin, *Die Sixtusaffare*, Enzersfeld, 2004. This did not prevent German accusations of Treachery. See Bülow, op. cit., p. 153.
9. Brook-Shepherd, *The Last Habsburg*, London, 1968, p. 241.
10. RB conversation KZ, August 1983
11. Ibid.
12. Brook-Shepherd, op. cit., p. 84.
13. Hantsch, *Leopold Graf Berchtold*, Graz, 1963, p. 594.
14. Stone, *The Eastern Front*, London, 1974, p. 282.
15. See Naval Air Station, Trieste, *War Diary*, 5 November 1916. Also Peter Schupita, *Die K.u.K. Seeflieger*, Vienna, 1983, p. 192.

16. M. Rauchensteiner (ed.), *Waffentreue: Die 12 Isonzoschlacht 1917*, Vienna, 2007, essay by Franz Felberbauer on gas deployment, pp. 13–33, idem., Felix Radax, pp. 49–63.
17. Wolfgang Zecha, *Unter der Masken: Giftgas auf den Kriegschauplätzen Oesterreich-Ungarn im Ersten Weltkrieg*, Vienna, 2000, p. 16 *et seq.*
18. Dieter Martinetz, *Der Gaskrieg 1914/18: Entwicklung, Herstellung und Einsatz chemischer Kampfstoffe*, Bonn, 1996, p. 100.
19. Rauchensteiner (ed.), op. cit., p. 45.
20. Zecha, op. cit., p.73. Clark I and Clark II were especially poisonons (Chlorarsenkampfstoff)
21. Schupita, op. cit., p. 180.
22. Fritz Weber, *Menschenmauer am Isonzo*, Vienna, 1932.
23. Ernest Bauer, *Der Löwe von Isonzo*, Graz, 1987, p. 99.
24. See Ernest Hemingway, *A Farewell to Arms*, New York, 1929.
25. Felberbauer, in Rauchensteiner (ed.), op. cit., p. 29.
26. Richard Fester, *Die Politik Kaiser Karls und der Wendepunkt des Weltkrieges*, Berlin, 1926, p. 186.
27. Both the Empress Zita and Czernin were aware of this. Oberst Max Bauer, a German officer on the German General Staff makes frequent references to this, notably to a German occupation of Prague. See Oberst Bauer, *Der Grosse Krieg in Feld und* Also Erich Feigl (ed.), *Kaiser Karl*, Vienna, 1984, p. 183. *Heimat: Erinnerungen und Betrachtungen*, Bauer Papers (Coblenz) Also Ronge, *Krieg und Industrie Spionage*, Vienna, 1930, p. 345 *et seq.*
28. Edmund Glaise-Horstenau, *Die Katastrophe*, Vienna, 1928, p. 221 *et seq.* Also see Erich Feigl (ed.) *Kaiser Karl*, Vienna, 1984, p. 183; Christopher Brennan, 'Reforming Austria-Hungary: The Domestic Policies of Emperor Karl I' (unpublished PhD thesis, LSE, London, 2012).
29. Schupita, op. cit., p. 196.
30. Bauer, *Der Löwe*, op. cit., p. 76.
31. Peter Feldl, *Das verspielte Reich*, Vienna, 1969, pp. 148–153.
32. Feigl, op. cit., p. 7–15. Also Szeps, op. cit., p. 46; and KZ to RB, conversation 25 August 1983, Waldstein, Styria.
33. Czernin, op. cit., p. 22.
34. Univ. Prof Hofrat Peter Broucek lecture, 19 February 2004, Vienna: 'Kaiser Karl als Staatsman'.
35. Glaise-Horstenau, op. cit., p. 223.
36. Bauer, *Der Löwe*, op. cit., p. 102.
37. Glaise-Horstenau, *Katastrophe*, op. cit., p. 136.
38. Ibid., p. 341.
39. Ibid., p. 344.
40. Feigl, op. cit., pp. 314–16.
41. Friedrich Funder quoted by Bauer, *Der Löwe*, op. cit., p. 126.
42. Brook-Shepherd, *The Last Habsburg*, London, 1968, p. 241. p. 186.

Chapter 26 Aftermath

1. *Grillparzer's Werke*, ed. Rudolf Frank, Leipzig, 1890, Vol. III, p. 346: *König Ottokar's Glück und Ende*, Act III.
2. Bauer, *Der Löwe von Isonzo*, Graz, 1987, p. 128.
3. RB in conversation with Gottfried Banfield, 28 January 1979, Trieste.
4. See Richard Bassett, *Hitler's Spy Chief*, London, 2005, p. 149.
5. See Ingomar Post, *Oesterreich in Feuer*, Graz, 2013.
6. See Brook-Shepherd, *The Last Habsburg*, London, 1968, op. cit., p. 267.
7. Schmidl, *Juden in der k. (u.) k. Armee 1788–1918*, Eisenstadt, 1989, p. 150.
8. See the superb Heeresgeschichtlichesmusuem (HGM) publication accompanying the exhibition 'Alexander Pock – Militärmalerei als Beruf', Vienna, 2012.
9. E. Schroedinger, *What is Life?*, Cambridge, 2001.
10. Fritz Kreisler, *Six Weeks in the Trenches*, New York, 1916.

SELECTED BIBLIOGRAPHY

Part 1 The Habsburg Connection

Vienna Kriegsarchiv

Altes Artillerie Archiv

Feldakten
Hofkriegsrätliche Akten: Allgemeine Korrespondenz des Hofkriegsrates
Kabinettsakten: Persönliche Korrespondenz zwischen Maria Theresia und ihren Offizieren (incl. FM Daun)
M.M.T.O. Archiv
Neustädter Akten: Schriftstücke
Ungarische Akten

Vienna Haus Hof und Staatsarchiv

Bratislava Štátny Ustredný Fond Pálfy-Daun
Budapest Hadtörteneti Intézet és Múzeum
Hadik Lévéltár
Staatskanzlei Vorträge: Kaunitz Memoranden
FM Lacy Nachlass
Wiener Stadt und Landarchiv
(MA 8) HA9009 Zur Belagerung Wiens

Pannonhalma (St Martinsberg) Hungary

Speculum Christiani Hominis et Jesuitae sive Vita et Virtutes P. Gulielmi Germam Lamormaini. 1619–32

Official publications of the Austrian Army

Generals-Reglement. Vienna, 1769
Regulament und Ordnung des gesammten Kaiserlich-Koeniglichen Fuss-Volcks, 2 volumes. Vienna, 1749
Regulament und Ordung für Gesammte Kaiserl. Koenigl. Husaren Regimenter. Vienna, 1751
Reglement für das Kaiserlich Königlich Gesammte Feld-Artilleriecorps. Vienna, 1757
Reglement für die sämmentlich Kaiserlich Königlich Infanterie. Vienna, 1769

Memoirs

Archenholz, Johann Wilhelm von, Geschichte des siebenjährigen Krieges in Deutschland. Vols 1–2. Frankfurt, 1788

——*Gemälde der preussichen Armee vor und in dem siebenjährigen Krieg*. Osnabrück, 1974

Arneth, Alfred (ed.), *Briefe der Kaiserin Maria Theresa an ihre Kinder und Freunde*. Vienna, 1881

Bisset, Andrew (ed.), *Memoirs and Papers of Sir Andrew Mitchell*. London, 1850

Cognazzo, J., *Freymütiger Beytrag zur Geschichte der Oesterreichen Militärdienstes*. Frankfurt, 1789

Lamormaini, Wilhelm S.J., *Virtutes Ferdinand II*. Graz, 1638

Lehman, Max, *Friedrich der Grosse und der Ursprung des sieben Jährigen Krieg*. Leipzig, 1894

Ligne, Prince Karl Joseph, *Mélanges militaires*. Leipzig, 1754

Memoirs of the House of Taaffe. Vienna, 1856

Militaerische Correspondenz des Koenigs Friedrich des Grossen mit dem Prinzen Heinrich von Preussen. Berlin, 1851–54

Podewils, Count Otto, *Friedrich der Grosse und Maria Theresa*. Berlin, 1937

Politische Correspondenz Friedrich der Grosse (ed. J.G. Droysen u.a.). Berlin, 1879–1939, Vols 1–43

Prittwitz und Gaffron, Christian Wilhelm, *Unter der Fahne des Herzogs von Bevern*. Berlin, 1955

Roper, William, *Life of Thomas More*. London, 1553

Tempelhoff, Georg Friedrich von, *Geschichte des siebenjährigen Krieges in Deutschland*, Vols 1–6, Berlin, 1783–1801

Wraxall, Nathaniel William, *Memoirs of the Courts of Berlin, Dresden, Warsaw and Vienna 1777–9*. London, 1800

Wrede, Alphons Frh. von, *Geschichte der k.u.k. Wehrmacht von 1618*. Vienna, 1898

Selected secondary sources

Adler, Viktor, *Protokoll der Internationale Arbeiter Congress zu Paris*. Vienna, 1890

Allmayer-Beck, J.C., *Die kaiserlichen Kriegsvoelker 1479–1718*. Munich, 1978

——*Der Aufbau des Oesterreichischen Heerwesens* (Catalogue 'Maria Theresa und ihre Zeit'). Vienna, 1980

——*Das Heer unter dem Doppeladler 1718–1848*. Munich, 1981

——*Das Heerwesen unter Josef II* (Catalogue Josef II). Melk, 1980

——*Die K. (u.) K.-Armee 1848–1914*. Vienna, 1974

Arneth, A. Geschichte, *Maria Theresia*, Vols 1–19. 1869–1879

Badone Giovanni, *Le Aquili e i gigli: una Storia mai scritta*. Milan, 1869

Balbinus, Bohuslaus, *Epitome rerum Bohemicarum*. Prague, 1677

Barker, Thomas M., *Double Eagle and Crescent: Vienna's Second Turkish Siege*. New York, 1967

Bassett, Richard, *The Austrians*. London, 1988

Bauer, F.H. *Der Hinterlad Carabin System Crespi*. Vienna, 1977

Beales, Derek, *A History of Joseph II*, Vol. 2. Cambridge, 2009

Belloc, Hilaire, *Six British Battles*. London, 1931

Benedikt, H., *Als Belgien Oesterreich war*. Vienna, 1965

Blanning, Timothy, *Joseph II and Enlightened Despotism*. Harlow, 1994

Blau, Friedrich, *Die deutschen Landsknechte*. Görlitz, 1882

Bobič, Pavlina., *War and Faith: The Catholic Church in Slovenia 1914–1918*. Boston, 2012

Boehm, Bruno, *Prinz Eugen als Feldherr* (bibliography). Vienna, 1943

Braubach, Max, *Prinz Eugen von Savoy*. Vienna, 1963

Broucek, Peter, *Der Schwedenfeldzug nach Niederoesterreich 1645/1646*. Vienna, 1967

Browning, Reed, *The War of the Austrian Succession*. New York, 1993

Caspar, M. and van Dyck, W. (eds), *Johannes Keppler in seinen Briefen*. Munich, 1930

Chambers, R.W., *Thomas More*. London, 1938

Christoph, Paul, *Maria Theresia und Marie Antoinette, Ihr Geheimer Briefwechsel*. Vienna, 1952

Cognazzo, J., *Freymütiger Beytrag zur Geschichte des Oesterreichen Militärdienstes*. Frankfurt, 1789

Coreth, Anna, *Pietas Austriaca*. Munich, 1982

Coxe, William, *A History of the House of Austria*, Vols 1–3. London, 1853

Craig, Gordon A., 'Command and Staff problems in the Austrian Army 1740–1866', in *The Theory and Practice of Wars: Essays presented to Capt.Basil Liddell Hart*. London, 1965

Crankshaw Edward, *The Fall of the House of Habsburg*. London, 1963

——*The Habsburgs*. London, 1971

——*Maria Theresa*. London, 1969

Czernin, K.E., *Die Einzig gerechte Sache*. Enzersfeld, 2013

——*Die Sixtusaffaire*. Enzersfeld (second reprint), 2004

Dolleczek, Anton, *Geschichte der oesterreichischen Artillerie von den früehesten Zeiten bis zur Gegenwart*. Vienna, 1887

——*K. u. K. Blank und Handwaffen*. Vienna, 1894

Droysen, J.G. (ed.), *Politische Korrespondenz Friedrich der Grosse*, Vols 1–43. Berlin, 1879–1939
Duffy, Christopher, *FM Browne*. Vienna, 1966
——*Sieben Jahre Krieg. Die Armee Maria Theresias*. Vienna, 2003
——*The Army of Maria Theresa: the Armed Forces of Imperial Austria 1740–1780*. London, 1977
——*The Military Experience in the Age of Reason*. London, 1987
——*The Wild Goose and the Eagle*. London, 1964
Egg, Erich, *Der Tiroler Geschutzguss 1400–1600*. Innsbruck, 1960
Eickhoff, Ekkehard, *Venedig, Wien und die Osmanen, 1645–1700*. Munich, 1970
Evans, R.J.W., *The Making of the Habsburg Monarchy*. Oxford, 1979
——*Rudolf II and his World*. Oxford, 1986
Fludd, Robert, *The Squesing of Peter Foster's Sponge*. London, 1631
Frauenholz, E. von, *Das Heereswesen in der Zeit der Dreissigjährigenkrieg*, Vols 1–2. Munich, 1938
Gestrich, Andreas, *Das Wiener Diarium in sieben jährigen Krieg*. Göttingen, 2006
Gindely, Anton, *Rudolf II und seine Zeit*. Prague, 1868
Gribeauval, Jean Baptiste, *Réglement concernant les fonts et les constructions de l'artillerie de France*, Vols 1–3. Paris, 1764–92
Grillparzer, Franz, *Grillparzers Werke*: ed. Rudolf Franz, Vol. 3. Vienna, 1903
Grünwald, M., *Samuel Oppenheimer und sein Kreis*. Vienna, 1928
——*Geschichte der Juden in Wien 1625–1740*. Vienna, 1913
Gunther, Franz, *Von Ursprung und Brauchtum der Landsknechte*: Institut für Oesterreichische Geschichts Forschung. Vienna, 1953
Habsburg, Otto von, *Zurück zur Mitte*. Vienna, 1991
Hamilton, Lord Frederick, *The Vanished Pomps of Yesterday*, London, 1921.
Hartley, M., *The Man Who Saved Austria*. London, 1912
Haythornthwaite, Philip, *The Austrian Army 1740–80*. London, 1991–95
Henderson, Nicholas, *Prince Eugen*. London, 1964
Hess, Gottfried, *Graf Pappenheim*. Leipzig, 1855
Hildebrandt, C., *Anekdoten und Characterzüge aus dem Leben Friedrichs der Grosse*, 6 vols. Halberstadt, 1829
Hirtenfeld, Jaromir, *Der Militaer-Maria Theresien Orden und seine Mitglieder*. Vienna, 1857
Historisches Museum der Stadt Wien, Catalogue to the 82nd special exhibition: *Die Türken vor Wien*. Vienna, 1983
Höbelt, Lothar, *Böhmen*. Vienna, 2013
Hochedlinger, Michael, *Austria's Wars of Emergence: War, State and Society in the Habsburg Monarchy 1683–1797*. London, 2003
——'Mars ennobled: the ascent of the military and the creation of a military nobility in mid 18th century Austria', *German History* XVII (1999), 141
Hoehn, Reinhard, *Revolution Heer*. Darmstadt, 1944
Hoyos, Philipp, *Die Kaiserliche Armee 1648–1650*. Vienna, 1976
Hurter-Ammann, F.E. von, *Geschichte Kaiser Ferdinands II und seiner Eltern bis zu dessen Krönung in Frankfurt*. Schaffhausen, 1850
Jedlicka, Ludwig, *Maria Theresia in ihren Briefen und Staatsschriften*. Vienna, 1955
Jobst, J., *Die Neustadter Burg und die k. u. K. Theresianische Militärakademie*. Wiener Neustadt, 1908
Kallbrunner, Josef, *Maria Theresia's Politisches Testament*. Vienna, 1952
Karajan, Th.G. von, *Maria Theresa und Graf Emmanuel Sylva-Tarouca*. Vienna, 1856
Karniel, Josef, *Die Toleranzpolitik Kaiser Josephs II*. Gerlingen, 1986
Kessel, Eberhard, 'Beiträge zu Loudon's Lebensgeschichte', in *Mitt. Des Instituts für Oest. Geschichtsforschung*, Vol. LIV. Vienna, 1942
Khevenhueller-Metsch, J.J., *Aus der Zeit Maria Theresas 1742–1766*, Vols 1–4. Vienna, 1907
Klopp, O., *Corrispondenza epistolare tra Leopoldo Imperatore*, ed. P. Marco d'Aviano, Vol. 1., Graz, 1888
Kohlrausch, Frederick, *A History of Germany*. London, 1844
Kotasek, Edith, *FM Graf Lacy*. Horn, 1956
Kriele, Johann, *Schlacht bei Kunersdorf*. Berlin, 1801
Krones, F., *Ungarn unter Maria Theresa und Josef II*. Graz, 1871
Kunisch, Johannes, *FM Laudon: Jugend und erste Kriegsdienste*. Vienna, 1972
Lamormaini S.J., Wilhelm, *Virtutes Ferdinand II Romanorum Imperatoris*. Graz, 1638
Leitner von Leitnertreu, T.I., *Ausführliche Geschichte der Wiener Neustädter Militaerakademie*. Hermannstadt, 1852
Loraine Petrie, F., *Napoleon's Conquest of Prussia 1806*. London, 1907
Lorenz, G., *Quelle zu Geschichte Wallensteins*. Vienna, 1987
Ludwigstorff, George, *Der Militär Maria Theresien Orden (Stolzer und Seeb Oesterreichs Orden vom Mittelalter bis zur Gegenwart*, Graz, 1996)

Lützow, Count Francis, *Bohemia*. London, 1919

Macaulay, Lord, *Essay on Frederick the Great*. Vol. VI of *Life and Works* (pp. 645 *et seq.*). London, 1897

Macmunn, George, *Prince Eugene*. London, 1934

Mann, Golo, *Wallenstein: Sein Leben erzählt*. Frankfurt, 1971

Matzner-Holzer, Gabriele, *Verfreundete Nachbarn*. Vienna, 2005

Mention, L., *L'Armée sous l'ancien régime*. Paris, 1900

Millar, Simon, *Kolin 1757: Frederick the Great's First Defeat*. Oxford, 2001

Mirabeau, Vicomte de, *Système militaire de la Prusse*. Paris, 1788

Mitranov, P. von, *Josef II*. Vienna, 1910

Montecuccoli, Raimondo, *Dell'arte militare*. Venice, 1657

Morris, E. E., *The Early Hanoverians*. London, 1886

Namier, Lewis, *Conflicts: Studies in Contemporary History*. London, 1942

Naude, Albert, *Zur Schlacht bei Kunersdorf: Forschungen zur Brandenburgishen und Preussichen Geschichte*, Vol. 6. Berlin, 1893

Ottenfeld, Rudolf, *Die Oesterreichische Armee von 1700 bis 1867*. Vienna, 1895

Paganel, Camillo, *Storia di Giuseppe Secondo*. Milan, 1843

Parrott, David, *The Business of War*. Cambridge, 2012

Patera, H. von (with Gottfried Pils), *Unter Oesterreichs Fahnen*. Vienna, 1960

Peball, Kurt, *Die Schlacht bei St Gotthard 1664*. Vienna, 1964

Pekař, Josef, *'Bila hora'*: Prague, 1922 (reprinted in Jaroslav Meznik, *Josef Pekař a historicke myty*. Pekajovske Studie. Prague, 1995)

Pereira S.J., Benedictus, *De Magia de observatione somniorum et de divination astrologia*. Cologne, 1598

Pesendorfer, Franz, *FM Loudon: Der Sieg und sein Preis*. Vienna, 1989

Poetner, Regina, *The Counter Reformation in Central Europe: Styria 1580–1630*. Oxford, 2001

Randa, Alex, *Das Weltreich: Wagnis und Auftrag Europas in 16 und 17 Jahrhundert*. Vienna, 1962

——*Oesterreich in Uebersee*. Vienna, 1966

Regele, Oskar, *Der Oesterreischiche Hofkriegsrat 1556–1848*. Cologne, 1949

Rilke, Rainer Maria, *Die Weise von Liebe und Tod des Cornets Christoph Rilke*. Leipzig, 1912

Robitschek, Norbert, *Hochkirch: Eine Studie*. Vienna, 1905

Rops, Daniel H., *History of the Church of Christ* in *The Church in the Eighteenth Century*, Vols 1–9, Vol. 7. London. 1964

Rosenkranz, G.J., *Graf Johann Sporck*. Paderborn, 1954

Rothenberg, Gunther E., *Die Oesterreichische Militärgrenze in Kroatien 1522–1881*. Vienna, 1970

Schefers, Johann, *Johann Graf von Sporck*. Delbrück, 1998

Schlag, Gerald, *Unser Leben und Blut*. Vienna, 1998

Schmidl, Erwin, *Juden in der k. (u.) k. Armee 1788–1918*. Eisenstadt, 1989

——*Habsburgs Jüdische Soldaten 1788–1918*. Vienna, 2014

Schmidt, Georg, *Bibliographie Literatur Wallensteins*. Graz, 1884

Schmieder, K.C., *Geschichte der Alchemie*. Halle, 1832

Schuschnigg, Kurt von, *Helden der Ostmark*. Vienna, 1937

Schwarz, H.F., *The Imperial Privy Council in the 17th Century*. Cambridge, Mass., 1943

Seton-Watson, R.W., *History of the Czechs and Slovaks*. London, 1943

Sokol, Hans, *Die k.u.k. Militärgrenze*. Vienna, 1967

Spencer, Charles Blenheim, *Battle for Europe*. London, 2005

Srbik, Heinrich Ritter von, *Wallenstein's Ende*. Vienna, 1920

Stadtmuseum Vienna, Catalogue to Exhibition *300 Jahrfeier der Entsatz Wiens*. Vienna, 1983

Stone, Norman, *The Eastern Front*. London, 1974

Stoye, John, *Siege of Vienna*. London, 2000

Sturminger, W., *Bibliographie und Ikonographie der Türkenbelagerungen Wiens 1529 und 1683*. Graz, 1955

Svoboda, J., *Die Theresianische Militärakademie zu Wiener Neustadt und ihre Zoeglinge*. Vienna, 1894

Szabo, Franz A.J., *The Seven Years War in Europe*. Harlow, 2008

——*Kaunitz and Enlightened Absolutism 1753–1780*. Cambridge, 1994

Taylor, A.J.P., *The Habsburg Monarchy*. London, 1948

Teply, K., *Die Einführung des Kaffees in Wien: Georg Franz Kolschitzky*. Vienna, 1980

Thadden, F.L., *FM Daun*. Munich, 1961

Thuerheim, Andreas, *FM Otto Ferdinand von Abensperg und Traun*. Vienna, 1877

Tietze, S., *Die Juden Wiens*. Leipzig, 1933

Tolstoy, L.N., *War and Peace*, Vols 1–2. London, 1964

Valentinisch, Helfried, *Ferdinand II, die Inneroesterreichischen Länder und der Gradiskanerkrieg 1615–1618*. Graz, 1975

Wandruszka, Adam, *The House of Habsburg*. New York, 1964

Watson, Francis, *Soldier under Saturn*. London, 1938

Wawro, Geoffrey, *A Mad Catastrophe: The Outbreak of World War One and the Collapse of the Empire of the Habsburgs*, Texas, 2014
Wheatcroft, G., *Enemy at the Gates*. London, 1997
Wilson, Peter H., *Europe's Tragedy*. London, 2009
Zoellner, Erich and Moecke, Hermann (eds), *Oesterreich im Zeitalter des aufgeklärten Absolutismus*. Vienna, 1992

Part 2: Revolution and Reaction

Primary sources

Feldakten
Haus Hof und Staatsarchiv (HHSA)
Kabinettsakten
Kriegsarchiv Vienna (KA)
Kriegswissenschaftliche Mémoires
Krieg 1809, 4 vols. Vienna, 1907–1910 (KA)
Oesterreichische Militärische Zeitschrift (ÖMZ), Vols 1–8
Oesterreichische Feldakten in 1866 (k.k. Generalstabsbureau für Kriegsgeschichte) Vienna, 1867
Public Record Office (PRO)
The Times, June 1866 (London Library, Times Room)

Selected secondary sources

Anon., *Schreiben eines Offiziers der Cavallerie: Memoires Kriege gegen Preussen II*. Vienna, 1791
Allmayer-Beck, J.C., *Der Feldzug der oesterreischichen Nord Armee nach Königgrätz in Entscheidung 1866*. Stuttgart, 1966
——*Die K. (u.) K. Armee 1848–1914*. Munich, 1974
——'Der Tiroler Volksaustand im Kriegeschehen 1809', in *Der Donauraum*, Vol. V, 1960
Amstaedt, Jakob, *Die k.k. Militärgrenze 1522–1888*. Würzburg, 1969
Anderson, J.H. *The Austro-Prussian War in Bohemia 1866*. London, 1908
Angeli, Moritz von, *Zur Geschichte des k.k. Generalstabes*. Vienna, 1876
Anger, Gilbert, *Illustrierte Geschichte der k.u.k. Armee*. Vienna, 1886
Archduke Charles (EZH Carl), *Gruendsaetze der Strategie 1796*. Vienna, 1804
Arnold, James, *Marengo & Hohenlinden*. London, 1999
——*Napoleon Conquers Austria*. London, 1995
Bahr, Hermann, *Wien*. Vienna, 1912
Bancalari, Gustav, *Quellen der oesterreichischen Kriegs und Organisations Geschichte Nr 2*. Vienna, 1872
Bartsch, Rudolf, *Der Volkskrieg in Tirol*. Vienna, 1905
Barus, Martin (Komitet pro udrzovani pamatek z valky roku 1866), *Das Denkmal des Kavalleriegefechtes bei Strezetice*. Hradec Králové, 2009
Benedek, Ludwig, *Benedeks nachgelassene Papiere*. Leipzig, 1901
Bieberstein, Marshall Oskar von (ed.), *Die Memoiren des general Rapp, Adjutanten Napoleon I*. Leipzig, 1902
Bleibtreu, Karl, *Das Geheimnis von Wagram und andere Studien*. Dresden, 1887
Bonnal, H., *La Manoeuvre de Landshut 1809*. Paris, 1905
—— *Sadowa*. London, 1907
Bowden, Scott (with Chas Tarbox), *Armies on the Danube*. Chicago, 1990
Boycott Brown, Martin, *The Road to Rivoli*. London, 2001
Brehm, Bruno, *1809: Zu früh und zu spät*. Salzburg, 1958
Carman, W.Y., *Headdress of the British Army: Yeomanry*. London, 1970
Castle, Ian, *Aspern and Wagram 1809*. London, 1994.
Craig, Gordon A., *Königgrätz*. Vienna, 1966
Crankshaw, Edward, *Bismarck*. London, 1981
Criste Oscar: *Erzherzog Carl von Oesterreich*. Vienna, 1912
——*FM Johannes Fürst von Liechtenstein*. Vienna, 1905
Daniel-Rops, H., *History of the Church of Christ*, Vols 1–9. London, 1965
Deák, István, *Der k. (u.) k. Offizier: 1848–1914*. Vienna, 1991
Debidour, Antonin, *Etudes critique sur la Révolution*. Paris, 1886
——*Recueil des Actes du Directoire Executif*, Vols 1–4. Paris, 1910
Dirrheimer, Gunther, *Die k.k. Armee des Biedermeiers*. Vienna, 1975

Drimmel, Heinrich, *Franz von Oesterreich*. Vienna, 1982
Duffy, Christopher, *Austerlitz 1805*. London, 1977
Ferrero, Guglielmo, *The Gamble: Bonaparte in Italy 1796-7*. London, 1939
Friedjung, Heinrich, *Der Kampf um der Vorherrschaft in Deutschland*. Stuttgart, 1897
Geehre, Richard S. (ed.), *'I decide who is a Jew': The Papers of Dr Karl Lueger*. Washington, DC, 1982
Gentz, Fr., *Briefe an Pilar*. Vienna, 1868
Gestrin, F., *Slovensk Zgovina 1813-1914*. Ljubljana, 1950
Gill, John, H., *Thunder on the Danube: Napoleon's Defeat of the Habsburgs, Vols 1-3*. Barnsley, 2010
Glaise Horstenau, Edmund von, *Franz-Josef's Weggefährte: Das Leben des Generalstabschefs Grafen Beck*. Zurich, 1930
Gogg, Karl, *Oesterreichs Kriegsmarine 1848-1918*. Salzburg, 1967
Groote, W., *Napoleon und das Heerwesen seiner Zeit*. Freiburg, 1968
Grosser Generalstab, *Der Feldzug von 1866 in Deutschland*. Berlin, 1867
Gruendorf, W. Ritter von, *Memoiren eines Oesterreichischen Generalstäblers*. Stuttgart, 1913
Guibert, François Apolline comte de, *Essai général de tactique*. Vols 1-3. Paris, 1773
Gunther, Martin, *Der Heldenberg*. Vienna, 1970
Hartley, M., *The Man Who Saved Austria*. London, 1927
Haslip, Joan, *Imperial Adventurer*. London, 1971
Haswell Miller, A.E. *Vanished Armies*. London, 2009
—— (and N.P. Dawnay), *Military Drawings and Paintings in the Royal Collection*. London, 1966
Holler, Gerd, *Gerechtigkeit für Ferdinand*. Vienna, 1986
Hormay zu Hartenburg, Josef, *Lebensbilder aus dem Befreiungskriege*. Jena, 1841
Horsetzky, Adolf von, *Kriegsgeschichtliche Übersicht der Feldzeuge seit 1792*. Vienna, 1914
Hüffer, Herman, *Quellen zur Geshichte des Krieges von 1799*. Leipzig, 1900
Jedlicka, Ludwig, *Erzherzog Carl, der Sieger von Aspern*. Vienna, 1962
—— *Von alten zum neuen Oesterreich*. St Pölten, 1975
—— *Hoch und Deutschmeister: 700 Jahre*. Vienna, 1944
Kodek, Gunter K., *Von der Alchemie bis zur Aufklärung: Chronik der Freimaurerei in Oesterreich und das Habsburgischen Kronländer, Vols I-IX*. Vienna, 1998
Kohlrausch, Frederick, *A History of Germany*. London, 1844
Krieglstein, Binder von, *Der Krieg Oesterreichs gegen Napoleon 1809*. Berlin, 1906
Kriegsgeschichtliche Abteilung des grossen Generalstabs, *Der Feldzug von 1866 in Deutschland*. Berlin, 1867
Langeron, comte, *Mémoires: Austerlitz, campagne de Russie et battaille de Berlin*. Paris, 1895
Lecomte, F., *Relation historique et critique de la campagne d'Italie en 1859*. Paris, 1860
Lentz, Thierry (ed.), *Correspondence de Napoleon Ier publiée par ordre du l'empreur Napoleon III, Vols 1-7*. Paris, 1858-1970
Lettow Vorbeck, Oscar, *Geschichte des Krieges in Deutschland im 1866*. Berlin, 1896
Loraine Petrie, F., *Napoleon and the Archduke Charles*. London, 1909
—— *Napoleon's Conquest of Prussia 1806*. London, 1907
Lorenz, Reinhold, *Volksbewaffnung und Staatsidee in Oesterreich (1792-1797)*. Leipzig, 1926
Loy, L., *La Campagne en Styrie en 1809*. Paris, 1908
Magenschab, Hans, *Andreas Hofer*. Graz, 2002
—— *Erzherzog Johann*. Graz, 2008
Malcolm, Neill, *Bohemia, 1866*. London, 1912
Malnig, Helmut W., *Venedig 2 Juli 1849: Die Erste Kombinierte Militär Operation der Welt* in *Pallasch*. 46 June 2013.
Marmont, Marshal A., *Mémoires de Maréchal Marmont duc de Raguse*. Paris, 1857
Miller, Frederick, *A Study of the Italian Campaign in 1859*. London, 1860
Mollinary, Anton Frh. von, *Sechshundvierzigjahre in Oesterreich-Ungarischen Heere*. Zurich, 1905
Moltke, Helmuth, *Krieggeschichtlichen Arbeiten*. Berlin, 1904
Montgomery Hyde, H., 'Geschichte des Feldzuges in Italien 1800', *Mexican Empire*. London, 1946
Mras, Karl, 'Geschichte des Feldzuges in Italien 1800', *Oesterreichische Militär Zeitschrift (OMZ)*. Vols 5-9. Vienna, 1822
Neuhold, Helmut, *Oesterreichs Kriegshelden*. Graz, 2012
Ottenfeld, Rudolf, *Die Oesterreichische Armee von 1700-1867*. Vienna, 1895
Pardoe, Miss, *The City of the Magyar*. London, 1840
Parkfrieder, Joseph Gottfried, *Der Heldenberg im Park zu Wetzdorf*. Augsburg, 1858
Picard, E. *La Campagne de 1800 en Allemagne*. Paris, 1907
Pridham, Charles, *Kossuth and Magyar Land*. London, 1851
Radetzky, Graf, *Der k.k. oesterreichische Feldmarshall Graf Radetzky: eine biographische Skizze nach den eigenen Dictaten, etc.*, ed. Heller von Hellwand. Stuttgart, 1858

Rapp, Jean Georges, *Mémoires*. Paris, 1821

Rauchensteiner, Manfried, *Kaiser Franz und Erzherzog Carl*. Vienna, 1972

——*Die Schlacht bei Deutsch-Wagram am 5 und 6 Juli 1809* (Militär Historische Studien (MHS) Nr 11). Vienna, 1977

——*Das sechste oesterreischiche Armeekorps im Kriege 1809* (Mitteilungen des Oesterreichischen Staats Archiv (OSA) Vol XVII). 1965

Regele, Oskar, *FM Mack*. Vienna, 1968

——*FZM Benedek und der Weg nach Königgrätz*. Vienna, 1960

Regimental Histories:

Geschichte des k.u.k. Peterwardeiner Infanterieregiment Nr 70. Peterwardein, 1898

Geschichte des k.u.k. Infanterieregiment Nr 4 Hoch und Deutschmeister. Vienna, 1908

Geschichte des k.u.k. Infanterieregiment Nr 27 Koenig der Belgier (2 vols). Graz, 1924

Reinalter, Helmut, *Aufgeklärter Absolutismus und Revolution: Zur Geschichte des Jakobinertums*. Vienna, 1980

Ritter, Gerhard, *Staatskunst und Kriegshandwerk*. Munich, 1965

Rodger, A.B., *War of the Second Coalition*. Oxford, 1961

Roider, Karl A., *Baron Thugut and Austria's Response to the French Revolution*. Princeton, 1987

Rössler, Helmuth, *Oesterreichs Kampf um Deutschlands Befreiung*. Hamburg, 1940

Rothenberg, Gunther, *The Army of Francis Joseph*. West Lafayette, 1998

——*The Emperor's Last Victory*. London, 2004

——*Napoleon's Great Adversaries: The Archduke Charles and the Austrian Army*. London, 1982

——*The Military Border in Croatia 1740-1881*. Chicago, 1966

Rumbold, Horace, *The Austrian Court in the Nineteenth Century*. London, 1904

——*Recollections of a Diplomatist*. London, 1902

——*Final Recollections of a Diplomatist*. London, 1905

Saint-Chamans, comte, *Mémoires du Général Comte de Sant-Chamans*. Paris, 1896

Schemfil, Viktor, *Das k.k. Tiroler Korps im Kriege 1809* (*Tiroler Heimat*, Vol. XXIII). Innsbruck, 1959

Schoenbichler, Herbert, *Radetzky's Stellungnahme zu den politischen Vorgängen 1847-1856*. Vienna, 1950

Schreiber, Georg, *Des Kaisers Reiterei: Oesterreichische Kavallerie in vier Jahrhunderten*. Vienna, 1967

Schrödinger, E., *What is Life?*. London, 1946

Schroeder Paul W., *Metternich's Diplomacy at its Zenith 1820-1823*. Austin, Texas, 1962

Scomparini Caesar, *Der Berufsoffizier der Jetztzeit: Sein Wissen seine Thätigkeit und seine soziale Stellung*, Pressburg, 1890

Scotti, G., *Lissa 1866*. Trieste, 2004

Ségur, Baron, *La Campagne de Russie*. Paris, 1936

——*Mémoires de comte de Ségur*. London, 1827

Ségur, Louis Philippe comte de, *Memoires*, Vols 1-3. Paris, 1824

Sked, Alan, *Radetzky: Imperial Victor and Military Genius*. London, 2011

Sokol, A.E., *Seemacht Oesterreich: Die k.u.k. Seemarine*. Vienna, 1972

Srbik, Heinrich Ritter von, *Aus Oesterreichs Vergangenheit*. Salzburg, 1949

——*Geist und Geschichte vom deutschen Humanismus bis zur Gegenwart*. Munich, 1950

——*Metternich*, 2 vols. Munich, 1925

Steinacker, Harold, *Der Tiroler Freiheitskampf von 1809 und die Gegenwart*. Brunn, 1943

Steiner, Hertha, *Das Urteil Napoleons I über Oesterreich*. Vienna, 1946

Stradal, Otto, *Der andere Radetzky*. Vienna, 1971

Strobel, Ferdinand, *Die Landwehr Anno Neun*. Vienna and Leipzig, 1909

Sybel von Heinrich, *Geschichte der Revolutionszeit*, Vol. 1. Düsseldorf, 1853

Tapié, Ludwig von, *Die Völker unter dem Doppeladler*. Graz, 1975

Taylor, A.J.P., *The Habsburg Monarchy*. London, 1941

Tritsch, Walter, *Franz von Oesterreich*. Leipzig, 1937

——*Metternich und sein Monarch*. Darmstadt, 1952

Vivenot, A., *Thugut, Clerfayt und Wurmser*. Vienna, 1870

Voykoswitch, A., *Castiglione*. Klagenfurt, 1997

Vriser, Sergej, *Uniforme v Zgodovini*. Ljubljana, 1987

Wagner, Walther, *Von Austerlitz bis Königgrätz: Oesterreichs Kampftaktik, etc*. Osnabrück, 1978

Wallisch, Friedrich, *Die Flagge Rot Weiss Rot*. Graz, 1956

Wandruszka, Adam, *The House of Habsburg*. New York, 1964

Wawro, Geoffrey, 'Austria versus the Risorgimento', *European History Quarterly* (*EHQ*, January 1996)

——*The Austro-Prussian War: Austria's War with Prussia and Italy 1866*. Cambridge, 1996

Wilhelm, John, *Erzherzog Karl: der Feldherr und seiner Armee*. Vienna, 1913

Winter, Eduard, *Der Josephismus*. Berlin, 1962

Wurmbrand, Ernst Graf von, *Ein Leben für alt-Oesterreich*. Vienna, 1988
Zimmer, Frank, *Bismarcks Kampf gegen Kaiser Franz Joseph*. Graz, 1996
Zorzi, Alvise, *Venezia Austriaca 1798–1866*. Bari, 1985
Zwehl, Hans Karl, *Der Kampf um Bayern*. Munich, 1939
Zwiedeneck-Suedenhorst, Hans von, *Erzherzog Johann von Oesterreich im Feldzüge von 1809*. Graz, 1892
——*Zur Geschichte des Krieges von 1809 in Steiermark*. Graz, 1892

Part 3 Imperial and Royal

Primary sources

Akten der Militaerkanzlei Seiner Majestaet
Akten der Militaerkanzlei des Thronfolgers EZH Franz Ferdinand
Akten des Evidenzbüros
Akten des k.u.k. Generalstabes
Alexander Freiherr von Krobatin Nachlass
Armeeoberkommando: Operationakten
——Detailabteilung
Detailbeschreibung von Serbien 1905 (mit Nachtrag 1909)
Dispatches Major Otto Gellinek Belgrade May 1914 (KA)
Feldakten:
Glaise-Horstenau Papers
Kriegsarchiv (KA) Vienna
Nachlass Erzherzog Franz Ferdinand (Austrian State Archives)
Oskar Potiorek Nachlass
E. Spannocchi Diaries

Diplomatic Papers
Haus-Hof-Staatsarchiv (HHSA)
Oe-U series
OeVA series
Foreign Office Documents Series 7/708
Public Record Office London
Szapáry Papers (Dobersberg Lower Austria)

Selected secondary sources

Albertini, Luigi, *Le Origini della Guerra del 1914: le relazioni europee dal Congresso di Berlino all' attentato di Sarajevo*, Vols 1–3. Milan, 1942–3
Andrassy, Julius, *Diplomatie und Weltkrieg*. Berlin, 1920
Andrič, Ivo, *Na Drini Curprija: Most na Drini*. Belgrade, 1945
Auffenberg-Komarow, M. Frh von, *Aus Oesterreichs Hoehe und Niedergang*. Munich, 1921
Baker, Kenneth (with Sergio degli Ivanissevich), *La Presenza Britannica a Trieste*. Trieste, 2004
Banfield, G. de, *L'Aquila di Trieste*. Trieste, 1984
Bardolff, Carl Frh. von, *Soldat in alten Oesterreich*. Jena, 1938
Bauer, Ernest, *Glanz und Tragik der Kroaten*. Vienna, 1969
——*Die Löwe von Isonzo*. Graz, 1985
——*Drei Leopardenköpfe in Gold: Oesterreich in Dalmatien*. Vienna, 1973
——*Der letzte Paladin des Reiches: General Oberst Sarkotic von Lovčen*. Vienna, 1988
——*Zwischen Halbmond und Doppeladler*. Vienna, 1971
Benedikt, Heinrich, *Monarchie der Gegensätze*. Vienna, 1947
Bittner, Ludwig (ed. u.a.), *Oesterreich-Ungarns Aussenpolitik von der bosnischen Krise 1908 bis zum Kriegausbruch 1914: Diplomatische Aktienstücke des Oesterreich-Ungarischen Ministeriums des Äussern*, ed. Luwig Bittner, Alfred Francis Pribram, Heinrich Ritter von Srbik and Hans Übersberger, 8 vols. Vienna, 1930
Bled, Jean Paul, *Franz Joseph*. Vienna, 1988
Bobič, Pavlina, *War and Faith: The Catholic Church in Slovenia 1914–1918*. Boston, 2012
Bogičevič, Miloš, *Dragoutin Dmitrievitsch*. Paris, 1918
——*Kriegsursachen*. Amsterdam, 1919
Boroevič, Svetozar von, *Proti Italiji*. Ljubljana, 1923
Boyer, John W., *Karl Lueger: Christlichesozial Politik als Beruf*. Vienna, 2010

Brennan, Christopher, 'Reforming Austria-Hungary: Beyond his Control or Beyond his Capacity? The Domestic Policies of Emperor Karl I November 1916–May 1917'. Unpublished Ph.D thesis LSE, London, 2012

Bridge, F.R., *Great Britain and Austria-Hugary, 1906–1914: A Diplomatic History*. London, 1972

Brook-Shepherd, G. *Between Two Flags*. London, 1972

——*The Last Habsburg*. London, 1968

——*Victims at Sarajevo*. London, 1984

Broucek, Peter, *Ein Generaal in Zwielicht: Die Errinerungen Edmund Glaise-Horstenau*. Vienna, 1980

——*Ezherzog Franz Ferdinand und sein Verhältnis zur Chef des Generalstabes Franz Frh. Conrad v. Hötzendorf*. Prague, 1995

——*Kaiser Karl: der politische Weg des letzten Herrschers*. Vienna, 1997

Buchanan, Sir George, *My Mission to Russia*. London, 1923

Bülow, Prince Bernard, *Memoirs*. London, 1931

Churchill, Winston, *The World Crisis*, Vols 1–5. London, 1923–31

Clark, Christopher, *The Sleepwalkers*. London, 2013

Clary, Aldringen Alfons, *Geschichten eines alten Oestereichers*. Vienna, 1984

Cooper, Robert, *The Breaking of Nations*. London, 2003

Coreth, Botho, *Aufwachsen in Spätherbst*. Vienna, 1976

Cornwall, Mark, 'Morale and Patriotism in the Austro-Hungarian Army in State, Society and Mobilisation' in *Europe during the First World War*. Cambridge, 1997

——Review of *Die Loewe von Isonzo* in *South Slav Journal*, London, 1988

Cramon, August von, *Unser Oesterreichische-Ungarische Bundesgenosse im Weltkrieg*. Berlin, 1922

Crankshaw, Edward, *The Fall of the House of Habsburg*. London, 1963

Czernin, K.E., *Gaswaffeneinsatz Oesterreich-Ungarns im Ersten Weltkrieg*. Enzersfeld, 2004

——*Die 'Sixtusaffaire'*. Enzersfeld, 2004

Czernin, O., *In the World War*. London, 1919

Damanski, Josef, *Die Militärkapellmeister Oesterreich-Ungarns*. Prague, 1904

Daniel-Rops, H., *A Fight for God*, Vol. 9 of *History of the Church of Christ*. London, 1965

Dedijer, Vladimir, *The Road to Sarajevo*. New York, 1966

Drzdowski, Georg, *Militärmusik: Geschichte in Moll und Dur*. Klagenfurt, 1967

Feigl, Erich (ed.), *Kaiser Karl: Personliche Aufzeichnungen, Zeugnisse und Dokumente*. Vienna, 1984

Feldl, Peter, *Das verspielte Reich*. Vienna, 1968

Fester, Richard, *Die Politik Kaiser Karls und die Wende des Weltkrieges*. Berlin, 1926

Fischer, Fritz, *Griff nach der Weltmacht*. Düsseldorf, 1962

Fleming, Peter, *The Siege at Peking*. Oxford, 1984

Forstner, Franz, *Przemyśl: Oesterreich-Ungarns bedeutendste Festung*. Vienna, 1987

France, Anatole, *Corrrespondence*. Paris, 1924

Giesl von Gieslingen, Wladimir, *Zwei Jahrzehnte im Nahen Orient*, ed. Eduard Ritter von Steinitz. Berlin, 1927

Glaise Horstenau, Edmund, *Die Katastrophe*. Vienna, 1928

——(ed.) *Oesterreich Ungarns letzte Krieg 1914–18*. Vienna, 1929

Gottlieb, W.W., *Studies in Secret Diplomacy during the First World War*. London, 1957

Habsburg, Otto, *Zurück zur Mitte*. Vienna, 1991

Hantsch, Hugo, *Leopold Graf Berchtold*. Graz, 1963

Haslip, Joan, *The Emperor and the Actress*. London, 1985

Hastings, Max, *Catastrophe 1914: Europe goes to War*. London, 2013

Hemingway, Ernest, *A Farewell to Arms*. New York, 1929

Herdtrich, S.J. Wilhelm, *Principii Confucia Vita*. Graz, 1687

Hill, Richard, *Slatin Pasha*. Oxford, 1965

Holler, Gerd, *Erzherzog Franz Ferdinand von Oesterreich-Este*. Vienna, 1991

Horvat, J., *Prvi Svjetski Rat*. Zagreb, 1967

Hötzendorf, Conrad Franz von, *Aus meiner Dienstzeit 1906–1918*, Vols 1–5. Vienna, 1921–25

——*Private Auzeichnungen*, ed. Kurt Peball. Vienna, 1977

——*Zum Studium der Taktik*. Vienna, 1912

Hoyos, F.A., *Der Deutsch-Englisch Gegensatz unf des Einfluss auf der Balkanpolitik Oesterreich-Ungarns*. Berlin, 1922

Jelavich, Barbara, *What Austria Knew about the Black Hand*, Austria History Yearbook. Vol. XXII, Minnesota, 1991

Jeřabek, Rudolf, *Potiorek: General im Schatten von Sarajevo*. Graz, 1991

Jung, Peter, *Austro-Hungarian Forces in World War I*. Botley, 2003

——*L'Esercito Austro-Ungarico nella Prima Guerra Mondiale*. Gorizia, 2014

Kemp, Paul J., *The Austrian Navy*. London, 1991

Kisch, Egon Erwin, *Der Rasende Reporter.* Prague, 1929
Kissinger, Henry, *Diplomacy.* London, 1992
Kiszling, Rudolf, *Oesterreich-Ungarns Anteil am Ersten Weltkrieg.* Vienna, 1958
Klessmann, Eckhart, *Napoleon und die Deutschen.* Berlin, 2007
Kober, Josef, Anniversary Catlaogue: *Zinnsoldaten einst und jetzt.* Vienna, 2012
Kokoschka, Oskar, *My Life.* London, 1971
Kraus, Karl, *Die letzten Tage der Menschheit.* Vienna, Vols 1–2. Munich, 1964
Kreisler, Fritz, *Six Weeks in the Trenches.* New York, 1916
Lernet-Holenia, Alexander, *Die Standarte.* Vienna, 1934
Lewin, E., *Germany's Road to the East.* London, 1916
Ludwig, Emil, *July 1914.* London, 1924
Lussu, Emilio, *Un anno sull'Altopiano.* Milan, 1938
Lützow, Count Heinrich, *Im diplomatischen Dienst der k.u.k. Monarchie.* Vienna, 1971
McMeekin, S., *The Russian Origins of the First World War.* Cambridge, Mass., 2011
Mann, Michael, *Regimental History of The 1st The Queen's Dragoon Guards.* London, 1993
Markus, Georg, *Der Fall Redl.* Vienna, 1984
Martinetz, Dieter, *Der Gaskrieg 1914/18: Entwicklung, Herstellung und Einsatz chemischer Kampfstoffe.* Bonn, 1996
Merry del Val, Card., *Memories of Pius X.* London, 1924
Meyer, Hermann Frank, *Blutiges Edelweiss.* Berlin, 2008
Millo, Alma, *L'Elite del Potere a Trieste.* Milan, 1989
Misič, Živojin, *Une Lutte dure et permanente.* Belgrade, 1987
Moneypenny, William Flavell (with George Earle Buckle), *Life of Disraeli,* Vols 1–6. London, 1910–20
Musulin, Alexander Freiherr von, *Das Haus am Ballplatz.* Munich, 1924
Novak, Karl F., *Der Weg zur Katastrophe.* Berlin, 1919
Ortner, C., *Oesterreich Ungarns Artillerie.* Vienna, 2007
Paleologue, Maurice, *An Ambassador's Memoirs 1914–1917.* London, 1973
Patka, Marcus G. (ed.), *Welt Untergang: Judisches Leben und Sterben im Ersten Weltkrieg.* Catalogue of exhibition. Jüdisches Museum Wien (JMW), Vienna, 2014.
Peball, Kurt (ed.), *Conrad von Hötzendorf: Private Aufzeichnungen.* Vienna, 1977
Pechma, Alexander (ed.), *Peking 1900 (Paula von Rosthorns Errinerungen).* Vienna, 2001
Pepernik, A., *Doberdob slovenskih fantov grob.* Celje, 1936
Pieri, Piero, *l'Italia Nella Prima Guerra Mondiale.* Turin, 1965
Pils, G. (with E. Brixen and G.Martin), *Das war Oesterreichs Militärmusik.* Graz, 1982
Portland, Duke of, *Men, Women and Things: Memories of the Duke of Portland K.G.G.C.V.O.* London, 1937
Pribram, A.F., *Austria-Hungary and Great Britain 1908–1914.* Oxford, 1951
——*England and the International Policy of the European Great Powers.* Oxford, 1931
Proks, Petr, *Habsburkove & Velka Valka.* Prague, 2011
Ranitovic, Branko (with Vanda Ladovic), *Zagreb 1900.* Zagreb, 1974
Rapp, Adolf, *Gross-Deutsch Klein-Deutsch.* Munich, 1922
Rauchensteiner, M., *Tod des Doppeladlers.* Graz, 1997
——(ed.), *Waffentreue: Die 12 Isonzoschlacht 1917.* Vienna, 2007
Redlich, Joseph, *Franz Josef.* London, 1926
——*Das politische Tagebuch 1908–1914.* Graz, 1953
Regimental Histories:
Geschichte des k.und k. Peterwardein Infanterie Regiment Nr. 70. Peterwardein, 1898
Reininghaus, Gina, *Mein Leben mit Conrad von Hötzendorf.* Leipzig, 1935
Rodd, Sir J. Rennell, *Social and Diplomatic Memories 1902–1919.* London, 1922
Rohl, J. C. G., *Delusion or Design?* London, 1973
Ronge, Max, *Krieg und Industrie Spionage.* Vienna, 1930
Rops, Daniel H., *A Fight for God.* New York, 1966
Roth, Joseph, *Radetzkymarsch.* Cologne, 1979
Rothenberg, Gunther, *The Army of Francis Joseph.* West Lafayette, 1998
Rumbold, Horace, *The Austrian Court in the Nineteenth Century.* London, 1909
Sazonov, S., *Fateful Years.* London, 1928
Schachinger, Werner, *Die Bosniaken kommen.* Graz, 1989
Schalek, Alice (pseud. Paul Michaely), *Am Isonzo: Maerz bis Juli 1916.* Vienna, 1916
Schierbrand, Wolf von, *Austria-Hungary: The Polyglot Empire.* New York, 1917
Schmidl, Erwin, *Juden in der k.(u.) k. Armee 1788–1918.* Eisenstadt, 1989
Schnitzler, Arthur, *Jugend in Wien.* Vienna, 1968
Schoenherr, Max, *Carl Michael Ziehrer: Sein Leben und seine Zeit.* Vienna, 1974

Schroedinger, E., *What Is Life?*. Cambridge, 2001

Schupita, Peter, *Die k.u.k Seeflieger*. Koblenz, 1983

Scomparini Caesar, *Der Berufsoffizier der Jetztzeit: Sein Wissen seine Thätigkeit und seine soziale Stellung*, Pressburg, 1890

Sema, Antonio, *La Grande Guerra sull fronte dell' Isonzo*. Gorizia, 1995

Simms, Brendan, *Unfinest Hour*. London, 1998

Singer, Ladislaus, *Ottokar Graf Czernin*. Graz, 1965

Slovenec (1915) *3.4.15*. Ljubljana, 1915

Slovensko (Anon.), *Slovenski liberalei in loza*. Ljubljana, 1893

Stationery Office London, *War 1914: Punishing the Serbs*. London, 1999

Steed, Henry V. Wickham, *The Habsburg Monarchy*. London, 1930

——*Through Thirty Years*. London, 1930

Steiner, Zara, *Decisions for War*. London, 1984

Steinitz, G. Eduard Ritter von (ed.), *Zwei Jahrzehnte im Nahen Orient: Aufzeichnungen des Generals der Kavallerie Baron Wladimir Giesl*. Berlin, 1927

——(ed.), *Erinnerungen an Franz Josef II*. Berlin, 1931

Suklje, F., *Iz mojeh Spominov*, Vol. 3. Ljubljana, 1929

Szeps, Bertha, *My Life and History*. London, 1938

Taylor, A.J.P., *The First World War*. London, 1967

Tolstoy, L.N., *War and Peace*. London, 1957

Vivian, Herbert, *Life of Emperor Charles*. London, 1932

Voghera, Giorgio, *Gli Anni di Trieste*. Gorizia, 1989

Wandruszka, Adam, *The House of Habsburg*. New York, 1964

Wawro, Geoffrey. *A Mad Catastrophe*. Austin, Texas, 2014

Weber, Fritz, *Menschenmauer am Isonzo*. Vienna, 1932

Wedel, Oswald, *Austro-German Diplomatic Relations 1908–1914*. Oxford, 1934

Williams, Joyce G., *Colonel House and Sir Edward Grey*. New York, 1984

Williamson, Samuel, *Austria-Hungary and the Outbreak of the First World War*. London, 1991

Windischgraetz, Lajos, *My Adventures and Misadventures*. London, 1965

Winterhalder, Th. Ritter von, *Kämpfe in China*. Vienna, 1902

Zecha, Wolfgang, *Unter der Maske: Giftgas auf den Kriegschauplatzen Oesterreich-Ungarn im Ersten Weltkrieg*. Vienna, 2000

Zweig, Stefan, *Die Welt von Gestern*. Stockholm, 1944

INDEX

Printed and bound by CPI Group (UK) Ltd, Croydon, CR0 4YY

01/11/2024

14584839-0001